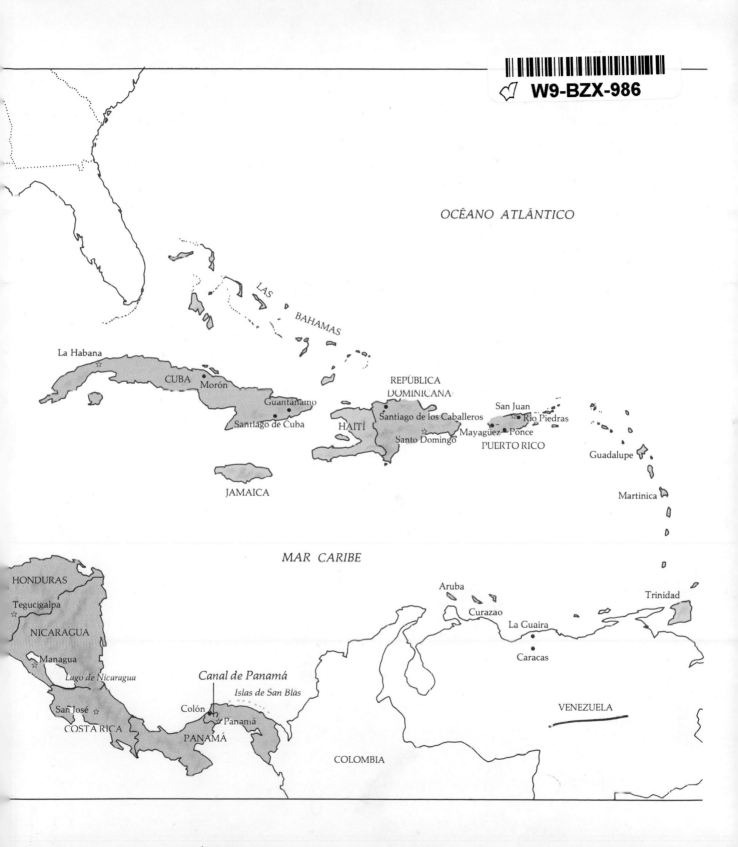

En contacto

A First Course in Spanish
Third Edition

Pablo Valencia
The College of Wooster

Franca Merlonghi
Pine Manor College

Maureen Weissenrieder
Ohio University

Houghton Mifflin Company   **Boston**

Dallas / Geneva, Illinois / Princeton, New Jersey / Palo Alto

The publisher would like to thank the following copyright holders for permission to use copyrighted material.

Appendix C, selected definitions. Copyright © 1982 by Houghton Mifflin Company. Reprinted and adapted by permission from *The American Heritage Dictionary, Second College Edition.*

Mexican tourism advertisement, © 1982. Used by permission of the Secretaría de Turismo de México.

Art credits appear following the Index.

Cover photograph by Ross Elmi

Printed in the U.S.A.

Student's Edition ISBN: 0-395-36950-9

Instructor's Edition ISBN: 0-395-44893-X

Library of Congress Catalog Card Number: 87-80580
DEFGHIJ-D-99876543210

Lección preliminar

Presentaciones

Una clase de esquí

Señor Romero: Buenos días. Me llamo Juan
Romero. Soy el instructor de esquí.
Y usted, ¿cómo se llama?

Luis: Buenos días, señor. Me llamo Luis
Pérez.

A skiing lesson

Mr. Romero: *Good morning. My name is Juan
Romero. I'm the ski instructor. And
you, what's your name?*

Luis: *Good morning, sir. My name is Luis
Pérez.*

En una discoteca

Pedro: ¡Hola! Me llamo Pedro Jiménez. Y tú,
¿cómo te llamas?

Alicia: Me llamo Alicia López. Mucho gusto.

Pedro: Encantado.

In a discotheque

Pedro: *Hi! My name is Pedro Jiménez. And you,
what's your name?*

Alicia: *My name is Alicia López. Nice to meet you.*

Pedro: *Pleased to meet you.*

En contacto

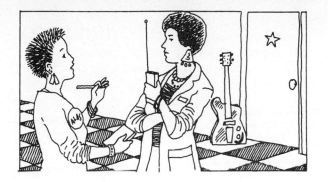

Después del concierto	After the concert
Señorita Murillo: Buenas tardes. Me llamo Guadalupe Murillo. Soy la agente de prensa del grupo musical Alas. Y usted, ¿cómo se llama?	Miss Murillo: *Good afternoon. My name is Guadalupe Murillo. I'm the press agent of the musical group Alas. And you, what's your name?*
Señorita García: Buenas tardes, señorita. Me llamo Cristina García. Soy aficionada del grupo Alas.	Miss García: *Good evening, miss. My name is Cristina García. I'm a fan of the group Alas.*

A. Introduce yourself to a classmate seated near you.
B. Play the role of an instructor and introduce yourself to a student.

Despedidas

En una cancha de tenis	At a tennis court
Elena: Pues, ¡adiós, Jorge! Hasta luego.	Elena: *Well, good-by, Jorge! See you later.*
Jorge: ¡Adiós, Elena! Hasta la vista.	Jorge: *Good-by Elena! See you.*

A. Pretend that class has ended. Say good-by to some classmates.
B. Now say good-by to your instructor.

Expresiones de cortesía

There are many courtesy expressions in Spanish, just as there are in English. Familiarize yourself with the following courtesy expressions and use them in appropriate situations until they come to you as automatically as do their English equivalents.

Con permiso.	*Excuse me.*
Por favor.	*Please.*
Lo siento.	*I'm sorry.*
Gracias (Muchas gracias).	*Thanks (Thanks a lot).*
De nada.	*You're welcome.*
No hay de qué.	*Don't mention it.*

Which courtesy expression would you use in each of the following circumstances?

1. You are entering a store, and someone holds the door open for you. You say: . . .
2. You see a customer leave an umbrella behind at a cash register and return it to him/her. He/she thanks you. You say: . . .
3. You need to borrow a pen from the clerk at the cash register to write out a check to pay for your purchases. You begin by saying: . . .
4. Upon leaving the store, you bump into a customer, and all his/her packages fall on the floor. You say: . . .

Expresiones para la clase

Here is a list of requests that your instructor will probably use in class. Familiarize yourself with them so that you will be able to follow the directions without hesitation.

To more than one student

Abran los libros en la página cinco (5).	*Open your books to page five (5).*
Miren el ejercicio.	*Look at the exercise.*
Cierren los libros.	*Close your books.*
Ahora escuchen.	*Now listen.*
Saquen papel / lápiz / pluma.	*Take out (a) paper / pencil / pen.*

To one student

Repita, por favor.	*Repeat, please.*
Vaya a la pizarra, por favor.	*Go to the blackboard, please.*
Siéntese, por favor.	*Sit down, please.*
Lea las instrucciones.	*Read the instructions.*

You can use the following expressions to ask for clarification of a word, a page number, etc., to tell someone that you do not understand what was said or know the answer to a question, or to ask your instructor to go more slowly.

¿Cómo se dice **singer** en español?   *How do you say singer in Spanish?*
¿Qué quiere decir **cómo** en inglés?   *What does cómo mean in English?*
¿Qué página, por favor?   *What page, please?*
No comprendo, (señora Miranda).   *I don't understand, (Mrs. Miranda).*
No sé, (señor Rivera).   *I don't know, (Mr. Rivera).*
(Señorita Almeida), más despacio, por favor.   *(Miss Almeida), more slowly, please.*

Find a partner and role-play the following situations, creating an appropriate dialogue. Which classroom expressions would you and your instructor use in each of the situations?

1. Your instructor asks you to go to the board. Tell him/her that you don't understand.
2. Your instructor asks the class to open their books. Ask him/her which page you should turn to.
3. Your instructor asks you how to say *fast* in Spanish. Tell him/her that you don't know.
4. You ask your instructor the meaning of the Spanish phrase **Buenos días.** Your instructor asks you to please repeat.
5. Your instructor asks the class to look at exercise 5. Ask him/her to go more slowly.

Palabras análogas

English and Spanish share many words that are derived from the same root word in Latin and Greek. These words are called cognates **(palabras análogas** or **cognados.)** Recognizing cognates is very useful in developing reading skills in Spanish, as they reduce considerably the language barrier and speed up understanding.

Close cognates are easily recognized in print, though their pronunciation differs in the two languages; for example, **universidad** / *university;* **filosofía** / *philosophy;* **medicina** / *medicine.* Some cognates are more difficult to recognize; for example, Spanish **lengua** *(language)* is related to English *lingual* and *language.*

There are a relatively small number of false cognates **(análogas falsas** or **cognados falsos)** whose meanings are not equivalent in the two languages. An example of a false cognate is **colegio,** which usually means *elementary school* or *high school,* not *college.* Context frequently will help you realize when you encounter a false cognate.

Read the following newspaper ads **(anuncios)** and see how much you are able to understand.

1

2

Listen carefully as your instructor gives you the equivalent of the numbers shown in the advertisements in Spanish. Then give the information requested, responding with a brief phrase.

Anuncio 1

1. Título del almanaque
2. Cada página contiene . . .
3. Cinco (5) tipos de información en el almanaque
4. El número de años de publicación del almanaque

Anuncio 2

1. Nombre de la estación
2. Tipos de música de la estación
3. Las horas de los programas musicales
4. País y ciudad donde está la estación

Acknowledgments

The authors and publisher would like to thank the following people for their comments on *En contacto*. Their many valuable suggestions for improvement have helped guide the development of this new third edition.

Professor Alurista, *California State Polytechnic University, San Luis Obispo*
Fernando Burgos, *Memphis State University*
Malcolm Compitello, *Michigan State University, East Lansing*
Octavio de la Suaree, *William Paterson College*
Lee Dowling, *University of Houston, University Park*
Alex Esparza, *San José City College*
Joseph R. Farrell, *California State Polytechnic University, Pomona*
Rosa M. Fernández, *The University of New Mexico, Albuquerque*
Herschel Frey, *University of Pittsburgh*
Rita Goldberg, *St. Lawrence University*
Lynn Gorrell, *The Pennsylvania State University*
Pedro Gutiérrez, *University of Houston, University Park*
Nicolás Hernández, *Georgia Institute of Technology*
Douglas R. Hilt, *West Georgia College*
Mario Iglesias, *The Ohio State University, Columbus*
Reynaldo Jiménez, *University of Florida*
John R. Kelly, *North Carolina State University, Raleigh*
Roberta Lavine, *University of Maryland*
Nitza Lladó-Torres, *University of Southern California*
Antonio Martínez, *Texas A & M University, College Station*
James C. Murray, *Georgia State University*
Frank Nuessel, *University of Louisville*
Hernán C. Quiñones, *University of California, Los Angeles*
Enrique Riveros-Schäfer, *Occidental College*
Nelson Rojas, *University of Nevada*
Nina Rukas, *University of Alaska, Fairbanks*
Paul Seavers, *University of Hawaii at Manoa*
Marie Sheppard, *University of Massachusetts, Amherst*
Cynthia Steele, *University of Washington*
Alain Swietlicki, *University of Wisconsin-Madison*

Ancillaries

The *Workbook/Lab Manual* consists of a workbook with writing exercises coordinated with the student text, and a lab manual that requires responses in writing to material on the recordings. The exercises in both the workbook and the lab manual parallel the presentation of content, structure, and vocabulary of the student text. End-of-unit review sections keyed to the student text are also included.

The *Recordings* accompanying *En contacto, Third Edition,* are available in both cassette (primarily for student purchase) and reel-to-reel (primarily for loan) format. They include listening comprehension materials, dictations, and other activities correlated with the lab manual, core material, and selected pronunciation, vocabulary, and grammar exercises from the text.

For a detailed description of the organization, purpose, and contents of each of the components of the *En contacto, Third Edition* program, see the Instructor's Annotated Edition.

En contacto, Third Edition, Student Evaluation Form

An evaluation form for *En contacto, Third Edition* is provided at the end of the student text. The authors and editors hope that students will share with them their experience with the third edition.

Introduction

En contacto, Third Edition, is a four-skills program designed for the introductory course in Spanish, with emphasis on communicative competence and contemporary culture. *En contacto* provides a sound basis for learning Spanish as it is spoken and written today. Practice is given in listening, speaking, reading, and writing, with opportunities for self-expression, sharing information, conversing on everyday topics, and role-playing in concrete situations. The program also introduces contemporary life and culture in various parts of the Hispanic world, including regions of the United States where there is a strong concentration of Spanish speakers.

Student Text

The student text is composed of a preliminary lesson that introduces salutations, leave-takings, courtesy and classroom expressions, cognates, the geography of the Hispanic world, and a full-color photo essay on the Hispanic world; eight units of three lessons each that focus on different geographical areas of the Spanish-speaking world; a section entitled *Lengua en acción* at the end of each unit that contains functional, proficiency-oriented activities; a section entitled *Otro mundo* that provides supplementary materials about young people's activities and cultural aspects of the Hispanic world; four full-color photo essays thematically organized; and a Reference Section.

Each of the 24 lessons is built around a theme and is divided into the following sections:

1. *Texto básico:* core material with a vocabulary list, related exercises and activities that include personalized questions *(Conversación),* role-playing and creative activities *(Práctica),* and cultural notes related to the theme of the basic text. Core material is varied in format and includes monologues, dialogues, interviews, TV and radio broadcasts, an opinion poll, a newspaper article, and a song.
2. *Pronunciación y ortografía:* explanations of sound-spelling correspondences with exercises and dictation practice, Spanish proverbs, poems, and tongue twisters. This section appears in the first 18 lessons.
3. *Estudio de palabras:* word sets and vocabulary expansion exercises and activities that stress functional use of the language. Word sets or exercises are often illustrated and include word-building activities with prefixes, suffixes, and word families.
4. *Estructuras útiles:* grammar explanations, often illustrated with drawings and captions to show grammar in context, numerous examples, charts, exercises, and activities. Each lesson generally contains three or four grammar topics.
5. *¿Comprende usted? (Lecciones 1–12)* and *¡Exprésese usted! (Lecciones 13–24):* readings related to the lesson themes designed to develop reading and writing skills, with exercises and activities.

Estudio de palabras: Palabras análogas falsas
Estructuras útiles: Present perfect subjunctive •
 Past perfect subjunctive • **Pero** and **sino** •
 Review of object and reflexive pronouns
¡Exprésese usted! El punto de vista / El billete de
 diez dólares

Lengua en acción 8   451

Otro mundo 455

La vida de los jóvenes
Países y paisajes

Reference Section   RI

English equivalents of core material *(Units 2–3)*
Sound-spelling correspondences
Glossary of grammatical terms
Verb charts
Spanish-English vocabulary
English-Spanish vocabulary
Index

Pronunciación y ortografía: Signos de puntuación
Estudio de palabras: Materiales • Sustantivos compuestos
Estructuras útiles: **Usted-, ustedes-,** and **nosotros-** commands • More on reflexive constructions • More on the imperfect versus the preterit • Verbs followed by **a** or **de** + infinitive
¡Exprésese usted! La oración clave / La República Dominicana: Una vista histórica

Lección 18: En Cuba   328

Texto básico: Una entrevista
Nota cultural: Los deportes en Cuba
Pronunciación y ortografía: Dictado
Estudio de palabras: Más actividades deportivas • Familias de palabras
Estructuras útiles: Review of the present subjunctive in noun clauses • Indicative versus subjunctive in adjectival clauses • Indicative versus subjunctive in adverbial clauses • Position of two object pronouns
¡Exprésese usted! El punto de vista / Otra revolución

Lengua en acción 6   345

Unidad 7: En México

Lección 19: En México   352

Texto básico: El pueblo o la ciudad
Nota cultural: La economía mexicana
Estudio de palabras: Muebles y decoración • Los prefijos **co-** y **re-**
Estructuras útiles: The imperfect subjunctive • The impersonal reflexive construction • Relative pronouns • **¿Qué?** versus **¿cuál(es)?**
¡Exprésese usted! La descripción / El parque de Chapultepec

Lección 20: En México   366

Texto básico: ¿Por qué somos lo que somos?
Nota cultural: El arte popular de México
Estudio de palabras: El correo • La correspondencia

Estructuras útiles: The future tense • The conditional tense (mood) • Future and conditional of probability • Review of **ser** and **estar** with adjectives
¡Exprésese usted! La carta formal

Lección 21: En México   382

Texto básico: Una imagen basada en estereotipos
Nota cultural: La mujer mexicana
Estudio de palabras: Ocupaciones y profesiones
Estructuras útiles: Commands with **tú** and **vosotros** • Softening requests and criticisms • **Si**-clauses • **Como si**-clauses
¡Exprésese usted! La autobiografía / Autobiografía de Josefina Salcedo J.

Lengua en acción 7   398

Unidad 8: En España

Lección 22: En España   404

Texto básico: Democracia bajo la monarquía
Nota cultural: El cine español
Estudio de palabras: La política
Estructuras útiles: Present perfect tense • Pluperfect and conditional perfect • Superlatives with **sumamente** and **-ísimo**
¡Exprésese usted! Las invitaciones

Lección 23: En España   419

Texto básico: Las tunas
Nota cultural: El arte y la música en España
Estudio de palabras: El amor, el matrimonio y el divorcio
Estructuras útiles: Present progressive tense • Preterit and imperfect progressive tenses • Use of reflexive verbs for unintentional actions
¡Exprésese usted! La descripción / Su cuarto

Lección 24: En España   434

Texto básico: Un folleto sobre Barcelona
Nota cultural: La región de Cataluña

Pronunciación y ortografía: El sonido [h]
Estudio de palabras: Las estaciones y los meses • Las fechas • ¿Qué tiempo hace? • Los años y las décadas
Estructuras útiles: Preterit of irregular verbs • Indirect-object pronouns • **Hace . . . que** in expressions of time
¿Comprende usted? Una llamada por teléfono

Lección 12: En Perú   211

Texto básico: Excursión a Machu Picchu
Nota cultural: Cuzco y los incas
Pronunciación y ortografía: Los sonidos [s] y [z]
Estudio de palabras: Artículos de ropa • Los viajes
Estructuras útiles: Preterit of **-ir** verbs with stem changes **o** > **u** and **e** > **i** • Nominalization • Reflexive constructions • Verbs like **gustar**
¿Comprende usted? Tarjetas postales

Lengua en acción 4   229

Unidad 5: En Colombia, Venezuela y Panamá

Lección 13: En Colombia   234

Texto básico: Las noticias del día
Nota cultural: La radio en Colombia
Pronunciación y ortografía: Los sonidos [s], [ks], [gs]
Estudio de palabras: Comidas y bebidas • Pequeños negocios
Estructuras útiles: Introduction to the subjunctive mood • Present subjunctive forms of **-ar** verbs • Uses of the subjunctive • Comparisons of inequality
¡Exprésese usted! Descripción de un evento / La noticia del año

Lección 14: En Venezuela   253

Texto básico: Una carta de Caracas
Nota cultural: La arquitectura en Caracas
Pronunciación y ortografía: Los sonidos [g] y [ǧ]

Estudio de palabras: Plano de una casa • Preposiciones compuestas
Estructuras útiles: Present subjunctive of **-er** and **-ir** verbs • Uses of the present subjunctive • Superlative of adjectives • Irregular comparatives and superlatives
¡Exprésese usted! El resumen / Venezuela y el petróleo

Lección 15: En Panamá   271

Texto básico: Los indios cunas
Nota cultural: El regateo y los precios fijos
Pronunciación y ortografía: Las letras **ll**, **y** + vocal y **hie**
Estudio de palabras: El cuerpo humano • Sustantivos que terminan en **-ma** y **-ta** • Sufijos en **-oso**
Estructuras útiles: Verbs with irregular present-subjunctive stems • Comparisons of equality • The neuter **lo**
¡Exprésese usted! La carta amistosa

Lengua en acción 5   286

Unidad 6: En Costa Rica, la República Dominicana y Cuba

Lección 16: En Costa Rica   292

Texto básico: La estación biológica de Monteverde
Nota cultural: La selva en Hispanoamérica
Pronunciación y ortografía: Consonantes con cambios ortográficos
Estudio de palabras: Algunos animales e insectos • Los números ordinales
Estructuras útiles: The imperfect • Imperfect versus preterit • Long forms of possessive adjectives • Possessive pronouns
¡Exprésese usted! Descripción de un viaje

Lección 17: En la República Dominicana   312

Texto básico: La Voz de los Jóvenes
Nota cultural: La República Dominicana

Pronunciación y ortografía: Flap [r] • More on linking
Estudio de palabras: El pueblo de Río Verde • Prefijos en **im-, in-** y **des-**
Estructuras útiles: Present tense and uses of **estar** • Present tense of **ir** • Contractions **al** and **del** • Word order in interrogative sentences
¿Comprende usted? En una agencia de turismo

Lección 6: En los Estados Unidos 99

Texto básico: ¿Cómo es tu primo?
Nota cultural: Hispanics in Florida
Pronunciación y ortografía: Trilled [R]
Estudio de palabras: Adjetivos descriptivos • Los colores
Estructuras útiles: Descriptive adjectives and agreement • Present tense of **-er** and **-ir** verbs • Use of **¡qué!** in exclamations • Adverbs in **-mente** • **Ser** and **estar** in contrast
¿Comprende usted? Hispanoamérica en la edad del jet

Lengua en acción 2   118

Unidad 3: En Argentina, Uruguay y Chile

Lección 7: En Argentina 122

Texto básico: ¡Contigo o sin ti!
Nota cultural: El lenguaje popular
Pronunciación y ortografía: El sonido [ñ] • La letra **h**
Estudio de palabras: Aparatos útiles • Los números 21–30 • Los números 31–199
Estructuras útiles: Present tense of **tener;** idioms with **tener** • **Tener que** and **hay que** in contrast • Prepositional pronouns • Present tense of verbs with irregular **yo**-forms
¿Comprende usted? Después del concierto

Lección 8: En Uruguay 138

Texto básico: ¿Te gusta aquel velero?
Nota cultural: Los deportes en el mundo hispánico

Pronunciación y ortografía: Los sonidos [b] y [β] • Más sobre los diptongos
Estudio de palabras: Medios de transporte • Los deportes
Estructuras útiles: Demonstrative adjectives and pronouns • Direct-object pronouns • Present tense of stem-changing verbs **e > ie** • Present tense of stem-changing verbs **o > ue**
¿Comprende usted? Regata en Punta del Este

Lección 9: En Chile 156

Texto básico: Una investigación sociológica
Nota cultural: La familia en la sociedad hispánica
Pronunciación y ortografía: Los sonidos [d] y [ð]
Estudio de palabras: Otros miembros de la familia • Los números de 200 y más
Estructuras útiles: Affirmative and negative counterparts • Present tense of stem-changing verbs **e > i** • Present tense of **conocer, dar, saber,** and **traducir** • **Saber** and **conocer** in contrast
¿Comprende usted? En casa de Patricia

Lengua en acción 3   172

Unidad 4: En Bolivia, Ecuador y Perú

Lección 10: En Bolivia 178

Texto básico. Una huelga inminente
Nota cultural: Lenguas indígenas
Pronunciación y ortografía: Los sonidos [p], [t] y [k]
Estudio de palabras: ¿Qué hora es? • Expresiones de tiempo en el pasado
Estructuras útiles: The preterit • **Para** and **por** in contrast • Adjectives with shortened forms
¿Comprende usted? Minicuento

Lección 11: En Ecuador 195

Texto básico: Un viaje de negocios
Nota cultural: Personalismo y palanca

iv

Contents

Lección preliminar 2

Presentaciones
Despedidas
Expresiones de cortesía
Expresiones para la clase
Palabras análogas
¿Qué es el mundo hispánico?
Panorama del mundo hispánico
Un poco de geografía

Unidad 1: El mundo hispánico

Lección 1: El mundo hispánico 14

Textos básicos: ¿Cómo se llama usted? • Hola, ¿qué tal?
Notas culturales: Spanish surnames • Formality in greetings
Pronunciación y ortografía: Sound/letter correspondence • Basic vowel sounds and Spanish syllables • Accent marks and punctuation marks
Estudio de palabras: Los días de la semana • Palabras análogas
Estructuras útiles: Subject pronouns • Present tense and uses of **ser**
¿Comprende usted? Estereotipos hispánicos

Lección 2: El mundo hispánico 30

Textos básicos: ¿Dónde vive usted? • Buenos días
Notas culturales: The term **americano/americana** • Use of first names and courtesy titles
Pronunciación y ortografía: Intonation patterns • Linking within breath groups
Estudio de palabras: Los números de 0 a 20 • Objetos de la clase
Estructuras útiles: Gender of nouns; the singular indefinite article • Plural of nouns and indefinite articles • Omission of the indefinite article • Agreement of adjectives of nationality
¿Comprende usted? ¡Anuncios especiales!

Lección 3: El mundo hispánico 47

Texto básico: ¿Te gusta bailar?
Nota cultural: Nicknames
Pronunciación y ortografía: Capitalization • The Spanish alphabet
Estudio de palabras: Asignaturas • Los sufijos **-ía** y **-dad**
Estructuras útiles: The infinitive • Present tense of regular **-ar** verbs • The definite article • **Me (te, le) gusta(n)**
¿Comprende usted? Los hispanos en los Estados Unidos

Lengua en acción 1 64

Unidad 2: En España, México y los Estados Unidos

Lección 4: En España 68

Texto básico: ¡Qué barbaridad!
Nota cultural: The university system
Pronunciación y ortografía: Diphthongs • Syllabication • Stress
Estudio de palabras: Etapas de la vida • La familia • Diminutivos
Estructuras útiles: Possession and close relationship with **de** • Possessive adjectives • Personal **a** • The invariable form **hay**
¿Comprende usted? Un permiso temporal

Lección 5: En México 84

Texto básico: ¿Hay un banco por aquí?
Nota cultural: Regional terms

El mundo hispánico

(a)

(b)

(c)

(d)

(e)

(f)

(g)

(h)

(i)

(j)

¿Qué es el mundo hispánico?

The color photo essay in this *Lección preliminar* presents a few glimpses of everyday life as well as some historic landmarks in Hispanic countries. It also depicts the presence of Hispanics in the United States. Each photograph focuses on a particular activity or cultural aspect found in Hispanic societies. Read the following captions without stopping to decipher every word. These captions contain many cognates that will enable you to understand the gist without difficulty. Now look at the photos and see how successful you are in matching the captions with the photos.

1. Caracas es una ciudad cosmopolita que combina la arquitectura moderna y tradicional. Es la capital de Venezuela.
2. La fuente luminosa de la Cibeles, frente al edificio de correos, está en el centro de una de las plazas de mayor tráfico de Madrid, España.
3. Los cafés al aire libre son típicos en la ciudad de Sevilla. Estos turistas y habitantes de la ciudad conversan en un café en el barrio de Santa Cruz.
4. Gran parte de la población en los Andes en Perú es de origen indio, descendiente de la cultura nazca. Las vistas de las montañas son maravillosas.
5. San Juan en Puerto Rico es un paraíso para los turistas por su clima tropical, con temperaturas ideales y preciosas vistas de palmeras.
6. Los vendedores ambulantes son muy típicos en la cultura hispánica. Este señor vende su mercancía en bicicleta por las calles de Cartagena, Colombia.
7. El espíritu de cooperación entre hispanos es muy evidente en esta fotografía de un mural en un barrio hispánico de Chicago.
8. La Pirámide de la Luna en Teotihuacán, México es un magnífico ejemplo de la arquitectura preazteca. Los aztecas construyeron grandes ciudades antes de la época de los españoles.
9. La artesanía de México y Centro América usa colores vivos y formas geométricas en telas y cerámica. (Oaxaca, México)
10. Las plazas hispánicas son sitios favoritos para reunirse, como indica esta foto de unas familias mexicanas. (Plaza de la Paz, Guanajuato, México)

Panorama del mundo hispánico

Spanish is the first language of an estimated 296 million people. It is spoken in Spain, Mexico, six Central American countries, Puerto Rico, Cuba, the Dominican Republic, and nine South American countries. It is also spoken as a first or second language by an estimated 15 million people in the United States. Spanish ranks fourth among the world languages, after Mandarin, English, and Hindi.

Because of economic, commercial, cultural, and political ties between the United States and its Hispanic neighbors to the south, a knowledge of Spanish is of great importance to United States citizens. English speakers who are proficient in Spanish gain great personal satisfaction in learning about the culture of Hispanic countries and in being able to speak to and understand the people from those societies, as well as those Hispanics living in numerous communities within the United States. Furthermore, a knowledge of Spanish opens job opportunities available to an individual, especially in the fields of business, education, merchandising, medicine, law, government, and diplomacy. Students interested in living abroad find that the knowledge of a foreign language is essential. With a mastery of Spanish, numerous possibilities for study within various academic disciplines present themselves, both in Hispanic America and Spain.

Hispanic Population in the United States, 1980

A. Refer to the map on the previous page. Which areas of the United States are most heavily populated by Hispanics? What reasons can you give as a possible explanation for this distribution?

B. Find your state on the map. What percentage of the population is of Hispanic origin?

C. According to the U.S. Department of Commerce, Bureau of the Census, the percentage of Hispanics in the United States population is expected to rise from 6% in 1980 to at least 9% by the year 2000. How do you think this will affect the population of your state? Why?

D. Refer to the maps of the Hispanic world on the inside of the text cover.

1. Pronounce the names of the Spanish-speaking countries after your instructor.
2. Repeat the names of the following capital cities. Then identify the name of the country that corresponds to each capital city.

Buenos Aires	San Salvador	Asunción
Santiago	La Paz	Quito
Madrid	Caracas	Managua
Tegucigalpa	Lima	Santo Domingo
San Juan	Bogotá	Ciudad de Panamá
San José	Montevideo	La Habana
Ciudad de México	Ciudad de Guatemala	

Un poco de geografía

Learn the following noun phrases that refer to geographical features and pronounce them after your instructor. Most of the nouns are Spanish-English cognates, but remember that cognates are pronounced differently in the two languages. Note that both **el** and **la** mean *the;* the form used depends on whether the noun that follows is masculine or feminine.

el canal   the canal
la capital   the capital city
el continente   the continent
la cordillera   the mountain range
la costa   the coast
la frontera   the frontier; the border
la isla   the island
el lago   the lake

el mapa   the map
el mar   the sea
la montaña   the mountain
el océano   the ocean
el país   the country
la península   the peninsula
el río   the river
la sierra   the sierra (mountain range)

Now learn the points of the compass **(los puntos cardinales)** in Spanish so that you can locate geographical areas in relation to one another.

México está **al sur de** los Estados Unidos.

Mexico is (to the) south of the United States.

El Mar Caribe está **al este de** Nicaragua.

The Caribbean Sea is (to the) east of Nicaragua.

El Océano Pacífico está **al oeste de** Sudamérica.

The Pacific Ocean is (to the) west of South America.

Barcelona está **en el noreste de** España.

Barcelona is in the northeast of Spain.

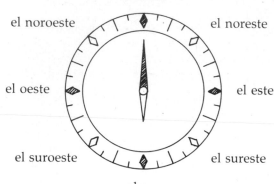

el norte

el noroeste   el noreste

el oeste   el este

el suroeste   el sureste

el sur

A. Refer to the maps as directed by your instructor as he/she says the following statements. Say **sí** if the statement is true; say **no** if it is false.

1. La capital de España es Madrid.
2. Colombia es un país de Europa.
3. España es una península.
4. Buenos Aires está en la costa del Océano Pacífico.
5. El Río Bravo está en la frontera entre México y Guatemala.
6. México es un país del continente norteamericano.

B. Look at the following illustrated map of southern Spain and listen as your instructor makes the following statements. Say **sí** if the statement is true and **no** if it is false.

1. Granada está al oeste de Sevilla.
2. La isla de Gibraltar está al norte de Córdoba.
3. Motril está al este de Cádiz.
4. Málaga está al sur de Granada.
5. Granada está al suroeste de Córdoba.
6. Sevilla está al sureste de Córdoba.

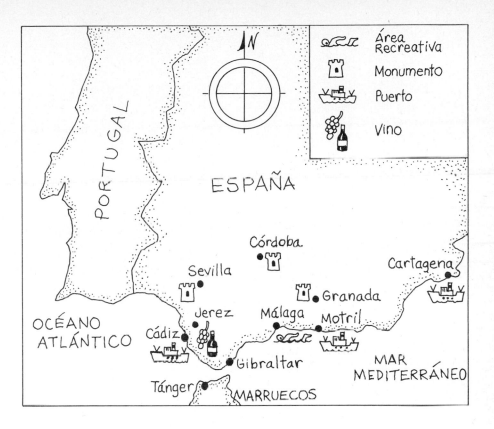

C. Look at the maps on the inside of the text cover. Complete the following statements, using the appropriate Spanish word referring to a point of the compass. Note that **al** means *to the*, and **en el** means *in the* in this exercise.

1. El Océano Atlántico está al _____ de México.
2. La República Dominicana está al _____ de los Estados Unidos.
3. Ciudad Juárez está en el _____ de México.
4. Punta Arenas está en el _____ de Chile.
5. La Costa Brava está en el _____ de España.

Unidad I
El mundo hispánico

Los habitantes de la capital mexicana llaman "angelito" a la representación de La Victoria que está en una columna de 150 pies. ¿Qué significa para ellos?

Lección I
El mundo hispánico

¿Cómo se llama usted?

Two students, Felipe Arrojo from Salamanca, Spain, and Cristina Marcano from Tucumán, Argentina, introduce themselves.

Monólogo 1
Me llamo Felipe Arrojo Ortiz.
Soy de Salamanca, España.
Soy estudiante.
Estudio ciencias políticas en la Universidad de Salamanca.

My name is Felipe Arrojo Ortiz.
I'm from Salamanca, Spain.
I'm a student.
I'm studying political science at the University of Salamanca.

Monólogo 2
Y yo me llamo Cristina Marcano Campos.
Soy de Tucumán, Argentina.
Soy estudiante también.
Estudio medicina en la Universidad de Buenos Aires.

And my name is Cristina Marcano Campos.
I'm from Tucumán, Argentina.
I'm a student also.
I'm studying medicine at the University of Buenos Aires.

Comprensión

Answer the following questions based on Monologues 1 and 2.

Preguntas sobre el Monólogo 1

1. ¿Es de Salamanca o de Madrid Felipe Arrojo?	Felipe es de . . .
2. ¿Es estudiante o profesor Felipe?	Felipe es . . .
3. ¿Es de Francia Felipe?	No, Felipe no es de . . .
4. ¿De qué país es?	Es de . . .
5. ¿Estudia en la Universidad de Salamanca?	Sí, Felipe estudia en . . .

Preguntas sobre el Monólogo 2

1. ¿Es de Salamanca Cristina Marcano?	No, Cristina no es de . . .
2. ¿Es de México Cristina Marcano?	No, Cristina no es de . . .
3. ¿De qué país es?	Es de . . .
4. ¿Es estudiante Cristina Marcano?	Sí, Cristina es . . .
5. ¿Estudia medicina o lenguas modernas?	Estudia . . .
6. ¿Estudia en la Universidad de Valencia?	No, no estudia en . . . Estudia en . . .

Conversación

Answer the following questions about yourself, according to the indications given.

1. ¿Es usted estudiante, señor (señora, señorita)?	Sí, soy . . .
2. ¿Cómo se llama usted, señor (señora, señorita)?	Me llamo . . .
3. Y usted, señorita (señor, señora), ¿cómo se llama?	Me . . .
4. ¿Es usted de España?	No, no soy de . . .
5. ¿De qué país es usted?	Soy de . . .
6. ¿Estudia usted en un colegio o en una universidad?	Estudio en . . .
7. ¿Qué lengua moderna estudia usted?	. . . español.
8. ¿Usted también estudia inglés?	Sí, . . . No, no . . .

Situaciones

1. Role-play one of the following people at a party. When someone asks you what you do and what country you come from, provide him/her with that information.

   —Soy . . . (estudiante, profesor/a, doctor/a, médico/a) y soy de . . . (los Estados Unidos, España, México).

2. Your advisor wants to know whether you are studying political science. Provide him/her with that information.

—¿Estudia ciencias políticas?
—No, estudio . . . (lenguas modernas, historia, medicina, inglés, geografía).

Práctica

A. Introduce yourself in Spanish to the student seated next to you, and say what city or town you are from. Then ask him/her for the same information, using the familiar form **Y tú, ¿cómo te llamas?** (And you, what's your name?).

▶ S1: *Me llamo _____. Soy de San Diego; y tú, ¿cómo te llamas?*
▶ S2: *Me llamo _____ y soy de _____.*

B. Pretend that you are in Buenos Aires and have just met a young person at the university. Find out what his/her full name is, whether he/she is a student or a teacher, and if he/she studies medicine, political science, or a modern language.

Nota cultural Spanish surnames

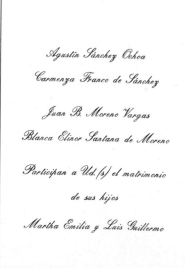

Agustín Sánchez Ochoa
Carmenza Franco de Sánchez

Juan B. Moreno Vargas
Blanca Elinor Santana de Moreno

Participan a Ud.(s) el matrimonio
de sus hijos

Martha Emilia y Luis Guillermo

English speakers are often surprised at the apparent complexity of Spanish family names **(apellidos)**. In the United States, the surname generally consists of the father's last name; for example, John *Smith*. Spanish last names are usually composed of the father's first surname followed by the mother's first family name. For example, in the full name **Felipe Arrojo Ortiz, Arrojo** is the father's first surname, and **Ortiz** is the mother's first family name. Felipe would probably be referred to as **Felipe Arrojo** in ordinary conversation. If clarification were requested or needed, as in introductions or formal job applications, both surnames would be used. Sometimes surnames may also be expressed by joining the names with **y** or a hyphen, as in **Arrojo y Ortiz** or **Arrojo-Ortiz.**

Legally, a woman or a man keeps the same name throughout his/her life. When a woman marries, she may choose to drop her mother's family name and add her husband's surname, which is generally preceded by **de.** For example, if **Cristina Marcano Campos** married **Felipe Arrojo Ortiz,** she would probably be referred to as **Cristina de Arrojo** or **Cristina Marcano de Arrojo.**

*Siempre hay estudiantes en la Plaza Mayor de Salamanca, España porque Salamanca
tiene una universidad importante. Otras personas del área también van a la Plaza Mayor
para pasar parte del día. Observe el tipo de personas en la plaza. ¿Es importante la plaza
en la cultura hispánica? ¿Por qué?*

Hola, ¿qué tal?

*Felipe Arrojo and Alicia Díaz, two students at the University of Salamanca,
greet each other and speak briefly before continuing on their way.*

Felipe: Hola, Alicia, ¿qué tal? ¿Cómo estás?
Alicia: Muy bien, gracias. ¿Y tú?
Felipe: Como siempre, gracias.
Alicia: Pues . . . es tarde. Adiós, Felipe. ¡Hasta el lunes!
Felipe: Ah, sí, hoy es viernes. ¡Hasta el lunes!

Felipe: *Hi, Alicia, how are things? How are you?*
Alicia: *Fine (Very well), thanks. And you?*
Felipe: *Same as usual, thanks.*
Alicia: *Well . . . it's late, good-by, Felipe. See you on Monday!*
Felipe: *Oh, yes, today is Friday. See you Monday!*

Comprensión

1. ¿Es estudiante o profesora Alicia?   Alicia es . . .
2. ¿Estudia Alicia en la Universidad   Sí, Alicia estudia . . .
   de Salamanca?
3. ¿Es estudiante Felipe?   Sí, Felipe es . . .

4. ¿Estudia Felipe en la Universidad de Madrid?

No, Felipe no estudia . . .

5. ¿Cómo está Alicia?

Alicia está . . .

6. ¿Cómo está Felipe?

Felipe está . . .

Conversación

1. ¿Es usted profesor (profesora)?

No, no soy . . .

2. ¿Estudia usted en la Universidad de Salamanca?

No, no estudio . . .

3. ¿Estudia usted en la Universidad de . . .?

Sí, estudio . . .

4. ¿Cómo está usted, señor (señora, señorita)?

Estoy . . .

5. ¡Adiós, señor (señora, señorita)!

¡Hasta . . ., (señor)!

Situaciones

1. You meet a friend on your way to the bank and ask him/her how he/she is.

—¿Qué tal, (Marta), cómo estás?
—(Muy bien, Bien, Regular, Así así, Como siempre), gracias.

2. It's the end of class. Say good-by to the student seated next to you.

—¡Adiós, (Miguel)!
—¡Chau, (Ana), hasta . . . (el lunes, pronto, luego, la vista, mañana).

Práctica

Role-play the dialogue on page 17, substituting your own first name for that of **Felipe** or **Alicia**. If you prefer, use one of the Spanish names **(nombres)** listed below. The names **José** (*Joseph*) and **María** (*Mary*) often form compound names, as in **José Luis** and **María Mercedes.**

Nombres de pila de muchachos (*First names of boys*)

Andrés	Enrique	José	Pedro	Antonio	Fernando
Luis	Raúl	Carlos	Jaime	Mario	Tomás

Nombres de pila de muchachas (*First names of girls*)

Alicia	Elena	Lisa	Patricia	Carmen	Inés
María	Pilar	Dolores	Isabel	Margarita	Rosa

Nota cultural Formality in greetings

In Spanish, as in English, speakers use different levels of formality in the language, depending on the situation, the person or persons with whom they are speaking, and regional variations. For example, in the dialogue *Hola, ¿qué tal?*, Felipe uses **hola** to say hello to his friend Alicia. If Felipe met a professor at the university, he would probably greet him/her with a more formal **Buenos días** (*Hello, good morning*).

In most Spanish-speaking countries, people shake hands more frequently than in the United States. Acquaintances often shake hands at the beginning of a conversation and when they say good-by. Young people often touch each other lightly on the arm or shoulder rather than shake hands. Older women tend to exchange a light kiss **(un beso)** on one or both cheeks. Older men may give each other an embrace or hug **(un abrazo)**, especially if they have not seen each other for a long time.

When two friends pass on the street, they may stop, shake hands, and talk for a while. If they do not intend to stop and talk, their greeting may be a simple **¡Hola!** or **¡Adiós!**, accompanied by a friendly raising of the hand. These expressions are a polite acknowledgement, equivalent to *Hi!* or nodding your head in English-speaking cultures.

Vocabulario

The *Vocabulario* contains the basic words and expressions used in the core material (monologues, dialogues, and corresponding questions and activities) of each lesson. Most close cognates are listed in alphabetical order at the beginning of each *Vocabulario* section.

El abrazo (embrace) *es común en el mundo hispánico y es una demostración de afecto especial. Estos hombres, ¿son familia o amigos? ¿Es frecuente el abrazo en los Estados Unidos? (Cali, Colombia)*

Palabras análogas

un adjetivo	una expresión	una variación
una comprensión	una historia	un verbo
una conversación	un monólogo	un vocabulario
un doctor	un profesor	
una doctora	una profesora	

Sustantivos

ciencias políticas political science
español Spanish (*language*)
los Estados Unidos the United States
un estudiante, una estudiante a student
inglés English (*language*)

una lección a lesson
una lengua moderna a modern language
lunes Monday
un médico a medical doctor
un país a country

una pregunta a question
un señor a gentleman; **señor** (+ last name) Mr. (+ last name)
una señora a lady; **señora** (+ last name) Mrs. (+ last name)
una señorita a young lady; **señorita** (+ last name) Miss (+ last name)
un sustantivo a noun
viernes Friday

Adjetivos
otro, -a other, another

Verbos
es he/she is; *(formal)* you are; it is
¿es usted? are you?
estoy I am
está he/she is; *(formal)* you are; it is
estudio I study, am studying
estudia he/she studies, is studying; you *(formal)* study, are studying
¿estudia usted? do you study?
soy I am

Otras palabras y expresiones
adiós good-by
así, así so-so
bien well
¿cómo? how?
¿cómo está usted? how are you? *(formal)*
¿cómo estás? how are you? *(familiar)*
¿cómo se llama usted? what's your name? *(formal)*
como siempre same as usual
¡chau! so long!, by!
de of, from
¿de qué país? from what country?
en in, at
es tarde it's late
gracias thanks, thank you
hasta luego see you later
hasta el lunes see you Monday
hasta mañana see you tomorrow
hasta pronto see you soon
hasta la vista see you later (I'll be seeing you)
hola hi, hello
hoy today
me llamo my name is (*literally,* I call myself)
muy bien very well
no no, not
o or
pues well
¿qué? what?
¿qué tal? how are things?
regular not bad
sí yes; **ah, sí** oh, yes
sobre about
también also, too
tú you *(familiar)*
usted you *(formal)*
y and
yo I

Pronunciación y ortografía

I. Sound/letter correspondence

In Spanish, as in English, sounds and letters do not always correspond. However, there are more consistent spelling patterns in Spanish than in English. As a guide to correct pronunciation, phonetic symbols within brackets will sometimes be used in this text to represent specific sounds. For example, the symbol [k] is used to represent the sound that is used at the beginning of the Spanish word **que**. A complete list of the phonetic symbols is given in Appendix B.

II. Basic vowel sounds and Spanish syllables

1. There are five basic vowel sounds in Spanish: **[a]**, **[e]**, **[i]**, **[o]**, and **[u]**. Spanish vowels are pronounced as short, quick, distinct sounds. They

are never pronounced as a *schwa* ("uh" sound), as in the second syllable of the word *vowel [vowuhl]*; nor are they pronounced as a glide, as in the first syllable of the word *basic [beysik]*.

2. A Spanish syllable always contains one vowel (**a, e, i, o,** or **u**) or a vowel combination (for example, a diphthong such as **ia, ie,** or **ue**). A syllable is considered *open* if it ends in a vowel or vowel combination (as in **Cla-ra**) and *closed* if it ends in a consonant (as in **An-drés**). For more on Spanish syllables, refer to *Lección 4.*

A. Listen to your instructor pronounce the following names of countries, first in Spanish, then in English. Your instructor will then say the Spanish names again. Repeat the Spanish names, being careful to imitate his/her pronunciation.

Costa Rica	Costa Rica	**Panamá**	Panama	**Cuba**	Cuba
Chile	Chile	**Perú**	Peru	**Honduras**	Honduras

B. Pronounce the following Spanish first names after your instructor. Pay special attention to the way you pronounce the letters **a, e, i, o,** and **u.** The names are divided into syllables, and the stressed syllable is shown in boldface type.

Cla-ra	E-**li**-sa	I-sa-**bel**	**Car**-los	Ar-**tu**-ro
Pa-blo	E-**le**-na	Ma-ri-**sol**	**Pe**-dro	Su-**sa**-na
Ro-sa	Fe-**li**-pe	An-**drés**	**Hu**-go	Ro-**ber**-to

C. Tell who comes from which country by combining the names of people in Exercise B with the names of countries listed in Exercise A.

▶ *[Clara] es de [Perú].*

III. Accent marks and punctuation marks

1. In written Spanish, an accent mark (called **acento** or **tilde**) occurs only on a vowel, as in **Perú.** Accent marks do not occur in words that are pronounced according to normal stress patterns. They are an important part of Spanish spelling because they indicate how a word is stressed. Note that the letter **ñ** is a separate letter in the alphabet and not the letter **n** with a **tilde,** as it is called in English.

Bárbara **Gó**mez   An**drés** Gon**zá**lez

2. An accent mark is sometimes used to distinguish between pairs of words that look and sound alike, but have different meanings and grammatical functions.

cómo	how	**qué**	what	**sí**	yes	**mí**	me
como	as	**que**	that	**si**	if	**mi**	my

3. An inverted question mark ¿ (**signo de interrogación**) or an inverted exclamation point ¡ (**signo de exclamación** or **admiración**) at the beginning of a sentence or phrase serves as a visual cue that a question or exclamation follows. A regular question mark or exclamation point also occurs at the end of the sentence or phrase.

¿Cómo se llama usted?   ¡Hasta el lunes, Alicia!
Y usted, ¿cómo se llama?   Pues . . . ¡adiós, Felipe!

D. Write the following sentences as dictated. Then exchange papers with a classmate and correct his/her accent marks and punctuation.

   1. Andrés, ¿estudias lenguas modernas?
   2. ¡Hasta el lunes, Bárbara!
   3. ¿Cómo estás, Antonio?
   4. Soy de Tucumán, Argentina.

Estudio de palabras

I. Los días de la semana *(The days of the week)*

1. The following are the days of the week in Spanish. Note that in Spanish-speaking countries, most calendars begin with Monday **(lunes)** as the first day of the week.

lunes   martes   miércoles   jueves   viernes   sábado   domingo

2. In Spanish, the days of the week are not usually capitalized unless they occur at the beginning of a sentence.

— ¿Qué día es hoy?	*What day is today?*
— **Viernes,** todo el día.	*Friday, all day long.*
— ¡Qué bien! **El viernes** es mi día favorito.	*How nice! Friday is my favorite* *day.*

A. Name the days that precede and follow the ones listed below.

▶ viernes   *jueves, sábado*

   1. domingo   2. martes   3. jueves   4. miércoles

B. Say good-by to your friend Luis. He will then say good-by to you. Use **el** and any day of the week you like.

▶ S1: *Adiós, Luis. Hasta el lunes.*   S2: *No, hasta el domingo. Chau.*

C. Answer the following questions.

   1. ¿Hoy es lunes? ¿martes? ¿miércoles? ¿Qué día es?
   2. ¿Qué día es mañana *(tomorrow)*?

3. Si (*If*) mañana es viernes, ¿que día es hoy?
4. Si hoy es sábado, ¿qué día es mañana?
5. Hoy es jueves, ¿no?
6. Mañana es domingo, ¿no?

II. Palabras análogas (*Cognates*)

As you read in the preliminary lesson (*Palabras análogas*), cognates are words in two languages that resemble each other in spelling and meaning, but are pronounced differently.

D. Listen carefully as your instructor pronounces the following words. Repeat each word and then give the meaning in English.

comprensión	lección	pronunciación	moderna
monólogo	medicina	diálogo	superior
vocabulario	ortografía	doctor	práctica
profesor	cultural	verbo	adjetivo

E. Complete each of the following sentences with an appropriate word. Note that the first letter of the word is already given.

1. Estudio la l _____.
2. El señor Ortiz es p _____ de historia.
3. ¿Estudia usted m _____?
4. ¿De qué país es el d _____ Campos?
5. ¿Qué lengua m _____ estudia Cristina?
6. No estudio el v _____ de la lección, estudio la nota c _____.

Estructuras útiles

I. Subject pronouns

—¿Es **usted** de España, señorita?
—¿Quién, **yo?**
—Sí, **usted.**
—No, no soy de España. Soy de los Estados Unidos.

On the following page is a chart of the subject pronouns in Spanish. Note that **tú, usted, vosotros,** and **ustedes** all mean *you.* Spanish has no equivalent for the subject pronoun *it.*

Singular	Plural	
yo I	**nosotros**	we *(m or group of m and f)*
	nosotras	we *(f)*
tú you *(fam.)*	**vosotros**	you *(m or group of m and f; fam.)*
	vosotras	you *(f) (fam.)*
usted you *(formal)*	**ustedes**	you *(fam. or formal)*
él he	**ellos**	they *(m or group of m and f)*
ella she	**ellas**	they *(f)*

1. The familiar pronoun **tú** is used to address someone you know on a first-name basis, such as a child, a close relative, a friend, or a fellow student. The more formal pronoun **usted** is normally used to address a person whom the speaker does not address on a first-name basis.
2. In Hispanic America, **ustedes** is used to address more than one person, whether the relationship is formal or familiar.
3. **Usted** and **ustedes** may be abbreviated to **Ud.** and **Uds.** or to **Vd.** and **Vds.** In this text, only the abbreviations **Ud.** and **Uds.** will be used.
4. In Spain, two different pronouns are used to address more than one person: **vosotros/as** and **ustedes.** The plural form of **tú** is **vosotros** and **vosotras;** the plural form of **usted** is **ustedes.**
5. The masculine plural forms **ellos, nosotros,** and **vosotros** may refer to an all-male group or to a mixed group of males and females. The feminine plural forms **ellas, nosotras,** and **vosotras** refer to an all-female group.

A. Which subject pronoun (**tú, usted, ustedes, vosotros,** or **vosotras**) would you be likely to use in addressing the following persons (a) if you were living in Madrid? or (b) if you were living in Mexico City?

▶ your friend Jorge   (a) *tú*, (b) *tú*

1. your uncle and aunt
2. a police officer
3. the dean of the university
4. a teacher
5. the governor of your state
6. two strangers
7. your younger sisters
8. your best friend
9. three good friends
10. your doctor

B. Give the subject pronoun that would be used to refer to the persons indicated.

▶ Ana y Luisa   *ellas*

1. Ricardo
2. María
3. Fernando y yo
4. señorita Martínez
5. Felipe y María
6. señor Blanco
7. usted y Linda
8. profesor Monte y profesora Caro

II. Present tense and uses of **ser**

—*¿Son ustedes de Ecuador?*
—*Sí, somos de Ecuador. Somos de Guayaquil.*

1. The verb **ser** is irregular in Spanish as is the verb *to be* in English. Note that **ser** has six different irregular forms in the present tense, while *to be* has only three *(am, are, is)*. Learn all the conjugated forms (the forms that agree with or match the subject pronouns) of **ser,** which are presented in the chart below.

	ser	
yo	**soy**	I am (I'm)
tú	**eres**	you *(fam.)* are
usted	**es**	you *(formal)* are
él, ella	**es**	he/she is
nosotros, -as	**somos**	we are
vosotros, -as	**sois**	you *(fam., in Spain)* are
ustedes	**son**	you *(fam. or formal)* are
ellos, ellas	**son**	they are

2. Subject pronouns are normally omitted in Spanish, especially when it is clear from the verb form or context who the subject is.

Soy Felipe Arrojo. *I'm Felipe Arrojo.*
Somos de Portugal. *We're from Portugal.*

3. Subject pronouns are generally used for clarity, contrast, or emphasis.

Son Luis y Marta. **Él** es de Panamá y **ella** es de Costa Rica. *It's Luis and Marta. He's from Panama and she's from Costa Rica.*

— **Tú** eres de Chile, ¿no? *You're from Chile, right?*
— No, **yo** no soy de Chile, soy de Argentina. *No, I'm not from Chile, I'm from Argentina.*

4. The subject pronouns **usted** and **ustedes** are often used for purposes of courtesy, as well as for clarity.

Buenos días. ¿Es **usted** el doctor?   *Good morning. Are you the doctor?*

5. A sentence is made negative by using **no** before the verb form. To make **ser** negative, use **no** before the verb forms **soy, eres, es,** et cetera.

Soy chileno, **no soy** colombiano.   *I'm Chilean, I'm not Colombian.*
¿No eres estudiante?   *Aren't you a student?*
No somos de Perú.   *We're not from Peru.*

6. The verb **ser** is one of the most commonly used verbs in Spanish. It is used to indicate:
a. nationality

— **¿Eres** colombiano o venezolano?   *Are you Colombian or Venezuelan?*
— **Soy** colombiano.   *I'm Colombian.*

b. occupation or profession, or membership in a group (such as religious or political affiliation). Note that the indefinite articles **un** and **una** are usually omitted before a noun of nationality or profession.

— **¿Es** Pedro profesor o médico?   *Is Pedro a professor or a doctor?*
— **Es** médico.   *He's a doctor.*

— **¿Es** capitalista o comunista?   *Is he a capitalist or a communist?*
— **Es** capitalista.   *He's a capitalist.*

c. place of origin, when accompanied by **de**

— **¿De** qué país **son** ustedes?   *What country are you from?*
— **Somos de** Perú.   *We're from Peru.*

C. Say that the following people are from the countries indicated.

▶ ellas / Costa Rica   *Ellas son de Costa Rica.*

1. tú / México
2. él / El Salvador
3. ellos / España
4. tú y él / Venezuela
5. ustedes / Perú
6. nosotras / Ecuador
7. ellas / Puerto Rico
8. yo / Argentina
9. usted / Colombia

D. Clarify whether the following people are or are not doctors, students, or professors, according to the cues. Use the occupation ending in **-a** when referring to a female.

▶ Teresa (sí)   *Teresa es [estudiante, doctora, profesora].*
▶ Alberto (no)   *Alberto no es [estudiante, doctor, profesor].*

1. usted (sí)	4. tú (no)
2. Miguel Gómez (no)	5. ella (sí)
3. Luisa (sí)	6. Paco (no)

E. Answer the following questions in the affirmative or in the negative. Remember to answer with the adjective of nationality ending in **-o** if you are a male, and **-a** if you are a female.

▶ ¿Es usted argentino/a? *Sí, soy argentino/a.*
No, no soy argentino/a; soy [norteamericano/a].

1. ¿Es usted puertorriqueño/a?	5. ¿Eres colombiano/a?
2. ¿Es usted boliviano/a?	6. ¿Eres mexicano/a?
3. ¿Es usted hondureño/a?	7. ¿Eres uruguayo/a?
4. ¿Es usted cubano/a?	8. ¿Eres norteamericano/a?

F. Ask your instructor and several classmates if they are from various Spanish-speaking countries. Use **usted** when addressing your instructor, and **tú** when addressing another student.

▶ *¿Es usted de Colombia, [señor]?*
▶ *¿Eres de Argentina, [Miguel]?*

¿Comprende usted?
Developing reading skills

The *¿Comprende usted?* selections are intended to help you develop the skill of understanding new reading materials in Spanish, improve your knowledge of the language, and open new interests. By the end of the program, you should be able to read a variety of materials in this section with little or no help from a dictionary.

As you read new material in Spanish, follow the steps given below. They will help you gain confidence in your ability to use the language, save you time and effort, and consolidate your other language skills as well.

1. Read the complete text and concentrate on what you do understand rather than on what you do not. Try to grasp the basic message of sentences and paragraphs, looking for cognates to help you understand the meaning.
2. Read the text a second time, trying to see how the parts that you understood the first time may clarify some of the parts that you did not understand.
3. Go back over the selection and underline key words that you still do not understand. There will be a few new, non-cognate words included

in the reading. Make an educated guess about the meaning of the
words you have underlined, trying to make global sense of the text,
rather than a word-for-word English rendition of it.

4. Look up your underlined words in the end vocabulary, or be more
   daring and move on to step 5 without checking the vocabulary until
   after you have finished doing the exercises.
5. Do the exercises, trying to create mental images of key words and
   phrases rather than flash English words in your mind.
6. Read the selection once more. Remember that you do not need to
   understand every individual word in order to understand the basic
   meaning of the selection.

Estereotipos hispánicos

Los estereotipos culturales describen parte de la realidad, pero no son la
realidad total. Para muchos norteamericanos, el estereotipo de México representa toda Hispanoamérica y España: tacos, enchiladas, mariachis, sombreros enormes. Para otros norteamericanos, los problemas políticos de un
5 país hispánico son una representación de todos los países hispánicos: el
dictador, la revolución, la guerrilla. Y finalmente, el estereotipo tradicional
del individuo hispánico es el Don Juan, el romántico, el macho, el matador.
   Los hispanos también crean estereotipos de los norteamericanos: millonarios, materialistas, cándidos, inocentes en la política, generosos. Natu-
10 ralmente, el estereotipo del norteamericano también se basa en la realidad,
pero no es la realidad en su totalidad. Los estereotipos son simplistas y la
realidad es compleja. ¡Es importante comprender la diferencia!

A. Match each Spanish word with its English equivalent in the right-hand
   column.

1. representa	is based
2. realidad	complex
3. crean	dictator
4. políticos	reality
5. tradicional	millionaires
6. millonarios	part
7. se basa	political
8. dictador	traditional
9. compleja	represents
10. revolución	create
11. parte	revolution

B. Read the following words and create a *detailed* mental picture of the person or thing they represent. Then compare your mental picture with that of a classmate.

millonario, dictador, norteamericano, hispano, guerrilla

C. *¿Verdad o falso?* Say whether the following statements are true or false, according to the reading.

1. Para muchos norteamericanos, los mexicanos simbolizan a los hispanos en general.
2. Los hispanos observan y comprenden la realidad norteamericana en su totalidad.
3. Unos estereotipos se basan en la tradición.
4. Unos estereotipos son parte de la realidad.

D. Write two sentences that summarize the reading (one for each paragraph).

(Arriba) Uno de los estereotipos del mundo hispánico es el baile flamenco. (Barcelona, España) (Abajo) También existe una realidad moderna, como lo confirma esta fotografía de un grupo artístico que prepara un vídeo de música contemporánea en San Juan, Puerto Rico. ¿Qué foto cree Ud. es más representativa de la cultura hispánica? ¿Por qué?

Lección 2
El mundo hispánico

¿Dónde vive usted?

An auto mechanic from Valencia, Spain, and a nurse from Nuevo Laredo, Mexico introduce themselves and mention their nationalities and occupations.

Monólogo 1
Me llamo Jorge Ramírez.
Soy español y vivo en Valencia.
Valencia es una ciudad industrial del este de España.
No tengo hijos: soy soltero.
Soy mecánico y trabajo en una fábrica de automóviles.

My name is Jorge Ramírez.
I'm Spanish and live in Valencia.
Valencia is an industrial city in the east of Spain.
I don't have any children: I'm single.
I'm a mechanic, and I work in an automobile factory.

Monólogo 2
Me llamo Rosa Jiménez de García.
Soy mexicana y vivo en Nuevo Laredo.
Nuevo Laredo es un pueblo del norte de México.
Soy casada y tengo tres hijos.
Soy enfermera y trabajo en un hospital.

My name is Rosa Jiménez de García.
I'm Mexican and I live in Nuevo Laredo.
Nuevo Laredo is a town in the north of Mexico.
I'm married and have three children.
I'm a nurse, and I work in a hospital.

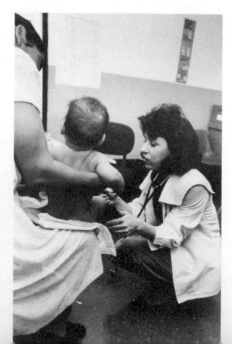

Comprensión

Preguntas sobre el Monólogo 1

1. ¿Es español o mexicano Jorge Ramírez?
2. ¿De qué país es, de España o de México?
3. ¿En qué ciudad vive?
4. ¿Es Valencia una ciudad del norte o del este de España?
5. ¿Es soltero o casado Jorge? ¿Tiene hijos?
6. ¿Es mecánico o enfermero Jorge?
7. ¿Dónde trabaja Jorge? ¿en una fábrica o en un hospital?

Preguntas sobre el Monólogo 2

1. ¿Es profesora o enfermera Rosa Jiménez de García?
2. ¿De qué nacionalidad es?
3. ¿En qué pueblo vive?
4. ¿Es Nuevo Laredo un pueblo del este o del norte de México?
5. ¿Es soltera o casada Rosa? ¿Tiene dos o tres hijos?
6. ¿Dónde trabaja Rosa? ¿en una fábrica, en un colegio o en un hospital?

Conversación

1. ¿Es usted norteamericano, señor?   Sí, soy . . ., (No, no soy . . .)
2. ¿Es usted norteamericana, señorita?   Sí, soy . . ., (No, no soy . . .)
3. ¿En qué país vive usted, señora?   Vivo en . . .
4. ¿En qué estado vive usted, señor?   Vivo en . . .
5. ¿Vive usted en un pueblo o en una   Vivo en . . .
   ciudad, señor?
6. ¿Es usted enfermera o estudiante,   Soy . . .
   señorita?
7. ¿Es usted mecánico o estudiante,   Soy . . .
   señor?
8. ¿Trabaja usted, señorita?   Sí, trabajo . . . (No, no trabajo . . .)
9. ¿Es usted casado/a o soltero/a?   Soy . . .

Situaciones

1. You're at a function of the Spanish Club. Respond to a guest who asks if you are Spanish.

   —¿Eres español?
   —No, soy . . . (norteamericano/a, americano/a, mexicano/a, canadiense).

2. You meet a young Mexican on a plane trip. Find out where he/she works.

   —¿Dónde trabaja usted?
   —Trabajo en . . . (una fábrica, un hospital, una universidad). Soy . . .
      (mecánico/a, enfermero/a, profesor/a).

Estos estudiantes madrileños toman café y charlan (chat) con los amigos en un bar cerca de la Universidad Complutense de Madrid. Es frecuente en España ir al bar entre las clases. ¿Dónde charlan los estudiantes norteamericanos: en un bar, en una cafetería, en un restaurante?

Práctica

Pretend that you are at the bar shown in the photo above and are speaking with a stranger. Ask his/her name, what country he/she is from, what city or town he/she lives in, whether he/she is Spanish or Mexican, and where he/she works. Use the vocabulary and structures from the monologues in this lesson.

Nota cultural The term **americano/americana**

The term **americano/americana** is used in formal language (books, classrooms, lectures) to refer to any person that has been born in the western hemisphere. In most other contexts it is used to refer to a citizen of the United States. To refer more precisely to someone born in the United States **(los Estados Unidos)**, a speaker may use the term **estadounidense** or **norteamericano/norteamericana.** The latter term could theoretically apply to a Mexican or a Canadian, however, since Mexico and Canada are also part of the North American continent. Spanish speakers usually use the term **mexicano/mexicana** to refer to a Mexican, and **canadiense** to refer to a Canadian.

Buenos días

Inés Gómez arrives at the hospital to visit her mother just as one of the doctors, Julio Martínez, is leaving. She asks about her mother's health and exchanges greetings with the doctor before he leaves.

Srta. Gómez: Buenos días, Dr. Martínez. ¿Cómo está mi mamá hoy?
Dr. Martínez: Buenos días, señorita. Está bastante bien y muy tranquila. Y usted, ¿cómo está?
Srta. Gómez: Muy bien . . . y muchas gracias, doctor.
Dr. Martínez: De nada, señorita.
Srta. Gómez: Pues, hasta luego, doctor.
Dr. Martínez: Hasta pronto, señorita. Aquí estoy a sus órdenes.

Srta. Gómez: *Good morning, Dr. Martínez. How is my mother today?*
Dr. Martínez: *Good morning, Miss (Gómez). She's feeling quite well and (is) very calm. And how are you?*
Srta. Gómez: *Very well . . . and thank you so much, doctor.*
Dr. Martínez: *That's quite all right, Miss (Gómez).*
Srta. Gómez: *Well, doctor, I'll see you later.*
Dr. Martínez: *I'll see you soon, Miss (Gómez). I'm (always) here at your service.*

Comprensión

1. ¿Cómo se llama el doctor?   Se llama . . .
2. ¿Dónde trabaja él?   Trabaja en . . .
3. ¿Cuál es el apellido de Inés?   El apellido de Inés es . . .
4. ¿Cómo está la mamá de Inés?   La mamá de Inés está . . .
5. ¿Cómo está Inés?   Inés está . . .

Conversación

1. ¿Cuál es su apellido, señor (señora, señorita)?   Mi apellido es . . .
2. ¿Dónde trabaja usted?   Trabajo en . . .
3. ¿Cómo está su mamá?   Mi mamá está . . .
4. ¿Cómo está usted?   Estoy . . .

Situaciones

1. You are at the hospital. Find out from the doctor how a member of your family is doing.

    —Doctor/a, ¿cómo está mi . . . (mamá, hijo, hija)?
    —Está . . . (bien, bastante bien, muy bien, muy tranquilo/a).

2. You are returning coats to the guests who checked them in before the annual student play at your college. They thank you.

—Muchas gracias, . . . (señor/a, señorita).
—. . . (De nada, A sus órdenes, A la orden, Para servirle),
. . . (señor/a, señorita). Buenas noches.

Práctica

A. Role-play the dialogue between Inés Gómez and Dr. Martínez. Change the names, if you like, to those of individuals you know.

B. Review the common expressions for saying good-by from *Lección 1*. Use some of them to say good-by to your friends and classmates when you see them on campus or at the end of the class period.

Nota cultural Use of first names and courtesy titles

The use of first names among adults is usually reserved for informal speech. Among friends, first and/or last names are used interchangeably with no special connotation of respect or distance. For example, if two friends, José Andino and Pedro Muñoz, are talking, they might call each other **José** and **Pedro** or **Andino** and **Muñoz.**

Often the courtesy titles **señor, señora,** and **señorita** (abbreviated in writing to **Sr., Sra.,** and **Srta.**) are used in place of a name. At present there is no universally accepted Spanish term for *Ms.*, as in *Ms. Smith,* though

Miguel Hernández López,
    Sra. e hijos
Calle 5 de mayo #89
Salta, Argentina

10 PESOS

JUAN B. AMBROSETTI

REPUBLICA ARGENTINA

Dra. Milagros Amador de Pereira
Avenida de la Independencia #36
Santiago de los Caballeros
República Dominicana

some people use **Sa.** in writing. Sometimes professional titles such as **doctor/a** or **profesor/a** are used as substitutes for names. Thus, it is correct to address a person with a polite **señor/a, doctor/a, profesor/a, licenciado/a** *(lawyer)*.

In most Spanish-speaking countries, the courtesy titles **don** and **doña** are used when speaking to adults and usually signify respect (whether of age or social position). **Don** is used with a man's first name (**don Miguel, don José**), and **doña** is used with a woman's first name (**doña Rosa, doña Carmen**). **Doña** may refer to a married or single woman.

Vocabulario

Palabras análogas

americano, -a	**industrial**	**mexicano, -a**
una clase	**mamá**	**norteamericano, -a**
un hospital	**un mecánico, una mecánica**	**tranquilo, -a**

Sustantivos

un apellido   a last name
una ciudad   a city
un enfermero, una enfermera   a nurse
un estado   a state
una fábrica   a factory
una fábrica de automóviles   an automobile factory
un hijo   a son; a child (as related to parents)
una hija   a daughter
hijos   sons; children (as related to parents)
una nacionalidad   a nationality
un pueblo   a town

trabajo   I work, am working
trabajas   you *(fam.)* work, are working
trabaja   he/she/it works, is working; you *(formal)* work, are working
vivo   I live, am living
vives   you *(fam.)* live, are living
vive   he/she lives, is living; you *(formal)* live, are living

Otras palabras y expresiones

a la orden   at your service;   *(pl.)* **a sus órdenes**
aquí estoy a sus órdenes   I'm (always) here at your service
bastante bien   quite well
buenas tardes (noches)   good afternoon (evening, night)
buenos días   good morning, hello
¿cómo está mi mamá?   how is my mother?
¿cuál?   which, what?
de nada   you're welcome, not at all
¿dónde?   where?
hasta   until
muchas gracias   thank you very much
muy   very
para servirle   at your service

Adjetivos

canadiense   Canadian
casado, -a   married
dos   two
español, -a   Spanish
mi   my;   *(pl.)* **mis**
soltero, -a   single
su   your *(formal)*;   *(pl.)* **sus**
tres   three

Verbos

se llama   his/her name is
tengo   I have
tienes   you *(fam.)* have
tiene   he/she/it has;   you *(formal)* have

Pronunciación y ortografía

I. Intonation patterns

1. Intonation refers to the rise and fall of the voice in speaking. In Spanish, a falling intonation pattern is normally used for statements, exclamations, commands, and for information questions (questions that begin with an interrogative word like **¿dónde?** and **¿quién?**).

Statement:	Me llamo Miguel.	*My name is Miguel.*
Exclamation:	¡Qué inteligente eres!	*How intelligent you are!*
Command:	¡Trabaje usted!	*Work!*
Information questions:	¿Quién es Jorge Ramírez?	*Who is Jorge Ramírez?*
	¿Dónde vive Rosa?	*Where does Rosa live?*

2. A rising intonation pattern is normally used for general questions (questions that can be answered with **sí** or **no**). In conversation, the verb form may precede or follow the subject.

General questions:	¿Eres de Madrid?	*Are you from Madrid?*
	¿Trabaja Miguel en un hospital?	*Does Miguel work in a hospital?*
	¿Miguel trabaja en un hospital?	

A. Read aloud the following sentences, using the correct intonation pattern.

1. Soy estudiante.
2. ¡Qué inteligente eres!
3. ¿Elena vive en Costa Rica?
4. ¿Quién vive en La Paz?
5. ¡Estudie usted!
6. ¿Eres de San Francisco?
7. ¿Dónde vive usted?
8. ¿De qué país es usted?

II. Linking within breath groups

In connected speech, words normally occur in breath groups (groups of words related to each other and usually followed by a slight pause). In Spanish, a breath group often sounds as though it were one long, multi-syllabled word. The following examples show where linking generally occurs in Spanish. You will learn more about linking in *Lección 5* after you have studied diphthongs.

1. A final consonant is linked to an initial vowel.

en un pueblo Él es español. ¿Es usted argentino?

2. If two consonants are identical, they fuse into one, slightly longer consonant.

un norteamericano   el lunes

3. If two vowels are identical, they fuse into one, slightly longer vowel.

Pepe es mecánico.   Es de Elena.

4. Since the letter **h** does not represent any sound in Spanish, linking occurs with the vowel that follows **h**.

un hospital   en Honduras   mi hijo

B. Read aloud the following sentences, linking the vowels and consonants as shown. Pronounce each breath group as though it were one long, multi-syllabled word.

1. María vive en España.
2. ¿Trabajas en un hotel?
3. Carmen está en Buenos Aires.
4. ¿Está Ana aquí?
5. No trabajo el lunes
6. Enrique estudia antropología.
7. ¡Es Sara!

Estudio de palabras

I. Los números de 0 a 20

The following are the Spanish names for the numbers **0** through **20**.

0 = **cero**			
1 = **uno**	6 = **seis**	11 = **once**	16 = **dieciséis**
2 = **dos**	7 = **siete**	12 = **doce**	17 = **diecisiete**
3 = **tres**	8 = **ocho**	13 = **trece**	18 = **dieciocho**
4 = **cuatro**	9 = **nueve**	14 = **catorce**	19 = **diecinueve**
5 = **cinco**	10 = **diez**	15 = **quince**	20 = **veinte**

A. Give the number that precedes and follows each number indicated.

▶ uno   *cero, dos*

1. cinco	4. cuatro	7. siete
2. nueve	5. dieciséis	8. seis
3. dos	6. diecinueve	9. doce

B. Ask another student to answer the following addition and subtraction problems. If your classmate makes an error, correct him/her.

▶ 3 + 3 = ?   S1: *¿Cuántos son tres y tres?*
             S2: *Tres y tres son seis.*
             S1: *Muy bien. ¿Y cuántos son . . . ?*
▶ 3 − 1 = ?   S1: *¿Cuántos son tres menos uno?*
             S2: *Tres menos uno son uno.*
             S1: *¡No, no, no! Tres menos uno son dos.*

1. 10 − 4 = ?	6. 8 − 4 = ?	11. 11 − 1 = ?
2. 6 + 3 = ?	7. 8 + 5 = ?	12. 10 + 4 = ?
3. 4 + 4 = ?	8. 7 + 8 = ?	13. 12 + 6 = ?
4. 9 − 7 = ?	9. 15 − 3 = ?	14. 14 + 5 = ?
5. 4 − 1 = ?	10. 13 − 8 = ?	15. 19 − 3 = ?

C. On a scale of 0 to 10, rate your ability to do activities like those indicated below.

▶ speak Spanish   *siete*

1. play the guitar	6. draw a portrait
2. spell in English	7. typewrite in English
3. handle a computer	8. sing the national anthem
4. drive a car	9. ride a motorcycle
5. dance	10. take color photos

II. Objetos de la clase

Learn the name of each classroom object shown in the drawing on page 39 and be prepared to identify it in Spanish. Note that both **un** and **una** mean *a, an,* or *one.*

D. Identify by number to another student each object in the drawing.

▶ S1: *[ocho]*   S2: *Es una mesa.*

E. Ask a classmate to identify an object in your classroom. If the object is close enough to you so that you can touch it, ask **¿Qué es esto?** *(What's this?).* Otherwise ask **¿Qué es eso?** *(What's that?).* Correct your classmate if he/she identifies the object incorrectly.

▶ S1: *¿Qué es esto?*   S2: *Es un libro.*
 S1: *Muy bien. Y ¿qué es eso?*   S2: *Es un bolígrafo.*
 S1: *No, no es un bolígrafo.*
   Es un lápiz.

1. un libro
2. un lápiz
3. un cuaderno
4. un escritorio
5. una calculadora
6. un papel
7. un bolígrafo, una pluma
8. una mesa
9. una regla
10. un cassette

11. una puerta
12. una ventana
13. una silla
14. una pizarra
15. un disco
16. una revista
17. un periódico
18. una papelera
19. un mapa
20. una computadora personal

F. Say that you have *one* of the items in the following pairs.

▶ revista o periódico   *Tengo una revista.*

1. lápiz o bolígrafo
2. calculadora o computadora
3. cuaderno o libro

4. cassette o disco
5. mesa o escritorio
6. mapa o papel

Estructuras útiles

I. Gender of nouns; the singular indefinite article

1. In Spanish, all nouns are either masculine or feminine, even those that refer to things, places, or ideas. Nouns that refer to males are masculine, and nouns that refer to females are feminine.

Masculine		Feminine	
actor	pueblo	actriz	ciudad
señor	lápiz	señora	mesa

2. The gender of a noun is important to recognize because it determines the form of the article or adjective that modifies it. In Spanish, there are two singular forms of the indefinite article: **un** and **una**. **Un** *(a, an)* precedes a masculine singular noun, and **una** *(a, an)* precedes a feminine singular noun.

un actor	una actriz
un señor	una señora

3. Most nouns that end in **-o** are masculine, and most nouns that end in **-a** are feminine. A few common exceptions are **una mano** *(hand),* **un día** *(day),* **un mapa** *(map),* **un problema** *(problem).*

un libro	una revista
un mecánico	una enfermera

4. Most nouns that end in the consonants **-l, -r,** or **-s** are masculine, and nouns that end in **-ad** or **-ión** are feminine.

un hospital	una ciudad	una región
un par	una facultad	una lección
un país	una universidad	una expresión

5. The gender of most other nouns must be learned. An effective way to remember the gender of a noun is to learn the article with it.

un continente	una clase
un lápiz	un cassette

A. Indicate whether the following nouns are masculine or feminine by using the appropriate indefinite article (**un** or **una**).

▶ hospital   *un hospital*
▶ enfermera   *una enfermera*

1. mecánico	3. profesor	5. papel	7. estudiante
2. fábrica	4. doctora	6. pueblo	8. periódico

9. médico	11. país	13. misión	15. cualidad
10. cassette	12. ciudad	14. situación	16. hotel

B. State whether each item is a person **(una persona)**, a thing **(una cosa)**, or a place you may go to **(un lugar / un sitio).**

▶ señora   *Una señora es una persona. No es una cosa y no es un sitio.*
▶ papel   *Un papel es una cosa. No es un sitio y no es una persona.*

1. puerta	4. ciudad	7. escritorio
2. enfermera	5. doctor	8. revista
3. profesor	6. señorita	9. hospital

C. Identify in Spanish at least ten items in the drawing shown below of Carlos' messy dorm room, using the appropriate indefinite article with each item. Then give their English equivalents.

▶ una silla   *a chair*

II. Plural of nouns and indefinite articles

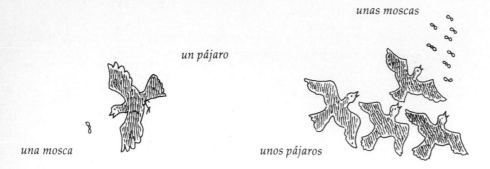

un pájaro

unas moscas

una mosca

unos pájaros

1. Most Spanish nouns form their plural by adding **-s** when the noun ends in a vowel, and **-es** when the noun ends in a consonant.

cuaderno	cuaderno**s**	doctor	doctor**es**
calculadora	calculadora**s**	papel	papel**es**
continente	continente**s**	ciudad	ciudad**es**
estudiante	estudiante**s**	país	país**es**

2. Nouns ending in **-z** undergo a spelling change in the plural. The final **z** changes to **c** before the plural ending **-es.**

lápiz	lápi**ces**	actriz	actri**ces**

3. Nouns ending in **-ión** drop their accent mark in the plural.

lecc**ión**	expres**ión**	relig**ión**
lecc**iones**	expres**iones**	relig**iones**

4. The indefinite article **un** becomes **unos** in the plural. The indefinite article **una** becomes **unas** in the plural. Both **unos** and **unas** are equivalent to *some* but often are not translated in English. The indefinite article in Spanish must agree with the noun in gender and number.

un periódico	*a newspaper*	**unos** periódicos	*(some) newspapers*
un profesor	*a professor*	**unos** profesores	*(some) professors*
una revista	*a magazine*	**unas** revistas	*(some) magazines*
una universidad	*a university*	**unas** universidades	*(some) universities*

D. Clarify that the items listed are not something else.

▶ cuadernos   *Son unos cuadernos. No son unos [papeles].*
▶ universidad   *Es una universidad. No es un [hospital].*

1. regla	3. mapa	5. papeles
2. revistas	4. calculadoras	6. papelera

E. When a classmate says that he/she has one of the following items, assure him/her that you have two or more of them.

▶ calculadora   S1: *Tengo una calculadora.*
                   S2: *¿Sí? Pues yo tengo [tres] calculadoras.*

1. mapa de España	4. cassette	7. periódico
2. silla	5. lápiz	8. lección de filosofía
3. problema	6. clase	9. revista de francés

III. Omission of the indefinite article

Ricardo es actor y Carmen es actriz.

1. The indefinite article is usually omitted when stating someone's profession, occupation, nationality, or organizational membership.

Elena es enfermera.	*Elena is a nurse.*
Soy estudiante.	*I'm a student.*
Jorge es español.	*Jorge is Spanish.*
Juana es demócrata.	*Juana is (a) democrat.*

2. The indefinite article is usually omitted after a negative with **tener** (to have).

No tengo (un) disco.	*I don't have a record.*
¡No tengo papel!	*I don't have (any) paper!*
No tengo periódicos aquí.	*I don't have (any) newspapers here.*

F. Admit that you do not have the following items; then mention something you do have.

▶ disco   *No tengo (un) disco; tengo [un libro].*

1. papelera	4. calculadora	7. mapa
2. cassette	5. papel	8. escritorio
3. revista	6. lápiz	9. bolígrafo

G. Identify someone you know who has the following occupation.

▶ profesor/a   *El señor Martínez es profesor.*

1. enfermero/a   4. actor/actriz
2. mecánico/a   5. doctor/a
3. estudiante   6. profesor/a

IV. Agreement of adjectives of nationality

1. Adjectives of nationality (like many other types of descriptive adjectives) agree in gender and number with the nouns they describe. An adjective of nationality whose masculine form ends in **-o** changes **-o** to **-a** in the feminine.

Pedro es **peruano.**	*Pedro is Peruvian.*
Clara es **peruana.**	*Clara is Peruvian.*

2. An adjective of nationality ending in **-e** does not change in the feminine.

Thomas es **canadiense.**	*Thomas is Canadian.*
Laura es **canadiense.**	*Laura is Canadian.*

3. If the adjective of nationality ends in a consonant, **-a** is added to the masculine form to refer to a female.

Carlos es **español.**	*Carlos is Spanish.*
Carmen es **española.**	*Carmen is Spanish.*

4. If an accent occurs in the last syllable of the masculine form of an adjective of nationality, the accent is dropped in the feminine form and an **-a** is added. Common adjectives of this type are **francés, inglés, portugués,** and **alemán** *(German)*.

Louis es **francés.**	*Louis is French.*
Renée es **francesa.**	*Renée is French.*

5. The plural of adjectives of nationality is formed by adding **-s** to a final vowel and **-es** to a final consonant. Note that the accent is dropped in the plural of adjectives like **francés, inglés, portugués,** and **alemán.**

Soy **argentino.**	*I'm Argentine.*
Pepe y yo somos **argentinos.**	*Pepe and I are Argentine.*
Hugo es **inglés.**	*Hugo is English.*
Hugo y Linda son **ingleses.**	*Hugo and Linda are English.*

6. Learn the adjectives of nationality below. Most are obvious cognates.

alemán	boliviano	canadiense	costarricense
argentino	brasileño	colombiano	chileno

chino	hondureño	nicaragüense	puertorriqueño
dominicano	inglés	norteamericano	salvadoreño
ecuatoriano	italiano	panameño	uruguayo
francés	japonés	paraguayo	venezolano
guatemalteco	mexicano	peruano	

H. Identify the nationality, occupation, or profession of the characters who appeared in the monologues and dialogues of *Lecciones 1* and *2,* using appropriate words from the lists below.

1. Jorge Ramírez
2. Rosa de García
3. Felipe Arrojo Ortiz
4. Cristina Marcano Campos

boliviano	enfermera
chileno	profesora
canadiense	mecánico
español	actor
inglés	médica
portugués	estudiante
argentino	
mexicano	

I. Specify the nationality of the individuals mentioned, according to the countries supplied.

► Laura / Canadá   S1: *¿De qué nacionalidad es Laura?*
                      S2: *¿Laura? Pues Laura es canadiense.*

1. Hugo y Ricardo / Panamá
2. Carmen / Costa Rica
3. Pedro, Carlos y Juanita / Chile
4. los señores Díaz / Nicaragua
5. la señorita / los Estados Unidos
6. doña Matilde / Bolivia

J. Find out whether the following individuals are French, German, English, Portuguese, or from the United States, according to the countries supplied in the cues. Use the appropriate forms of **francés, alemán, inglés, portugués,** or **estadounidense.**

► María / Portugal   S1: *María, ¿eres portuguesa?*
                      S2: *Sí, soy portuguesa.*
                             No, no soy portuguesa. Soy española.

1. Karl / Alemania
2. Jane / Inglaterra
3. Renée y François / Francia
4. Diego y Manolo / Portugal
5. Heidi / Alemania
6. John / los Estados Unidos

¿Comprende usted?

Review the suggestions for developing reading skills given in *Lección 1* and then read the following four advertisements about automobiles. Look for cognates to help you understand what the ads mean without looking up words in a dictionary. Then do the exercises that follow, looking back at the ads to clarify any words or expressions that you did not understand the first time.

¡Anuncios especiales!

1. **Panda de SEAT**
   Un coche español . . . ¡estupendo!
     veloz, económico, suave, dinámico . . .
   Facilidades de crédito

2. **En Argentina . . . un FIAT**
   Un automóvil que construye un argentino y que
     ¡todo argentino usa!

3. **Volkswagen**
   ¡de calidad alemana!
   ¡de construcción nacional mexicana!
   ¡de fama mundial!
     . . . El carro ideal para todos . . .

4. **Autos usados,** pero . . . ¡en excelentes condiciones!
   garantía absoluta
   servicio de calidad
   gran selección de marcas y modelos

A. Locate the Spanish cognates and equivalents of the following words and expressions in the advertisements and write them as they appear in the text of the ads.

   1. quality of service
   2. car (four different words)
   3. completely guaranteed
   4. swift
   5. of German quality

B. Choose four or five expressions from the ads, and use them to create your own advertisement for an automobile.

Lección 3
El mundo hispánico

¿Te gusta bailar?

Francisco (Paco) Uribe and Cristina (Tina) Gómez are students at City College in New York. Their parents are from Puerto Rico, but Paco and Tina were born in the United States. They discuss a forthcoming party at the Club Borinquen to celebrate the end-of-semester exams. **Boriquén** *(origin of the word* **Borinquen***) was the name given to the island of Puerto Rico by the native Taino Indians.*

Paco: El sábado hay una fiesta latina en el Club Borinquen. ¿Te gusta bailar?

Tina: Sí, sobre todo me gusta la salsa.°

Paco: ¿Y cantar?

5 Tina: En grupo, sí. Pero no canto muy bien.

Paco: ¡Pues yo sí! Escucha: «Adiós, adiós, adiós, Borinquen querido, tierra de mi amor . . .»

Tina: Bueno, bueno. ¡Por favor! No me gustan las canciones nostálgicas.

Paco: Entonces el sábado olvidamos los exámenes, bailamos la salsa y . . .

10 cantamos canciones alegres.

Tina: ¡Estupendo!

° very popular dance in most parts of Hispanic America

¿Le gusta a Ud. la música latina? En Nueva York, con su enorme comunidad puertorriqueña, la música latina es muy popular. Aquí un grupo musical participa en la celebración del Día de Puerto Rico en Nueva York. ¿Qué conjuntos hispánicos conoce Ud.?

Paco: *On Saturday there's a Latin (Hispanic) party at the Club Borinquen. Do you like to dance?*

Tina: *Yes, most of all I like (to do) the salsa.*

Paco: *And (do you like) to sing?*

Tina: *In a group, yes. But I don't sing very well.*

Paco: *I do. Listen: "Good-by, good-by, good-by, beloved Borinquen, land of my love . . ."*

Tina: *Okay, okay. Please! I don't like nostalgic songs.*

Paco: *Then Saturday we'll forget exams, dance the salsa, and . . . sing happy songs.*

Tina: *Great!*

Comprensión

¿Verdad o falso?

1. Según Paco, hay una fiesta latina el viernes.
2. A Tina le gusta bailar el tango.
3. Paco canta una canción puertorriqueña (borinqueña).
4. A Tina le gustan las canciones nostálgicas.
5. El sábado Paco y Tina estudian para los exámenes.

Conversación

1. ¿Le gusta bailar en las fiestas? (Sí, me gusta . . .)
2. ¿Baila usted bien? ¿mal? ¿así así? (Bailo . . .)
3. ¿Le gustan las fiestas de la universidad? (Me gustan . . .)
4. ¿Canta usted bien? ¿muy bien? ¿mal? ¿así así? (Canto . . .)
5. ¿Hay una fiesta el sábado o el domingo? (Sí, hay . . . No, no hay . . .)
6. ¿Le gustan las canciones nostálgicas? ¿Le gustan más las canciones alegres? (Me gustan . . .)

Situaciones

1. You want to get better acquainted with a classmate. Find out if he/she likes or dislikes certain things and activities.

   —¿Te gusta . . . (el baile, la música, el arte, bailar, cantar)?
   —Sí, me gusta. (No, no me gusta.)

2. Find out some of your instructor's likes and dislikes.

   —¿Le gustan . . . (las canciones nostálgicas, las fiestas, los bailes latinos)?
   —Sí, me gustan. (No, no . . . .)

Vocabulario

Palabras análogas

el arte	**el grupo**	**la salsa**
el club	**la música**	**el tango**
el examen	**nostálgico, -a**	

Sustantivos

el amor   love
el baile   dance
la canción   song
la fiesta   party
la tierra   land

Adjetivos

alegre   happy
estupendo, -a   great, wonderful
latino, -a   Latin, Hispanic
querido, -a   beloved, dear

Verbos

bailar   to dance
cantar   to sing
escuchar   to listen; **¡escucha!**   listen!
estudiar   to study
olvidar   to forget
trabajar   to work

Otras palabras y expresiones

a [Tina] le gusta(n)   (Tina) likes (*literally,* it is pleasing to Tina)
bueno, bueno   good, good; okay, okay
entonces   then
hay   there is, there are
mal   badly
más   more
me gusta(n)   I like
te gusta(n)   you like (*fam.*)
le gusta(n)   he/she likes, you like (*formal*)
para   for
pero   but
por favor   please
según   according to
sobre todo   especially, most of all
¿verdad o falso?   true or false?
¡yo sí!   I do!

GRAN
BAILE

Día: Viernes 10 de febrero
Sitio: Auditorio Colegio San Carlos
Hora: 7:30 P. M.
Amenizará: "Tabasco"
PRECIO: $5.00 PAREJA

Práctica

In groups of two or three, prepare a short dialogue based on the information given below, using structures and vocabulary from the dialogue in this lesson and previous monologues and dialogues.

Ricardo, a student from Madrid, meets Linda, a student from Dallas, at a dorm for international students. Ricardo greets her and asks her what her name is, where she lives, and so on. Then he asks her if she likes to dance or to sing Spanish songs, and Linda replies that she does. Ricardo tells her that there is a party in the Club de Sevilla on Friday, and Linda says, "Great! See you Friday."

READ ✓

Nota cultural Nicknames

Many Spanish-speaking people use nicknames (**sobrenombres** or **apodos**) for their friends and relatives; for example, **Paco** or **Pancho** for **Francisco,** and **Tina** for **Cristina.** English counterparts are *Frank* and *Chris.*

Sometimes nicknames are based on a characteristic trait of an individual. For example, **el Chato** may be used to refer to a person with a flat nose, and **el Tacaño** (or **el Taca**) may be used to refer to a person who is considered stingy. Some of these nicknames become so associated with the individual that the real name of the person may be forgotten. Usually these nicknames are used affectionately or humorously and are not considered offensive as they might be in Anglo cultures.

Here are a few common nicknames often used in place of a first name.

Moncho: Ramón
Lucho: Luis
Gabi: Gabriel
Pepe: José
Quique: Enrique
Rafa: Rafael
Nacho: Ignacio

Lola: Dolores
Concha: Concepción
Betina: Beatriz
Mari: María
Mencha: Carmen
Chela: Graciela
Lucha: Lucía *or* Luisa

Pronunciación y ortografía

I. Capitalization

1. The first word in a sentence, as well as proper nouns that refer to persons or places, are capitalized in Spanish as they are in English. Nouns or adjectives that refer to nationality or to languages, the pronoun **yo** *(I),* days of the week, and months of the year are generally *not* capitalized in Spanish, in contrast with English usage.

Él es boliviano; yo soy peruano.   *He's Bolivian; I'm Peruvian.*
Estudio español.   *I'm studying Spanish.*
¡Hasta el lunes!   *Until Monday!*
Es el dos de noviembre.   *It's November 2 (the second of November).*

2. To express a capital or a small letter, the terms **mayúscula** and **minúscula** are used: **A = a mayúscula; a = a minúscula.**

II. The Spanish alphabet

Learn the names of the letters (las letras) of the Spanish alphabet and how they are pronounced. Note that the digraphs ch, ll, and rr are treated as single letters. The letters k and w occur only in words of foreign origin.

El alfabeto:

Letra	Nombre	Letra	Nombre	Letra	Nombre
a	a	j	jota *hoeta*	r	ere
b	be	k	ka	rr	erre (doble ere)
c	ce	l	ele	s	ese
ch	che	ll	elle	t	te
d	de	m	eme	u	u
e	e	n	ene	v	ve (uve)
f	efe	ñ	eñe	w	doble ve (doble uve) *dough blay vay*
g	ge *hay*	o	o	x	equis
h	hache	p	pe	y	i griega (ye)
i	i	q	cu	z	zeta (zeda)

1. When a written accent occurs over a vowel, the expression **con acento** or **con tilde** is used; for example, **a con acento = á.**
2. The letters of the Spanish alphabet are feminine in gender: **la a, la be.**
3. In vocabularies and dictionaries, words and syllables beginning with **ch, ll,** and **ñ** follow those beginning with **c, l,** and **n** respectively. **Ch** follows **cu, ll** follows **lu,** and **ñ** follows **nu.** Note the alphabetical order of the following word groups.

cómo	lengua	nota
cubano	luna	nudo
chileno	llama	ñandú

A. Spell your name in Spanish and that of a student seated near you.

▶ Felipe Gómez   Felipe: *efe mayúscula, e, ele, i, pe, e*
Gómez: *ge mayúscula, o con acento, eme, e, zeta*

B. Dictate to a classmate or to your instructor, letter by letter, the name of a friend or relative, your favorite movie or TV actor, a well-known individual in town, or a day of the week.

C. Alphabetize properly the following unfamiliar Spanish words.

1. ángulo, andar, año, anotar
2. allegar, altura, altavoz, altiplano
3. araña, archivo, arco, arena, arrestar
4. chocolate, coco, curioso, coche, charlar
5. llama, lista, lobo, lluvia, luna

Estudio de palabras

I. Asignaturas (*Course subjects*)

Learn some of the common course subjects in Spanish.

la antropología anthropology
el arte *(m or f)* art
el arte dramático dramatic arts
la biología biology
las ciencias de computación
    computer science
las ciencias políticas political science
la contabilidad accounting
la economía economics
la filosofía philosophy
la física physics
la geología geology
la historia history

la ingeniería engineering
las lenguas modernas modern
    languages
    el alemán German
    el español Spanish
    el francés French
    el inglés English
    el italiano Italian
la literatura literature
las matemáticas mathematics
la psicología psychology
la química chemistry
la sociología sociology

A. Identify which subject you like in preference to the other.

▶ química / alemán *Me gusta la química, pero me gusta más el alemán.*

    1. sociología / psicología
    2. historia / antropología
    3. química / física
    4. francés / inglés
    5. economía / filosofía
    6. ciencias políticas / arte
    7. matemáticas / geología
    8. contabilidad / ingeniería

B. Identify the general type of course in which you would be likely to study the following items or topics.

    1. la multiplicación y la división
    2. la flora y la fauna de los Estados Unidos
    3. Picasso y Renoir
    4. la construcción de calles y avenidas
    5. la revolución mexicana
    6. las costumbres de las tribus primitivas
    7. los principios del capitalismo
    8. las ideas de Platón y Sócrates

II. Los sufijos **-ía** y **-dad**

1. Many Spanish nouns ending in **-ía** have English equivalents ending in -*y*. You have learned in this lesson the names of several class subjects whose English equivalents end in -*y* (**la antropología, la biología,** et cetera).

2. Many Spanish nouns ending in **-dad** have English equivalents ending in *-ty;* for example, **la dificultad** *(difficulty).*

C. Give the English equivalents of the following Spanish nouns.

la cortesía	la categoría	la refinería
la galería	la fantasía	la lotería
la facilidad	la cantidad	la capacidad
la sociedad	la cualidad	la comunidad

D. Ask another student if he/she likes these subjects.

► la biología S1: *¿Te gusta la biología?*
 S2: *Sí, me gusta la biología.*
 No, no me gusta la biología.

1. la sociología   5. la filosofía
2. la antropología   6. la historia
3. la geología   7. la teología
4. la economía   8. la psicología

E. Read the following sentences aloud. Can you grasp their meaning?

1. La cortesía es una cualidad necesaria en la sociedad moderna.
2. En esa comunidad hay dos galerías de arte.
3. La Refinería del Norte tiene capacidad para refinar grandes cantidades de petróleo.

Estructuras útiles

I. The infinitive

1. The basic form of a Spanish verb (the form listed in dictionaries and in vocabularies) is the infinitive. A Spanish infinitive consists of one word; for example, **hablar.** An English infinitive is made up of two words; for example, *to speak.*
2. Spanish infinitives consist of a stem and an ending, as shown below.

Infinitive	Stem	Ending
cantar	cant	-ar
aprender	aprend	-er
describir	describ	-ir

3. Most Spanish infinitives end in **-ar,** but many also end in **-er** and **-ir.**

bailar   to dance   **aprender**   to learn   **decidir**   to decide
cantar   to sing   **leer**   to read   **describir**   to describe
hablar   to speak   **prometer**   to promise   **recibir**   to receive

A. Give the English equivalent of the following verbs without referring to any vocabulary list. Then give their infinitive stem and ending.

► visitar   *to visit*   *Stem: visit   Ending: -ar*

1. decidir   4. continuar   7. prometer
2. comprender   5. recibir   8. describir
3. bailar   6. entrar   9. cantar

II. Present tense of regular **-ar** verbs

¿*Habla* usted chino?

No, *hablo* ruso.

Nosotros *hablamos* portugués, ¿y ustedes?

Nosotros *hablamos italiano.*

En la torre de Babel hablan muchas lenguas.

1. The present tense of regular **-ar** verbs is formed by adding a set of present-tense endings to the infinitive stem. The verb endings change according to the subject of the sentence. They must agree with (match) the subject, whether the subject is expressed or not.

(Yo) bailo muy bien.   *I dance very well.*
Pablo baila mucho.   *Pablo dances a lot.*

2. Below is a chart showing the present-tense forms of the verb **hablar.**

	hablar		
yo	habl	**o**	Hablo español.
fam. — tú	habl	**as**	¿Hablas francés?
form. — Ud., él, ella	habl	**a**	Ud. habla mucho en clase.
nosotros, -as	habl	**amos**	No hablamos mucho.
vosotros, -as	habl	**áis**	¿Habláis italiano?
Uds., ellos, ellas	habl	**an**	Hablan dos lenguas.

3. In Spanish, a single verb form may be used to express an action that may require several words in English. There is no Spanish equivalent of the auxiliary verbs *do/does* and *don't/doesn't*, which are used in interrogative and negative sentences or as emphatic markers in English.

Hablo inglés.
- *I speak English.*
- *I'm speaking English.*
- *I do speak English.*

¿Hablas español?
- *Do you speak Spanish?*
- *Are you speaking Spanish?*

No **hablamos** alemán.
- *We don't speak German.*
- *We are not speaking German.*

¿No **hablas** español?
- *Don't you speak (Aren't you speaking) Spanish?*

4. The present tense may be used in Spanish to express actions intended or planned for the near future.

¿Trabajas mañana? — *Are you working (Will you work) tomorrow?*

Bailo con Jorge esta noche. — *I'm dancing (I'm going to dance) with Jorge tonight.*

Llegan más tarde. — *They're arriving (They will arrive) later.*

5. Here is a list of common regular **-ar** verbs, a number of which you have seen and used in some forms of the present tense. Learn the infinitives now, as you will need to use them in the exercises.

bailar to dance	**llegar** to arrive
buscar to look for	**mirar** to look (at)
caminar to walk	**necesitar** to need
cantar to sing	**olvidar** to forget
comprar to buy	**pasar** to spend (time)
contestar to answer	**preguntar** to ask
desear to want; to wish	**tomar** to take; to have (food, drink), to eat
entrar to enter	
escuchar to listen (to)	**trabajar** to work
esperar to wait (for)	**usar** to use
estudiar to study	**viajar** to travel
hablar to speak	**visitar** to visit
llamar to call; to phone	

Quiz Wed. & Conjugation Spell spanish Know english meaning

6. The verbs **buscar** (*to look for*), **escuchar** (*to listen to*), **esperar** (*to wait for*), and **mirar** (*to look at*) do not require a preposition in Spanish.

Busco unos libros de español.
Escucho la radio.

Esperan el autobús.
Miramos unas fotos.

7. Some verbs like **desear** and **necesitar** may be followed by a dependent infinitive. In this "double-verb construction," the first verb is conjugated, and the second is an infinitive.

Deseo ir al teatro.   *I want to go to the theater.*
Necesito viajar a Panamá.   *I need to travel to Panama.*

B. Tell what items or places the following people are or are not looking for. Use the appropriate present-tense form of **buscar.**

▶ ella / el mapa   *Ella busca el mapa.*
                     Ella no busca el mapa.

1. tú / el lápiz   5. ellas / el hotel
2. él / las fotografías   6. ustedes / la clase de física
3. nosotros / el periódico   7. usted / las revistas
4. ellos / la costa   8. yo / el colegio San Juan

C. Do Exercise B again, but this time tell what items the people indicated are or are not looking at. Use the appropriate present-tense form of **mirar.**

▶ ella / el mapa   *Ella mira el mapa.*
                     Ella no mira el mapa.

D. Tell what languages the following people do or do not speak. Use the appropriate present-tense form of **hablar** and choose from the languages **inglés, español, francés, alemán, ruso** *(Russian),* **italiano,** or **portugués.**

▶ tú   *Tú hablas alemán, pero no hablas portugués.*

1. Antonella y Paola   4. nosotros
2. la profesora de francés   5. los señores Padilla
3. Pepe y tú   6. yo

E. Ramón is having a party at the Club Borinquén. Tell who is arriving with whom, using the appropriate present-tense form of **llegar.**

▶ tú / Pepe   *Tú llegas con Pepe.*

1. Ana / Ernesto
2. tú / tu hermana
3. yo / mi hermano
4. ustedes / Ricardo
5. nosotros / los señores Castellano
6. la señorita Aguirre / el señor Gómez

F. Report what the following people wish to do. Use the cues indicated and the appropriate form of the verb **desear.**

▶ Juan / comprar los libros   *Juan desea comprar los libros.*

1. Pedro y Sonia / trabajar en la universidad
2. nosotros / mirar el periódico de Bogotá
3. ellas / buscar cosas en la librería
4. tú / escuchar música hispanoamericana
5. yo / viajar a España
6. Josefina / usar la computadora personal
7. usted / escuchar la radio
8. él y ella / esperar un taxi
9. ustedes / olvidar los exámenes
10. tú y Pedro / bailar mucho

SKip 6.

G. Exchange information with another student about where the following people work. In the responses, use the appropriate form of the verb **trabajar** and the names of the capitals of any Spanish-speaking country. Refer to the maps on the inside cover of your text if necessary.

▶ el señor Herrera   S1: *¿Dónde trabaja el señor Herrera?*
                      S2: *Trabaja en [Managua].*

1. los señores Blanco   3. Carlos y Rodrigo   5. yo
2. tú   4. la señorita Ruiz   6. ustedes

H. Complete each statement with the appropriate form of the verb in parentheses.

1. (tomar)   Yo ____ té *(tea)*, pero Paco ____ café *(coffee).*
2. (pasar)   Nosotros ____ las vacaciones en San Juan; ellos ____ las vacaciones en Santo Domingo.
3. (usar)   Tú ____ un lápiz, y ella ____ un bolígrafo.
4. (preguntar)   Nicolás ____ mucho; sus hermanas ____ poco.
5. (escuchar)   Tú y Marta ____ música clásica en la radio; nosotros ____ música rock en una discoteca.
6. (contestar)   Yo ____ la pregunta; tú ____ el teléfono.
7. (visitar)   Ellos ____ Nueva York; tú ____ San Antonio.
8. (esperar)   Nosotros ____ un taxi; tú ____ un autobús.

I. Answer the following questions about everyday activities.

1. ¿Escuchas la radio, discos o cassettes?
2. ¿Qué bailas, la salsa? ¿y [Alberto]? ¿y [Juanita]?
3. ¿Toman ustedes café o té por la mañana *(morning)*?

4. ¿Qué uso yo en clase, un bolígrafo o un lápiz?
5. ¿Qué hablas en la clase de español? ¿y en la clase de historia?
6. ¿Tú no deseas bailar? ¿Y [Clemencia] no desea bailar?
7. ¿Todos ustedes trabajan? ¿Quién trabaja? ¿Y quién no trabaja?

III. The definite article

Es **el** pueblo de San Jacinto.   Es **la** ciudad de San Francisco.

	Singular	Plural	
Masculine *the*	el	los	Male
Feminine	la	las	female

1. In Spanish there are two singular forms of the definite article: **el** and **la**. The definite article **el** is used with a masculine singular noun. The definite article **la** is used with a feminine singular noun. Both **el** and **la** mean *the*.

   el pueblo   *the town*   **la** ciudad   *the city*
   el país   *the country*   **la** fiesta   *the party*

2. There are also two plural forms of the definite article: **los** and **las.** The definite article **los** is used with a masculine plural noun. The definite article **las** is used with a feminine plural noun. Both **los** and **las** mean *the*.

   los estados   *the states*   **los** países   *the countries*
   las costas   *the coasts*   **las** fiestas   *the parties*

3. The definite article is used to *specify* a particular person, place, or thing.

   Es **el pueblo** de San José.   *It's the town of San José.*
   Es **la canción** que canta Pepe.   *It's the song that Pepe sings.*

4. The definite article precedes nouns used in a general sense and abstract nouns.

El español es importante.   *Spanish (in general) is important.*
Los libros son necesarios.   *Books (in general) are necessary.*
Me gusta **el café.**   *I like coffee (in general).*
El amor es extraordinario.   *Love is extraordinary.*

5. The definite article is used with days of the week to indicate *on.* Days of the week ending in **-s** have the same singular and plural forms; **-s** is added to **sábado** and **domingo** to form the plural. The plural definite article with the days of the week is used for habitual or repeated actions.

Hay fiesta **el sábado.**   *There is a party on Saturday.*
Trabajo **los lunes.**   *I work on Mondays.*

6. The definite article is used with the courtesy titles **señor, señora,** and **señorita,** and with professional titles such as **doctor/a** and **profesor/a** when talking *about* an individual or yourself. It is omitted, however, when talking *directly to* the individual.

La señorita Suárez es enfermera.   *Miss Suárez is a nurse.*
El doctor Martínez trabaja mucho.   *Dr. Martínez works very hard.*
Yo soy **la profesora Ruiz.**   *I am Professor Ruiz.*
But:
Buenos días, **señorita Suárez.**   *Good morning, Miss Suárez.*
Hasta mañana, **doctor.**   *Until tomorrow, doctor.*

J. Complete each sentence with the correct form of the definite article.

► Es _____ ciudad de San Francisco.   *la*

1. Busco _____ cuaderno de biología.
2. Es _____ enfermera de Hermosillo, México.
3. Ahí está _____ Océano Pacífico.
4. Victoria es _____ estudiante que habla alemán y francés.
5. Aquí está _____ ciudad de Caracas, Venezuela.
6. ¿Es _____ Club Borinquén?

K. Give an opinion about whether the following people or things are important, very important, or not important. Use the plural form in your answers.

► libro   *Los libros son [muy] importantes.*
          Los libros no son [muy] importantes.

1. computadora   4. automóvil   7. papelera
2. silla   5. calculadora   8. escritorio
3. médico   6. hospital   9. profesor

L. Announce that there is a party in the places mentioned on the day indicated.

▶ sábado / Club Latino   *El sábado hay una fiesta en el Club Latino.*

1. lunes / residencia de estudiantes   3. martes / universidad
   (*student housing*)   4. viernes / pueblo
2. miércoles / casa de Jorge

M. Make complete statements about the following persons, using the cues given.

▶ señor Padilla / viajar al Perú   *El señor Padilla viaja al Perú.*

1. señorita Hernández / no bailar el tango
2. señor y la señora Campos / cantar muy bien
3. profesor Díaz / trabajar los lunes y los martes
4. doctora García / desear llegar pronto

N. Complete the sentences in the following paragraphs with the appropriate form of the indefinite or the definite article, as needed.

Me llamo Vicente Aranguren Villareal. Trabajo en _____ fábrica de automóviles. Para mí, _____ automóviles son importantes para el trabajo. También me gusta viajar en automóvil. _____ día deseo viajar a _____ Florida y también a _____ América del Sur: a Colombia, a Chile, a todos _____ países de América del Sur, porque mi papá y mi mamá son suramericanos.

   Tengo _____ novia (*girlfriend*) cubana, María López. Ella es para mí _____ persona más querida del mundo. _____ sábado hay _____ fiesta en _____ casa de mi novia. _____ sábados siempre bailamos, cantamos y olvidamos _____ automóviles y _____ trabajo. ¡ _____ sábado es un día estupendo!

IV. **Me (te, le) gusta(n)**

Me gusta la leche.
Me gusta el café.
¡Pero más me gustan
los ojos de usted!

1. The following patterns with **gustar** are used to express *I like, you like,* and *he/she likes.*

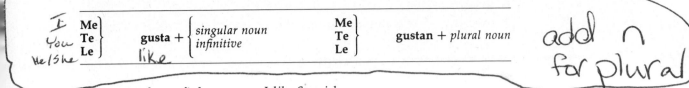

| I You He/She | Me Te Le } | gusta + *like* | { singular noun infinitive | Me Te Le } | gustan + *plural noun* | add n for plural |

Me gusta el español.   *I like Spanish*
¿**Te gusta** bailar?   *Do you like to dance?*
Le gustan las canciones.   *You (formal) like the songs. (He/she likes the songs.)*

¿No **te gustan** los bailes? *Don't you (familiar) like dances?*

2. Because **le** can refer to *you* (formal), as well as to *he* and *she,* a prepositional phrase with **a** may be used to clarify the meaning of **le**. Context will, however, usually make the desired meaning clear.

¿No **le gusta** el arte
{ **a** usted?   *Don't you like art?*
a él?   *Doesn't he like art?*
a ella?   *Doesn't she like art?*
a José?   *Doesn't José like art?*

O. State whether or not you like the following things.

▶ el español   *Me gusta el español.*
▶ las ciencias políticas *No me gustan las ciencias políticas.*

1. la medicina   5. los pueblos tranquilos
2. la universidad   6. las lenguas modernas
3. la química   7. los lunes
4. los sábados   8. el hospital

P. State whether or not you like to do the following things.

▶ comer   *Me gusta comer.*
          No me gusta comer.

1. hablar y escribir en español
2. vivir en los Estados Unidos
3. leer novelas en inglés
4. cantar canciones populares
5. visitar la familia
6. comprar libros

Q. Ask the following people whether they like various things and activities.

▶ Pepe / el café   *Pepe, ¿te gusta el café?*
▶ profesor / los bailes latinos   *Profesor, ¿le gustan los bailes latinos?*

1. Luis / cantar
2. Doctor Pérez / computadoras personales
3. Manuel / fiestas
4. profesor / bailar
5. señor Gómez / programas de televisión
6. señora Márquez / España

R. Ask fellow classmates whether the people in Exercise Q like or do not like the various things and activities.

▶ Pepe / el café   S1: *¿Le gusta a Pepe el café?*
                 S2: *Sí, le gusta el café.*
                      No, no le gusta el café.

¿Comprende usted?

Review the suggestions for developing reading skills on pages 27 and 28 and then read the following passage for general understanding.

Los hispanos en los Estados Unidos

Los hispanos que viven en los Estados Unidos son de grupos lingüísticos muy diferentes. Hay hispanos que hablan exclusivamente español, y consideran el inglés como una lengua extranjera y difícil. Hay hispanos que no hablan español porque viven en ciudades donde no hay muchos hispanos y donde la lengua común es el inglés. Entre los dos extremos hay un enorme número de hispanos que usan el español y el inglés en diferentes proporciones. La educación bilingüe es una posible solución para educar a los hispanos (y a otros individuos) en las dos culturas y las dos lenguas.

A. Complete the answers to the questions, according to the reading.

1. ¿Es homogéneo el grupo de hispanos que vive en los EEUU?
2. ¿Qué lengua hablan los hispanos que viven en ciudades de los EEUU donde no hay muchos hispanos?

3. ¿Son completamente bilingües los hispanos que hablan español e inglés en los EEUU?
4. ¿Es posible o imposible educar a los hispanos en las dos lenguas y las dos culturas?

B. Complete the sentences with appropriate Spanish words without looking at the reading.

Los hispanos que viven en los _____ son de grupos _____ . Los hispanos que viven en las _____ grandes generalmente _____ español, y muchos de ellos _____ el inglés como _____ extranjera. La _____ bilingüe es una _____ para educar a los _____ en las dos _____ y en las dos _____ .

C. Re-read the completed passage in Exercise B. Practice reading it aloud several times until you are satisfied with your speed and your reading proficiency.

Los niños en esta clase bilingüe en Washington, D.C. tratan de aprender y apreciar dos lenguas y dos culturas. Muchos estudios demuestran que un niño que inicia sus estudios en la lengua materna aprende más rápidamente que si se le priva de su cultura original. ¿Ud. qué piensa?

Lengua en acción I

A. Un calendario personal (Lección 2)

Prepare your social calendar for October. Referring to the activities listed and following the model dialogue, find classmates to go with you. On the calendar, note the activity and name of the person who will accompany you.

Día	Actividad
10 de octubre	la conferencia de historia medieval
15 de octubre	el concierto de [your favorite singer]
5 de octubre	la reunión (meeting) del Club de Español
15 de octubre	la fiesta de [name of a friend]
16 de octubre	la exposición de arte abstracto
2 de octubre	el partido (game) de béisbol
10 de octubre	la película (film) Cocodrilo Dundee

Octubre						1988
L	M	M	J	V	S	D
					1	2
3	4	5	6	7	8	9
10	11	12	13	14	15 *Rubén Blades*	16
17	18	19	20	21	22	23
24/31	25	26	27	28	29	30

▶ S1: *El concierto de Rubén Blades es el 15. ¿Vamos?*
S2: *¿Qué día es el 15?*
S1: *Es sábado.*
S2: *Pues bien, vamos. (Lo siento; el sábado es la fiesta de [María].)*
S1: (If your classmate will go, reply appropriately and take leave. If your classmate can't go, ask about another activity or take leave and find someone else.)

B. ¿Qué tiene en el maletín? (What do you have in the briefcase?) *(Lección 2)*

You have flown to Chile to work with an international news agency. Your briefcase is missing upon your arrival in Santiago. Specify to the airline representative (a classmate) what your briefcase contains and the approximate value **(valor)** of each article in dollars **(dólares).** The airline representative will note the information on the form.

Artículo perdido	Cantidad	Valor
_____	_____	_____
_____	_____	_____
_____	_____	_____
_____	_____	_____
_____	_____	_____
_____	_____	_____
_____	_____	_____

C. Vamos a hablar (Let's talk) *(Lección 3)*

You want to get to know a classmate that you don't know well. Greet him/her and find out the following information. Then, alternate roles.

1. Find out his/her first and last name.
2. Find out how he/she is.
3. Find out where he/she is from.
4. Find out about his/her likes and dislikes **(bailar, viajar, fiestas informales, música romántica, . . .)**
5. Now say good-by.

D. ¿Qué tienen en común? (What do you have in common?)
(Lección 3)

Ask two classmates about their interests and habits so that you can find a potential housemate. Write down their names and responses so that you can choose the most compatible person. Add several items of your own choosing if you wish.

Yo	*Compañero/a 1*	*Compañero/a 2*	
_____	_____	_____	usar una computadora personal
_____	_____	_____	gustarle estudiar de día/noche (*night*)
_____	_____	_____	fumar (*to smoke*)
_____	_____	_____	tomar bebidas (*drinks*) alcohólicas
_____	_____	_____	escuchar música rock/clásica
_____	_____	_____	mirar televisión hasta muy tarde
_____	_____	_____	gustarle los animales

Persona más compatible: _____

E. ¿En qué le puedo servir? (How may I help you?) *(Wrap-up)*

You have gone to various places to make a request of the person in charge (a classmate). Use the dialogue cues to accomplish what you need to get done.

Usted

1. Greet and identify yourself.
2. State what you need or want.
3. Thank the person in charge and say good-by.

La persona encargada (the person in charge)

Return the greeting and offer your services.
Apologize and say it's impossible to do.
Acknowledge the visitor's thanks and say good-by.

ver a la Sra. López sobre un apartamento

buscar trabajo para el verano

visitar a . . . en el hospital

Unidad 2
En España, México y los Estados Unidos

Madrid, la capital de España, es una ciudad moderna, cosmopolita y elegante. Alrededor de Plaza Cibeles en el centro comercial de la ciudad, hay muchos bancos y negocios y una intensa actividad. Diga si la arquitectura de los edificios en esta foto es como la de su ciudad o de alguna ciudad que Ud. conoce.

Lección 4
En España

¡Qué barbaridad!

Ricardo Solana y Marisol del Valle son estudiantes de la Universidad Complu-
tense de Madrid. En este momento Ricardo ve a su amiga Marisol en una li-
brería del centro de la capital.

Ricardo: Hola, Marisol. ¿Qué haces por aquí?
Marisol: Busco un libro de arte. Y tú, ¿qué haces?
Ricardo: Pues yo busco unos libros para el curso de inglés.
Marisol: ¿Hay libros de texto aquí?
5 Ricardo: Sí, pero en el segundo piso.
Marisol: Ah, bueno. ¿Y quién es tu profesor de inglés este año?
Ricardo: El profesor Duarte . . . el padre de Anita.
Marisol: Ah, sí. Es estupendo, ¿no?
Ricardo: Sí, pero muy severo.
10 Marisol: ¿Es verdad que habla francés y alemán?
Ricardo: Sí, y también un poco de italiano y ruso.
Marisol: ¡Cinco lenguas extranjeras! ¡Qué barbaridad!

El metro de Madrid es muy
práctico para los estudiantes de
la Ciudad Universitaria.
Observe al fondo (background)
de esta foto la Facultad de
Farmacia. ¿Usa Ud. el metro?
¿el autobús? ¿el automóvil?
¿Cuándo?

Comprensión

1. ¿Dónde está la librería?
2. ¿Quiénes son Ricardo y Marisol?
3. ¿A quién ve Ricardo?
4. ¿Qué busca Marisol?
5. ¿Qué busca Ricardo en la librería?
6. ¿Quién es el señor Duarte?
7. ¿Es severo o indulgente el señor Duarte?
8. ¿Cuántas lenguas extranjeras habla? ¿cuáles?

Conversación

1. ¿Cuántos idiomas habla Ud.? ¿uno? ¿dos?
2. ¿Habla usted francés? ¿alemán? ¿italiano?
3. ¿Habla usted español perfectamente? ¿así así? ¿un poquito?
4. ¿Cómo se llama su profesor/a de inglés? ¿y de español?
5. ¿A quién ve Ud. en la clase? (Veo . . .)
6. ¿Qué busca Ud. en una librería?
7. ¿Hay muchas librerías en su ciudad?

Situaciones

1. You are at a large party and have lost sight of some people. Respond to a friend who asks whom you're looking for.

   —¿A quién buscas?
   —Busco . . . (a mi amigo, a mis padres, a nuestro compañero, a tus hermanos).

2. You have gone to the library to listen to a record, but the librarian tells you there is no record player there. React with an appropriate exclamation.

   —No hay tocadiscos en la biblioteca.
   —¡Qué . . . (problema, lástima)!

Vocabulario

Palabras análogas
el momento   **el texto**

Sustantivos
el/la amigo/a friend
el año year
la biblioteca library
el centro downtown, center
el/la compañero/a companion, pal

el curso course (of study)
la hermana sister
el hermano brother; **los hermanos** *(pl.)* brothers, brother(s) and sister(s)
el idioma language
la librería bookstore

el libro de texto textbook
el padre father; **los padres** parents
el piso floor
el ruso Russian (language)
el tocadiscos record player

Adjetivos

¿cuánto, -a? how much; **¿cuántos, -as?** *(pl.)* how many?
este, -a this; **estos, -as** *(pl.)* these
extranjero, -a foreign
indulgente lenient
mucho, -a much; **muchos, -as** many, a lot of
nuestro, -a our; **nuestros, -as** *(pl.)*
segundo, -a second
severo, -a strict, demanding
tu your *(fam.);* **tus** *(pl.)*

Verbos

estar *(irreg.)* to be; **estoy, estás, está**
hacer *(irreg.)* to do; to make; **hago, haces, hace**
ver to see; **veo, ves, ve**

Otras palabras y expresiones

¿a quién? whom? to whom?
ah, bueno oh, good
aquí here
del (de + el), de la of the, from the
en este momento at this moment
¿es verdad que . . . ? is it true that . . . ?
perfectamente perfectly
por aquí around here
que that
¡qué barbaridad! how amazing!
  (how dreadful, *etc. depending on context*)
¡qué bien! how nice!
¡qué horror! how dreadful!
¡qué lástima! what a pity!
¡qué problema! what a problem!
¿quién? who? **¿quiénes?** *(pl.)*
un poco de (inglés) a little (English)
un poquito a little bit

Práctica

A. Imagine that you are a student at the University of Madrid and you meet a friend at a bookstore. After shaking hands and greeting each other, carry on a conversation about your courses. Discuss the books you are getting for a language course and the name of your professor. Then shake hands again and say good-by. Use the vocabulary and structures from the dialogue in this lesson.

B. Prepare a brief talk about your city or town. Indicate whether there is one hospital or none, one or two bookstores, et cetera, using the expression **hay** or **no hay.** Use the vocabulary from previous lessons.

Nota cultural The university system

Most universities in Spanish-speaking countries are financed by the national or state government. A prerequisite for admission to the university is the **bachillerato,** a diploma earned by students after they have passed a series of government-controlled examinations that are administered at the end of their secondary-school studies.

Universities in Spain and Hispanic America are usually comprised of several **facultades** *(colleges/schools),* such as **la facultad de medicina** or **la facultad de ciencias.** Students must choose their major when they register and must take all their courses at their respective **facultades.**

There are over twenty state universities in Spain, of which **la Universidad Complutense de Madrid** is the largest and also one of the few European universities with a campus. The campus **(la ciudad universitaria),** located away from downtown Madrid, contains the buildings of the many **facultades** and also numerous **colegios mayores** *(student dormitories).* Most students, however, live off campus.

Pronunciación y ortografía

I. Diphthongs

1. In Spanish, the vowels **a, e,** and **o** are traditionally called *strong;* the vowels **i** (sometimes **y**) and **u** are traditionally called *weak.* A diphthong is a complex sound consisting of two vowels within one syllable. In Spanish, diphthongs are formed when a strong vowel (**a, e,** or **o**) combines with an unstressed weak vowel (**i, y,** or **u**), or when two weak vowels combine with each other within one syllable.

2. Diphthongs occur frequently in Spanish. Examples of common words
   containing diphthongs are listed below.

ai (ay)	ia	ie	io	ei (ey)
hay	estudiante	bien	estadio	rey
Jaime	importancia	diez	Julio	reina

iu	oi (oy)	ua	ue	ui
ciudad	hoy	lengua	buenos	Suiza
viuda	oigo	Eduardo	pueblo	cuidado

3. A written accent on the weak vowel in a two-vowel combination
   indicates that the two vowels do not form a diphthong; they belong to
   separate syllables.

biología	Valparaíso	país	Raúl
policía	Río Verde	día	dúo

II. Syllabication

A strong foreign accent is noticed in non-Spanish speakers who separate
syllables in the wrong places when speaking Spanish. The most important
rule to remember is that in Spanish a single consonant always goes with the
following vowel, in contrast to English.

vo-ca-bu-la-rio   *vo-cab-u-lar-y*

In writing, a knowledge of syllable division is most useful when separating
words at the end of a line.

1. Every Spanish syllable must contain either a single vowel or a
   diphthong. Most Spanish syllables end in a vowel sound.

   Es-pa-ña   pro-fe-so-ra   i-ta-lia-no   ciu-dad

2. Two strong vowels, or an accented weak vowel in combination with a
   strong vowel, form separate syllables.

   ca-er   dí-a   pa-ís

3. A single consonant (including ch, ll, and rr) between vowels always
   forms a syllable with the second vowel.

   pe-lí-cu-la   i-ta-lia-no   no-che   e-lla   ca-rro

4. Two consonants between vowels are divided into separate syllables; the
   first consonant goes with the preceding vowel, the second one with the
   following vowel.

   al-to   Car-los   con-no-ta-ción

However, when the second consonant is **l** or **r,** the two consonants remain together with the vowel that follows.

ha-blar   pa-la-bra   a-gra-de-cer

5. In a three-consonant group, the first two consonants go with the preceding vowel, and the third goes with the following vowel.

ins-tan-te   ins-pi-ra-ción

However, when the third consonant is **l** or **r,** the last two consonants remain together with the vowel that follows.

as-tró-no-mo   ex-pli-car   des-cri-bir

III. Stress

1. Spanish words of more than one syllable have a definite spoken stress, or emphasis, on one of the syllables. Most words that end in a vowel, **-n,** or **-s** are stressed on the *next-to-the-last* syllable.

lla-mo   es-**tu-**dian   **bue-**nos
len-gua   **ha-**blan   **ha-**ces

2. Most words that end in a consonant other than **-n** or **-s** are stressed on the *last* syllable.

u-ni-ver-si-**dad**   pro-fe-**sor**   cul-tu-**ral**

3. Words that are pronounced contrary to the preceding statements are written with an accent mark on the vowel of the stressed syllable.

lec-**ción**   **mú-**si-ca   a-**sí**   **lá-**piz   in-**glés**

4. Spanish stress is very important because the meaning of a word or sentence may depend on proper stress.

la **pa**pa   *the potato*   **En**tre.   *Come in.*
el pa**pá**   *the father*   En**tré.**   *I came in.*

A. Listen and repeat the following words after your instructor. Each one contains a diphthong.

cuadra   vocabulario   Luisa   bien   lengua
vacaciones   cambiar   italiano   pueblo   muy

B. Read aloud the following sentences, paying attention to diphthongs and to vowel combinations that are not diphthongs.

1. Luisa habla italiano muy bien.
2. Jaime vive en la ciudad de Valparaíso.

3. No es un pueblo importante.
4. La biología es una ciencia muy interesante.

C. Divide the following words into syllables. Then pronounce them correctly.

segundo	estupendo	profesor	verdad
barbaridad	extranjero	también	buscamos
coche	padre	pizarra	hablamos

D. Which syllable of the following words is stressed in Spanish? How can you tell?

len-guas	es-tu-dio	prác-ti-ca	Cór-do-ba
no-ta	cul-tu-ral	pre-gun-ta	Bo-go-tá
se-ñor	fan-tás-ti-co	diá-lo-go	Ca-ra-cas

Estudio de palabras

I. Etapas de la vida (*Stages of life*)

el bebé

el niño
little boy

el muchacho
el chico *Boy*

el joven
young

el hombre
man

el anciano
el viejo *elderly man*

la bebé

la niña

la muchacha
la chica
girl

la joven

la mujer
woman

la anciana
la vieja

74 Lección 4

A. Give a nationality to each person shown in the previous illustrations.

▶ *El muchacho es chileno.*

B. Use your imagination and identify the following people by giving them names (see list of proper names in *Lección 1*). Then indicate how they are related to each other.

▶ el bebé *El bebé se llama [Luis] y es el hermano de [Tomás].*

1. la chica
2. el hombre
3. la niña
4. la mujer
5. el muchacho
6. el joven

II. La familia

el padre (el papá) father
la madre (la mamá) mother
los padres parents; fathers
las madres mothers
el hermano brother
la hermana sister
los hermanos brothers and sisters; brothers
las hermanas sisters

el hijo son
la hija daughter
los hijos children; sons
las hijas daughters
el hermano mayor (menor) older (younger) brother
el hijo mayor (menor) older (younger) son
la hija mayor (menor) older (younger) daughter

Note that the masculine plural noun for **padre, hermano,** and **hijo** may refer to a group containing both males and females, or to a group containing males only. The meaning is usually made clear by context.

C. Give the names of your family members (real or imaginary) to a classmate.

▶ *Mi mamá se llama _____ ; mi papá se llama _____ ;*
mi hermano mayor se llama _____ ; mi hermana menor se llama _____ .

D. Answer the following questions about your family.

1. ¿Tiene usted hermanos? ¿cuántos?
2. ¿Tiene usted hermanas? ¿cuántas?
3. ¿Cuántos hijos hay en su familia?
4. ¿Tiene usted un/a hermano/a mayor? ¿un/a hermano/a menor?
5. ¿Trabajan sus hermanos? ¿sus hermanas?

III. Diminutivos

1. The suffixes **-ito/-ita** and **-(e)cito/-(e)cita** are often added to Spanish nouns and adjectives to form diminutives. A diminutive suffix generally implies <u>smallness in size</u> or indicates <u>affection</u> on the part of the speaker toward the person or object mentioned.

Manolito y yo somos amigos de toda la vida.	*Manny and I are lifelong friends.*
Mi hermana mayor se llama Luisa, y mi **hermanita** se llama Leonor.	*My older sister's name is Luisa, and my younger sister is Leonor.*
Este libro es un texto de química, y este **librito** es una colección de poemas.	*This book is a chemistry textbook, and this little book is a collection of poems.*

2. You will hear, especially in Hispanic America, the adjectives **chiquito/a** and **poquito/a** much more frequently than their base forms, **chico/a** and **poco/a**. Further diminutive endings are often added to these diminutives, forming the words **chiquitito/a** and **poquitito/a**.

3. Although there are regional and personal preferences, the most common diminutive endings are as follows:

   a. <u>**-ito/-ita (-itos/-itas)** added to words ending in **-o, -a, -l.**</u>

libro	⟶ libr**ito**	*book*
hermana	⟶ herman**ita**	*sister*
papeles	⟶ papel**itos**	*papers*

   b. <u>**-cito/-cita (-citos/-citas)** added to words that end in **-e** or consonants other than **l.**</u>

café	⟶ cafe**cito**	*(cup of) coffee*
joven	⟶ joven**cito**	*young man*
joven	⟶ joven**cita**	*young woman*

Since regional and personal usage may follow rules that are different from the ones given above, you should use only those forms that you have heard used by native speakers or by your instructor as you develop a feeling for the language.

E. Restate the following sentences in their base form. The diminutives given here follow the rules stated above.

1. ¿Cómo está el **niñito**?
2. ¿Cómo se llaman los **hermanitos** de Raúl?
3. Vivo con mi **hermanita**.
4. **Rosita** es mexicana.
5. El **papelito** no es importante.
6. ¿Tomamos un **cafecito**?

F. Restate the following sentences, changing the diminutives to their base form. These diminutives represent common variations of the rules previously mentioned, but you should easily see the base word.

1. Eres **buenecito,** ¿verdad, Miguel?
2. ¿Tienes un **lapicito?**
3. Santa Ana es un **pueblecito** al norte de Sevilla.
4. Un **poquitico** de paciencia, ¡por favor!
5. Es una **viejecita** muy inteligente.
6. ¡Hasta muy **prontico!**

Estructuras útiles

I. Possession and close relationship with **de**

*Es el carro **de Luisito.***

1. The pattern **de** + *a noun* is used in Spanish to express possession or close relationship. The pattern *noun* + *apostrophe* + *s* does not exist in Spanish.

Es la silla **de la muchacha.**	*It's the girl's chair.*
Son **las plumas de Linda.**	*They are Linda's pens.*
El hermano de Pablo es muy inteligente.	*Pablo's brother is very smart.*

2. The interrogative expression **¿de quién?** is equivalent to *whose?* and is used when asking a question about the possession of an object or about a relationship. The plural expression **¿de quiénes?** may be used if the person asking the question knows that there are several owners.

—**¿De quién** es el cuaderno?	*Whose notebook is it?*
—Es **de Eduardo.**	*It's Eduardo's. (It belongs to Eduardo.)*
—**¿De quién(es)** son los papeles?	*Whose papers are they?*
—Son **de María** y **de David.**	*They are María's and David's.*

A. Make up questions about ownership using the following nouns. In your responses, use **de** plus the names of students in your class.

▶ bolígrafo   S1: *¿De quién es el bolígrafo?*
              S2: *Es de [Esteban].*

▶ periódicos   S1: *¿De quién(es) son los periódicos?*
              S2: *Son de [Patricia] y de [Guillermo].*

1. sillas	4. papel	7. computadora
2. libro	5. cuaderno	8. calculadora
3. lápiz	6. revistas	9. cassettes

B. Identify two items that belong to a classmate and two items that do *not* belong to the classmate. Use the nouns in Exercise A or others that you know.

▶ *La computadora y la calculadora son de Ricardo. El cuaderno y el lápiz no son de Ricardo.*

II. Possessive adjectives

1. The following chart shows the forms of the possessive adjectives in Spanish and their English equivalents.

Possessive adjectives

mi, mis	my
tu, tus	your *(fam.)*
su, sus	his, her, their, your *(fam. and formal)*, its
nuestro/a nuestros/as	our
vuestro/a vuestros/as	your *(fam.)*

—Profesor Gómez, ¿son **sus** libros?   *Professor Gómez, are they your books?*
—Sí, son **mis** libros.   *Yes, they're my books.*

—¿Es **vuestro** hijo?   *Is he your son?*
—Sí, es **nuestro** hijo.   *Yes, he's our son.*

2. Possessive adjectives (like definite and indefinite articles) precede the noun they modify. **Mi, tu,** and **su** agree in number with the noun possessed. **Nuestro** and **vuestro** agree in number and gender with the noun possessed.

Es **mi libro**.   *It's my book.*
Son **mis hijas**.   *They're my daughters.*

Es **nuestro amigo.**   *He is our friend.*
Son **nuestras hermanas.**   *They are our sisters.*

3. The possessive adjective **tu** is written without an accent mark. This distinguishes it from the subject pronoun **tú.**

¿Tu hermano se llama Carlos?   *Is your brother named Carlos?*
¿Tú trabajas mucho?   *Do you work a lot?*

4. The possessive forms **su** and **sus** may mean *his, her, their,* and *your.* **De + él, ella, usted, ustedes, ellos** or **ellas** or the person's name may be used to clarify the meaning of **su/sus.**

¿Es **su** casa?   ¿Es la casa **de David?**

C. Say that these things belong or do not belong to the people indicated in parentheses.

▶ el cuaderno (yo)   *Es mi cuaderno.*
                       No es mi cuaderno.

1. la calculadora (tú)   4. los lápices (él)
2. los discos (tú)   5. los papeles (nosotros)
3. la revista (tú y Marta)   6. las fotos (ella)

D. Answer each question in the affirmative, using the appropriate form of the possessive adjective.

▶ ¿Es de Diego el automóvil?   *Sí, es su automóvil.*

1. ¿Es de doña Marina y de don Pepe la casa?
2. ¿Son de los señores Blanco los libros?
3. ¿Es de tu papá el periódico? .
4. ¿Son de Carmen las revistas?
5. ¿Es de tu amiga la calculadora?
6. ¿Son de tu hermano los discos?
7. ¿Es de Guillermo el televisor?
8. ¿Es de la señora de Martínez el bolígrafo?

E. Answer each question in the negative, using the appropriate form of the possessive adjective and the cues indicated.

▶ El hermano de María es mecánico,   *No, su hermano es médico.*
¿no? (médico)

1. Los amigos de ustedes son franceses, ¿verdad? (canadienses)
2. Tu padre es de Costa Rica, ¿no? (Nicaragua)
3. La hermana de Jorge y Marta es estudiante, ¿no? (artista)
4. Tu amiga se llama Julia, ¿no? (Ángela)
5. Las hermanas de Paco son enfermeras, ¿no? (dentistas)
6. Tus padres son alemanes, ¿verdad? (portugueses)

III. Personal a

Escucha los gatos.

Escucha a "Los Gatos".

1. The preposition **a** is used before a direct-object noun that refers to a specific person or persons. Sometimes it is used with a personified noun like a city or a pet.

Invito **a** mi novia.	*I invite my fiancée.*
Busco **a** mi hija.	*I'm looking for my daughter.*
Visitamos **(a)** Quito todos los años.	*We visit Quito every year.*

2. The personal **a** is not normally used after the verb **tener.**

Tengo una hermana.	*I have one sister.*
No tengo (un) hijo.	*I don't have a (one) son.*

F. Complete each sentence with **a,** if appropriate.

▶ Busco _____ dos cuadernos.   *Busco dos cuadernos.*

1. Busco _____ mi hermano.
2. ¿Invita Ud. _____ Ricardo?
3. Esperamos _____ un automóvil.
4. Llaman _____ sus padres.
5. Tengo _____ un hijo.
6. Visitamos _____ el hospital.
7. Veo _____ mi amiga Pepita.
8. Escuchan _____ los discos.
9. Las muchachas esperan _____ las niñas.

G. Make up five questions or statements, using verbs from the first column and people, places, and objects from the second column. Use the personal **a** if needed.

▶ llamar [Marisol]   *¿A quién llamas? ¿a Marisol?*

1. buscar	tu novia
2. llamar	un hospital
3. visitar	el libro de Hemingway
4. escuchar	Marisol
5. esperar	mis padres
6. invitar	Madrid

IV. The invariable form **hay**

1. The invariable form **hay,** derived from the verb **haber,** is used in Spanish to express *there is* or *there are.* When used with a singular noun, **hay** is usually followed by the indefinite article **un/a,** an indefinite modifier **(mucho, poco),** or no modifier at all.

Hay un hospital en el pueblo.	*There is a (one) hospital in town.*
Hay mucha gente en Ciudad de México.	*There are lots of people in Mexico City.*
En mi casa **hay** (un) jardín, pero no **hay** (un) patio.	*At my house there is a (one) garden, but there isn't a (one) patio.*

2. When used with a plural noun, **hay** may be followed by the indefinite article **unos/as,** a cardinal number **(dos, tres),** an indefinite modifier **(muchos, pocos),** or no modifier at all.

Hay unas señoras a la puerta.	*There are some women at the door.*
En el centro **hay** tres restaurantes.	*There are three restaurants downtown.*
Aquí **hay** pocas clases de idiomas.	*There are few language classes here.*
Perdón, señor, ¿**hay** libros de inglés aquí?	*Excuse me, sir, are there any English books here?*

H. Ask a classmate whether there are the following things in the classroom.

▶ discos S1: *¿Hay discos en la clase?*
S2: *Sí, sí hay (No, no hay) discos en la clase.*

1. una cesta	4. una puerta	7. tres pizarras
2. una mesa	5. estudiantes	8. dos computadoras
3. sillas	6. unos papeles	9. un/a profesor/a

I. Tell a classmate some of the items that are in your room **(cuarto)** or in your dormitory **(dormitorio).** Then ask him/her if the same things are in his/her room.

▶ *Hay (un) escritorio en mi cuarto. ¿También hay (un) escritorio en tu cuarto?*

¿Comprende usted?

Deriving meaning from cognates

By now, you should know which of the suggestions given in *Lección 1* are most helpful to you and which steps you may skip as you develop speed and confidence in reading for general understanding. Refer back to them as needed.

Un permiso temporal

En España y en Hispanoamérica, los estudiantes generalmente usan un **carnet de identidad** que sirve para identificar a un individuo como alumno (estudiante) de un colegio o universidad. El carnet es el documento oficial de identificación y sirve para entrar en la biblioteca, la cafetería y otras instalaciones de la universidad. A veces el horario oficial de un estudiante sirve como permiso temporal hasta la emisión de un carnet con la fotografía y el número oficial de identidad del estudiante.

Permiso temporal

Permiso temporal de admisión a la biblioteca e instalaciones de la *Universidad de Córdoba* hasta emisión del carnet de identidad oficial.

Estudiante: Sandra Coronado
Curso: Medio
Año: 1985

Horario

Inglés	lunes, miércoles, viernes	Prof. Rafael Montes
Historia musulmana	martes, jueves	Prof. Gamal Karim
Historia moderna	lunes, miércoles, viernes	Prof. Soledad Cuenca
Filología	martes, jueves	Prof. Feliciano Delgado
Dialectología	lunes, miércoles, viernes	Prof. Inmaculada Martín
Arqueología	martes, jueves	Prof. Ma. Dolores Fernández

Armando Ramos S.

el secretario, Armando Ramos S.

A. You can understand many words on the schedule card without recourse to a dictionary. What are the English equivalents of the following words from the schedule card?

el permiso	la identidad	la arqueología	oficial
el secretario	la instalación	la filología	temporal
la admisión	musulmana	medio	la emisión

B. Ask for information from your classmates about Sandra's schedule and teachers at the University of Córdoba by asking questions such as the following.

1. ¿Cuántas veces por semana (*How many times a week*) es la clase de [inglés]?
2. ¿Quién es el profesor de [historia musulmana]?
3. ¿Quién es [la profesora Soledad Cuenca]?
4. ¿Estudia Sandra geología? ¿psicología? ¿arqueología?
5. ¿La profesora Fernández es su profesora de filología?

C. Complete the following sentences with appropriate words and expressions from the reading.

1. El carnet de identidad es un . . . .
2. Los estudiantes usan el carnet para . . . .
3. Sandra usa las instalaciones de la Universidad de . . . con un . . . .
4. La profesora Inmaculada Martín dicta clase (*gives class*) de . . . .
5. No hay clase de historia moderna los . . . .

En la Universidad Complutense de Madrid, pocos estudiantes viven en los colegios mayores de la Ciudad Universitaria. Muchos estudiantes van a sus clases en motocicleta o en coche. ¿Vive Ud. en un colegio mayor? ¿Cómo va a clase?

Lección 5
En México

¿Hay un banco por aquí?

Carlos Guzmán, un joven venezolano, está en Ciudad de México, donde va a pasar las vacaciones. Está cansado, pero necesita ir al banco ahora para cambiar bolívares° por pesos° antes de regresar al hotel. Habla con un agente de policía en la acera cerca del hotel.

monetary unit of Venezuela / monetary unit of Mexico

Carlos: Perdón, señor policía. ¿Hay un banco por aquí? Necesito cambiar dinero.

Policía: Sí, señor, hay uno en la Calle Madero. Se llama el Nuevo Banco de Comercio.

5 Carlos: ¿Está cerca?

Policía: No, está bastante lejos. A unas ocho cuadras de aquí.

Carlos: ¡Tanto! . . . ¿Es posible ir en autobús?

Policía: Sí, cómo no. El camión pasa por aquí, pero hay mucho tránsito. Es más fácil ir en metro. La entrada del metro está allí en la

10 esquina.

Carlos: Entonces voy en metro. ¡Muchas gracias!

Policía: De nada, señor.

Estas personas esperan el metro en Ciudad de México, donde siempre hay mucho tránsito en las calles. El metro de Ciudad de México es famoso por su excelente servicio, por sus estaciones modernas y atractivas y por sus trenes silenciosos y rápidos. ¿Hay metro en su ciudad? Comente Ud. sobre el metro como medio de transporte.

Comprensión

1. ¿Quién es Carlos Guzmán?
2. ¿Por qué está en Ciudad de México? (Porque . . .)
3. ¿Qué necesita hacer Carlos?
4. ¿Dónde está el banco?
5. ¿Es posible o no es posible ir al banco en autobús?
6. ¿Qué palabra usa el policía para **autobús?**
7. ¿Carlos va al banco en autobús o en metro? ¿por qué?
8. ¿Qué dice Carlos al policía al final de la conversación? ¿Qué responde el policía?

Conversación

1. ¿Va Ud. a la universidad en metro, en coche o a pie?
2. ¿Necesita dinero en este momento? ¿Necesita mucho o poco dinero?
3. Si hay un banco cerca de aquí, ¿cómo se llama?
4. ¿Cuántos bancos hay en su ciudad o en su pueblo? ¿cuatro? ¿diez? ¿muchos?
5. ¿A cuántas cuadras está su casa (su apartamento, su dormitorio) de aquí?
6. ¿Usted va a ir a pie a su casa (su apartamento, su dormitorio) después de clase? ¿Va a tomar un taxi?
7. ¿Está Ud. cansado/a en este momento? (Estoy . . . No estoy . . .)
8. ¿Cómo se dice «muchas gracias» en inglés? ¿y «de nada»?

Situaciones

1. A passer-by asks you where the Bank of Commerce is. Tell him/her where it is.

   —¿Dónde está el Banco de Comercio, por favor?
   — Bastante cerca. (A unas dos cuadras del centro. En la Avenida Juárez. En la Plaza Central.)

2. When you say it's impossible to go now to the theatre, your friend wants to know why. Tell him/her why you can't go.

   —¡Qué lástima! Es imposible ir al teatro ahora.
   —¿Por qué?
   —Hay mucho tráfico y estoy . . . (nervioso/a, rabioso/a, triste).

Vocabulario

Palabras análogas

el apartamento	**el comercio**	**el/la policía**
el automóvil	**el dormitorio**	**posible**
el banco	**el hotel**	**el taxi**
central	**nervioso, -a**	**las vacaciones**

Sustantivos

la acera   sidewalk
el/la agente de policía   police officer
el autobús   bus
la avenida   avenue
el avión   airplane
la calle   street
el camión   city bus *(Mexico)*; truck
la casa   house
el coche   car
la cuadra   block
el dinero   money
la entrada   entrance
la esquina   corner
el metro   subway
la plaza   square
el teatro   theater
el tránsito   traffic

Adjetivos

cansado, -a   tired
enfermo, -a   sick
fácil   easy
joven   young
nuevo, -a   new
poco, -a   little
rabioso, -a   furious, very angry
triste   sad

Verbos

cambiar   to exchange, change
decir *(irreg.)*   to say;   **digo, dices, dice**
dirigir   to direct;   **dirijo, diriges, dirige**

ir *(irreg.)*   to go;   **voy, vas, va**
regresar   to return
responder   to respond, answer;   **respondo, respondes, responde**

Otras palabras y expresiones

a   to;   **al (= a + el), a la**   to the
a pie   on foot
a unas [ocho] cuadras de aquí   (at) about [eight] blocks from here
ahora   now
al final de   at the end of
allí   there
antes de *(+ inf.)*   before . . . — ing
cerca (de)   near
cómo no   of course
¿cómo se dice . . . ?   how does one say . . . ?
con   with
de nada   you are welcome
después   after
donde   where
en [autobús]   by [bus]
lejos (de)   far (from)
pasar las vacaciones   to spend one's vacation
perdón   excuse me
por   for, in exchange for
por aquí   around here
porque   because
¿por qué?   why?
¿qué quiere decir . . . ?   what does . . . mean?
si   if
¡tanto!   so much! so far!

Práctica

A. Make up a dialogue between yourself and a policeman in Mexico. Ask if there is a restaurant **(restaurante)** or a café **(café)** in the vicinity. Then ask where it is and how to get to it. Use the vocabulary and structures from the dialogue in this lesson.

B. Choose five Spanish cognates from the dialogue in this lesson. Imagine that you are helping a student from Mexico to pronounce and spell the English equivalents. Explain in what ways the English equivalents differ from the Spanish cognates.

La vida diaria

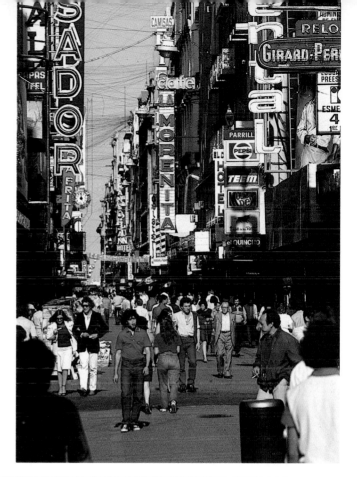

(Derecha) El ritmo de vida de una gran metrópoli como Buenos Aires contrasta drásticamente con el de los pueblos del altiplano boliviano (abajo). En el centro comercial de la capital argentina se vive una vida moderna, elegante e internacional. Por el contrario, el aislamiento de muchos pueblos bolivianos situados en las montañas de los Andes mantiene a los habitantes unidos a su pasado precolombino, que se ve incluso en sus vestidos tradicionales.

Actividades

1. Identifique en la foto de Buenos Aires algunas palabras que indiquen los productos y servicios que se ofrecen en este centro comercial.
2. Nombre un pueblo rural y una ciudad cosmopolita de Estados Unidos. Compárelos con Buenos Aires y el altiplano boliviano.

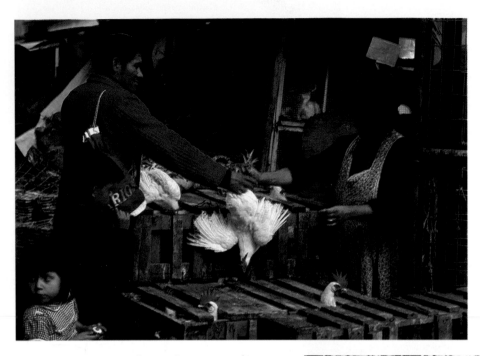

Los grandes supermercados son frecuentes en las ciudades del mundo hispánico. En ellos se puede comprar de todo. Sin embargo, con ellos coexisten todavía pequeñas tiendas como ésta (arriba) en Paloquemado, Venezuela, donde pueden comprarse animales vivos que garantizan la frescura y el buen sabor de la comida. También se sirven los productos de puerta en puerta, como este vendedor de pan en Córdoba, España (derecha). Este conveniente servicio a domicilio puede extenderse a otros productos como el queso, la leche o las frutas y verduras.

Actividades

1. ¿Qué productos se sirven de puerta en puerta en su pueblo/ciudad? ¿A cuántas casas cree Ud. sirve este señor?
2. ¿Se compran animales vivos en algún mercado que usted conozca en los Estados Unidos? ¿Y en las ferias rurales?

Cada ciudad o pueblo hispánico, ya sea grande o pequeño, tiene dos edificios principales. Uno es la iglesia, el otro, el mercado. Este mercado de Guanajuato, México es un ejemplo típico. Aquí se venden toda clase de alimentos, traídos cada día del campo a la ciudad. Los clientes son familias, dueños de pequeños restaurantes o vendedores ambulantes. A veces también se venden algunos productos de artesanía.

Actividades

1. Haga una lista de lo que Ud. y su familia necesitan diariamente para comer. ¿Qué productos cree Ud. que podría encontrar en el mercado de la foto?
2. Nombre algunas frutas, verduras y objetos que aparecen en la foto. ¿Qué más cree Ud. que venden en este mercado?

La vida social en la cultura hispánica es bastante diferente a la vida social en Estados Unidos. Tradicionalmente la familia hispánica permanece unida hasta que los hijos se casan. Los paseos se hacen en familia o en grupo, como muestra la foto en la Playa Boca Grande en Cartagena, Colombia (arriba). Sin embargo, las parejas de novios prefieren salir solas en sus tardes libres, como estos jóvenes en Málaga, España (abajo).

Actividades

1. Normalmente, ¿cuándo se independiza un joven de su familia en los Estados Unidos?
2. ¿Cuáles eran las reglas en su casa con respecto a horas, visitas, etc. para los hijos?

Entre los entretenimientos más populares del mundo hispánico se encuentran los juegos de azar y los deportes. (Arriba) No es raro ver personas, mayormente hombres, jugando juegos como el dominó, las cartas, o apostando a la lotería en las calles (Colombia). (Abajo) Entre los deportes, el fútbol es sin duda el más popular. Para los aficionados, el fútbol es una pasión a la vez que un deporte (Estadio Azteca, Ciudad de México).

Actividades

1. ¿Hay afición a los juegos de azar en los Estados Unidos?
2. ¿Ha visto Ud. alguna vez un juego de fútbol? ¿Qué le pareció?

Las corridas de toros tienen su origen en deportes practicados en Creta, Grecia y Roma hace más de veinte siglos. Las plazas de toros en las grandes ciudades se parecen a los antiguos coliseos romanos. Sin embargo, cualquier plaza puede servir como escenario para una corrida, como ésta de la foto en el estado de Yucatán, México. En España y en México la corrida acaba con la muerte del toro, pero en Portugal y ciertas partes de Hispanoamérica no se mata el toro al final de la corrida.

Actividades

1. ¿Cree Ud. que las corridas son arte o deporte? Busque información sobre las distintas partes de una corrida.
2. ¿Qué animales se usan en los Estados Unidos en deportes?

READ

Nota cultural Regional terms

Some terms in the Spanish language vary considerably from one country or region to another. For example, the Spanish equivalent for *bus* is **un autobús** in many areas, but it is also called **un camión** in Mexico and **una guagua** in Puerto Rico, Cuba, and the Canary Islands. An *automobile* may be universally referred to as **un automóvil**, but it is also called **un coche** in Spain and **un carro** in many Hispanic American countries.

Pronunciación y ortografía
I. Flap [r]

Spanish has both a single flap [r] and a trilled [R] sound. The single flap [r] is pronounced toward the front of the mouth, with the tip of the tongue making one quick "flap" against the gum ridge behind the upper front teeth. It is a very different sound from English [r], which is pronounced toward the back of the mouth without the assistance of the tip of the tongue. Spanish [r] resembles the sound an English speaker often makes when pronouncing the *tt* in words such as *bitter, better, butter*. The Spanish sound is spelled with a single letter **r**.

A. Close your book and listen to your instructor say the following pairs of words. Repeat only the word that contains the sound [r]. Then repeat the exercise with your book open.

loro / lodo	moro / modo	pudo / puro
codo / coro	cara / cada	muro / mudo

B. Repeat the following words after your instructor. Each word contains one or more flap [r] sounds.

escritorio	obrero	Carlos	Nicaragua
profesora	trabaja	Carmen	Paraguay
acero	enfermera	Clara	Argentina

C. Read the following sentences aloud. Pay careful attention to the way you pronounce [r].

1. Clara Suárez es enfermera.
2. Carlos trabaja en una fábrica.
3. El señor Duarte es profesor.

II. More on linking

1. In *Lección 2* you learned that linking occurs in breath groups when a final consonant is linked to an initial vowel and when two consonants or two vowels are identical.

   es‿español   un‿norteamericano
   en‿un pueblo   es de‿Elena
   el‿lunes   está‿aquí

2. Linking also occurs when one word ends in a weak vowel (**i, u**) and the following word begins with a strong vowel (**a, e, o**) or vice versa, thus forming a diphthong. Final **y** is considered a weak vowel at the end of a syllable.

   Necesito‿una pluma.   Hoy‿es lunes.   Es mi‿hermano.

3. Linking tends to occur even when the final vowel and the initial vowel are both strong vowels.

   Trabajo‿en México.   Ana‿está‿en casa.   No‿es difícil.

   To avoid a strong foreign accent that may interfere with communication, do not stop the flow of your voice between adjacent vowels. Practice reading aloud, with proper linking, to develop good, clear pronunciation.

   D. Read aloud the following sentences, linking the vowels and consonants where indicated. Pronounce each breath group as though it were one, multi-syllabled word.

   1. Estudio‿en‿un colegio.
   2. Hay‿una revista‿en la mesa.
   3. Necesito‿unos dólares para comprar dos‿sándwiches.
   4. No‿habla‿alemán.
   5. Está cerca del‿hospital.

Refranes

Lo barato es caro y lo caro es barato.   Inexpensive things are costly and expensive things are cheap.

Secreto de uno, secreto es;
Secreto de dos, secreto de Dios;
Secreto de tres, de todos es.

Estudio de palabras

I. El pueblo de Río Verde

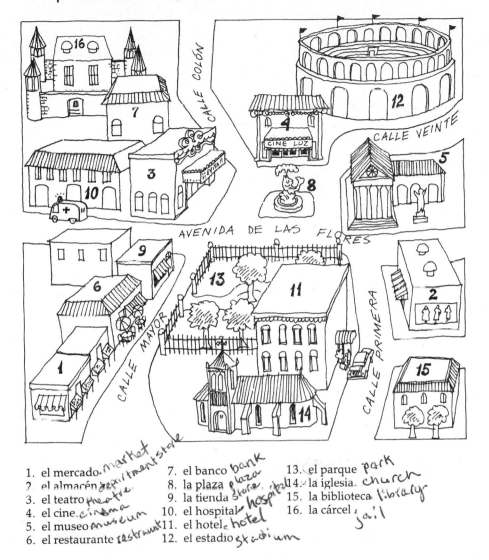

1. el mercado *market*
2. el almacén *department store*
3. el teatro *theatre*
4. el cine *cinema*
5. el museo *museum*
6. el restaurante *restaurant*
7. el banco *bank*
8. la plaza *plaza*
9. la tienda *store*
10. el hospital *hospital*
11. el hotel *hotel*
12. el estadio *stadium*
13. el parque *park*
14. la iglesia *church*
15. la biblioteca *library*
16. la cárcel *jail*

A. Look at the map of Río Verde and ask another student on which street the buildings listed below the drawing are located.

▶ S1: *¿Dónde está [el restaurante]?*   S2: *Está en la Calle Mayor.*

B. Ask another student whether or not any of the following buildings or places are near his/her house.

▶ hotel   S1: *¿Hay un hotel cerca de tu casa?*
            S2: *Sí, hay un hotel cerca de mi casa. Se llama Hotel Plaza.*
                    Está en la Calle 10.
                    No, no hay un hotel cerca de mi casa.

1. mercado   3. parque   5. almacén
2. iglesia   4. cine   6. tienda

II. Prefijos en **im-, in-** y **des-**

The prefixes **im-, in-,** and **des-** are often used with Spanish adjectives and nouns to mean *not,* to indicate *lack of,* or to mean the opposite of the original word.

posible possible	**imposible** impossible
acción action	**inacción** inaction
contento satisfied	**descontento** dissatisfied

C. Read aloud each word, giving its English equivalent. Then add the prefix indicated and give the English equivalent of the new word.

im-	**in-**	**des-**
paciente	tranquilo	animado
parcial	alterable	aparición
personal	coherente	armar
preciso	competente	equilibrio

Estructuras útiles

I. Present tense and uses of **estar**

Roberto **está** *en el hospital.* **Está** *muy enfermo.*

1. There are two verbs in Spanish that mean *to be:* **ser,** which you studied in *Lección 1,* and **estar.** The present-tense forms of **estar** are shown in the chart below. Note that the **yo-**form, **estoy,** is irregular.

	estar	
yo	**estoy**	Estoy muy cansado.
tú	**estás**	¿Cómo estás?
Ud., él, ella	**está**	Está en el mercado.
nosotros, -as	**estamos**	Estamos aquí.
~~vosotros, -as~~	~~estáis~~	~~Estáis en la clase de español.~~
Uds., ellos, ellas	**están**	Están en México.

2. **Estar** is used:
   a. to express how someone feels.

   —¿Cómo **estás** hoy?   *How are you today?*
   —**Estoy** muy nervioso porque   *I'm very nervous because there's an*
     hay examen.   *exam.*

   b. to indicate the location of someone or something.

   —¿Dónde **está** el Banco   *Where's the International Bank?*
     Internacional?
   —**Está** a unas cuadras de   *It's a few blocks from here.*
     aquí.

A. Ask the following people how they feel today. They should respond with the proper form of the adjectives **cansado/a, triste, contento/a, rabioso/a, tranquilo/a, nervioso/a.**

▶ Mariluz   S1: *¿Cómo estás hoy, Mariluz?*
             S2: *Estoy [contenta].*

1. Prof. García	3. Srta. Goya	5. Doña Luz
2. Dra. Robledo	4. Catalina	6. Carlos

B. Some of the following people are well, others are ill. State whether they are at home or in the hospital.

▶ Jorge (bien)   *Jorge está bien. Está en casa.*
▶ Luisa (mal)   *Luisa está mal. Está en el hospital.*

1. la secretaria (bien)	4. los señores Álvarez (bien)
2. tú (bien)	5. yo (mal)
3. nosotros (mal)	6. tú y Luisa (bien)

C. When a classmate asks where different people are from, tell him/her where they are from and where they are now. Use the names of the cities and countries indicated or other Hispanic place names.

► Jaime / Bilbao (Quito)   S1: *¿De dónde es Jaime?*
                            S2: *Jaime es de Bilbao, pero está en Quito ahora.*

1. Luisa / Buenos Aires (San José)
2. Ana y tú / España (los Estados Unidos)
3. los señores Alarcón / Cuba (Asunción)
4. Ricardo y Miguel / Puerto Rico (Santo Domingo)
5. el doctor Gonsálvez / Chile (La Paz)
6. tú / México (Caracas)

D. When a classmate asks for the following items, tell whether they are here, at home, in the library, or elsewhere.

► libro de inglés   S1: *¿Tienes un libro de inglés?*
                     S2: *Sí, aquí está.*
                         No, mi libro de inglés está [en casa].

1. regla   4. periódico
2. papeles   5. pluma
3. mapa   6. revista de automóviles

II. Present tense of **ir**

1. The verb **ir** is irregular in the present tense. Its endings are like those of **estar,** but they do not have a written accent.

		ir	
yo	**voy**	Voy a clase.
tú	**vas**	¿Vas a México o a España?
Ud., él, ella	**va**	Va a un café.
nosotros, -as	**vamos**	Vamos a un restaurante.
~~vosotros, -as~~	~~vais~~	~~Vais mañana.~~
Uds., ellos, ellas	**van**	Van a la clase de inglés.

2. The interrogative expression **¿adónde?** is usually used in asking questions about where one is going.

—**¿Adónde van** ustedes?   *Where are you going?*
—**Vamos** al teatro.   *We're going to the theater.*

3. Future action can be expressed in Spanish by the **ir a** + *infinitive* construction.

Voy a visitar el pueblo de Río Verde.	*I'm going to visit the town of Río Verde.*
Vamos a pasar las vacaciones en Uruguay.	*We're going to spend our vacation in Uruguay.*

4. In addition to being used to indicate a future action, **vamos a** + *infinitive* may also be used to express a suggestion, equivalent to *let's* in English.

—¿Qué hacemos ahora?	*What should we do now?*
—**Vamos a estudiar.**	*Let's study.*
—Pepe no está aquí.	*Pepe isn't here.*
—Pues, **vamos a esperar** cinco minutos.	*Well, let's wait for five minutes.*

E. Say that the people indicated are going to the countries mentioned.

▶ Ignacio / Panamá   *Ignacio va a Panamá.*

1. los estudiantes / Chile
2. yo / Colombia
3. tú y yo / México
4. Jorge y tú / Venezuela
5. Marta / Costa Rica
6. tú / Bolivia

F. Ask where the following people are going for a vacation.

▶ tú   *¿Adónde vas para las vacaciones?*

1. Miguel
2. tus padres
3. ustedes
4. nosotras
5. Elena y tú
6. las niñas
7. tú
8. Andrea

G. Answer the following questions, saying that the activities are going to take place tomorrow, not today.

▶ ¿Esteban estudia hoy?   *No, va a estudiar mañana.*

1. ¿Tú y yo trabajamos hoy?
2. ¿Alicia escucha la radio hoy?
3. ¿Los estudiantes van al café hoy?
4. ¿Tomás va en taxi al centro hoy?
5. ¿Miras la televisión hoy?
6. ¿Ángel y tú van a la biblioteca hoy?
7. ¿Carmen y Ricardo van al mercado hoy?

H. Say which of the following activities you or someone you know of is going to do and when.

▶ estudiar la lección   *[Esteban] va a estudiar la lección [el jueves].*

1. mirar la televisión
2. estudiar para un examen
3. hablar con la familia
4. trabajar en otro país

5. cantar en el coro
6. bailar en una discoteca
7. preparar una fiesta
8. regresar a casa

I. Accept or refuse the following invitations from a friend. Use the **vamos a** + *infinitive* construction in your responses to signify *let's*. If you refuse, offer an alternative.

▶ ¿Cambiamos el dinero ahora?   *Bueno, ¡vamos a cambiar el dinero!*
No, ¡vamos a cambiar el dinero [otro día]!

1. ¿Tomamos el metro pronto?
2. ¿Miramos las revistas mañana?
3. ¿Escuchamos el disco en mi casa?

4. ¿Esperamos el autobús aquí?
5. ¿Tomamos un taxi al centro?
6. ¿Estudiamos en la biblioteca?

III. Contractions **al** and **del**

*Pepe le habla **al** profesor.*

*Pepe habla **del** profesor.*

There are two written contractions in Spanish. The prepositions **a** and **de** contract with the definite article **el** to form **al** and **del**. They do *not* contract with **la, los,** or **las.**

Voy **al** teatro el sábado.
El teatro está frente **al** museo.

I'm going to the theater on Saturday.
The theater is opposite the museum.

—¿Dónde está la mamá **del** niño?
—Está cerca **del** escritorio.

Where is the child's mother?
She's near the desk.

esta – always used for location

J. Tell where the following people are going, and specify the day on which they are going.

▶ yo / el cine   *Voy al cine [el lunes].*

　　1. tú / el aeropuerto
　　2. ellos / la capital de Argentina
　　3. él / el Banco Nacional
　　4. nosotras / la tienda San Miguel
　　5. tú y Jaime / el parque Balboa
　　6. yo / el mercado de San José

a + el = al

a la

K. Ask three individuals in the class on which days of the week they go to different places in town. Use vocabulary from the map of Río Verde in the *Estudio de palabras.* Then report the information to the class.

▶ S1: *¿Qué día vas [al cine]?*　　S2: *Voy [al cine] los sábados.*
　　S1: *[Pepe] dice que va [al cine] los sábados.*

L. You are trying to correct misinformation about the identity of the owner(s) of the items mentioned. Answer each question in the negative, using the opposite gender form of the noun, with the correct definite article.

▶ ¿El cuaderno es de la niña?　　*No, es del niño.*

　　1. ¿El bolígrafo es de la joven?
　　2. ¿Los lápices son de los estudiantes?
　　3. ¿La revista es de la señorita?
　　4. ¿El escritorio es del profesor?
　　5. ¿Los libros son de las muchachas?
　　6. ¿La calculadora es del hombre?

de + el = del

de la

M. Show where the different buildings and places shown on the map of Río Verde in the *Estudio de palabras* are located in reference to each other. Use the following expressions, and remember to use the contractions **al** and **del** when necessary.

cerca de　near	**frente a**　facing
lejos de　far from	**a la izquierda de**　to the left of
delante de　in front of	**a la derecha de**　to the right of
detrás de　behind	**junto a**　next to

▶ *El teatro está [frente a la plaza].*
▶ *El restaurante está [junto al mercado].*

IV. Word order in interrogative sentences

1. Interrogative sentences that may be answered by **sí** or **no** are formed in several ways:

   a. by using rising intonation at the end of a statement.

   ¿Usted es americano?
   { *Are you (an) American?*
   { *You're (an) American?*

   b. by adding a tag phrase like **¿no?**, **¿verdad?**, or **¿no es verdad?** to the end of a sentence. Note that **¿sí?** is never used as a tag phrase in Spanish.

   | Ud. habla inglés, **¿no?** | *You speak English, don't you?* |
   | No está aquí Raúl, **¿verdad?** | *Raúl isn't here, is he?* |

   c. by changing the word order and using rising intonation at the end of a statement. In this case, the subject follows either the verb or the construction **ser** + *predicate adjective*.

   | **¿Viaja usted** a Panamá? | *Are you traveling to Panama?* |
   | **¿Es** mexicano **el banco?** | *Is the bank Mexican?* |

2. Interrogative sentences that ask for specific information are introduced by an interrogative word or expression that is usually followed immediately by the verb.

¿Cómo está usted?	*How are you?*
¿Qué haces tú por aquí?	*What are you doing around here?*
¿Dónde vive Elena?	*Where does Elena live?*
¿De qué país **son** ustedes?	*What country are you from?*
¿Cuándo necesitas las revistas?	*When do you need the magazines?*
¿Adónde va María?	*Where's Maria going to?*

   (handwritten margin notes: How, What, where, from what, when, to where)

   N. Change the following statements to questions, using two or more of the ways of forming questions.

   ▶ Tú eres estudiante.   *¿Tú eres estudiante?*
                            ¿Eres estudiante tú?
                            Tú eres estudiante, ¿no?

   1. Ud. vive en Valencia.
   2. Uds. trabajan en una fábrica.
   3. María estudia medicina.
   4. Alberto es mecánico.
   5. Ellas hablan español perfectamente.
   6. Vamos al cine el sábado.

O. Change the following statements to questions, using the interrogative words indicated.

▶ Roberto vive en Guadalajara. (¿dónde?)   *¿Dónde vive Roberto?*

1. Elvira habla tres lenguas extranjeras. (¿cuántas?)
2. Los muchachos están en la biblioteca. (¿quiénes?)
3. La profesora mira el tránsito. (¿qué?)
4. Inés está triste hoy. (¿cómo?)
5. El joven necesita comprar un carro. (¿quién?)
6. Roberto y yo vamos al aeropuerto hoy. (¿cuándo?)
7. Carlos va a la oficina porque necesita información. (¿por qué?)
8. Mi número de teléfono es el 13-19-07. (¿cuál?)

P. Ask your classmates as many questions as you can about the opening dialogue of this lesson to see how much of it they can remember.

¿Comprende usted?

Read the following dialogue between Carlos García and a travel agent without stopping to look up unfamiliar words. Then do the exercises.

En una agencia de turismo

Carlos García está en Ciudad de México, y desea viajar al estado de Yucatán en el sureste de México. Va a una agencia de turismo y habla con la agente.

Agente: Buenos días, señor. ¿En qué puedo servirle?
  Carlos: Buenos días, señorita. Pues . . . busco información sobre una excursión a Yucatán.
Agente: ¿Desea viajar en avión?
5 Carlos: No, no me gusta viajar en avión. ¿Es posible ir en autobús?
  Agente: Sí, cómo no. El lunes hay una excursión muy buena con visitas a Mérida, las zonas arqueológicas de Uxmal y muchos otros sitios interesantes. Aquí hay un folleto con detalles y muchas fotografías del área.
10 Carlos: ¿Cuánto cuesta la excursión?
  Agente: Hay varias posibilidades. En mi opinión, la excursión número tres es excelente y es relativamente económica.
  Carlos: Gracias. Voy a estudiar los folletos y mañana hablamos. ¿Está bien?
15 Agente: Sí, señor. Aquí está mi nombre y mi número de teléfono. Estoy a sus órdenes.

A. Indicate whether the following statements are true or false, based on the reading.

1. Yucatán está cerca de Estados Unidos, en el norte de México.
2. Un folleto turístico tiene información ilustrada de áreas geográficas.
3. Si algo cuesta mucho, es económico.
4. Hay que ir a Uxmal en avión.
5. Según la agente de turismo, hay dos excursiones a Yucatán.

B. Choose the most appropriate rejoinders from the second column to complete these five exchanges.

1. —¿Le gusta viajar por autobús?
2. —¿Hay excursiones económicas?
3. —¿En qué puedo servirle?
4. —Deseo ir a Yucatán. ¿Hay excursiones?
5. —Miro los folletos y mañana hablamos.

a. La semana que viene hay unas excursiones a Mérida.
b. No, prefiero viajar en avión.
c. Bien. Aquí está mi número de teléfono.
d. Pues, necesito información sobre autobuses y trenes.
e. Sí, hay varias posibilidades.

C. Complete the following statements with appropriate words and expressions from the reading.

1. En una agencia de turismo es posible encontrar . . . .
2. Para una persona que no desea viajar en avión es posible . . . .
3. Algunos sitios de interés en el sureste de México son . . . .
4. Para hacer un viaje es buena idea primero estudiar unos folletos y después hablar con . . . .

Las ruinas arqueológicas de Palenque en el sur de México son una demostración del estado avanzado de la civilización maya. Visite Ud. las ruinas de Palenque con la imaginación y discuta con sus compañeros de clase la posible tecnología de los mayas. ¿Conoce Ud. unas ruinas interesantes? ¿Dónde están?

Lección 6
En los Estados Unidos

¿Cómo es tu primo?

Daniel Briceño y su novia Carolina Ortiz están en un café en el aeropuerto de Miami, Florida. Beben café y té, y comen sándwiches mientras esperan la llegada en avión de un primo de Daniel que vive en Los Ángeles.

Translate

Carolina: ¿Te gustan los sándwiches? Están riquísimos, ¿verdad?

Daniel: Sí, pero ¡qué café más terrible! Está muy fuerte . . . Camarero, una cerveza, por favor.

Camarero: Sí, señor. Inmediatamente.

5 Carolina: Dime, Daniel, ¿cómo se llama tu primo?

Daniel: Enrique Briceño Cárdenas. Es técnico en computadoras.

Carolina: ¡Qué interesante! ¿Y cómo es? ¿alto y moreno como tú?

Daniel: No, al contrario, Quique es bajo y rubio . . . pero muy simpático, igual que yo.

10 Carolina: Y también muy humilde como tú, ¿eh?

Daniel: Sí, claro. Como todos los Briceño . . .° ¡Oye, Carolina, ya anuncian la llegada del vuelo de Los Ángeles.

todos . . . all the Briceños

Carolina: Y llega a tiempo. ¡Qué suerte!

Daniel: Camarero, la cuenta, por favor.

15 Camarero: En seguida, señor.

En muchas ciudades de los Estados Unidos vive un gran número de hispanos. La influencia hispánica está presente en la radio y la televisión, la educación, el comercio y en otros aspectos de la vida diaria como en el arte de este mural en un parque infantil de San Francisco, California. Describa brevemente algunos aspectos de este mural. ¿Qué significado cree Ud. que tienen algunos símbolos del mural para los hispanos de este barrio?

Lección 6   99

Comprensión

1. ¿Dónde están Daniel Cárdenas y Carolina Ortiz en este momento?
2. ¿Qué hacen allí?
3. ¿Son novios o amigos Daniel y Carolina?
4. ¿Es buena o mala la comida del café?
5. ¿Por qué desea Daniel una cerveza?
6. ¿Quién llega de Los Ángeles en avión?
7. ¿Qué hace Quique en Los Ángeles? ¿Cuál es su profesión?
8. Según Daniel, ¿cómo es su primo?
9. Y según Carolina, ¿es Daniel simpático, humilde o arrogante?

Conversación

1. ¿Tiene Ud. primos? ¿Cómo se llaman? ¿Cuál es su apellido? ¿Cuál es su nombre de pila? ¿Tienen sobrenombres o apodos?
2. ¿Dónde viven sus primos? ¿Viven en los Estados Unidos o en otro país? Si viven en los Estados Unidos, ¿en qué estado y en qué ciudad o pueblo viven?
3. ¿Tiene Ud. hermanos o hermanas? ¿Son muy jóvenes? ¿Son estudiantes? ¿Trabajan?
4. ¿Le gusta a Ud. viajar? ¿Viaja Ud. mucho en avión?
5. ¿Hay un aeropuerto internacional en su ciudad? ¿Cómo se llama?
6. ¿Hay vuelos internacionales a países hispánicos? ¿a qué países?

Situaciones

1. You are in a restaurant and ask a friend what he/she will have to drink.

   —(Daniel), ¿qué bebes?
   —Bebo . . . (café, agua, vino, leche, té).

2. You see a friend eating in the cafeteria. Ask him/her how the food is.

   —¿Cómo está . . . (la ensalada, el helado, la fruta, el taco)?
   —Está . . . (delicioso/a, exquisito/a, rico/a, muy bueno/a, terrible).

Vocabulario

Palabras análogas

arrogante	el interés	la profesión
la computadora	interesante	el sándwich
delicioso, -a	internacional	el taco
exquisito, -a	la opinión	terrible

do not need to know

Sustantivos

el aeropuerto airport
el agua *(f)* water
el apodo nickname
el café coffee; café
el camarero waiter
la cerveza beer
la comida meal; food
la compañía company
la cuenta check, bill
la ensalada salad
la fruta fruit
el helado ice cream
la leche milk
la llegada arrival
el nombre de pila first name
la novia fiancée, sweetheart
el novio fiancé, sweetheart
la prima female cousin
el primo male cousin
el sobrenombre nickname
el té tea
el técnico en computadoras computer technician
el vino wine
el vuelo flight

Adjetivos

alto, -a tall
antipático, -a unpleasant, disagreeable
bajo, -a short *(in stature)*
bueno, -a good
fuerte strong

humilde humble, modest *stop finish*
malo, -a bad
moreno, -a dark-complexioned
rico, -a delicious; rich
riquísimo, -a very delicious; very rich
rubio, -a blond
simpático, -a attractive, nice, friendly
todo, -a all

Verbos

anunciar to announce
beber to drink
comer to eat
decir *(irreg.)* to tell; **dime** tell me

Otras palabras y expresiones

a tiempo on time
al contrario on the contrary
claro of course
como like
¿cómo es él? what's he like?
en seguida right away
igual que (yo) just like (me)
inmediatamente immediately, right away
mientras while
mucho a lot
¡oye! hey, listen!
¡qué café más terrible! what terrible coffee!
¡qué interesante! how interesting!
¡qué suerte! what luck!
ya already; now

Práctica

A. Describe the girl in the photo at the left. Tell what kind of a person she is. Tell where she lives (in a house, an apartment, or dormitory), what she does for a living, what her nationality is, and what she looks like. Use at least five adjectives from the dialogue in this lesson.

B. Imagine that you are in a snackbar. Order a sandwich and coffee with milk. The coffee is not good, so request something else to drink.

Estos estudiantes de Buenos Aires, Argentina desarrollan un proyecto con la ayuda de computadoras.

Nota cultural Hispanics in Florida

Ever since its discovery, Florida has always had a very special meaning for Hispanics. The region was discovered by Juan Ponce de León in 1513 on the day of **Pascua Florida** *(Easter Sunday)*, and received its name from that Christian holy day. Saint Augustine **(San Agustín),** one of the oldest cities in the United States, was founded in 1565 by another Spaniard, Pedro Menéndez de Avilés.

Today many Hispanics from the Caribbean, Central America, and South America live in Florida, especially in the Miami area. The largest group is comprised of Cubans who arrived there in great numbers in the late fifties and early sixties. Because of the presence of many Hispanics in Florida, other Spanish-speaking people have been attracted to the state, which has resulted in a constantly expanding Hispanic population.

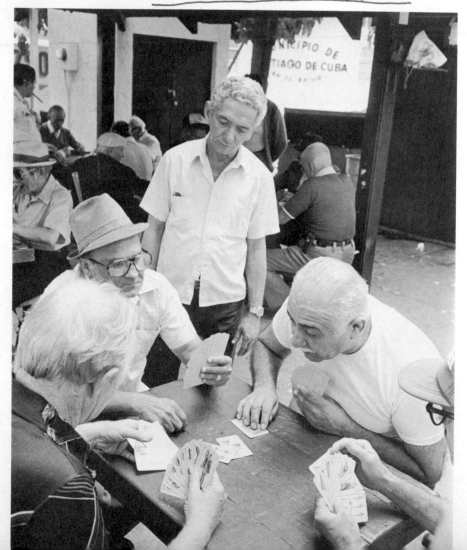

Estos inmigrantes cubanos de "la pequeña Habana", Miami, juegan a las cartas con una baraja española. Hay muchos clubes sociales hispánicos en los Estados Unidos como éste, adonde los mayores van para charlar y socializar. ¿Qué actividades o centros para mayores hay en su ciudad?

Pronunciación y ortografía
Trilled [R]

When pronouncing the trilled [R], the tongue tip is in the same position as when pronouncing the flap [r], on the upper gum ridge. However, when you pronounce the trilled [R], the tip of your tongue should *vibrate* against the gum ridge, as you force air through your mouth.

The trilled [R] is spelled **r** at the beginning of a word or after **l**, **n**, or **s**. It is spelled **rr** between vowels.

Enrique   rápido   ca**rr**o   **r**ubio

A. Escuche a su profesor/a y repita las palabras siguientes. *(Listen and repeat the following words or expressions after your instructor.)*

Ramón	pizarra	terrible	Enrique
Rosa	correcto	horrible	Israel

B. Escuche a su profesor/a pronunciar los siguientes pares de palabras. Repita sólo la palabra que tiene el sonido [R]. *(Listen to your instructor say the following pairs of words. Repeat only the word that contains the sound [R]).*

perro / pero	cero / cerro	coro / corro
caro / carro	parra / para	barrios / varios

C. Lea las siguientes oraciones en voz alta. Preste atención a la pronunciación de las palabras con **r** y **rr**. *(Read the following sentences aloud. Pay careful attention to the way you pronounce the words that contain the letters **r** and **rr**.)*

1. Enrique y Ramón van a cambiar dinero.
2. Rosa habla portugués y francés. No habla ruso.
3. ¿Hay una pizarra en la clase de arte romano?

D. Escuche a su profesor/a pronunciar las siguientes palabras. Si la palabra tiene el sonido [r], cámbiela a una palabra con [R], y viceversa. *(Listen to your instructor pronounce the following words. If the word contains the sound [r], change it to a word with [R], and vice versa.)*

▶ perro   *pero*
▶ pero   *perro*

1. cero	4. caro	7. carro
2. parra	5. coro	8. para
3. corro	6. pera	9. barrio

Trabalenguas *(Tongue twister)*

Por la Calle Carretas pasó un perrito.
Pasó una carreta y le cortó el rabito.
¡Pobre perrito!

A small dog passed through
Carretas Street. A cart passed
by and cut off its small tail.
Poor little dog!

Estudio de palabras

I. Adjetivos descriptivos

[handwritten: Know for test Fri. 6th M & F]

gordo   flaco   activa   perezoso   grande   pequeño

rica   pobre   generosa   tacaño

guapo   feo   vieja   joven   inteligente   tonto

[handwritten: Bonita - pretty]

1. There are many adjectives in Spanish that express the idea of *pretty* or *handsome*. However, the terms **hermosa, linda, guapa,** and **bonita** are often used to describe a female, and **guapo** and **bien parecido** are often used to describe a male. The words are not always interchangeable, and their use varies from country to country.

2. The following are other useful descriptive words and phrases.

de estatura mediana   of medium height
delgado, -a   slim, slender
de cierta edad   middle-aged
usa gafas   he/she wears glasses
de pelo negro   black-haired
de pelo castaño   brown-haired
pelirrojo, -a   red-headed

3. **Optimista** and **pesimista** end in **-a** whether they refer to a male or a female.

A. Conteste las siguientes preguntas, usando la forma correcta del adjetivo. (*Answer the following questions, using the appropriate form of the descriptive adjective.*)

1. ¿Cuál es el contrario de **alto?** ¿de **viejo?**
2. ¿Cuál es un sinónimo de **bonita?**
3. ¿Es Ud. optimista o pesimista? En su opinión, ¿es optimista o pesimista su profesor/a de español? ¿y su profesor/a de inglés?
4. ¿Es usted rubio/a? ¿moreno/a? ¿viejo/a?
5. ¿Es muy guapo/a su novio/a? ¿Es simpático/a?

B. Describa a las personas del siguiente dibujo, usando el mayor número posible de adjetivos de las listas anteriores. (*Describe the people in the following drawing, using as many adjectives as you can from the preceding lists.*)

Carlos Garcia   el señor Gutiérrez   la señora Gómez de Valencia   Pepito el mendigo

C. Descríbase a sí mismo/a, usando algunos adjetivos y otras expresiones útiles de las listas anteriores. *(Describe yourself, using some of the adjectives and other useful descriptive words and phrases from the preceding lists.)*

II. Los colores

amarillo, -a	yellow	**azul**	blue
anaranjado, -a	orange	**gris**	gray
blanco, -a	white	**verde**	green
morado, -a	purple	**(de color) café**	brown
negro, -a	black	**azul claro**	light blue
rojo, -a	red	**azul marino**	navy blue
rosado, -a	pink	**verde oscuro**	dark green

1. The adjectives **azul, gris,** and **verde** do not change when used with a feminine noun.

   el lápiz **azul**   la mesa **azul**

2. The adjectives **claro** and **oscuro** are often used with **de color,** either stated or understood, and the adjective is then invariable.

   el papel azul **claro**   las reglas de color azul **oscuro**

3. **(De color) café,** and **(de color) marrón,** which are invariable, represent the color *brown.* Other words for brown are **pardo,-a, castaño,-a** *(for hair)* and **moreno,-a** *(for complexion).*

   Mi madre es **morena,** pero tiene pelo **castaño.**   *My mother is dark-complexioned but has brown hair.*

D. Pregúntele a otra persona de la clase de qué color son los siguientes objetos. *(Ask another person in the class to specify the color of the following items.)*

   ► tu casa / ¿azul o blanca?   S1: *¿De qué color es tu casa, ¿azul o blanca?*
                                        S2: *Es [blanca].*

   1. el bolígrafo de Pepe / ¿negro o anaranjado?
   2. la puerta de la clase / ¿blanca o café?
   3. el libro de Juan / ¿rojo o amarillo?
   4. el papel / ¿blanco o rosado?
   5. la pizarra / ¿verde oscuro o gris?
   6. la silla / ¿amarilla o morada?

Estructuras útiles

I. Descriptive adjectives and agreement

Las ciudades son **agitadas.** *El campo es* **tranquilo.**

1. In Spanish, adjectives must agree in gender and number with the nouns they modify. There are two main classes of adjectives: four-form and two-form.

   a. Adjectives whose masculine singular form ends in **-o** have four forms.

	Singular	Plural
Masculine	alt**o**	alt**os**
Feminine	alt**a**	alt**as**

   El muchacho es **alto.**   Los muchachos son **altos.**
   La muchacha es **alta.**   Las muchachas son **altas.**

   b. Adjectives that end in a consonant or in a vowel other than **-o** usually have two forms. They agree *only* in number with the noun they modify. Note that a written accent is required on the plural form of **joven** in order to reflect its proper stress.

Singular	Plural
fácil	fáciles
pobre	pobres
joven	jóvenes
pesimista	pesimistas

   El ejercicio es **fácil.**   Los ejercicios son **fáciles.**
   La señora es **pobre.**   Las señoras son **pobres.**
   La muchacha es **joven.**   Las muchachas son **jóvenes.**
   El director es **pesimista.**   Los directores son **pesimistas.**

2. When an adjective modifies two or more nouns of different gender, the masculine plural form is used.

Pedro y Lucía son **bajos**.   *Pedro and Lucía are short.*
Carlos y Mercedes son **activos**.   *Carlos and Mercedes are active.*

3. Descriptive adjectives may precede or follow the noun.
   a. Adjectives of size, color, shape, and nationality usually follow the noun.
   b. Limiting adjectives such as definite and indefinite articles, possessive adjectives, and adjectives of quantity, such as **poco** and **mucho,** precede the noun.

Pepe es **un** niño **perezoso**.   *Pepe is a lazy child.*
La señora **rubia** es técnica en computadoras.   *The blonde woman is a computer technician.*
Mi novio compra **un** carro **rojo.**   *My fiancé is buying a red car.*
El señor López es **un** hombre **pesimista.**   *Mr. López is a pessimistic man.*
Hay **muchas** personas en mi clase de español.   *There are many people in my Spanish class.*

A. Describa el color de algunos objetos de la clase que pertenecen a diferentes personas. *(Describe the color of some classroom items that belong to different people.)*

▶ *Mi cuaderno es [azul claro].*
▶ *El cuaderno de Miguel es [verde oscuro].*

B. Cambie al plural las oraciones siguientes. *(Change the following sentences to the plural.)*

▶ La lección es fácil.   *Las lecciones son fáciles.*

1. El aeropuerto es grande.
2. El joven es simpático.
3. La señora es flaca.
4. El niño es simpático.
5. La chica es morena.
6. El señor es arrogante.

C. Pregúntele a otro estudiante su opinión sobre las siguientes personas. Responda con la forma correcta de uno de los adjetivos indicados. *(Ask a classmate to give his/her opinion about the following people. Answer with the correct form of one of the adjectives given.)*

▶ la señora Gutiérrez / ¿viejo o joven?   S1: *¿Es muy vieja o muy joven la Sra. Gutiérrez?*
S2: *En mi opinión, es muy [vieja].*

1. los señores Guzmán / ¿humilde o arrogante?
2. tu primo Juan / ¿pobre o rico?
3. tu hermana Concha / ¿perezoso o activo?
4. doña Rosa / ¿gordo o flaco?
5. Pepe y Ángela / ¿simpático o antipático?
6. los estudiantes de la clase / ¿optimista o pesimista?

D. Describa las siguientes personas, usando por lo menos dos adjetivos de la lista para describir a cada una. (*Describe the following persons, using at least two adjectives from the list to describe each one.*)

rubio	moreno	tacaño	generoso	simpático
joven	viejo	pobre	rico	grande
alto	bajo	inteligente	pequeño	antipático

► tu tía y su hija   *Mi tía [Teresa] y su hija son altas y generosas.*

1. uno de tus amigos
2. dos hermanas o primas
3. tu primo
4. dos de tus amigas
5. dos estudiantes de la clase
6. tú y yo

E. Escoja entre los adjetivos de la lista u otros originales el adjetivo apropiado para describir cada cosa, según su opinión. Puede usar más de un adjetivo. (*Choose from among the adjectives in the list, or other original ones, the proper adjective to describe each item according to your opinion. You may use more than one adjective.*)

bueno	terrible	exquisito	importante
fantástico	horrible	excelente	especial

► los deportes   *Los deportes son excelentes, importantes y fantásticos.*

1. los aviones
2. los amigos
3. los espaguetis
4. los exámenes
5. las vacaciones
6. las novelas
7. las lenguas extranjeras
8. los libros de historia
9. las hamburguesas

F. Diga que los objetos mencionados son franceses, españoles, italianos, etc. (*State that the objects mentioned are French, Spanish, Italian, etc.*)

► ¿La revista es de Italia?   *Sí, es una revista italiana.*
► ¿Los periódicos son de España?   *Sí, son unos periódicos españoles.*

1. ¿El vino es de Francia?
2. ¿Las sillas son de Italia?
3. ¿El avión es de España?
4. ¿Las mesas son de Alemania?
5. ¿Los autobuses son de Inglaterra?
6. ¿Los libros son de Portugal?

II. Present tense of -er and -ir verbs

1. The present tense of regular -er and -ir verbs is formed by adding the present-tense endings (indicated in boldface in the chart below) to the infinitive stem. The endings of -er and -ir verbs are identical except for the **nosotros-** and **vosotros-**forms.

aprender	*er verbs*	escribir	*ir Verbs*
aprend **o**		escrib **o**	– *Yo*
aprend **es**		escrib **es**	– *Tu*
aprend **e**		escrib **e**	– *El Ella Ud*
aprend **emos**		escrib **imos**	– *nosotros*
aprend **éis**		escrib **ís**	–
aprend **en**		escrib **en**	

Quiz Wed. Nov. 27 *translate er & ir verbs Spanish to English*

2. Here is a list of some common -er verbs.

aprender to learn	Tú **aprendes** inglés y español.
beber to drink	Usted **bebe** té por la mañana.
comer to eat	Ustedes **comen** mucha fruta.
comprender to understand	Yo no **comprendo**, María.
leer to read	Tú **lees** una revista y un periódico.
prometer to promise	**Prometemos** ser puntuales.
vender to sell	Mi hermana **vende** su coche.

3. Here is a list of some common regular -ir verbs.

asistir (a) to attend	**Asisto** a la clase de español todos los días.
decidir to decide	Mañana **decido** si voy a la conferencia.
describir to describe	Ellas **describen** la ciudad de Caracas.
dividir to divide	**Divido** diez entre cinco.
escribir to write	Eduardo **escribe** muchos trabalenguas en la pizarra.
recibir to receive	¿**Recibes** dinero el lunes?
vivir to live	Mi primo y yo **vivimos** en San Francisco.

change forms   *conjugate beber*   *conjugate beber*

G. Diga que estas personas siempre, nunca o algunas veces beben vino cuando comen. *(Say that these persons always, never, or sometimes drink wine when they eat.)*   *Come*

▶ usted   *Usted siempre bebe vino cuando come.*

1. tú	3. ellas	5. Carlos y Jaime	7. tú y Consuelo
2. él	4. nosotros	6. las jóvenes	8. Carmen

110   Lección 6

H. Diga que las siguientes personas leen mucho, pero aprenden poco. *(State that the following people read a lot, but learn little.)*

▶ tú   *Tú lees mucho, pero aprendes poco.*

1. Paco y tú
2. los estudiantes
3. yo
4. el muchacho grande
5. nosotras
6. ellas

I. Diga qué prometen hacer las personas siguientes. *(Tell what the following people promise to do.)*

▶ papá / comprar un auto   *Papá promete comprar un auto.*

1. los jóvenes / estudiar mucho
2. tú / vender la casa
3. usted / llamar el sábado
4. yo / trabajar el lunes
5. él / comer con nosotros
6. nosotras / llegar a tiempo

J. Conteste las siguientes preguntas. Luego haga las mismas preguntas a un/a compañero/a de clase, pero use la forma de **tú**. *(Answer the following questions. Then ask a classmate the same questions, but use the* ***tú****-form of the verb.)*

1. ¿Vive usted en una casa, un dormitorio o un apartamento?
2. ¿Qué días de la semana asisten ustedes al curso de español?
3. ¿Dónde comen sus amigos generalmente?
4. ¿Bebe usted leche, agua, vino o cerveza?
5. ¿Comprende su hermana el ruso? ¿el chino? ¿otros idiomas?
6. ¿Leen ustedes periódicos o revistas?
7. ¿Vende usted sus libros? ¿a quién(es)?
8. ¿Promete Pepe ser puntual al profesor o a la profesora?
9. ¿Recibe usted dinero de sus padres? ¿en dólares o en pesos?

K. Complete cada una de las siguientes oraciones con la forma apropiada de **asistir, decidir, describir, escribir, recibir** o **vivir**, según el significado. *(Complete each of the following sentences with the appropriate form of* ***asistir, decidir, describir, escribir, recibir***, *or* ***vivir****, according to the context.)*

1. Mi prima y yo _____ a la universidad los lunes, martes y jueves.
2. ¿Quién _____ qué cursos ofrece el departamento de idiomas?
3. Yo no _____ composiciones muy buenas para la clase de inglés.
4. Guillermo _____ una «Λ» porque habla español muy bien.
5. Nosotros _____ la fotografía de la plaza en la clase.
6. Los López _____ en Santiago de Chile.
7. ¿Tú _____ dinero de tus padres todos los viernes?

III. Use of ¡qué! in exclamations

1. **¡Qué!** + *adjective* or *noun* is used to express surprise, approval, rejection, or astonishment in exclamatory sentences. The equivalent in English is **how!** + *adjective* or **what a!** + *noun*.

¡Qué inteligente!	*How intelligent!*
¡Qué chico!	*What a boy!*
¡Qué horrible!	*How horrible!*
¡Qué chévere!	*Terrific!*

2. The pattern **¡qué!** + *noun* + **más** or **tan** + *adjective* is very common in conversational Spanish.

¡Qué café más terrible!	*What terrible coffee!*
¡Qué aeropuerto tan grande!	*What a huge airport!*

L. Pregúntele a un/a compañero/a de clase cómo se dicen las siguientes expresiones en español. (*Ask a classmate how to say the following expressions in Spanish.*)

▶ How nice!   S1: *¿Cómo se dice «How nice!» en español?*
　　　　　　　　S2: *Se dice «¡qué bueno!»*

1. What a hotel!	3. What a waiter!
How terrible!	How nice!
What a terrible hotel!	What a nice waiter!
2. What a day!	4. What a lesson!
How beautiful!	How easy!
What a beautiful day!	What an easy lesson!

M. Reaccione a las siguientes situaciones con una exclamación, usando **qué**. (*React to the following situations, using an expression with **qué**.*)

1. El/la profesor/a de español dice que no hay examen hoy.
2. Tu primo dice que hay una fiesta el sábado.
3. El Sr. Gallego dice que viaja a Puerto Rico.
4. Tu amiga dice que habla cuatro lenguas modernas.
5. Un niño de tres años dice que sabe contar (*knows how to count*) hasta 20.

IV. Adverbs in **-mente**

Adverbs that end in **-mente** in Spanish are usually equivalent to adverbs that end in *-ly* in English.

1. The suffix **-mente** is added to the *feminine singular* form of four-form adjectives. Note that accents are retained when the suffix **-mente** is added to an adjective.

generosa ⟶ generosamente
típica ⟶ típicamente

2. The suffix **-mente** is added to the *singular* form of two-form adjectives.

fácil ⟶ fácilmente
inteligente ⟶ inteligentemente

3. When <u>two</u> or more adverbs with <u>**-mente**</u> are used, the suffix appears attached to the <u>*last adverb only*</u>. If the adjectives used are four-form, the feminine form of the adjective is used for both.

Paco lee **fácil, rápida** y **atentamente**.   *Paco reads easily, rapidly, and carefully.*

If ends in O change O to a before adding mente

N. Cambie los adjetivos siguientes a adverbios, usando **-mente**. *(Change the following adjectives to adverbs, using -mente.)*

▶ difícil   *difícilmente*
▶ claro   *claramente*

1. activo
2. arrogante
3. generoso
4. perezoso
5. humilde
6. horrible

O. Complete las oraciones siguientes con un adverbio apropiado. Use los adjetivos de la lista para formar los adverbios. Usted debe poder comprender el significado de los adjetivos nuevos. *(Complete the following sentences with an appropriate adverb. Use the adjectives from the list to form the adverbs. You should be able to understand the meaning of the new adjectives.)*

evidente   personal
frecuente   inmediato
general   tradicional

1. _____ escucho la radio cuando estudio.
2. _____ comen en el restaurante «Sancho Panza».
3. Voy _____ al hospital.
4. _____ los norteamericanos son muy generosos.
5. _____ el señor López no vive en San Diego ahora.
6. Voy a llamar _____ a la señora Gutiérrez.

V. Ser and estar in contrast

No, gracias, ¡para mí el café **es** horrible!

¡Este café **está** horrible!

A Pepe no le gusta el café.

A Doris le gusta el café, pero no bebe el café del aeropuerto.

Both **ser** and **estar** mean *to be* in English, but they cannot be used interchangeably.

1. **Ser** is used:
    a. to link (to equate or show the sameness of) two nouns, or a pronoun and a noun.

Diego **es** estudiante.	*Diego is a student.*
La joven **es** cantante.	*The young girl is a singer.*
Yo **soy** arquitecto.	*I'm an architect.*

    b. with a **de-**phrase to express origin, possession, or close relationship, or to state the material something is made of.

Mi novio **es** de Perú.	*My fiancé is from Peru.*
El televisor **es** de Anita.	*The TV set is Anita's (belongs to Anita).*
La mesa **es** de plástico.	*The table is (made of) plastic.*

    c. with adjectives to describe the normal attributes or characteristics of a noun, when these attributes can be verified objectively by anyone.

El señor López **es** antipático.	*Mr. López is unpleasant.*
Tu casa **es** grande.	*Your house is big.*

    d. to indicate the location of an event.

La fiesta **es** en mi casa.	*The party is at my house.*
La reunión **es** en la sala.	*The meeting is in the living room.*

2. **Estar** is used:
    a. to indicate location or position.

¿Dónde **están** Luis y tu primo?	*Where are Luis and your cousin?*
Mi automóvil **está** en la Calle San José.	*My car is on San José Street.*

b. to indicate health.

—¿Cómo **estás**, Juan?   *How are you, Juan?*
—No **estoy** muy bien.   *I'm not very well.*

c. with the following adjectives to express condition or state of being.

cansado	tired	**dormido**	asleep
ocupado	busy	**sentado**	seated
triste	sad	**abierto**	open
contento	happy	**cerrado**	closed
vacío	empty	**lleno**	full

—**¿Estás** triste o **estás** cansada?   *Are you sad or are you tired?*
—No **estoy** triste. **Estoy** contenta.   *I'm not sad. I'm happy.*

d. with adjectives to give a subjective appraisal of how someone or something seems, or to describe how someone's behavior impresses the speaker.

¡Este café **está** horrible!   *This coffee is (tastes) horrible (in my opinion)!*

Pepe **está** muy joven.   *Pepe looks very young (to me).*
Lucha **está** antipática.   *Lucha is acting disagreeably.*

(handwritten margin notes: "match adj with noun O or a"; "Estar: location, feeling ×"; "Ser: All helse")

P. Diga si estas personas son o no son lo que se indica. *(Say whether these people are or are not what is indicated.)*

▶ mi padre / mecánico   *Sí, mi padre es mecánico.*
                           No, mi padre no es mecánico.

1. yo / estudiante
2. ustedes / profesores
3. tú / arquitecto
4. tu mamá / alta
5. tu médico / una persona simpática
6. nosotros / el futuro del país

Q. Complete cada oración con varias frases con **de** para indicar lugar de origen, posesión o material. *(Complete each statement with several **de**-phrases to indicate place of origin, possession, or material.)*

de Nicaragua	de mi amiga	de papel
de otros materiales	de la ciudad	de una familia humilde
de plástico	de un profesor	de metal

▶ El cassette . . .   *El cassette es de plástico, de metal y de otros materiales.*

1. Mi profesor de español . . .
2. El cuaderno . . .
3. Un amigo de mi papá . . .
4. La papelera . . .
5. La calculadora . . .
6. El dinero . . .

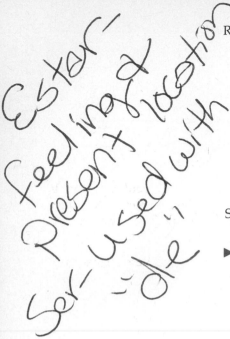

R. Use la forma correcta de **ser** o **estar**, según el contexto. *(Use the appropriate form of **ser** or **estar**, according to the context.)*

1. Mi primo _____ en Madrid, pero no _____ de Madrid.
2. Mis amigas no _____ en la biblioteca. _____ en el café.
3. Yo no _____ argentina. _____ de México.
4. El periódico _____ del profesor.
5. —¿Cómo _____ ? —Muy bien, gracias, ¿y tú?
6. Tú y tu amiga _____ enfermeras, ¿verdad?
7. ¡Estos sándwiches _____ riquísimos!
8. ¡Los exámenes _____ horribles! Me gustan más las vacaciones.

S. Explique cómo son estas personas y cómo están algunas veces. *(Explain what these people are like and how they feel or act sometimes.)*

▶ tú   *Yo soy alegre y simpático/a, pero algunas veces estoy triste y furioso/a.*

1. tus hermanas
2. tus primas
3. tu profesor/a favorito/a
4. tu dentista
5. un/a amigo/a especial
6. tú

¿Comprende usted?

The following reading tells you about the familiar and the unfamiliar as you take an imaginary trip to a Hispanic country. Read for general meaning, then answer the true-false questions about the reading. Then re-read the passage before you do *Exercise B.*

Hispanoamérica en la edad del jet

Los grandes aeropuertos internacionales de los países hispanoamericanos dan una apariencia de fabricación en serie. El viajero que llega al aeropuerto internacional de Ciudad de México, de Bogotá, de Lima o de Buenos Aires recibe la falsa impresión de que los países de México, Colombia, Perú
5 o Argentina son copias de los Estados Unidos. Los viajeros, elegantes o ridículos, altos o bajos, ricos o pobres, rubios o morenos, parecen idénticos a los viajeros que vemos en los aeropuertos norteamericanos: pasan rápidamente de un avión a otro, de una puerta de entrada a una puerta de salida, de un restaurante o cafetería a un taxi o autobús.
10   El norteamericano que llega a un país hispanoamericano generalmente sufre una gran desilusión en el aeropuerto: ¿dónde está la diferencia? ¿dónde están los famosos contrastes de Hispanoamérica? Las diferencias aparecen poco a poco: el aroma del café es diferente; muy pocas personas

hablan inglés; las tiendas elegantes venden otros productos, diferentes para
15 el extranjero; los restaurantes ofrecen un menú con nombres indescifrables
en Chicago, Minneapolis o Detroit. Y cuando iniciamos el viaje a la ciudad
en taxi o autobús, escuchamos la diferencia en la conversación de los otros
viajeros o del chofer, leemos la diferencia en los avisos de tránsito y de los
comercios, y vemos la diferencia en una ciudad con edificios altos y casas
20 coloniales, en los automóviles de último modelo y los carros de caballos, en
los contrastes de riqueza y miseria. ¡Estamos en Hispanoamérica!

A. *¿Verdad o falso?* Diga si las oraciones siguientes son verdaderas o falsas
según la lectura. Si son falsas, dé la información correcta. *(Say whether
the following statements are true or false, according to the reading. If they
are false, give the correct information.)*

1. México, Colombia, Perú y Argentina son copias de los Estados
Unidos.
2. Los aeropuertos internacionales parecen fabricados en serie.
3. Los viajeros son similares en todas partes.
4. Las diferencias entre los EEUU y el mundo hispánico son
inmediatamente obvias para el viajero de la edad del jet.
5. Unos nombres de los platos y especialidades de los restaurantes
de los aeropuertos son familiares y otros son diferentes para el
viajero norteamericano.
6. El viaje del aeropuerto a la ciudad ofrece contrastes increíbles.
7. Es obvio que estamos en Hispanoamérica porque la lengua
española está en todas partes.

B. Busque en la lectura un sinónimo para cada una de las palabras
siguientes *(Find the synonym used in the reading for each of the following
words.)*

1. ilegible   3. manufactura   5. prosperidad
2. aspecto   4. turista   6. pobreza

*El paso de Bolivia a Perú en las
regiones andinas es difícil y, en
unos casos, primitivo. El
transbordador manual (ferry)
de la fotografía pasa automóviles
y autobuses por la frontera
entre Bolivia y Perú en el lago
Titicaca, el lago más alto del
mundo. Observe los diferentes
medios de transporte. ¿Qué
posibles problemas encuentran
los conductores al usar este
transbordador manual?*

Lengua en acción 2

A. Clases favoritas (*Lección 4*)

Ask three of your classmates what classes they are taking besides **(además de)** Spanish. Find out which one they like best, who the professor is, and what he/she is like. Take notes so that you can talk about your findings.

Nombre de compañero/a	*Carlos*			
Otras asignaturas	*inglés cálculo*			
Asignatura favorita	*inglés*			
Apellido de profesor/a	*Barnett*			
Descripción de profesor/a	*interesante*			

B. Una presentación (*Lección 4*)

Imagine that you are downtown and meet a classmate, Andrés, who is talking with an older woman and two children. He stops you to introduce his grandmother, Sra. Julia Aguirre. Talk briefly with her.

Usted

1. Tell her you are glad to meet her.
2. Respond and ask her whose children she is with.
3. Ask what the children's names are.
4. Respond, then change the subject and give an excuse for having to leave **(Bueno, Sra. Aguirre . . .)**

Sra. Aguirre

Respond, and ask where he/she is from.
Explain that the children are the son and daughter of a friend.
Respond, and ask him/her if he/she has any brothers or sisters.
Respond, say where you are going with the children, and take leave.

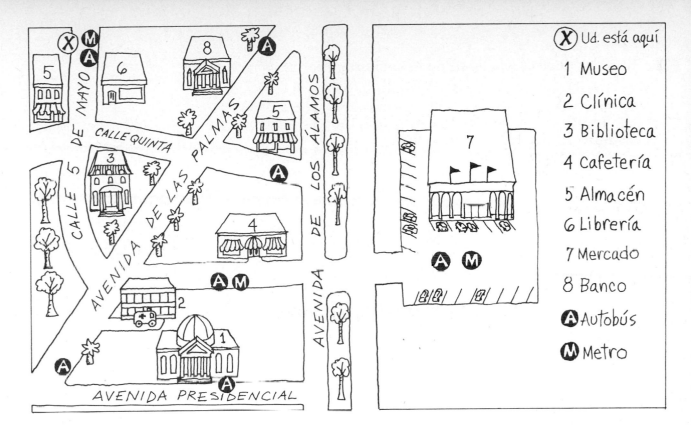

	X Ud. está aquí
	1 Museo
	2 Clínica
	3 Biblioteca
	4 Cafetería
	5 Almacén
	6 Librería
	7 Mercado
	8 Banco
	Ⓐ Autobús
	Ⓜ Metro

C. ¿Adónde vas? *(Lección 5)*

You are new to the town shown in the above map. Ask classmates where you can go to do some things and what means of transportation are available to go there. Be sure to thank them for their help.

1. depositar un cheque
2. comprar cuadernos
3. comprar unos suéteres
4. comer *(to eat)* tacos
5. ver una exposición de arte
6. comprar frutas
7. consultar con un médico
8. consultar una enciclopedia

D. Planes para las vacaciones *(Lección 5)*

You are looking for a place to spend your term break. Find out from a few classmates what their plans are to see if that sparks some ideas.

¿Adónde vas?				
¿Cuándo vas? ¿Cuándo regresas?				
¿Con quién viajas?				
¿Cómo viajas? ¿en auto?				

E. El amor (love) en la edad de la computadora (Lección 6)

You want to join Radio Fiesta's computerized dating service. Answer the radio announcer's (a classmate's) questions so that he/she can enter appropriate information into the system. Then, alternate roles.

1. ¿Cómo se llama Ud.?
2. ¿Cuál es su profesión?
3. ¿De qué color es su pelo?
4. ¿Y sus ojos?
5. ¿Qué le gusta hacer en su tiempo libre (spare time)?
6. ¿Cómo es su carácter y personalidad?
7. ¿Qué tipo de persona busca?

F. Expresiones y rutinas (Wrap-up)

Role-play the following situations with a classmate by completing each dialogue with appropriate phrases and expressions.

Asking the waiter for the check

—Camarero, _____ , por favor. (el menú, la cuenta, el mapa)
—Sí, _____ Sr./Srta. (inmediatamente, en diez minutos, ah bueno)
—Gracias.
—_____ . (Cómo no, Gracias a ti, Para servirle)

Getting a policeman to repeat directions

—_____ , señor policía. ¿Hay un hotel por aquí? (Hola, Perdón, Buenos días)
—Sí, hay uno en la _____. (Avenida Miraflores, Calle Segunda, Cárcel Constitución)
—_____ No comprendo español bien. (Repítalo, por favor., ¡Cómo no!, ¿Cómo se dice eso en español?)
—En la _____. Hay un hotel en la _____. (Avenida Miraflores, Calle Segunda, Cárcel Constitución)
—Ahora sí comprendo. _____ por la información. (De nada, Gracias, lgualmente)

Reacting to startling news

—_____ , Marisol. ¿Qué tal? (Perdón, Buenos días, Hola)
—Bien, ¿y tú? _____ (¿Cómo está Ud.?, ¿Cómo estás?, ¿Qué haces por aquí?)
—Estoy muy _____ . Tengo tres exámenes hoy. (bien, rabiosa, contenta)
—¡Tres exámenes! _____ (¡Qué bien!, ¡Qué sorpresa!, ¡Qué barbaridad!)
—Sí, tengo uno _____ . (en seguida, a tiempo, al contrario)
—Pues, _____ (¿estás segura/o?, cómo no., ¡buena suerte!)

Unidad 3
En Argentina, Uruguay y Chile

En el área recreativa de Las Leñas, Argentina se puede esquiar y gozar de comodidades sumamente modernas, que incluyen diez hoteles y nueve telesquíes (ski lifts). ¿Le gusta esquiar? ¿En qué meses del año cree Ud. que se puede esquiar en Las Leñas? ¿Qué facilidades busca Ud. cuando va a esquiar? ¿Qué otros deportes practica Ud. en el invierno?

Lección 7
En Argentina

¡Contigo o sin ti!

Sergio Ramírez tiene una cita con su amiga Carmen en la taquilla° del Luna
Park, gran estadio donde presentan los conciertos de música rock y popular en
Buenos Aires. Ahora los dos jóvenes van a comprar sus entradas.

box office

Escena 1

Sergio: Dos entradas, por favor. ¿Tiene numeradas° económicas?

numbered seats

Empleada: No, ya no quedan. Sólo tengo para la «popu»,° a partir de la
fila treinta.

area of Luna Park where
unnumbered seats are sold

5   Sergio: Entonces, dos para la «popu», por favor.

Carmen: ¡Qué lástima! No me gusta la «popu».

Sergio: Bueno, Mencha, por lo menos tenemos entradas . . . . Y, ¿qué
hacen Luis y tu prima? ¿Vienen al concierto?

Carmen: No, no vienen. Mi prima no está bien, y mi hermano tiene

10   que estudiar para el próximo examen de filosofía.

Sergio: Vamos, che.° Hay que entrar al estadio. *(Paga las entradas y*
entran.)

Vamos . . . Listen, man!
(Argentinian interjection)

Un grupo de músicos callejeros
de los Andes entretiene a los
transeúntes (passers-by) en
Buenos Aires, Argentina con la
música de su tierra. ¿Se imagina
Ud. por qué toca su música este
grupo en esta parte de la
ciudad? ¿Qué día de la semana
y qué época del año cree Ud.
que es? ¿Por qué?

Escena 2

Locutor: Ahora presentamos al conjunto español Alas° en «¡Contigo   Wings

15   o sin ti!»

Grupo Alas: Tengo que hablar contigo, contigo, contigo

No puedo vivir sin ti, sin ti, sin ti

Si no deseas pasar tu vida conmigo, conmigo, conmigo,

¡El mundo va a ser fatal para mí, para mí, para mí!

20   *(Gran aplauso)*

Carmen: ¡Tremendo! ¡Qué canción más estupenda!

Sergio: ¡Fenomenal! ¡Otro fabuloso éxito del conjunto Alas!

Comprensión

1. ¿Qué es el Luna Park? ¿Por qué van Sergio y Carmen allí?
2. ¿Qué tipo de entradas compran los jóvenes?
3. ¿Quiénes no van al concierto? ¿Por qué no van?
4. ¿Cuál es el apodo de Carmen?
5. ¿Quién paga las entradas?
6. ¿Quiénes son los Alas? ¿Cuál es el título de la canción que cantan?
7. ¿Le gusta la canción a Sergio? ¿y a Carmen?
8. ¿De qué habla la canción?

Conversación

1. ¿A qué tipo de concierto le gusta ir a usted? ¿Le gustan los conciertos de música rock, o los conciertos de música clásica, folklórica o popular?
2. ¿A qué otros espectáculos va usted? ¿al teatro? ¿al cine? ¿a concursos televisados? ¿al ballet?
3. Cuando usted va a un concierto, ¿va solo/a o con amigos/as?
4. ¿Cómo se llama su canción favorita? ¿Quién/es canta/n la canción?
5. ¿Qué cantantes (conjuntos) son muy populares en los Estados Unidos? ¿en Europa? ¿Qué conjunto le gusta más a usted?
6. ¿Qué tipo de música le gusta? ¿Le gusta cantar? ¿Canta Ud. en el coro de la universidad?

Situaciones

1. You are at the movies with a friend. Suggest a solution when he/she says the following:

—Tengo . . . (hambre, sed, miedo); siempre ocurre cuando veo películas de terror.

—¿Por qué no . . . (comes algo, bebes algo, salimos del cine)?

2. A friend calls you to invite you to a folk concert. Tell him/her why you can't go.

—¿Por qué no vamos al concierto de música folklórica? Empieza en 15 minutos.

—No puedo; tengo que . . . (esperar a mi hermana, terminar de estudiar, volver al trabajo).

Vocabulario

Palabras análogas

el aplauso	fabuloso, -a	popular
el ballet	fatal	presentar
clásico, -a	favorito, -a	televisado, -a
el concierto	¡fenomenal!	el terror
económico, -a	folklórico, -a	el tipo
el examen	la música rock	tremendo, -a

Sustantivos

el/la cantante singer
la cita date; appointment
el concurso competition
el conjunto musical group
el coro chorus
el/la empleado/a sales clerk, employee
la entrada ticket
la escena scene
el espectáculo show
el éxito hit, success
la fila row
el locutor speaker, announcer
el lugar place
la película film
el título title
la vida life

Adjetivos

grande (gran) big, large; great
próximo, -a next
solo, -a alone
treinta thirty

Verbos

empezar (ie) to begin; **empiezo** I begin, I'm beginning
ocurrir happen; occur
pagar to pay
poder *(irreg.)* to be able; can; **puedo** I can, I'm able to

quedar to remain; to be left
salir *(irreg.)* to go out; **salgo** I go out, I'm going out
tener *(irreg.)* to have; **tener que** + *inf.* to have to + *inf.*
terminar to end, finish
venir *(irreg.)* to come; **vengo** I come, I'm coming
volver (ue) to return; **vuelvo** I return, I'm returning

Otras palabras y expresiones

a partir de from
algo something
conmigo with me
contigo with you *(fam.)*
cuando when
¿de qué? about what?
en tren by train
entre between, among
para mí for me
por ejemplo for example
por lo menos at least
siempre always
sin without; **sin ti** without you *(fam.)*
sólo only
tener . . . años to be . . . years old
tener hambre to be hungry
tener miedo to be afraid
tener sed to be thirsty
ya no no longer; **ya no quedan** there aren't any left

Práctica

A. Prepare un diálogo con un/a compañero/a de clase. Suponga (*Suppose*) que está con un/a amigo/a en la taquilla de un teatro y desea comprar entradas económicas. El empleado dice que sólo quedan entradas caras a partir de la fila diez. Su amigo/a dice que no tiene suficiente dinero, y usted tiene que pagar las dos entradas.

B. Suponga que usted tiene que preparar un programa de actividades musicales y teatrales para un semestre en su universidad. Usted presenta sus sugerencias (*suggestions*) al director de programas especiales y explica los tipos de conciertos y espectáculos.

Nota cultural El lenguaje popular

Native speakers of Spanish can often identify the nationality of a speaker by their use of certain expressions. For example, speakers using **bárbaro** and **che** would probably be identified as Argentinians. Slang terms (for example, **la popu**) might further indicate the speaker is from a certain age group (youth) within Argentina. Other Argentinian expressions, such as **chau** (from the Italian *ciao,* meaning *good-by*), have passed the national frontier and spread throughout the Hispanic world by means of the media or the entertainment industry.

Use of the **vos**-form may also identify the national origin of the speaker. Instead of the **tú**-form of the verb, people throughout Hispanic America, but mainly Argentinians and Uruguayans, may use a special **vos**-form (not to be confused with the plural **vosotros**-form used in Spain). For example, they would say **vos necesitás** instead of **tú necesitas,** and **vos bailás** or **comés** instead of **tú bailas** or **comes.** Like the **tú**-form, the **vos**-form is used among close friends and relatives, and rarely, if ever, used with strangers.

Pronunciación y ortografía

I. El sonido [ñ]

The Spanish [ñ] is pronounced with the front of the tongue pressed flat against the palate (the roof of the mouth). It resembles the sound of *ny* in *canyon* and is spelled **ñ.** Remember that **ñ** is a separate letter in the Spanish alphabet; words or syllables beginning with **ñ** are alphabetized after words or syllables beginning with **n.**

A. Escuche a su profesor/a y repita las siguientes palabras. Todas las palabras tienen el sonido [ñ].

español doña niño
señor Briceño España

B. Ahora cierre su libro. Escuche a su profesor/a y repita sólo las palabras que tienen el sonido [ñ].

cuna cuña caña cana
sueño sueno napa ñapa

C. Ponga en orden alfabético las siguientes palabras.

1. canal, caña, cansado, cantar, capital
2. anuncio, antiguo, antes, año, antipático
3. pino, piñón, pinchazo, pintar, piña

II. La letra h

The letter **h** is orthographic in Spanish; that is, it is used in spelling, but does not represent any sound. It is often referred to as "silent h".

D. Escuche a su profesor/a y repita las siguientes palabras. Recuerde no pronunciar la **h**.

ahora hotel Hugo hoy hace hermano
Honduras hospital Hortensia hay habla hola

E. Dicte las siguientes oraciones en voz alta a la clase.

1. Hugo está en el hospital.
2. ¿Hay un hotel por aquí?
3. Ahí está la hermana de Herminia.
4. ¡Hola, Hortensia! ¿Cómo estás hoy?

F. Complete las oraciones siguientes con palabras lógicas con **h**.

▶ Horacio es _____ ; no es arrogante. *humilde*

1. ¡Camarero! ¡Este café está _____ !
2. Mi hermana está muy enferma; está en el _____ .
3. Cuando viajo a México, voy siempre al _____ San Carlos.
4. En los países de América del Sur, no todos _____ español.
5. La capital de _____ es Tegucigalpa.
6. ¿ _____ un estadio en la ciudad donde usted vive?

Refranes

1. **Con arte y con engaño se vive la mitad del año.**
   With guile and deceit one can live only half a year.
2. **Hoy por ti, mañana por mí.**
   I'll help you out today and you'll help me tomorrow.

Estudio de palabras

I. Aparatos útiles

el altoparlante loudspeaker
la cámara (fotográfica) camera
la copiadora copier
el estéreo stereo
la filmadora movie camera
la grabadora tape recorder
la máquina de escribir typewriter

el micrófono microphone
la procesadora de palabras word processor
el televisor (en blanco y negro, a colores) (black-and-white, color) TV set
el vídeo video
el videodisco videodisk

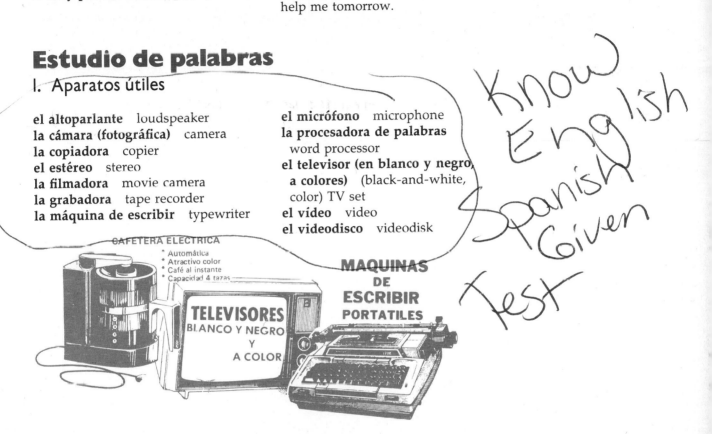

A. Diga si usted tiene los siguientes aparatos.

▶ copiadora / procesadora de palabras

Tengo copiadora, pero no tengo procesadora de palabras.
No tengo copiadora, y no tengo procesadora de palabras.

1. tocadiscos / estéreo
2. radio / televisor
3. televisor / estéreo
4. cámara fotográfica / filmadora
5. vídeo / videodisco
6. grabadora / máquina de escribir
7. máquina de escribir / calculadora
8. micrófono / altoparlante

B. Conteste las siguientes preguntas.

1. ¿Tiene Ud. un televisor a colores o en blanco y negro?
2. ¿Es bueno usar la grabadora para aprender el español? ¿por qué?
   ¿Tiene usted cassettes en español?
3. ¿Escribe Ud. sus composiciones en la máquina de escribir o usa
   la procesadora de palabras?
4. ¿Le gusta más usar la cámara fotográfica o la filmadora? ¿por qué?
5. ¿Tiene Ud. una computadora? ¿Le gusta usar las computadoras?
   ¿Tiene que aprender a usar las computadoras para alguna de sus
   clases? ¿para cuáles?

II. Los números 21 – 30

21 = **veintiuno**	25 = **veinticinco**	29 = **veintinueve**
22 = **veintidós**	26 = **veintiséis**	30 = **treinta**
23 = **veintitrés**	27 = **veintisiete**	
24 = **veinticuatro**	28 = **veintiocho**	

1. Numbers from twenty-one to twenty-nine can be written as a single
   word or as three words: **veinte y seis, veinte y ocho,** et cetera.
2. **Veintiuno** becomes **veintiún** before a masculine plural noun and
   veintiuna before a feminine plural noun.

veintiún muchachos   **veintiuna** muchachas
veintiún días   **veintiuna** lecciones

III. Los números 31 – 199

31 = **treinta y uno**	39 = **treinta y nueve**	80 = **ochenta**
32 = **treinta y dos**	40 = **cuarenta**	90 = **noventa**
33 = **treinta y tres**	41 = **cuarenta y uno**	100 = **cien (ciento)**
34 = **treinta y cuatro**	50 = **cincuenta**	101 = **ciento uno**
35 = **treinta y cinco**	51 = **cincuenta y**	150 = **ciento cincuenta**
36 = **treinta y seis**	**uno**	199 = **ciento noventa**
37 = **treinta y siete**	60 = **sesenta**	**y nueve**
38 = **treinta y ocho**	70 = **setenta**	

1. Compound numbers above thirty are usually written as three words (in
   contrast to numbers from **dieciséis** to **veintinueve**).

cincuenta y dos   **sesenta y tres**

2. In compound numbers above thirty, **uno** becomes **un** before a masculine
   plural noun and **una** before a feminine plural noun.

treinta y un libros   **treinta y una** revistas

3. **Cien** becomes **ciento** before numerals one through ninety-nine.

cien sillas	**ciento cincuenta** pesos
cien cuadernos	**ciento tres** páginas

4. In Spanish, commas are used instead of periods in expressing numerical amounts with decimals.

un dólar con treinta centavos = $1,30	*one dollar and thirty cents* = $1.30
cien dólares con noventa y un centavos = $100,91	*one hundred dollars and ninety one cents* — $100.91

C. Usted necesita comprar los siguientes artículos. Pregúntele a la empleada de una tienda cuánto cuestan los objetos indicados *(how much these things cost).* Después diga cuánto cuestan.

▶ el estéreo ($179,60) S1: *¿Cuánto cuesta el estéreo?*
S2: *Cuesta ciento setenta y nueve dólares con sesenta centavos.*

1. la computadora ($99,99)
2. la grabadora ($72,50)
3. la cámara ($94,25)
4. la máquina de escribir ($153,95)
5. la calculadora ($21,70)
6. cinco discos ($38,40)
7. diez cassettes ($40,55)
8. el televisor en blanco y negro ($80,60)

D. Suponga que usted trabaja en un almacén de Puerto Rico. A causa de *(Due to)* la inflación, usted tiene que subir los precios *(prices).* Diga el precio de los siguientes aparatos antes *(before)* y después de añadir *(after adding)* 10 pesos.

Almacén San Marcos

Lista de precios   ¡Hoy! ¡Precios razonables!

micrófonos	15 pesos cada uno
altoparlantes	85 pesos cada uno
filmadoras	140 pesos cada una
grabadoras	100 pesos cada una
máquinas de escribir	158 pesos cada una
televisores en blanco y negro	152 pesos cada uno
tocadiscos	133 pesos cada uno

▶ *Hoy un micrófono cuesta 15 pesos; mañana cuesta 25 pesos.*

Estructuras útiles

I. Present tense of **tener**; idioms with **tener**

1. The verb **tener** *(to have)* is irregular in the present tense. The **yo**-form ends in **-go,** and the stem changes from **e** to **ie** in the **tú**-form and in the third person singular and plural.

	tener		
yo	ten	**go**	Tengo dos hermanas.
tú	tien	**es**	¿Tienes una prima?
Ud., él, ella	tien	**e**	Tiene una grabadora muy buena.
nosotros, -as	ten	**emos**	Tenemos un tocadiscos viejo.
vosotros, -as	ten	**éis**	¿Tenéis una cámara alemana?
Uds., ellos, ellas	tien	**en**	No tienen televisor a colores.

2. In Spanish, the indefinite article is often omitted after **tener,** unless the numeral *one* is meant. Note that in replies to questions, a direct object is not required after **tener.**

—¿Tienes estéreo, Sara?   *Do you have a stereo, Sara?*
—Sí, tengo un estéreo en casa. *Yes, I have one stereo at home.*
—¿Y tu amigo Rafael?   *And your friend Rafael?*
—No, no tiene.   *No, he doesn't (have one).*

3. The verb **tener** is followed by a noun in many common idiomatic expressions. Note that the verb *to be + adjective* is used in English for these expressions.

tener . . . años to be . . . years old	**tener razón** to be right
tener calor to be warm *(persons)*	**no tener razón** to be wrong
tener éxito to be successful	**tener sed** to be thirsty
tener frío to be cold *(persons)*	**tener sueño** to be sleepy
tener hambre to be hungry	**tener suerte** to be lucky
tener miedo to be afraid	

Tengo un **frío** terrible, pero no *I'm terribly cold, but I'm not*
 tengo hambre.   *hungry.*
Hace calor, **tengo** mucha **sed.** *It's hot; I'm very thirsty.*

(handwritten note: Know for test)

A. Diga cuántos años tienen las siguientes personas.

▶ Guillermo / 30 *Guillermo tiene treinta años.*

1. mi madre / 55   4. la novia de Juan / 22
2. yo / 44   5. tú / 66
3. nosotros / 99   6. tú y Sandra / 77

B. Conteste las preguntas siguientes, usando la forma apropiada de **tener.**

▶ Jaime tiene un estéreo estupendo. ¿y tú?

Yo también tengo un estéreo estupendo.
No, no tengo estéreo.

1. Yo tengo quince discos del grupo Alas. ¿y usted?
2. El señor Ruiz tiene una calculadora japonesa. ¿y tus primos?
3. Marta y Susana tienen muchas amigas. ¿y tu mamá?
4. Ciudad de México tiene muchos restaurantes. ¿y el pueblo de Río Verde?
5. El señor Pinzón no tiene automóvil. ¿y tu familia?

C. Diga que las personas siguientes tienen **frío, calor, sed, miedo, razón, sueño, hambre** o **suerte,** según la lógica.

▶ Raúl acaba de encontrar cien dólares.
  En mi opinión _____ .   *tiene suerte*

1. No me gustan los leones; _____ de ellos.
2. Quiero beber una cerveza porque _____ .
3. Mencha va a comer un sándwich porque _____ .
4. Raúl dice que _____ . Entonces, ¿por qué no se pone un suéter?
5. Nosotros _____ . ¿Quieren abrir las ventanas, por favor?
6. Trabajo día y noche. Por eso estoy cansado y siempre _____ en la clase.
7. Ustedes _____ cuando dicen que cincuenta menos diez son cuarenta.

II. **Tener que** and **hay que** in contrast

Hay que trabajar para vivir.

Sí, pero yo tengo que trabajar menos para vivir más.

1. The expression **tener que** *(to have to, must)* + *infinitive* is used in Spanish to express obligation by a specific person.

Tengo que comprar dos entradas.
No **tenemos que pagar** ahora.

I have to (must) buy two tickets.
We don't have to pay now.

2. The expression **hay que** + *infinitive* is used to express general need or obligation to do something. It is never used with a subject.

—¿A dónde **hay que ir** para cambiar dinero?
—**Hay que ir** a un banco.

Where must one (do you have to) go to change money?
One must (You have to) go to a bank.

D. ¿Qué hace Ud. esta semana? Forme oraciones completas, usando los sujetos indicados y la forma apropiada del verbo **tener.**

▶ (lunes) yo / comer en la cafetería   *El lunes yo tengo que comer en la cafetería.*

1. (lunes) Luisa / usar mi máquina de escribir
2. (martes) yo / llamar al aeropuerto
3. (miércoles) Pedro / comer conmigo y con Joselito
4. (jueves) Manuel / pagarme por los cassettes
5. (viernes) Manuel y yo / estudiar en la biblioteca
6. (sábado) los profesores / discutir los trabajos con nosotros
7. (domingo) Luisa y yo / ir al teatro

E. Explique lo que hay que hacer para alcanzar *(reach)* los siguientes objetivos.

▶ para sacar buenas notas *(grades)*   *Para sacar buenas notas hay que estudiar mucho.*

1. para ver la Estatua de la Libertad
2. para ser millonario *(millionaire)*
3. para ser feliz
4. para comprender a un amigo
5. para tener éxito en la vida
6. para comprender el mundo hispánico

III. Prepositional pronouns

¿Te gustan los calamares?   ¡A **mí** me gustan!
No, no me gustan.   ¡A **nosotros** nos gustan también!

1. Prepositional pronouns (also called disjunctive pronouns) are used principally as the objects of a preposition. They are the same in form as the subject pronouns except for the **yo-** and **tú**-forms.

¿Este radio es **para mí** o **para ti?**	*Is this radio for me or for you?*
Me gusta salir **con él**, pero no **con ella.**	*I like to go out with him, but not with her.*

Subject pronouns	Prepositional pronouns
yo	mí, (conmigo)
tú	ti, (contigo)
él, ella, Ud.	él, ella, Ud.
nosotros, -as	nosotros, -as
vosotros, -as	vosotros, -as
ellos, ellas, Uds.	ellos, ellas, Uds.

2. The pronoun **mí** has a written accent to distinguish it from the possessive adjective **mi** (*my*).

El tocadiscos es para **mí.**	*The record player is for me.*
Es **mi** tocadiscos.	*It's my record player.*

3. When used with **con**, the pronouns **mí** and **ti** form **conmigo** and **contigo.**

—¿Quieres salir **conmigo?**	*Do you want to go out with me?*
—No, no quiero salir **contigo.**	*No, I don't want to go out with you.*

4. **A** or **de** + *prepositional pronoun* is often used for clarity or emphasis.

—¿**A ti** te gusta la música clásica? Pues **a mí** me gusta mucho.	*Do you like classical music? Well, I like it a lot.*
—¿Es el carro **de él** o **de ella?**	*Is it his car or hers?*

5. Subject pronouns are used instead of prepositional pronouns after **entre, menos** (*except*), and **como,** in contrast to English usage.

Entre tú y yo no hay secretos.	*Between you and me there are no secrets.*
Todos van al teatro **menos yo.**	*Everyone is going to the theater except me.*
Como ella, quiero viajar a Chile.	*Like her, I want to travel to Chile.*

F. Durante sus vacaciones en Buenos Aires, Raúl va a muchos lugares interesantes con diferentes personas. Haga el papel de (*Play the part of*) Raúl, y conteste las preguntas siguientes.

▶ ¿Vas al Luna Park con Alberto?   *Sí, voy con él.*

1. ¿Vas al Teatro Colón con la hermana de Rico?
2. ¿Vas a la playa con tu amigo Antonio?

3. ¿Vas a la Universidad de Buenos Aires conmigo?
4. ¿Vas a la Casa Rosada con nosotros?
5. ¿Vas a la Plaza San Martín con Virginia y conmigo?
6. ¿Vas al Museo Nacional con tus padres?

G. Mucha gente habla de otros y viceversa. Cambie las oraciones según el modelo.

▶ Felipe habla de nosotros . . .   *y nosotros hablamos de él.*

1. Alma habla de ti . . .   4. Yo hablo de ellas . . .
2. Usted habla de ella . . .   5. Tú hablas de ellos . . .
3. Ellos hablan de usted . . .   6. Ustedes hablan de nosotros . . .

H. Conteste las siguientes preguntas. Use la forma apropiada del pronombre preposicional.

▶ ¿A ti te gusta bailar?   *Sí, a mí me gusta mucho.*
                             No, a mí no me gusta bailar.

1. ¿A Roberto le gusta cantar?
2. ¿A tu hermana le gusta estudiar?
3. ¿A tus amigos les gusta trabajar?
4. ¿A usted le gusta viajar?

I. Exprese en español.

1. Between you *(fam.)* and me, Pepe is very lazy.
2. There are no problems between them and her.
3. Everyone is going to the concert except me.
4. Everyone has a nickname except him.
5. Like me, they don't want to go to the party.
6. Like her, I want to study in Buenos Aires.

IV. Present tense of verbs with irregular **yo**-forms

*Hoy **salgo** en noche de estrellas*
*porque **vengo** a tu balcón.*
*Te **traigo**, hermosa Mirella,*
en la mano, el corazón.

1. The following verbs end in **-go** in the **yo**-form of the present tense. This group of verbs includes **tener,** which you have just studied in this lesson. Note that some of the verbs listed below have stem and spelling changes in addition to the irregular **yo**-form that ends in **-go.**

decir	*to say, tell*	di**go**, dic**es**, dic**e**, dec**imos**, dec**ís**, dic**en**
hacer	*to do, make*	ha**go**, hac**es**, hac**e**, hac**emos**, hac**éis**, hac**en**
oír	*to hear*	oi**go**, oy**es**, oy**e**, o**ímos**, o**ís**, oy**en**
poner	*to put*	pon**go**, pon**es**, pon**e**, pon**emos**, pon**éis**, pon**en**
salir	*to leave*	sal**go**, sal**es**, sal**e**, sal**imos**, sal**ís**, sal**en**
tener	*to have*	ten**go**, tien**es**, tien**e**, ten**emos**, ten**éis**, tien**en**
traer	*to bring*	trai**go**, tra**es**, tra**e**, tra**emos**, tra**éis**, tra**en**
venir	*to come*	ven**go**, vien**es**, vien**e**, ven**imos**, ven**ís**, vien**en**

2. Compounds formed with these verbs normally follow the same pattern. For example:

distraer	*to distract*	distrai**go**, distra**es**, . . .
prevenir	*to prevent*	preven**go**, previen**es**, . . .
proponer	*to propose*	propon**go**, propon**es**, . . .

J. Diga que usted también hace las mismas actividades que las personas indicadas.

▶ Carlos y Ricardo traen sándwiches a la fiesta.   *Yo también traigo sándwiches a la fiesta.*

1. Hoy mi papá viene tarde a casa.
2. Pedro trae la guitarra a la reunión.
3. Mi hermana sale con los amigos hoy.
4. Elena pone los discos en la mesa.
5. Mi hermano hace mucho y dice poco.
6. Los jóvenes oyen música en la Calle Siete.
7. Los hijos de los Briceño dicen que van al estadio.
8. Ustedes tienen mucho sueño.

K. Complete las conversaciones siguientes con la forma apropiada de uno de los verbos de la lista.

decir	salir	oír	traer
hacer	tener	poner	venir

1. —¿_____ usted la canción «Guadalajara» en este momento?
   —No, ahora _____ la canción «En mi viejo San Juan».
2. —¿Con quién _____ usted de la clase?
   —_____ con mis amigas de San Juan.

3. —¿Qué _____ tú a la fiesta mañana?
   —¿Yo? _____ la cerveza.
4. —Yo _____ tres primos. ¿y ustedes?
   —¡Nosotros _____ muchísimos!
5. —¿Cuándo _____ otra vez a mi casa, Rosita?
   —_____ otra vez el lunes, si quieres.
6. —¿Qué _____ los domingos, Paco?
   —¿Yo? _____ muy poco. Descanso mucho.
7. —¿Qué _____ en la mesa?
   —_____ mis libros de inglés.
8. —¿Qué _____ cuando estás furiosa?
   —_____: «¡Al diablo con todo!»

¿Comprende usted?

Sergio y Carmen conversan en un café después del concierto. Lea su conversación, observando la reacción de ellos a cada *(each)* comentario. Luego conteste las preguntas.

Después del concierto

Sergio: ¡Qué lata! Estos conciertos son demasiado populares. ¡Qué cantidad de gente!

Carmen: Vos tenés razón. Si tenés entradas numeradas, bueno. Pero en «la popu» siempre es difícil encontrar un buen puesto.

5 Sergio: Pues no tengo la culpa. Cuando no hay entradas económicas, no hay; y ya está.

Carmen: La próxima vez necesitás comprar las entradas con anticipación. No podés esperar hasta el último momento.

Sergio: Oye, Mencha; con un grupo tan popular como los Alas es

10 imposible comprar asientos buenos a un precio económico.

Carmen: Claro pero, ¿qué decís si la próxima vez pagamos por partes iguales? Yo pago mi entrada, vos pagás la tuya y así podemos comprar entradas numeradas.

Sergio: No me gusta ir "a la americana", pero vamos a ver qué pasa la

15 próxima vez.

A. Conteste las siguientes preguntas sobre la lectura.

1. Además de Sergio y Carmen, ¿quiénes están en el concierto?
2. Según Carmen, ¿qué problema hay con «la popu»?
3. Según Sergio, ¿qué problema hay con las entradas numeradas?
4. ¿Qué solución tiene Sergio para el próximo concierto?

B. Estas palabras pueden tener distintas connotaciones. Escoja (*Choose*) el significado que más se aproxime a su uso en el diálogo.

1. último: final, fantástico, exterminado
2. a la americana: con mucho dinero, pagar individualmente, en inglés
3. claro: naturalmente, el contrario de oscuro, un día excelente
4. razón: justificación, causa, inteligencia
5. culpa: censura, falta, acusación
6. concierto: presentación musical, acuerdo, al mismo tiempo

C. Escoja una de las expresiones siguientes de la lectura para responder a cada situación. Recuerde el contexto en que ocurren y la emoción con

Debes ir con anticipación.	¡Qué lata!
¿Qué dices si vamos a la americana?	No puedes esperar hasta
No tengo la culpa.	el último momento.

1. —¿Tu automóvil no funciona? ¿Entonces no podemos salir a ninguna parte?
2. —Realmente quiero invitarte a una discoteca pero tengo muy poco dinero.
3. —Estoy un poco enferma y no quiero salir a ninguna parte hoy.
4. —No sé si invitar a Marisa o a Leonor para la fiesta de mañana.
5. —Quiero comprar entradas numeradas para la partida porque va mucha gente.

Como en los EEUU, los teatros de cine de Buenos Aires, Argentina muchas veces tienen tres o más salas donde ofrecen diferentes películas para todos los gustos. ¿Cuál de los tres títulos le atrae más a Ud.? ¿Por qué?

Lección 8
En Uruguay

¿Te gusta aquel velero?

Eduardo García y Raúl Díaz son dos jóvenes amigos que viven en Montevideo, capital de Uruguay. Ahora están en Punta del Este, centro de turismo internacional cerca de la capital. Este fin de semana hay una regata de gran colorido con setenta veleros, y los jóvenes los miran desde la orilla del mar.

Escena 1

Eduardo: Mira, ¡qué increíble! ¿Te gusta aquel velero rojo, Raúl?

Raúl: ¿El número cuarenta y dos? Sí, me gusta, pero prefiero aquel otro de velas azules.

5 Eduardo: Voy a ver si puedo sacar algunas fotos. Sobre todo quiero una de aquel rojo.

Raúl: No la puedes sacar bien desde aquí.

Eduardo: Podemos ir al Club Marino donde están los fotógrafos y reporteros oficiales . . . pero las entradas son muy caras.

10 *Escena 2*

Raúl: Mira, allí va mi vecina Pilar. ¿La recuerdas?

Eduardo: No, no la recuerdo. ¿Quién es?

Raúl: Es Pilar Guzmán, la reportera de *La Nación.* ¿Vamos a saludarla? Creo que ella puede llevarnos al Club. Así puedes sacar tus

15 fotos desde allí con buena luz. . . . Y ¡no tenemos que pagar las entradas!

Eduardo: ¡Bárbaro! ¿Qué esperamos?

Las ciudades grandes del mundo hispánico son todas muy distintas. Compare esta foto de Montevideo, la moderna capital de Uruguay, con la foto de Madrid (p. 67) y de Santo Domingo (p. 315). ¿Qué puede Ud. decir de la vida de los habitantes de Montevideo?

Comprensión

1. ¿Quiénes son Eduardo y Raúl?
2. ¿Qué es Punta del Este?
3. ¿Qué hay este fin de semana en Punta del Este?
4. ¿Desde dónde miran los jóvenes los veleros?
5. ¿Qué quiere hacer Eduardo?
6. ¿Cómo son las entradas para el Club Marino, caras o baratas?
7. ¿Quién es Pilar Guzmán? ¿Por qué quiere saludarla Raúl?

Conversación

1. ¿Le gustan los veleros o prefiere los botes de motor?
2. ¿Le gusta sacar fotos en la playa o prefiere dibujar o pintar?
3. ¿Qué prefiere ser usted: reportero, fotógrafo, artista o deportista profesional? ¿por qué?
4. ¿Quién cree Ud. que tiene una vida más interesante: el reportero, el fotógrafo, el artista o el deportista? ¿por qué?
5. ¿Le gustan los deportes? ¿Prefiere participar en ellos o ser espectador/a? ¿Es usted aficionado/a a algún deporte?

Situaciones

1. You're at a boat show with a friend who asks if you like the models displayed. Say you prefer those shown in a book that you are holding.

   —¿Te gusta . . . (aquel bote, aquella vela, esos veleros, esas barcas)?
   —No, prefiero . . . (éste, ésta, éstos, éstas).

2. You're at a wedding reception. A friend suggests that you go with him/her to greet some people. Agree with his/her suggestion.

   —¿Vamos a saludar . . . (a la vecina, a los cantantes, a tus primas)?
   —Sí, vamos a . . . (saludarla, saludarlo, saludarlos, saludarlas).

Vocabulario

Palabras análogas

el/la artista	increíble	oficial	profesional
la foto	marino, -a	participar	el/la reportero/a
el/la fotógrafo/a	la nación	preferir (ie)	el turismo

Sustantivos

el/la aficionado/a fan
la barca small boat
el bote de motor motor boat
el deporte sport
el/la deportista sportsman, sportswoman
el/la espectador/a spectator
la luz light

el mar sea
la orilla del mar seashore
la playa beach
la regata boat race, regatta
el/la vecino/a neighbor
la vela sail
el velero sailboat

Study only words from Quiz for test

Adjetivos

algún/alguno, -a some
aquel, aquella that (over there); **aquellos, aquellas**
 (pl.) those (over there)
barato, -a cheap, inexpensive
caro, -a expensive
ese, -a that; **esos, -as** *(pl.)* those
este, -a this; **estos, -as** *(pl.)* these

Verbos

creer to believe; to think
dibujar to draw, sketch
llevar to take; to carry
pintar to paint
querer (ie) to want; to wish; to love

recordar (ue) to remember
sacar (fotos) to take (pictures)
saludar to greet

Otras palabras y expresiones

así (in) that (this) way, thus, so
¡bárbaro! great!
de gran colorido very colorful
desde from
este fin de semana this weekend
la her, it; **lo** him, it
las them *(f)*; **los** them *(m)*
¡mira! (from **mirar**) look! *(fam.)*
¿qué esperamos? what are we waiting for?
vamos a saludarla let's go greet her

Práctica

Prepare un diálogo basado en la siguiente información, usando las palabras y las expresiones en el diálogo al comienzo de esta lección.

Julia y Ricardo miran unos botes de motor en una sala de exposición. Julia quiere comprar un bote rojo, pero Ricardo dice que es mejor comprar un velero porque los veleros cuestan *(cost)* menos. Julia y Ricardo discuten los precios y si es mejor comprar el bote de motor o el velero.

Nota cultural Los deportes en el mundo hispánico

A popular sport in most Hispanic countries is soccer **(fútbol)**. Most young men play it, and everyone follows the scores of their favorite teams with great interest and enthusiasm.

Many cities and towns have teams **(equipos)** which compete in national championships. Players from the best teams are selected for international competition, such as the **Copa de Europa** or the **Copa Mundial**. Hispanic teams have often been finalists in international competitions; Uruguay won the **Copa Mundial** in 1930 and in 1950. Argentina won the **Copa Mundial** in 1978 and 1986, and narrowly lost to Italy in the 1982 competition.

Hispanics are well known the world over in other sports, such as tennis, polo, jai alai (a sport that originated in the Basque provinces of Spain), swimming, and baseball. While women participate in such tradi-

(Izquierda) El deporte de pista (Universidad de Santiago de Chile) es igualmente popular entre hombres y mujeres; pero el de jai-alai (derecha) parece atraer más a los hombres. Describa los beneficios para la salud que tiene el correr.

tional sports as basketball **(baloncesto)** and volleyball **(vóleibol),** they are also becoming better known in sports that used to be considered the realm of men, such as fencing **(esgrima),** shot-put **(lanzamiento de peso),** and throwing the discus and javelin **(lanzamiento del disco y de la jabalina).**

Pronunciación y ortografía

I. Los sonidos [b] y [ƀ]

1. In Spanish, the stop sound [b] (spelled **b** or **v**) is pronounced much like the *b* in *boy*. It occurs at the beginning of a breath group or after a pause, and after **m** or **n**. Note that **n** is pronounced [m] before [b].

barato	**v**elero	tam**b**ién
busco	**v**iernes	in**v**itar

2. There is no English equivalent of the fricative [ƀ] (also spelled **b** or **v**), which occurs most often after a vowel. It is pronounced with the lips barely touching as air is forced out.

di**b**ujar	sá**b**ado	re**v**ista
auto**b**ús	tra**b**ajo	uni**v**ersidad

3. Since both [b] and [ƀ] are spelled either **b** or **v**, it is necessary to memorize the spelling of words containing these sounds.

A. Escuche y repita las palabras o frases que dice su profesor/a.

un **v**elero	es posi**b**le	¿**V**ive usted en **B**ogotá?
un **b**ote	es horri**b**le	¿**V**a usted a **B**olivia?

B. Lea las oraciones siguientes en voz alta. Ponga atención a la pronunciación de la [b] y [ɓ].

1. **V**oy a **v**er a **B**ár**b**ara.
2. ¿Es el **b**anco de **B**ogotá?
3. **B**enito **v**iaja a **V**enezuela.
4. ¿Es posi**b**le ir en auto**b**ús?

II. Más sobre los diptongos

1. Diphthongs consist of a combination of a strong vowel (**a, o, e**) with a weak vowel (**i** or **u**), or a combination of the two weak vowels (**i** and **u**). These groupings are pronounced as a single syllable. The letter **y** is considered a weak vowel at the end of a word or syllable.

Ed**ua**rdo	internac**i**onal	pref**i**ero	p**ue**do	r**ui**señor
c**ua**renta	of**i**cial	qu**i**ero	b**ue**na	m**uy**

2. The following words contain vowel combinations that are *not* diphthongs, and thus are pronounced as separate syllables. The weak vowel has a written accent to show this pronunciation.

Raúl   increíble   Díaz   ahí

3. The letter **u** after **q** when followed by **e** or **i** is only orthographical and does not represent a diphthong.

que   a**qu**el   **Qu**ito   **qu**into

C. Diga si las siguientes palabras contienen diptongos y pronúncielas.

1. treinta	5. concierto	9. quedan	13. filosofía
2. taquilla	6. Luis	10. estadio	14. deseamos
3. cuatro	7. tienen	11. día	15. seis
4. puedo	8. creo	12. hoy	16. querer

Un verso fácil: *Burros y sabios*

La «v» de vaca y la «b» de burro
son diferentes cuando se escriben.°   they are written
(Algunos «burros»° siempre confunden°   dumb people / confuse
su transcripción.)
Pero los sabios,° siempre despiertos,°   wise people / alert
las reconocen y las separan.
Aunque estos sabios, en otras cosas . . .
¡muy burros son!

Estudio de palabras

I. Medios de transporte

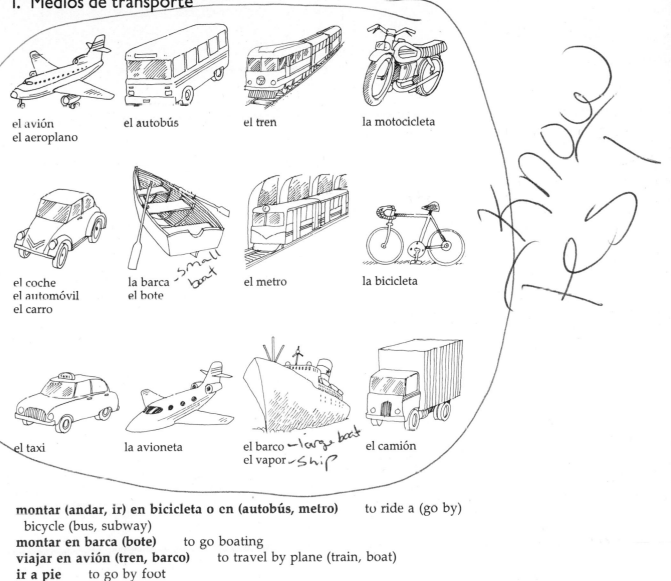

el avión
el aeroplano

el autobús

el tren

la motocicleta

el coche
el automóvil
el carro

la barca —small boat
el bote

el metro

la bicicleta

el taxi

la avioneta

el barco —large boat
el vapor —ship

el camión

montar (andar, ir) en bicicleta o en (autobús, metro)   to ride a (go by)
  bicycle (bus, subway)
montar en barca (bote)   to go boating
viajar en avión (tren, barco)   to travel by plane (train, boat)
ir a pie   to go by foot

A. ¿Qué medios de transporte utilizamos en las siguientes
   situaciones?

1. en el agua
2. en el aire
3. en la ciudad
4. para el transporte público
5. para una sola persona
6. para transportar comida

B. ¿Cómo va usted a los siguientes lugares? ¿Qué medio de transporte usa y por qué?

▶ la ciudad: ¿tren o coche? *Voy a la ciudad en tren. No me gusta ir en coche.*

1. el parque: ¿bicicleta o a pie?
2. el mercado: ¿carro o motocicleta?
3. el estadio: ¿motocicleta, carro o autobús?
4. Las Bahamas: ¿avioneta o bote?
5. la biblioteca: ¿metro, taxi o a pie?
6. la tienda: ¿autobús, metro o taxi?
7. Punta del Este: ¿vapor, velero o avión?
8. el hospital: ¿taxi o coche?

II. Los deportes

Nombres de deportes

el alpinismo   mountain climbing
el baloncesto (el básquetbol)   basketball
el béisbol   baseball
el esquí   skiing
el fútbol   soccer
el fútbol americano   football
la natación   swimming
el patinaje   skating
la pista y campo   track and field
el tenis   tennis
la vela   sailing

Otras palabras y expresiones

el árbitro   referee
el/la campeón/ona   champion
la cancha   (tennis, basketball) court
el equipo   team
el gimnasio   gym
el maratón   marathon
el partido   game
la piscina   swimming pool
la pista   ski slope; race track

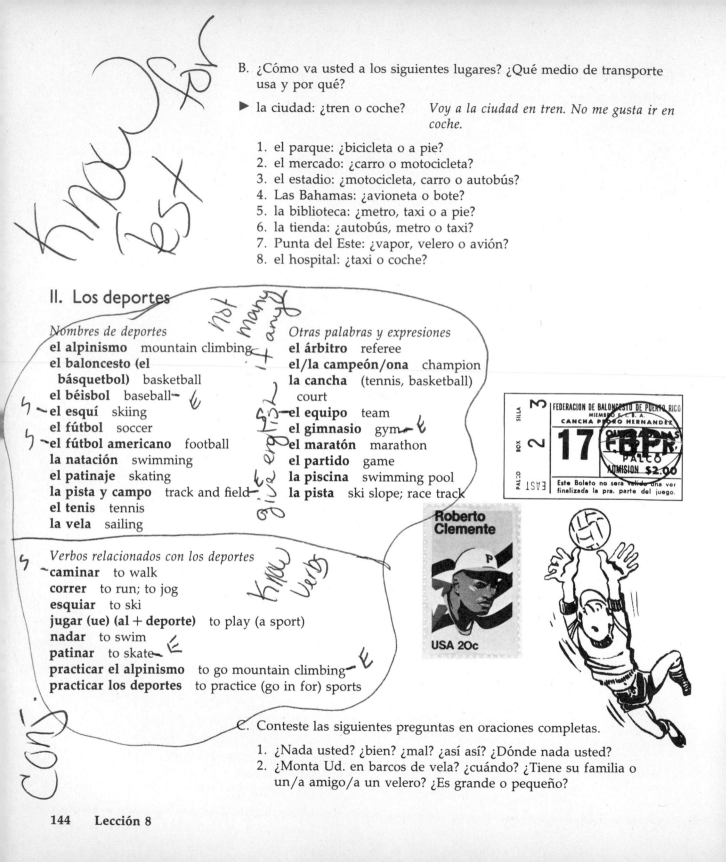

Verbos relacionados con los deportes

caminar   to walk
correr   to run; to jog
esquiar   to ski
jugar (ue) (al + deporte)   to play (a sport)
nadar   to swim
patinar   to skate
practicar el alpinismo   to go mountain climbing
practicar los deportes   to practice (go in for) sports

C. Conteste las siguientes preguntas en oraciones completas.

1. ¿Nada usted? ¿bien? ¿mal? ¿así así? ¿Dónde nada usted?
2. ¿Monta Ud. en barcos de vela? ¿cuándo? ¿Tiene su familia o un/a amigo/a un velero? ¿Es grande o pequeño?

3. ¿Tiene una bicicleta o una motocicleta? ¿Monta todos los días? ¿De qué marca *(brand)* es su moto o bicicleta?
4. ¿Hay equipos de fútbol o de béisbol en su universidad o ciudad? ¿Ganan muchos partidos?
5. ¿Le gusta caminar o correr? ¿Dónde y cuándo camina o corre? ¿Quiere correr en un maratón? ¿Cuántos kilómetros corre al día?
6. ¿Practica la pista y campo? ¿Es usted campeón o campeona? ¿Practica usted este deporte solo/a o con amigos?
7. ¿Es usted aficionado/a al baloncesto? ¿Qué equipo nacional o internacional le gusta más?
8. ¿Prefiere los equipos profesionales o los equipos de las universidades?
9. ¿Le gusta más esquiar, patinar o practicar el alpinismo? ¿Dónde practica estos deportes?

Estructuras útiles

I. Demonstrative adjectives and pronouns

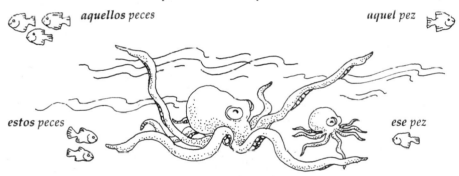

aquellos peces *aquel pez*

estos peces *ese pez*

La madre pulpo enseña los adjetivos demostrativos al pulpito.

A. Demonstrative adjectives

1. Demonstrative adjectives demonstrate or point out specific persons or things. The chart below summarizes the forms of the demonstrative adjectives.

	Masculine Singular	Feminine Singular	Masculine Plural	Feminine Plural
este-group	este	esta	estos	estas
ese-group	ese	esa	esos	esas
aquel-group	aquel	aquella	aquellos	aquellas

2. Spanish has three groups of demonstrative adjectives in contrast to English, which has two groups *(this/these* and *that/those)*. Demonstrative adjectives precede the noun they modify and agree with it in number and gender.

   a. The **este**-group indicates someone or something close to the speaker.

Este carro es nuevo.	*This car is new.*
Estas bicicletas son viejas.	*These bicycles are old.*

   b. The **ese**-group indicates someone or something close to the person spoken to.

Esa revista es buena.	*That magazine is good.*
Esos periódicos son interesantes.	*Those newspapers are interesting.*

   c. The **aquel**-group indicates someone or something distant from both speakers.

Aquel avión es grande.	*That airplane (over there) is big.*
Aquellos aviones son grandes.	*Those airplanes (over there) are big.*

B. Demonstrative pronouns

There are two different kinds of demonstrative pronouns:

a. When the referent is a specific person, place, or thing, the demonstrative pronoun always agrees in number and gender with its referent. These pronoun forms are the same as the adjective forms, except for a written accent on the stressed vowel.

—**Este coche** es caro, ¿verdad?	*This car is expensive, isn't it?*
—Sí, y **ése** es caro también.	*Yes, and that one is expensive, too.*
—**Estos modelos** son baratos, ¿no?	*These models are inexpensive, aren't they?*
—Sí, pero **aquéllos** son más baratos.	*Yes, but those (over there) are cheaper.*

b. When the referent is an abstract idea or concept, or an unknown or unidentified object, the invariable forms **esto, eso,** and **aquello** are used. These demonstrative pronouns do not change in number or gender and do not require a written accent.

—¿Qué es **esto?**	*What's this?*
—¿**Eso?** No sé.	*That? I don't know.*
—¿Qué es **aquello?**	*What's that?*
—**Aquéllas** son las revistas nuevas.	*Those are the new magazines.*

A. Diga que las personas del sexo femenino hacen más que las siguientes personas del sexo masculino.

▶ Ese niño dibuja mucho.   *Sí, pero esa niña dibuja más.*

1. Esos señores trabajan mucho.
2. Este chico patina mucho.
3. Estos jóvenes esquían mucho.
4. Aquel hombre nada mucho.
5. Aquellos muchachos juegan mucho.
6. Ese viejo camina mucho.
7. Este joven corre mucho.

B. Complete cada oración de los mini-diálogos con **esto, eso** o **aquello,** según el contexto.

1. —_____ que digo yo es importante. Debes considerarlo.
   —Tienes razón. _____ es verdad.
2. —¿Qué es _____ que está al norte muy lejos, un avión?
   —Yo no sé qué es _____ . Pero _____ que está aquí cerca sí es un avión.
3. —¿Qué es _____ que tienes en la mano, Julio?
   —¿ _____ ? Es un videocassette del grupo «Alas».

C. Busque (*Look for*) los siguientes objetos en la clase y descríbalos a su profesor/a. Use los adjetivos y pronombres demostrativos adecuados, según la posición de los objetos.

mapa	silla	puerta	bolígrafos
pizarra	mesa	lápiz	papelera
cuaderno	libros	ventanas	escritorio

▶ *Ese mapa es de Sur América. Aquél es de Europa y es más grande.*

II. Direct-object pronouns

—¿Puedes ver bien la película desde aquí?
—Bueno, realmente no **la** veo nada bien.

1. The direct object receives the action of the verb by completing the meaning of the verb phrase and answering the question *whom?* or *what?*

In the sentence, **Antonio desea unas camisas, unas camisas** is the direct object and tells what the speaker wants. Note that when the direct object refers to a specific person, it requires the personal **a**.

Tú hablas **español**.	*You speak Spanish.*
Rosa busca **trabajo**.	*Rosa is looking for work.*
Ellos invitan **a María Teresa**.	*They invite María Teresa.*

2. The direct-object noun may be replaced by a direct-object pronoun when the context is clear. Below is a chart of the direct-object pronouns in Spanish.

Singular		Plural	
me	me	**nos**	us
te	you *(fam.)*	**os**	you *(fam.)*
lo	you *(formal)*, him, it	**los**	you *(formal, m)*, them *(m)*
la	you *(formal)*, her, it	**las**	you *(formal, f)*, them *(f)*

—¿Tú hablas **español?**	*Do you speak Spanish?*
—**Lo** hablo un poco.	*Yes, I speak it a little.*
—¿Rosa busca a **su hermano?**	*Is Rosa looking for her brother?*
—No, no **lo** busca ahora.	*No, she's not looking for him now.*
—¿Visitan a **su mamá?**	*Do they visit their mother?*
—Sí, **la** visitan con frecuencia.	*Yes, they visit her frequently.*
—¿Recuerdas a **mis vecinos?**	*Do you remember my neighbors?*
—No, no **los** recuerdo. ¿Quiénes son?	*No, I don't remember them. Who are they?*

3. Note that the direct-object pronoun normally *precedes* the verb in Spanish, while it follows the verb in English.

La comprendo.	*I understand her.*
No **lo** necesito.	*I don't need it.*

4. **Le** is used instead of **lo** in certain areas of Spain and Hispanic America to refer to *you (formal, masculine singular)* and *him*. In the same areas, **les** is used instead of **los**. In this text, the direct-object forms shown in the chart will be used.

5. In double-verb constructions (see *Lección 3*) or in constructions with **ir a** + *infinitive*, the direct-object pronoun may be attached to the infinitive or may precede the conjugated verb. Both structures are common.

Puedes sacarlas desde aquí. **Las puedes sacar** desde aquí.	*You can take them (the photos) from here.*
¿Vamos a saludarla? **¿La vamos a saludar?**	*Shall we go greet her?*

D. Diga que Ud. comprende estas cosas o a estas personas perfectamente. Use la forma correcta de los pronombres de objeto directo.

▶ ¿Comprendes al señor Llano?   *Sí, lo comprendo perfectamente.*

1. ¿Comprendes el español?
2. ¿Comprendes la lección?
3. ¿Comprendes a tus padres?
4. ¿Nos comprendes a nosotros?
5. ¿Comprendes a las muchachas?
6. ¿Comprendes las instrucciones?

E. Unos amigos de Ud. se mudan *(are moving)* a Venezuela y venden estas cosas por los precios indicados. Diga si Ud. va a comprarlas o no.

▶ el tocadiscos ($50)   *Sí, lo compro.*
                          No, no lo compro.

1. la cámara fotográfica ($200)
2. el televisor a colores ($80)
3. la computadora japonesa ($1.200)
4. los discos nuevos ($7 cada uno)
5. la motocicleta roja ($890)
6. la bicicleta amarilla ($20)
7. la calculadora norteamericana ($14)

F. Diga que piensa o que no piensa hacer las siguientes actividades esta noche.

▶ leer estas revistas   *Sí, pienso leerlas esta noche.*
                          No, no pienso leerlas esta noche.

1. escribir unas cartas
2. mirar la televisión
3. visitar a tus padres
4. esperar a los amigos
5. escuchar las noticias
6. tocar el piano

G. Álvaro y Nina son novios. Haga el papel de Nina y conteste las preguntas de Álvaro en forma afirmativa o negativa.

▶ Álvaro: Nina, ¿me crees siempre?   Nina: *Claro que te creo siempre.*
                                             No, no te creo siempre.

1. Nina, ¿me invitas a tu casa hoy?
2. ¿Prefieres a otros chicos?
3. ¿Escuchas a otras personas?
4. Nina, ¿tú me admiras?
5. ¿Llevas a Roberto en tu coche hoy?
6. Nina, ¿tú me quieres mucho?

H. Complete las siguientes oraciones con frases lógicas. Use un pronombre de objeto directo.

1. —¿Ves esos veleros rojos? —Sí, ...
2. Ricardo siempre nos saluda a nosotras cuando . . . .

3. Las entradas son muy caras; por eso no . . . .
4. —Tengo un nuevo disco para el estéreo. —¿Puedo . . . ?
5. —¿Recuerdas a mi vecina Julia Romero? —No, ...
6. —Estas entradas son las últimas para el concierto. —¡Qué bien! Quiero . . . .
7. —¿Quién va a llevarnos a nosotros? —. . . .

III. Present tense of stem-changing verbs **e > ie**

1. In certain present-tense verb forms, the stem vowel changes from **e** to **ie** when it is stressed (that is, in all forms except the **nosotros-** and **vosotros**-forms). Note that the endings of stem-changing verbs are regular.

pensar	entender	preferir
pienso	entiendo	prefiero
piensas	entiendes	prefieres
piensa	entiende	prefiere
pensamos	entendemos	preferimos
~~pensáis~~	~~entendéis~~	~~preferís~~
piensan	entienden	prefieren

—¿En qué **piensan** ustedes?   *What are you thinking about?*
—**Pensamos** en las vacaciones.   *We're thinking about vacation.*

—¿**Entienden** ustedes al señor?   *Do you understand the man?*
—No, no lo **entendemos.**   *No, we don't understand him.*

—¿**Preferís** esta revista?   *Do you prefer this magazine?*
—No, **preferimos** ésa.   *No, we prefer that one.*

2. Below is a list of common verbs that have a stem-vowel change **e > ie** in the present tense.

-ar	**-er**	**-ir**
cerrar to close	**encender** to turn on	**mentir** to lie
empezar to begin	(*lights or equipment*)	**preferir** to prefer
negar to deny	**entender** to understand	**sugerir** to suggest
pensar to think;	**perder** to lose	
to intend	**querer** to want; to wish;	
	to love	

3. The verb **empezar** takes **a** before an infinitive.

Empiezo **a** entenderte bien.   *I'm beginning to understand you well.*
¿Quieres empezar **a** comer?   *Do you want to start to eat?*

4. The verb **pensar** + **en** = *to think about;* **pensar** + **de** = *to have an opinion of;* **pensar** + *infinitive* = *to intend* + *infinitive.*

Pienso en el fin de semana.	*I'm thinking about the weekend.*
¿Qué **piensas de** ella?	*What do you think of her?*
Pienso ir al centro.	*I intend to go downtown.*

I. Un amigo dice que no hace estas cosas. Dígale *(Tell him)* que usted y otro/a amigo/a tampoco *(not . . . either)* las hacen.

▶ ¡No entiendo a Lucho!   *¡Nosotros tampoco lo entendemos!*

1. ¡No niego el problema!
2. ¡No entiendo a los aficionados!
3. ¡No quiero esa situación!
4. ¡No prefiero el velero!
5. ¡No sugiero las preguntas!
6. ¡No miento!

J. Diga cuál de las actividades mencionadas probablemente prefieren hacer las personas indicadas.

▶ los jóvenes: escuchar música   *Los jóvenes probablemente prefieren*
clásica o música popular   *escuchar [música popular.]*

1. Elena: estudiar o salir con un amigo
2. nosotros: ir al centro a pie o en metro
3. yo: escuchar la radio o mirar la televisión
4. usted: leer un libro o leer el periódico
5. nosotras: esquiar o patinar *to ski* *to skate*
6. una muchacha de veinte años: ir a un baile o ir a un ballet
7. una persona que viaja mucho: cambiar dinero en un banco nacional o internacional
8. tú: jugar al tenis o jugar al fútbol

K. Conteste las siguientes preguntas, usando la forma apropiada de los verbos indicados.

▶ Yo **pienso** en las vacaciones. ¿y   *Nosotros también pensamos en las*
ustedes?   *vacaciones.*

1. Nosotros **empezamos** a leer. ¿y ellos?
2. Paco **quiere** ir a las montañas. ¿y tú y tu novio/a?
3. Yo **sugiero** leer muchas revistas interesantes. ¿y tú?
4. Tina siempre **pierde** dinero. ¿y Ud.?
5. Nosotros **negamos** eso. ¿y ellas?
6. **Enciendo** el televisor. ¿y ella?
7. Esos niños **mienten.** ¿y ese niño?

L. Haga ocho oraciones lógicas con las siguientes palabras y expresiones. No use los verbos más de una vez.

nosotros	mentir	las puertas y las ventanas
tú y tu amiga	cerrar	los veleros blancos
ustedes	empezar	buscar los discos
ellas	encender	todos los juegos de baloncesto
yo	pensar	la lección de cálculo
tú	perder	ir a la playa
él	sugerir	a (mis) hermanos
ella	querer	la luz del cuarto

IV. Present tense of stem-changing verbs o > ue

1. Certain verbs change the stem vowel **o** to **ue** in the present tense when the stem vowel is stressed. The endings remain regular.

almorzar	volver	dormir
almuerzo	vuelvo	duermo
almuerzas	vuelves	duermes
almuerza	vuelve	duerme
almorzamos	volvemos	dormimos
almorzáis	volvéis	dormís
almuerzan	vuelven	duermen

—¿**Almuerzas** al mediodía?   *Do you have lunch at noon?*
—No, **almuerzo** a la una y media.   *No, I have lunch at 1:30 P.M.*

—¿**Volvéis** a la oficina pronto?   *Are you returning soon to the office?*
—Sí, **volvemos** en cinco minutos.   *Yes, we are returning in five minutes.*

—¿**Duermes** bien en tu cuarto?   *Do you sleep well in your room?*
—No **duermo** bien porque mi   *I don't sleep well because my*
   vecino hace mucho ruido.   *neighbor makes a lot of noise.*

2. Below is a list of common verbs that have a stem change **o > ue** in the present tense. Note that the verb **costar** is generally used in the third person singular and plural only: **cuesta, cuestan.** The verb **llover** generally occurs in the third person singular only: **llueve.**

-ar	**-er**	**-ir**
almorzar to have lunch	**llover** to rain	**dormir** to sleep
aprobar to approve	**poder** to be able, can	**morir** to die
contar to count; to tell	**volver** to return	
costar to cost		
encontrar to find; to meet		
mostrar to show		
recordar to remember		

3. In the present tense, the verb **jugar** changes the stem vowel **u > ue** in
all forms except the **nosotros-** and **vosotros-**forms: j**ue**go, j**ue**gas, j**ue**ga,
jugamos, jugáis, j**ue**gan.

M. Algunas personas tienen mala memoria. Diga quién no recuerda la
información indicada.

▶ Pepe / mi apodo   *Pepe no recuerda mi apodo.*

1. yo / el nombre de ese campeón de tenis
2. mi hermanito / cuántos son dos y dos
3. mis amigas / qué día es hoy
4. tú / cuándo viene el próximo examen
5. ese joven / cómo se dice «weekend» en español
6. tú y ella / cuánto cuesta una motocicleta
7. nosotras / el color del velero número doce
8. ustedes / cómo sacar buenas fotografías

N. Diga que estas personas buscan los siguientes artículos, pero no los
encuentran. Después explique por qué no los encuentran.

▶ Ana / filmadora   *Ana no encuentra una filmadora barata.*
Cuestan demasiado.

1. nosotros / grabadoras
2. Raúl / estéreo
3. yo / raqueta de tenis
4. mis hermanas / entradas
5. tú / esquís
6. tú y Mario / vuelos
7. el empleado / dinero
8. tu tío y tu primo / metro

O. Complete las siguientes oraciones con frases lógicas, usando el infinitivo o el tiempo presente del verbo indicado.

▶ Luis **puede** ir al partido; yo no. . .   *puedo ir porque tengo una cita*
médica.

1. Yo **duermo** muy bien; Pepe . . .
2. Pablo **cuenta** historias absurdas; nosotros . . .
3. **Llueve** mucho en Puerto Rico; creo que también . . .
4. Hoy **vuelves** a la playa con Carlos; mañana nosotros también . . .
5. Yo **apruebo** tu decisión, pero tu papá no . . .
6. **Muestro** mis dibujos a Clara; no quiero . . .
7. Yo no **almuerzo** en casa; prefiero . . .
8. Este bote **cuesta** cien pesos; esos botes . . .
9. Nosotros **jugamos** al tenis, pero ellas . . .

P. Conteste las preguntas siguientes con la forma apropiada del verbo. Note que los verbos pueden tener cambios en la raíz *(stem)* de **e > ie** y de **o > ue.**

1. ¿Duerme usted bien o mal generalmente?
2. ¿Vuelven sus amigos a casa o al dormitorio después de las clases?
3. ¿Pierde su novio/a muchas cosas?
4. ¿Miente usted a veces para no ofender a alguna persona?
5. ¿Usted y su familia prefieren viajar en coche, en autobús o en tren?

¿Comprende usted?

Lea el artículo del periódico *La Prensa* de Buenos Aires. Note los datos *(facts)* más importantes y después haga los ejercicios.

Regata en Punta del Este

Luis A. Medús, corresponsal

BUENOS AIRES—Este domingo, 2 de febrero, se celebra la regata anual a beneficio del Hospital del Niño de Montevideo. Numerosos deportistas y aficionados del país se trasladan al país vecino para participar en la regata y
5 sólo piensan en el triunfo propio o del favorito que acompañan a la regata.

La Prensa tiene proyectado para el lunes un número extraordinario con los detalles de esta regata, que es uno de los eventos deportivos más importantes del año.

Las autoridades uruguayas estiman un incremento de un 20% sobre el
10 número de espectadores del año pasado, y varias aerolíneas anuncian vuelos extraordinarios para aliviar la demanda en el transporte.

Como siempre, los entusiastas de la regata no viajan solamente para presenciar el famoso evento: los restaurantes, las discotecas y todos los establecimientos comerciales van a recibir el beneficio directo del entusiasmo
15 que inspira la regata. Algunos de ellos ofrecen entradas gratis al Club Náutico, o a precios reducidos, para los clientes afortunados. Los nombres de estos establecimientos comerciales aparecen en nuestras ediciones de hoy y de mañana.

A. Sin mirar la lectura, indique si las siguientes declaraciones son verdaderas o falsas, según el contexto de la lectura. Después verifique sus respuestas en la lectura.

1. El Hospital del Niño de Montevideo participa en la regata.
2. La regata es el domingo, 2 de febrero, en Buenos Aires.
3. La regata es en Uruguay.

4. *La Prensa* va a publicar un número especial después de la regata.
5. Este año van a ir a la regata más espectadores que el año pasado.
6. La gente va exclusivamente para presenciar la regata.
7. Todas las entradas al Club Náutico son gratis.
8. La regata beneficia a los comerciantes de Montevideo.
9. *La Prensa* participa en la promoción de la regata.

B. Escoja la definición de la segunda columna que mejor describe cada palabra de la primera columna, según el significado que tiene en la lectura.

1. anual	a. nación cercana
2. triunfo	b. cantidad de dinero que se paga por un producto
3. proyectado	c. de todos los años
4. incremento	d. planeado, contemplado
5. aliviar	e. éxito
6. país vecino	f. especial
7. establecimiento comercial	g. aumento
8. precio	h. acompañar
9. extraordinario	i. lugar que vende artículos
	j. disminuir, reducir

Estas playas estupendas de Montevideo, Uruguay atraen a muchos turistas, especialmente uruguayos y argentinos. A lo largo de la playa hay edificios de apartamentos donde los visitantes ricos pueden pasar las vacaciones o fin de semana. Comente sobre los problemas de construir edificios altos en la playa y por qué le gusta o no le gusta la idea. ¿Dónde existen condominios como éstos en los Estados Unidos?

Lección 9
En Chile

Una investigación sociológica

Patricia Torres es estudiante de sociología de la Universidad Nacional de Santiago. Este semestre tiene un proyecto interesante de investigación con otros estudiantes. Con ellos trata de averiguar el nivel de vida de la clase media de uno de los barrios de la capital de Chile. Los estudiantes preparan
5 un cuestionario y luego salen a entrevistar a los habitantes del barrio.

Las respuestas al cuestionario dan a conocer información interesante sobre las condiciones de vida de la gente de ese barrio. Por ejemplo, entre los habitantes entrevistados, algunas familias no tienen ni teléfono, ni lavadora, ni estéreo. Todas tienen televisor, radio y nevera, pero ninguna fa-
10 milia tiene más de dos automóviles. La mayoría de las madres de familia son amas de casa. Algunas madres trabajan como empleadas u obreras; solamente el dos por ciento de ellas siguen profesiones. Todos los entrevistados necesitan más ayuda económica del gobierno.

Santiago de Chile, como muchas otras ciudades del mundo hispánico, tiene serios problemas urbanos. Sin embargo, la clase media es un importante factor en el progreso del país. Observe las personas en esta fotografía. ¿En qué se parecen a personas de la clase media en EEUU? ¿En qué son diferentes?

Cuestionario

1. ¿Cuántas personas en total viven en la casa?

    una _____ dos _____
tres _____ más de tres _____

2. ¿Quién trabaja en la familia?

    el padre _____ la madre _____
los hijos _____ las hijas _____

3. ¿En qué categoría trabaja el padre?

    empleado _____ obrero _____
en casa _____ profesional _____

4. ¿En qué categoría trabaja la madre?

    empleada _____ obrera _____
en casa _____ profesional _____

5. ¿Hay estudiantes en casa?

    sí _____ no _____ ¿cuántos? _____

6. ¿Dónde estudian los hijos?

    en una escuela pública _____
en la universidad _____
en un colegio particular _____
en un instituto técnico _____

	sí	no
7. ¿Tienen ustedes teléfono?	_____	_____
radio	_____	_____
televisor	_____	_____
nevera	_____	_____
estéreo	_____	_____
lavadora	_____	_____
lavaplatos	_____	_____
acondicionador de aire	_____	_____
secadora de ropa	_____	_____

8. ¿Tienen ustedes automóvil en la familia?

    no _____ uno _____ dos _____
más de dos _____

9. ¿Usan el transporte público?

    siempre _____ nunca _____
raras veces _____

10. Para vivir bien, ¿necesitan ustedes más ayuda económica del gobierno?

    no _____ sí, un poco _____
sí, mucha ayuda _____

Comprensión

1. ¿Quién es Patricia Torres?
2. ¿En qué proyecto participa?
3. ¿Qué clase de documento preparan los estudiantes?
4. ¿A quiénes entrevistan?
5. ¿Qué tipo de información dan a conocer las respuestas de los cuestionarios?

Conversación

1. ¿Estudia Ud. sociología u otra disciplina en las ciencias sociales? ¿cuál/es?
2. ¿Para qué cursos tiene Ud. que hacer proyectos? ¿Cómo son sus proyectos: interesantes, monótonos, creativos?
3. ¿Qué aparatos eléctricos tienen usted o su familia? ¿Tiene teléfono?
4. ¿Tiene automóvil su familia? ¿ninguno? ¿uno? ¿dos? ¿más de dos? ¿De qué marca/s es/son?
5. ¿Hay transporte público en su ciudad o pueblo? ¿Usa el transporte público? ¿raras veces? ¿frecuentemente? ¿nunca?
6. En su opinión, ¿qué aparatos eléctricos son esenciales y qué aparatos son superfluos?

Situaciones

1. You and a friend are looking for an apartment. Find out what your friend thinks about an apartment advertised in the newspaper.

   —¿Qué piensas de este apartamento; vamos a verlo?
   —No, porque no tiene . . . (lavaplatos, ni secadora de ropa ni lavadora, nevera, acondicionador de aire).

2. Inform a classmate of the results of a recent survey on the economy.

   —¿Qué tal los resultados de la investigación de la economía?
   —Interesantes; . . . (los obreros no consiguen empleo, la clase media pide más ayuda, el gobierno repite sus errores).

Vocabulario

Palabras análogas

la categoría	el documento	el instituto	público, -a	sociológico, -a
la condición	eléctrico, -a	monótono, -a	el/la radio	superfluo, -a
creativo, -a	esencial	la persona	el/la representante	técnico, -a
el cuestionario	la información	el proyecto	el semestre	el teléfono

Sustantivos

el acondicionador de aire   air conditioner
el ama de casa   housewife (f)
la ayuda   help
el barrio   neighborhood
la clase   kind
la disciplina   subject; discipline
el empleo   work, job
el/la entrevistado/a   the person interviewed
la escuela   school
la gente   people
el gobierno   government

el/la habitante   inhabitant
la investigación   survey, research, investigation
la lavadora   washing machine
el lavaplatos   dishwasher
la marca   brand
la mayoría   majority
la nevera   refrigerator (with freezer section)
el/la obrero/a   (blue collar) worker
la respuesta   answer
la secadora de ropa   clothes dryer

Adjetivos

entrevistado, -a   interviewed
ningún/ninguno, -a   no, not any
particular   private

Verbos

averiguar   to find out; to verify
conseguir (i)   to get, obtain
dar *(irreg.)*   to give
elegir (i)   to elect
entrevistar   to interview
pedir (i)   to ask for
repetir (i)   to repeat
seguir (i)   to follow
tratar (de)   to try to

Otras palabras y expresiones

la clase media   middle class
dar a conocer   to show, make clear, reveal
en total   in total, in all
frecuentemente   frequently
luego   then
más de (tres)   more than (three)
ni . . . ni   neither . . . nor
el nivel de vida   standard of living
nunca   never
por ciento   percent
raras veces   rarely
solamente   only
todos/as   everybody
el transporte público   public transportation
u (= o before **o** or **ho)**   or

Práctica

A. Imagine que Ud. trabaja para el censo *(census)*, y tiene que ir de casa en casa para obtener información de la gente que vive en un barrio. Haga una investigación entre varios compañeros de clase y pregúnteles información sobre su familia. Use las preguntas del cuestionario de la página 157.

B. Informe a la clase sobre los resultados de la investigación. Ponga en la pizarra las estadísticas de las preguntas de 1 a 7.

Nota cultural   La familia en la sociedad hispánica

In Spanish-speaking countries, **la familia** generally refers to the extended family which includes not only mother, father, and children, but also many close and distant relatives **(los parientes)**. Traditionally, the family unit has been an important institution in Hispanic society. All family members feel a particular bond for each other and a strong sense of loyalty to the family.

The Hispanic family is currently undergoing many changes, due primarily to industrialization. Young people from small towns and rural areas are moving to the cities in search of better-paying jobs, leaving behind parents and relatives. In large urban areas the nuclear family is becoming increasingly more prevalent; and, in some instances, both husband and wife

Una familia en Cali, Colombia celebra la Primera Comunión de uno de los niños. Observe la atención que recibe el niño por parte de la familia. ¿Podemos decir que es una ocasión importante? Diga quiénes imagina Ud. que son las personas de la foto con relación al niño.

hold jobs. These changes are creating many conflicts in a culture where traditionally the male has had the leading role as financial provider, and where individual members have depended upon and benefited from the support of large family units.

Pronunciación y ortografía
Los sonidos [d] y [ð]

1. The sounds [d] and [ð] are both spelled **d,** but they are pronounced differently. The stop sound [d] is pronounced with the tip of the tongue pressed flat against the back of the upper teeth, not against the gum ridge as in English. It occurs after a pause and after **n** and **l.**

don	acon**d**icionador	**D**on Martín **d**esea ir con **D**olores.
del	con**d**ición	**D**oña Luisa va al **d**entista.
dos	til**d**e	Fernan**d**o habla con **d**on **D**iego.

2. The fricative sound [ð] is pronounced much like the *th* in *mother,* but more relaxed, with the tip of the tongue protruding slightly between the teeth and barely touching them. It occurs after a vowel, at the end of a word, and after a consonant other than **n** or **l.** In some regions, final **d** and the **d** of words ending in **-ado** (with a stressed **a**) disappear in speech.

to**d**o	Ma**d**ri**d**	los Esta**d**os Uni**d**os	cansa**d**o
vi**d**a	uste**d**	que**d**an tres entra**d**as	pasa**d**o
rápi**d**o	ciu**d**a**d**	Ricar**d**o está en Ma**d**ri**d**.	la**d**o

A. Escuche a su profesor/a y repita estas palabras. Todas tienen el sonido [d] o [ð].

buenos días	de nada	el sábado	la empleada	el padre
buenas tardes	es grande	el domingo	la lavadora	la madre

B. Lea en voz alta las siguientes oraciones.

1. Buenos días, doña Matilde.
2. ¿Estudia usted medicina, Daniel?
3. ¿Dónde está el estadio?
4. Diego vive en Madrid.
5. Voy a pedir una lavadora de la tienda.

Refranes

1. **Poderoso caballero es don Dinero.**   Money talks.
2. **Peso ahorrado, peso ganado.**   A penny saved is a penny earned.
3. **Quien mucho duerme poco aprende.**   He who sleeps a lot learns little.

Estudio de palabras

I. Otros miembros de la familia

el abuelo grandfather
la abuela grandmother
los abuelos grandparents
el esposo (marido) husband
la esposa wife
el sobrino nephew
la sobrina niece
el tío uncle
la tía aunt
el primo male cousin
la prima female cousin

el nieto grandson
la nieta granddaughter
los nietos grandchildren
el suegro father-in-law
la suegra mother-in-law
el cuñado brother-in-law
la cuñada sister-in-law
el yerno son-in-law
la nuera daughter-in-law
el padrino godfather
la madrina godmother

Otras expresiones relacionadas
estar casado/a to be married
estar divorciado/a to be divorced
el matrimonio married couple, matrimony

el pariente relative
el soltero bachelor
la soltera single woman
vivir juntos to live together

1. Masculine plural nouns (like **los primos** and **los cuñados**) can refer to all-male groups, or to a mixed group of males and females. Context will help make the meaning clear.

Mario tiene tres **nietos:** Marta, Josefa y Enrique.

Mario has three grandchildren: Marta, Josefa, and Enrique.

Mis cuatro **abuelos** viven en Buenos Aires.

My four grandparents live in Buenos Aires.

2. **Los parientes** means *relatives* (not *parents*). The Spanish word for *parents* is **padres.**
3. The terms **padrino** and **madrina** refer to *godparents* at a baptism or confirmation, or to *witnesses* at a wedding.

A. Conteste las siguientes preguntas sobre su familia verdadera o una familia imaginaria.

1. ¿Cuántos tíos tiene usted? ¿cuántas tías? ¿Dónde viven?
2. ¿Tiene usted sobrinos o sobrinas? ¿Viven cerca o lejos de usted?
3. ¿Cuántos años tiene su abuelo? ¿su abuela? ¿Viven todavía todos los abuelos?
4. ¿Tiene usted un hermano o una hermana que está casado/a? ¿divorciado/a?
5. ¿Cuál es el nombre y cuáles son los apellidos de su abuelo o tío? ¿de su abuela o tía?
6. ¿Cuántas personas hay en su familia? ¿Cuántos parientes tiene en total?

B. Complete las siguientes oraciones con palabras apropiadas.

1. El padre de mi padre es mi _____ .
2. Mi _____ Ramón es el hermano de mi madre.
3. Los hijos de mis padres son mis _____ .
4. Mis _____ son los padres de mis padres.
5. Mis _____ Paco y Rosita son los hijos de mi tía Mercedes.
6. La hermana de mi papá es mi _____ .
7. La hermana de mi esposa es mi _____ .
8. Mis _____ son los padres de mi marido.

II. Los números de 200 y más

Numbers beyond 200 are quite easy to learn, for they are based on the cardinal numbers you already know. In writing numbers 1,000 and above, a period is used in Spanish (1.000) where a comma is used in English.

200 = doscientos, -as	1.000 = mil
300 = trescientos, -as	2.000 = dos mil
400 = cuatrocientos, -as	2.050 = dos mil cincuenta
500 = quinientos, -as	10.000 = diez mil
600 = seiscientos, -as	100.000 = cien mil
700 = setecientos, -as	1.000.000 = un millón
800 = ochocientos, -as	6.000.000 = seis millones
900 = novecientos, -as	10.000.000 = diez millones

1. Plural hundreds show gender and number agreement.

trescientos lápices   **setecientas** fotos
cuatrocientos hombres   **novecientas** mujeres

2. **Mil** does not change in the plural when preceded by a cardinal number. In the plural, **miles** is followed by **de** + noun.

dos **mil** hombres	*2,000 men*
dos **mil** mujeres	*2,000 women*
miles de hombres	*thousands of men*
miles de mujeres	*thousands of women*

3. **Millón (millones)** requires a **de**-phrase to quantify other nouns when no other number follows.

un millón de dólares	*$1,000,000*
dos millones de dólares	*$2,000,000*
un millón doscientos mil habitantes	*1,200,000 inhabitants*

C. Diga y luego escriba las siguientes combinaciones en español.

▶ 200 male workers   *doscientos obreros*

1. 500 magazines
2. 1,000 places
3. 1 million questions
4. 700 chairs
5. 3,000 students
6. 900 banks
7. 100,000 years
8. 3,400,000 dollars

D. Pregúntele a otra persona de la clase el precio de los artículos siguientes.

▶ bicicleta ($200)   S1: *¿Cuánto cuesta esa bicicleta?*
                      S2: *Cuesta doscientos dólares.*

1. coche ($13.900)
2. motocicleta ($5.400)
3. computadora ($2.560)
4. grabadora ($375)
5. televisor a colores ($694)
6. estéreo ($1.745)
7. máquina de escribir ($530)
8. velero ($3.200)

E. Conteste las preguntas siguientes. Calcule el número aproximado si no lo sabe.

1. ¿Cuántos estudiantes hay en esta universidad?
2. ¿Cuánto cuesta la matrícula en esta universidad?
3. ¿Cuánto paga usted por mes por su apartamento?
4. Si usted desea viajar a México, ¿cuánto dinero necesita más o menos?
5. Si usted desea comprar una casa, ¿cuántos dólares necesita?
6. ¿Cuántos habitantes tiene su ciudad (pueblo)? ¿y los EEUU?
7. ¿Cuántos hispanohablantes más o menos viven en los EEUU?
8. Si un dólar vale 120 pesos, ¿cuántos pesos son $250?

Estructuras útiles

I. Affirmative and negative counterparts

Yo *siempre* viaja en avión.   Yo *nunca* viajo en avión.

1. The chart below shows common affirmative and negative expressions in Spanish and their English equivalents.

sí	yes	no	no
algo/todo	something/everything	nada	nothing (at all)
alguien	someone, somebody	nadie	nobody, no one
alguno, -s, alguna, -s	some (*pronoun*)	ninguno, -s ninguna, -s	none (*pronoun*)
algún, alguno, -a, algunos, -as	some (*adjective*)	ningún, ninguno, -a, ningunos, -as	(not) any (*adjective*)
también	also	tampoco	neither, not . . . either
o . . . o	either . . . or	ni . . . ni	neither . . . nor
siempre/alguna vez	always/sometimes, on occasion	nunca/jamás	never, not . . . ever

2. The negative expressions **nada, nadie, nunca,** and **jamás** may precede or follow the verb. When they follow the verb, **no** must precede the verb. In general, the use of the negative expressions **nada, nadie, nunca,** and **jamás** before the verb is more emphatic.

Nadie me comprende. ⎫
No me comprende **nadie.** ⎭   *Nobody (No one) understands me.*

Nunca (Jamás) voy al cine. ⎫
No voy **nunca (jamás)** al cine. ⎭   *I never go to the movies.*

3. **Alguno** and **ninguno** may be used as pronouns or as adjectives. When used as adjectives, **alguno** becomes **algún,** and **ninguno** becomes **ningún** before a masculine singular noun. The adjective **ninguno** is seldom used in the plural.

Algunos estudiantes trabajan, pero **ninguno** trabaja en una profesión técnica.   *Some students work, but not one (of them) works in a technical profession.*

Vamos a ir a México **algún** día.   *We are going to Mexico some day.*

Algunas (de ellas) tienen dos automóviles.   *Some (of them) have two cars.*

Ningún pariente (nuestro) vive con nosotros.   *No relative (of ours) lives with us.*

4. The expressions **o . . . o** and **ni . . . ni** normally require a plural form of the verb, in contrast to English usage.

O tú **o** ella **deben** ir a la fiesta.   *Either you or she must go to the party.*

Ni su tío **ni** su tía **están** en casa.   *Neither your uncle nor your aunt is at home.*

5. Note the use of **tampoco** in the following expressions.

—Jorge no va al museo.   *Jorge isn't going to the museum.*
—(Ni) yo **tampoco.**   *Neither am I. (I'm not going either.)*

—A mí no me gusta bailar.   *I don't like to dance.*
—A mí **tampoco.**   *Neither do I. (I don't either.)*

A. Diga que usted no tiene ninguno de los artículos siguientes.

▶ lápices   *No tengo ningún lápiz.*

1. plumas	4. entradas	7. cassettes
2. revistas	5. motocicletas	8. televisores
3. mapas	6. coches	9. computadoras personales

(handwritten, left margin top) Put what is before V after V and "No" at Beginning

B. Ponga la expresión negativa después del verbo.

▶ Nadie me comprende.   *No me comprende nadie.*
▶ Ninguno de ellos trabaja.   *No trabaja ninguno de ellos.*

1. Ningún estudiante me saluda.
2. Nunca escucho música clásica.
3. Jamás compramos discos.
4. Tampoco voy al teatro.
5. Nada pasa en esta ciudad.
6. Nadie tiene estéreo.

C. Usted está muy pesimista hoy y contradice a todos sus amigos. Empiece (Begin) cada respuesta con la expresión ¡Qué va! (Nonsense!)

▶ En la vida todo es bueno.   *¡Qué va! ¡En la vida nada es bueno!*

1. Todo es fácil en esta clase.
2. Alguien quiere ser tu amigo.
3. Tú siempre aprendes tus lecciones muy bien.
4. O tú o tu hermano pueden pasar las vacaciones en México.
5. La novia de Pablo también va a la fiesta.
6. Algún amigo te comprende.
7. Hay algo aquí para ti.

(handwritten, left margin) Translate as is

D. Exprese en español.

1. —He never works.
   —I don't work either!
2. —He never drinks wine.
   —I don't drink wine either!
3. —Nobody loves him.
   —That's not true. Somebody loves him.
4. —There's nothing in my refrigerator.
   —There's nothing in our refrigerator either!
5. —There isn't any park or museum in that town.
   —There is either a park or a museum in every town!

II. Present tense of stem-changing verbs e > i

1. Some **-ir** verbs have a stem-vowel change from **e** to **i** in the present tense when the stem vowel is stressed. The endings are regular.

pedir	conseguir	reír
pido	consigo	río
pides	consigues	ríes
pide	consigue	ríe
pedimos	conseguimos	reímos
pedís	conseguís	reís
piden	consiguen	ríen

Nunca **consigo** entradas baratas.
Oscar **ríe** mucho en la clase.
¿A quién **pides** consejo? ¿a tu
padre?

I never (can) get cheap tickets.
Oscar laughs a lot in class.
Who(m) do you ask advice from,
  your father?

2. The following are common **-ir** verbs that have a stem vowel change
from **e** to **i** in the present tense.

conseguir   to get, obtain
despedir   to say good-by to
elegir   to elect; to choose
pedir   to ask (for); to request
reír   to laugh

repetir   to repeat
seguir   to follow
servir   to serve
sonreír   to smile

3. **Elegir, seguir,** and **conseguir** have a spelling change in the **yo**-form of
the present tense to preserve the pronunciation of the stem ending.

conseguir: (gu > g before **o)** consi**g**o, consi**gu**es, . . .
seguir: (gu > g before **o)** si**g**o, si**gu**es, . . .
elegir: (g > j before **o)** eli**j**o, eli**g**es, . . .

4. **Reír** and **sonreír** have an accent on the **í** in every form of the present
tense. The two vowels are pronounced as separate syllables.

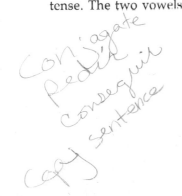

E. Diga que estas personas piden mucho pero no consiguen nada.

▶ yo   *Pido mucho, pero no consigo nada.*

1. nosotros
2. tú
3. tú y tu hermana
4. mis padres

5. Ángel
6. María y Pedro
7. todos ellos
8. todos nosotros

F. Complete las oraciones lógicamente.

▶ Ángel consigue muchas cosas, pero yo . . .   *no consigo nada.*

1. Yo río mucho, pero mi hermano . . . .
2. Carlos despide a su abuelo, y nosotros . . . .
3. Si tú pides un empleo en la biblioteca, yo . . . .
4. Ustedes sirven té en las recepciones; nosotras . . . .
5. Ellos no consiguen hablar con el director, pero yo siempre . . . .
6. En Puerto Rico eligen a un gobernador cada cuatro años; en este
   estado también . . . .
7. Cuando estamos juntos nosotros sonreímos mucho, pero tú y tu
   amigo . . . .
8. Yo repito la poesía para aprenderla, pero pocas personas . . . .

G. Haga seis oraciones lógicas, escogiendo palabras de las tres columnas. No use los verbos más de una vez.

tú	reír	sus errores
todos	conseguir	comida buena
mis amigos	servir	a un director
nadie	despedir	favores
alguno de ellos	seguir	en esa película
nosotros	elegir	a mi hermana
pocas personas	repetir	la mayoría

Only one Ud. person (handwritten)

III. Present tense of conocer, dar, saber, and traducir

The following verbs are irregular in the **yo**-form of the present tense.

conocer *to know person*	dar *to give*	saber *to know facts*	traducir *to translate*
conozco	**doy**	**sé**	**traduzco**
conoces	das	sabes	traduces
conoce	da	sabe	traduce
conocemos	damos	sabemos	traducimos
conocéis	dais	sabéis	traducís
conocen	dan	saben	traducen

—**Traduzco** estas páginas para el nuevo profesor de química. ¿Lo conoces?
—No, no lo **conozco** todavía.

I'm translating these pages for the new chemistry professor. Do you know him?
No, I don't know him yet.

Cuando **doy** mi opinión en casa, siempre **sé** que mis padres me van a escuchar.

When I give my opinion at home, I always know my parents are going to listen to me.

H. Diga si usted y otras personas que Ud. conoce hacen lo siguiente. Use los pronombres de objeto directo cuando el contexto lo requiere (*requires*).

▶ conocer España   *Yo no conozco España. Mis padres y mis hermanos la conocen.*

1. dar conferencias
2. traducir del francés al inglés
3. saber usar la computadora
4. dar conciertos
5. conocer a alguien en Centroamérica
6. saber tres lenguas extranjeras

Use verb in sentence. Make 2 sentences (handwritten)

IV. **Saber** and **conocer** in contrast

Sé muchas cosas . . .

*¡pero no **conozco** a muchas personas!*

1. **Saber** and **conocer** both mean *to know,* but they are associated with different types of knowledge and therefore cannot be used interchangeably. Remember that the **yo**-forms **sé** and **conozco** are irregular in the present tense.

—¿**Sabes** esquiar?	*Do you know how to ski?*
—No, no **sé** esquiar.	*No, I don't know how to ski.*
—¿**Conoces** a mi novia?	*Do you know my fiancée?*
—No, no la **conozco.**	*No, I don't know her.*

2. **Saber** is used to refer to knowledge of factual information (names, numbers, directions). This information is of the type that can be *imparted to someone else.*

Pilar **sabe** el nombre del artista.	*Pilar knows the artist's name.*
No **sé** tu número de teléfono.	*I don't know your telephone number.*
¿**Sabes** quién es el presidente de México?	*Do you know who is the president of Mexico?*

3. **Saber** + *infinitive* refers to knowledge in the sense of *knowing how to do something.*

Joaquín **sabe tocar** el piano.	*Joaquín knows how to play the piano.*
Yo **sé escribir** a máquina.	*I know how to type.*
Ustedes no **saben nadar,** ¿verdad?	*You don't know how to swim, do you?*

4. **Conocer** refers to knowledge in the sense of *knowing a person, a place, a thing,* or some other subject of knowledge that is acquired firsthand.

Note that personal **a** is sometimes used before the name of a city or country.

¡Es increíble! ¿Tú **conoces** bien a Luisa, pero no sabes dónde vive?

That's incredible! You know Luisa well, but don't know where she lives?

Conocemos (a) San Juan.

We know San Juan (well).

No **conozco** esa novela de Cervantes.

I don't know that novel by Cervantes.

I. Piense en personas que han viajado *(have travelled)* a otros países: su papá, sus primos, usted y su familia, unos tíos, sus abuelos, un/a amigo/a. Diga qué países conocen y si saben o no saben el idioma del país.

▶ *Mi papá conoce Francia y sabe (pero no sabe) francés.*

J. Pregúntele a otra persona de la clase si conoce algunos sitios o algunas personas y si sabe cierta información.

▶ ¿Conoces París?   *Sí, lo conozco muy bien.*
▶ ¿Sabes hablar francés?   *Sí, sé hablar francés.*

K. Exprese en español.

1. —Do you know Buenos Aires?
   —Yes, I know it very well.
2. —Does Milagros know Pilar? ~use personal a
   —No, she doesn't know her.
3. —Do you and your brother know how to swim?
   —Yes, but we don't know how to skate.
4. —Do you know the song «Cielito lindo»?
   —No, but I know «La cucaracha».
Skip→ 5. —Do you know where the train station is?
6. —Do you know today's date?

¿Comprende usted?

Patricia Torres habla con su familia sobre los problemas de su investigación sociológica. Hay diferentes actitudes entre los miembros de la familia. Uno de ellos no está contento con la participación de Patricia en el proyecto; otro es comprensivo y muestra interés en los problemas de Patricia; otro tiene una solución fácil. ¿Cómo son diferentes el padre y la madre de Patricia? Y Luisito, ¿cuántos años aproximadamente cree usted que tiene? Piense un poco y observe las palabras y expresiones que le ayudan a contestar las preguntas.

En casa de Patricia

Patricia: El proyecto es muy interesante, pero los problemas del investigador son tremendos.

Madre: ¡Claro! Seguramente piensan que eres empleada del gobierno y
quieres poner más impuestos.

5 Patricia: Exactamente. Ése es el obstáculo más grande.

Padre: Seguramente tienes problemas de todas clases. No me gustan las
benditas investigaciones sociológicas. ¿Por qué tienes que entrar
en esas casas? Nunca sabes a quién vas a encontrar.

Patricia: No te preocupes, papá. La universidad lo tiene todo muy bien
10 organizado, y yo nunca voy sola. Hoy voy a entrevistar a las
familias del barrio con otros dos estudiantes que participan en el
proyecto.

Luisito: Yo también voy a ser un gran investigador social, y si alguien
causa problemas, saco la pistola y ¡pum! ¡pum!

15 Patricia: ¡Ay, ese niño me vuelve loca!

Madre: Ya está bien, Luis. ¡A comer y nada de pistolas!

A. Conteste las preguntas siguientes.

1. ¿Quién no está muy contento con la participación de Patricia en
el proyecto?
2. ¿Quién muestra interés y comprende los problemas de Patricia?
3. ¿Está interesado en la conversación Luisito? ¿Qué solución tiene?
4. ¿Cuántos años aproximadamente cree usted que tiene Luisito?
5. ¿Patricia va a continuar a participar en la investigación?

B. Escoja entre las palabras de la lista siguiente las que mejor describen a
las personas de la lectura.

preocupado	paciente	idealista
despreocupado	alegre	optimista
comprensivo	joven	pesimista
serio	impaciente	

▶ Patricia es . . .   *seria, idealista y optimista.*

Lengua en acción 3

A. ¿Quién está libre? (Lección 7)

Usted trata de reunir a un grupo de compañeros para practicar español cada miércoles o jueves. Averigüe (Find out) quién quiere participar y qué día están libres (free) sus compañeros, usando las siguientes frases y expresiones. Pregúnteles su número de teléfono para llamarlos después. Escriba la información en la libreta de direcciones (address book).

¿Estás libre?	Hay que estudiar para español en grupo.
número de teléfono	Bien. Te llamo si formamos un grupo.
estar ocupado/a	Lo siento.

	Comentario		Comentario
Nombre *María*	*libre*	Nombre _____	
Dirección _____	*jueves/*	Dirección _____	
Teléfono *5-43-58-39*	*viernes*	Teléfono _____	
Nombre _____	Comentario	Nombre _____	Comentario
Dirección _____		Dirección _____	
Teléfono _____		Teléfono _____	
Nombre _____	Comentario	Nombre _____	Comentario
Dirección _____		Dirección _____	
Teléfono _____		Teléfono _____	

B. Una reservación en un buen restaurante (Lección 7)

Ud. quiere comer con unos amigos en el restaurante La Rambla. Haga una reservación por teléfono con el dueño (owner) del restaurante (su compañero/a de clase). Después, alternen los papeles (roles).

El/La dueño/a	Usted
—Muy buenas noches. La Rambla.	_____
¿En qué puedo servirle?	_____
—¿Para qué día, Sr./Srta.?	_____
—¿Para qué hora? ¿Quieren a las [seis]?	_____

El/La dueño/a	Usted
—¿Para cuántas personas?	_____
—¿A nombre de quién?	_____
—¿Y su número de teléfono?	_____
—Muy bien. [Seis] personas para el	_____
[lunes] a las [ocho]. Muchas gracias.	_____

C. Una excusa cortés (courteous) (Lección 8)

Ud. tiene tres entradas para una de las siguientes actividades. Invite a varios/as compañeros/as hasta encontrar a dos que puedan ir con usted. Si tiene que rechazar (refuse) una invitación, sea cortés: **Lo siento mucho, pero . . . . No puedo. Tengo que . . . .** Apunte (Jot down) a qué actividad Ud. va y con quién.

▶ S1: *Tengo tres entradas [para el concierto de Lionel Richie]. ¿Quieres ir conmigo?*
S2: *¿Cuándo es [el concierto]?*
S1: *Es [el domingo].*
S2: *Lo siento mucho, pero [Carlos y yo vamos a la fiesta latina ese mismo día]. (Sí, me gusta mucho ese cantante.)*

De interés general

Actividades, fin de semana

- Partido de Fútbol
(El Central Español contra El Nacional)
Sábado, 12:00 p.m.
Estadio Centenario

- Presentación Especial
"Casablanca"
Sábado, 7:30 p.m.
Cine Clásico

- Concierto de Lionel Richie
(solamente entradas numeradas)
Domingo, 8:00 p.m.
Auditorio Central

- Fiesta Latina
(Música y comida típicas)
Domingo, 7:00 p.m.
Café Internacional

D. Una guía turística (Lección 8)

Ud. llega a la estación de trenes de Puerto Lobo y consulta el mapa de la ciudad. Pídale (Ask) a un/a desconocido/a (un miembro de la clase) que le muestre (show) en el mapa cómo se llega a los sitios turísticos y dónde hay transporte público. Después, alternen los papeles.

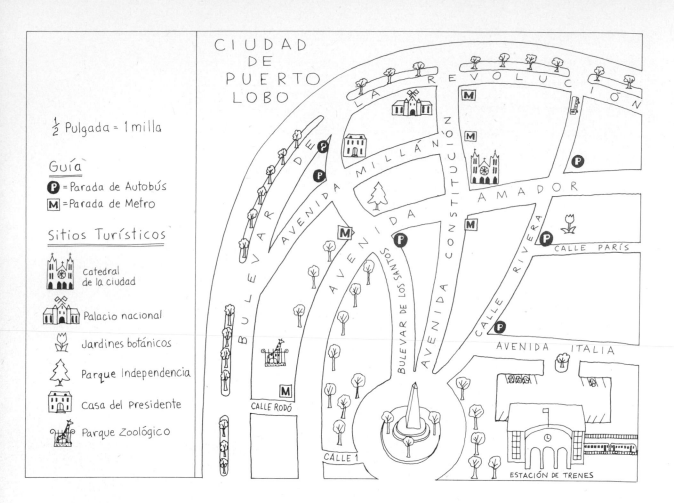

CIUDAD DE PUERTO LOBO

½ Pulgada = 1 milla

Guía
P = Parada de Autobús
M = Parada de Metro

Sitios Turísticos

Catedral de la ciudad

Palacio nacional

Jardines botánicos

Parque Independencia

Casa del Presidente

Parque Zoológico

▶ S1: *Perdón, [señor], ¿me puede mostrar en este mapa dónde está . . . ?*
　 S2: *Cómo no. Está aquí en . . . .*
　 S1: *¿Es posible ir a pie?*
　 S2: *No, está bastante lejos. ¿Por qué no toma Ud. . . . ?*
　 S1: *Muy bien, ¿y dónde tomo . . . ?*
　 S2: *La parada está . . . . Hay que . . . . Está cerca.*
　 S1: *Muchas gracias, ... Muy amable.*

E. Un sondeo telefónico (A telemarketing survey) *(Lección 9)*

Ud. trabaja en un sondeo telefónico para averiguar el tipo de persona que compra varios aparatos electrónicos. Llame a las personas de los dibujos (sus compañeros/as de clase) por teléfono y saque apuntes sobre sus respuestas. Sus compañeros/as indican, según los dibujos, qué aparatos creen que cada persona posee o quiere comprar.

Gladys Barrera

Pablo Antola

Los Gómez

Nombre			
Edad			
Estado civil			
Número de hijos			
Profesión			
Aparatos que posee			
Aparato que quiere comprar y por qué			

F. Los fines de semana (On the weekends) *(Lección 9)*

Entreviste a varios compañeros de clase sobre lo que hacen generalmente los fines de semana. Apunte sus respuestas para después hacer
una descripción general a la clase.

¿Sales por la noche los viernes? ¿los sábados? ¿los domingos?	*a veces* *casi siempre* *raras veces*		
Cuando sales, ¿adónde vas?	*al cine o a* *una fiesta*		
¿Quién te acompaña?	*mi mejor* *amigo/a*		

(continues)

¿Qué día haces la limpieza (cleaning)?	el sábado		
¿Tienes otros quehaceres (chores)?	Sí, voy al mercado		
¿Qué programas de televisión miras?	películas, deportes		
¿Compras el periódico los domingos?	frecuentemente		
¿Qué piensas hacer este fin de semana?	dormir porque estoy cansado		

G. Una serenata romántica (Wrap-up)

Ud. piensa contratar los servicios de Ramón, un músico que tiene el siguiente anuncio en el periódico. Llámelo, averigüe más sobre sus servicios, y haga un trato (deal) con él. Saque apuntes sobre sus respuestas.

SERENATAS ROMÁNTICAS

Recuerde Ud. a esa persona especial con la sorpresa perfecta. Conmemore su aniversario, cumpleaños u otro día festivo con la música apropiada. Desde las 12:00 p.m., llegamos a su casa (solo o en grupo) con su música preferida. Tocamos canciones tradicionales y populares, y tenemos guitarras, violines, flautas y trompetas.
Para más información: Ramón 5-24-56.

Ud. necesita saber

El costo por canción _____

Tipo de música que toca _____

_____

El costo por músico _____

Hasta qué hora trabajan _____

Ramón necesita saber

Nombre del cliente _____

Número de teléfono _____

Dirección de la casa _____

Día de la serenata _____

Tipo de música que quiere _____

Número de canciones _____

Solo o en grupo _____

Unidad 4
En Bolivia, Ecuador y Perú

La ciudad de Cuzco, Perú, centro del antiguo imperio inca, atrae visitantes por su proximidad a ruinas incaicas importantes y por el encanto (charm) de sus calles y de sus edificios coloniales en excelente estado de conservación. ¿Dónde hay una ciudad colonial bien conservada en EEUU? ¿Cómo es y qué importancia tiene?

Lección 10
En Bolivia

Una huelga inminente

Bolivia es un país de considerables recursos minerales. Sus minas de estaño son de importancia tradicional para obtener los ingresos° del país. Por eso las noti-cias sobre un cambio en el precio del estaño o la intranquilidad en las minas son de interés nacional. Hoy apareció en un periódico de La Paz este artículo sobre la situación laboral en las minas de estaño de Potosí.

income

Esta familia boliviana avienta (winnows) estaño en Potosí para obtener la mayor pureza posible del mineral. ¿Cree Ud. que este trabajo es peligroso para la salud? ¿Por qué?

¡Huelga inminente de mineros!

Potosí, 8 de julio. En la tarde de ayer se celebró° una importante reunión entre los líderes del sindicato° de los mineros y el representante del gobierno, el Sr. Jorge Martínez Gutiérrez. Durante la reunión celebrada en la oficina del sindicato, los líderes obreros presentaron al delegado del gobierno una lista de demandas con las firmas de unos quinientos mineros. Los representantes discutieron las más importantes: un aumento de sueldo de no menos del diez por ciento, la reducción en las horas de trabajo, el mejoramiento inmediato de las condiciones de trabajo en todas las minas del país y sobre todo, el no al cierre de las minas por el gobierno.

Los líderes sindicales transmitierron al representante gubernamental su preocupación por la intención del gobierno de cerrar permanentemente las minas principales. Exigen inmediata adopción de medidas° de seguridad preventivas de accidentes desastrosos como el del pasado mes de marzo, donde murieron más de sesenta mineros. Los líderes obreros afirmaron «si el gobierno no accede° a nuestras demandas para fines de mes, vamos a declarar una huelga general con el objeto de paralizar la producción de estaño en todo el país.»

El Sr. Martínez mencionó varias posibles reformas que, según él, pueden ayudar a resolver los problemas. Los mineros, sin embargo, no quedaron satisfechos, y decidieron reunirse de nuevo el lunes próximo para continuar las negociaciones y evitar una huelga con grandes repercusiones para la economía boliviana.

was held

labor union/measures

agree

Comprensión

1. ¿De qué trata el artículo que apareció en el periódico de La Paz?
2. ¿Quiénes participaron en la reunión en la oficina del sindicato?
3. ¿Qué entregaron los líderes de los mineros al Sr. Martínez?
4. ¿Cuáles son los problemas principales de los mineros?
5. ¿Qué piensan hacer los mineros si el gobierno no accede a sus demandas para fines de mes?
6. ¿Qué mencionó el Sr. Martínez como posible solución a las dificultades?
7. ¿Por qué quieren los mineros otra reunión para el lunes próximo?

Conversación

1. ¿Qué tipo de minas hay en los Estados Unidos? ¿Hay minas de oro (*gold*)? ¿de plata (*silver*)? ¿de cobre (*copper*)? ¿En qué estado o en qué región están?
2. ¿Hay frecuentes huelgas en los Estados Unidos? ¿Qué tipo de cosas protesta la gente en las huelgas?

3. ¿Cómo es la vida de los estudiantes en general? ¿dura? ¿fácil? ¿compleja? ¿cómoda?
4. ¿Cuáles son algunos problemas de la vida estudiantil?
5. ¿Qué recomiendan ustedes para mejorar la vida estudiantil? Por ejemplo, ¿recomiendan ustedes una reducción en el número de clases?

Vocabulario

Palabras análogas

el accidente	la economía	mencionar	el problema
la adopción	frecuente	la mina	la producción
afirmar	general	mineral	protestar
el artículo	la importancia	el minero	recomendar (ie)
celebrado, -a	importante	la negociación	la reducción
considerable	inmediato, -a	obtener *(irreg.)*	la reforma
continuar	inminente	la oficina	la región
declarar	la intención	paralizar	la repercusión
el delegado	la intranquilidad	la parte	resolver (ue)
la demanda	laboral	permanentemente	la situación
desastroso, -a	el líder	la preocupación	tradicional
la dificultad	la lista	preventivo, -a	transmitir

Sustantivos

el aumento   increase
el cambio   change
el cierre   closing, shutdown
el estaño   tin
la falta   lack
la firma   signature
la huelga   strike
julio   July
marzo   March
el mejoramiento   improvement
el mes   month
la noticia   news
el objeto   purpose
el precio   price
el recurso   resource
la reunión   meeting
la seguridad   security
el sueldo   salary
el trabajo   work

Adjetivos

cómodo, -a   comfortable
complejo, -a   complex
duro, -a   difficult, hard
estudiantil   student

gubernamental   government(al)
pasado, -a   last
principal   main
satisfecho, -a   satisfied
sindical   labor
varios, -as   several

Verbos

aparecer (zc)   to appear
ayudar   to help
discutir   to discuss
entregar   to deliver; to hand over
evitar   to avoid
exigir   to demand
mejorar   to better, improve
reunirse   to get together

Otras palabras y expresiones

ayer   yesterday
de nuevo   again
¿de qué trata (el artículo)?   what is (the article) about?
durante   during
el fin de mes   end of the month
la mayor parte de   most of
para fines de mes   by the end of the month
por ciento   percent
sin embargo   nevertheless

Práctica

Imagine que usted es un/a reportero/a de radio o televisión que está entrevistando a la gente que pasa por una calle en La Paz. Pregúnteles a varias personas cómo se llaman, cuál es su profesión, si creen que va a haber una huelga, qué piensan de la vida de los obreros, y si el gobierno va a mejorar las condiciones de vida de los trabajadores. Prepare por lo menos seis preguntas para la entrevista.

Nota cultural   Lenguas indígenas

La mayoría[1] de la gente en los países de Hispanoamérica habla castellano, es decir,[2] español. Sin embargo, hay áreas pobladas de indios que hablan además su propio[3] idioma como, por ejemplo, el quechua en Perú, Ecuador y Bolivia, el náhuatl en México y el guaraní en Paraguay. Hay otras áreas pobladas de tribus indígenas que hablan solamente su propio idioma, como en las selvas del Amazonas o en los Andes.

1. majority   2. **es** ... that is to say   3. **su** ... their own

Observe el interior de esta casa humilde del altiplano de Bolivia. La gente que habita en esta región (la mayoría india), habla el quechua o el aymará más que el español, dependiendo de la importancia de sus contactos con las ciudades y el mundo moderno. ¿Qué piensa Ud. que hace la muchacha en la mesa? ¿En qué lenguaje cree Ud. que recibe su educación?

Algunos países tienen programas oficiales para establecer comunicación con los indios que ni hablan ni entienden el español. En algunos casos el gobierno facilita radios transistores y ofrece programas educativos por la radio. También ofrece alimentos y artículos de producción industrial.[4] Así el gobierno ayuda a integrar a los indios a la vida nacional del país. Sin embargo, esta intervención del gobierno puede traer malas consecuencias si se lleva a un extremo, pues podría[5] destruir la cultura del indio al hacerlo demasiado dependiente del sistema industrial moderno.

---

4. **artículos** . . . factory-made articles   5. could

Pronunciación y ortografía
Los sonidos [p], [t] y [k]

1. In English, the sounds [p], [t], and [k] are usually aspirated (that is, they are pronounced with a slight puff of air, like the [p] in the word *pot*). In Spanish, however, these sounds are not aspirated. The Spanish [p] is like the [p] in the word *spot*, which is not aspirated.

   Potosí   **p**apá   **p**eligro   re**p**resentante

2. The Spanish [t] is like the [t] in the word *stew* and not like the one in the word *two*. The sound is made with the tip of the tongue touching the back of the upper front teeth (not the gum ridge).

   trabajo   **t**anto   **t**iempo   par**t**icular

3. The Spanish [k] is also an unaspirated sound. It is spelled **c** before **a, o** and **u,** and **qu** before **e** and **i.**

   cultural   **qu**e   cara**c**ol   **qu**ien

Lea las siguientes oraciones en voz alta. Preste atención a la pronunciación de los sonidos [p], [t] y [k].

1. Los mineros presentaron las peticiones ayer por la tarde.
2. Vamos a discutir los problemas más ampliamente mañana.
3. ¿A qué hora comen aquí?
4. ¿Quién viene contigo a la cafetería?

Refrán

¡Qué bonita es la paciencia!   All things come to he who waits.
   Mucho vale y poco cuesta.

Festivales y celebraciones

El calendario de fiestas y celebraciones del mundo hispánico está marcado por fechas de carácter religioso, histórico o tradicional. En México, una de esas celebraciones tiene lugar el 2 de noviembre y se conoce con el nombre de "El día de los muertos". La gente decora las tumbas de sus familiares y deja comida para los espíritus. En la foto vemos a los habitantes de Janitzio, Michoacán en una vigilia que dura toda la noche.

Actividad

¿En qué día honran la memoria de los muertos en su pueblo/ciudad? Compare las actividades de ese día con lo que se ve en la foto.

La Plaza de la Constitución en Ciudad de México, también conocida como el Zócalo, es una de las más grandes del mundo (sólo la Plaza Roja en Moscú la supera). En ella se celebran los momentos históricos más significativos de la historia mexicana. En la foto vemos el gran mural humano que conmemora el Día de la Revolución. Se celebra el 20 de noviembre y recuerda la rebelión del pueblo mexicano contra el dictador Porfirio Díaz, en 1910. El mural representa el logo del PRI (Partido Revolucionario Institucional), el partido en el poder.

Actividad
¿Qué fechas históricas se celebran en los Estados Unidos? ¿Cómo se celebran?

Estudio de palabras

I. ¿Qué hora es?

Es mediodía.

Es la una.

Es la una y media.

Es la una menos cinco.

Es medianoche.

Son las dos.

Son las dos y cuarto.

Son las nueve menos diez.

Quiz March 18

1. In Spanish, two forms of the verb **ser** are used to express time. **Es** is used with singular expressions, such as **es la una, es mediodía,** and **es medianoche. Son** is used with plural expressions, as in **son las dos** and **son las cinco.**

2. The feminine definite articles **la** and **las** modify the unexpressed nouns **hora** or **horas.**

   Es **la** una (hora).   Son **las** tres (horas) y quince.

3. Time between the full hour and the half hour is expressed by *adding* minutes to the hour.

   Son las **nueve y diez.**   *It's 9:10.*

4. Time after the half hour is expressed by *subtracting* minutes from the next full hour.

   Son las **cinco menos veinte.**   *It's 4:40.*

5. **¿A qué hora?** is used to ask at what time an event is going to occur. **A la (a las)** + *a number* is used in the reply.

6. Specific morning, afternoon, and evening hours (A.M./P.M.) are expressed with **de la mañana, de la tarde,** and **de la noche.**

   Los mineros trabajan a las siete   *The miners work at 7 A.M.*
   de la mañana.

7. When no specific time is mentioned, the expressions **por la mañana (tarde, noche)** are used.

   Los mineros trabajan **por la**   *The miners work in the morning*
   mañana y **por la tarde.**   *and in the afternoon.*

8. Useful time expressions

una hora an hour
un minuto a minute
un segundo a second
en punto sharp, exactly
tarde late
temprano early
a tiempo on time
a eso de (las dos) at about (two o'clock)

el reloj watch, clock
el reloj corriente regular watch (clock)
el reloj digital digital watch (clock)
el reloj de pulsera wrist watch
el reloj de pared wall clock
estar atrasado (adelantado) to be running slow (fast)

Use names
conjagate
llegar
in every sentence

A. Usted y varios amigos llegan a un ~~balneario~~ *iglesia* (*beach resort*) a distintas horas. Diga a qué hora llega cada persona.

▶ Miguel / 3:00 P.M.   *Miguel llega a las tres de la tarde.*

1. Marta y Teresa / 11 A.M.
2. yo / 12:00 noon
3. Patricia / 2:15 A.M.
4. tu novia / 8:25 P.M.
5. Felipe y tú / 10:30 P.M.
6. Jaime / 9:40 A.M.
7. José y Antonio / 1:45 P.M.
8. Alicia y su hermano / 12:00 P.M.

B. Conteste las siguientes preguntas.

1. ¿Tiene usted un reloj de pulsera? ¿Está atrasado o adelantado su reloj, generalmente?
2. ¿Cuántos segundos hay en un minuto? ¿en dos minutos?
3. ¿A qué hora estudia generalmente?
4. Cuando usted tiene una cita con alguien, ¿llega usted siempre tarde? ¿temprano? ¿a tiempo?
5. ¿Tiene usted una cita con alguien esta tarde o esta noche? ¿A qué hora? ¿A eso de [las siete] o a [las siete] en punto? ¿A dónde van ustedes?
6. ¿Qué tipo de reloj [relojes] tiene usted en su casa? ¿Cómo son?
7. ¿Qué hora es? ¿Es hora de salir? ¿de comer?

II. Expresiones de tiempo en el pasado

Learn the following expressions referring to time in the past.

ayer yesterday
ayer por la mañana yesterday morning
ayer por la tarde yesterday afternoon
ayer por la noche yesterday evening
anteayer the day before yesterday
anoche last night

el año pasado last year
el mes pasado last month
la semana pasada last week
el sábado (domingo, etcétera, pasado) last Saturday (Sunday, et cetera)

C. Diga cuándo hizo (*did*) Ricardo las siguientes actividades. Use las expresiones de tiempo en el pasado.

► bailó con Isabel   *Bailó con Isabel [anoche].*

1. estudió en la biblioteca
2. escuchó la radio
3. trabajó en una oficina
4. compró discos
5. viajó a La Paz
6. pasó las vacaciones en Bolivia
7. habló con su abuelo
8. invitó a Carlota al cine

D. Diga cuándo fue la última vez que Ud. llamó por teléfono a: sus padres, sus hermanos, sus tíos, su mejor amigo/a, sus abuelos, etcétera.

► *(Yo) llamé por teléfono a mi hermano/a [ayer].*

Estructuras útiles

I. The preterit

—¿Qué **pasó**? ¿Necesitas ayuda?
—No es nada. Es la primera vez que esquío . . .

There are two aspects of the past tense in Spanish: the preterit and the imperfect. The preterit represents a completed action in the past and views the past action in its beginning stage, in its ending stage, or in its entirety.

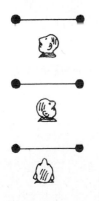

a. The beginning stage

Anoche **miré** televisión desde las ocho.
Last night I watched television from eight o'clock on.

b. The ending stage

Anoche **miré** televisión hasta las diez.
Last night I watched television until ten o'clock.

c. The entire action

Anoche **miré** televisión por dos horas.
Last night I watched television for two hours.

Quiz
March 18 '92

1. The preterit of regular verbs is formed by adding the preterit endings to the infinitive stem. The chart below shows the preterit forms of regular **-ar, -er,** and **-ir** verbs.

entrar	comer	vivir
entr **é**	com **í**	viv **í**
entr **aste**	com **iste**	viv **iste**
entr **ó**	com **ió**	viv **ió**
entr **amos**	com **imos**	viv **imos**
entr ~~asteis~~	com ~~isteis~~	viv ~~isteis~~
entr **aron**	com **ieron**	viv **ieron**

2. Note the following:
   a. The **-er** and **-ir** verbs have identical preterit endings.
   b. The **yo**-form and the **Ud.-, él-, ella-**forms are stressed on the last syllable: **tomé, tomó; salí, salió.**

3. The **nosotros-**forms of **-ar** and **-ir** verbs are identical in the present and preterit. The meaning is usually made clear by the context of each sentence.

Normalmente **escuchamos** la radio todos los días, pero ayer no la **escuchamos.**	*We usually listen to the radio every day, but yesterday we didn't listen to it.*
Este año **vivimos** en una casa, pero el año pasado **vivimos** en un apartamento.	*This year we live in a house, but last year we lived in an apartment.*

4. The **-ar** and **-er** verbs that change the stem vowel from **e > ie** or **o > ue** in the present tense do not have a stem change in the preterit.

—¿**Volvió** Ud. tarde o temprano?	*Did you return early or late?*
—**Volví** tarde.	*I returned late.*
—¿**Cerraste** las ventanas?	*Did you close the windows?*
—Sí, las **cerré.**	*Yes, I closed them.*

5. Verbs that end in **-car, -gar,** and **-zar** undergo regular spelling changes in the **yo-**form of the preterit. The **c** becomes **qu,** and **g** becomes **gu** to maintain the [k] or [g] sound of the infinitive before the **-é** ending. Also, **z** becomes **c** before the **-é** ending.

Llegué a las doce, **busqué** un restaurante y **almorcé** a la una.	*I arrived at noon, looked for a restaurant, and had lunch at one.*
Practiqué el alpinismo.	*I practiced mountain climbing.*
Analicé el problema.	*I analyzed the problem.*

6. **-Er** and **-ir** verbs whose infinitive stem ends in a strong vowel, such as **creer, leer,** and **oír,** have a **y** in the third-person singular and plural of the preterit. Note that the **i** of the preterit endings has a written accent.

creer	leer	oír
creí	leí	oí
creíste	leíste	oíste
creyó	leyó	oyó
creímos	leímos	oímos
creísteis	leísteis	oísteis
creyeron	leyeron	oyeron

Tomás **leyó** la noticia en *El Tiempo*. *Tomás read the news in El Tiempo.*
¿**Creyeron** esa barbaridad? *Did they believe that absurdity?*
¿Ustedes **oyeron** la música *Did you hear the music last night?*
anoche?

A. Diga si estas personas escucharon o no las noticias esta mañana.

▶ yo *Sí, escuché las noticias esta mañana.*
No, no escuché las noticias esta mañana.

1. esta chica
2. su compañero/a de cuarto
3. todos nosotros
4. su papá
5. tú y tu amigo
6. tú
7. la empleada
8. mis parientes

B. Explique que las siguientes personas esperaron a sus amigos o parientes por varias horas y luego volvieron al club.

▶ mis padres / mi tío *Mis padres esperaron a mi tío por [dos horas].*
Luego volvieron al club.

1. María y Juana / su prima
2. Julio y yo / nuestras cuñadas
3. Carmen / su suegra
4. sus abuelos / sus nietos
5. tú / tus hermanas
6. yo / mi primo
7. Pepe / su novia
8. tú y Ángela / sus sobrinos

C. Contraste lo que las siguientes personas hacen normalmente con lo que hicieron ayer. Use las formas apropiadas del presente y del pretérito.

▶ yo / normalmente llegar a las *Normalmente llego a las tres de*
tres de mis clases *mis clases pero ayer llegué a las*
cinco.

1. nosotros / siempre beber limonada
2. yo / nunca olvidar mis llaves
3. tú / normalmente salir con tus sobrinos
4. ustedes / generalmente comer a las ocho de la noche
5. su esposo / siempre regresar a la casa a almorzar
6. los muchachos / siempre entrar temprano a casa

D. Gabriela y Jaime no están de acuerdo (don't agree). Haga el papel de Jaime, y conteste negativamente usando los verbos en el pretérito.

► Gabriela: Yo escribí la composición anoche.   Jaime: *No es verdad. Tú no la escribiste anoche. La escribiste hoy.*

1. Yo preparé las tareas anteayer.
2. Ayer yo hablé español en la clase.
3. Ustedes llegaron tarde a la clase el lunes.
4. La semana pasada empecé a trabajar en la cafetería.
5. El año pasado mis padres compraron una casa.
6. Ayer por la mañana leímos el periódico.
7. El mes pasado participé en un proyecto interesante.

E. Pregúnteles a las siguientes personas cómo pasaron el sábado pasado. Después conteste la pregunta según el modelo, usando el pretérito.

► Gabriela / tocar la guitarra (piano, trompeta)
S1: *Gabriela, ¿tocaste la guitarra el sábado pasado?*
S2: *No, toqué el piano, ¿y tú?*
S1: *Toqué la trompeta.*

1. Jaime y Roberto / comprar una nevera (secadora, lavaplatos)
2. Marcos / escribir un cuestionario (carta, composición)
3. Ana / practicar el tenis (fútbol, básquetbol)
4. Patricia y Elena / comer en un restaurante (café, cafetería)
5. Carlos y su hermano / trabajar dos horas (hasta la una, con Pepe)
6. Marta y Roberto / describir la playa (la costa, los veleros)

F. Escriba de nuevo el siguiente párrafo. Cambie el sujeto de **yo** a **nosotros.** Luego escríbalo otra vez, usando **ellas** como sujeto.

El mes pasado yo escribí un cuestionario sobre el nivel de vida de la clase media en nuestro barrio. Entrevisté a cincuenta personas; les pregunté sobre el uso de aparatos eléctricos, como neveras, secadoras y lavaplatos. Luego analicé las respuestas. Aprendí muchas cosas interesantes sobre las condiciones de vida de la gente del barrio.

G. Diga dos cosas que usted hizo (did) la semana pasada. Use los verbos siguientes en el pretérito. Luego diga dos cosas que hizo un/a amigo/a o pariente anteayer.

tomar	pagar	comer	asistir	practicar
saludar	analizar	aprender	escribir	ver
entrevistar	buscar	leer	recibir	salir

► *La semana pasada escribí una carta a mis amigos y comí en un buen restaurante.*
► *Anteayer mi primo Roberto asistió a un concierto de música clásica y entrevistó al director de la orquesta.*

II. **Para** and **por** in contrast

*Salgo **para** España.* ~~I am leaving for spain~~

*Viajo **por** España.* ~~I am traveling through Spain~~

You have been using the prepositions **para** and **por** in various contexts from the beginning of this course. Although both **para** and **por** are often used to express *for,* they have other English equivalents and are not interchangeable.

A. *Para*

1. The preposition **para** is commonly used to express *motion* or *direction toward a final goal or destination.* The English equivalents may be:

   a. *in order to*

Trabajo **para** pagar mis gastos.	*I'm working in order to pay for my expenses.*

   b. *destined for a place or person*

Salgo **para** Caracas la semana entrante.	*I'm leaving for Caracas next week.*
María tiene muchas fotos **para** usted.	*María has many photos for you.*

   c. *for or by a specific time*

Los documentos deben estar listos **para** la reunión.	*The documents must be ready for (by the time of) the meeting.*
Tienes que terminar esto **para** las diez.	*You have to finish this by ten o'clock.*

2. **Para** is also used in structures with the meaning of *considering (the fact that)* and *in the opinion of.*

Para ser español, Luis habla bien el inglés.	*Considering that he is Spanish, Luis speaks English well.*
Para mí, Lucía es la mejor estudiante de los dos.	*In my opinion, Lucía is the better student of the two.*

Para toda la familia...

B. Por

1. **Por** has a wide variety of meanings, but many of them stem from the concept of *motion through or by a place* or *through a segment of time.*

¿Te gusta pasear **por** el parque?   *Do you like to walk through the park?*
El festival dura **(por)** una semana.   *The festival lasts for a week.*
Viví en Colombia **(por)** quince   *I lived in Colombia for fifteen years.*
   años.

no quiere más amor... por el momento

2. **Por** is also used to express the following meanings:
   a. *because of*

   Hoy no juegan **por** el calor.   *They are not playing today because of the heat.*

   b. *by (agent or means)*

   Mando las fotografías **por** correo.   *I'm sending the photographs by mail.*

DEPORTES POR TELEVISION

   c. *for (stopping or passing by to get someone or something)*

   Mañana paso **por** ella a las diez.   *Tomorrow I'll stop by for her at ten.*

   d. *in exchange for*

   Compramos un televisor **por**   *We bought a television set for a hundred dollars.*
      cien dólares.

   e. *in appreciation for*

   ¡Muchas gracias **por** el reloj!   *Thank you very much for the watch!*

H. ¿Qué va a hacer usted en los siguientes lugares?

▶ Esta noche voy al cine . . .   *para ver una película.*

1. Mañana por la tarde voy a la playa . . .
2. Siempre voy al almacén García . . .
3. En octubre voy a Argentina . . .
4. Me gusta la música clásica. Voy al concierto . . .

I. Exprese su opinión acerca de las siguientes cosas o actividades.

▶ ¿Qué es más interesante: un libro   *Pues, para mí es más interesante*
de historia o un libro de arte?   *[un libro de historia].*

1. ¿Qué es más difícil: un examen de matemáticas o un examen de español?
2. ¿Qué es más fácil: patinar o nadar?

3. ¿Qué es más rico: el pudín de vainilla o el pudín de chocolate?
4. ¿Qué es más económico: vivir en un apartamento, vivir con la familia o vivir en un dormitorio de la universidad?

J. Usted tiene varios objetos de segunda mano (*secondhand*) y decide cambiarlos por otros. Diga a un/a amigo/a cuál de los siguientes objetos quiere cambiar. Use algunos adjetivos descriptivos.

un radio	una filmadora	una computadora
un tocadiscos	una motocicleta	una calculadora
una bicicleta	unas revistas	una cámara
unos cassettes	unos discos	una máquina de escribir

▶ *Cambio mi bicicleta azul por tu bicicleta roja.*

K. Calcule el tiempo que necesita para pasar por algunos de sus amigos y llegar a tiempo a las siguientes actividades. Use la imaginación.

▶ la película / 7:00 P.M. S1: *La película empieza a las siete de la tarde.*
S2: *Entonces paso por Roberto a las seis y veinte y por ti a las seis y media.*

1. la conferencia / 9:00 A.M. 3. el concierto / 4:00 P.M.
2. la reunión / 2:30 P.M. 4. la comida / 6:00 P.M.

L. Diga por qué son famosos los siguientes países o ciudades.

▶ Buenos Aires tiene muchos teatros excelentes, ¿verdad? *Sí, es famoso por sus teatros.*

1. Puerto Rico tiene muchas playas bonitas, ¿no?
2. Madrid tiene muchos museos interesantes, ¿verdad?
3. Chile tiene muchos centros de esquí, ¿no?
4. Granada tiene muchos monumentos históricos, ¿no?

M. Complete las oraciones siguientes con **para** o **por,** según el contexto.

1. Vamos a la oficina del sindicato _____ presentar la lista de demandas.
2. Me gusta tu bolígrafo. ¿Quieres cambiarlo _____ éste?
3. Si el coche de Pablo no funciona, pasamos _____ él a las dos.
4. Trabajas _____ vivir mejor algún día, ¿no?
5. ¡Diego muestra mucha inteligencia _____ ser tan joven!
6. Te esperé ayer en el café _____ veinticinco minutos.
7. Este documento debe estar preparado _____ las doce en punto.
8. Estoy muy agradecido _____ su ayuda.
9. Daniel no vino hoy _____ estar enfermo.
10. Tenemos que pasar _____ varios pueblos _____ llegar a Sevilla.

III. Adjectives with shortened forms

*Jaime es un **gran** amigo mío.*

*Mi amigo Miguel es un hombre **grande** y fuerte.*

1. In Spanish, some adjectives drop their final **-o** before a masculine singular noun. Among these adjectives are **bueno, malo, primero,** and **tercero.**

Hablé con un **buen** amigo. Hablé con un amigo **bueno.**	*I talked with a good friend.*
Pasamos una **mala** semana. Pasamos una semana **mala.**	*We had a bad week.*
El **primer** niño se llama Juan. Es el ejercicio **primero.**	*The first boy is called Juan.* *It's the first exercise.*
La **primera** niña se llama Juana. Es la lección **primera.**	*The first girl is called Juana.* *It's the first lesson.*

2. The adjectives **alguno** and **ninguno** are shortened to **algún** and **ningún** before a masculine singular noun. Note that **ninguno** is rarely used in the plural.

Leyó eso en **algún** libro.	*He read that in some book.*
Leyó eso en **alguna** revista.	*He read that in some magazine.*
No tengo **ningún** amigo.	*I don't have a single (any) friend(s).*
No tengo **ninguna** amiga.	*I don't have a single (any) friend(s).*

3. The adjective **grande** becomes **gran** before a noun of either gender. When used before a noun, **gran** means *great, fine, famous;* when used after the noun, **grande** means *big* or *large.*

Es un **gran** artista.	*He's a great (fine) artist.*
Es una **gran** escuela.	*It's a great (famous) school.*
Es un artista **grande.**	*He's a big artist.*
Es una escuela **grande.**	*It's a large school.*

4. The adjective **cualquiera** becomes **cualquier** before a singular noun of either gender.

Lo comprende **cualquier**   *Any student can understand it.*
  estudiante.
Lo comprende **cualquier** persona.   *Any person can understand it.*

N. Dé la forma apropiada de cada adjetivo entre paréntesis.

1. un (grande) problema
2. un (bueno) estudiante
3. el (primero) asunto
4. (alguno) agencia
5. una (malo) comida
6. una (grande) ciudad
7. (ninguno) idea
8. (tercero) lugar

O. Complete las oraciones siguientes con la forma apropiada del adjetivo entre paréntesis.

1. (primero) ¿Cuál es el _____ día del mes?
2. (tercero) El _____ edificio es un almacén.
3. (alguno) ¿Tienes _____ fotos de Machu Picchu?
4. (ninguno) No hay _____ problema.
5. (bueno) Jorge es un _____ muchacho.
6. (malo) Hace _____ tiempo hoy.
7. (grande) Nueva York es una ciudad _____ .
8. (malo) Pasé unas vacaciones _____ en Perú.
9. (primero) La *Lección* _____ es muy difícil para mí.
10. (cualquiera) _____ niño puede hacerlo.

¿Comprende usted?

Lea el siguiente cuento, fijándose en las actitudes y modos de pensar de los personajes. Prepárese a dar un título que resuma el cuento y que llame la atención.

Minicuento

—¿Por qué no termina la huelga?— preguntó ansiosamente la mujer.
—Sabes que ya no hay comida y no podemos vivir del aire.
    Lorenzo pensó en la huelga y en sus compañeros de trabajo.
—No sé,— respondió casi automáticamente. —Queremos más dinero,
5 más seguridad, más tiempo libre con nuestras familias.
—Sí, sí, entiendo todo eso— gritó Remigia, casi desesperada. —Pero tú sabes que nunca vamos a tener una vida mejor aquí en las minas de Potosí.

Siempre vamos a ser pobres. ¡Hay que trabajar para comer, para vivir, para
todo! Si la huelga no termina . . .

10   —Mira, Remigia, si quieres, podemos ir a vivir a la capital. Puedo buscar empleo en una fábrica en La Paz, o . . .

—No, Lorenzo, eso no. Tu padre y mi padre trabajaron en las minas, tu
abuelo y mi abuelo también. Todos vivieron aquí y todos están enterrados
aquí. No quiero abandonarlos.

15   Lorenzo pensó otra vez en Jaime y en todos los compañeros muertos.
Vio su futuro y el futuro de sus hijos y sus nietos . . . y guardó silencio.

A. Conteste las preguntas, según la lectura.

1. ¿Quién es más flexible en su actitud? ¿Remigia o Lorenzo?
2. ¿Por qué no quiere Remigia ir a la capital?
3. Al final del cuento, Lorenzo guarda silencio. ¿Cree Ud. que
    muestra resignación? ¿Qué futuro cree Ud. que imagina Lorenzo?

B. Escoja entre los siguientes títulos el más apropiado, o escriba el que
    usted creó (created).

«Si la huelga no termina . . .»   «Mañana es otro día»
«El laberinto de Potosí»   «Vamos a la capital»
«El último accidente»

C. Escoja la expresión que más se aproxima en significado a las palabras
    indicadas.

1. no podemos vivir **del aire:** fuera de casa, sin casa, sin comer,
    con frío
2. **gritó** Remigia, casi desesperada: habló en voz baja, habló en voz
    alta, pensó, explicó
3. nunca vamos a tener una vida **mejor:** perfecta, difícil, más
    cómoda, diferente
4. están **enterrados** aquí: bajo tierra, vivos, tristes, felices

Lección II
En Ecuador

Un viaje de negocios

En Ecuador hay dos ciudades importantes: Quito, la capital y sede° del gobierno; y Guayaquil, un gran puerto en la costa, que es el centro económico del
país. En la escena siguiente, Consuelo Molina, coordinadora de la Sección de
Investigaciones de una gran compañía petrolera ecuatoriana, habla con su jefe,
el Sr. Martínez. Éste le mostró una carpeta de documentos hace un minuto.

seat

Sr. Martínez: Señorita, los planes para la investigación de los nuevos
campos petrolíferos° del Oriente ya están listos. Ahora es
necesario llevar estos documentos al Ministerio de Industrias,° como usted sabe.

5 Consuelo: Sí, señor. ¿Cuándo va usted a la capital?

Sr. Martínez: Yo no puedo ir a causa de la Conferencia Internacional de
Petróleo aquí en Guayaquil. ¿Puede ir usted en mi lugar?

Consuelo: ¡Qué lástima! ¡Y pensar que yo estuve en Quito la semana
pasada visitando° a mis parientes!

10 Sr. Martínez: Es que sólo hoy terminamos los planes de investigación.
Tuve que cancelar mi viaje a Quito a última hora por la
Conferencia.

oilbearing

Ministerio . . . Ministry of
Commerce

visiting

La ciudad de Quito, Ecuador
está a más de 8.000 pies de
altura sobre el nivel del mar.
¿Cómo cree Ud. que es el clima
allí? Observe el paisaje
(landscape) en esta foto tomada
desde la Plaza Independencia,
en la parte colonial de la
ciudad. ¿Qué características
topográficas tiene el área?

Consuelo: Está bien, Sr. Martínez. ¿Cuánto tiempo cree usted que
debo permanecer en la capital para arreglar el asunto?

15 Sr. Martínez: Un mínimo de tres días. Es urgente obtener la firma del
ministro lo más pronto posible. Me parece que Ud. puede
tener problemas con la burocracia y el papeleo.

Consuelo: ¡Claro! A propósito, ¿con quién debo hablar en el Ministerio
de Industrias?

20 Sr. Martínez: Con el jefe de la Sección Comercial. ¿Lo conoce? Es Gilberto
Jiménez, mi cuñado. Siempre nos ayuda en estas cosas.
Trabaja en esa sección y tiene mucha palanca. Esta misma
tarde le mando un telegrama.

Consuelo: Entonces voy a hacer reservaciones para el vuelo del
25 martes, y regreso el primero o el dos de junio.

Comprensión

1. ¿Qué puesto tiene Consuelo en la compañía petrolera en Guayaquil?
2. ¿Qué necesita del Ministro de Industrias la compañía?
3. ¿Por qué no puede ir a Quito el jefe de Consuelo?
4. ¿Cuánto tiempo debe permanecer Consuelo en la capital?
5. ¿Por qué va a mandarle un telegrama el jefe a su cuñado Gilberto Jiménez?
6. ¿Cuándo va a Quito Consuelo y cuándo piensa volver?

Conversación

1. ¿Qué tipo de problemas tiene usted con la burocracia y el papeleo en la universidad?
2. En los Estados Unidos, ¿hay muchos problemas con la burocracia y el papeleo en el gobierno federal o estatal?
3. ¿Conoce usted a alguien con mucha palanca en el gobierno federal o estatal?
4. ¿Tiene usted parientes que hacen viajes de negocios? ¿Viajan mucho o poco? ¿A qué continentes o países viajan?
5. ¿Tiene usted algún pariente que trabaja en una compañía industrial o petrolera? ¿Cuál es su puesto?

Vocabulario

Palabras análogas

la burocracia	federal	petrolero, -a
cancelar	imaginar	el plan
comercial	el ministro	la reservación
la conferencia	necesario, -a	la sección
la coordinadora	el petróleo	el telegrama

Sustantivos

el asunto   matter, business
el campo   field
la carpeta   file
el/la jefe/a   boss
junio   June
mayo   May
el Oriente   eastern region (of Ecuador)
la palanca   leverage, "pull"
el papeleo   "red tape"
el puerto   port
el puesto   position, appointment
el tiempo   time
el viaje de negocios   business trip

Adjetivos

estatal   state
listo, -a   ready

Verbos

deber   should, have to, must
mandar   to send
parecer (zc)   to seem
permanecer (zc)   to remain

Otras palabras y expresiones

a causa de   because of
a propósito   by the way
a última hora   at the last minute
antes   before
es urgente   it's essential
esta misma tarde   this very afternoon
hace un minuto   a minute ago
hacer reservaciones   to make reservations
lo más pronto posible   as soon as possible
un mínimo de   a minimum of

Práctica

Usted es jefe/a de la Sección de Investigaciones de una gran compañía bananera con sede en Guayaquil. Usted le da las instrucciones siguientes a un/a empleado/a:

a. Es necesario llevar algunos papeles al Ministerio de Industrias en Quito.
b. Es necesario obtener la firma del ministro para estos papeles.
c. Es importante hacer esto para poder continuar el proyecto de investigaciones en la ciudad de Esmeraldas en la costa.

Escriba su conversación. Mencione el nombre de algunos amigos o parientes que pueden ayudar al/a la empleado/a con el papeleo y la burocracia del gobierno.

Nota cultural   Personalismo y palanca

Una costumbre muy tradicional en las sociedades hispánicas es **el personalismo.** En los países hispánicos se le da una atención especial a las relaciones personales. Todo el mundo[1] fomenta los lazos[2] entre parientes y entre amigos.

---

1. **todo** . . . everybody   2. ties

Este cultivo de las relaciones humanas empieza a una edad temprana. Los padres les enseñan a sus hijos a ser gregarios[3] y extrovertidos en su trato[4] con otras personas. Cuando los hijos son mayores aprecian estas conexiones personales porque resultan esenciales en las sociedades hispánicas, donde la burocracia y el papeleo son realidades del diario vivir.[5]

Un individuo que cuenta con buenas conexiones personales puede obtener favores de todas clases. Muchas veces el buen puesto de una persona y su buena posición social dependen de las conexiones personales y de **la palanca.** Se dice que[6] una persona tiene palanca cuando puede obtener favores para sí[7] o para otras personas.

---

3. talkative   4. **en** . . . in their dealings   5. **del** . . . of daily life   6. **Se** . . . It is said that   7. himself/herself

Pronunciación y ortografía
El sonido [h]

The Spanish [h] has no English equivalent and should not be confused with the English [h] in *hat,* which is much softer. The Spanish [h], often referred to as the "jota sound," is pronounced at the back of the throat, with air forced through a narrow opening.

The sound [h] is spelled **j** before **a, o** and **u** and either **j** or **g** before **e** and **i.** A few proper nouns that contain an [h] sound, such as **México** and **Ximena,** have retained the old Spanish spelling with an **x,** but can also be spelled with the letter **j,** as in **Méjico** and **Jimena.**

A. Escuche y repita las palabras que dice su profesor/a.

hijo	viaje	urgente	lejos	bajo
hija	jefe	general	joven	jirafa
junio	julio	Jiménez	Gilberto	heraldo
agil	lejos	Jorge		

B. Lea las siguientes oraciones en voz alta. Preste atención a los sonidos representados por las letras **j** y **g.**

1. Gilberto Jiménez es cuñado del jefe.
2. Mi hija Josefa vive en Argentina.
3. Juanita hace un viaje de negocios en julio.
4. El jefe es el general Jorge Luján.
5. Hugo Sánchez es de México.

Refranes

1. **Cada oveja con su pareja.**
2. **Quien no oye consejo, no llega a viejo.**

Birds of a feather flock together.
If you don't follow advice, you'll never reach a ripe old age.

Estudio de palabras

I. Las estaciones y los meses

la primavera
abril   mayo   junio

el verano
julio   agosto   septiembre

el otoño
octubre   noviembre   diciembre

el invierno
enero   febrero   marzo

The names of the months are usually not capitalized in Spanish.

A. Conteste las preguntas siguientes acerca de las estaciones.

1. ¿En qué estación estamos?
2. ¿Cuáles son los meses de la primavera?

3. ¿Qué estación viene antes de la primavera?
4. ¿Qué estación sigue al verano?
5. ¿En qué estación juegas al tenis? ¿practicas el alpinismo? ¿montas en bicicleta? ¿patinas?
6. ¿Te gusta el invierno? ¿Te gusta la primavera? ¿Qué estación te gusta más?

B. Lea este verso y después diga el equivalente en inglés.

Treinta días trae noviembre
con abril, junio y septiembre
De veintiocho hay sólo uno,
los demás de treinta y uno.

II. Las fechas

—¿Cuál es la fecha de hoy?   *What's the date today?*
—El primero de marzo.   *The first of March (March 1).*

—¿Cuál es la fecha de su   *What's the date of your birthday?*
   cumpleaños?
—El dos de abril.   *The second of April (April 2).*

1. The first day of the month is expressed with the ordinal number **primero.**

   el **primero** de febrero   *the first of February (February 1)*

2. The other days of the month are expressed with cardinal numbers.

   el **cuatro** de agosto   *the fourth of August (August 4)*
   el **tres** de mayo   *the third of May (May 3)*

C. Diga en español las siguientes fechas.

▶ April 1   *el primero de abril*
▶ June 10   *el diez de junio*

1. July 7   3. May 9   5. January 14
2. December 5   4. March 31   6. September 11

D. Conteste las siguientes preguntas.

1. ¿Cuál es la fecha de hoy?
2. ¿Cuál es la fecha de mañana?
3. ¿Cuál es el primer día de la primavera?
4. ¿Qué día comienza el nuevo año?
5. ¿Qué día celebramos la independencia de Estados Unidos?

III. ¿Qué tiempo hace?

Hace buen tiempo.   The weather is nice.
Hace mal tiempo.   The weather is bad.
Hace mucho calor.   It's very hot.
Hace mucho frío.   It's very cold.
Hace fresco.   It's cool.
Hace un día estupendo.   It's a great day.
Hace sol.   It's sunny.

Hace viento.   It's windy.
Llueve.   It's raining.
Nieva.   It's snowing.
Está nublado.   It's cloudy.
Hay neblina.   It's misty.
   (It's foggy.)

E. Describa el tiempo de hoy. Use por lo menos cuatro expresiones de la lista anterior. Empiece la descripción con la palabra **hoy.**

F. Describa el siguiente dibujo en ocho o diez oraciones. Incluya en su descripción cuál es la fecha, cómo está el tiempo, quiénes van de viaje, adónde van y por qué. Use la imaginación en su descripción.

IV. Los años y las décadas

1. Calendar years are expressed in Spanish as a single breath group, as in English. Listen to your instructor pronounce the following dates. Stressed syllables are shown in boldface type.

   1983 = mil nove**cien**tos ochenta y **tres**
   1999 = mil nove**cien**tos noventa y **nueve**

2. Calendar years in the present century are sometimes shortened to **el** + *the last two digits.*

En **el setenta y dos** visité
Guayaquil.

In '72 I visited Guayaquil.

3. A decade is normally expressed as **los años** + *numeral.*

Trabajé en Quito en **los años
sesenta.**

I worked in Quito in the sixties.

G. Lea en voz alta los siguientes años en español.

▶ 1492   *mil cuatrocientos noventa y dos*

1. 1663	3. 1880	5. in '85	7. in the 80s
2. 1776	4. 1982	6. in '87	8. in the 90s

H. Diga en qué años nació *(was born)* y murió cada uno de los siguientes escritores famosos del mundo hispánico.

1. Miguel Ángel Asturias (Guatemala): 1899–1974
2. Sor Juana Inés de la Cruz (México): 1651–1695
3. Miguel de Cervantes (España): 1547–1616
4. José Martí (Cuba): 1853–1895
5. Gabriela Mistral (Chile): 1889–1957
6. Alfonsina Storni (Argentina): 1892–1938

Estructuras útiles

I. Preterit of irregular verbs

*Vanessa **fue** a Quito el año pasado.*

*Vanessa **fue** estudiante en Quito el año pasado.*

Many common Spanish verbs, although irregular in the preterit, follow certain patterns that make them easier to learn by groups. Note that the stress in the first and third persons singular of irregular preterit forms falls on the next-to-last syllable, and not on the last syllable, as it does in the case of regular preterits.

1. The verbs **ir** and **ser** have identical forms in the preterit. The context in which they are used will clarify whether the preterit form refers to **ir** or to **ser.** Note that **ir** is normally followed by the preposition **a.**

ir and ser	
fui	—¿Adónde **fuiste** en abril?
fuiste	—**Fui** a la Florida.
fue	
fuimos	—¿Quién **fue** el último en llegar?
~~fuisteis~~	—No sé, creo que **fui** yo.
fueron	

2. Although the verb **dar** ends in **-ar,** it follows the same pattern as regular **-er** and **-ir** verbs in the preterit. Note that the first and third persons singular have no written accents.

dar	
di	—¿**Diste** una contribución al Hospital del Niño?
diste	
dio	—Sí, **di** cincuenta pesos esta mañana.
dimos	
~~disteis~~	
dieron	

3. The following chart shows three sets of irregular verbs in the preterit. Note that the endings of the first two groups are identical. The endings of verbs with **j** in the stem differ from the first two sets only in the third person plural form, which ends in **-eron** (not **-ieron**).

stem vowel **u**	stem vowel **i**	**j** in the stem
estar	**venir**	**decir**
estuve	vine	dije
estuviste	viniste	dijiste
estuvo	vino	dijo
estuvimos	vinimos	dijimos
~~estuvisteis~~	~~vinisteis~~	~~dijisteis~~
estuvieron	vinieron	dijeron

4. The chart below shows common verbs that follow the same patterns as **estar, venir,** and **decir** in the preterit. The verb **hacer** has a spelling change from **c** to **z** in the third person singular **(hizo).**

verbs like **estar**	verbs like **venir**	verbs like **decir**
andar: anduve	hacer: hice, hiciste, hizo	traducir: traduje
haber: hube	querer: quise	traer: traje
poder: pude		
poner: puse		
saber: supe		
tener: tuve		

No **pudimos** salir, pero **hicimos** el trabajo. — *We couldn't go out, but we did the work.*

—¿Dónde **pusiste** los discos? ¿Los **trajiste?** — *Where did you put the records? Did you bring them?*

—**Tuve** que dejarlos en mi cuarto. — *I had to leave them in my room.*

5. The preterit of **hay** *(there is, there are)* is **hubo.**

—No **hubo** muchas dificultades. — *There weren't many difficulties.*

—Sí, pero **hubo** mucho papeleo. — *Yes, but there was a lot of red tape.*

6. Most compounds of the verbs shown in the preceding charts form their preterit in the same way.

proponer: Miguel **propuso** la mejor opción.
retener: El agente **retuvo** nuestros billetes.
predecir: Los reporteros **predijeron** el resultado de la regata.

A. Diga que las personas mencionadas fueron a varios lugares el otro día, pero no hicieron nada especial allí. Use el pretérito de **ir** y **hacer.**

▶ Pepe: capital   *Pepe fue a la capital, pero no hizo nada especial allí.*

1. yo / Nueva York
2. Alicia y Elena / centro
3. tu prima / reunión del departamento
4. nosotros / oficina
5. ustedes / costa
6. tú / puerto de Guayaquil

B. Mariela llamó a Felipe por teléfono después de las vacaciones y le preguntó dónde estuvieron él y otros/as amigos/as. Haga el papel *(role)* de Mariela o el papel de Felipe.

► tu primo (Caracas)   Mariela: *¿Dónde estuvo tu primo en las vacaciones?*
                          Felipe: *Estuvo en Caracas.*

1. Mencha (Ecuador)   4. tú (en la playa)
2. ustedes (el Caribe)   5. Juan y Manuel (en las montañas)
3. tu hermana (en el campo)   6. tú y Margarita (en casa)

C. Diga que las personas mencionadas no pudieron ayudar a sus padres el sábado pasado por distintas razones. Use el pretérito del verbo.

► Julián / ir a la biblioteca   *Julián no pudo ayudarlos porque tuvo que ir a la biblioteca.*

1. Tomás y tú / arreglar el carro
2. tú / comprar muchas cosas
3. usted / hacer una investigación
4. yo / escribir una composición
5. nosotras / estudiar para un examen
6. ellas / jugar al tenis

D. A Juan le gusta contradecir a Elvira. Haga el papel de Juan, y exprese el verbo en el pretérito.

► Elvira: Yo siempre digo la verdad.   Juan: *No es cierto. ¡Ayer no dijiste la verdad!*

1. Yo siempre quiero participar en las conversaciones.
2. Yo siempre vengo a las clases a tiempo.
3. Yo siempre traigo mi libro a la clase.
4. Yo siempre traduzco del español al inglés perfectamente.
5. Yo siempre propongo ideas buenas.

E. Complete las oraciones siguientes con la forma apropiada del pretérito del verbo entre paréntesis.

1. (traducir) El mes pasado yo _____ el artículo del español al inglés, y Alicia lo _____ al francés.
2. (traer) Anoche tú _____ discos de música italiana a mi fiesta, y ellas _____ discos de música alemana.
3. (venir) Mi tío Enrique _____ anoche, y mis abuelos _____ anteayer para la reunión anual de la familia.
4. (proponer) En la última reunión el representante del gobierno _____ varias reformas, y los mineros _____ otras.
5. (saber) Nosotros no _____ nada de la reunión hasta hoy.
6. (haber) Ayer _____ una reunión importante en Potosí.
7. (andar) Anoche mi novia y yo _____ cerca del mar.
8. (dar) Mis padres me _____ un reloj de oro, y mi hermano me _____ un libro de arte.

II. Indirect-object pronouns

—¿*Me* das cincuenta pesos?
—¿Por qué?
—Porque mañana es el Día de San Valentín y quiero compra*rte* unos chocolates . . .

1. The following chart shows the indirect-object pronouns in Spanish and their English equivalents.

Singular	Plural
me me	**nos** us
te you (*fam.*)	**os** you (*fam.*)
le him, her, you (*formal*)	**les** you, them

2. Indirect-object pronouns generally indicate *to whom* or *for whom* something is done, given, et cetera. They follow the same rules of position as direct-object pronouns. They *precede* the conjugated verb form, and may precede the conjugated verb form or be attached to the infinitive in double-verb constructions.

Los ministros están en Quito y hay que llevar**les** los documentos.	*The ministers are in Quito and we have to take the documents to them.*
Me gusta el helado.	*I like (= To me is pleasing) ice cream.*
Voy a explicar**le** el problema. ⎫ **Le** voy a explicar el problema. ⎭	*I'm going to explain the problem to you.*

3. The meaning of the indirect-object pronouns **le** and **les** often may be clarified by using **a** + *a noun* or *prepositional pronoun.*

Le doy la información **a ella,** no a José.	*I'm giving the information to her, not to José.*
¿Qué **les** parece **a ustedes** si salimos ahora?	*What do you think; should we leave now?*

4. The indirect-object pronouns **le** and **les** are often used in sentences that have **a** + *a noun phrase,* even though they might sound redundant to

the English speaker. To many speakers of Spanish, the omission of the pronoun sounds unnatural or stilted.

(Le) escribo una carta **a Pablo.**	*I am writing a letter to Pablo.*
(Les) doy dinero **a mis padres.**	*I give money to my parents.*

5. The indirect-object pronouns are also used with **a** for emphasis.

—¿**Te** interesa el jazz?	*Are you interested in jazz?*
—**A mí** me fascina pero a mi novia no.	*I love it but my fiancée doesn't.*

F. Exprese cada oración o pregunta de otra manera, según el modelo.

▶ No puedo darte el dinero.   *No te puedo dar el dinero.*

1. Vamos a escribirles hoy.
2. No queremos hablarte.
3. No voy a telefonearles ahora.
4. ¿Puedes mostrarnos la casa?
5. ¿Puedes traerme el periódico?
6. Voy a describirte el cuadro.

G. Explique si usted preparó una comida mexicana para las siguientes personas.

▶ ¿a María?   *Sí, le preparé una comida mexicana.*
     No, no le preparé una comida mexicana.

1. ¿a nosotras?
2. ¿a mí?
3. ¿a tus parientes?
4. ¿a los amigos?
5. ¿a la clase de español?
6. ¿a Antonio?

H. Las siguientes personas lo/la invitaron a usted a participar en varias actividades. Diga si usted aceptó o no aceptó la invitación.

▶ tú / a un baile   *Tú me invitaste a un baile y te acepté la invitación.*
     Tú me invitaste a un baile y no te acepté la invitación.

1. María / al cine
2. Pepe y tú / a nadar
3. Rafael / a estudiar
4. José y Rosa / a su casa
5. tú / a la playa
6. Andrés / a jugar al tenis

I. ¿Qué les parece lo siguiente a las personas indicadas? ¿fantástico? ¿fabuloso? ¿estupendo? ¿interesante? ¿horrible? ¿simpático? ¿antipático?

▶ los viajes de negocio / a Ud.   *Me parecen [interesantes].*

1. los estudiantes de la clase / al profesor
2. el papeleo del gobierno / a todo el mundo
3. la compañía / a los nuevos empleados

4. el comercio de Guayaquil / a los turistas
5. los turistas norteamericanos / al gobierno peruano
6. el viaje por tren / a un amigo

J. Hoy vamos a intercambiar *(exchange)* artículos de poco valor *(value)*. Hable con otra persona de la clase y pregúntele cuáles de sus cosas les regala a diferentes personas. Use los pronombres apropiados.

▶ a mí   S1: *¿Qué me regalas a mí?*
             S2: *A ti te regalo mi lápiz.*

1. a Guillermo   4. a tus primas
2. a tu hermano/a   5. a Luisa
3. a mí y a Luisa   6. al profesor

III. **Hace . . . que** in expressions of time

Hace dos horas que tomo este examen.   *Hace dos horas que tomé el examen.*

1. **Hace** + *a time expression* + **que** + *a verb in the present tense* is used in Spanish to express the idea that an action has been (and still is) going on for a given length of time.

Hace dos meses que Carlos   *Carlos has been working for a*
   trabaja para una compañía   *Spanish company for two months.*
   española.
Hace mucho tiempo que viven   *They have been living in this*
   en este país.   *country for a long time.*

2. Another way of expressing the same idea is to use **hace** + *a time expression,* or **(desde) hace** + *a time expression* at the end of the sentence.

Carlos trabaja para esa compañía **(desde) hace dos meses.**
Viven en este país **(desde) hace mucho tiempo.**

3. **Hace** + *a time expression* (+ **que**) + *a verb in the preterit* is used to express *ago*.

Hace un mes (que) compraron este coche.
They bought this car a month ago.

Raúl me **visitó hace una semana.**
Raúl visited me a week ago.

K. Explique el tiempo que usted lleva en las siguientes situaciones.

▶ Usted estudia el español.   *Hace dos años que estudio el español.*

1. Usted no ve a su familia.
2. Usted y su familia viven en la misma ciudad.
3. Usted no está enfermo/a.
4. Usted desea aprender español.
5. Usted está en esta clase.

L. Ernesto desea saber cuándo ocurrieron las siguientes cosas y le pide la información a Margarita. Haga el papel de uno de los dos.

▶ empezar los estudios   Ernesto: *¿Cuánto (tiempo) hace que empezaste los estudios?*

Margarita: *Empecé hace siete meses. (Hace siete meses que empecé.)*

1. visitar al dentista
2. tener vacaciones
3. leer una novela interesante
4. escribir una carta a alguien
5. llamar a tu casa
6. montar en bicicleta
7. ir a una buena película
8. comer en un restaurante chino

¿Comprende usted?

Hay ciertas expresiones que son muy aptas para usar en determinadas circunstancias, ya que todo el mundo las entiende y comprende el sentimiento que expresan. Lea la conversación siguiente entre Consuelo Molina, que está en Quito, su marido Rafael, y su hijo Rafa. Trate de reconocer estas expresiones y entender lo que cada una trata de expresar.

Una llamada por teléfono

Consuelo: ¿Aló? ¿Rafael?
Rafael: Sí, Coni, ¿cómo van las cosas?
Consuelo: Ya ves, mi vida, no puedo volver mañana jueves. El Ministro de Industrias salió en un viaje urgente y regresa mañana.

5   Tengo que esperarlo. Voy a permanecer en Quito hasta el
       viernes o el sábado.
Rafael: ¡Qué lata! Y mañana tenemos invitados a los Urrutia. En fin,
       los llevo a un restaurante. ¿Cambio tu cita con el dentista del
       viernes a la semana próxima?
10 Consuelo: Todavía no. La cita es por la tarde y si las cosas van bien,
       regreso el viernes al mediodía. Yo te llamo mañana por la
       noche otra vez. La prima Isabel y el cuñado Pepe te mandan
       recuerdos. Dicen que la próxima vez debes venir tú también.
Rafael: Pues les das mis saludos también. Le dices a Isabelita que si
15   prepara otro arroz como el del Año Nuevo, hago el viaje
       inmediatamente. Espera, Rafa quiere saludarte. Aquí está.
Rafa: ¿Mamá? Salí de campeón de tenis del colegio, y mis amigos
       están aquí para celebrarlo.
Consuelo: ¡Hombre, felicitaciones! Y la aritmética, ¿cómo va?
20 Rafa: Eso . . . pues . . . ¿Cuándo vuelves, mamá?
Consuelo: El viernes o el sábado. Adiós, hijo.
Rafa: Adiós, mamá . . . ¡Hasta el viernes!

A. Busque la siguiente información en la lectura *Una llamada por teléfono.*

1. ¿Por qué llama Consuelo a su marido?
2. ¿Qué dos complicaciones causa el cambio de planes de Consuelo?
3. ¿Cuáles son las soluciones a las dos complicaciones?
4. Rafa, el hijo de Rafael y Consuelo, ¿es buen estudiante de
   aritmética? ¿Es buen deportista? ¿Cómo lo sabe usted?
5. ¿Quién es Isabelita?

B. Escriba una reacción lógica para cada situación, usando una frase del
   diálogo.

1. Usted está irritado/a porque no puede ir a comer en casa de
   unos amigos.
2. Usted llama a su primo/a por teléfono y hablan por largo rato.
   Al final Ud. quiere decirle que sus padres le mandan saludos.
3. Un profesor le pregunta a usted si ya terminó la tarea. Usted no
   hizo la tarea y no quiere responderle.
4. Su mejor amigo/a recibió un premio en el departamento de
   física. Usted está muy contento/a. ¿Qué le puede decir a él/ella?

Lección 12
En Perú

Excursión a Machu Picchu

Alberto Falla, un joven panameño, pasa un mes de vacaciones en Lima, Perú, en casa de su buen amigo, Tomás Rivera. En la escena siguiente, Alberto se entusiasma con un posible viaje a las ruinas incaicas de la ciudad de Machu Picchu al ver las fotos de Tomás.

Tomás: Pero hombre, ¡no puedes irte a Panamá sin visitar Machu Picchu! Te repito otra vez: ¡es un lugar realmente extraordinario y misterioso! ¿Sabes que el explorador norteamericano Hiram Bingham lo descubrió en 1911?

Es extraordinario observar las ruinas de Machu Picchu desde un alto pico de los Andes, imaginando esa ciudad fortaleza de los incas en la época de su gloria. Imagínese en el lugar de los jóvenes de la foto y explique sus pensamientos al mirar las ruinas.

5 Alberto: Me encantan las ruinas, pero ya conozco las de Copán en
Honduras y las de Chichén Itzá en Yucatán. Me imagino que las
incaicas son muy similares a las mayas.

Tomás: ¡No, no, son completamente distintas! Ni en México ni en
Honduras quedan restos° de una ciudad entera a dos mil metros   remains

10 o más de altura. ¿Ves esta foto del panorama? ¿Y la de la ciudad
misma?° ¡Machu Picchu se encuentra dentro de las nubes!   **de** . . . of the city itself

Alberto: Tienes razón. Pero, ¿por qué dices que es misterioso?

Tomás: Con el terreno° tan abrupto, lleno de precipicios y montañas, es   terrain
difícil imaginar cómo los indios consiguieron llevar a ese lugar

15 las gigantescas piedras para las construcciones.

Alberto: Bueno, tengo que confiar en ti y en tu opinión. ¿Pero no es
Machu Picchu un sitio comercializado y lleno de turistas?

Tomás: Bueno, en Cuzco sí hay miles de turistas y mucho comercialismo,
pero Machu Picchu es un monumento nacional. Te aseguro que

20 te va a gustar mucho.

Alberto: Entonces debemos ir este sábado, porque me quedan sólo diez
días. ¿Cómo hacemos el viaje?

Tomás: Podemos ir en avión hasta Cuzco, y luego en tren hasta las
ruinas mismas. Tenemos que hacer las reservaciones inmediata-

25 mente porque sólo hay un hotel en Machu Picchu.

Alberto: Si quieres, vamos a consultar con un agente de viajes sobre
horarios y vuelos. Al mismo tiempo la agencia puede hacer las
reservaciones del hotel. Así que, ¡manos a la obra!

Comprensión

1. ¿Qué le muestra Tomás a su amigo Alberto?
2. ¿Le impresionan las fotos a Alberto? ¿por qué sí o no?
3. ¿Con qué ruinas compara Alberto las ruinas incaicas?
4. Según Tomás, ¿son similares las ruinas incaicas de Machu Picchu a las
   ruinas mayas (*Mayan*) de Honduras y Yucatán?
5. ¿Quién descubrió las ruinas de Machu Picchu? ¿en qué año?
6. Según Tomás, ¿por qué hay poco comercialismo en Machu Picchu?
7. ¿Cuándo piensan ir a Machu Picchu los dos jóvenes?

Conversación

1. ¿Le interesa a usted la arqueología? ¿Conoce algunas ruinas arqueológicas interesantes? ¿dónde?
2. ¿Saca usted fotos de los lugares que visita? ¿Qué tipo de fotografías le
   gusta sacar? ¿de personas? ¿de edificios? ¿de paisajes?
3. Cuando usted viaja, ¿consulta con una agencia de viajes, o hace todas
   las reservaciones usted mismo/a?
4. ¿Cuáles son algunas de las ventajas y desventajas de usar los servicios
   de una agencia de viajes?

Vocabulario

Palabras análogas

la agencia	el/la explorador/a	misterioso, -a
la arqueología	extraordinario, -a	el monumento
arqueológico, -a	fascinar	nacional
comercializado, -a	gigantesco, -a	el precipicio
comparar	impresionar	la ruina
la construcción	el indio	el servicio
consultar (con)	interesar	similar
la excursión	el metro	el/la turista

Sustantivos

el/la agente de viajes travel agent
la altura height, altitude
la desventaja disadvantage
el edificio building
el horario schedule, timetable
la nube cloud
el paisaje countryside
la piedra stone
el siglo century
la ventaja advantage

Adjetivos

abrupto, -a rough *(terrain)*
difícil difficult
distinto, -a distinct, different
entero, -a entire, whole
siguiente following

Verbos

asegurar to assure
confiar (en) to trust
descubrir to discover
encantar to like something very much
encontrarse (ue) to be located
enfermarse to get sick, fall ill
entusiasmarse (con) to get enthusiastic (about)
irse *(irreg.)* to go (away)

Otras palabras y expresiones

al mismo tiempo at the same time
al ver on seeing
completamente completely
dentro de within
¡manos a la obra! to work!
me quedan [diez días] I have [ten days] left
otra vez again
realmente really
tan so

Práctica

A. Imagínese que usted trabaja en una agencia de viajes y tiene que informar a varios clientes sobre un viaje desde Miami hasta Lima y Machu Picchu. Explique a los clientes los horarios de aviones.

Posibilidades de vuelos Miami-Lima-Cuzco

	Aerolínea	*Vuelo*	*Hora Salida*	*Hora Llegada*	*Frecuencia*
Miami-Lima	Eastern	518	17:10	21:26	Sáb./Dom.
	AeroPerú	605	18:15	23:55	Domingo
Lima-Cuzco	AeroPerú	431	6:30	7:30	Diario
	Faucett	215	7:00	8:00	Domingo

B. Enseñe a la clase algunas fotos de un sitio que visitó y le gustó. Diga por qué le interesó el lugar y qué medios de transporte usó para ir allí. Diga si allí van normalmente muchos turistas y si el sitio está muy comercializado. Use expresiones y estructuras del diálogo.

Nota cultural Cuzco y los incas

Cuzco, la antigua capital de los incas, está situado en los Andes a una altura de más de 3.000 metros. Entre las principales ruinas incaicas que se conservan allí están la Casa de las Mujeres del Sol y el Templo del Sol, lugar re-

La representación del gran Inca durante las celebraciones del Festival del Sol en Cuzco parece originarse en tiempos remotos. ¿Por qué cree Ud. que se celebra este festival en junio? ¿Cree Ud. que esta representación es legítima o turística? Apoye (support) su respuesta con sus observaciones sobre la fotografía.

servado a los sacerdotes[1] y centro de los ritos religiosos del pueblo. Una de las leyendas sobre la fundación de la ciudad de Cuzco y del templo la atribuye a los hijos del dios del sol. El dios les mandó buscar un lugar fértil donde establecer un templo en su honor, y ésta fue su selección. Otra leyenda explica que en la antigüedad, los sobrevivientes[2] de una gran inundación[3] se establecieron en el sitio que es hoy día Cuzco.

En el mes de junio se celebra el Festival del Sol en Cuzco. Los trajes de colores vivos de los indios, la música, los bailes y las comidas recuerdan la antigua tradición de rendir homenaje al sol y celebrar la llegada de la primavera.

Cerca de Cuzco está el pueblo de Pisac. Allí hay un mercado muy antiguo donde los indios venden sus productos agrícolas y su artesanía.[4] Ofrecen productos muy variados—frutas y legumbres,[5] ropa,[6] lana[7] de alpaca, joyas,[8] artículos de plata y utensilios de cocina.[9] Reina un ambiente[10] festivo entre la multitud que compra y regatea.[11]

---

1. priests 2. survivors 3. flood 4. crafts 5. vegetables 6. clothing 7. wool
8. jewelry 9. **utensilios** . . . kitchen utensils 10. environment 11. bargains

Pronunciación y ortografía
Los sonidos [s] y [z]

1. The Spanish consonant sound [s], as in *Sue,* is usually represented by the letters **c** (before **e** and **i**), **s** (before any vowel), or **z**.

   cero   cien   solo   azul

2. The Spanish consonant sound [z], as in *zoo,* is represented by the letter **s** when it is followed by another voiced consonant sound such as [m], [d], or [l].

   mismo   desde   isla

3. In Spain, the letter **c** before **e** or **i** and the letter **z** represent a sound similar to the sound of *th* in the word *thin.*

   cero   ciudad   lápiz

A. Escuche a su profesor/a y repita las palabras siguientes.

[s]			[z]	
cero	sabe	azul	mismo	asimismo
hace	según	azteca	entusiasmado	desmejorar
cien	sitio	almuerzo	desde	Islandia
edificio	casa	abrazo	isla	Ismael
corazón	dices			

B. Escuche y repita las siguientes oraciones que lee su profesor/a.

1. La ciudad de Cuzco está en el sur de Perú.
2. Debemos consultar con una agencia de viajes para hacer las reservaciones.
3. Hay un refrán que dice: «Cielo azul en marzo, cielo gris en abril».
4. Se entusiasmó con la visita a Islandia.

Refranes

No es oro todo lo que reluce.   All that glitters is not gold.
No hay cosa segura en esta vida.   Nothing is certain in this life.

Estudio de palabras

I. Artículos de ropa

1. la camisa *shirt*	9. los zapatos *shoes*	17. el impermeable *raincoat*
2. la corbata *tie*	10. las sandalias *sandals*	18. el sombrero *hat*
3. los pantalones *pants*	11. las botas *boots*	19. el gorro *cap*
4. la billetera *wallet*	12. los calcetines *socks*	20. la chaqueta *jacket*
5. el vestido *dress*	13. las medias *stockings*	21. el abrigo *coat*
6. la bolsa, el bolso *purse*	14. los guantes *gloves*	22. el traje *suit*
7. la blusa *blouse*	15. el suéter *sweater*	
8. la falda *skirt*	16. la bufanda *scarf*	

Expresiones útiles
ir de compras   to go shopping
llevar   to wear
el número   size *(of shoes)*
quedar bien (grande, pequeño)   to fit well (to be large, small)
la ropa de (verano)   (summer) clothing
la talla   size *(of clothing)*
el tamaño   size *(general term)*
usar   to wear

A. Conteste las siguientes preguntas acerca de su manera de vestir.

1. ¿Qué lleva usted cuando va a una entrevista?
2. ¿Qué ropa lleva en la primavera? ¿en el verano?
3. ¿Lleva usted sombrero cuando hace calor?
4. ¿Qué lleva usted cuando llueve?
5. ¿Qué usa cuando hace frío?
6. ¿De qué talla es su camisa?
7. ¿Qué número de zapatos usa usted?

B. Describa la ropa que usted lleva en este momento. Mencione el color, el tamaño y si quiere el precio *(price)*.

II. Los viajes

Sustantivos
la aduana   customs
el/la aduanero/a   customs officer
la agencia de viajes   travel agency
el aterrizaje   landing
el billete (boleto) de ida   one-way ticket
el billete de ida y vuelta   round-trip ticket
la carretera   highway
el despegue   takeoff
el destino   destination
el equipaje   baggage
la estación de ferrocarril   train station
la línea aérea   airline *(also,* **aerolínea***)*
la maleta   suitcase
el/la pasajero/a   passenger
el pasaporte   passport
el/la viajero/a   traveler

Verbos
alojarse   to lodge
aterrizar   to land (in a plane)
conducir (zc)   to drive (a car) *(also,* **manejar***)*
despegar   to take off (in a plane)
volar (ue)   to fly

Otras palabras y expresiones

¡buen viaje!   have a good trip!
hacer escala   to make a stop (on the way to a destination)
hacer las maletas   to pack the suitcases
hacer un viaje   to take a trip
tomar el tren   to take the train
¡que le (te) vaya bien!   have a good time!
¡que se (te) divierta(s) mucho!   enjoy yourself!

C. Usted participa en una encuesta *(survey)* de una agencia de viajes. Tiene que dar la información siguiente sobre su último viaje.

1. ¿Adónde viajó usted?
2. ¿En qué mes o estación del año viajó usted?
3. ¿Con quién viajó?
4. ¿Qué medio de transporte usó?
5. ¿Qué pasó cuando usted llegó a su destino?
6. ¿Estuvo en un hotel? ¿en cuál? ¿por cuánto tiempo?

D. Complete las oraciones de la primera columna con una frase apropiada de la segunda columna.

1. Cuando mi amiga hace un viaje,
2. Tuvimos que esperar en la estación de ferrocarril
3. Cuando fui a Quito,
4. ¿Compraste un billete de ida solamente,
5. Cuando viajaron con esa línea aérea,
6. No nos permiten fumar
7. ¿Le mostraste tu pasaporte
8. Cuando salió le dijimos,
9. Cuando hay mucho tráfico en la carretera,
10. Después de aterrizar,

a. el avión hizo escala en Bogotá y en Lima.
b. al aduanero?
c. o uno de ida y vuelta?
d. no es posible conducir rápidamente.
e. lleva siempre mucho equipaje.
f. tuvieron que esperar una hora en la aduana.
g. porque el tren tardó mucho.
h. durante el despegue y el aterrizaje.
i. «¡Buen viaje! ¡Que se divierta!»
j. perdieron sus maletas.

Estructuras útiles

I. Preterit of **-ir** verbs with stem changes **o** > **u** and **e** > **i**

1. The **-ir** verbs that have a stem-vowel change **o** > **ue** in the present tense (see pages 152–153) also have a stem-vowel change **o** > **u** in the third person singular and plural forms of the preterit.

dormir	morir
dormí	morí
dormiste	moriste
durmió	**murió**
dormimos	morimos
dormisteis	moristeis
durmieron	**murieron**

Todos **durmieron** como unos troncos. *They all slept like logs.*
¿Cuándo **murió** la abuela? *When did grandmother die?*

2. The **-ir** verbs that have a stem-vowel change **e > ie** or **e > i** in the present tense (see pages 150, 166–167) have a stem change **e > i** in the third person singular and plural forms of the preterit.

pedir	conseguir	reír	mentir
pedí	conseguí	reí	mentí
pediste	conseguiste	reíste	mentiste
pidió	**consiguió**	**rió**	**mintió**
pedimos	conseguimos	reímos	mentimos
pedisteis	conseguisteis	reísteis	mentisteis
pidieron	**consiguieron**	**rieron**	**mintieron**

—Al jefe le **pedimos** un millón *We asked the boss for one million*
de pesos.   *pesos.*
—¿Y por qué le **pidieron** tanto? *And why did you ask him for so much?*

Other common **-ir** verbs with a stem-vowel change **e > i** in the preterit are:

despedir   perseguir   sugerir
divertir   preferir   vestir
elegir   repetir

A. Diga por qué no durmieron anoche las personas indicadas, usando las expresiones siguientes.

hizo frío   alguien roncó *(snored)*
la persona tuvo insomnio   la persona estuvo enferma

▶ yo   *Anoche no dormí porque tuve insomnio.*

1. tú
2. el profesor de ingeniería
3. mi amiga Hilda y su mamá
4. tú y tu hermano
5. Silvia y yo
6. yo

B. Haga oraciones completas, usando el pretérito de los verbos.

▶ yo / conseguir / tres entradas / ópera   *Yo conseguí tres entradas para*
                                             la ópera.

1. ¿tú / despedir / a tu hermano / ayer en el aeropuerto?
2. el policía / perseguir / hombre / por las calles de la ciudad
3. nosotros / nunca / pedir / dinero / a nuestros padres
4. él / repetir / las palabras / en español
5. tú y Olga / elegir / un buen trabajo
6. las plantas / morir / durante las vacaciones

C. Diga qué piden este año las siguientes personas, escogiendo (*choosing*)
   una opción de la segunda columna. Luego diga qué pidieron el año
   pasado.

▶ los mineros   *Este año los mineros piden [más dinero].*
                 El año pasado pidieron [menos horas de trabajo].

1. los estudiantes   a. más dinero
2. la doctora   b. mejor comida
3. el empleado   c. menos horas de trabajo
4. los profesores   d. mejores condiciones
5. los policías   e. atención médica
6. las mujeres   f. buenos servicios

II. Nominalization

—¿El muchacho alto es hermano
 de Ángela?
—Sí, **el alto** es su hermano
 Carlos.

1. In Spanish, a noun is often distinguished from other nouns by means
   of an adjective, a **de**-phrase, or a **que**-clause.

—¿Ya conoces a algunos   *Do you know any students this*
 estudiantes este año?   *year yet?*
—Sí, conozco a los estudiantes *Yes, I know the students in this*
 de esta clase y a casi todos los *class and most of the students*
 estudiantes **que viven en el**   *who live in the dorm.*
 dormitorio.

2. In normal conversation, when the context is clear, a noun modified by an adjective, a **de-**phrase, or a **que-**clause used as an adjective can be omitted in a response, as long as the *article* modifying the noun is retained. This is often referred to as nominalization; that is, the adjective phrase functions as a noun.

—¿El libro verde es tu libro de química?

—Sí, **el verde** es mi libro de química.

—¿La mujer del sombrero azul es hermana de Ángela?

—No, **la del sombrero azul** es su tía.

Is the green book your chemistry book?

Yes, the green one is my chemistry book.

Is the woman with the blue hat Angela's sister?

No, the one with the blue hat is her aunt.

3. Nominalization is often used to avoid repetition.

El edificio blanco y **el azul** fueron construidos en 1911.

El libro de ciencia y **el de cálculo** cuestan $20 cada uno.

La calculadora que yo tengo y **la que** tú tienes son iguales.

The white building and the blue one were built in 1911.

The science book and the calculus one cost $20 each.

The calculator I have and the one you have are the same.

4. The neuter article **lo** may be used with an adjective, a **de-**phrase, or a **que-**clause in nominalization to refer to an abstract quality or characteristic.

Lo difícil es que no entienden español.

¡Lo del accidente fue terrible!

Lo que dijo usted no es verdad.

The hard part is that they do not understand Spanish.

The whole business about the accident was terrible!

What you said isn't true.

5. The indefinite article **un** changes to **uno** when it appears in nominalization. **Una** remains the same.

—Compré un automóvil de dos puertas.

—¡Qué casualidad! Ayer yo compré **uno** de dos puertas también.

—Conozco a una señora que trabaja en Chile.

—Pues yo conozco a **una** que trabaja en Argentina.

I bought a car with two doors.

What a coincidence! Yesterday I bought one with two doors, too!

I know a woman who works in Chile.

Well, I know one who works in Argentina.

D. Exprese de otra manera la siguiente información, usando el nombre adjetivo (nominalization).

▶ Los viajeros que tienen dinero   *Los que tienen dinero van a*
van a mejores hoteles.   *mejores hoteles.*

1. La muchacha rubia que habla con Ricardo tiene razón.
2. El hombre de la cámara fotográfica es nuestro profesor.
3. Me gustan las fotos de monumentos nacionales.
4. La señora que está cerca de la ventana tiene frío.
5. La agente que hace las reservaciones es muy simpática.
6. Las jóvenes colombianas llegaron a Nueva York.

E. Haga preguntas y respuestas lógicas en el pretérito con las frases indicadas, sin usar los sustantivos en las respuestas.

▶ turistas alemanes / salir en avión   S1: *¿Es verdad que los turistas*
                                            alemanes salieron en avión?
                                       S2: *Sí, los alemanes salieron en*
                                            avión a las siete.

1. señora chilena / visitar / Lima
2. señor que regresó a Panamá / olvidar / maleta
3. jefe de la compañía petrolera / viajar / Quito
4. muchacho guapo / conseguir / reservaciones
5. muchacha alta / pedir / información
6. turista norteamericana / consultar con / un agente de viajes
7. señora del sombrero / ir / aeropuerto

III. Reflexive constructions

La vi en la calle. ¡Qué simpática es!

Me vi en el espejo. ¡Qué viejo estoy!

1. A reflexive construction is one in which the direct or indirect object of the verb refers to or represents the same person or thing as the subject.

Reflexive
Alicia **se mira.**
Me veo en el espejo.

Alicia *is looking at herself.*
I see myself in the mirror.

Non-reflexive
Alicia **los mira.**
Te veo en el espejo.

Alicia *is looking at them.*
I see you in the mirror.

2. The chart that follows shows two Spanish verbs used reflexively, the first in the present and the second in the preterit. Note that the reflexive pronouns **me, te, nos,** and **os** are identical to the direct and indirect-object pronouns. Only the third person singular and plural reflexive forms, **se,** are different.

	llamarse	divertirse
yo	me llamo	me divertí
tú	te llamas	te divertiste
Ud., él, ella	se llama	se divirtió
nosotros, -as	nos llamamos	nos divertimos
vosotros, -as	os llamáis	os divertisteis
Uds., ellos, ellas	se llaman	se divirtieron

3. The reflexive object pronouns follow the same rules of position as non-reflexive object pronouns. Note that the reflexive pronoun **se** appears in dictionaries and vocabulary lists attached to the infinitive **(llamarse, divertirse)** to indicate the reflexive usage of the verb.

4. The following verbs are frequently used reflexively in Spanish.

acordarse (ue) de to remember
acostarse (ue) to go to bed
afeitarse to shave
arrepentirse (ie) to repent, to be sorry
bañarse to take a shower, bathe
decidirse (a) to make up one's mind
despertarse (ie) to wake up
divertirse (ie) to have a good time, enjoy oneself
dormirse (ue) to fall asleep
enamorarse (de) to fall in love (with)
enfermarse to become sick
enojarse (de) to get mad (about), get angry (about)
equivocarse to make a mistake

imaginarse to imagine
irse to go away
lavarse to wash oneself
levantarse to get up
llamarse to be called
negarse (ie) a to refuse to
peinarse to comb one's hair
ponerse to put on (*clothing*)
preocuparse (de) to worry (about)
quejarse (de) to complain (about)
quitarse to take off (*clothing*)
reírse (i) (de) to laugh (about)
sentarse (ie) to sit down
sentirse (ie) to feel
vestirse (i) to get dressed

5. Reflexive constructions are much more common in Spanish than they are in English. Often a verb that is used reflexively in Spanish is not used reflexively in English. A few Spanish verbs are always used reflexively but many may be used in both non-reflexive and reflexive constructions, depending on the situation.

Me imagino que son similares. *I imagine that they are similar.*
Me llamo Eduardo. *My name is Eduardo (literally, I call **myself** Eduardo).*

Llamo a Bernardo esta noche. *I'm calling Bernardo tonight.*

6. **Poner** *(to put)* and **quitar** *(to take away)* are used in their reflexive forms with articles of clothing to mean *to put on* or *to take off*. When used with a reflexive construction, the definite article, not the possessive adjective, is used in Spanish with articles of clothing.

—¿Qué **te pones** cuando hace frío? *What do you put on when it's cold?*
—**Me pongo** el abrigo. *I put on my coat.*

F. Las siguientes personas no conocen las ruinas incaicas, pero le dicen a usted que se imaginan que son estupendas.

▶ yo *Me imagino que las ruinas incaicas son estupendas.*

1. tú	3. tú y Tomás	5. los turistas
2. usted	4. ella	6. Carlos y yo

G. Diga en qué pasatiempos se divierten algunas personas que usted conoce. Escoja un pasatiempo de la lista o diga uno original.

jugar al fútbol	nadar	jugar al béisbol
ir al cine	patinar	jugar al tenis
cantar	sacar fotos	ir al museo
bailar	leer libros	escribir poesía

▶ *Mi primo [Daniel] se divierte mucho cuando saca fotos.*

H. Complete las oraciones siguientes con una frase lógica, usando el presente o el pretérito de los verbos de la lista según el contexto.

decidirse (a)	enfermarse	equivocarse	quejarse
enamorarse (de)	enojarse	imaginarse	sentirse

1. Cuando vi a esa chica simpática, _____ .
2. Ricardo se negó a ayudarme, por eso _____ mucho.
3. Tuve que ir al hospital porque comí algo malo y_____ .
4. ¿Cómo _____ hoy, señorita? ¿Mejor que ayer?
5. Nosotros no _____ cómo ustedes consiguieron las entradas para el concierto.

6. Ayer mis amigos y yo _____ ir a la playa este fin de semana.
7. Esos muchachos siempre _____ de la comida de la cafetería.
8. Si yo no _____ , Pedro y Diego son primos.

IV. Verbs like **gustar**

1. Sentences with the verb **gustar** follow the pattern *indirect-object pronoun + third person verb form + noun* or *infinitive*.

Les gusta viajar.	*They like to travel.*
¿Te gustan los deportes?	*Do you like sports?*

2. The following verbs follow the same sentence pattern as **gustar**.

doler (ue)	to hurt	**interesar**	to interest
encantar	to love	**molestar**	to bother
faltar	to need	**quedar**	to have left

Me interesa mucho **la política.**	*Politics interests me a lot.*
Les encanta viajar por barco.	*They love to travel by boat.*

3. In constructions with **gustar** and verbs like **gustar,** prepositional **a**-phrases are often used for emphasis or clarification.

A mí me faltan dos pesos.	*I need two pesos.*
A ella le quedan tres lápices.	*She has three pencils left.*

I. A las siguientes personas les faltan muchas cosas. Diga si a usted le faltan las mismas cosas.

▶ Tomás: un reloj   *A Tomás le falta un reloj, pero a mí no me falta ninguno.*
          A Tomás le falta un reloj, y a mí también me falta uno.

1. a ustedes: los documentos de identificación
2. a ti y a Luis: tres discos
3. a ellas: dinero
4. a él: tiempo
5. a esos señores: dos buenos diccionarios
6. a esa señora: un buen sueldo

J. Las personas siguientes se fueron de compras al almacén con cien pesos y compraron varias cosas. ¿Cuánto dinero les queda?

▶ Yo compré una camisa por veinte pesos.   *Me quedan ochenta pesos.*

1. Ángela compró una camisa por ochenta pesos.
2. Alberto y Luis compraron dos corbatas por diez pesos.
3. Nosotras compramos unas botas por treinta y tres pesos.
4. Eduardo compró unos zapatos por veintidós pesos.
5. Yo compré un gorro por dos pesos.

K. Complete con frases lógicas. Use los verbos **doler, encantar, faltar, interesar, molestar** o **quedar** y el objeto indirecto apropiado.

1. A Grisel _____ la mano, y tiene que ir al médico.
2. A mí _____ ver esas fotos de Yucatán porque pienso viajar a México en julio.
3. A ustedes _____ pintar y dibujar, ¿no es verdad?
4. Mi papá me dio diez dólares, pero ya sólo _____ dos.
5. A mi madre _____ el comercialismo de los lugares históricos.
6. ¿A ti _____ más los libros de historia o los libros de filosofía?
7. Tengo dos pesos, y _____ dos más para comprar ese sombrero.

L. Diga a cuáles de estas personas les interesan (o no) las siguientes cosas o actividades.

a un vecino   al presidente de los EEUU
a tus padres   a tu mejor amiga
a una prima   a uno de tus profesores
a tu mejor amigo   a un compañero de clase

1. la política   5. las novelas de detectives
2. viajar a Europa   6. los animales domésticos
3. los deportes   7. la profesión que tiene
4. la biología   8. las lenguas modernas

¿Comprende usted?

Tarjetas postales

Todo escritor tiene un público particular en mente *(mind)* cuando escribe. La consideración de ese público lo limita en cuanto a la selección de palabras y al estilo que utiliza al escribir. Alberto Falla envía *(sends)* estas tarjetas postales a sus amigos panameños. Una tarjeta es para su novia. Otra es para una amiga que le ayudó a conocer amigos en Perú. Dos son para unos amigos. Descubra cuál es cuál.

Lucha de mi vida:

El Perú es un país de encanto, pero aquí no está mi Lucha para salir y pasear con ella. Algún día tú y yo tenemos que venir juntos y ver esta maravilla. ¿Piensas mucho en mí? Yo no te olvido un instante.

Tuyo,

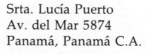

Srta. Lucía Puerto
Av. del Mar 5874
Panamá, Panamá C.A.

Querido Cuco:

Afortunadamente Tomás me convenció de visitar Machu Picchu. Esta foto te da una idea de la maravilla que es este lugar, pero la realidad es mucho mejor. El mes de vacaciones pasa rápidamente y la semana entrante vuelvo a Panamá.

Tu amigo,

Alberto

Sr. Antonio Tovar
Calle Torrijos 1, 2°B
Panamá, Panamá C.A.

Mi querida Mencha:

¡Tienes toda la razón! Perú es una maravilla. Ya visité a tus amigos los Romero y son simpatiquísimos. Te mandan saludos afectuosos. Me invitaron a comer, y otro día me llevaron a las ruinas de Pachacámac cerca de Lima, donde los incas tuvieron un gran templo.

Te recuerda siempre,

Alberto

Srta. Clemencia Pinzón
Calle de las Flores 2367
Panamá, Panamá C.A.

Mi queridísimo Pepe:

Estoy pasando un mes fantástico. Lima tiene su sector moderno y su parte colonial. Hoy estuve en el cambio de guardia del Palacio Presidencial. Los guardias tienen este mismo uniforme que ves en la postal. Es realmente imponente.

Te recuerda tu amigo,

Alberto

Sr. José María Agudelo
Apartado 79
Panamá, Panamá C.A.

A. Complete las oraciones según el contenido de las postales.

1. La novia de Alberto se llama _____ .
2. _____ son amigos de Alberto.
3. _____ le ayudó a Alberto a conocer gente en Perú.
4. A Alberto le queda _____ de vacaciones.
5. Alberto quiere regresar a Perú para _____ .
6. Una de las postales es una fotografía de _____ .

B. Usando las tarjetas postales, haga un resumen del viaje de Alberto.

1. Diga cuánto tiempo dura el viaje.
2. Mencione tres sitios que Alberto visitó en Perú.
3. Explique cómo es Lima según Alberto.
4. Diga cuándo piensa regresar Alberto a Perú y con quién.
5. Explique por qué decidió Alberto visitar Machu Picchu.

C. Suponga que usted está en Perú y escribe tarjetas postales a dos personas (por ejemplo a un/a amigo/a y a un pariente). Escoja algunos datos de las tarjetas de Alberto para escribir sus tarjetas.

(Izquierda) Observe cómo algunas de estas casas de Cuzco incorporan partes de antiquísimas construcciones incaicas en su edificación. (Derecha) La catedral con algunos edificios del gobierno eclesiástico y civil en la Plaza de Armas de Lima muestra la organización característica de la ciudad colonial española. La plaza en el centro es como el corazón de la ciudad. ¿Cuáles son las características esenciales de la ciudad norteamericana?

Lengua en acción 4

A. Un horario (*Lección 10*)

Ud. se encuentra de viaje en La Paz, Bolivia. Compre dos boletos de
autobús para ir a otra ciudad boliviana. La persona que vende los
boletos (un/a compañero/a de clase) le informa sobre las horas y los
precios. Después, alterne los papeles.

Compañía Copacabana			
Horario de autobuses: a partir del 15 de noviembre			
Destino	**Horas**	**Precios**	**Duración**
Oruro	5:00; 7:00; 15:00; 20:00	$4 (bolivianos)	3 horas
Cochabamba	6:00; 18:00; 21:00	$5	10 horas
Sucre	7:00; 10:00; 14:00; 15:00; 18:00	$20	16 horas
Potosí	8:00; 11:00; 12:00; 14:00	$30	18 horas

Empleado/a

1. Salude y ofrezca sus servicios.

2. Diga que no hay boletos para
   esa hora.
3. Diga que sí.
4. Conteste.

5. Conteste.

Usted

Salude y explique lo que quiere
   comprar.
Pregunte si hay boletos para otra
   hora.
Pregunte el costo de los boletos.
Pregunte a qué hora llega el
   autobús a _____ .
Compre los boletos y despídase
   (*say good-by*).

B. Demandas estudiantiles (*Lección 10*)

En grupos de 3 a 5 personas, decidan cuáles de las siguientes demandas son las más importantes. Clasifiquen las demandas en una
escala de 1 a 4; luego prepárense para decirle al presidente de la
universidad (su profesor/a) lo que es necesario cambiar.

_____ una reducción en el costo
de la educación universitaria
a. rebaja en la matrícula
   (*tuition*)
b. rebaja en el costo de los
   alojamientos (*lodging*)
c. ?

_____ más variedad en los
cursos ofrecidos
a. más cursos tecnológicos
b. más cursos para los
   estudiantes de primer
   año
c. ?

_____ mejor comida en la cafetería
  a. más variedad
  b. mejor nutrición
  c. ?

_____ más actividades culturales
  a. un concierto de . . .
  b. una conferencia de . . .
  c. ?

C. ¿Qué tal tu viaje? *(Lección 11)*

Ud. le muestra a un miembro de la clase unas fotos de un viaje
reciente al Ecuador. Su compañero/a le hace varias preguntas a Ud.
sobre el viaje:

¿Quiénes son estas personas? **¿Qué día y a qué hora**
¿Te gustó . . . ?   **salieron Uds.?**
¿Cómo son las playas,   **¿Qué hiciste (hicieron) . . . ?**
  las tiendas . . . ?

Cuéntele lo que pasó y cuándo, usando como guía los dibujos y las
indicaciones y conteste las preguntas de su compañero/a. Use expresiones de tiempo como **el [lunes] pasado, la semana pasada, después,**
luego, más tarde.

1. llegar al aeropuerto de Guayaquil, saludar a mis amigos

2. ir a la playa de Salinas, tomar
el sol, nadar, salir en bote

3. ir a un club, hablar con
gente interesante, bailar

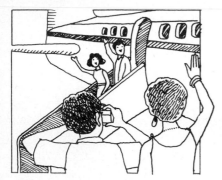

4. ir a una tienda, comprar
regalos para . . .

5. llover un día, ir al
cine/museo, ver . . .

6. [¿Qué más hizo Ud.?]

D. ¿Tiene Ud. una habitación? *(Lección 11)*

Paso (Step)*1:* Ud. visita Quito, Ecuador y necesita encontrar una habitación en un hotel por unos días. Indique con una equis (X) el tipo de habitación que quiere, la fecha de su llegada y salida y el precio que puede pagar.

_____ habitación sencilla, 2–9 de mayo, no más de 5.000 sucres por noche

_____ habitación doble, 15–17 de mayo, no más de 10.000 sucres por noche

Paso 2: Ud. va de hotel en hotel en busca de una habitación. Pregúntele al/a la hotelero/a (un miembro de la clase) si tiene la habitación que Ud. quiere. Si no la tiene, encuentre otro/a hotelero/a y repita el proceso. El/La hotelero/a con una habitación disponible *(available)* debe completar el siguiente formulario.

Fecha de llegada _____   **Hotel Emperador**

Fecha de salida _____   Av. Robles y Av. Amazonas

Profesión _____   Tel. 230-440

Procedencia _____   Quito, Ecuador

Nacionalidad _____

Sr/a. _____

Tipo de habitación   ☐ sencilla   ☐ doble

Forma de pago   ☐ en efectivo *(cash)*

☐ cheque de viajero

☐ tarjeta de crédito

Número de tarjeta de crédito o carnet de identidad _____

_____

E. Unas maletas perdidas *(Lección 12)*

Ud. llegó al aeropuerto de Cuzco, pero sus maletas no llegaron. Infórmele al/a la oficial del aeropuerto (un miembro de la clase) de su pérdida y contéstele sus preguntas. Después, alternen los papeles. El/La oficial completa el siguiente informe.

Descripción del equipaje perdido

Indique con una equis (x) el tipo de maleta.

Nombre del pasajero _____

Hotel en Cuzco _____

Número de vuelo _____

Número de maletas _____

Color _____

Tamaño: pequeño   regular   grande

Material: plástico   cuero   tela

Contenido: Ropa   Efectos personales   Aparatos

_____   _____   _____

_____   _____   _____

_____   _____   _____

_____   _____   _____

F. En el Almacén Flores (Wrap-up)

Un/a amigo/a va a celebrar su cumpleaños (birthday) este mes. Ud. quiere comprarle un regalo (gift), pero no sabe qué escoger (choose). El/La vendedor/a de la tienda (su compañero/a de clase) le ayuda.

Vendedor/a	Usted
1. Salude al/a la cliente.	Conteste e infórmele que busca un regalo y explique para quién es.
2. Pregunte cuánto dinero quiere gastar (spend).	Conteste.
3. Pregunte sobre su amigo/a: ¿Le gusta la ropa moderna, deportiva, elegante? ¿Es activo/a?, etc.	Conteste.
4. Recomiende un regalo y dígale el precio.	Déle las gracias y decida si lo quiere comprar o no.

Unidad 5
En Colombia, Venezuela y Panamá

Los habitantes de Caracas sienten legítimo entusiasmo cuando hablan de la modernidad de su ciudad. El Centro Simón Bolívar de esta fotografía con sus bellas fuentes y mucho espacio para caminar lejos del tránsito de las calles es especialmente importante para los caraqueños (inhabitants of Caracas). ¿Le sorprende el entusiasmo que sienten los hispanos por su modernidad? ¿Cómo es diferente del punto de vista de un norteamericano?

Lección 13
En Colombia

Las noticias del día

Son las siete de la mañana en Medellín, ciudad del noroeste de Colombia. El señor Alonso Fernández enciende la radio para escuchar las noticias del día antes de salir a trabajar. Mientras escucha las noticias, toma una taza de café con leche y saborea una arepa antioqueña.°

Locutor: Muy buenos días, señoras y señores. Desde Medellín, éste es su noticiero Todecol, «El primero con las últimas».° Y . . . quiero que recuerden . . . para el dolor de cabeza, ¡mejor mejora Mejoradina!

5 *Bogotá.* —Anoche llegó a Bogotá el Secretario de Estado de los Estados Unidos para asistir a la Conferencia Interamericana de Desarrollo Económico. El Secretario expresó su interés en encontrar cuanto antes° una solución justa y efectiva a los problemas monetarios que agobian° a varias naciones del

10 hemisferio occidental.

Cali. —El conocido ciudadano Dr. Pedro Ayala, jefe de la compañía Plasticol de Colombia, fue secuestrado° ayer en la tarde de su automóvil en la Calle Quince. La policía afirma que con la cooperación de los ciudadanos es probable que se

15 encuentre a los culpables.

Cartagena. —El festival mundial de cine causa sensación internacional en esta ciudad. En una entrevista exclusiva con

saborea . . . he savors an **arepa,** a large, thin Antioquian corn griddle wafer

El . . . the first one with the latest news

cuanto . . . as soon as possible

overwhelm

kidnapped

En esta estación de radio en Bogotá, Colombia los locutores trabajan en equipo. ¿Qué experiencia personal y personalidad cree Ud. que necesita tener un locutor?

20 esta estación, la señorita Oldtown, una de las actrices más
admiradas, declaró que le encanta Colombia y que espera que
la comisión del festival le conceda° un premio por su actuación°   awards / performance
en la película *Doble pasión*. Esta película despertó más interés
entre el público que *Amor sin dolor*, de la misma actriz.

Locutora: ¿Ya compró su billete para el sorteo° extraordinario de la   drawing
Lotería de Antioquia? ¡Puede ganar más de veinticinco millones
25 el viernes de la semana entrante!

Locutor: Y ahora seguimos con las noticias deportivas.—Todo el país
sigue de cerca° la Vuelta a Colombia en Bicicleta.° Raúl To-   **sigue**... follows closely /
millo, favorito de la Vuelta, parece tener serias dificultades. La   **Vuelta**... Colombian
etapa de hoy termina en Medellín, y si las noticias sobre   cross-country bicycle race
30 Tomillo resultan ciertas, es posible que Matamoros llegue a ser
el nuevo líder de la Vuelta.

Locutora: Y ahora, señoras y señores, otra vez ... para el dolor de
cabeza, ¡mejor mejora Mejoradina! Hasta las noticias del mediodía, éste es su noticiero Todecol, «El primero con las últimas».

El señor Fernández apaga el radio, mira su reloj, abre la puerta y sale para la
oficina en carrera.°   **en**... in a rush

Comprensión

1. Describa las primeras acciones del señor Fernández por la mañana.
2. ¿Para qué es buena la Mejoradina?
3. ¿Por qué llegó anoche el Secretario de Estado de los Estados Unidos a Bogotá?
4. ¿Qué le pasó al Dr. Pedro Ayala ayer por la tarde?
5. ¿En qué ciudad colombiana celebran los festivales mundiales de cine este año?
6. ¿Cuánto dinero puede uno ganar en la lotería de Antioquia el viernes de la semana entrante?
7. ¿De qué evento deportivo habla el locutor?
8. Dé algunos detalles de la Vuelta a Colombia en Bicicleta.
9. ¿Qué hace el señor Fernández después de escuchar las noticias del día?

Conversación

1. ¿A qué hora desayuna usted? ¿y almuerza? ¿y cena?
2. ¿A qué hora del día escucha usted la radio?
3. ¿Generalmente escucha usted música o las noticias del día en la radio?
4. ¿Prefiere usted escuchar las noticias en la radio o mirarlas en la televisión?
5. ¿Participa usted en carreras de bicicletas? Si no, ¿en qué deportes participa?
6. ¿Qué le parecen los anuncios comerciales en la radio? ¿Qué le parecen los anuncios comerciales en la televisión?

Vocabulario

Palabras análogas

la acción	exclusivo, -a	la pasión
el actor	expresar	probable
admirado, -a	el festival	resultar
causar	el hemisferio	el/la secretario/a
la comisión	interamericano, -a	la sensación
la cooperación	justo, -a	serio, -a
efectivo, -a	la lotería	la solución
el evento	monetario, -a	

Sustantivos

la actriz actress
el anuncio announcement
la carrera race
el/la ciudadano/a citizen
el/la culpable guilty person
el desarrollo development
el detalle detail
el dolor de cabeza headache
la entrevista interview
la estación station (as in *radio station*)
el noticiero newscast
el premio prize
la taza cup

Adjetivos

cierto, -a true
conocido, -a well-known
deportivo, -a sporting; referring to sports
doble double
mundial world
occidental western

Verbos

abrir to open
apagar to turn off
cenar to have dinner
desayunar to have breakfast
esperar to hope (for)
ganar to win
pasar to happen
secuestrar to kidnap
terminar to end, finish

Otras palabras y expresiones

al + *inf.* on *or* upon (doing something)
después de + *inf.* after (doing something)
generalmente generally
llegar a ser to become
¿qué le pasó? what happened to him?
la semana entrante the coming week
todo el país the whole country

Práctica

A. Prepare un diálogo con otro/a estudiante entre el Sr. Fernández y su hijo/a. Al entrar en el comedor *(dining room)* para tomar el desayuno con su padre, el hijo o hija le pregunta cuáles son las noticias del día. El Sr. Fernández le cuenta los últimos acontecimientos *(events)*. Usen expresiones apropiadas del diálogo en esta lección.

B. Imagine que usted es locutor/a de radio o de televisión. Prepare un breve comentario de dos o tres sucesos recientes, reales o imaginarios, ocurridos en su pueblo o ciudad. Luego presente las noticias en la clase.

Nota cultural La radio en Colombia

Para comprender la importancia de la radio en la educación colombiana, es necesario darse cuenta de[1] lo difícil que es el transporte debido a[2] las enormes cordilleras de los Andes que atraviesan[3] el país. Hay muchas regiones que no reciben comunicación televisiva y donde el correo[4] llega solamente una vez a la semana o al mes. Llevar la educación a estas regiones aisladas es un problema de tremendas dimensiones.

El padre José Joaquín Salcedo encontró en la radio una solución que contribuye a resolver el problema de proporcionar educación a todos. Fundó el programa de «Acción Cultural Popular» en 1947 para llevar la educación a zonas rurales aisladas. El programa tuvo tanto éxito que los educadores de otros países de Hispanoamérica siguieron el ejemplo del padre Salcedo y empezaron programas similares. Los programas de radio no sólo enseñan[5] a leer y a escribir, sino que[6] llevan a la población conocimientos[7] de historia, arte, música, higiene, agricultura y otros campos de interés práctico o de enriquecimiento[8] cultural. Así la radio ocupa un lugar esencial en las comunicaciones de Colombia. Sirve una función multifacética como medio de entretenimiento,[9] de difusión de las noticias y de educación.

---

1. **darse** . . . to realize 2. **debido** . . . owing to 3. cross 4. mail 5. teach
6. **sino** . . . but (also) 7. knowledge 8. enrichment 9. entertainment

Dos indios colombianos escuchan las noticias del día por radio. ¿En qué lengua cree Ud. que reciben las noticias? ¿Qué otro tipo de programa cree Ud. que les interesa a estas personas?

Pronunciación y ortografía
Los sonidos [s], [ks] y [gs]

1. The sounds [s], [ks], and [gs] may all be spelled **x,** depending in part on the origin of the word or on regional pronunciation. The letter **x** is pronounced [ks] or [gs] when followed by a vowel. It is pronounced [s] when followed by a consonant sound, and also in a few common words like **exacto.**

x = [ks] or [gs]
examen	exorbitante	existir
éxito	exuberante	exagerar

x = [s]
expectativa	extraordinario	explicar
exclamación	excepcional	excusar

2. Remember that the letter **x** in some family and place names sometimes represents [h]; for example, in **Xavier, México, Oaxaca.**

A. Escuche a su profesor/a leer las siguientes oraciones. Después repítalas, poniendo atención a la pronunciación de la **x.**

1. Hay gran expectativa entre los estudiantes de México.
2. Usted exagera cuando dice que su experiencia es excepcional.
3. Hiram Bingham exploró las extraordinarias ruinas de Machu Picchu.
4. Los precios de las excursiones son exorbitantes.

B. El siguiente poema muestra un poco exageradamente algunos posibles malentendidos (*misunderstandings*) interculturales. Complete el poema con las palabras de la lista. Luego, léalo en voz alta.

México	exótico	mexicano
exorbitantes	expresa	exagera

_____ con gran dolor
un _____ de Chiapas
que una dama americana
_____ la situación:

al pobre lo encuentra _____
y al rico peripatético;°   extravagant
los precios _____ ,
¡y _____ encantador!

Estudio de palabras
I. Comidas y bebidas

There are various regional terms for food in Hispanic countries, but the following words and expressions will be understood in most Spanish-speaking areas. Learn the following food terms, including the categories into which they have been grouped.

Las comidas

el almuerzo   lunch, late mid-morning meal
la cena   supper, evening meal
la comida   main meal of the day
el desayuno   breakfast

Utensilios

la cuchara   spoon
el cuchillo   knife
el plato   plate
la servilleta   napkin
el tenedor   fork
el vaso   glass

Los mariscos y el pescado

la almeja   clam
el atún   tuna
el camarón   shrimp
el cangrejo   crawfish, crab
la langosta   lobster
el langostino   prawn
el lenguado   sole

Las frutas

la banana   banana
el durazno   peach
la fresa   strawberry
el limón   lemon
la manzana   apple
la naranja   orange
la pera   pear
la piña   pineapple
la toronja   grapefruit
las uvas   grapes

La carne y las aves de corral

el bistec   beefsteak
la carne de cerdo   pork
la carne de res   beef
el cordero   lamb
el jamón   ham
el pavo   turkey
el pollo   chicken
la ternera   veal
el tocino   bacon

Las legumbres, las verduras o los vegetales

el aguacate   avocado
la alcachofa   artichoke
la cebolla   onion
las espinacas   spinach
los frijoles   kidney beans
los guisantes   peas
las judías verdes   stringbeans
la lechuga   lettuce
la papa   potato
el tomate   tomato
la zanahoria   carrot

Los postres

los caramelos   candy
el flan   baked custard
la gelatina   gelatin
el helado   ice cream
el pastel   pie, pastry
la torta   cake

Las bebidas

el agua (mineral)   (mineral) water
las gaseosas   soda, pop
el jugo   juice
la limonada   lemonade
el refresco   soda
el vino (tinto o blanco)   (red or white) wine

Otros productos

el aceite (de oliva)   (olive) oil
el arroz   rice
el azúcar   sugar
los cereales   cereals
la crema   cream
la ensalada   salad
los huevos   eggs
la mantequilla   butter
la margarina   margarine
el pan   bread
la pimienta   pepper
el queso   cheese
la sal   salt
la tostada   toast

A. Conteste las siguientes preguntas.

1. ¿Qué come usted para el almuerzo? ¿para la comida?
2. ¿Le gusta la carne? ¿Qué clase de carne le gusta más?
3. ¿Le gustan los mariscos? ¿Le gustan más los camarones o la langosta?
4. ¿Le gustan los sándwiches de atún? ¿Los come para el desayuno, el almuerzo o la cena?
5. Imagine que usted va a comer pavo para la comida. ¿Qué legumbres le gusta comer con el pavo?
6. Imagine que usted va a prepararse una ensalada de frutas para el almuerzo. ¿Qué clase de frutas va a poner en la ensalada?
7. ¿Qué bebidas toma usted con el desayuno? ¿con el almuerzo? ¿con la cena?

B. Imagine que usted fue a una comida muy elegante anoche. Identifique las cosas enumeradas sobre la mesa que Ud. se sirve del buffet. Use palabras de esta sección.

C. Pregúntele a un/a compañero/a de clase qué tomó para el desayuno esta mañana. Luego dígale qué tomó usted.

D. Imagínese que usted está a dieta (on a diet). Prepare un menú para el día.

II. Pequeños negocios

In many cities and towns of Spain and Hispanic America people often buy food every day in small stores or markets rather than weekly or biweekly in big supermarkets.

Learn the names of small stores where foods are sold and the names of the people who work in these places. Notice that nouns referring to small stores often end in **-ía,** and nouns referring to employees often end in **-ero** and **-era.**

Negocios
la carnicería   butcher shop
la frutería   fruit shop
la lechería   dairy, creamery
la panadería   bakery
la pastelería   pastry shop
la pescadería   fish market
la tienda de comestibles   grocery store

Empleados (o dueños)
el/la carnicero/a
el/la frutero/a
el/la lechero/a
el/la panadero/a
el/la pastelero/a
el/la pescadero/a
el/la tendero/a

E. Usted está en uno de los negocios mencionados arriba, y necesita comprar algunas cosas. En ese país, $1 US = 100 pesos. Prepare un diálogo apropiado entre usted y un/a empleado/a del negocio. Por ejemplo:

En una frutería
El frutero: ¿En qué puedo servirle?
   Usted: Necesito un kilo de manzanas y medio kilo de uvas.
El frutero: Muy bien, [señor].
   Usted: ¿Cuánto cuestan las manzanas?
El frutero: Cien pesos el kilo.
   Usted: ¿Y las uvas?
El frutero: Ochenta pesos el kilo.

Estructuras útiles
I. Introduction to the subjunctive mood

1. Up to this point you have studied verbs in the indicative mood, which is used when the speaker relates facts or supplies information.

   I *know* that Paul *is* at home at this moment.
   We *returned* home early last night.

2. In this lesson you will begin to study the *subjunctive mood*. In English, only a few subjunctive forms of the verb are left that are clearly different from the indicative forms.

I insist that Paul *be* at home at five o'clock sharp.
My mother wishes that I *were* a better student.

3. In Spanish, the subjunctive mood is used more frequently than in English. It is used most often in dependent **que-**clauses when a speaker attempts to influence someone's actions, expresses emotion, doubt, denial, or uncertainty, or expresses a subjective judgment.

Mi padre prefiere que yo **trabaje,** pero dudo que **pueda** encontrar trabajo.	*My father prefers that I work, but I doubt that I can find work.*
Es necesario que **almorcemos** temprano.	*It is necessary that we eat early.*

II. Present subjunctive forms of **-ar** verbs

1. The present subjunctive forms of regular **-ar** verbs are made up of a stem based on the **yo-**form of the present indicative and a set of endings that have a characteristic vowel **e** in all persons. Note that verbs that end in **-car** and **-gar** change **c** > **qu** and **g** > **gu** in accordance with regular Spanish spelling changes.

hablar		buscar		llegar	
habl	**e**	busqu	**e**	llegu	**e**
habl	**es**	busqu	**es**	llegu	**es**
habl	**e**	busqu	**e**	llegu	**e**
habl	**emos**	busqu	**emos**	llegu	**emos**
habl	**éis**	busqu	**éis**	llegu	**éis**
habl	**en**	busqu	**en**	llegu	**en**

María quiere que yo la **busque.**	*María wants me to look for her.*
Es importante que **llegues** a tiempo.	*It is important that you arrive on time.*

2. Verbs in **-ar** with stem changes **e** > **ie** and **o** > **ue** in the present indicative undergo the same stem-vowel changes in the present subjunctive. Remember that the **z** in **almorzar, comenzar,** and **empezar** changes to **c** before the **e** of the ending in accordance with regular Spanish spelling changes. For examples of common **-ar** verbs with stem-vowel changes **e** > **ie** and **o** > **ue,** see *Lección 8.*

cerrar	encontrar	almorzar
cierre	encuentre	almuerce
cierres	encuentres	almuerces
cierre	encuentre	almuerce
cerremos	encontremos	almorcemos
cerréis	encontréis	almorcéis
cierren	encuentren	almuercen

3. The present subjunctive forms of **dar** and **estar** have the same endings as other **-ar** verbs, but accents occur in the first and third persons singular of **dar** and in all forms except the first person plural of **estar**.

dar	estar
dé	esté
des	estés
dé	esté
demos	estemos
deis	estéis
den	estén

A. Diga que usted quiere que las siguientes personas hagan *(do)* las cosas indicadas.

▶ David busca su cuaderno.   *Quiero que David busque su cuaderno.*

1. Tú compras el periódico.
2. Nosotros terminamos el trabajo hoy.
3. Marta nos espera en el café.
4. Tú y Pablo pagan la cuenta.
5. Josefina me llama por teléfono esta tarde.
6. Tú y Manuel llegan a las dos.

B. Añada *(Add)* el sujeto indicado a cada una de las oraciones siguientes, según el modelo.

▶ Es necesario estudiar   *Es necesario que tú estudies para los exámenes.*
para los exámenes.   *Es necesario que ella estudie para los exámenes.*
(tú, ella)

1. Es difícil trabajar el domingo. (nosotros, tú)
2. Es importante firmar estos papeles. (el jefe, nosotros)
3. Es necesario participar en el festival. (todos, los jóvenes)
4. Es fácil arreglar el asunto. (él, tú y Pepe)
5. Es absurdo comprar un nuevo televisor. (ellos, yo)
6. Es difícil ganar la lotería. (ella, nosotras)

C. Exprese su reacción personal acerca de los siguientes acontecimientos. Empiece cada oración con los verbos **desear, querer, insistir (en), preferir** o **esperar** y use el presente del subjuntivo de los verbos indicados.

▶ Carlos y Carlota **dan** una buena excusa.

[Insisto en que] Carlos y Carlota den una buena excusa.

1. **Piensan** ir al museo.
2. El carro **cuesta** menos de diez mil dólares.
3. **Nieva** todo el día.
4. Ricardo **busca** trabajo.
5. Ustedes **están** en casa a las once.
6. Hoy **llegamos** a clase a tiempo.

III. Uses of the subjunctive

Insisto (en) que Pablo está en casa en este momento.

Insisto (en) que Pablo esté en casa a las cinco en punto.

1. When the verb of the main clause expresses a *desire to influence,* and the subject of the main clause is different from the subject of the dependent clause, the subjunctive must be used in the dependent clause. The following verbs express a desire to influence.

aconsejar   to advise
decir   to say, tell
desear   to desire, want
insistir (en)   to insist (on)
mandar   to order
pedir (i)   to ask for
permitir   to permit

preferir (ie)   to prefer
prohibir   to prohibit, forbid
querer   to want
recomendar (ie)   to recommend
rogar (ue)   to beg
sugerir (ie)   to suggest

Quiero que **tú** me **ayudes.**
Insisto en que **ustedes investiguen** el asunto.

I want you to help me.
I insist that you investigate the matter.

2. When the verb of the main clause expresses an *emotion* or *hope*, the subjunctive is required in the dependent clause. The following verbs express emotion or hope.

alegrarse de   to be glad
enojarse de   to be angry
esperar   to hope
gustar   to like
lamentar   to regret
molestar   to bother

ojalá   (I) hope
sentir (ie)   to regret
sorprender   to surprise
temer   to fear
tener miedo de   to be afraid of

Esperamos que **paguen** las cuentas.

We hope that they pay the bills.

Temo que ellos no **arreglen** el asunto.

I fear that they won't take care of the matter.

3. When the verb in the main clause expresses *doubt, denial,* or *uncertainty,* the subjunctive is required in the dependent clause. However, when the verb in the main clause expresses certainty or a lack of doubt or denial, the indicative is generally used in the dependent clause.

Followed by subjunctive
dudar   negar
no es cierto   no estoy seguro
es dudoso   puede ser

Followed by indicative
no dudar   no negar
es cierto   estoy seguro
es verdad

Dudo que Teresa **esté** en casa ahora.

I doubt Teresa is home now.

No estoy segura de que **regrese** mañana.

I'm not sure he's going to return tomorrow.

But:

No dudo que Teresa **está** en casa. La vi entrar.

I don't doubt Teresa is home. I saw her go in.

Estoy segura de que **regresa** mañana.

I'm sure he's going to return tomorrow.

4. When the verb **creer** is used in the main clause, the speaker's intent determines whether the subjunctive or the indicative is used in the dependent clause.

a. In affirmative sentences, **creer** is usually followed by the indicative.

b. In questions or in negative sentences, if there is doubt on the part of the speaker, the subjunctive is used. If there is certainty on the part of the speaker, the indicative is used.

—Hay muchas nubes y **creo** que **va** a llover. ¿**Cree** usted que **va** a llover? *(opinion: no doubt)*

—No **creo** que **va** a llover. *(opinion: no doubt)*

—Hay muchos problemas en las minas. **¿Cree** Ud. que los mineros
declaren una huelga? *(doubt)*

—No, **no creo** que **declaren** una huelga. *(answer indicates doubt)*

—No estoy de acuerdo. **No creo** que **declaran** una huelga. *(answer does
not indicate doubt)*

5. The following impersonal expressions require the subjunctive in the
dependent clause because they express *a subjective judgment, an emotion,
doubt or uncertainty, denial, or a desire to influence on the part of the speaker.*

es difícil	es importante	es preferible
es dudoso	es (im)posible	es triste
es estupendo	es increíble	es una lástima
es fácil	es mejor	no es cierto
es horrible	es necesario	puede ser

Es mejor que ayudes a Jaime. *It's best for you to help Jaime.*

Es dudoso que pasemos las *It is doubtful (that) we'll spend our*
vacaciones en Colombia.   *vacation in Colombia.*

6. If there is no change in subject, the infinitive construction is used.

Quiero comprar una bicicleta. *(no change in subject)*
Quiero que tú me compres una bicicleta. *(different subjects)*

Es bueno usar la imaginación. *(no change in subject)*
Es bueno que los niños usen la imaginación. *(different subjects)*

D. Diga que usted no quiere que ocurran las siguientes situaciones.

▶ Esa señorita llama a la policía.   *¡No quiero que llame a la policía!*

1. Fernando viaja con cinco maletas.
2. Beatriz compra pollo para la comida todos los días.
3. Los tíos están tristes.
4. Carmen y yo hablamos inglés en la clase de español.
5. Nosotros trabajamos sin ganar dinero.
6. Buscamos más libros en la biblioteca.

E. Usted es una persona extrovertida. Exprese su reacción personal
acerca de los siguientes acontecimientos. Empiece cada oración con
**me alegro de que, me enojo de que, siento que, me parece extraño
(bueno, natural, raro) que, temo que** o **tengo miedo de que** y el
presente del subjuntivo de los verbos.

▶ Rosarito gana el premio.   *[Me alegro de que] Rosarito gane el premio.*

1. Mejoradina mejora los dolores de cabeza.
2. La conferencia dura tres días.

3. Un grupo terrorista secuestra al Dr. Pedro Ayala.
4. Los policías no investigan la situación.
5. El festival mundial de cine causa sensación internacional.
6. La actriz inglesa declara que le encanta Colombia.
7. La etapa de hoy de la Vuelta termina en Medellín.

F. Demuestre esperanza de que los siguientes acontecimientos ocurran. Empiece cada oración con **espero que** u **ojalá (que)** y use el presente del subjuntivo de los verbos indicados.

▶ Pedro no te niega nunca la verdad.   *Espero [Ojalá] que Pedro no te niegue nunca la verdad.*

1. Encontramos la respuesta.
2. Te cuentan algo más interesante esta vez.
3. Ada almuerza con sus amigos en el café.
4. Volamos directamente a Bogotá.
5. Recuerdas la dirección exacta.
6. Encuentran los billetes de la lotería.
7. Mi hermano me presta su carro.

G. Diga si **es necesario (importante, estupendo)** o si **no es necesario (importante, estupendo)** que las siguientes personas hagan las acciones indicadas. Haga oraciones completas.

▶ Jorge piensa estudiar ahora.   *Pues (no) es necesario que estudie ahora.*

1. Yo pienso volar a mi casa esta tarde en el vuelo de las 8:00.
2. Ellos piensan contarnos una historia interesante.
3. Nosotros pensamos cerrar la puerta y las ventanas.
4. Los profesores piensan dar exámenes mañana.
5. Isabel piensa tocar la guitarra y cantar.
6. Esos chicos piensan encontrar a las amigas en el restaurante.

H. Jorge afirma muchas cosas interesantes, pero Pablo no siempre está de acuerdo con Jorge. Haga el papel de Pablo y empiece cada oración con **dudo que** o **no dudo que.** Termine la oración con una razón apropiada.

▶ Jorge: Luisa gana cien dólares   Pablo: *Dudo que gane cien dólares*
        a la semana.   *a la semana [porque parece*
                                           muy rica].

1. Yo me levanto a las seis.
2. Pepe y su mujer compran un Fiat.
3. Mi profesor trabaja en el Ministerio de Industrias.
4. Nadie me llama por teléfono.
5. Mario y Linda bailan en el Club Marino todos los sábados.

6. La hermana de Luis da clases de cerámica.
7. Lucía y Manuel le consultan su futuro a un astrólogo.
8. Tú y yo no necesitamos estudiar.

I. Diga si usted cree que van a ocurrir o no los siguientes acontecimientos. Empiece con **(no) estoy seguro/a de, es verdad, es dudoso,**
o **(no) es cierto** y use el presente del indicativo o del subjuntivo,
según el contexto.

▶ Raúl gana la Vuelta, ¿verdad?   *Estoy seguro de que Raúl la gana.*

1. El presidente viaja a Colombia, ¿no?
2. Ud. compra un nuevo automóvil.
3. Sus padres regresan de Cali.
4. Una amiga lo/la visita este fin de semana.
5. Los alumnos de esta clase están entusiasmados, ¿no?
6. La comisión del festival le da un premio al actor francés, ¿no?
7. Ud. toma un café en la cafetería, ¿verdad?
8. Ud. termina su trabajo de la semana el viernes, ¿no?

J. Haga oraciones con las siguientes frases. Use el presente del indicativo
o del subjuntivo en la cláusula subordinada, según el contexto.

▶ nosotros / creer / mineros   *Creemos que los mineros declaran una*
declarar una huelga   *huelga.*

1. yo / lamentar / el trabajo / no estar listo
2. ¿no creer / tú / ellos / pagar demasiado por ese apartamento?
3. tú / saber / nosotras / siempre viajar en el verano
4. Raquel / pedir / yo / mirar este artículo
5. Carlos / sugerir / Susana / jugar primero
6. ¿es verdad / Fernando / hablar tres idiomas?
7. nosotros / alegrarse de / tú y él / cambiar la fecha de la / reunión
8. yo / pensar / tú / gastar demasiado dinero

IV. Comparisons of inequality

—Estas cataratas son **más altas que**
 las del Niágara.
—Sí, y aquí hay **menos turistas**
 que en el Niágara.

1. Comparisons of inequality of adjectives, adverbs, and nouns are usually expressed in Spanish with the patterns **más ... que** (*more ... than*) and **menos ... que** (*less ... than*).

Caracas es **más** moderna **que** Bogotá.	*Caracas is more modern than Bogotá.*
Este actor es **menos** popular **que** Gloria Valencia.	*This actor is less popular than Gloria Valencia.*
Tú siempre haces todo **más** rápidamente **que** yo.	*You always do everything more quickly than I (do).*
Enrique conduce **menos** cuidadosamente **que** tú.	*Enrique drives less carefully than you (do).*
En Perú hay **más** llamas **que** en Colombia.	*In Peru there are more llamas than in Colombia.*
En general, leo **menos** revistas **que** periódicos.	*In general, I read fewer magazines than newspapers.*

2. Comparisons of inequality of quantity that involve a specified number of items or a specific amount are expressed by the following patterns.

más de + *noun phrase*	*more than* + noun phrase
menos de + *noun phrase*	*less than* / *fewer than* } + noun phrase
Me tomé **más de cuatro aspirinas** y todavía tengo dolor de cabeza.	*I took more than four aspirins and I still have a headache.*
Hay **menos de quince personas** aquí para escuchar al orador.	*There are fewer than fifteen people here to listen to the speaker.*

3. In negative sentences, **no ... más que** usually expresses the idea of *only*.

No puedo darte **más que** dos dólares.	*I can only give you two dollars.*

K. Diga cómo hace la primera persona las siguientes cosas en comparación con la segunda.

▶ David / hablar / claramente / Manuel   *David habla más (menos) claramente que Manuel.*

1. Ángela / escuchar / atentamente / José
2. Felipe / leer / rápidamente / Carmen
3. Pedro / responder / frecuentemente / Antonio
4. Julia / explicar / pacientemente / Paco
5. Félix / escribir / fácilmente / Raquel
6. Rosa / contestar / imaginativamente / Pancho

L. Compare las cosas o personas de cada dibujo. Use **más** o **menos** + la forma apropiada del adjetivo + **que.**

gordo/a   rico/a   nuevo/a
alto/a   moderno/a   bonito/a
viejo/a   pequeño/a   joven

Mónica es más bonita que Marta.
Marta es menos bonita que Mónica.

▶   Mónica   Marta

1.   el Sr. Ruiz   el Sr. Gómez

5.   mi bicicleta   su bicicleta

2.   Dolores   Carmen

6.   estas flores   esas flores

3.   don Ricardo   su hijo

7.   el carro azul   el carro verde

4.   nuestra casa   su casa

8.   doña Matilde   su prima

M. Compare sus propias acciones con las de su mejor amigo/a.

▶   tomar medicina   *Yo tomo menos medicina que [Eduardo].*
                    [Eduardo] toma más medicina que yo.

1. participar en deportes   5. asistir a conciertos
2. mirar televisión   6. ganar premios
3. salir con amigos   7. comer cosas exóticas
4. beber cerveza   8. comprar ropa

N. Compare sus propias acciones con las de las siguientes personas. Use **más de** o **menos de** en sus respuestas.

▶ Susana leyó tres libros el mes pasado.

Pues yo leí más (menos) de tres libros.
Leí [cuatro].

1. Juan les pidió diez dólares a sus padres.
2. Ricardo comió seis huevos para el desayuno.
3. Julia fue al cine seis veces la semana pasada.
4. Marta compró veinte discos el año pasado.
5. Ana y María pasaron dos semanas en La Florida la primavera pasada.
6. Gonzalo escribió diez cartas ayer.

O. Las personas mencionadas quieren comprar las siguientes cosas. Diga que ellos no quieren pagar más del precio indicado. Emplee la expresión **no . . . más que.**

▶ yo / $4 / una comida española

No quiero pagar más que cuatro dólares por una comida española.

1. ellos / $3 / dos pollos
2. tú / $15 / un pavo
3. nosotras / $1 / diez manzanas
4. Miguel / $5 / tres pasteles

Los Arrayanes

Comida criolla
preparada al carbón.
Disfrute un ambiente
tradicional.
Música de cuerda.

¡Exprésese usted!

Descripción de un evento

Cuando usted desea describir un evento, debe concentrarse en los detalles que puedan resultar interesantes para el lector: el **qué**, el **quién**, el **cuándo**, el **cómo** y el **por qué**.

Lea el siguiente artículo y escriba los cuatro o cinco puntos que el corresponsal, Miguel Uribe, posiblemente consideró más importantes al escribirlo.

La noticia del año
Miguel Uribe, corresponsal.
Bogotá, 11 de octubre. Ayer a las tres de la tarde Raúl Tomillo ganó la Vuelta a Colombia en Bicicleta. Raúl, favorito de la Vuelta por su magnífica actuación del año pasado, tuvo un serio accidente antes de llegar a Medellín. Pudo terminar la etapa muy difícilmente, pero los médicos que lo atendieron declararon inmediatamente: «Es obvio que Raúl Tomillo necesita descanso, y es casi seguro que tenga que retirarse de la competencia». Sin embargo, cuando empezó la etapa del día siguiente, Raúl se presentó, con algunas obvias laceraciones, pero en alto estado de espíritu, decidido a ganar el gran evento deportivo.

La Vuelta continuó y todo el país la siguió minuto a minuto en

El ciclismo es el deporte por excelencia de los colombianos. En 1987 el presidente de Colombia dio una condecoración al triunfador colombiano, Lucho (Luis) Herrera, en la Vuelta a España, y declaró fiesta nacional el día del triunfo. ¿Cómo celebran los triunfos deportivos en su pueblo/ciudad?

la televisión, en los periódicos, en los radios transistores que hasta en las regiones más remotas del país informaron al público del progreso diario de los participantes de la Vuelta.

El triunfo de Raúl Tomillo con un escaso margen de un minuto tiene que recordarse para siempre en los anales del deporte colombiano. Es un triunfo personal y un triunfo del espíritu tenaz de competencia de nuestros atletas.

¡Felicitaciones, Raúl! Tu triunfo es nuestro triunfo. Tus laureles son los laureles de Colombia entera.

A. Conteste las siguientes preguntas que resumen la información básica sobre el artículo, basando sus respuestas en las notas que tomó.

1. ¿Por qué es particularmente emocionante (exciting) la Vuelta a Colombia este año?
2. ¿Dónde y cuándo tuvo el accidente Raúl?
3. ¿Qué declararon los médicos?
4. ¿Cómo estaba Raúl al día siguiente?
5. ¿Por qué es obvio que todo el país tiene gran interés en la Vuelta?
6. ¿Cómo considera el autor el triunfo de Raúl?

B. Escriba un artículo imaginario para la revista o periódico de su universidad. Describa un evento deportivo, musical o teatral que ocurrió allí recientemente. Incluya la siguiente información en un máximo de diez oraciones.

1. ¿Quién o quiénes participaron?
2. ¿Qué momentos especiales tuvo?
3. ¿Dónde y cuándo tuvo lugar?
4. ¿Cómo resultó?
5. ¿Por qué es memorable?

Lección 14
En Venezuela

Una carta de Caracas

*Enrique (Quique) Pérez, un joven arquitecto colombiano, está en Caracas,
adonde lo envió su gobierno para estudiar unos proyectos de vivienda del gobierno venezolano. Después de un mes en Venezuela, escribe una carta a su
hermano Miguel, estudiante de la Universidad Nacional de Colombia, para
contarle sus impresiones sobre Caracas.*

Caracas, 15 de marzo

Querido Miguel:

    Por fin encuentro tiempo para escribirte unas líneas, y te aseguro que
estoy «vivito y coleando».° El problema más grande es que, entre el ajetreo
de las reuniones de trabajo, la preparación de informes y un poco de tu-
5 rismo, ¡no paro! Pero no te olvido, ni a papá ni a mamá tampoco.

    Dudo que pueda volver a Bogotá el mes próximo. Es necesario que lea
unos informes del gobierno venezolano sobre el desarrollo urbanístico y
que escriba un informe de todo para la oficina del Ministerio de Desarrollo°
en Bogotá. De todos modos, te doy algunas de mis impresiones de estas
10 primeras semanas en Venezuela.

    La ciudad de Caracas me parece sumamente moderna, aunque tiene
muchos barrios pobres. La industrialización, que es evidente por todas
partes, es más reciente que en Bogotá. La arquitectura me parece buena,

«vivito . . . "alive and kicking"

Ministerio . . . Ministry of
Development

*Los centros comerciales
ultramodernos, con sus negocios,
bares y cafés, son hoy día parte
integral de la ciudad de
Caracas. ¿Qué elementos de la
vida diaria moderna espera Ud.
encontrar en una ciudad como
Caracas?*

pero la de Bogotá es mejor, en mi opinión. Puede ser prejuicio personal,
15 pero me parece que Bogotá tiene uno de los mejores estilos urbanísticos del
hemisferio.

La semana pasada tus amigos Luis y Rosa Pinzón me recibieron muy
gentilmente en su casa. Con ellos fui a visitar varios sitios de interés en los
alrededores de la capital, como el puerto de La Guaira y Macuto. De ca-
20 mino, pude ver las famosas autopistas que nuestros ingenieros civiles estiman tanto, y balnearios y magníficas playas venezolanas. Quizás pueda
practicar mi pasatiempo favorito: la natación.

Tengo muchas ganas de conocer la vida del llano venezolano ahora, y
es posible que tenga la oportunidad de ir este fin de semana. Los Pinzón
25 tienen una hacienda de ganado cerca de San Carlos, y me invitaron a hacer
el viaje con ellos. Espero que pueda montar a caballo y comer ternera a la
llanera° al estilo venezolano. Me dicen que es fabulosa.

Por favor, le das mis saludos a Pilar. Todavía sales con ella, ¿verdad?
Debes mantenerme al tanto porque ¡no quiero llegar a Bogotá y encontrarte
30 casado y con hijos!

Te abraza tu hermano,

Quique

ternera . . . veal roasted on a spit

Comprensión

1. Explique quién es Enrique Pérez y por qué está en Caracas.
2. ¿A quién le escribe la carta? ¿Por qué le escribe?
3. ¿Qué tipo de carta escribe? ¿Es una carta comercial? ¿personal? ¿amistosa? ¿íntima?
4. ¿Por qué duda Enrique que pueda volver a Bogotá el mes próximo?
5. ¿Cómo es Caracas, según Enrique? ¿Le impresiona la ciudad? ¿En qué
   aspectos prefiere él a Caracas? ¿a Bogotá?
6. ¿Quiénes son los Pinzón? ¿Qué lugares en los alrededores de Caracas
   visitó Enrique con ellos?
7. ¿Qué piensa hacer Enrique este fin de semana? ¿Con quiénes va?
8. ¿Quién es Pilar? ¿Qué quiere saber Enrique de ella?
9. ¿Es «Quique» un nombre de pila, un apodo o un apellido?

Conversación

1. ¿Hay autopistas grandes en los alrededores de su ciudad o pueblo? ¿Le
   gusta conducir por las autopistas o prefiere conducir por las calles más
   tranquilas?

2. ¿Qué ciudad moderna o antigua conoce usted en los Estados Unidos? ¿Prefiere usted la arquitectura moderna o la antigua?
3. ¿Tiene usted hermanos o hermanas? ¿Les escribe cartas? ¿frecuentemente? ¿raras veces? ¿una vez al mes o a la semana?
4. ¿Escribe usted cartas íntimas o sólo cosas de interés general a su familia? ¿A quién más le escribe usted cartas con frecuencia?
5. Cuando usted viaja a otra ciudad o país, ¿le gusta visitar lugares turísticos o prefiere visitar amigos y parientes? ¿por qué?

Vocabulario

Palabras análogas

el/la arquitecto/a	la impresión	moderno, -a
la arquitectura	la industrialización	la oportunidad
el aspecto	íntimo, -a	personal
el estilo	invitar	la preparación
estimar	la línea	reciente
evidente	magnífico, -a	turístico, -a
famoso, -a		

Sustantivos

el ajetreo   hustle and bustle
los alrededores   outskirts
la autopista   high-speed highway
el balneario   bathing resort
la carta   letter
el ganado   cattle
la hacienda   ranch
el informe   report
el ingeniero civil   civil engineer
el llano   plain
el pasatiempo   hobby
el prejuicio   bias, prejudice
el saludo   greeting

Adjetivos

amistoso, -a   friendly
antiguo, -a   ancient, old
urbanístico, -a   referring to the city

Verbos

abrazar   to hug, embrace
conducir (zc)   to drive
enviar   to send
explicar   to explain

mantener *(irreg.)*   to maintain, keep
olvidar(se) (de)   to forget (about)
parar   to stop

Otras palabras y expresiones

al tanto   up to date
aunque   although
con frecuencia   frequently
de camino   on the way
de todos modos   at any rate, anyway
el fin de semana   weekend
gentilmente   kindly
montar a caballo   to ride horseback
por fin   finally
por todas partes   everywhere
proyectos de vivienda   housing projects
quizás   perhaps
sumamente   very
tener ganas (de)   to want, feel like
todavía   still

Práctica

A. Entreviste a otra persona de la clase sobre un viaje que hizo recientemente. Haga cinco o seis preguntas sobre el lugar que visitó, cuánto
tiempo permaneció allí, cómo fue, qué vio y cuándo regresó.

B. Imagínese que usted está en Caracas o en otra ciudad hispánica para
pasar el fin de semana. Escriba una tarjeta postal a un/a compañero/a
de clase, y cuente lo que hizo el sábado o el domingo. Lea la tarjeta a la
clase.

Nota cultural La arquitectura en Caracas

Caracas, la capital de Venezuela, es un ejemplo notable de ciudad en desarrollo, en la que se mezclan[1] los estilos arquitectónicos de siglos pasados con
las construcciones modernas. En el centro antiguo de la ciudad está la
Plaza Bolívar, cuyo[2] nombre rinde homenaje[3] al héroe de la independencia
venezolana. Alrededor de la plaza están la Catedral, de estilo colonial,
construida en el siglo XVI, y la Casa Amarilla, antigua residencia presidencial y ahora Ministerio de Relaciones Exteriores.[4]

1. **se** . . . are mixed   2. whose   3. **rinde** . . . pays homage   4. **Ministerio** . . .
Ministry of Foreign Affairs

*La casa natal de Simón Bolívar
en Caracas es de gran interés
histórico para los suramericanos,
que veneran su memoria. ¿Sabe
Ud. quién es Simón Bolívar?
¿Cuál país lleva el nombre de
este héroe famoso? Encuentre
Ud. información sobre la vida de
este fascinante héroe de la
independencia de gran parte de
Suramérica.*

La ciudad moderna se ha desplegado[5] en torno al[6] centro antiguo y se caracteriza por sus rascacielos,[7] estructuras ultramodernas, centros comerciales y amplias[8] avenidas y autopistas.

Entre los edificios modernos se destacan[9] las torres gemelas[10] del Centro Simón Bolívar, centro comercial y sede de muchas oficinas de gobierno.

_____

5. **se** ... has spread out   6. **en** ... around the   7. skyscrapers   8. wide
9. **se** ... stand out   10. **torres** ... twin towers

Pronunciación y ortografía
Los sonidos [g] y [ǥ]

The strong Spanish [g], as in **gané,** is similar to the hard [g] in *go*. It occurs after a pause and after [n]. The soft Spanish [ǥ], as in **amigo,** is similar to the [g] in *egg* (that is, without a complete closure at the velum.). It occurs after a vowel and (depending on the regional variation) after consonant sounds other than [n].

Both [g] and [ǥ] are spelled **g** before **a, o,** and **u**. Since g before **e** or **i** is pronounced like [h], the strong [g] and soft [ǥ] sounds are represented by the spelling **gu** before the letters **e** and **i**. The sounds [gwe] and [gwi] are spelled **güe** and **güi** respectively.

A. Escuche y repita las siguientes oraciones leídas por su profesor/a. Cada oración tiene los sonidos [g] o [ǥ].

[g]	[ǥ]
Gano mucho.	Te aseguro que sí.
Guillermo está aquí.	Hay mucho ganado.
Tengo dos pesetas.	Es la ciudad de Bogotá.
Es un grupo terrorista.	Apagué el radio.
María es bilingüe.	Él es muy elegante.

B. Complete este verso de una canción colombiana tradicional con las siguientes palabras. Después, léalo en voz alta.

llegar   Magdalena
Bogotá   tengo
aguas

_____ que subir,° subir   to go up
las _____ del _____
pa'° _____ a _____   = **para**
¡y besar° a mi morena!   to kiss

C. Lea las siguientes oraciones en voz alta. Ponga atención especial a la pronunciación de las palabras con **g** o **gu.**

1. Me gusta mucho la ciudad de Bogotá.
2. Tengo ganas de ir a Aragón.
3. Llegué a Santiago en agosto.
4. El lago de Nicaragua es magnífico.

Estudio de palabras

I. Plano de una casa

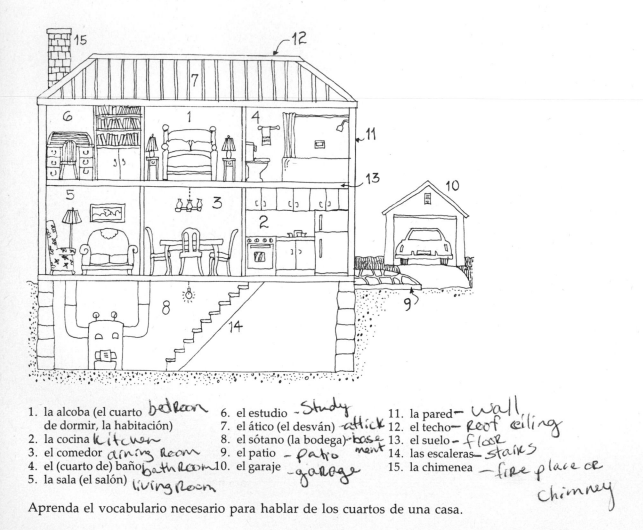

1. la alcoba (el cuarto ~~bedroom~~ de dormir, la habitación)
2. la cocina ~~kitchen~~
3. el comedor ~~dining Room~~
4. el (cuarto de) baño ~~bathroom~~
5. la sala (el salón) ~~living Room~~
6. el estudio – ~~study~~
7. el ático (el desván) ~~attick~~
8. el sótano (la bodega) ~~basement~~
9. el patio – ~~patio~~
10. el garaje – ~~garage~~
11. la pared– ~~wall~~
12. el techo– ~~Roof ceiling~~
13. el suelo– ~~floor~~
14. las escaleras– ~~stairs~~
15. la chimenea – ~~fire place or chimney~~

Aprenda el vocabulario necesario para hablar de los cuartos de una casa.

A. Imagine que uno/a de sus compañeros/as de clase es dueño/a *(owner)* de una casa. Pregúntele acerca de su casa.

1. ¿Cuántos cuartos tiene la casa? ¿cuántos pisos?
2. ¿En qué cuarto de la casa cocina? ¿En qué cuarto duerme? ¿mira la televisión? ¿se baña?
3. ¿En qué piso de la casa está la sala? ¿la cocina? ¿el comedor? ¿las alcobas?
4. ¿Cómo es la sala, grande o pequeña? ¿y los otros cuartos de la casa?
5. ¿Tiene garaje la casa? ¿Para cuántos coches hay lugar?
6. ¿Tiene patio la casa? ¿Es grande o pequeño? ¿Tiene flores *(flowers)* y plantas?
7. ¿Tiene chimenea la casa? ¿sótano? ¿ático? ¿Dónde se guardan *(keep)* las cosas que no se usan cada día?

su gran OPORTUNIDAD

lo tienen todo

de 1 a 5 dormitorios con calidades de primera, chimenea, energía solar

B. Usted quiere alquilar *(rent)* su apartamento a estudiantes hispanoha-blantes. Prepare una tarjeta para poner en el tablero *(bulletin board)* de la cafetería, en la que describe el apartamento y el precio del alquiler.

> Cuatro dormitorios, dos baños, aseo, salón con chimenea, comedor, cocina, garaje para dos coches

II. Preposiciones compuestas

In Spanish, as in English, prepositions are used to indicate the relationship in time or in space of a person, place, or thing to another person, place, or thing. Here is a list of frequently used compound prepositions (prepositions consisting of more than one word).

a la derecha de to the right of
a la izquierda de to the left of
al lado de next to, beside
cerca de near
debajo de under, below
delante de in front of

dentro de within
detrás de behind
encima de above, over
enfrente de facing, opposite
fuera de outside of
lejos de far from

C. Imagínese que usted tiene que darle instrucciones a un estudiante nuevo sobre cómo llegar a diversos lugares en la universidad. Dígale dónde están lugares como la biblioteca, la cafetería, la oficina del rector, el teatro, el gimnasio, las canchas de tenis, etcétera.

▶ *Los dormitorios están enfrente [del gimnasio].*

D. Esta señora necesita algunas cosas y las busca en la tienda de comestibles que está cerca de su casa. Mire el dibujo y describa la posición de por lo menos cinco objetos con relación a otros cinco objetos.

Estructuras útiles

I. Present subjunctive of **-er** and **-ir** verbs

1. The present subjunctive forms of most **-er** and **-ir** verbs are made up of a stem based on the **yo**-form of the present indicative and a set of endings that have a characteristic vowel **a** in *all* persons.

comer		vivir	
com	**a**	viv	**a**
com	**as**	viv	**as**
com	**a**	viv	**a**
com	**amos**	viv	**amos**
~~com~~	~~**áis**~~	~~viv~~	~~**áis**~~
com	**an**	viv	**an**

2. Verbs in **-er** with stem-vowel changes **e > ie** or **o > ue** in the present indicative undergo the same stem-vowel change in the present subjunctive. For examples of common **-er** verbs with stem-vowel changes **e > ie** or **o > ue,** see pages 150 and 152.

entender (e > ie)		volver (o > ue)	
entiend	a	vuelv	a
entiend	as	vuelv	as
entiend	a	vuelv	a
entend	amos	volv	amos
~~entend~~	~~áis~~	~~volv~~	~~áis~~
entiend	an	vuelv	an

3. Verbs in **-ir** with stem-vowel changes **e > ie, e > i,** or **o > ue** in the present indicative undergo the same stem-vowel changes in the present subjunctive. For examples of common **-ir** verbs with stem-vowel changes **e > ie, e > i,** and **o > ue**, see pages 150, 167, and 152, respectively.

Unlike their corresponding forms in the present indicative, these verbs have an additional stem-vowel change in the **nosotros-** and **vosotros-**forms of the subjunctive.

preferir (e > ie)		pedir (e > i)		dormir (o > ue)	
prefier	a	pid	a	duerm	a
prefier	as	pid	as	duerm	as
prefier	a	pid	a	duerm	a
prefir	amos	pid	amos	durm	amos
~~prefir~~	~~áis~~	pid	áis	~~durm~~	~~áis~~
prefier	an	pid	an	duerm	an

Don't learn Vosotros form (handwritten)

A. Las siguientes personas van a hacer varias actividades. Pregúntele a alguien de la clase si quiere que otras personas también participen en estas actividades.

▶ Susana va a comer en casa. (yo, ellos)   *¿Quieres que yo también coma en casa?*
¿Quieres que ellos también coman en casa?

1. Lucho va a leer el periódico. (Tomás y yo, Beto)
2. Quique va a discutir los problemas contigo. (Luisa, yo)
3. Anita va a aprender chino. (ellas, tú y yo)
4. Maricarmen va a asistir al ballet. (Mario y Pepe, Lucha)
5. Raúl va a vender revistas. (nosotros, Marta y Jorge)
6. Tomás y yo vamos a comer comida mexicana. (Fernando, tú y yo)

B. Complete las siguientes oraciones lógicamente. Use el presente del subjuntivo de los verbos entre paréntesis. Si puede, explique su afirmación (statement).

▶ (correr) Me gusta que (tú) . . . .   *Me gusta que (tú) corras todos los días. El ejercicio es bueno.*

1. (sentirse) Quiero que usted . . . .
2. (sufrir) Temo que mi hermano mayor . . . .
3. (comprender) Me alegro de que tú . . . .
4. (beber) Dudo que mis amigos . . . .
5. (divertirse) Es posible que nosotros . . . .
6. (decidir) No es probable que mis parientes . . . .
7. (pedir) Espero que mi mejor amigo . . . .
8. (responder) Ojalá que el presidente . . . .

C. Complete las siguientes oraciones lógicamente. Use el presente del subjuntivo de los verbos de la lista.

encender	mentir	conseguir	dormir
entender	repetir	despedir	morir
volver	seguir	reír	servir

1. ¡Es increíble que tus padres . . . !
2. Me enojo de que mi hermano mayor . . . .
3. Es mejor que el profesor . . . .
4. No estoy segura de que la señora Gutiérrez . . . .
5. Es una lástima que Lucha y tú . . . .
6. ¡Es horrible que ese muchacho . . . !
7. Tengo miedo de que mi prima . . . .
8. Me alegro de que esa niña . . . .

II. Uses of the present subjunctive

Le recomiendo que no vaya muy lejos en ese carro . . . .

Here are some examples showing the present subjunctive of **-er** and **-ir** verbs in dependent clauses grouped according to the main uses of the subjunctive. For further details concerning the uses of the present subjunctive, see *Lección 13*, pages 244–246.

1. *Desire to influence:* ¡Es mejor que tú **comas** las espinacas!
2. *Emotion or hope:* Me alegro de que me **escriba** una vez al mes.
3. *Doubt, denial, uncertainty:* Dudamos que nos **comprendan.**

D. Recomiende lo que deben hacer las personas indicadas. Use verbos y expresiones como **recomiendo que, prohibo que, sugiero que, pido que** y **aconsejo que.**

► Esos jóvenes no leen nada.   *[Sugiero que] esos jóvenes lean mucho.*

1. Ese chico no duerme ocho horas al día.
2. Mis padres no me escriben mucho.
3. Tú prometes más de lo que puedes hacer.
4. Siempre respondemos mal a las preguntas.
5. Miguel y yo no corremos todos los días.
6. Mi hermano de 10 años no aprende sus lecciones.
7. Nunca comemos a mediodia.
8. No vuelve usted a tiempo con sus compañeros a clase.

E. Trate de influir en el comportamiento *(behavior)* de alguien, usando verbos y expresiones como **quiero que, deseo que, insisto en que, prefiero que, es necesario que, es importante que.**

► Creo que no voy a reunirme con   *[Quiero que] te reúnas con*
ustedes ahora.   *nosotros inmediatamente.*

1. Voy a encender todas las luces de la casa.
2. Pensamos elegir al mismo presidente en las elecciones próximas.
3. Mi papá piensa dormir ahora.
4. Pablo y yo esperamos conseguir entradas económicas para el concierto.
5. Ellos dicen que no van a despedirse de Josefina esta tarde.
6. Voy a mentirles a mis padres acerca de la fiesta.

F. Su amiga Consuelo habla de lo que varios amigos y parientes quieren hacer. Comente sobre sus preferencias y ofrezca una alternativa.

► Jorge desea vivir en Ciudad   *No es bueno que viva en Ciudad de*
de México.   *México. Es mejor que viva en [Guadalajara] porque hay menos tránsito.*

1. Luz no piensa asistir a la universidad este año.
2. Elena y Fernando quieren pedir trabajo en Santiago.

3. Yo espero conseguir tres coches nuevos.
4. Mi prima Alicia y yo deseamos vender carros.
5. Mi cuñado espera vivir en Bogotá.
6. Mi suegra quiere volver a Panamá.

G. Suponga que usted es padre o madre de una familia numerosa.
Exprese la esperanza (**espero que . . .**), la duda (**no creo que . . . , dudo
que . . .**) o la certeza (**estoy seguro/a de que . . .**) que sus hijos hagan
ciertas cosas. Use su imaginación y algunos de los siguientes verbos.

dormir	mentir	servir	volver
seguir	vivir	encender	repetir

▶ *Carlos, estoy seguro/a que duermes muy poco. Dudo que estudies en la
biblioteca hasta las tres de la mañana. Espero que tus amigos . . .*

H. Complete las siguientes oraciones con la forma apropiada de los
verbos indicados. Use el presente del indicativo o subjuntivo, según el
contexto.

1. (aprender, querer) Creo que tú no _____ venir porque no te gusta
bailar. Te aconsejo que _____ a bailar y así vas a divertirte más.
2. (querer, poder) Es verdad que Laura _____ tocar el piano, pero
no creo que _____ dedicarse a la música.
3. (poder, beber) Es una lástima que nadie _____ traer los refrescos
a la fiesta. Yo no tengo carro, y ¡temo que finalmente (nosotros)
no _____ nada!
4. (reír, querer) Es obvio que todo el mundo se _____ con ese
programa de televisión. Me sorprende que tú no _____ verlo esta
noche.
5. (comprender, hablar) No creo que él _____ inglés, pero es
posible que (él) _____ un poco el ruso.

III. Superlative of adjectives

1. The superlative of adjectives is usually expressed with the following
patterns. Note that after the superlative construction, **de** is used to
express *in* or *of*.

el (la, etc.) más + adjetivo	*the most* + adjective *the* + an adjective ending in *-est*
el (la, etc.) menos + adjetivo	*the least* + adjective
Enrique es **el más inteligente** de la clase.	*Enrique is the most intelligent (one) in the class.*
Margarita es **la menos imaginativa** de todas.	*Margarita is the least imaginative (one) of all.*

2. If the superlative construction includes a noun, the noun immediately
   follows the definite article in Spanish.

   Raúl es **el muchacho más alto**
     del grupo.
   Raúl is the tallest boy in the group.

   Ésas son **las iglesias más
   bonitas** de la ciudad.
   *Those are the most beautiful
   churches in the city.*

I. Comente sobre las cualidades de los siguientes sitios. Use el superlativo del adjetivo.

▶ Esa hacienda es más atractiva
que la otra, ¿verdad?
*Sí, es la hacienda más atractiva de
todas.*

1. Esos edificios son más altos que éstos, ¿no?
2. Esa entrevista fue más interesante que las otras, ¿no es verdad?
3. Este puerto es más moderno que el otro, ¿no crees?
4. Estos restaurantes son más caros que los otros, ¿no?
5. Esta huelga fue más larga que aquélla, ¿no te parece?
6. Este barrio es más exclusivo que los otros, ¿verdad?

J. Usted quiere comentar sobre las siguientes afirmaciones. Use el superlativo del adjetivo y los sustantivos indicados.

▶ Muchos productos de Venezuela
son importantes. (el petróleo)
*Sí, pero el petróleo es el producto
más importante de todos.*

1. La mayoría de los países centroamericanos son pequeños. (El Salvador)
2. Algunas ciudades de Venezuela son modernas. (Caracas)
3. Muchos ríos de Suramérica son largos. (el Amazonas)
4. Todas las minas de Colombia son importantes. (las minas de esmeraldas)
5. Hay muchas montañas altas en Chile. (el Aconcagua)
6. Hay algunas universidades antiguas en Perú. (Universidad de San Marcos)

K. ¿Qué o quién considera Ud. superior dentro de las siguientes categorías?

▶ escritor *Para mí Shakespeare es el escritor más [importante de
Inglaterra].*

1. actriz
2. actor
3. tipo de comida
4. deportista
5. cantante
6. grupo musical
7. programa de televisión
8. estación del año

IV. Irregular comparatives and superlatives

*¿Es esta manzana **más buena** que
la otra? Sí, es mucho **mejor**.*

1. The adjectives **bueno, malo, grande,** and **pequeño** have both regular
   and irregular comparative and superlative forms.

Adjectives	Comparative	Superlative
bueno	más bueno/a mejor	el/la más bueno/a el/la mejor
malo	más malo/a peor	el/la más malo/a el/la peor
grande	más grande mayor	el/la más grande el/la mayor
pequeño	más pequeño/a menor	el/la más pequeño/a el/la menor

Estas manzanas son $\begin{cases} \textbf{mejores} \\ \textbf{más buenas} \end{cases}$ que ésas.   *These apples are
better than those.*

Ese durazno es $\begin{cases} \textbf{el mejor} \\ \textbf{el más bueno} \end{cases}$ de todos.   *That peach is the best
one of all.*

2. **Mejor (el mejor)** and **peor (el peor),** which are generally used in the
   sense of *better (best)* and *worse (worst),* refer to quality; **más bueno** and
   más malo usually refer to taste.

Este automóvil es **mejor** que aquél.	*This car is better than that one.*
La cosa **más barata** es a veces **la peor.**	*The cheapest thing is sometimes the worst.*
Los postres son **más buenos** que las verduras.	*Desserts are better (-tasting) than vegetables.*
Esta medicina es **más mala** que el vinagre.	*This medicine is worse (-tasting) than vinegar.*

3. **Mayor (el mayor)** and **menor (el menor)** generally refer to age; **más grande** and **más pequeño** usually refer to size.

Alicia es **mayor** que yo, pero es **más pequeña.**
Alicia is older than I (am), but she's smaller.

Tú eres **el menor** del grupo.
You are the youngest (boy) in the group.

4. The adverbs **bien, mal, mucho,** and **poco** have irregular comparative forms. They have no superlative forms.

Adverbs	Comparative
bien well	**mejor** better
mal badly	**peor** worse
mucho much	**más** more
poco little	**menos** less

Manuel canta **bien,** pero Ramona canta **mejor** que Manuel.
Manuel sings well, but Ramona sings better than Manuel.

David escribe **mal** en español, pero tú escribes **peor.**
David writes poorly in Spanish, but you write worse.

L. Julio y Alicia comparan varias cosas. Haga el papel de Julio o el de Alicia, y use las formas irregulares de **bueno** y de **malo.**

▶ tren / avión   Julio: *Viajar en tren es mejor (peor) que viajar en avión.*
                  Alicia: *No, viajar en tren es peor (mejor) que viajar en avión.*

1. la música clásica / la música moderna
2. las novelas españolas / las novelas inglesas
3. los sándwiches de jamón / los sándwiches de pollo
4. las novelas de misterio / las novelas de aventuras
5. los automóviles japoneses / los automóviles alemanes
6. la arquitectura moderna / la arquitectura tradicional

M. Ricardo y Victoria comparan varios sitios en un mapa. Haga el papel de Ricardo o de Victoria, y use las formas regulares o irregulares de **grande** y de **pequeño.** Verifique las respuestas en los mapas de las tapas *(covers)* del libro.

▶ Bogotá / Ciudad de México   Ricardo: *Bogotá es más grande (mayor) que Ciudad de México.*
                              Victoria: *No, Bogotá es más pequeña (menor) que Ciudad de México.*

1. Ciudad de México / Mérida
2. Guatemala / Colombia

3. el Río Amazonas / el Río Negro
4. el Lago Izabal / el Lago de Nicaragua
5. la isla de Cuba / la isla de Puerto Rico
6. Portugal / España
7. El Mar Caribe / el Golfo de México

N. Diga quién es mayor o menor entre las personas mencionadas.

▶ Paco tiene catorce años; Luisa tiene quince.   *Paco es menor que Luisa. Luisa es mayor que Paco.*

1. El señor Gómez tiene ochenta años; su esposa tiene noventa.
2. El hermano de Jorge tiene veintiún años; el hermano de Luisa tiene treinta.
3. María Concepción tiene doce años; María de Lourdes tiene diecisiete; y María Isabel tiene once años.
4. Mi marido tiene treinta y ocho años; yo tengo veintiocho años.
5. La doctora Díaz tiene cuarenta años; su hijo Enrique tiene diez; y su hija Linda tiene diecinueve.
6. Todos nosotros tenemos veinticinco años; todos ustedes tienen veinticuatro años.

O. Compare lo que hace Lupita con lo que hace Miguel.

▶ cantar: ¿bien o mal?   *Lupita canta bien, pero Miguel canta mejor (que Lupita).*

1. nadar: ¿mucho o poco?
2. cocinar: ¿bien o mal?
3. dormir en clase: ¿mucho o poco?
4. escribir en español: ¿mucho o poco?
5. conducir: ¿bien o mal?
6. viajar: ¿mucho o poco?

P. Dé su opinión acerca de qué cosas tienen buen sabor y qué cosas son mejores para la salud *(health)*.

▶ las verduras / los postres   *Para mí los postres son más buenos que las verduras, pero las verduras son mejores para la salud.*

1. los caramelos / el arroz
2. la carne / las verduras
3. el pan / las tortas
4. los helados / la carne
5. los refrescos / los jugos de fruta
6. el pollo / el pescado
7. los huevos / la sopa
8. la leche / el vino

¡Exprésese usted!

El resumen

El primer paso al hacer un resumen escrito u oral es tomar notas en sus propias palabras de los puntos más importantes de la lectura. Se deben citar *(quote)* sólo aquellas frases de la lectura que usted piense usar luego para apoyar *(support)* esos puntos principales.

Lea la siguiente selección sobre la importancia del petróleo en Venezuela, y tome nota en sus propias palabras de los seis o siete puntos más importantes de la selección.

Venezuela y el petróleo

El petróleo forma la base de la economía venezolana desde los años 60. Venezuela paga la importación de la gran mayoría de los productos manufacturados necesarios para la vida económica del país con las ventas de petróleo en Europa y en los Estados Unidos.

Durante los años 60, el gobierno del presidente Rafael Caldera comenzó a nacionalizar las compañías de petróleo para establecer una base industrial totalmente venezolana. También durante los 60, el gran político venezolano Juan Pablo Pérez Alfonzo promovió la fundación de la OPEP (Organización de Países Exportadores de Petróleo), conocida internacionalmente como OPEC. Esta organización trató de controlar los precios mundiales del petróleo y de proteger los intereses de sus miembros. Aunque varias crisis internacionales durante la década de los 70 y a principios de los 80 causaron mucha fluctuación en los precios mundiales del petróleo, la participación de Venezuela en la OPEP benefició grandemente al país.

Venezuela terminó de nacionalizar las compañías petroleras en los años 70, pero no llegó a diversificar mucho la producción industrial del país y hoy día sigue dependiente de los países más industrializados para maquinaria, automóviles y otros productos manufacturados importantes. Sin em-

LA OPEP Y AMÉRICA LATINA

OPEP y el Tercer Mundo
Otro milagro del petróleo

bargo, gracias a la exportación del petróleo, Venezuela tiene la renta per cápita más alta de Hispanoamérica, según los censos de 1978 a 1982. Si consigue hacerse más autosuficiente con la diversificación de su economía, puede llegar a ser uno de los países más prósperos del mundo.

A. Escriba un resumen de la lectura sobre la importancia del petróleo en Venezuela. Use los apuntes que Ud. tomó para resumir los puntos siguientes.

  1. ¿Cuándo empezó la nacionalización del petróleo en Venezuela?
  2. ¿Para qué nacionalizó Venezuela la producción de petróleo?
  3. ¿Quién participó en la fundación de la OPEP?
  4. ¿Qué trató de hacer la OPEP y qué efectos tuvo en la economía venezolana?
  5. ¿Cuál es la situación actual (presente) de la producción industrial venezolana?
  6. ¿Qué posible futuro tiene Venezuela?

B. Escriba dos citas (quotations) de la selección que posiblemente puedan apoyar (support) su resumen sobre la importancia del petróleo en Venezuela.

El petróleo creó en Venezuela una prosperidad inimaginable, pero esa prosperidad no llegó por igual a todos los sectores de la población. Por eso existen contrastes de riqueza y miseria como los que vemos en esta fotografía de la capital venezolana. ¿Qué soluciones sugiere Ud. para aliviar este terrible problema?

Lección 15
En Panamá

Los indios cunas

Los indios cunas viven a lo largo de la costa oriental de Panamá y en las numerosas islas de San Blas en el Caribe. Hablan una lengua derivada del chibcha, la lengua extinta de los antiguos pobladores° de la región central inhabitants de Colombia. Lo interesante es que poco a poco los indios cunas aceptan la
5 lengua española para comunicarse con el mundo exterior en un tipo de bilingüismo.

Los indios cunas, que viven en pequeñas aldeas° bajo el mando de un villages jefe, se sienten muy orgullosos de sus costumbres y tradiciones. Para ser jefe es necesario que un hombre conozca muy bien todas las tradiciones de
10 la tribu y que sea de una familia poderosa.

Aunque la pesca es la base de la economía, los cunas también cultivan plátanos, maíz, caña de azúcar, cacao y cocos. Usan los cocos como dinero entre sí, pero usan y exigen dinero panameño para comerciar con otra

Observe la apariencia de estos jóvenes indios cunas que viven en las islas de San Blas, Panamá, y los instrumentos musicales que tocan. ¿Puede distinguir entre los muchachos y muchachas? ¿Por qué? ¿Qué instrumentos musicales tocan?

gente. Son excelentes artesanos: tallan° madera, hacen canastas y tejen° they carve/weave
15 hamacas. Las mujeres cunas, además de preparar otras piezas de artesanía,
hacen encajes° y molas. La palabra "mola" quiere decir *blusa*, pero en ge- laces
neral, se refiere al tipo de tela multicolor que representa pájaros, reptiles,
plantas y símbolos religiosos indios y cristianos. Las molas que hacen para
la venta no son tan delicadas ni tan bien trabajadas° como las propias, pero done
20 a los turistas y a los coleccionistas de arte de todo el mundo les encantan.

La mujer cuna desempeña un papel importante en esta sociedad matriarcal, porque la herencia y la posición social de una persona dependen de
la descendencia por línea materna. Al casarse es necesario que el hombre
vaya a vivir con la familia de su esposa y que trabaje para el padre de ella.
25 Sin embargo, en la vida política y social, las mujeres no ejercen tanta autoridad como los hombres.

En los últimos años la civilización occidental rompe poco a poco el ais-
lamiento° cultural de los cunas. Las ocasiones en que los cunas se ven más isolation
expuestos a la introducción de costumbres y valores ajenos a los suyos° son theirs
30 cuando los hombres trabajan por dinero en el istmo,° cuando las mujeres Isthmus (Panama)
cunas van a Ciudad de Panamá para vender sus molas, y cuando los frecuentes visitantes de otros países van a las islas de San Blas. En otras palabras, las necesidades económicas y el deseo de mejorar su nivel de vida
causan un impacto y cambios al sistema tradicional de valores de esta tribu.

Comprensión

1. ¿Dónde viven los cunas?
2. ¿Qué lenguas hablan estos indios?
3. ¿Qué es necesario saber para ser jefe?
4. ¿Cuáles son algunos productos que cultivan los cunas?
5. Mencione algunos productos de artesanía de los cunas.
6. Describa la mola cuna.
7. ¿Qué papel importante desempeña la mujer en la sociedad cuna?
8. ¿A qué se debe el cambio de valores tradicionales entre los cunas?

Conversación

1. ¿Le interesa a usted la vida de los cunas? ¿por qué sí o por qué no?
2. Desde su punto de vista, ¿por qué es bueno o malo que los indios
   cunas cambien sus valores?
3. ¿Quiere usted mejorar su propio nivel de vida? ¿por qué sí o por qué no?
4. Si usted mejora su nivel de vida, ¿van a sufrir algún cambio sus
   valores? Explique su opinión.
5. Identifique algunas cosas que causan un impacto en su nivel de vida
   (por ejemplo, el barrio donde usted vive).

Vocabulario

Palabras análogas

aceptar
la autoridad
el bilingüismo
la civilización
comunicarse (con)
cristiano, -a
cultivar
delicado, -a
depender (de)

derivado, -a
excelente
extinto, -a
la hamaca
identificar
el impacto
la introducción
materno, -a

matriarcal
multicolor
numeroso, -a
la ocasión
la planta
político, -a
la posición
preparar

religioso, -a
representar
el reptil
el sistema
social
la sociedad
la tradición
tradicional

Sustantivos

la **artesanía**   artisanry
el/la **artesano/a**   artisan
la **base**   basis
el **cacao**   cocoa (bean)
el **cambio**   change
la **canasta**   basket
la **caña de azúcar**   sugar cane
el **coco**   coconut
el/la **coleccionista**   collector
la **costumbre**   custom
la **descendencia**   ancestry, lineage
el **deseo**   desire, wish
la **herencia**   inheritance
la **madera**   wood
el **maíz**   corn
el **mando**   command
la **necesidad**   need, necessity
el **papel**   role
la **pesca**   fishing
la **pieza**   piece
el **plátano**   plantain
el **punto de vista**   point of view
el **símbolo**   symbol
la **tela**   cloth
la **tribu**   tribe
el **valor**   value
la **venta**   sale
el/la **visitante**   visitor

Adjetivos

exterior   outside, exterior
orgulloso, -a   proud
oriental   eastern

poderoso, -a   powerful
propio, -a   one's (their) own
último, -a   last

Verbos

casarse   to marry
comerciar   to trade
desempeñar   to play (a role)
ejercer   to exercise (one's rights); to practice (a profession)
referirse (ie) a   to refer to
romper   to break

Otras palabras y expresiones

a lo largo de   along (the length of)
además de   in addition to
ajeno a   foreign to
bajo   under
en general   generally
en los últimos años   recently
entre sí   among themselves
expuesto a   exposed to
poco a poco   little by little
se debe (a)   is due to
tan . . . como   as (so) . . . as
tanto . . . como   as many (much) . . . as
todo el mundo   the whole world, everyone

Práctica

A. Usted entrevista a algún turista acerca de su visita reciente a las islas de San Blas. Pregúntele cómo son los indios cunas, qué hacen, qué lengua hablan, etcétera.

B. Imagine que usted tiene que preparar un itinerario para dos amigos que quieren visitar algunos lugares interesantes cerca de su ciudad o pueblo. Dígales cuáles son los lugares de interés, cómo pueden ir, qué cosas pueden ver allí y dónde pueden comer y dormir.

Nota cultural   El regateo y los precios fijos

Una costumbre característica de casi todos los países hispánicos es el regateo.[1] Es el arte de negociar[2] el precio de un objeto entre el vendedor y el comprador. Esta costumbre bastante antigua se practica principalmente en los mercados al aire libre,[3] donde las costumbres tradicionales prevalecen. La persona que quiere comprar pregunta el precio del producto que le interesa y puede pasarse hasta media hora mientras conversa con el vendedor, y tratan de llegar al precio que les conviene a ambos.[4] Para regatear es necesario saber conversar y tratar con la gente sin perder de vista el propósito del intercambio de palabras.

Sin embargo, el regateo generalmente no se practica en las tiendas, almacenes y supermercados modernos donde existen precios fijos que se indican en la etiqueta.[5] Bajo estas circunstancias el contacto entre el comprador y el vendedor es mínimo y se limita al intercambio de un objeto por cierta cantidad de dinero.

---

1. bargaining   2. negotiating   3. **al** . . . in the open air   4. **les** . . . is agreeable to both of them   5. price tag

Este vendedor regatea (bargains) con los peregrinos (pilgrims) que van al Santuario del Señor de Monserrate, localizado en la punta de un cerro (hill) con una vista preciosa de Bogotá, Colombia. Observe la mercancía. ¿Dónde cree Ud. que está el puesto de este vendedor: al final o al comienzo del peregrinaje? ¿Por qué?

Pronunciación y ortografía
Las letras ll, y (+ vocal) y hie

The Spanish spellings **ll**, **y** (+ *vowel*), and **hie** are pronounced differently in various parts of Spain and Hispanic America. Some speakers of Spanish distinguish between the [L] sound reflected by the **ll** spelling, as in **calle**, and the [y] sound spelled **y** (+ *vowel*), as in **yo**, or **hie**, as in **hierba**. The [L] sound is close to the English *ly* in *halyard;* the [y] sound is close to the English *y* in *yes*. Note that some speakers of Spanish have only one sound [y] reflected by all three spellings **ll**, **y** (+ *vowel*), and **hie**.

[L]		[y]	
calle	anillo	yo	leyes
orgulloso	llevar	cayeron	hierba
collares	llamar	¡huyuyuy!	hierro

    Specific pronunciations of these sounds often signal the place of origin of the speaker, but they are all understood without difficulty among Spanish speakers. The best policy is to follow your instructor's pronunciation.

A. Escuche y repita las palabras leídas por su profesor/a.

ll	y (+ *vowel*)	hie
llego	ya	hierba
llamo	ayer	hielo
lleno	ayudo	hiena
detalle	oyen	hierro

B. Escuche las siguientes oraciones leídas por su profesor/a y repítalas con atención especial a las palabras escritas con **ll**, **y** (+ *vowel*) y **hie**.

1. Allí en las islas de San Blas, los cunas llevan molas y tallan figuras de madera.
2. Ya no creo que haya hielo en el lago.
3. Cuando llueve en mayo, prospera la hierba.
4. Mi apellido es Yánez y voy en avión a Yucatán.

C. Aprenda a leer correctamente la siguiente balada. Ponga atención a las palabras escritas con **ll**, **y** (+ *vowel*) y **hie**.

En Sevilla hay un balcón
que tiene rejas de hierro.°   **rejas** ... iron grill work
Detrás del hierro una niña,
con cabello de azabache,°   **cabello** ... jet-black hair
entre las flores de mayo
esconde° mi corazón.   hides

Estudio de palabras

I. El cuerpo humano

Aprenda los términos para las partes del cuerpo en el dibujo que aparece abajo.

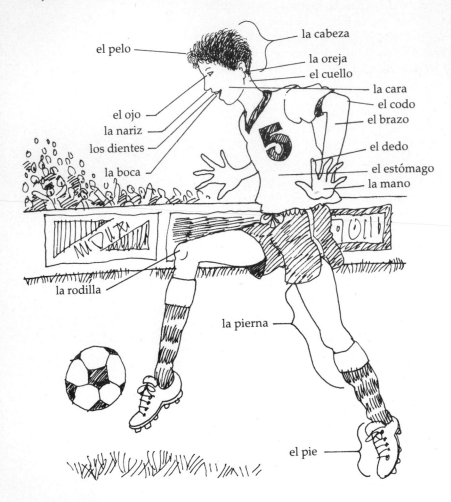

el pelo

la cabeza
la oreja
el cuello

el ojo
la nariz
los dientes
la boca

la cara
el codo
el brazo

el dedo
el estómago
la mano

la rodilla

la pierna

el pie

A. Escriba una breve descripción del muchacho en el dibujo. Diga si es alto o bajo, gordo o flaco, etcétera. Mencione también el color de su pelo y de sus ojos. Añada otros detalles imaginarios (por ejemplo, su nombre, su nacionalidad, los miembros de su familia).

B. Pregúntele a sus compañeros de clase si les duele alguna parte del cuerpo en las situaciones indicadas.

► los pies / andar mucho   S1: ¿Te duelen los pies después de andar
                                 mucho?
                            S2: ¡Sí, me duelen bastante!

1. la cabeza / leer mucho   5. los dientes / visitar al dentista
2. los ojos / mirar mucho la tele 6. las rodillas / hacer ejercicios
3. el estómago / comer mucho   7. los dedos / escribir a máquina
4. el brazo / jugar al tenis   8. el pie izquierdo / correr

II. Sustantivos que terminan en **-ma** y **-ta**

Nouns of Greek origin that end in **-ma** and **-ta** are masculine. Most of them
are cognates.

el clima   el poema   el sistema   el cometa
el drama   el problema el telegrama   el planeta

C. Complete las oraciones siguientes con sustantivos lógicos que terminen
en **-ma** o **-ta** de la lista que precede.

1. El _____ de Guayaquil es muy caluroso.
2. Algunas personas tienen miedo cuando ven un _____ en el cielo (*sky*).
3. Me gustan más los _____ que los cuentos (*stories*).
4. Espero recibir un _____ de Guillermo, que vuelve de Madrid el
   siete de agosto.
5. Tengo un _____ con el estéreo. ¡No funciona!
6. El _____ de tejer de los cunas es muy complicado.
7. ¿Quiere usted viajar al _____ Marte algún día?

III. Sufijos en **-oso**

The adjectival suffix **-oso/a (-osos/as)** means *full of*. Many adjectives ending in **-oso** have English equivalents ending in **-ous**. Other adjectives
ending in **-oso** have English equivalents ending in **-ful** or **-ic**.

maravilloso/a marvelous   **temeroso/a** fearful
nervioso/a nervous   **majestuoso/a** majestic

D. Dé los equivalentes en inglés de los adjetivos siguientes que terminan
en **-oso**.

1. fabuloso   4. desastroso   7. poderoso
2. peligroso   5. hermoso   8. delicioso
3. dudoso   6. curioso   9. religioso

E. Complete las oraciones siguientes con la forma correcta de un adjetivo lógico del Ejercicio D.

1. Mi viaje a Costa Rica fue _____ . Quiero volver a ese país el verano próximo.
2. Para mí, Puerto Rico es una isla muy _____ .
3. Las minas de estaño son muy _____ . Cada año ocurren muchos accidentes allí.
4. Jorge Rivas es un hombre _____ ; es jefe de una gran compañía.
5. ¡El examen de química fue _____ ! ¡No pude contestar ninguna de las preguntas!
6. Doña Margarita es una persona muy _____ . Va mucho a la iglesia.
7. Ese hombre es muy _____ . Quiere saber muchas cosas.
8. Las manzanas que acabo de comprar son _____ . ¿Quiere Ud. comer una?

Estructuras útiles

I. Verbs with irregular present subjunctive stems

No te preocupes, es posible que el ruido no sea nada . . . .

1. The following verbs have irregular present subjunctive stems, although the *endings* are regular.

haber: haya, hayas, haya, hayamos, hayáis, hayan
ir: vaya, vayas, vaya, vayamos, vayáis, vayan
saber: sepa, sepas, sepa, sepamos, sepáis, sepan
ser: sea, seas, sea, seamos, seáis, sean

Es posible que **haya** mucha gente, pero no creo que éste **sea** el grupo que buscamos.	*There may be many people, but I don't think this is the group that we are looking for.*
No quiero que **vayas** a la playa sin mí.	*I don't want you to go to the beach without me.*

2. Verbs with a special **yo-**form in the present indicative that ends in **-go** or **-zco** have a subjunctive stem based on this form. Their present subjunctive *endings*, however, are regular.

tener: tenga, tengas, tenga, tengamos, tengáis, tengan
poner: ponga, pongas, ponga, pongamos, pongáis, pongan
decir: diga, digas, diga, digamos, digáis, digan

conocer: conozca, conozcas, conozca, conozcamos, conozcáis, conozcan
parecer: parezca, parezcas, parezca, parezcamos, parezcáis, parezcan
conducir: conduzca, conduzcas, conduzca, conduzcamos, conduzcáis, conduzcan

Other verbs that fall in this category include: **caer** *(to fall)*, **hacer, oír, pertenecer** *(to belong to)*, **salir, traducir, traer,** and **venir.**

Espero que **conozcamos** pronto a tu novio.	*I hope we meet your boyfriend soon.*
No creo que **tenga** importancia.	*I don't think it has any importance.*

A. Usted habla con Roberto y cree que él exagera mucho. Exprese sus dudas con cortesía, usando el presente del subjuntivo de los verbos.

▶ Roberto: Tengo un coche rojo, uno blanco y otro azul.   *Me parece increíble que tengas un coche rojo, uno blanco y otro azul.*

1. En México los trenes siempre salen tarde.
2. Conozco bien todos los países de Hispanoamérica.
3. Mis padres van a Europa todos los años.
4. Pablo y yo tenemos doscientos discos.
5. Siempre vengo a clase a tiempo.
6. Yo sé la fecha de nacimiento de todos los héroes de mi país.
7. Salgo de casa todos los días a las siete de la mañana.
8. Pongo todo mi dinero en un banco.

B. Exprese sus deseos de que todo salga bien para un picnic que prepara con unos amigos y familiares. Use **ojalá que** con el presente del subjuntivo de los verbos indicados.

▶ Carmen / traer / refrescos   *Ojalá que Carmen traiga los refrescos.*

1. Jorge / salir / temprano
2. mi hermana / venir / a tiempo
3. Juan y Emilia / hacer / su famoso arroz con camarones
4. tú / traer / sandalias cómodas
5. todos / tener / hambre

6. Guillermo / conducir / bien
7. haber / un buen sitio junto al río
8. hacer / un día estupendo

C. Exprese su opinión acerca de los siguientes pares de afirmaciones. Use expresiones de la lista y el presente del indicativo o del subjuntivo, según la lógica de la situación.

es cierto   es posible   es probable
es dudoso   no es posible   no es probable
no es cierto   es increíble   es claro

▶ Hay sesenta minutos en una   *Es cierto que hay sesenta minutos en*
hora. Hay veintitrés horas   *una hora. No es cierto que haya vein-*
en un día.   *titrés horas en un día.*

1. Hace buen tiempo hoy. Va a hacer mal tiempo mañana.
2. Los artistas son inteligentes. Los políticos son astutos.
3. Si tengo calor, nado en la piscina. Si tengo frío, voy al parque.
4. Hay pocos puertorriqueños en Nueva York. Hay muchos cubanos en Miami.
5. Estos muchachos no saben nada. Aquellos muchachos lo saben todo.
6. Tus abuelos vienen a verte mañana. Tus primos vienen a visitarte el año próximo.

II. Comparisons of equality

*En mi balcón tengo **tantos** geranios **como** rosas.*

1. Comparisons of equality are expressed with the following patterns:

tan + *adjective* + **como**   as (so) . . . as
tan + *adverb* + **como**   as (so) . . . as
tanto/a (tantos/as) + *noun* + **como**   as much (many) . . . as

Ella es **tan tacaña como** él.	*She is as stingy as he (is).*
Yo conduzco **tan rápidamente como** él.	*I drive as fast as he (does).*
Tengo **tantas amigas como** amigos.	*I have as many women friends as men friends.*
Tenemos **tanto tiempo como** ellos.	*We have as much time as they (do).*

2. When the adjective, adverb, or noun is omitted, the pattern **tanto como** is used.

| Tú eres ágil, pero ella lo es **tanto como** Ud. | *You're agile, but she's as agile as you.* |
| Nosotros trabajamos **tanto como** ustedes. | *We work as much as you.* |

D. Raúl y su novia Julia son muy semejantes *(similar)*. Compárelos, usando la fórmula **tan + adjetivo + como.**

▶ sincero   *Raúl es tan sincero como su novia.*
               Julia es tan sincera como su novio.

1. generoso   5. joven
2. pobre   6. simpático
3. optimista   7. alto
4. imaginativo   8. rubio

E. Luisa y su hermana hacen las mismas actividades de la misma forma. Compare su manera de hacer las cosas, usando la fórmula **tan + adverbio + como.**

▶ comer rápidamente   *Luisa come tan rápidamente como su hermana.*

1. esperar pacientemente   5. patinar bien
2. hablar fácilmente   6. nadar mal
3. responder cordialmente   7. trabajar constantemente
4. bailar alegremente   8. cantar tristemente

F. Compare varias personas y objetos que usted conoce muy bien. Use la expresión **tan ... como** en sus comparaciones.

▶ *Consuelo y Ramón son tan simpáticos como Alicia Aragón.*
▶ *Este mapa de Hispanoamérica es tan grande como el otro.*

G. Haga oraciones comparativas, usando la información dada.

▶ Isabel e Inés tienen muchas faldas.   *Isabel tiene tantas faldas como Inés.*

1. Vivian e Ignacio tienen muchas plantas.
2. El señor Ruiz y el señor Gómez tienen muchas hijas.
3. Los artesanos y los pescadores tienen mucha paciencia.

4. Pilar y yo tenemos mucho tiempo libre.
5. Los cunas y los mayas conservan muchas tradiciones.
6. El director y el presidente ejercen mucha autoridad.
7. Tú y tus amigos tienen muchas vacaciones.
8. Ismael y Alberto son muy estudiosos.

H. Pregúntele a un/a compañero/a de clase si quiere tener **más que,
menos que** o **tanto como** las personas mencionadas.

▶ dinero / señor González

S1: *¿Quiere Ud. tener tanto dinero como el
señor González?*

S2: *Sí, quiero tener tanto como él.
No, quiero tener más (menos) que él.*

1. discos / sus amigos
2. oportunidades de trabajo / sus padres
3. fama / algunos científicos
4. éxito / su actriz favorita
5. inteligencia / Einstein
6. habilidad / Picasso
7. amigos / su primo
8. posibilidades en la vida / cualquiera

III. The neuter **lo** (pronoun and article)

1. The neuter pronoun **lo** is often used before a verb to replace a whole
thought or fact already mentioned or understood.

—¿Sabes que Pepita sale con
  Ricardo?
—Sí, **lo** sé.

*Do you know that Pepita is going
  out with Ricardo?*
Yes, I know (all that).

—¿Crees que Jorge es inteligente?
—Sí, creo que **lo** es.

Do you think Jorge is intelligent?
Yes, I think he is.

2. As mentioned in *Lección 12,* the neuter article **lo** can be used with an
adjective to refer to an abstract quality or characteristic. The English
equivalent often contains the word *thing* or *part.*

Lo interesante es que los cunas
aceptan poco a poco la lengua
española.
Lo difícil es comprender algunas
de sus costumbres.

*The interesting thing is that the
Cunas are slowly accepting the
Spanish language.*
*The difficult part is to understand
some of their customs.*

3. **Lo +** *de-phrase* is often used to refer to a recent situation or event. The
equivalent in English would be the expression *that matter of, that (whole)
business about,* or *that thing about.*

Lo de la huelga de mineros es muy serio.	*That matter of the miners' strike is very serious.*
¡Lo del secuestro en Bogotá es terrible!	*That business about the kidnapping in Bogotá is terrible!*

4. **Lo** + *que-clause* is used to refer to the totality of a past, present, or future event or situation. It does not refer to a specific noun. The equivalent in English is *what* or *that which*.

No sé **lo que voy a hacer.**	*I don't know what I'm going to do.*
Lo que pasó es que olvidé invitarlos.	*What happened is that I forgot to invite them.*
Lo que me dice usted es muy interesante.	*What you're telling me is very interesting.*

I. Conteste las siguientes preguntas según el modelo, usando el verbo **saber** y el pronombre **lo.**

▶ ¿Sabe usted que los cunas son bilingües? *Sí, lo sé.*
¿De verdad? Pues ahora lo sé.

1. ¿Sabe usted que Anthony Quinn es hispano?
2. ¿Saben ustedes que el fútbol es el deporte más popular en Hispanoamérica?
3. ¿Sabe usted que Cristobal Colón hizo cuatro viajes de exploración al Nuevo Mundo?
4. ¿Sabe usted que El Salvador es el país más pequeño de Centroamérica?
5. ¿Sabe usted que el sol es la moneda de Perú?

J. Complete las oraciones siguientes con frases lógicas.

▶ Lo malo es que . . . . *Lo malo es que no puedo ir al partido de fútbol hoy.*

1. Lo interesante es que . . . .
2. Lo bueno es que . . . .
3. Lo difícil es que . . . .
4. Lo fácil es que . . . .
5. Lo probable es que . . . .
6. Lo curioso es que . . . .

K. Empiece las oraciones siguientes con **lo de** + una expresión apropiada, usando la imaginación.

▶ . . . es muy interesante. *Lo del sistema de comercio de los cunas es muy interesante.*

1. . . . es estupendo.
2. . . . es horrible.
3. . . . es dudoso.
4. . . . es serio.
5. . . . es ridículo.
6. . . . es necesario.

L. Complete cada oración con una cláusula que empiece con **lo que.**

▶ No sé . . . .   *No sé lo que quieres decir.*
▶ Quiero aprender . . . .   *Quiero aprender lo que enseña Roberto.*

1. ¿No deseas comer . . . ?   4. Usted lee . . . .
2. Comprendemos . . . .   5. No te voy a vender . . . .
3. Le prometo . . . .   6. Vamos a pedirles . . . .

¡Exprésese usted!

La carta amistosa

Para escribir una carta amistosa en español se usa un formato diferente al formato en inglés. Considere la siguiente carta: notará que el encabezamiento *(heading)* incluye el nombre de la ciudad o pueblo de donde se escribe y la fecha que se escribe con mención del día antes que el mes. En español se usan los dos puntos *(colon)* después del saludo *(salutation)*, en vez de una coma *(comma)*. Normalmente se incluye el cierre o despedida *(closing)* de una carta en español dentro del párrafo final o en un nuevo párrafo, pero es posible escribirlo encima de la firma, al igual que en inglés.

Lea la siguiente carta de un estudiante panameño que desea establecer correspondencia con una estudiante norteamericana. Note el uso de preguntas y otros comentarios que muestran el interés de Juan Ramón en la persona a quien escribe.

Ciudad de Panamá, 7 de marzo

Querida Leslie:

Hace poco conocí a una compañera universitaria tuya, Karen Hobart, que pasó el mes de febrero aquí en Panamá. Me dijo que te interesa establecer correspondencia con algún estudiante universitario. Me llamo Juan
5 Ramón Alonso, pero todos me llaman Juancho. Estudio primer año de biología, y espero estudiar medicina tropical más tarde. Aquí en Panamá tenemos un buen centro de investigaciones de enfermedades tropicales.

No sé mucho de ti, ni de la universidad donde estudias. ¿Cómo es tu universidad? ¿Tiene estudios de medicina general y de especializaciones?
10 ¿Por cuál disciplina es más famosa? ¿Qué estudias allí?

Karen me contó que quieres aprender algo de mi país, de sus costumbres, su población, su geografía, etc. Pues, te cuento que Panamá no es muy grande en tamaño. Su capital, Ciudad de Panamá, es la ciudad más poblada con más de medio millón de habitantes. Otra ciudad más o menos
15 importante es Colón, que queda, al igual que Ciudad de Panamá, a orillas del Canal. Muy pocos extranjeros saben que la entrada del Pacífico al Canal queda al este de la entrada del Atlántico. (Si miras en un mapa, puedes entender eso mejor.) A finales de 1999, el canal y la zona del canal quedarán totalmente en manos panameñas.

20   Mi país es importante también como centro financiero internacional. Ya
tenemos 122 bancos internacionales establecidos en Ciudad de Panamá.

¿Qué otras cosas puedo contarte de Panamá? Pues, es un país muy
pintoresco con las Ruinas del Panamá Viejo, la ciudad que destruyó el
pirata inglés Morgan en 1671. Son de interés también las islas de San Blas,
25   donde viven los famosos indios cunas.

Ahora de mi vida social, pues paso mucho tiempo cuando mis estudios
me lo permiten de visita con mis amigos. Nos gusta ver cines en español de
Venezuela, México, Argentina y España y claro, los cines de EEUU. Mi
cantante favorito es Rubén Blades que también es compositor de música
30   popular. Es un verdadero tesoro panameño. Pero me gusta la música de
todo el mundo y me encanta bailar. Y tú, ¿cómo prefieres pasar tu tiempo?
¿Cuáles son tus pasatiempos favoritos?

Bueno, no escribo más por hoy. Espero que me escribas muy pronto y
que puedas venir algún día a Panamá como tu amiga Karen, para así cono-
certe personalmente. Hasta la próxima, recibe un saludo de tu amigo,

Juancho

A. Conteste las siguientes preguntas.

1. ¿Qué especialización piensa estudiar Juan Ramón y por qué?
2. ¿Qué puede Ud. mencionar de interés sobre Ciudad de Panamá?
    ¿y sobre el Canal?
3. ¿Qué quiere saber Juan Ramón de Leslie?
4. ¿Cuáles son los pasatiempos de Juancho?

B. Imagínese que Ud. recibió la carta de Juan Ramón. Contéstela con una
carta similar e incluya lo siguiente.

1. Conteste las preguntas que él le hace.
2. Hágale tres o cuatro preguntas más, pero no las escriba en forma
    de lista. Mézclelas (*mix them*) con la información que usted da en
    su carta.
3. Use la forma correcta de la fecha y las fórmulas de saludo y
    despedida.

*Muchos expertos opinaron que era (it was) imposible construir el Canal de Panamá con
recursos que hoy consideramos primitivos y con serios problemas técnicos y médicos. El
éxito de la empresa (enterprise) cambió la dirección de la historia. ¿Puede Ud. pensar por
qué fue tan importante este evento?*

Lengua en acción 5

A. En un restaurante *(Lección 13)*

Ud. va a un restaurante donde selecciona una bebida, un plato *(dish)* y un postre del siguiente menú. Un camarero (su compañero/a de clase) toma su pedido *(order)* y lo/la atiende según las indicaciones.

Camarero/a	Cliente
1. Salude al/a la cliente y pregúntele qué desea comer.	Pídale al/a la camarero/a que le recomiende algo.
2. Recomiéndele un plato.	Explique que no le gusta ese plato y pida otra cosa. Si Ud. no entiende algo en el menú, pida una explicación.
3. Respóndale al/a la cliente. Pregúntele qué quiere beber.	Conteste.
4. Responda de una forma apropiada: **Muy bien (señor), ahora mismo vengo con su comida./Sí, (señora), en seguida.**	Después que el/la camarero/a le trae su comida, Ud. encuentra que necesita un tenedor/cuchillo/vaso, etc. Llame al/a la camarero/a para pedirlo.

Camarero/a	Cliente
5. Pida disculpas (*Apologize*) por la falta de(l) . . .	Responda.
6. Pregúntele si desea algo más.	Pida un postre/café/té/agua y después, pida la cuenta.
7. Traiga lo que le pidió el/la cliente y después traiga la cuenta.	

B. El candidato perfecto (*Lección 13*)

Ud. y un/a compañero/a de clase son vicepresidentes de una compañía que produce textos universitarios. Uds. tienen que seleccionar una persona para un puesto de representante de ventas. Ud. prefiere al candidato A y su compañero/a a la candidata B. Comparen los dos candidatos y lleguen a un acuerdo (*agreement*). Después, dé las conclusiones a la clase y explique cómo llegaron al acuerdo.

Descripción del puesto: Representante de ventas
Tiene las siguientes obligaciones: Visitar cada mes unas 20 universidades. Presentar los libros de la compañía. Tomar pedidos (*orders*) y ayudar a los clientes. Supervisar a 4 personas. Preparar un informe (*report*) anual. Ser responsable y creativo.

A. *Ernesto Sánchez Ávila*

Dos años como profesor de educación física en una universidad.
Maestría en Administración Comercial.
Miembro de un equipo de natación.
Se lleva bien con la gente; simpático; dinámico
Espera tener la oportunidad de usar su preparación académica.

B. *Julia Monte Gómez*

Cinco años en una librería; dos años como supervisora en la compañía telefónica.
Licenciada en Bellas Artes; estudia computadoras en cursos nocturnos.
Miembro de la Sociedad Literaria de la capital.
Meticulosa; seria; profesional

Quiere volver a la profesión de vendedora.

C. Por teléfono *(Lección 14)*

Ud. busca un apartamento para alquilar *(rent)*. Le interesa ver uno anunciado en el periódico. Llame al dueño del apartamento (su compañero/a de clase) para informarse sobre:

a. el alquiler mensual *(monthly)*
b. si está amueblado *(furnished)*
c. el depósito inicial
d. si se permite tener animales domésticos
e. quién paga la luz y la calefacción *(heat)*
f. cuándo puede Ud. ir a verlo

No olvide ser cortés en su conversación.

D. Su casa ideal *(Lección 14)*

Ud. quiere comprar una casa y ahora habla con un/a corredor/a de bienes raíces *(realtor)*. Con un miembro de la clase, represente la siguiente conversación, siguiendo los pasos indicados.

Estilo colonial, cerca del centro comercial, 4 alcobas grandes, 2 comedores, 1 baño, necesita arreglos. $110.000,00

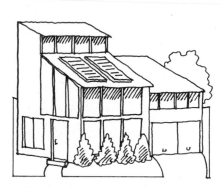

Estilo moderno, en suburbio, 6 alcobas pequeñas, cocina-comedor, 3 baños, energía solar, garaje doble. $150.000,00

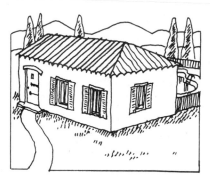

Estilo rústico, área rural, 3 habitaciones, 2 baños, cocina moderna, comedor, piscina. Mejor oferta sobre $125.000,00.

Paso 1: El/La corredor/a le hace preguntas sobre el tipo de casa que Ud. quiere y le muestra las fotos de tres casas en venta.

Paso 2: El/La corredor/a trata de venderle una de las casas. Ud. le hace por lo menos cinco preguntas sobre las casas, basadas en las fotos. El/La corredor/a contesta sus preguntas según la información debajo de las fotos.

Paso 3: Ud. decide cuál de las tres casas prefiere ir a ver y le explica por qué al/a la corredor/a.

E. ¿Qué opina Ud.? *(Lección 15)*

Entreviste a tres o cuatro compañeros/as de clase, preguntándoles su opinión sobre los tres temas indicados u otros de su elección. Cuente el número de opiniones positivas, negativas e indiferentes y prepare un resumen de los comentarios, usando el cuadro siguiente.

1. La marihuana se usa cada día más entre los estudiantes universitarios.
2. La persona que sirve bebidas alcohólicas en las fiestas debe ser responsable si cualquiera de sus invitados *(guests)* tiene un accidente automovilístico por estar borracho/a *(drunk)*.
3. Los fumadores *(smokers)* no deben tener el derecho *(right)* de fumar en sitios públicos.

Tema 1	*Tema 2*	*Tema 3*	*Tema 4*
positiva	positiva	positiva	positiva
negativa	negativa	negativa	negativa
indeciso/a	indeciso/a	indeciso/a	indeciso/a
Sugerencias	*Sugerencias*	*Sugerencias*	*Sugerencias*
_____	_____	_____	_____
_____	_____	_____	_____
_____	_____	_____	_____
_____	_____	_____	_____
_____	_____	_____	_____

Si Ud. es el/la entrevistado/a, use algunas de las siguientes frases u otras similares para expresar su opinión.

Opinión positiva

Me parece bien que . . .
Me alegro de que . . .
Me gusta que . . .

Sugerencias y comentarios

Creo que se debe . . .
Recomiendo que . . .
Este problema no tiene
  solución. Es dudoso que . . .

Opinión negativa

Me parece mal que . . .
Es triste que . . .
No me gusta que . . .

Indeciso/a

No estoy seguro/a que . . .

F. Una consulta con el médico *(Lección 15)*

Ud. no se siente muy bien y va a consultarse con el/la doctor/a
Antola (un miembro de la clase). Dígale cómo se siente, siguiendo las
indicaciones. Después, alternen los papeles.

Doctor/a Antola   *Usted*

1. Salude al/a la paciente y pregúntele cómo se   Salude al/a la doctor/a y explíquele cómo se
   siente.   siente.
2. Pregunte cuánto tiempo hace que se siente así.   Conteste.
3. Pregúntele si tiene algún otro problema   Conteste negativamente.
   médico.
4. Recomiéndele algo al/a la paciente.   Déle las gracias.

G. ¿Quién quiere hacer esto? *(Wrap-up)*

Ud. y dos amigos/as (sus compañeros/as de clase) viven en la misma
casa. Uds. tratan de decidir quién debe hacer las siguientes tareas
durante las próximas cuatro semanas. Apunte quién va a hacer cada
tarea y ¡no permita que le asignen demasiado trabajo!

Tarea	Semana I	Semana 2	Semana 3	Semana 4
ir de compras				
preparar las comidas				
lavar los platos				
pagar la luz y el teléfono				
limpiar los cuartos de baño				
pasar la aspiradora *(vacuum)*				

Expresiones útiles

No es justo que . . .   No sé cómo . . .
No me gusta/Me gusta . . .   No puedo porque . . .
Prefiero . . . porque . . .

Unidad 6
En Costa Rica, la República Dominicana y Cuba

En las ciudades hispánicas, los mercados se llenan de gente a toda hora en busca de frutas y vegetales frescos, carne y pescado, canastas y otros productos de primera necesidad. Son una atracción fascinante para los turistas con su ambiente de bullicio (hubbub) y vigor. ¿Qué artículos puede comprar Ud. en este mercado de Santo Domingo, República Dominicana?

Lección 16
En Costa Rica

La estación biológica de Monteverde

La estación biológica de Monteverde, situada al norte de San José, está financia-
da por organizaciones nacionales e internacionales. Allí se ofrece° un amplio   se . . . is offered
campo de investigación para científicos interesados en el estudio de la riquísima
fauna y flora de la selva y en la preservación del medio ambiente. En esa esta-
ción Alicia Benavides, una estudiante costarricense, participa en el estudio de
los hábitos de una gran variedad de insectos y pájaros. En este momento, Lo-
renzo Díaz, un amigo suyo, llega con Pedro Ruiz, un biólogo de la estación.

El gobierno costarricense provee un poco de tierra a los ciudadanos de San José para
sembrar (plant) ¿Cómo se beneficia la comunidad cuando hay áreas verdes en las
ciudades?

Alicia: ¡Hola, Lorenzo, hola, Pedro! Ya estábamos preocupados porque tardaban tanto en llegar. Los esperábamos ayer por la mañana. ¿Qué pasó?

Pedro: Nada. Que se dañó el bendito° jeep y tuvimos que regresar a San José por repuestos para arreglarlo. Por eso no pudimos llegar ayer. Pero cuéntanos, ¿cómo van las cosas?   darn

Alicia: Pues, ¡muy bien! Pude observar muchos tipos de pájaros y saqué fotos muy interesantes, ¡incluso una de un quetzal!°   a rare tropical bird

Pedro: Hablando de fotos, compré las películas que querías . . . y también creo que hay otras cosas para ti en el correo que trajimos. ¿Acabaste de clasificar las mariposas que fotografiamos la semana pasada?

Alicia: Las diapositivas° mías, sí. Todavía necesito clasificar las tuyas. Como no estabas, decidí esperar hasta tu regreso para consultarte sobre algunas. ¿Podemos reunirnos más tarde para hablar de eso?   slides

Pedro: De acuerdo. Ahora voy a ver si me limpio y me organizo un poco. Mientras tanto, ¿puedes mostrarle la estación a Lorenzo?

Alicia: Sí, cómo no. Lorenzo, creo que te va a entusiasmar lo que hacemos aquí. Me imagino que sabes que ahora tenemos un grupo internacional de expertos en el medio ambiente aquí, en la estación. Vas a aprender mucho sobre la preservación del ambiente, que es lo que más te interesa.

Lorenzo: Sí, vine precisamente por eso. ¿Y tú? . . . Es evidente que te gusta mucho la estación, pero, ¿no echas de menos la vida cómoda de la capital?

Alicia: No mucho. El trabajo de investigación biológica es realmente interesante, y a la falta de comodidades te acostumbras muy pronto. Por lo menos tenemos las cosas esenciales: buenas camas, un comedor, un salón pequeño y varios baños y duchas. Y claro, el laboratorio de biología.

Lorenzo: ¡Caramba! ¡Esto es mejor de lo que esperaba!

Comprensión

1. ¿Dónde está Alicia y qué hace ella allí?
2. ¿Qué ofrece la estación biológica de Monteverde? ¿Dónde está situada?
3. ¿Por qué llegaron tarde a la estación biológica Pedro Ruiz y Lorenzo?
4. Identifique algunos de los animales que se observan en Monteverde.
5. ¿Qué trajo Pedro Ruiz para Alicia?
6. ¿Qué comodidades hay en la estación, según Alicia?
7. ¿Qué es lo que más le interesa a Lorenzo?

Conversación

1. ¿Hay selvas en los Estados Unidos? ¿en qué estado o región?
2. ¿De qué animales tiene miedo usted? ¿de las culebras? ¿de las ranas? ¿de los ratones?
3. ¿Qué tipos de pájaros hay en el estado donde usted vive? ¿Cuál es el pájaro oficial de su estado?
4. ¿Qué hace su estado para proteger las especies de animales en peligro de desaparecer? ¿y para preservar regiones naturales?
5. ¿Prefiere Ud. más los lugares primitivos o los lugares civilizados para vivir? ¿por qué?
6. ¿Le gusta ir de camping en los bosques? ¿Le gusta dormir en tiendas de campaña o al aire libre?
7. ¿Qué comodidades considera usted esenciales para su felicidad?

Vocabulario

Palabras análogas

el animal
biológico, -a
el/la biólogo/a
civilizado, -a
clasificar
considerar
el/la experto/a
la fauna

financiado, -a
la flora
fotografiar
el hábito
el insecto
interesado, -a
el jeep
el laboratorio

natural
observar
la organización
organizar
preservar
primitivo, -a

Sustantivos

el bosque   woods
la cama   bed
el/la científico/a   scientist
la comodidad   comfort, convenience
el correo   mail
la culebra   snake
la ducha   shower
la especie   species
la estación biológica   biological research station
la felicidad   happiness
la mariposa   butterfly
el medio ambiente   environment
el peligro   danger
la preservación del ambiente   environmental conservation
la rana   frog
el ratón   mouse
el regreso   return
el repuesto   spare (part)
la selva   jungle

la tienda de campaña   tent
la variedad   variety

Adjetivos

amplio, -a   wide, full
mío, -a   my
preocupado, -a   worried
situado, -a   located
suyo, -a   his, her, your *(formal)*
tuyo, -a   your *(fam.)*

Verbos

acabar de (+ *inf.*)   to have just done something, finish doing something
acostumbrarse a   to get used to, be accustomed to
arreglar   to fix
dañarse   to become damaged
desaparecer (zc)   to disappear
limpiar   to clean
ofrecer (zc)   to offer
proteger   to protect

Música, baile y teatro

A Buenos Aires se le conoce como "la ciudad que nunca duerme". Una muestra de esa ciudad alegre está en la calle Lavalle que muestra la foto. En ella se encuentran diversiones para todos los gustos. Estas incluyen una variedad de cines y teatros que presentan lo nuevo y lo tradicional, lo experimental y lo clásico, lo exótico y lo famoso.

Actividad

Con otra persona de la clase planee pasar una noche en la calle Lavalle. Elijan un restaurante y una diversión; reserven mesas y compren boletos. Inviten a otras personas si quieren.

*Para la gente que se interesa en "las tablas" (el teatro) existen lugares como el Teatro
Colón de Buenos Aires, donde se presentan obras, ballets, óperas, zarzuelas (un teatro
musical más ligero) y presentaciones de música clásica, entre otras cosas. La literatura
hispánica cuenta con muchos dramaturgos famosos, cuyas obras se representan con éxito
en teatros como éste. También se presenta en el Teatro Colón talento extranjero de fama
mundial.*

Actividad
*Compare una obra de teatro y una película de televisión. Diga cuáles son los pros y los
contras de uno y otro medio artístico.*

Otras palabras y expresiones
al aire libre   in the open air
¡caramba! *(interj.)*   hah!
de acuerdo   agreed
e   and (before words beginning with **hi** or **i**)
echar de menos   to miss (someone or something)

incluso   including
ir de camping   to go camping
mientras tanto   meanwhile
por eso   for that reason
precisamente   precisely
pronto   quickly, soon

Práctica

A. Escriba una tarjeta desde Monteverde a un/a amigo/a. Dígale si le gusta la selva costarricense y por qué. Explíquele lo que usted vio en la selva.

B. Usted discute con un/a compañero/a de clase sobre algunos animales que están en peligro de desaparecer. ¿Cuáles son? ¿Qué se puede hacer para salvarlos *(save them)?*

Nota cultural   La selva en Hispanoamérica

Tradicionalmente los hispanoamericanos que viven en los pueblos y en las ciudades ven la selva como su enemigo natural y no sienten deseos de conservarla. Esta actitud negativa de resentimiento hacia una naturaleza hostil se refleja en muchas obras de la literatura hispanoamericana. Entre los animales peligrosos que viven en las selvas de Hispanoamérica están el jaguar, las serpientes, las hormigas carniceras[1] y aun ciertas clases de ranas,

1. **hormigas ...** meat-eating ants

Costa Rica es uno de los primeros países del mundo en demostrar una preocupación ecológica. Lea el letrero (sign) de la foto y diga qué tipo de estudios pueden realizarse en el bosque de Monteverde. ¿Conoce Ud. algún grupo ecologista? ¿Cómo se llaman? ¿Qué pretenden proteger?

que a pesar de[2] su apariencia tranquila pueden matar[3] a un individuo en pocos minutos con su potente veneno.[4] Algunas de las plantas también pueden ser venenosas y destructoras del esfuerzo[5] civilizador humano.

Sin embargo, las selvas tienen un papel muy importante en el balance ambiental de la tierra. Si las selvas desaparecen, la vida humana en todo el planeta se va a afectar irreparablemente. Pero a pesar de las grandes campañas[6] de los expertos en el medio ambiente por protegerlas, las selvas van desapareciendo rápidamente. Costa Rica es uno de los pocos países que se preocupa por preservar muchas de sus selvas y las declara parques o reservas nacionales.

A través de[7] los esfuerzos de varias organizaciones internacionales se trata de despertar hoy en día el interés por la protección y conservación del medio ambiente. Esto es a pesar de que en muchos casos, estos esfuerzos compiten frente a frente con nuestra idea del "progreso".

------

2. **a** . . . in spite of   3. kill   4. poison   5. effort   6. campaigns   7. **A** . . . Through

Pronunciación y ortografía

Consonantes con cambios ortográficos

The following chart summarizes the different spellings of some of the consonant sounds you have had in this course. It will be especially useful in learning to anticipate regular spelling changes that occur in Spanish verbs, nouns, and adjectives.

Sound and spelling	Before *a*	Before *o*	Before *u*	Before *e*	Before *i*
	Spelling-changing consonant sounds				
[k] = **c** or **qu**	**c**arta	**co**sa	**cu**rar	**que**rer	**qui**en
[s] = **s, z,**	**sa**ludo	**so**lo	**su**bida	**se**mana	**si**no
or **c**	**za**pato	**zo**rro	a**zu**l	**ce**ntro	**ci**ne
[g] = **g** or **gu**	**ga**to	**go**rro	**gu**sto	**gue**rra	**guí**a
[ǧ] = **g** or **gu**	ami**ga**	ami**go**	se**gu**ro	si**gue**	se**guí**
[h] = **j** or **g**	de**jar**	**jo**ven	**ju**lio	mu**jer**	**ji**rafa
	—	—	—	reco**ge**	pá**gi**na
[gw] + [ǧw] = **gu** and **gü**	**gua**pa	a**guo**so	—	pin**güe**	**güi**ro

A. Escriba las siguientes oraciones dictadas por su profesor/a. Luego corrija los errores, comparando sus oraciones con las del libro.

1. Mi amigo participa en un programa de investigación.
2. Te traigo los libros que querías de San José.

3. El jaguar es una especie en peligro de desaparecer.
4. ¿Cuál es la casa de Cuco?
5. Organizaron un viaje a Zaragoza.

B. Complete cada oración con la forma correcta del verbo indicado.

1. Ayer yo **conseguí** dos billetes y Pablo _____ tres.
2. Hoy **averigüé** dónde vive Carlota; mañana voy a _____ dónde vive Pepita.
3. Alicia **buscó** un quetzal; yo _____ unas mariposas.
4. Yo **llegué** a la estación a las dos, pero Jorge no _____ hasta las tres.
5. Carlos **abrazó** a mi mamá y yo también la _____ .

Estudio de palabras

I. Algunos animales e insectos

Animales salvajes

el caimán alligator	**el lobo** wolf
la cebra zebra	**el mono** monkey
el ciervo wild deer	**el oso** bear
el cocodrilo crocodile	**la rana** - frog
el elefante elephant	**la serpiente (culebra)** snake
el jaguar jaguar	**el tigre** tiger
la jirafa giraffe	**el zorro** fox
el león lion	

Insectos comunes

la abeja bee	**la mariposa** butterfly
la cucaracha cockroach	**la mosca** fly
la hormiga ant	**el mosquito** mosquito

Animales domésticos

el burro donkey	**el gato** cat
la cabra goat	**la oveja** sheep
el cerdo pig	**el pato** duck
el conejo rabbit	**el perro** dog

Some animals have different names for the male and female species; for example:

el caballo horse	**el gallo** rooster
la yegua mare	**la gallina** hen
el toro bull	
la vaca cow	

A. Busque una descripción apropiada en la columna de la derecha para cada animal salvaje.

1. el caimán
2. el zorro
3. el tigre
4. el mono
5. el león
6. la jirafa
7. la cebra
8. el ciervo
9. el elefante
10. el oso

a. Es el rey (king) de la selva.
b. Tiene el cuello largo (long).
c. Hay unos de color blanco que viven en el círculo polar ártico.
d. Es similar al burro, pero tiene rayas (líneas) blancas y negras.
e. Es un animal muy listo (clever), y le gusta comer pollos.
f. Es un animal enorme, y tiene fama de tener una memoria excelente.
g. Vive casi siempre en el agua.
h. Le encanta imitar a las personas.
i. Es fuerte, elegante, agresivo y tiene el pelo casi anaranjado con rayas negras.
j. Vive en los bosques, es tímido y corre muy rápidamente.

B. Identifique los animales domésticos del dibujo siguiente, y descríbalos en pocas palabras, como se hizo en el Ejercicio A.

C. Describa un animal para que un/a compañero/a de clase pueda identificarlo.

▶ S1: *Es un animal que vive en casa, come pescado y le gusta salir por la noche.*
S2: *El gato.*

II. Los números ordinales

1. Ordinal numbers indicate position or order in a series. Below are listed the ordinal numbers from *first* to *tenth* in Spanish.

primero, -a	first	**sexto, -a**	sixth
segundo, -a	second	**séptimo, -a**	seventh
tercero, -a	third	**octavo, -a**	eighth
cuarto, -a	fourth	**noveno, -a**	ninth
quinto, -a	fifth	**décimo, -a**	tenth

2. Use of the first ten ordinal numbers is very common in Spanish. After **décimo,** however, cardinal numbers are generally used instead of ordinal numbers and are placed after the noun.

la lección cuarenta   **la unidad veinte**

3. Ordinal numbers agree in gender and number with the noun they modify.

la quinta calle   **las primeras lecciones**
el octavo piso   **los primeros libros**

4. **Primero** and **tercero** drop the final **-o** before a masculine singular noun.

el primer día   **el tercer cuarto**

5. Ordinal numbers are abbreviated with the use of a cardinal number and a raised **o** or **a**, depending on the gender of the noun modified.

1° = primero 2° = segundo
1^a = primera 2^a = segunda

6. Ordinal numbers often precede the noun they modify. Important exceptions are when they are part of the name of a street and the title of a chapter.

El **primer capítulo** que leí es el **capítulo quinto.**   *The first chapter I read is Chapter Five.*

Mi mejor amiga vive en la **Calle Novena.**   *My best friend lives on Ninth Street.*

Note the English influence in the following exception.

La **Quinta Avenida** es muy elegante.   *Fifth Avenue is very elegant.*

D. Haga oraciones completas, usando la forma apropiada del número ordinal.

▶ quinto / revista / leer   *Es la quinta revista que leo.*

1. tercero / canción / escuchar   4. primero / vaso / romper
2. segundo / película / ver   5. décimo / programa / preparar
3. cuarto / casa / comprar   6. octavo / concurso / ganar

E. Identifique dónde se sientan varios estudiantes de la clase, indicando el asiento *(seat)* y la fila.

▶ S1: *¿Dónde se sienta [Marta]?*
S2: *[Marta] se sienta en el primer asiento de la primera fila.*

F. Estudie el siguiente dibujo de un edificio de apartamentos. Diga en

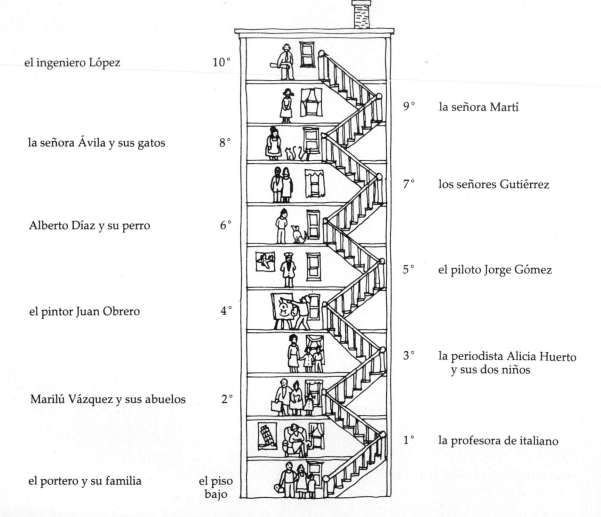

el ingeniero López   10°

9°   la señora Martí

la señora Ávila y sus gatos   8°

7°   los señores Gutiérrez

Alberto Díaz y su perro   6°

5°   el piloto Jorge Gómez

el pintor Juan Obrero   4°

3°   la periodista Alicia Huerto
      y sus dos niños

Marilú Vázquez y sus abuelos   2°

1°   la profesora de italiano

el portero y su familia   el piso
                             bajo

qué piso del edificio de apartamentos viven las personas mencionadas. Note que en algunas regiones, **el piso bajo = la planta baja** o **el primer piso.**

▶ la señora Martí   *Vive en el noveno piso.*

1. Alicia Huerto con sus dos niños
2. Marilú Vázquez y sus abuelos
3. Alberto Díaz y su perro
4. los señores Gutiérrez
5. el pintor Juan Obrero
6. el ingeniero López
7. el piloto Jorge Gómez
8. la profesora de italiano
9. la señora Ávila y sus gatos
10. el portero y su familia

Estructuras útiles

I. The imperfect tense

*De niña yo **vivía** en una casa grande y **tenía** un perro y un gato.*

In *Lección 10* you learned that there are two simple past tenses in Spanish. The *preterit* refers to the beginning or the end of an action or to a whole action that was completed in the past. The *imperfect* refers to an habitual action or to an action in progress viewed at a given moment in the past.

A. Forms of the imperfect for all verbs

1. The imperfect tense of almost all Spanish verbs is formed by adding the imperfect endings to the infinitive stem. The imperfect endings of -**ar** verbs have a characteristic **b** and an accent mark on the stressed **a** of the **nosotros**-forms. The imperfect endings of -**er** and -**ir** verbs have a characteristic stressed **í**.

escuchar		comer		vivir	
escuch	**aba**	com	**ía**	viv	**ía**
escuch	**abas**	com	**ías**	viv	**ías**
escuch	**aba**	com	**ía**	viv	**ía**
escuch	**ábamos**	com	**íamos**	viv	**íamos**
escuch	**abais**	com	**íais**	viv	**íais**
escuch	**aban**	com	**ían**	viv	**ían**

El año pasado, mientras **vivía** en un dormitorio, **escuchaba** muchos programas de nutrición en la radio.

Last year while I lived in a dorm, I listened to many programs about nutrition on the radio.

Por eso, **comía** una comida balanceada: vegetales y frutas, proteínas, leche y cereales.

For that reason, I ate balanced meals: vegetables and fruit, proteins, milk, and cereals.

2. Only three verbs in Spanish are irregular in the imperfect: **ir, ver,** and **ser.**

ir	ver	ser
iba	veía	era
ibas	veías	eras
iba	veía	era
íbamos	veíamos	éramos
ibais	veíais	erais
iban	veían	eran

Cuando yo **era** pequeño, **iba** al colegio y allí **veía** a todos mis amigos.

When I was young, I went to school and there I saw all my friends.

B. Uses of the imperfect

1. The imperfect tense describes an action in progress in the past or a situation or condition that existed over an indefinite period of time in the past. The equivalent in English is usually given as *was (were)* + the *-ing* form of the verb.

¿Qué **hacían** Uds. a las diez anoche?

What were you doing at ten last night?

Mientras mi hermana **miraba** la televisión, yo **leía** el periódico.

While my sister was watching (watched) television, I was reading (read) the newspaper.

Trabajábamos día y noche en el proyecto.

We were working (worked) day and night on the project.

2. The imperfect tense describes a habitual or repeated past action. Words or expressions such as **con frecuencia, muchas veces,** and **siempre** often serve as cues for the imperfect. The English equivalents of these kinds of action are *used to + verb* or *would + verb*.

De joven, yo **iba** a la playa con frecuencia.	*When I was young, I used to (would) go to the beach frequently.*
Visitaba a mis abuelos todas las semanas.	*I used to (would) visit my grandparents every week.*

3. The imperfect tense is often used to describe the background of an event or to tell what was happening when an event took place.

Hacía un tiempo excelente, y no **había** viento.	*The weather was excellent, and there wasn't any wind.*
¡Qué jóvenes **éramos** entonces!	*How young we were then!*

4. The imperfect expresses clock time and age in the past.

Eran las cinco de la tarde.	*It was five o'clock in the afternoon.*
Tenías veintiséis años.	*You were twenty-six years old.*

A. Diga que antes estas personas hacían las cosas mencionadas, pero ya no las hacen.

▶ (leer) Antes yo _____ fotonovelas, pero ya no las _____ . *leía; leo*

1. (estudiar) Antes tú y Pepe _____ francés, pero ya no lo _____ .
2. (caminar) Antes nosotras _____ a la universidad, pero ya no _____ .
3. (recibir) Antes Lucía _____ muchas visitas, pero ya no _____ tantas.
4. (tocar) Antes Gonzalo _____ el piano como pasatiempo, pero ahora nunca lo _____ .
5. (escribir) Antes tú _____ poemas, pero ya no los _____ .
6. (salir) Antes Catalina _____ con muchos amigos, pero ya no _____ con nadie.

B. Explíquele a un amigo o a una amiga qué hacía ayer mientras él/ella hacía otra cosa.

▶ jugar al tenis / estudiar   *Yo jugaba al tenis mientras tú estudiabas.*
Yo estudiaba mientras tú jugabas al tenis.

1. comer en casa / comer en la cafetería
2. fotografiar las culebras / observar sus hábitos
3. montar a caballo / patinar
4. asistir a un concierto / bailar en el club
5. ver una exposición de fotos / ir a un partido de básquetbol
6. dirigir el seminario / escribir notas
7. conducir el carro / leer el mapa
8. preparar café / lavar los platos

C. Dígale a su profesor/a qué actividades hacía o no hacía cuando era joven. Use verbos de la lista siguiente u otros verbos que conoce.

cantar	cocinar	nadar	dormir	dibujar
bailar	tocar	esquiar	leer	caminar
pintar	jugar	comer	salir	correr

▶ *Cuando era joven, dibujaba mucho pero no pintaba nunca.*

D. Exprese en español las siguientes conversaciones.

1. —What were you doing yesterday afternoon?
   —I was painting the bathroom.
2. —Where did you use to live when you were young?
   —I used to live in Puerto Rico.
3. —Who was studying while you were watching television?
   —Ricardo and Anita were studying. Pepe was listening to the radio.
4. —When you lived in a dorm, what did you use to do every day?
   —I would get up at seven, study until ten o'clock, and then go to classes.
5. —What time was it when you had lunch?
   —It was twelve o'clock.
6. —How old were you in 1978?
   —I was twelve.

II. Imperfect versus preterit

The preterit and the imperfect reflect different ways of looking at the past. They enable the Spanish speaker to express from different perspectives an action or an event that took place in the past.

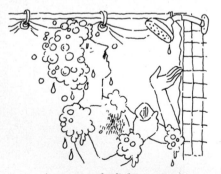

*Ayer mientras **me bañaba**, cortaron el agua...*

A. The preterit refers to:

1. a single, completed past event, as well as a completed series of past events, actions, or situations.

Llegué al museo antes que los otros.

I arrived at the museum before the others.

Les **pregunté** varias veces, hasta que me **respondieron.**

I asked them several times, until they answered me.

2. the beginning or the end of a past event or action.

El programa de radio **empezó** a las ocho y **terminó** a las nueve.

The radio program began at eight o'clock and ended at nine.

B. The imperfect refers to:

1. actions that were occurring at a particular time in the past.

Pepe **dormía** a las once anoche.

Pepe was sleeping at eleven last night.

En 1982, ¿**estabas** en Santo Domingo?

In 1982, were you in Santo Domingo?

2. customary actions in the past or a series of actions whose end is not indicated.

Usted siempre **iba** a la playa los veranos.

You always used to go to the beach in the summer.

De joven, yo **comía** mucho.

When (I was) young, I used to eat a lot.

3. what *used to happen* in the past in contrast to what happens now.

Piedad **estudiaba** lenguas, pero ahora estudia química.

Piedad used to study languages, but now she studies chemistry.

Yo **vivía** en la Calle Real, y ahora vivo en la Avenida Caracas.

I used to live on Real Street, and now I live on Caracas Avenue.

4. what was going on when something occurred to interrupt it.

El detective **investigaba** el crimen cuando **ocurrió** una explosión.

The detective was investigating the crime when an explosion occurred.

The diagram below contrasts the uses of the preterit and the imperfect. Keep in mind that Spanish speakers can express the same past event or action with the preterit or the imperfect, depending on their point of view.

action begun at some point in the past   *action ends*

preterit tense   imperfect tense   preterit tense

Miguel { **escribió** muchas cartas.
            escribía muchas cartas.

Miguel { *wrote many letters.*
            wrote (was writing, used to write) many letters.

E. Lea las siguientes oraciones. Identifique cada verbo y diga si está en el pretérito o en el imperfecto. Después diga por qué requiere el pretérito o el imperfecto.

1. Cuando **llegué** a la estación de Monteverde, Alicia me **esperaba.** Yo le **entregué** el correo y algunas cosas que ella **necesitaba.**
2. Pedro Ruiz **llegó** a la estación conmigo. Pedro le **dijo** a Alicia que él **iba** a organizar sus cosas y que no **tenía** tiempo de mostrarme la estación.
3. Alicia me **dijo** que la estación **era** primitiva, pero que **tenía** buenos laboratorios. Me **mostró** el comedor y el salón y me **llevó** a mi cuarto.

F. Complete los siguientes párrafos con la forma apropiada del pretérito o del imperfecto de los verbos entre paréntesis, según el contexto.

1. Cuando yo (ser) _____ joven, con frecuencia (visitar) _____ a un amigo que (vivir) _____ cerca.
2. Un día yo (ir) _____ a verlo, y su madre me (decir) _____ que mi amigo (estar) _____ en el hospital, pero que no (estar) _____ muy enfermo.
3. Yo (decidir) _____ ir a visitarlo, pero una enfermera del hospital me (explicar) _____ que yo (ser) _____ muy joven. Entonces, yo (ir) _____ a otra puerta y (entrar) _____ con un grupo de gente mayor, y así (poder) _____ visitar a mi amigo.

G. Explique que las primeras personas hacían algo cuando las segundas los interrumpieron. Use la imaginación para explicar las circunstancias.

▶ yo / dormir / tú / despertarme   *Yo dormía tranquilamente cuando tú me despertaste con la música.*

1. Pepe / comer / Luisa / llamarlo
2. nosotros / salir / tú y tu hermana / llegar
3. tú / visitar / yo / descubrir
4. Eugenia / estar / Margarita / mostrar
5. tú / vivir / yo / ir
6. Anita y yo / discutir / Pedro / entrar

H. Exprese en español los siguientes diálogos.

1. —Hi, John, where did you go yesterday?
   —I went to see Luisa, but she wasn't home.
   —What did you do then?
   —I returned home and watched an old movie on television.
2. —Was it raining when you went out?
   —Yes, that's why I called a taxi.
   —Did it arrive soon?
   —No, there weren't any taxis!

3. —I didn't live in Costa Rica when I was a child.
   —Where did you live?
   —I lived in Colombia until 1970.
   —Did you speak Spanish then?
   —A little, but I improved my Spanish when I worked in Costa Rica later.

III. Long forms of possessive adjectives

1. The following chart compares the short and long forms of the possessive adjectives. Note that the short and long forms of the possessives **nuestro (nuestra, etc.)** and **vuestro (vuestra, etc.)** are the same.

Owner	Short forms	Long forms
yo	mi, mis	**mío/a, míos/as**
tú	tu, tus	**tuyo/a, tuyos/as**
él, ella, Ud.	su, sus	**suyo/a, suyos/as**
nosotros, -as	nuestro/a, nuestros/as	**nuestro/a, nuestros/as**
vosotros, -as	vuestro/a, vuestros/as	**vuestro/a, vuestros/as**
ellos, ellas, Uds.	su, sus	**suyo/a, suyos/as**

2. The long forms of the possessive adjectives follow the noun and are more emphatic than the short forms. They agree in gender and number with the noun they modify.

Aquí está la chaqueta **mía.** Y ahora, ¿dónde está la corbata **tuya?**	*Here is my jacket. Now, where is your tie?*
Mi carro es pequeño y viejo, pero el carro **tuyo** es grande y moderno.	*My car is small and old, but your car is big and modern.*

3. Note how Spanish expresses the English construction *a friend of mine, an aunt of hers,* et cetera.

Carlos es **un amigo mío.**	*Carlos is a friend of mine.*
Esa señora es **una tía suya.**	*That woman is an aunt of hers.*

I. Usted, sus parientes y sus amigos tienen diferentes cosas. Piense en una de esas personas y describa las cosas que tiene, usando la forma larga del adjetivo posesivo.

► una tía / los sombreros   *Pienso en mi tía Juana. Los sombreros suyos son elegantes pero un poco pasados de moda (old-fashioned)*

1. un amigo / el automóvil
2. una amiga / el cuarto

3. su compañero de cuarto / los programas de estudio
4. dos amigas / la cámara fotográfica
5. usted / trabajo
6. un primo / la casa
7. un chico de esta clase / el pelo
8. dos chicas de esta clase / los ojos

J. Usted trabaja en un campamento (camp) de verano. Tiene que asegurarse de quiénes son los dueños (owners) de los siguientes artículos con la ayuda de un jovencito. Él contesta sus preguntas de forma enfática, usando una forma larga de los adjetivos posesivos.

▶ ¿Son de Rosita estos zapatos?   *Sí, son los zapatos suyos.*

1. ¿Son míos aquellos libros?
2. ¿Es de Sofía la maleta que está sobre la mesa?
3. ¿Es de José Manuel ese cassette?
4. ¿Es de Sandra aquella cámara?
5. ¿Son de ustedes aquellas camas?
6. ¿Es tuya aquella carta?
7. ¿Son nuestros esos botes?
8. ¿Son de Ramón y de Carlos los trajes de baño (bathing suits) que están ahí?

K. Exprese en español los siguientes diálogos.

1. —Who is Javier?
   —He's a friend of ours.
2. —Do you know that woman?
   —Yes, she's an aunt of mine.
3. —Is that *your* dog?
   —No, it belongs to a neighbor of mine.
4. —Whose cups are those?
   —They belong to a cousin of mine.

IV. Possessive pronouns

The possessive pronouns are identical in form to the long forms of the possessive adjectives. They agree in gender and number with the thing possessed. The possessive pronouns are most commonly preceded by a definite article. After the verb **ser,** however, the article may be omitted.

—¿Tienes los discos de Pepe?	*Do you have Pepe's records?*
—No, sólo tengo **los tuyos.**	*No, I only have yours.*
—¿Hablabas con mi profesor de inglés?	*Were you talking with my English professor?*
—No, hablaba con **el mío.**	*No, I was talking with mine.*

—¿Entonces, aquella casa es
  tuya?
—Sí, es **mía** ¡y **tuya!**

Then, that house is yours?

Yes, it's mine . . . and yours!

L. Cambie las oraciones siguientes, usando los pronombres posesivos apropiados.

▶ Tenemos sus reservaciones.   *Tenemos las suyas.*
▶ Pedro tiene los cuadernos de Jorge. *Tiene los suyos.*

1. Tengo mi bicicleta.
2. Tiene las sandalias de Anita.
3. Tenemos nuestras entradas.
4. Tiene el carro de mis padres.
5. Tiene su calculadora.
6. Tiene tu máquina de escribir.
7. Tienes los lápices de Eduardo.
8. Tiene sus papeles.

M. Suponga que come en un restaurante con varias personas y su hermano, Roberto, no sabe de quién es cada cosa. Ayúdele a encontrar al dueño *(owner).*

▶ ¿Estos frijoles son para Tomás o para mí?   *Creo que no son suyos.*
                                                Son tuyos.

1. ¿Ese pollo es para mí o para ti?
2. ¿Esas enchiladas son para Luis o para nosotros?
3. ¿Esos tacos son para ti o para Beto?
4. ¿Y estas verduras son para tus amigas o para ustedes?
5. ¿Esa cerveza es para mí o para Francisca?
6. ¿Este arroz con pollo es para Mariela o para ti?

¡Exprésese usted!

Descripción de un viaje

Cuando una persona viaja, siempre tiene experiencias nuevas y aprende cosas de interés para otros. Con frecuencia las personas escriben cartas o diarios de sus viajes, contando el tipo de cosas que sus amigos y familiares pueden encontrar entretenidas *(entertaining).*

Lea el siguiente extracto del diario de viaje de María Ester Correa, una joven costarricense que viaja por Colombia para visitar amigos y conocer el país. Al regresar a Costa Rica, ¿cómo cree Ud. que María Ester piensa usar el diario? ¿Quién va a leerlo?

Bogotá, sábado 15 de febrero

Estoy encantada con Bogotá. Mi amiga Inés Arias me acompaña a todas partes y me muestra los sitios más interesantes de la ciudad. Ayer subimos a Monserrate, una montaña muy alta que ofrece una vista panorámica es-
5 tupenda del altiplano, que aquí llaman la «Sabana de Bogotá». Hizo un día de sol maravilloso, y vimos toda la ciudad, muchísimo más grande que San José. Como San José tiene sólo un millón de habitantes, el tamaño de Bogotá verdaderamente me impresionó. La única cosa que no me gustó del viaje a Monserrate fue el teleférico, aunque otros lo encuentran emocio-
10 nante. Tengo horror de las alturas y sólo iba pensando en qué hacer si se rompía el cable . . . .

Medellín, lunes 17 de febrero

El sitio que más me gusta de Medellín hasta ahora es «El Ranchito». Como en Costa Rica, aquí tienen muchísimas orquídeas. «El Ranchito», que es la
15 antigua casa de un presidente de Colombia, tiene una colección fabulosa. Chela Llano, mi querida amiga, y yo fuimos con su primo Ignacio que sabe mucho de orquídeas y me explicó que ¡tienen cinco mil especies diferentes! En el museo de la casa vimos una carta del emperador del Japón que da las gracias por unas orquídeas muy raras que recibió de aquí.

20 *Popayán, domingo 23 de febrero*

Mañana vuelvo a Bogotá para tomar el avión para San José. Esta ciudad es ideal para pasar el último día de mi visita en Colombia porque es muy tranquila. Es una reliquia colonial muy bien conservada. El terremoto de 1982 destruyó muchas casas e iglesias, pero poco a poco reconstruyen lo más
25 importante. Mi amigo Juan Mosquera es de una de las familias originales de Popayán, y la antigua casa de su familia es un museo oficial con documentos históricos de la época de la independencia. El mes entrante va a venir mucha gente de todo el país para celebrar la Semana Santa y la Pascua de Resurrección que son fiestas tradicionales muy famosas en esta ciu-
30 dad.

A. Escoja entre las posibilidades de la segunda columna la mejor explicación para las palabras de la primera columna, según el contexto de la lectura.

1. encantado
2. maravilloso
3. altiplano
4. teleférico
5. raro
6. terremoto
7. Semana Santa
8. subir

a. que va de un lugar más bajo a uno más alto
b. transporte aéreo por cable
c. terreno alto y llano
d. fascinado
e. movimiento fuerte de tierra
f. extraordinario
g. celebración de la pasión y muerte de Jesús
h. que no es común

B. Escriba un párrafo sobre un viaje corto que usted hizo dentro o fuera de los Estados Unidos, o sobre un viaje imaginario. Considere lo siguiente:

1. Al escribir, piense en la persona o personas que van a leer su descripción.
2. Concéntrese en una o dos experiencias o ideas (positivas o negativas).
3. Mencione dos o tres sitios relacionados a sus experiencias. ¿Cómo se sintió usted en ese sitio? ¿por qué?

Esta plaza en San José, Costa Rica es diferente a la mayoría de las plazas de Hispanoamérica. Diga cómo es diferente a la Plaza de Armas en Lima (página 228).

Lección 17
En la República Dominicana

La Voz° de los Jóvenes

Voice

La Voz de los Jóvenes es un radioprograma de La Estación Musical 56 de Santo Domingo que se dirige principalmente a la juventud. Entre los anuncios y la música, la estación se dedica a enseñar y a aconsejar a sus radioyentes° sobre cualquier problema que tengan. A menudo la estación ofrece premios a través de concursos publicitarios. Este mes el concurso «¡Entendámonos!» ofrece un radiorreloj al joven o a la joven que envíe la mejor carta explicando por qué quiere ganar el premio. Aquí tiene usted la carta que escribió un joven radioyente.

radio listeners

La caña de azúcar es la principal fuente de ingresos para la República Dominicana y algunos otros países del Caribe. El trabajo en la caña es arduo y requiere mucha labor manual. ¿Qué destrezas (skills) cree Ud. que requiere este oficio?

10 de octubre

Muy estimada Voz:

Me llamo Rafael de los Santos y tengo dieciocho años. Trabajo en una central azucarera al noreste de Santo Domingo. Mi horario es muy estricto y requiere que me levante a las seis para empezar a trabajar a las ocho, por-
5 que vivo a unos 30 kilómetros de la refinería. A veces me despierto tarde y no tengo tiempo para desayunarme. Tengo que levantarme, lavarme, vestirme de prisa y salir corriendo para coger la guagua.° Mi mamá me dice   bus que no es bueno trabajar sin tomar el desayuno, que voy a morirme de hambre. Pero . . . ¿qué hacer?
10 Esta mañana, por ejemplo, me desperté a las siete y media y tuve que salir corriendo para coger la guagua de las ocho. Llegué a la refinería a las ocho y media y me puse a trabajar inmediatamente. Cuando llego tarde, el jefe siempre me dice: «No sea perezoso; llegue temprano mañana; haga esto y haga lo otro.» ¡Es terrible! ¡No me atrevo a decirle nada! Hoy por la
15 mañana, mientras trabajaba, empezaron a dolerme la cabeza y el estómago. A pesar de eso, no podía descansar ni comer nada porque el jefe me miraba mucho.

Espero ser dueño del radiorreloj porque estoy seguro de que con él voy a dejar de tener dificultad en despertarme. Y con tiempo para desayu-
20 narme, voy a sentirme mejor y a trabajar más.

Su seguro servidor,°   Sincerely yours

Rafael de los Santos

Comprensión

1. ¿A quiénes se dirige el radioprograma?
2. ¿Qué tipo de programas ofrece la estación?
3. ¿Cuál es el premio que ofrece este mes *La Voz de los Jóvenes*?
4. ¿Qué deben hacer los radioyentes para ganar el premio?
5. ¿Cómo se gana la vida Rafael de los Santos?
6. ¿Por qué no se desayuna a veces Rafael?
7. ¿Qué le pasó a Rafael esta mañana?
8. ¿Qué le dice el jefe cuando llega tarde?
9. Según Rafael, ¿cómo le va a ayudar el radiorreloj?

Conversación

1. ¿Escucha usted radioprogramas para los jóvenes? ¿cuáles?
2. ¿Ofrecen premios los radioprogramas que usted escucha?
3. En su opinión, ¿cuál es la estación musical de radio más popular?

4. ¿Es usted mayor o menor que Rafael de los Santos?
5. ¿Cuántas horas al día o a la semana trabaja usted?
6. ¿Se despierta usted solo/a o con la ayuda de un despertador? ¿A qué hora se levanta usted?
7. ¿Le duele a usted la cabeza o el estómago si no toma el desayuno?

Vocabulario

Palabras análogas

estricto, -a
el kilómetro

musical
publicitario, -a

el radioprograma
la refinería

Sustantivos

la **central**   plant
el **despertador**   alarm clock
el/la **dueño/a**   owner
la **juventud**   youth
el **radiorreloj**   clock radio

Adjetivos

azucarero, -a   sugar
estimado, -a   esteemed
seguro, -a   certain

Verbos

atreverse (a)   to dare (to)
coger   to catch, get
dedicarse (a)   to devote oneself (to)
dejar de   to stop
desayunarse   to have breakfast
descansar   to rest

dirigirse (a)   to direct oneself; to be aimed (at)
enseñar   to teach
ponerse *(irreg.)* **(a** + *inf.)*   to begin (to), start (to)
requerir (ie)   to require, need

Otras palabras y expresiones

a menudo   often
a pesar de   in spite of
a través de   through
a veces   sometimes
corriendo   running
de prisa   quickly, hurriedly
explicando   explaining
ganarse la vida   to earn one's living
haga esto y haga lo otro   do this and do that
morirse de hambre   to starve (literally, to die from hunger)
principalmente   mainly

Práctica

A. Llame por teléfono a *La Voz de los Jóvenes* para explicar por qué quiere ganar el radiorreloj. Dé algunos detalles de su rutina *(routine)* por la mañana.

B. Imagínese que Ud. trabaja para La Estación Musical 56 y tiene que preparar un intermedio *(break)* de tres minutos en un programa musical. Prepare lo que va a decir, incluyendo algún anuncio publicitario, el nombre de un cantante y la canción que van a escuchar los radioyentes de la estación.

Nota cultural La República Dominicana

La República Dominicana, con una población de más de 6 millones de habitantes, se encuentra en La Española. Esta isla, segunda en tamaño[1] en el Mar Caribe, está situada entre Cuba y Puerto Rico. La República Dominicana ocupa dos terceras partes de la isla, y la República de Haití ocupa el resto. La Española es una isla muy hermosa, con montañas altas cubiertas de[2] bosques, valles verdes y playas de arena[3] blanca. Cristóbal Colón descubrió la isla en 1492, y su hermano Bartolomé fundó la ciudad de Santo Domingo, la capital actual del país.

La economía de la República Dominicana está basada principalmente en la agricultura. La cosecha[4] más importante y el producto principal de exportación es la caña de azúcar. Se exportan también el café, el cacao, el arroz y el tabaco. Para que el país tenga una economía más variada, el gobierno fomenta[5] las industrias ligeras,[6] como la del cemento, los textiles, los productos farmacéuticos y los productos de madera. Fomenta también el turismo, que cada año da más empleos a los dominicanos.

---

1. size 2. **cubiertas** ... covered with 3. sand 4. crop 5. is promoting (encouraging) 6. light

(Izquierda) Santo Domingo, la capital de la República Dominicana es una ciudad próspera y activa, con muchos negocios nacionales y multinacionales. La población urbana llega al 54% del total de la isla. (Derecha) La estatua de Cristobal Colón preside la plaza del mismo nombre en Santo Domingo. Al fondo se ve la primera iglesia construida por los españoles en el Nuevo Mundo (Catedral Basílica Menor de Santa María). ¿Cuándo cree Ud. que fue construida la iglesia, antes o después del siglo XV? ¿Por qué?

Pronunciación y ortografía

Signos de puntuación

1. Here is a list of the most common punctuation marks in Spanish.

.	punto	( )	paréntesis
,	coma	–	guión
;	punto y coma	. . .	puntos suspensivos
:	dos puntos	¿ ?	signos de interrogación
´	acento (tilde)	¡ !	signos de exclamación
¨	diéresis		(admiración)
« » o " "	comillas	—	raya

2. For the most part, punctuation marks are used in Spanish as they are in English. Exceptions, in addition to use of the upside down question mark and exclamation point, include the following:

a. The dash (—) is used to introduce the lines said by each speaker in a dialogue.

b. The " " quotation marks are used mostly for direct quotations from written texts. The « » quotation marks are used mostly to give quotations from conversations, and sometimes also to set off the title of a publication, such as a book or a magazine.

A. Dicte la siguiente conversación entre Ramón y Teresa a otra persona de la clase. Luego corrija las oraciones. Use las indicaciones **raya, punto,** etcétera al dictar las oraciones.

1. —¿Qué le dijiste a ése?
2. —Le dije: «¡Estás loco!»
3. —Y luego, ¿hablaste de . . . lo que sabemos?
4. —No, ya no hubo tiempo para más.

B. Escriba el siguiente párrafo al dictarlo su profesor/a. Luego corríjalo, comparándolo con el párrafo del libro.

Doña Matilde Pedregón (la señora de don Jacinto Pedregón y Toneles) dijo: «¿Quién me cogió la cartera?» Pero su protesta sólo encontró un silencio absoluto. «¡Ah, sí, miserables!» protestó nuevamente. «¿Quieren que lo averigüe yo, o que lo averigüe el policía que . . . ? No me digan que no saben o que no quieren saber; o que mi cartera no les interesa.»

C. Identifique todos los signos de puntuación que aparecen en el Ejercicio B de esta sección.

Estudio de palabras

I. Materiales

el acero steel	**la lana** wool
el adobe adobe	**el lino (hilo)** linen
el algodón cotton	**la madera** wood
el cemento cement	**el nilón** nylon
el cobre copper	**el oro** gold
el cristal glass, crystal	**el plástico** plastic
el cuero leather	**la plata** silver
el dril denim	**el poliéster** polyester
el hierro iron	**la seda** silk
el ladrillo brick	

A. Describa la ropa que usted lleva en este momento. Mencione el color, el material, y (si quiere) cuánto le costó.

B. Imagínese que usted trabaja para un gran almacén y está encargado de (*in charge of*) la sección de publicidad. Prepare un anuncio para el periódico local. Haga una lista de los artículos rebajados (*at a discount*). Dé algunos detalles descriptivos de cada artículo.

C. ¿De qué material(es) están hechos (*are made*) los siguientes objetos?

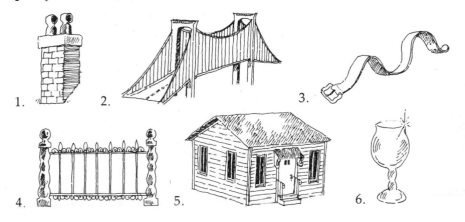

1.   2.   3.

4.   5.   6.

II. Sustantivos compuestos

Many compound nouns in Spanish are made up of a *verb form + noun*. They are always masculine in gender.

el abrelatas   **abre** (from **abrir**) + **latas** (*cans*) = can opener
el parabrisas   **para** (from **parar**) + **brisas** (*breezes*) = windshield

D. Lea las oraciones, tratando de comprender el significado de los sustantivos compuestos.

1. el lavamanos — Si quieres lavarte las manos, allí está el lavamanos.
2. el lavaplatos — Dejemos los platos por ahora; después los lavamos en el lavaplatos.
3. el paracaídas — ¡Mira! Dos personas cayeron de aquel avión con paracaídas.
4. el paraguas — Llueve mucho. ¡Qué lástima! No tengo conmigo ni impermeable ni paraguas.
5. el sacacorchos — No puedo servir el vino porque no encuentro el sacacorchos para abrir la botella.
6. el salvavidas — En todos los barcos hay que llevar por lo menos un salvavidas para cada pasajero.
7. el sacapuntas — Espera. Tengo que sacarle punta a mi lápiz. ¿Dónde está el sacapuntas?

Estructuras útiles

I. Usted-, ustedes-, and nosotros-commands

—*¡Declaremos una huelga de hambre!*
—*Ay, no digan tonterías...*

1. When using a command, a speaker is attempting to influence someone's behavior. The command forms for **Ud., Uds.,** and **nosotros/as** (*let's* + verb) are identical to the corresponding present subjunctive forms. The pronouns **usted** and **ustedes** *follow* the verb form in commands when they are expressed; the pronouns **nosotros/as** are rarely stated.

¡Trate (usted) de llegar temprano!   *Try to arrive early!*
Compren (ustedes) una casa   *Buy a house nearer the refinery.*
  más cerca de la refinería.
¡Ofrezcamos un premio!   *Let's offer a prize!*

No compre (usted) ese radiorreloj.	*Don't buy that clock radio.*
No digan (ustedes) tonterías.	*Don't say such foolish things!*
¡No vendamos el coche!	*Let's not sell the car!*

2. In affirmative commands, single object pronouns (including reflexive pronouns) are attached to the end of the verb form, and a written accent is required on the stressed syllable.

—¿Investigo la situación?	*Shall I investigate the situation?*
—Sí, **investíguela** en seguida.	*Yes, investigate it at once.*
—¿Me olvido del asunto?	*Shall I forget about that business?*
—Sí, **olvídese** de eso.	*Yes, forget about it.*
—¿Compramos la casa?	*Shall we buy the house?*
—Sí, **comprémosla.**	*Yes, let's buy it.*

3. In negative commands, single object pronouns (including reflexive pronouns) precede the verb form.

—¿Firmo esta carta?	*Shall I sign this letter?*
—No, **no la firme** todavía.	*No, don't sign it yet.*
—¿Me siento allí?	*Shall I sit there?*
—No, **no se siente** en esa silla.	*No, don't sit in that chair.*
—¿Discutimos el asunto?	*Shall we discuss the matter?*
—No, **no lo discutamos.**	*No, let's not discuss it.*

4. The affirmative **nosotros**-command of **ir** is **vamos.** The negative form is **vayamos.**

¡Vamos!	*Let's go!*
¡No vayamos!	*Let's not go!*

5. The affirmative **nosotros**-command followed by **se** or by the reflexive **-nos** loses the final **-s** of the verb form.

Démoselo a ellos ahora. No se lo demos mañana.	*Let's give it to them now. Let's not give it to them tomorrow.*
Sentémonos aquí. No nos sentemos allí.	*Let's sit here. Let's not sit there.*

6. In the affirmative, *let's* + verb can also be expressed in Spanish by the construction **vamos a** + *infinitive.*

¡Vamos a comer!	*Let's eat!*
¡Vamos a bailar!	*Let's dance!*

A. Usted da consejos a un matrimonio que visita su pueblo o ciudad por primera vez. Use mandatos con **usted** o **ustedes** en el afirmativo o en el negativo. Si puede, dé razones lógicas para explicar su consejo.

▶ Mi esposa y yo queremos comer en ese restaurante.

No coman ustedes en ese restaurante. [No sirven buena comida.] Sí, coman ahí. [La comida es excelente.]

1. Yo pienso visitar el Museo de Bellas Artes esta tarde.
2. Mi esposa y yo pensamos comprar algunas cosas en el Almacén San Carlos.
3. Deseo sacar fotos de la Iglesia Santa María.
4. Mi esposa y yo deseamos salir por la noche.
5. Mañana vamos a consultar con un agente de viajes.
6. Pensamos volver a casa el sábado a mediodía.

B. Usted trabaja en la oficina de una central azucarera en Puerto Rico. Conteste las preguntas de la secretaria según las indicaciones. Use pronombres para expresar los objetos directos o indirectos en sus respuestas.

▶ ¿Quiere usted que yo lleve estos documentos al jefe? (sí)

Sí, llévelos al jefe, por favor.

1. ¿Quiere que yo escriba estos papeles a máquina ahora? (no)
2. ¿Desea que yo cierre la puerta de la oficina? (no)
3. ¿Desea que yo revise este artículo? (sí)
4. ¿Quiere usted que mi asistente y yo terminemos este trabajo antes de salir? (sí)
5. ¿Quiere usted que yo le dé la cita al señor Ruiz? (sí)
6. ¿Desea usted que yo llame a la coordinadora esta tarde? (no)

C. Haga mandatos con **usted** o **ustedes** y algunos de los verbos indicados.

▶ escuchar   *¡Escuchen la música!*

asistir	negar	pagar
comenzar	entrar	apagar
investigar	saborear	tomar
demostrar	encender	aprender

D. Miguel y Carlos están de vacaciones en Lima, Perú. Miguel propone varias actividades interesantes, pero Carlos quiere hacer algo diferente. Haga el papel de Miguel o de Carlos y use la forma apropiada del verbo con **nosotros.**

▶ ¿visitar el museo o la biblioteca?

Miguel: *Visitemos el museo, ¿quieres?*
Carlos: *No, no lo visitemos; visitemos la biblioteca.*

1. ¿ir al mercado o al almacén?
2. ¿comer en un café o en un restaurante?
3. ¿escuchar la radio o mirar televisión?
4. ¿comprar libros o revistas?
5. ¿beber un refresco o agua?
6. ¿tomar el metro o el autobús?

E. Usted no está de acuerdo con las sugerencias de un amigo o una amiga. Conteste en forma negativa y use un objeto directo o indirecto en sus respuestas.

▶ ¿Vamos a leer el periódico?   *No, no lo leamos ahora.*

1. ¿Vamos a escribirle a Grisel?
2. ¿Vamos a comer unos helados?
3. ¿Vamos a darle los discos a Pepe?
4. ¿Vamos a mostrarle el radiorreloj a Ricardo?
5. ¿Vamos a seguir a esos hombres?
6. ¿Vamos a llamar a la policía?

II. More on reflexive constructions

Manuel ayuda a Gabriel.

*Manuel y Gabriel **se ayudan.***

1. The plural reflexive forms **nos, os,** and **se** (*plural*) are used to express reciprocal meaning (*each other, one another*).

Tú y yo **nos comprendemos** bien.	*You and I understand each other well.*
Marta y Pepe **se escriben** a menudo.	*Marta and Pepe write one another often.*
¿Por qué no **os saludáis?**	*Why don't you greet each other?*

2. The following verbs are often used with a reciprocal meaning.

ayudarse to help each other
comprenderse to understand
  one another
conocerse to know (one
  another); to be or become
  acquainted

encontrarse to meet, come
  across (one another)
escribirse to write to each other
saludarse to greet one another
verse to see each other

3. Some verbs, mostly ones that do not take a direct object, have a special
   meaning when used reflexively. Note that the verb **morir** is used in
   idioms such as **morirse de hambre** *(to starve to death)* and **morirse de
   sed** *(to die of thirst)*.

caer to fall
dormir to sleep
ir to go
morir to die
salir to go out
subir to go up

caerse to fall down
dormirse to fall asleep
irse to leave
morirse to die
salirse to leave, escape
subirse to climb (with effort)

F. Usted conoce a Beatriz hace bastante tiempo. Tomás quiere saber más
   acerca de su amistad con Beatriz.

▶ ¿Ustedes se sientan juntos/as en clase?   *Sí, nos sentamos juntos/as
                                                en clase.*

1. ¿Ustedes dos se hablan en español?
2. ¿Ustedes se encuentran en la biblioteca?
3. ¿Ustedes dos se ven los sábados?
4. ¿Ustedes dos se comprenden bien?
5. ¿Ustedes se ayudan a hacer las tareas *(homework; chores)*?
6. ¿Ustedes se escriben cuando están de vacaciones?

G. Complete las oraciones siguientes con el presente o el pretérito de uno
   de los verbos de la lista. Use la forma recíproca del verbo.

ayudar   encontrar   saludar
comprender   escribir   ver
conocer

▶ Pepe y yo _____ por casualidad en el Museo   *nos encontramos*
  Antropológico.

1. Mi madre y yo no _____ . Ella no confía en mí.
2. Mi novia y yo _____ por lo menos dos veces a la semana.
3. Mi abuelo paterno y mi padre _____ una vez al mes. Les gusta
   escribir cartas largas.

4. El profesor de inglés y la profesora de español _____ en el comedor de la universidad.
5. Esa chica y Carlos _____ la semana pasada en el Club Marino, ¿verdad?
6. ¿Tu compañero de clase y tú _____ con las tareas?

H. Complete las oraciones con la forma correcta del verbo apropiado.

caer / caerse   salir / salirse
dormir / dormirse   subir / subirse
morir / morirse

1. Mi abuelita _____ el mismo año que _____ el presidente Suárez.
2. No encontré la clase interesante y por eso yo _____ por la puerta de atrás. Todos los otros estudiantes _____ al terminar la clase.
3. Ayer _____ mucha nieve toda la tarde y mi hermana _____ en la acera.
4. Como no había escaleras para _____ al techo de la casa, el obrero _____ por un poste de la luz que había cerca.
5. Anoche yo _____ muy poco porque mi hermanito estaba enfermo y _____ muy tarde.

III. More on the imperfect versus the preterit

1. The basic uses of the imperfect and the preterit are contrasted in the following chart.

Imperfect	Preterit
1. Describes an event in progress, or a situation or condition that existed over an indefinite period of time in the past. 2. Describes habitual or repeated past events. 3. Describes the background or tells what was happening when an event took place. 4. Expresses clock time and age in the past.	1. Talks about a completed past event or a completed series of past events. 2. Focuses on the beginning or end of a past event.

2. Use of the imperfect and the preterit of **conocer, saber, querer,** and **poder** depends upon the special meaning that the speaker wishes to convey. Note how the English equivalents change with use of the imperfect and the preterit of these verbs.

Conocí a Jaime en tu casa.	*I met (was introduced to) Jaime at your house.*
Ya lo **conocía**.	*I knew him already.*
Supe que estabas enferma.	*I learned (found out for the first time) that you were sick.*
Sabía que estabas enferma.	*I knew (was aware at the time) that you were sick.*
Quise ir, pero no **pude**.	*I wanted (tried) to go, but I didn't succeed.*
Quería ir, pero no **podía**.	*I wanted to go (felt like going), but I couldn't (was unable to due to circumstances).*
Inés **no quiso** ir al baile.	*Inés refused to go to the dance.*

I. Complete con el pretérito o el imperfecto de los verbos **conocer, saber, querer** y **poder.**

1. —¿Cuándo _____ usted a Carlos? —Lo _____ en casa de Roberto.
2. —Roberto está en el hospital. —Ah, ¿sí? Pues yo no _____ que estaba enfermo.
3. De joven, yo siempre _____ hacer muchas cosas.
4. Traté de abrir la puerta, pero no _____ .
5. El profesor hizo una de aquellas preguntas horribles, y nadie _____ la respuesta.
6. Yo ya _____ a todos los que estaban allí.

J. Exprese en español los siguientes diálogos.

1. —Do you know Patricia Santamaría?
   —Yes, I met her at Juan's house.
   —Did you know that her sister is in the hospital?
   —Yes, I found it out yesterday.
2. —Did you invite Rosita to go with you to the party?
   —Yes, I invited her, but she refused to go.
   —Did you go to the party anyway?
   —I wanted to go, but I couldn't.

IV. Verbs followed by **a** or **de** + *infinitive*

1. Verbs that refer to the beginning of an action or state, or to something that is (or was) about to happen, often require the preposition **a** before an infinitive. The following verbs use **a** and are often associated with actions about to begin.

atreverse a	¡**Atrévete a** decirlo!
ayudar a	¿Me **ayudas a** llevar esto?
comenzar a	**Comienzo a** comprender.
decidirse a	Me **decidí a** aceptar la invitación.
dedicarse a	Nos **dedicamos a** trabajar.
empezar a	**Empezamos a** trabajar.
enseñar a	Le **enseño a** hablar español.
ir a	**Van a** visitar a Juan.
negarse a	Nos **negamos a** hacerlo.
ponerse a	Se **puso a** cantar en el baño.

2. Verbs that refer to something that has already happened or is coming to an end often require the preposition **de** before an infinitive. The following verbs use **de** and are often associated with actions that have already occurred.

acabar de	¡**Acabemos de** reparar este aparato!
alegrarse de	Me **alegro de** saber que has encontrado empleo.
arrepentirse de	Se **arrepintió de** comprar la cámara.
dejar de	**Dejó de** tocar el piano.
terminar de	**Terminamos de** estudiar tardísimo.

K. Una persona de la clase empieza a hacer lo siguiente. Diga que usted ya acabó de hacerlo.

► estudiar para los exámenes

S1: *Empiezo a estudiar para mis exámenes.*
S2: *Pues yo ya acabé de estudiar para los míos.*

1. organizar un experimento
2. prepararme para salir
3. leer una novela
4. ayudar con la comida
5. escribir una tesis
6. explicar el asunto

L. Muchas personas no se atreven a hacer ciertas cosas. Diga si Ud. se atreve a hacer lo siguiente. O, suponiendo *(assuming)* que Ud. ya las hizo, diga si Ud. se arrepintió de hacerlas.

► dar un concierto

No me atrevo a dar un concierto.
Una vez me atreví a dar un concierto, y no me arrepentí de hacerlo.

1. correr diez kilómetros sin parar
2. sobrepasar *(to exceed)* el límite de la velocidad al conducir
3. presentarse a un examen sin estudiar
4. hacerse artista
5. bañarse con el grupo «Los Osos Polares»
6. viajar a Alemania solo/a sin saber alemán

M. Diga si es necesario usar **a** o **de** antes de los infinitivos en las siguientes oraciones.

1. Ya empezábamos _____ comprender este lío.
2. Siempre me arrepiento _____ decir estupideces.
3. No creo que Memo se atreva _____ actuar en el drama.
4. Me dijo que quiere ir _____ ver a su amiga esta tarde.
5. Mi hermana me va _____ contar la historia.
6. ¡Nos alegramos _____ recibir buenas noticias tuyas!
7. Un amigo me enseñó _____ esquiar en el agua.
8. ¿A qué te dedicas ahora? ¿ _____ vender radiorrelojes?

N. Imagínese que usted es un famoso actor o actriz. Hable de su vida y de sus planes futuros, usando verbos que requieren las preposiciones **a** o **de** antes del infinitivo.

▶ *Me llamo [John Wayne]. Quiero empezar a trabajar en películas más realistas, pero no me niego a trabajar en películas de aventuras.*

¡Exprésese usted!
La oración clave

En las *Lecciones 13* y *14* usted aprendió a resumir en sus propias palabras los puntos más importantes de una lectura. Es de mucha utilidad ahora aprender a reconocer la oración clave (*topic sentence*) de una selección. La oración clave representa un resumen del párrafo y es posible usarla como título de éste. Puede ocurrir en forma explícita, cuando una oración en particular del párrafo lo resume, o en forma implícita, cuando no aparece directamente en el párrafo, pero se puede deducir de la lectura.

Lea la siguiente selección histórica sobre la República Dominicana. Busque y tome nota de la oración clave explícita de cada párrafo, o escriba una original si la oración clave es implícita.

La República Dominicana: Una vista histórica

Cuando Cristóbal Colón descubrió la Isla de Haití (nombre nativo), la llamó «La Española». Esta isla forma parte de las Antillas y hoy en día está dividida entre la República de Haití y la República Dominicana.

5   Desde su descubrimiento por Colón hasta el presente, la historia de la República Dominicana muestra innumerables problemas políticos. España perdió interés en la isla por los descubrimientos en el continente, y la cedió a Francia en 1795. En 1801 empezó a formar parte de Haití, luego de la invasión dirigida por el líder haitiano, Toussaint L'Ouverture.

10   Después de su independencia de Haití en 1844, la República Dominicana sufrió tres dictaduras (1844–1916). Estuvo bajo el control de España
(1861–1863) y el de los Estados Unidos (1916–1924). Finalmente, después
de un breve período de un gobierno constitucional pero impotente (1924–
1930), tuvo la terrible dictadura del general Rafael Trujillo (1930–1961).
15   Trujillo todavía es recordado con admiración por algunos y con terror
por otros. Su poder se extendía por la República Dominicana, y también por
otros países de América y Europa (incluso en los Estados Unidos), donde
algunos refugiados políticos morían asesinados a manos de agentes secretos
de su gobierno. Bajo Trujillo hubo progreso material y social; sin embargo,
20 el gobierno bajo su mano fuerte le quitó al pueblo grandes cantidades de
dinero y actuó con extrema crueldad con los prisioneros políticos.
    Hoy en día los dominicanos tienen un gobierno constitucional, y tratan
de establecer una democracia moderna y progresista. Se celebran elecciones
presidenciales cada cuatro años, y la constitución garantiza los derechos
25 personales y políticos de los dominicanos.

A. Compare sus oraciones claves con las siguientes. Sus oraciones claves
    para cada párrafo deben aproximarse a éstas.

Primer párrafo:	La República Dominicana es uno de dos países que forman la isla de La Española. (implícita)
Segundo párrafo:	"La historia de la República Dominicana muestra innumerables problemas políticos." (explícita)
Tercer párrafo:	Entre 1844 y 1961 la República Dominicana tuvo sólo seis años de gobierno constitucional pero impotente. (implícita)
Cuarto párrafo:	Trujillo tuvo un gobierno dictatorial con progreso material y social. (implícita)
Quinto párrafo:	"Hoy en día los dominicanos tienen un gobierno constitucional, y tratan de establecer una democracia moderna y progresista." (explícita)

B. Usando sus oraciones claves, escriba un resumen corto de la historia
    de la República Dominicana. Si quiere, añada dos o tres cosas más de
    la lectura. Recuerde que debe usar comillas para las citas copiadas
    directamente de la selección original.

Lección 18
En Cuba

Una entrevista

El periodista mexicano Andrés Ramos está en el gimnasio de la Universidad de La Habana, donde se entrenan los atletas para los próximos Juegos Panamericanos. Ahora entrevista a Ángela Molina, una joven atleta cubana.

Periodista: Señorita, mañana usted va a participar en la competencia de esgrima. ¿Cómo se siente usted? ¿Un poco nerviosa?

Ángela: No, me siento muy en forma. Estoy acostumbrada al espíritu competitivo de los campeonatos.

5 Periodista: Todo el mundo tiene ganas de verla a usted, la campeona de Cuba que tuvo tanto éxito en los últimos Juegos Panamericanos. Y todos esperan que usted tenga éxito mañana.

Ángela: Muchas gracias. Espero no desilusionarlo a usted ni a los demás aficionados.

10 Periodista: Veo que aquí en Cuba hay mucho interés por las competencias deportivas. ¿Por qué las toman tan en serio? ¿Puede decírmelo?

Ángela: Sí. Se lo explico. Nuestros atletas pertenecen a un sinnúmero de equipos regionales y practican los deportes con mucha

Algunos héroes revolucionarios aparecen diseñados por el público del Estadio Latinoamericano de La Habana durante el Festival Mundial de la Juventud. El primero a la izquierda es José Martí. ¿Reconoce Ud. a alguno de los otros?

seriedad. Hay un creciente interés por parte del público
15   porque ven los éxitos de los deportistas y jugadores cubanos
casi como un triunfo personal.

Periodista: Hay muchos campeones famosos entre los cubanos. ¿Cómo
puede explicar Ud. una tradición de tanto éxito en el atletismo?

Ángela: Lo que pasa es que no hay muchos gobiernos que fomenten el
20   atletismo tanto como el nuestro, o que construyan instalaciones deportivas buenas como este gimnasio, por ejemplo.
Además, el clima maravilloso nos permite entrenarnos al aire
libre. Y claro, los espectadores siempre nos animan mucho.

Periodista: ¿Piensa dejar el atletismo algún día?
25   Ángela: En absoluto. El atletismo es todo para mí, y cuando no pueda
practicarlo más, pienso dedicarme a entrenar a otros atletas.

Comprensión

1. ¿Por qué está Andrés Ramos en Cuba?
2. ¿Quién es Ángela Molina? ¿Qué deporte practica Ángela?
3. ¿Por qué no está nerviosa Ángela ese día?
4. ¿Qué es un aficionado? ¿Qué esperan los aficionados de Ángela?
5. Según Ángela, ¿cuáles son las razones para el éxito del atletismo cubano?
6. ¿Qué piensa hacer Ángela cuando no pueda practicar más el atletismo?

Conversación

1. ¿Es usted deportista? ¿Qué deportes practica?
2. ¿Cuántas horas a la semana se entrena?
3. ¿Le gusta la esgrima? ¿Es éste un deporte popular en los Estados Unidos?
4. ¿Piensa Ud. participar alguna vez en un campeonato deportivo? ¿En
qué clase de campeonato deportivo?
5. ¿Le interesan los Juegos Panamericanos?
6. Nombre tres campeones deportivos hispanoamericanos o norteamericanos.
7. ¿Cree usted que la universidad debe dar una preparación deportiva
además de una preparación académica?
8. En su opinión, ¿se le da demasiada importancia a los deportes en el
sistema educativo de Estados Unidos?

Vocabulario

Palabras análogas

académico, -a   fantástico, -a   panamericano, -a
la administración   maravilloso, -a   regional
competitivo, -a

Sustantivos

el/la atleta athlete
el atletismo athletics
el campeonato championship
el clima weather, climate
la competencia competition
la derrota defeat
la esgrima fencing
el/la espectador/a spectator
el espíritu spirit
la instalación deportiva sports facility
el juego game
el/la jugador/a player
el/la periodista journalist
la razón reason
la seriedad seriousness
el sinnúmero endless number
el triunfo triumph

Adjetivos

acostumbrado, -a accustomed
creciente growing
demasiado, -a too much, too many

Verbos

animar to encourage, cheer
construir to build, construct
construir to build, construct
dejar to leave behind; to let, allow
desilusionar to disappoint, disillusion
entrenarse to train
fomentar to promote, encourage
nombrar to name
pertenecer (zc) to belong to

Otras palabras y expresiones

casi almost
los demás the other, the rest of
en absoluto not at all
en forma in good shape
por parte de on the part of
tan en serio so seriously

Práctica

BÉISBOL

*el Club Habana
contra el Club
Pinar del Río*

Fecha: Domingo, 3 de abril
Hora: 2,00 p.m.
Lugar: Estadio Latinoamericano

A. Entreviste a un/a compañero/a de clase sobre los deportes en su universidad. Pídale que nombre los deportes que practican los atletas, los deportes que más le interesan y en cuáles espera poder participar este año. Refiérase a la lista de deportes de la página 332.

B. Mire el anuncio de un partido de béisbol. Discuta con su profesor/a qué equipos van a jugar, cuándo y dónde va a tener lugar el partido. Diga qué equipo va a ganar, en su opinión, y por qué.

Nota cultural Los deportes en Cuba

La educación física en Cuba es obligatoria en todas las escuelas y universidades y se le da gran importancia a la competencia deportiva. Sin embargo, las escuelas no descuidan[1] otros aspectos de la educación. Los estudiantes que demuestran talento deportivo reciben su preparación académica al

---

1. **no . . .** do not neglect

Los equipos cubano y estadounidense participan en una
competición de básquetbol.
¿Dónde cree Ud. que es posible
ver un partido entre estos dos
equipos? ¿Qué cree Ud. que
significa "El deporte es un
derecho del pueblo", el lema
(slogan) que aparece al fondo
(background) de esta fotografía?

mismo tiempo que reciben entrenamiento[2] deportivo. Si uno de estos jóvenes (hombre o mujer) sobresale[3] en algún dep... llega a ser un atleta
nacional, un héroe de la juventud.

No existe el deporte profesional en Cuba, ...an muchos
deportes, como el béisbol, el boxeo, el polo y ...ía política de Cuba, la oportunidad de participa... ...omo
atleta o como espectador pertenece a todo ...n ver
un partido de béisbol, el deporte nacio... ...trada,
porque lo subvenciona[4] el gobierno. ¡Lo... ...el estadio!

---

2. training 3. excels 4. subsidizes

Pronunciación

Dictado

Escuche la siguiente sele... ...r/a mientras la sigue
usted en el libro. Luego ... ...su profesor/a en frases
cortas. No olvide los acen... ...puntuación.

¡No es fácil tener paciencia, cre... ...er posible que yo sea excesivamente impaciente? No me gusta ... ...n autobús por más de cinco
minutos. Detesto esperar en la sala de esp... de un médico. Me desespera

JUEGOS
CENTROAMERICANOS
Y DEL CARIBE

esperar semanas y meses por una fiesta, un viaje, una operación—cualquier cosa. Hay quienes prefieren esperar. Dicen algunos que mientras esperan, los problemas se resuelven solos o desaparecen. Yo creo que se multiplican, y después me devoran vivo. Dicen otros que «el mejor maestro es el tiempo y la mejor maestra la experiencia». ¡Hermoso refrán! Pero más real y verdadero para mí es este otro: «Él que espera desespera».

Estudio de palabras

I. Más actividades deportivas

el baloncesto
(el básquetbol)

los bolos

el fútbol

el ciclismo

la pelota
(el béisbol)

el jai alai

la equitación

el voleibol

el boxeo

Expresiones relacionadas con los deportes

jugar al baloncesto   to play
  basketball
jugar a los bolos   to bowl, go
  bowling
jugar al fútbol   to play soccer
jugar a la pelota   to play baseball
jugar al voleibol   to play volleyball

marcar un gol   to score a goal
montar a caballo   to ride horseback
practicar el boxeo   to box
practicar el ciclismo   to go
  cycling
practicar el jai alai   to play jai
  alai

In current usage, **jugar** can be used without **a** + *the definite article.*

¿Quieres **jugar al tenis?**
¿Quieres **jugar tenis?**   *Do you want to play tennis?*

A. Diga en qué estación del año se practica cada deporte en la región donde usted vive o en otras regiones de los Estados Unidos.

B. Pregúntele a un grupo pequeño de compañeros de clase acerca de los deportes. ¿Cuáles son sus tres deportes preferidos y en qué orden de preferencia? ¿Cuántos practican un deporte? ¿Cuántos son espectadores o aficionados del deporte? ¿Prefieren asistir al deporte o mirarlo en la televisión?

C. Lea el párrafo siguiente y luego prepare cinco preguntas basadas en el texto, usando palabras interrogativas. Después hágales sus preguntas a algunos compañeros de clase.

Ayer los aficionados del Club Atlético de Madrid fueron al estadio para ver el último partido de fútbol de este año. Cerca de diez mil personas se reunieron en el estadio Vicente Calderón para presenciar el juego entre el equipo madrileño y el Betis de Sevilla. Los jugadores del Betis se defendieron muy bien, pero no pudieron marcar ni un gol frente a la agresión de los rojiblancos, que resultaron ser una vez más el orgullo de los espectadores de la capital.

II. Familias de palabras

Sometimes it is possible to form several types of words from the same word stem. The word stem **interés,** for example, can appear as the noun **el interés,** in the verb **interesar,** in the adjective **interesante** and in the adverb **interesantemente.** These sets of related words belong to *word families.* Not all word stems can be formed into so many variations. Some, such as **escuela,** can only be used as a noun (**escolaridad, escolasticismo**) or as an adjective (**escolar, escolástico**).

D. Dé Ud. todas las variaciones que pueda de las siguientes palabras.

1. asistir
2. el trabajo
3. comercial
4. civil
5. la pesca
6. público
7. industrializar
8. la visita
9. mineral

E. Usted ya conoce algunos de los verbos y sustantivos siguientes. Diga lo que quiere decir en inglés cada par *(pair)* de palabras.

1. servir / el servicio
2. secar / la secadora
3. viajar / el viaje
4. practicar / la práctica
5. nevar / la nevera
6. mejorar / el mejoramiento
7. mandar / el mando
8. importar / la importancia
9. firmar / la firma
10. emplear / el empleo

Estructuras útiles

I. Review of the present subjunctive in noun clauses

The following is a review of the principal uses of the present subjunctive that you have previously studied on pages 244–246.

1. The present subjunctive is used in a dependent noun clause after a main clause in which the speaker expresses a *desire to influence,* or indicates *emotion, hope, doubt,* or *denial.* Remember that if there is no change in subject the infinitive construction is used.

Desire to influence: No me gusta que **tomes** gaseosas, ni me gusta tomarlas a mí tampoco.
Hope: Espero que no me **olvides.**
Ojalá (que) **puedas** ir a la fiesta conmigo.
Doubt: Con esta lluvia dudo que el avión **llegue** a tiempo.

2. The present subjunctive is used in a dependent noun clause after an *impersonal expression* that reflects a *subjective judgment, a desire to influence, an emotion, doubt,* or *denial.*

Es absurdo
Es necesario
Es horrible
Puede ser   } que tú no **vuelvas** a tu casa.
Es incomprensible
Es preferible
Es una lástima

A. Dígale a su hermano que Ud. espera que mañana haga las actividades mencionadas una hora más temprano.

▶ Te despiertas generalmente a las ocho. *Espero que mañana te despiertes a las siete.*

1. Te levantas generalmente a las ocho y media.
2. Generalmente te bañas a las nueve menos cuarto.
3. Te desayunas generalmente a las nueve.
4. Te pones a trabajar generalmente a las nueve y diez.
5. Generalmente te sientas a ver la televisión a las seis.
6. Te acuestas generalmente a las once de la noche.

B. Exprese una emoción **(siento, me alegro, no me gusta, me molesta, temo)** hacia las siguientes situaciones, y añada *(add)* otros detalles o comentarios.

▶ La profesora está enferma. *Siento mucho que esté enferma, pero me alegro de que no haya clase porque tengo una cita.*

1. Este año no hay vacaciones.
2. Tenemos una conferencia importante hoy.
3. Nunca recibo dinero de mis padres.
4. Mañana tu amigo/a no puede visitarte.
5. El español es una lengua muy fácil.
6. Mucha gente muere de hambre en el mundo.
7. Tenemos un equipo de fútbol excelente, pero no construyen un estadio.
8. Practicas muy pocos deportes y comes demasiado.

C. Exprese cinco deseos para el año entrante, usando la expresión **¡Ojalá (que)!**

▶ *¡Ojalá que yo pueda ir a México el año entrante!*

D. Termine las oraciones siguientes en forma original e imaginativa. Use el presente del subjuntivo o del indicativo, según el sentido de la oración.

▶ Es imposible que . . . . *un loco como yo piense lógicamente.*

1. Todos saben que . . . .
2. Es extraordinario que . . . .
3. Es maravilloso que . . . .
4. Es obvio que . . . .
5. Dicen que . . . .
6. Es verdad que . . . .
7. Es estupendo que . . . .
8. Es algo increíble que . . . .
9. Creo que . . . .
10. Es necesario que . . . .

II. Indicative versus subjunctive in adjective clauses

Deseo conocer un/a muchacho/a que **pueda** *comprenderme, que* **se interese** *en los deportes y que no* **fume**.

1. An adjective clause (**que**-clause) is a dependent clause that modifies a noun or pronoun. When the noun or pronoun modified by the **que**-clause refers to someone or something that is not a part of the speaker's knowledge or experienced reality or is non-existent, the verb in the dependent **que**-clause is in the subjunctive. This is often the case after a main clause that includes verbs and expressions such as **no hay . . .**, **necesito . . .**, **no puedo imaginar . . .**, and **¿dónde encuentro . . . ?** When the noun or pronoun is definite and exists, the indicative is used in the dependent **que-**clause. Compare the following pairs of sentences:

El nuestro es un gobierno que **fomenta** el atletismo.
Ours is a government that promotes athletics.

No hay muchos gobiernos que **fomenten** el atletismo tanto como el nuestro.
There aren't many governments that promote athletics as much as ours.

Allí está la secretaria que **escribe** bien a máquina.
There is the secretary who types well.

Necesito una secretaria que **escriba** bien a máquina.
I need a secretary who types well.

Mario compró una casa maravillosa, que **tiene** siete habitaciones.
Mario bought a marvelous house, which has seven bedrooms.

No puedo imaginar una casa que **tenga** tantas habitaciones.
I can't imagine a house that has so many bedrooms.

Aquí hay una profesora que **enseña** bien.
There's a teacher here who teaches well.

¿Dónde encuentro un profesor que **enseñe** mejor?
Where can I find a teacher who teaches better?

2. Note that when the direct-object noun in a sentence refers to a person unknown to the speaker, the personal **a** is usually omitted.

Conozco a un director que **comprende** todos los problemas.

I know a director who understands all the problems.

No conozco un director que **comprenda** todos los problemas.

I don't know a director who understands all the problems.

E. Responda negativamente a estos comentarios de un/a amigo/a.

► Tú tienes una amiga que es campeona olímpica, ¿verdad?

No, no tengo una amiga que sea campeona olímpica.

1. Aquí hay un estudiante que sabe todas las respuestas, ¿no?
2. En Cuba hay muchos atletas que prefieren otra vocación, ¿verdad?
3. Tenemos amigos que nos dan regalos (*gifts*) todos los días, ¿no?
4. En los Estados Unidos hay pobres que tienen tres autos, ¿verdad?
5. En esta clase hay una chica que habla español perfectamente, ¿no?
6. Conoces un país que produce tantos productos agrícolas como los Estados Unidos, ¿no es cierto?
7. En esta universidad hay atletas que participan en los Juegos Panamericanos, ¿no?
8. Tú y yo conocemos a un periodista que dice siempre la verdad, ¿no es cierto?

F. Diga a quién conoce (o no conoce) usted que sabe hacer las siguientes cosas. Complete con frases lógicas.

bailar   cantar   reparar coches   reparar televisores

► una mujer   *Conozco a una mujer que sabe cantar; no conozco ninguna mujer que sepa bailar.*

1. un joven   4. una señora
2. dos chicos   5. una atleta
3. tres muchachas   6. un periodista

G. Complete las oraciones lógicamente, según su experiencia.

1. Tengo un magnífico amigo que . . ., pero no tengo uno que . . . .
2. Necesito un/a compañero/a de cuarto que . . ., pero no necesito uno/a que . . . .
3. En esta clase tenemos un/a profesor/a que . . ., pero no tenemos uno/a que . . . .

4. La película que vi el otro día es una película que . . .. No hay una película que . . .
5. ¿Dónde hay un buen restaurante que . . .?
6. Quiero viajar a un país que . . ..

H. Diga qué tipo de persona le gusta, pero que usted no conoce ahora.

▶ *Me gustan las personas que participan en todos los deportes, pero no conozco personalmente un hombre o una mujer que practique el alpinismo.*

III. Indicative versus subjunctive in adverbial clauses

*Pongo los paquetes donde Ud. **diga**.*

*Sí, señora. Los pongo donde Ud. **dice**.*

1. Adverbial clauses are dependent clauses introduced by a conjunction, such as **como, cuando, para que.** The verb in the dependent adverbial clause is in the *indicative* when the action, situation, or event expressed in the clause is factual or has already occurred at the time when the action expressed in the main clause takes place. Adverbial clauses introduced by the following conjunctions are *always* in the indicative.

ahora que now that, since	**puesto que** because, since
desde que since	**ya que** now that, since
porque because	

Podemos empezar **ahora que todos estamos** aquí.

We can begin now that we are all here.

Ha mejorado su salud **desde que empezó** a vivir en el campo.

His health has improved since he has been living in the country.

Te quiero **porque eres** extraordinario.

I love you because you are extraordinary.

2. The verb in the dependent adverbial clause is in the *subjunctive* when the action, situation, or event expressed in the clause is uncertain or has not yet taken place. Adverbial clauses introduced by the following conjunctions are *always* in the subjunctive.

a menos que unless
antes (de) que before
con tal que provided, as long as

para que so that, in order that
(*purpose, goal*)
sin que without

Vamos a comprar esa casa **a
menos que cueste** demasiado.
Termina tu trabajo **antes que tu
padre vuelva** a casa.
Es necesario llevarlos **para que
vean** el apartamento.

*We're going to buy that house
unless it costs too much.*
*Finish your work before your
father returns home.*
*It is necessary to take them to see
the apartment.*

3. The conjunctions listed below may be followed by either the indicative
or the subjunctive depending on whether the action, situation or event
expressed in the clause is factual and has taken place or is uncertain
and has not yet taken place.

aunque although, even though
cuando when, whenever
de manera que so that, in such
a way that
de modo que so that, in such a
way that
después de que after

donde where, wherever
en cuanto as soon as
hasta que until
luego que as soon as
tan pronto como as soon as

Trabajo aquí **aunque me pagan**
poco. (*Action has taken place.*)
Voy a trabajar aquí **aunque me
paguen** poco. (*Action is
uncertain.*)

*I work here, although they pay me
little.*
*I'm going to work here even
though they may pay me little.*

Todos los días se lo explico
cuando la veo. (*Action has taken
place.*)
Voy a explicárselo a Rosita
cuando la vea. (*Action has not
taken place.*)

*Every day I explain it to her when
I see her.*

*I'll explain it to Rosita when I see
her.*

Siempre salgo **después de que
llegas.** (*Action has taken place.*)
Pienso salir **después de que
llegues.** (*Action has not taken
place.*)

I always go out after you arrive.

*I'm thinking about going out after
you arrive.*

I. Complete las siguientes oraciones con **te dan permiso** (*permission*) o **te
den permiso,** según el sentido de la cláusula principal.

1. Te pido que mañana vengas tan pronto como . . . .
2. Puedes salir conmigo esta noche ya que . . . .
3. Debes viajar a Puerto Rico cuando . . . .

4. Entonces, ¿tú siempre pasas las vacaciones donde . . . ?
5. Entonces, vas a casarte con Guillermo sin que . . . .
6. Es buena idea explicarles tus motivos para que . . . .

J. Oscar y su hermana, Inés, se ayudan mucho. Oscar piensa hacer estas cosas mañana, a menos que su hermana las haga primero. Haga el papel de Oscar.

► lavar el carro   Oscar: *Lavo el carro mañana a menos que tú lo laves primero.*

1. limpiar el garaje
2. llevarle un regalo a Raquel
3. hacer la compra *(do the shopping)*
4. anunciarle la noticia a papá
5. arreglarle el radiorreloj a mamá
6. escribir una carta a la estación de radio

K. Termine las siguientes frases de una manera original. Use las conjunciones **ahora que, porque, puesto que, desde que** y **ya que.**

► ir a la fiesta   *Teresa va a la fiesta ahora que sabe que tú vas también.*

1. El profesor va a explicarle el problema de química . . . .
2. Yo les ayudo este fin de semana . . . .
3. Le vendemos el estéreo . . . .
4. Ana no puede comprar otra motocicleta . . . .
5. No olvido la fiesta de aniversario de mi tía . . . .
6. Es importante estar en casa a tiempo para la entrevista . . . .

L. Explique lo que piensa hacer después de cumplir *(fulfill)* distintas condiciones. Use las conjunciones **cuando, donde, sin que, con tal que, antes (de) que, ahora que, a menos que** y **porque.**

► *Pienso ser un/a artista famoso/a cuando termine la universidad, a menos que encuentre una profesión más interesante.*

M. Dígales a sus compañeros/as lo que piensa hacer un/a amigo/a en el futuro, según las circunstancias. Use las conjunciones **cuando, donde, sin que, con tal que, a menos que, desde que** y **puesto que.**

► *[Elena] quiere estudiar en esta universidad, a menos que gane el premio de lenguas para estudiar en Madrid.*

IV. Position of two object pronouns

1. The chart below shows the order of appearance of direct- and indirect-object pronouns when they are used together in the same clause.

1st position	2nd position
me te se nos os se	lo, la, los, las

—¿Me das ese cuaderno?   *Will you give me that notebook?*
—Sí, **te lo** doy.   *Yes, I'll give it to you.*

—¿Quién les envió la calculadora   *Who sent you the calculator?*
   a Uds.?
—Enrique **nos la** envió.   *Enrique sent it to us.*

—¿Alberto les compró los discos?   *Did Alberto buy you the records?*
—No, **nos los** compró Mercedes.   *No, Mercedes bought them for us.*

2. The indirect-object pronouns **le** and **les** become **se** before **lo, la, los,** and **las.** A prepositional phrase with **a** is often used to clarify the meaning of **se.**

—¿Quién le preparó la torta?   *Who prepared the cake for him?*
—**Se la** preparé yo.   *I prepared it for him.*

—Estos vasos son para tu prima,   *These glasses are for your cousin,*
   ¿no?   *aren't they?*
—Sí, voy a dár**selos a ella.**   *Yes, I'll give them to her.*

3. Be sure not to confuse the indirect-object **se** with the reflexive or the reciprocal **se.** Context will help you determine the meaning.

Se lo explican a Eloísa.   *They explain it to Eloísa.*
Se lo explican el uno al otro.   *They explain it to each other.*

4. In double-verb constructions or in *verb + preposition + infinitive* constructions, the two pronouns may precede the conjugated verb or they may be attached to the infinitive. When the two pronouns are attached to the infinitive, a written accent is required on the final syllable of the infinitive.

Me los puede mostrar. }   *You can show them to me.*
Puede **mostrármelos.**

Te lo acabé de arreglar. }   *I just finished fixing it for you.*
Acabé de **arreglártelo.**

5. When two pronouns are used with commands, they are attached to direct affirmative commands, but precede negative ones.

¡Escríbamelo mañana.   *Write it for (to) me tomorrow.*
¡No **me lo escriba!**   *Don't write it for (to) me.*

N. Moncho tiene un amigo que quiere enseñarle muchas cosas nuevas en su apartamento. Haga el papel de Moncho o del amigo.

▶ la nevera   S1: *¿Te enseño la nevera?*
              S2: *Sí, quiero que me la enseñes ahora.*

1. el lavaplatos
2. la secadora
3. las sillas
4. el reloj de pared
5. el televisor a colores
6. el tocadiscos

O. Usted necesita ayuda para terminar un proyecto de economía. Pídale a un/a profesor/a que le dé los siguientes artículos, pero que no se los dé en este momento.

▶ la calculadora   *Démela, por favor, pero no me la dé en este momento.*

1. los lápices de colores
2. el mapa de Centroamérica
3. las revistas mexicanas
4. los libros de economía
5. la pluma verde
6. su cuaderno

P. Dos estudiantes discuten los planes para la fiesta de Graciela. Conteste las preguntas, usando dos pronombres (objeto directo e indirecto).

▶ ¿Puedes prepararme una torta?   *Sí, te la puedo preparar con mucho gusto.*

1. ¿Le compras los flanes al pastelero?
2. ¿Puedes prepararme los sándwiches?
3. ¿Me traes los discos?
4. ¿Quieres conseguirme las gaseosas?

Q. Alberto decide distribuir regalos (*gifts*) entre varios amigos. Haga el papel de Alberto. Para diferenciar entre los amigos, use una expresión con **a (a ti, a él, a ella,** etcétera).

▶ Este regalo es para ti.   *Voy a dártelo a ti.*
▶ Estos regalos son para ustedes.   *Voy a dárselos a ustedes.*

1. Este regalo es para ella.
2. Estos regalos son para usted.
3. Este regalo es para él.
4. Este regalo es para ellos.
5. Estos regalos son para Clemencia.
6. Estos regalos son para ti.

¡Exprésese usted!

El punto de vista

El protagonista de la siguiente selección considera dos opciones para solucionar su dilema. Aunque su decisión no se da explícitamente, usted puede tener una preferencia por una de las posibles soluciones.

Lea la siguiente selección para comprensión general y haga el Ejercicio A. Luego lea de nuevo la selección para tener una idea más precisa de su contenido y entonces haga los Ejercicios B y C.

Otra revolución

«¡No me dejes, Clarencio, que tu hija y yo te necesitamos!» Las palabras de la mujer resonaban en su memoria mientras cabalgaba hacia Morón, donde debía reunirse con los otros. La guerra era repugnante, una porquería. ¿Para qué servía? ¿para mejorar su vida o la de su hija? ¿para acabar
5 con las injusticias? Nada. El mundo iba a continuar igual, y quizás él y su hija y su mujer, y todos . . . ¡todos! iban a morir en el enorme cataclismo del fin del mundo.

Pero entonces, ¿por qué seguir hacia Morón? Recuerdos de los amigos de muchos años se precipitaron al mismo tiempo a su memoria: Juanito,
10 ahora muerto; Oscar, aquel Oscar jovial, idealista, que quería cambiar el mundo, iba a estar en Morón, y lo iba a recibir con los brazos abiertos; Maruja, la mujer realista y dedicada, que creía en el destino de la revolución con un entusiasmo contagioso. Otros, caras sin nombre y nombres sin caras, pasaban por su memoria, héroes todos, mientras el caballo cambiaba
15 del trote al galope hacia Morón. El caballo sabía de memoria el camino, como sabía también el camino de su casa . . . .

A. Escoja las palabras o expresiones de la segunda columna que mejor reflejan el significado de las palabras de la primera columna. Es posible que Ud. quiera verificar algunas opciones con el contexto del cuento.

1. dejar	a. desastre
2. resonar	b. llegar en tumulto
3. cabalgar	c. abandonar
4. porquería	d. cosa desagradable
5. cataclismo	e. ir a caballo
6. precipitarse	f. hacer eco

B. Haga una lista con los argumentos que tiene Clarencio a favor de permanecer en casa y otra con los argumentos a favor de participar en la revolución.

Con el clima cálido de Cuba es maravilloso tomar uno de los famosos helados cubanos en un café al abierto como éste, en la parte antigua de La Habana. ¿Qué sabores piensa Ud. que se pueden comprar en este café?

C. Entre las dos alternativas, seleccione la más atractiva para usted. Imagínese en la misma situación de Clarencio y escriba una breve explicación de su decisión, defendiendo su punto de vista. Use algunas de las siguientes expresiones de transición útiles.

por el momento	desde entonces	porque
después	primero	finalmente
pronto	luego	en otras palabras

▶ *Es natural que Clarencio quiera . . . , pero creo que debe . . . porque . . . .*

Lengua en acción 6

A. Unas quejas del hotel *(Lección 16)*

Ud. viaja por Hispanoamérica. Tiene poco dinero, y por eso se aloja en un hotel muy barato. Ud. encuentra algunas deficiencias en su cuarto. Quéjese cortésmente con el/la hotelero/a *(innkeeper)*, siguiendo las indicaciones.

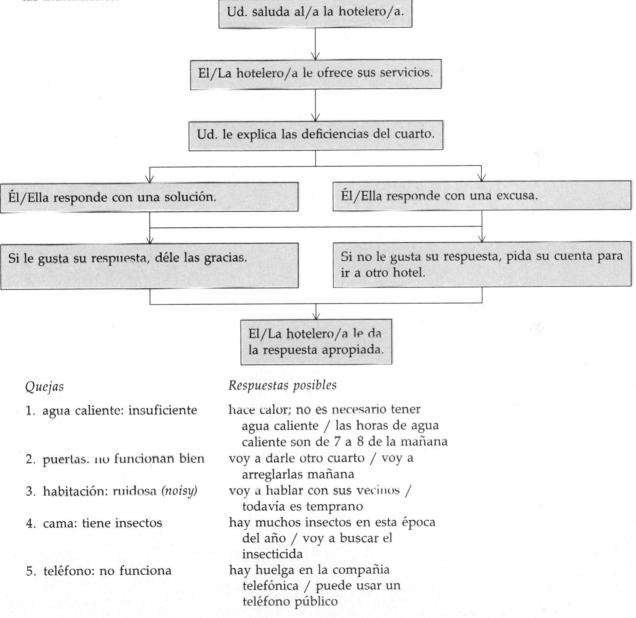

Ud. saluda al/a la hotelero/a.

El/La hotelero/a le ofrece sus servicios.

Ud. le explica las deficiencias del cuarto.

Él/Ella responde con una solución.

Él/Ella responde con una excusa.

Si le gusta su respuesta, déle las gracias.

Si no le gusta su respuesta, pida su cuenta para ir a otro hotel.

El/La hotelero/a le da la respuesta apropiada.

Quejas	*Respuestas posibles*
1. agua caliente: insuficiente	hace calor; no es necesario tener agua caliente / las horas de agua caliente son de 7 a 8 de la mañana
2. puertas: no funcionan bien	voy a darle otro cuarto / voy a arreglarlas mañana
3. habitación: ruidosa *(noisy)*	voy a hablar con sus vecinos / todavía es temprano
4. cama: tiene insectos	hay muchos insectos en esta época del año / voy a buscar el insecticida
5. teléfono: no funciona	hay huelga en la compañia telefónica / puede usar un teléfono público

B. De compras en el almacén *(Lección 16)*

Usted quiere comprar varios artículos en un almacén, pero no sabe cómo se llaman en español ni en qué piso están. Explíquele a un/a dependiente/a (un miembro de la clase) lo que Ud. busca, describiendo su apariencia física y su función. Use gestos *(gestures)* si es necesario y sea cortés con el/la dependiente/a.

Directorio		
1er *piso* Bolsos Joyería Perfumes y cosméticos	3er *piso* Ropa para damas Zapatos para damas Ropa de casa	5to *piso* Librería Departamento de música
2do *piso* Ropa para caballeros Equipo deportivo	4to *piso* Muebles Aparatos electrodomésticos	6to *piso* Equipaje Departamento de fotografía

▶ S1: *Con permiso, señor(ita). Busco algo, pero no sé cómo se llama en español.*
   S2: *¿Para qué se usa?*
   S1: *Para secar el pelo después de lavarlo.*
   S2: *Creo que lo que Ud. busca es una toalla. Es de tela, ¿no? Están en el departamento de ropa de casa en el tercer piso.*
   S1: *¿El departamento de ropa de casa? No puede ser. Este aparato es eléctrico.*
   S2: *Ah, sí. Ahora entiendo. Usted quiere un secador de pelo. Están en el cuarto piso, con los aparatos electrodomésticos.*
   S1: . . .

C. Celebraciones *(Lección 16)*

Explíquele a un/a visitante costarricense (su compañero/a de clase) cómo se celebran los días de fiesta en los Estados Unidos. Cuéntele qué hacía su familia cuando usted era niño/a y conteste las preguntas que le haga su amigo/a. Según sea apropiado, incluya información acerca de los siguientes temas:

ocasión que se celebraba   lugar de la celebración
fecha de la celebración   comida que se preparaba
gente que se invitaba   otras actividades que había

Celebraciones

El Día de los Enamorados   los cumpleaños
La Navidad   Halloween
El Año Nuevo   El Día de Acción de Gracias

Comidas especiales

| helados | chocolates | galletas *(cookies)* | gaseosas | tortas |
| caramelos | pavo | champán | jamón | pastel |

Actividades

adornar un árbol
cantar villancicos *(carols)*
tener juegos *(games)*
disfrazarse de . . . *(to dress up as)*

mandar tarjetas *(cards)*
dar regalos *(gifts)*
adornar con globos *(balloons)*

D. Un paquete misterioso *(Lección 17)*

Durante un viaje en autobús, usted encuentra un paquete con dinero.
Cuéntele a su amigo/a (un miembro de la clase) el incidente. Dé la
información indicada basándose en los dibujos. Su amigo/a le hace
preguntas y expresa sus reacciones mientras escucha.

1. adónde ibas, con quién ibas,
cuántos pasajeros había
delante, cómo eran, qué hacían

2. dónde estaba el paquete
cuando lo notaste, de quién
crees que era el paquete

3. adónde fuiste con el paquete, qué
les dijiste, cuánto dinero había
en el paquete, quién lo reclamó

4. Y ahora que tienes una
recompensa *(reward)* de $ . . . ,
¿qué piensas hacer?

E. Quehaceres (Chores) *(Lección 17)*

Ud. tiene que hacer varias cosas hoy. Va a la tintorería *(dry cleaners)*, al banco y al mecánico. En cada lugar Ud. le dice al/a la empleado/a (un miembro de la clase) lo que quiere, pero siempre hay un problema y el/la empleado/a no puede hacer lo que Ud. pide. Decida si Ud. prefiere ir a otro lugar. Después, alternen los papeles.

Tareas

En la tintorería: (1) quitarle una mancha *(spot)* a un traje de lana (2) limpiar y planchar *(to iron)* un vestido de seda
En el banco: (1) cambiar un cheque de $2.000,00 (2) mandar un giro postal *(money order)* a Europa
Con el mecánico: (1) reparar el silenciador *(muffler)* (2) cambiar las llantas *(tires)*

Expresiones útiles

no puedo garantizar que . . .   es mejor . . . porque . . .
es imposible . . . porque . . .   lo siento, pero hoy no puedo . . . porque . . .
es difícil . . . porque . . .

F. El/La novio/a ideal *(Lección 18)*

Entreviste a 3 ó 4 compañeros/as de clase para averiguar su opinión sobre las cinco características más importantes que debe tener el/la novio/a perfecto/a. Pídales que las clasifiquen en una escala de 1 a 5, donde 1 es la más importante. Después dé los resultados a la clase.

▶ S1: *¿Qué cinco características principales debe tener el/la novio/a ideal?*
S2: *Primero, busco a [un hombre] que sea guapo. Segundo, es importante que tenga altos ideales.*

Características	Modelo	S1	S2	S3
saber bailar	5			
ser guapo/a	1			
ganar mucho dinero				
ser sincero/a	3			
tener buen sentido del humor	4			
???	tener altos ideales 2			

G. Cinco preguntas (Lección 18)

Forme un equipo con 3 ó 4 compañeros de clase. Traten de adivinar (*guess*) el nombre del deporte en que piensa otro equipo de la clase. Su equipo tiene cinco oportunidades para hacer preguntas. El otro equipo sólo puede contestar **sí** o **no.** El equipo que adivine más deportes en la menor cantidad de tiempo es el ganador.

Vocabulario útil

Dónde se juega/practica	*Equipo que se usa*	*Número de personas*
piscina	una raqueta	solo/a
cancha	una pelota	en equipo
pista	un bate	1 – 4 – 9 personas
estadio	unos guantes especiales	
nieve	unos zapatos especiales	

▶ *Su equipo*   *Otro equipo*

—¿Practicamos ese deporte en la nieve?   No.
—¿Necesitamos una cancha para practicar ese deporte?   No.
—¿Se practica en el agua ese deporte?   Sí.
—¿Se puede practicar ese deporte solo?   Sí.
—Ya sabemos. Es la natación.   Correcto. Ahora es su turno.

(Completado con 4 preguntas.)

H. ¿Quiere Ud. aceptar las consecuencias? (*Wrap-up*)

Ud. no cumplió con una de sus responsabilidades y tiene que darle una explicación a la persona encargada (su compañero/a de clase). Si él/ella no acepta su excusa, le dice a Ud. las consecuencias. Si Ud. quiere protestar las consecuencias, defienda sus excusas, pero no olvide ser cortés. Después, alternen los papeles.

¿Me puede decir por qué no entregó el informe final a tiempo?

Posibles explicaciones

tener tres exámenes esa semana
estar enfermo/a
no saber nada del informe

Posibles consecuencias

bajarle la nota a una [B, C, . . .]
asignarle [1, 2, . . .] informes extras
ir a ver al decano (*dean*)

Posibles explicaciones

no recibir las multas en el correo
perder las multas
no saber dónde pagar las multas

Posibles consecuencias

darle otra multa de $ . . .
suspenderle el carnet *(license)* de conducir
mandarle a tomar un curso especial de conducir

Ud. no pagó estas multas *(fines)*.
¿Por qué?

I. Cómo controlar la tensión nerviosa *(Wrap-up)*

Ud. participa en un estudio sobre las presiones y tensiones que sufren
los universitarios. Pregúntele a un/a compañero/a de clase con qué
frecuencia hace las siguientes cosas. Apunte *(Jot down)* sus respuestas.
Después, recomiéndele lo que debe hacer para mejorar su estilo de
vida y así evitar la tensión nerviosa.

	Siempre	Generalmente	A veces	Nunca
¿fumar?				
¿tomar alguna medicina?				
¿poder concentrarse bien?				
¿ponerse nervioso/a por cualquier cosa?				
¿comer comidas equilibradas *(balanced)*?				
¿comer a horas regulares?				
¿dormir bien?				

Posibles recomendaciones

dejar de fumar
tomar vitaminas
encontrar un pasatiempo
leer un libro de nutrición
tomar un vaso de leche antes de
  acostarse

hacer más ejercicio
buscar ayuda profesional
aprender a meditar
comer tres veces al día
no tomar medicinas innecesarias

Unidad 7
En México

La vida (muy idealizada) de los aztecas en su ciudad de Tenochtitlán aparece en este maravilloso mural de Diego Rivera en el Palacio Nacional de Ciudad de México. Compare este mural con el de la página 99 en la ciudad de San Francisco. Vea el movimiento y trate de imaginar el colorido de los dos. ¿Cree Ud. que le gustaban los aztecas a Rivera? ¿Ve Ud. en la misma forma a los indios de su país? Explique.

Lección 19
En México

¿El pueblo o la ciudad?

Se dice que la ciudad ofrece más oportunidades de trabajo y una vida más interesante que el pueblo. Diego Palmas, un joven mexicano de veintiún años, decidió comprobar este hecho.° Diego nació y recibió su educación primaria y secundaria en Tlapa, un pequeño pueblo que está a unos cien
5 kilómetros de Ciudad de México. Después de terminar el bachillerato, trabajó dos años como empleado en la mueblería de su tío Juan. Pero Diego no estaba satisfecho ni con el trabajo ni con su sueldo. Su padre le sugirió que fuera a trabajar en los campos petrolíferos° de Chiapas; pero Diego prefirió ir a la capital, donde hay más oportunidades de trabajo. Su novia
10 prefería que Diego se estableciera en Tlapa.
   ¿Qué decisión tomar? Diego dejó su pueblo natal y se fue a la capital a buscar empleo. Durante los primeros cuatro meses, vivió con unos parientes

matter

campos . . . oilfields

Las familias de algunos de estos niños en Ciudad de México pueden ser parte de un enorme número de familias de inmigrantes del campo a la ciudad. Imagínese que Ud. es uno de estos niños y piense en su opinión del cambio. ¿Qué le gusta y qué no le gusta de Ciudad de México?

suyos en un pequeño apartamento en el centro. Temía que le fuera imposible acostumbrarse al ruido, al tráfico y al gentío.° Echaba de menos tam-   crowd, mob
15 bién los árboles y las flores alrededor de la plaza de recreo de Tlapa. Al principio, no pudo conseguir empleo porque, como él, eran muchas las personas que llegaban a la capital cada día con la esperanza de mejorar su vida. Pero al fin consiguió trabajo en una mueblería del barrio donde vivía, y empezó a acostumbrarse a la vida agitada de la ciudad.
20   Hoy, después de un año en la capital, Diego tiene un puesto mejor en la mueblería, y vive en un cuarto pequeño cerca de sus parientes. Los domingos va con unos amigos al parque de Chapultepec, a un partido de fútbol o a una corrida de toros. Una vez al mes vuelve a Tlapa a ver a sus padres y a su novia, con quien espera casarse pronto. Le cuenta a su novia
25 de la vida urbana y de las posibilidades de ganar suficiente dinero para mejorar la vivienda y para mantener una familia en el ambiente de la ciudad.

Comprensión

1. ¿Quién es Diego Palmas? ¿Dónde nació?
2. ¿Qué hizo después de terminar su bachillerato?
3. ¿De qué no estaba satisfecho el joven?
4. ¿Qué le sugirió su padre? ¿Qué decidió hacer Diego?
5. ¿Con quiénes vivió cuando llegó a la capital? ¿Dónde vivió?
6. ¿Dónde consiguió trabajo al fin?
7. ¿Mejoró el nivel de vida de Diego?
8. ¿Qué hace los domingos? Y, una vez al mes, ¿adónde va?
9. ¿Qué le cuenta Diego a su novia?

Conversación

1. ¿Vive usted en el campo, en un pueblo o en una ciudad?
2. ¿Dónde cree usted que existen más oportunidades de empleo?
3. ¿Le parece muy complicada la vida de la ciudad? ¿por qué?
4. ¿Qué ventajas tiene la vida del campo? ¿la vida de la ciudad?
5. ¿Dónde trabajó usted después de graduarse de la escuela secundaria? ¿por cuántas horas al día? ¿por cuántos días al mes?
6. Cuando usted siente nostalgia por algo, ¿qué hace? ¿Llama por teléfono a alguien? ¿Escribe cartas?

Vocabulario

Palabras análogas

agitado, -a	la educación	la posibilidad	secundario, -a
complicado, -a	existir	primario, -a	el tráfico
la decisión	graduar(se)		

Sustantivos

el ambiente   atmosphere
el árbol   tree
el bachillerato   secondary school education
el campo   country, countryside
la corrida de toros   bullfight
la esperanza   hope
la flor   flower
la mueblería   furniture store
el recreo   recreation
el ruido   noise
la vivienda   housing

Adjetivos

cada   each
suficiente   enough, sufficient
urbano, -a   city, urban

Verbos

comprobar (ue)   to check, verify
establecerse (zc)   to settle down; to set up (in business)
ganar   to earn
nacer (zc)   to be born

Otras palabras y expresiones

al día (mes)   daily (monthly)
al fin   finally
al principio (de)   at the beginning (of)
alrededor (de)   around
el pueblo natal   home town
sentir nostalgia (por)   to be homesick (for)
una vez al mes   once a month

Práctica

A. Usted tiene que hacer una encuesta *(take a poll)* sobre las ventajas y las desventajas de la vida en la ciudad. Prepare usted diez preguntas para entrevistar a los estudiantes de la clase. Después, haga un resumen de los resultados.

B. Haga una lista de los atractivos de su ciudad o pueblo, mencionando el ambiente, los recursos económicos y las actividades culturales, entre otras cosas. Después, evalúe *(evaluate)* los atractivos, usando una escala *(scale)* de uno a diez.

Nota cultural La economía mexicana

Los recursos naturales de México son variados y algunos, especialmente el petróleo y el gas natural, tienen tal potencial de desarrollo que pueden permitir al país un asombroso[1] crecimiento[2] económico, pero también pueden hacer que la economía del país dependa excesivamente de los precios internacionales del petróleo.

El gobierno mexicano nacionalizó su producción petrolera en 1938. Actualmente esta industria está controlada por PEMEX, Petróleos Mexicanos,

---

1. astonishing   2. growth

Estos trabajadores de los pozos de petróleo de México reciben relativamente buen sueldo, pero trabajan mucho en labores difíciles. ¿Qué tipo de persona piensa Ud. que busque trabajo en los campos petrolíferos? ¿Qué destrezas y educación se necesitan para este tipo de trabajo?

un organismo gubernamental. Los grandes campos petrolíferos están situados en el norte en Tampico y en el sur en los estados de Tabasco y Chiapas, donde se ha descubierto una gran abundancia de gas natural. La presencia de estos recursos, junto con los yacimientos[3] de carbón en el norte del país, favorecen el desarrollo de la industria petroquímica y siderúrgica.[4]

Además del petróleo y del gas natural, también existen en México yacimientos de cobre, hierro, plata y oro, así como de plomo,[5] estaño y azufre.[6]

---

3. **junto** . . . together with the deposits   4. **industria** . . . petrochemical and iron and steel industry   5. lead   6. sulphur

Estudio de palabras

I. Muebles y decoración

The following is a list of common household furniture terms in Spanish.

la alfombra   rug
el armario   wardrobe
la cama   bed
la cómoda   chest of drawers
la cortina   curtain
el cuadro   painting
el espejo   mirror

el estante (la estantería)   bookcase
la lámpara   lamp
la mesa   table
la mesita de noche   night table
la (silla) mecedora   rocking chair
el sillón   armchair
el sofá   sofa

A. Una compañía de bienes raíces (*real estate*) de Ciudad de México acaba de comprar un nuevo edificio de apartamentos. Usted trabaja para esta compañía y tiene que amueblar (*furnish*) dos apartamentos para que sirvan de apartamentos modelos. Escoja algunos de los muebles necesarios, y complete una forma de pedido.

B. Usted quiere darle más ambiente a su alcoba. Discuta con otro/a estudiante qué muebles necesita comprar, dónde va a comprarlos, si va a comprarlos nuevos o de segunda mano y qué artículos decorativos va a poner.

II. Los prefijos **co-** y **re-**

Many Spanish words are formed with prefixes derived generally from Greek or Latin words. The following prefixes are encountered frequently in Spanish words.

1. The prefix **co-** means *together, joint(ly), with*.

   el coautor: una persona que es autor con otro u otros
   cooperar: trabajar en unión con otros
   copiloto: una persona que asiste al piloto

2. The prefix **re-** means *again, back (to an earlier state)*.

   redistribuir: distribuir otra vez
   reelegir: elegir otra vez
   releer: leer otra vez

C. Complete las siguientes frases con una palabra apropiada de la lista.

coeducación   reestructuración   releer
coexistir   reexaminar

1. Muchos empleados protestaron la ____ de la oficina.
2. Espero que nuestros países puedan ____ porque la alternativa es horrible.
3. En Hispanoamérica muchos jóvenes asisten a escuelas que no son mixtas. La ____ es relativamente moderna.
4. Me gustó mucho esa novela, y pienso ____la este verano.
5. Si quiere prosperar en el mundo del negocio, debe ____ su método de producción.

Estructuras útiles
I. The imperfect subjunctive

1. The imperfect subjunctive of all regular as well as irregular verbs is formed by dropping the **-ron** from the third person plural of the preterit and adding the imperfect subjunctive endings to this stem. A written accent is required in the stem of the **nosotros**-form.

	entrar	poder	venir
Third person plural of preterit:	[entra ron]	[pudie ron]	[vinie ron]
	entra **ra**	pudie **ra**	vinie **ra**
	entra **ras**	pudie **ras**	vinie **ras**
	entra **ra**	pudie **ra**	vinie **ra**
	entrá **ramos**	pudié **ramos**	vinié **ramos**
	entra **rais**	pudie **rais**	vinie **rais**
	entra **ran**	pudie **ran**	vinie **ran**

Esperaba que **llegaran** a tiempo.
Temían que Ud. no **escribiera.**

I hoped they would arrive on time.
They were afraid you wouldn't
write.

2. The imperfect subjunctive is used in dependent clauses under the same circumstances that call for the present subjunctive, provided that:
a. the verb in the main clause is in the past, or;
b. the main verb is in the present, but the dependent clause refers to an action in the past.

El padre esperaba que Diego **ganara** más dinero en la ciudad.
Necesitábamos a alguien que nos **ayudara** a terminar el proyecto.
Es una lástima que no **vinieran** anoche.

The father hoped that Diego would earn more money in the city.
We needed someone who could help us finish the project.
It's a shame that they didn't come last night.

A. Las personas indicadas fueron a vivir en la ciudad. Diga lo que la familia esperaba para cada uno.

▶ Ramiro / vivir mejor   *Su familia esperaba que Ramiro viviera mejor.*

1. tú / encontrar trabajo
2. nosotros / acostumbrarnos pronto a la ciudad
3. yo / conocer mucha gente importante
4. Celia / ser feliz
5. Esperanza y su marido / ponerse más contentos
6. tú y José / tener un apartamento cómodo

B. Diga qué le parecen a usted los siguientes acontecimientos (*events*). Use expresiones como **es magnífico, es terrible, es desastroso, es extraordinario.**

▶ El mes pasado ese país eligió un nuevo gobierno.

Es magnífico que ese país eligiera un nuevo gobierno el mes pasado.

1. Anoche nadie fue a la conferencia sobre ecología.
2. Ayer cayó el gobierno de esa república.
3. La semana pasada hubo un accidente horrible en la autopista.
4. Hace poco se descubrió un remedio *(cure)* contra el cáncer.
5. El año pasado la Academia de Arte le dio un premio a esa actriz.
6. En mayo llegaron dos mil inmigrantes hispanoamericanos.

C. Diga cómo se sentía usted frente a varias situaciones o eventos de la semana pasada. Haga oraciones completas, usando los verbos **esperaba, quería, dudaba, no creía, me alegré de, me enojé de** u otros similares.

▶ ustedes / venir tan pronto   *Me alegré de que ustedes vinieran tan pronto.*

1. Sara / conseguir un empleo en la mueblería
2. tú / leerme el poema que escribiste
3. nosotros / poder terminar el informe a tiempo
4. Clara / decirme lo que pasó en la reunión
5. Julio / saber tanto de computadoras
6. Eduardo y tú / reírse de mí
7. tú / echar de menos a la familia
8. Elena y Pilar / no jugar al tenis con nosotros

II. The impersonal reflexive construction

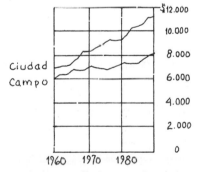

*Según las estadísticas, **se vive** mejor en la ciudad que en el campo.*

1. The reflexive pronoun **se** + *a third-person singular form* of the verb is often used in Spanish to form impersonal constructions that express a situation in which no one in particular performs the action. The English equivalent may be expressed with the subject *one, they, people, you,* or a passive-voice construction such as *English is spoken here.* Note that the

same impersonal situation is sometimes expressed in Spanish by using **uno** or a third-person plural form of the verb.

¿Se compra la harina en el almacén o en la pastelería?	*Does one buy flour in the grocery store or in the pastry shop?*
En Latinoamérica **se juega** al fútbol.	*Soccer is played throughout Latin America.*
¿A qué hora **comen** en España?	*At what time do they eat in Spain?*

2. **Se** + *a third-person plural form* of the verb is preferred with a following noun in the plural.

Aquí **se venden carros** usados.	*Used cars are sold here.*
Se abren las tiendas a las cuatro.	*They open the stores at four.*

D. En México Tom Mead habla con Elvira, una joven mexicana que tiene ideas basadas en estereotipos de los Estados Unidos. Haga el papel de Tom y use la construcción impersonal reflexiva en sus respuestas.

▶ Elvira: Creemos que todos los norteamericanos son ricos.   Tom: *Se cree que todos son ricos, pero no es verdad.*

1. Decimos que todos los norteamericanos tienen dos autos.
2. Pensamos que todos los norteamericanos viven bien.
3. Creemos que todos los norteamericanos estudian en la universidad.
4. Creemos que todas las ciudades norteamericanas son grandes.
5. Pensamos que en los Estados Unidos nadie habla español.
6. Decimos que en los Estados Unidos nadie ayuda a su vecino.

E. Al final del año usted decide vender todo lo que no necesita, y anuncia lo siguiente en la cartelera *(bulletin board)* de la Unión Estudiantil. Use una construcción impersonal reflexiva en sus anuncios.

▶ una bicicleta   *¡Se vende una bicicleta por cincuenta dólares!*

1. diez discos	4. dos textos de filosofía
2. una máquina de escribir	5. un estéreo
3. un televisor a colores	6. tres abrigos de lana

F. Compare algunas actividades y experiencias de su generación con las de la generación de sus padres. Use la construcción impersonal reflexiva con verbos como:

preferir	querer	aprender	hacer
exigir	enseñar	ver	escuchar

▶ *Antes se prefería la música clásica, pero ahora se prefiere la música popular.*

III. Relative pronouns

*El señor Martínez es el hombre **que** lleva el perro en los brazos.*

1. Relative pronouns connect (or relate) a dependent clause to a main clause and refer to a specific noun (the antecedent) in the main clause. The most common relative pronoun in Spanish is **que** *(who, whom, that, or which)*. **Que** may designate persons, things, or abstract ideas.

Elvira es la amiga **que** me regaló este bolso.	*Elvira is the friend who gave me this handbag.*
La libertad **que** tiene este país no existe en muchos otros.	*The freedom which this country has doesn't exist in many others.*

2. When the dependent clause is introduced by a preposition, **quien/es** is preferred if the antecedent is a person. If the antecedent is a noun referring to a thing, **el que (la que, los que, las que)** is preferred.

El abogado **con quien** hablé no aceptó mis ideas.	*The lawyer with whom I spoke didn't accept my ideas.*
Hay pocas personas **a quienes** escribo.	*There are few people to whom I write.*
Éstos son los libros **con los que** aprendí español.	*These are the books with which I learned Spanish.*
Ésa es la noticia **de la que** te hablaba.	*That's the news item about which I was talking to you.*

G. Diga qué hacían las personas siguientes que usted vio ayer en su pueblo o ciudad. Use el pronombre relativo **que**.

▶ Vi a una mujer muy elegante . . . .   *[que manejaba un Cadillac].*

  1. Vi a un hombre muy pobre . . . .
  2. Vi a un niño pequeño . . . .

3. Vi a dos señoritas altas . . . .
4. Vi a un señor mayor . . . .
5. Vi a unos muchachos grandes . . . .
6. Vi a mi amiga Josefina . . . .

H. Explíquele a un amigo que el verano pasado usted trabajó para las siguientes personas o negocios. Use el pronombre relativo **que** o **quien**.

▶ aquella pastelería   *Aquélla es la pastelería para la que trabajé el verano pasado.*

▶ ese médico   *Ése es el médico para quien trabajé el verano pasado.*

1. ese hospital
2. aquella zapatería
3. esas señoras
4. este mercado

5. aquella frutería
6. esos hombres
7. ese abogado
8. esa fábrica de cemento

I. Complete las oraciones siguientes con frases lógicas. Use el pronombre relativo **quien/es** y las preposiciones **para, de, con, a, sin** o **por**.

▶ El médico . . . .   *[a quien consulté me dijo que descansara más].*

1. El zapatero . . . .
2. La mujer . . . .
3. Los empleados . . . .

4. Las señoras . . . .
5. El mecánico . . . .
6. La locutora . . . .

IV. ¿Qué? versus ¿cuál/es?

—¿*Qué* vestido vas a ponerte para la fiesta?
—No sé, ¿*cuál* te gusta más?

1. The interrogatives **¿qué?** and **¿cuál/es?** may both be used before nouns. However, strictly speaking, there is a difference in meaning between these two interrogatives. **¿Qué?** + *noun* calls for an unlimited number of possible answers, and **¿cuál/es?** + *noun* calls for a choice among a few possibilities.

¿Qué fruta prefieres?	*What fruit do you prefer?*
¿Cuál fruta prefieres, la manzana o la pera?	*Which fruit do you prefer, the apple or the pear?*

2. **¿Qué?** with the verb **ser** (often followed by the indefinite article) usually asks for a definition. **¿Cuál/es?** with the verb **ser** (often followed by the definite article) asks for other types of information.

—**¿Qué es** una «panadería»? *What is a "panadería"?*
—Es una tienda donde se vende *It's a store where they sell bread.*
  el pan.

—**¿Cuál es** tu número de teléfono? *What's your phone number?*
—Es el 28-34-56. *It's 28-34 56.*

J. Conteste las siguientes preguntas con una definición o con la información que se pide.

▶ ¿Qué es un sofá? *Un sofá es un mueble que se usa en la sala de la casa.*

1. ¿Qué es un armario?
2. ¿Qué es un sillón?
3. ¿Cuál es el país hispánico más grande?
4. ¿Qué es un escritorio?
5. ¿Cuál es la fecha de su cumpleaños?
6. ¿Qué es un tigre?

K. Trate de obtener la información deseada de sus compañeros de clase, usando los interrogativos **¿qué?, ¿cuál?** o **¿cuáles?**

▶ el título de tu libro de química   S1: *¿Cuál es el título de tu libro de química?*
                                       S2: *Es «Química orgánica».*

1. tu dirección   5. el nombre de esa canción
2. tus pasatiempos favoritos 6. tu apellido
3. una amiga   7. un disco
4. tu número de teléfono   8. una zapatería

L. Pregúntele a otra persona **qué** o **cuál/es** le gustan más. Si usa **cuál/es,** dé dos opciones en su pregunta.

▶ bebida   *¿Cuál bebida te gusta más: el té o el café?*
▶ coche   *¿Qué coche te gusta?*

1. comida   3. deportes   5. música
2. películas   4. deporte   6. conciertos

M. Complete los siguientes diálogos, usando **¿qué?** o **¿cuál/es?** según el contexto.

1. —¿_____es mío? —El grande.
2. —¿_____ quieres tomar? —Un té, nada más.

3. —¿_____ discos vas a traer? —Los últimos que compré.
4. —¡Mira aquellos carros! —¿_____ , los rojos? ¡Qué elegantes!
5. —¿_____ es una mueblería? —Es un negocio donde se venden muebles.
6. —¿_____ es tu canción favorita? —«Contigo o sin ti».

¡Exprésese usted!

La descripción de un lugar

No se puede describir algo o alguien en su totalidad. Es necesario seleccionar los datos físicos e históricos y la información que mejor ilustre un aspecto en particular de esa cosa, lugar o persona.

Lea la siguiente selección fijándose en cómo mezcla el narrador sus impresiones subjetivas con datos históricos y físicos del parque. También observe cómo él contrasta el ambiente del parque durante los días de semana con el del fin de semana.

El parque de Chapultepec

Hay varios parques en Ciudad de México, pero yo recordaré siempre el parque de Chapultepec como uno de los parques más hermosos no sólo de la ciudad, sino del hemisferio. El parque de Chapultepec es el pulmón que da respiración a la ciudad, el refugio de sus habitantes, el centro de recreo 5 de ricos y pobres.

Los aztecas tuvieron una fortaleza en este lugar, y luego se construyó un palacio que fue residencia del gobierno español. El palacio pasó a ser un colegio militar y finalmente residencia de presidentes mexicanos y museo.

Los domingos la capital de México entera parece dirigirse al enorme Bosque de Chapultepec, un parque que se convierte en un paraíso para los niños y sus familias. Allí se pueden hacer actividades como montar en bote, armar una tienda de campaña (tent), asistir a cursos ofrecidos por el gobierno, celebrar una fiesta de cumpleaños o sencillamente descansar entre los árboles y las flores. Observe a la gente en esta escena y describa algunas de sus actividades.

Es, pues, un parque histórico, que refleja momentos importantes de la his-
10 toria de México. Pero es también un parque de flores y árboles, de caminos
que siguen líneas curvas de subidas y bajadas alrededor del promontorio
que le dio su nombre. Es un pequeño paraíso en medio del conglomerado
anónimo y amorfo de la capital.

El silencio del parque desaparece los domingos, cuando la ciudad en-
15 tera parece abandonar la casa para ir allí. Los silenciosos caminos de un
lunes o de un jueves se llenan de niños. Y los globos de colores que se
venden por todas partes flotan en el aire y parecen buscar a los niños, en-
contrarlos y llevarlos de la mano a un país encantado de juegos y flores,
donde no hay tristezas, ni injusticias, ni tragedias, ni hambre.

A. Dé la siguiente información, según la lectura.

1. Mencione dos datos históricos y dos datos físicos del parque de
   Chapultepec.
2. Diga qué cambios ocurren en el parque entre los días de la
   semana y los domingos.
3. Dé su opinión de por qué se habla de tristezas, injusticias,
   tragedias y hambre en la última línea.

B. Escoja un edificio o lugar de su universidad, ciudad o pueblo, y
descríbalo, incluyendo la siguiente información.

1. Mencione una o dos razones por qué lo escogió.
2. Explique uno o dos datos históricos del sitio.
3. Describa su aspecto exterior.
4. Describa cómo se siente usted cuando está allí.
5. Diga cómo cambia este sitio en alguna época del año (durante
   las vacaciones, por ejemplo, cuando no hay estudiantes; o al
   contrario, el primer día de clases, cuando todo el mundo regresa).

La Zona Rosa de Ciudad de
México tiene fama internacional
por su riqueza y su elegancia.
Aquí predominan los teatros,
bares, salones y boutiques con
nombres en lenguas extranjeras.
¿Por qué cree Ud. que vinieron
las personas de la foto a la Zona
Rosa?

Lección 20
En México

¿Por qué somos lo que somos?

El canal de la Teleducación Mexicana presenta una serie de programas sobre el mexicano y su identidad. Hoy el señor Emiliano Gómez, Director del Museo Nacional de Antropología, explica la importancia del museo para el mexicano moderno. El señor Obregón es el locutor.

Sr. Obregón: Señor Gómez, como director del museo, ¿podría usted explicarles a nuestros televidentes por qué el Museo de Antropología es tan importante para el pueblo mexicano de hoy?

5   Sr. Gómez: El pueblo mexicano desea conocerse mejor. Quiere encontrar y definir su identidad nacional. Fue esta preocupación existencial° la que contribuyó a la creación y desarrollo del Museo de Antropología.

Sr. Obregón: ¿Por qué cree Ud. que existe tal preocupación?

10   Sr. Gómez: Será por la experiencia histórica que ha vivido° el país desde la revolución hasta hoy. Será también por la influencia de las obras de artistas como Diego Rivera y José Clemente Orozco y de escritores como Octavio Paz y Carlos Fuentes, que despertaron la conciencia del mexicano y lo
15   hicieron detenerse a pensar en sus raíces.

preocupación . . . concern with the (Mexican nation's) existence itself

ha . . . has lived

Al Museo Nacional de Antropología de Ciudad de México se le considera como uno de los museos más modernos e interesantes del mundo. Es un museo del pasado y también del presente como proceso continuo de transformación. Exprese su opinión de lo que son y de lo que deberían ser (should be) algunos de los museos que Ud. conoce.

Sr. Obregón: ¿Podría usted precisar más este punto?

Sr. Gómez: ¡Cómo no! Primero existieron ricas culturas indias que la conquista española casi destruyó. Luego recibimos la influencia europea, y finalmente hoy tratamos de aceptar el impacto tecnológico norteamericano sin que nos destruya. Los artistas y pensadores° mexicanos de nuestro siglo tratan de hacernos comprender esta compleja herencia para que nos comprendamos más profundamente a nosotros mismos.

thinkers

Sr. Obregón: ¿Diría usted que el museo ayuda al joven mexicano a conocerse a sí mismo?

Sr. Gómez: Sí. Ya tenemos en el museo una colección impresionante de la historia del pueblo mexicano. Además, los continuos descubrimientos arqueológicos permitirán nuevas exhibiciones en un futuro próximo que nos enseñarán más sobre nuestro pasado.

Sr. Obregón: ¿Podría decirnos con mayor detalle qué se propone hacer?

Sr. Gómez: Sí, tendremos algunas muestras de los descubrimientos más recientes de las varias culturas indígenas que nos componen, como la azteca, la maya y la tolteca. Habrá salones especiales para exhibiciones, conferencias y películas educativas sobre estas culturas.

Sr. Obregón: ¿Deberían visitar el museo con mayor frecuencia los estudiantes de las universidades y los colegios?

Sr. Gómez: Nuestras relaciones con las instituciones educativas son excelentes. Pero la radio y la televisión podrían ayudarnos a informar al público en general sobre el interés y el valor de nuestros programas y colecciones.

Sr. Obregón: Ya termina nuestro programa. Le estamos muy agradecidos, Sr. Gómez, por su visita. Usted muy elocuentemente nos recuerda quiénes somos. Todos los mexicanos estamos muy orgullosos del papel que desempeña el Museo Nacional de Antropología en la búsqueda de nuestra identidad nacional. Su obra vale cualquier apoyo que podamos darle.

Comprensión

1. ¿Qué presenta el canal de la Teleducación Mexicana?
2. ¿Quién es el Sr. Emiliano Gómez? ¿De qué habla?
3. ¿Por qué se preocupa el pueblo mexicano por su identidad?
4. ¿Quiénes son Octavio Paz y Carlos Fuentes?
5. ¿Cuáles son algunas de las culturas indígenas de México? ¿Qué otras culturas forman parte de la herencia mexicana?
6. ¿Qué exhibe el Museo de Antropología? Aparte de sus exhibiciones, ¿qué más ofrece el museo al público?

Conversación

1. ¿Mira usted programas educativos en los Estados Unidos? ¿cuáles? ¿por qué?
2. ¿Recuerda usted algún documental interesante que vio en la televisión? ¿De qué se trataba?
3. ¿A qué tipo de museos le gusta ir? ¿a museos de arte? ¿a museos de ciencias? ¿por qué?
4. ¿Qué influencia tuvieron los indios norteamericanos en la herencia cultural de los Estados Unidos?
5. ¿De qué país/es vino su familia? ¿Conserva su familia tradiciones especiales de sus antepasados? ¿Qué tipo de tradiciones son éstas?

Vocabulario

Palabras análogas

azteca	definir	el futuro	el programa
la colección	el/la director/a	histórico, -a	la relación
la conciencia	elocuentemente	la identidad	la revolución
la conquista	especial	la influencia	la serie
conservar	europeo, -a	informar	tecnológico, -a
continuo, -a	la exhibición	la institución	tolteca
la creación	exhibir	maya	la visita
la cultura	la experiencia		

Sustantivos

el antepasado ancestor
la búsqueda search
el canal channel
el descubrimiento discovery
el documental documentary
el/la escritor/a writer
la muestra display, sample
la obra work
el pueblo people, nation
el punto point
la raíz root
el salón hall, salon
la teleducación educational TV
el/la televidente TV viewer

Adjetivos

educativo, -a educational
impresionante impressive
indígena native, indigenous

Verbos

componer *(irreg.)* to make up; to compose
contribuir to contribute
destruir to destroy
detener(se) *(irreg.)* to stop
precisar to specify, state exactly
recordar (ue) to remind

Otras palabras y expresiones

nosotros/as mismos/as ourselves
aparte de besides, in addition
sí mismo/a himself, herself
estar agradecido, -a to be grateful
finalmente finally
formar parte to make up
profundamente deeply, profoundly
el público en general general public
tal such (a)

Práctica

A. Entreviste a un/a compañero/a de clase sobre un museo que él o ella conozca. Pídale información sobre qué tipo de museo es, qué cuadros, esculturas, artefactos u objetos exhibe y qué exhibiciones o programas especiales ofrece. Pídale también su opinión del museo.

B. Refiérase a las láminas en colores en el texto que tratan el tema de la herencia cultural hispánica. Describa brevemente una de las fotografías que aparecen allí, usando palabras o expresiones de esta lección y otras que usted ya domina.

Nota cultural El arte popular de México

Este escaparate (shopwindow) en Ciudad de México atrae las miradas de todos con maravillosos ejemplares de la artesanía mexicana. Trate de describir y valorar artísticamente algunos de los objetos del escaparate. ¿Cuáles le gustan más? ¿Para qué y dónde pueden usarse?

La tradición del arte popular en México se remonta a[1] más de tres mil años, como lo muestran los artefactos expuestos[2] en los museos antropológicos y culturales del país. Los artesanos de hoy, como los de ayer, se sirven del barro,[3] de la madera, del cristal y de los metales para sus creaciones artísticas. Una de las artes manuales más apreciadas en todo el mundo son los tejidos.[4] Los tejedores[5] mexicanos producen telas de variados colores y diseños que sirven para ropa, petates[6] y bolsas. Para fomentar el arte popular mexicano, el gobierno ha establecido la agencia Fonart, que sirve como estímulo para los artesanos y centro de distribución para su trabajo.

FONART
FONDO NACIONAL PARA EL
FOMENTO DE LAS ARTESANIAS

___

1. **se ...** goes back to 2. exhibited 3. clay 4. woven fabrics 5. weavers
6. sleeping mats

Estudio de palabras

I. El correo

la estampilla
el sello

el correo

la carta

el sobre

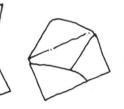
el papel de escribir
el papel de carta

el paquete

el cartero

el buzón

el telegrama

la tarjeta postal

la dirección
las señas

el remitente

echar al correo

A. Conteste las preguntas siguientes.

1. ¿Cuántas cartas escribe usted al mes?
2. ¿Cuántas cartas recibe al mes? ¿Cuántas le gustaría recibir?
3. ¿Cuándo viene el cartero a su casa? ¿por la mañana? ¿por la tarde? ¿una o dos veces al día? ¿Pasa todos los días?
4. ¿Cuánto cuesta un sello ordinario para enviar una carta dentro de los Estados Unidos?
5. ¿A quién le envía usted tarjetas postales? ¿cuándo?
6. ¿Recibió un telegrama alguna vez? ¿de quién?

II. La correspondencia

In Spanish as in English there are certain set phrases that are suitable for writing informal or personal letters, and other set phrases that are more appropriate in formal or business correspondence. The first phrases in the following groups of expressions are used in informal or personal letters and the remaining phrases are used in formal or business correspondence.

Expresiones de saludo

(Mi) querido/a (Pedro, amigo/a, etcétera):	*(My) dear (Pedro, friend, et cetera):*
Estimado/a señor (señora, señorita) González:	*Dear Mr. (Mrs., Miss) González:*
Apreciados señores (Apreciada señora, etcétera):	*Dear Sirs (Madam, et cetera):*

Expresiones de despedida

Un abrazo,	*An embrace,*
Recibe un abrazo fuerte de tu (amigo/a),	*Receive a strong embrace from your friend,*
Con mucho cariño,	*With much affection,*
Muchos besos,	*Many kisses,*
Su servidor/a,	*At your service, (Your servant),*
(Muy) atentamente (cordialmente),	*(Very) courteously (cordially),*
Quedo de usted (ustedes), atentamente,	*Cordially yours,*

B. Dé un saludo y una despedida apropiados para cada una de las siguientes cartas.

1. a su novio/a que lleva dos meses en España
2. al jefe de departamento en una compañía donde Ud. busca empleo

3. a un almacén grande para devolver una secadora de ropa que no funciona
4. a sus abuelos, a quienes no escribe desde hace varios meses
5. a unos amigos de sus padres que usted no conoce, pero a quienes va a visitar
6. a la universidad para pedir una beca *(scholarship)*

Estructuras útiles

I. The future tense

Habrá *muchos vehículos extraños en el año 2200.*

1. In Spanish, future meaning can be expressed in three ways: with the present indicative of the verb, with the present indicative of **ir a** + *infinitive,* or with the future tense.

¿Trabajas en mi casa esta tarde?	*Are you working (Will you work) at my house this afternoon?*
Voy a trabajar mañana por la tarde en tu casa.	*I'm going to work (I will work) tomorrow afternoon at your house.*
Trabajaremos en casa de Pepe esta tarde.	*We'll work at Pepe's house this afternoon.*

2. The future of most Spanish verbs is formed by adding the future endings to the infinitive of the verb.

almorzar		creer		sentir	
almorzar	**é**	creer	**é**	sentir	**é**
almorzar	**ás**	creer	**ás**	sentir	**ás**
almorzar	**á**	creer	**á**	sentir	**á**
almorzar	**emos**	creer	**emos**	sentir	**emos**
almorzar	**éis**	creer	**éis**	sentir	**éis**
almorzar	**án**	creer	**án**	sentir	**án**

—¿**Almorzaremos** pronto?   *Will we have lunch soon?*

—Sí, creo que así nos **sentiremos**   *Yes, I think we'll feel better that*
mejor.   *way.*

3. The future endings are added to the modified stem of the following verbs. These verbs may be divided into three groups.

Infinitive	Change	Modified Stem
caber	*Drops the e of the infinitive ending*	cabr-
haber		habr-
poder		podr-
querer		querr-
saber		sabr-
poner	*Drops the e of the infinitive ending, and*	pondr-
salir	*inserts a* **d**	saldr-
tener		tendr-
valer		valdr-
venir		vendr-
decir	*Uses a special stem*	dir-
hacer		har-

—¿**Habrá** otra reunión mañana?   *Will there be another meeting*
    tomorrow?

—Sí, **saldremos** para la reunión   *Yes, we'll leave to go to the*
a las 3:00 en el carro de José.   *meeting at 3:00 in José's car.*

—¿**Cabrán** dos personas más en   *Will two more people fit in the car?*
el carro?

A. En el verano usted y sus amigos irán a diferentes sitios. Usted cuenta los planes de todos. Use el tiempo futuro de **ir** y de los otros verbos en cada oración. Complete las oraciones de una forma original.

▶ tú / Florida / visitar . . .   *Tú irás a Florida, y visitarás Cabo Cañaveral*
    y las playas de Miami.

1. yo / Costa Rica / subir . . . .
2. Carmencita / la playa / nadar . . . .
3. Miguel y tú / un pueblo en Yucatán / ver . . . .
4. Manuel y Rosa / las montañas / estar . . . .
5. tú / tu casa / trabajar . . . .
6. usted y yo / el sur de California / divertirse . . . .

B. Usted va a vivir en un apartamento nuevo, y sus amigos vienen a ayudarle. Conteste las preguntas que le hacen. Use el tiempo futuro y una expresión apropiada, como **mañana, esta tarde, esta noche, pasado mañana, la semana entrante,** etcétera.

▶ ¿Roberto va a poner esos mue-   *Sí, los pondrá en la sala esta tarde.*
bles en la sala?

1. ¿César va a tener tiempo para ayudarnos?
2. ¿José y Conchita van a limpiar la cocina?
3. ¿Vas a traer toda la ropa hoy?
4. ¿Ramón y tú van a salir para comprar una nueva nevera?
5. ¿Van a venir María Dolores y Ricardo con tu colección de libros?
6. ¿Susana va a arreglar la cortina en el cuarto de baño?

C. ¿Piensa usted que las siguientes cosas que ocurrían en el pasado
seguramente ocurrirán en el futuro?

▶ Antes era difícil vivir en paz *(peace).*   *Creo que será difícil vivir en*
paz en el futuro.
Creo que no será difícil vivir en
paz en el futuro.

1. Antes había muchos pobres.
2. Antes se podía viajar fácilmente.
3. Antes se ofrecían buenos cursos en universidades en otros países.
4. Antes la gente quería tener mucho dinero.
5. Antes se pensaba en los problemas humanos.
6. Antes se decía que la vida era mejor en el pasado.

D. Diga usted por lo menos tres actividades que usted piensa hacer el
próximo sábado o domingo. Use el tiempo futuro.

▶ *El sábado me levantaré temprano, jugaré al tenis con Manuel y comeré*
con Alicia en la cafetería.

II. The conditional tense (mood)

1. In Spanish, the conditional (expressed in English by *would/should +*
verb) of most verbs is formed by adding the conditional endings to the
infinitive (the same stem as the future). Note that the conditional
endings are identical to the imperfect endings of **-er** and **-ir** verbs.

estudiar	comer	ir
estudiar **ía**	comer **ía**	ir **ía**
estudiar **ías**	comer **ías**	ir **ías**
estudiar **ía**	comer **ía**	ir **ía**
estudiar **íamos**	comer **íamos**	ir **íamos**
estudiar **íais**	comer **íais**	ir **íais**
estudiar **ían**	comer **ían**	ir **ían**

—¿Te **atreverías** a decirle que   *Would you dare tell him he's crazy?*
    está loco?
—¡Jamás! ¡Se **sentiría** ofendido!   *Never! He'd feel offended!*

2. The verbs that have modified stems in the future have the same
modified stems in the conditional.

—¿Qué **harías** en mi lugar?   *What would you do in my place?*
—Probablemente **tendría** las   *I'd probably have the same doubts*
    mismas dudas que tú.   *as you.*

3. The conditional is used in Spanish to express:
   a. what would occur under certain conditions or circumstances.

Visitaríamos el museo, pero   *We would visit the museum, but*
    está cerrado.   *it's closed. (The action would*
    occur if the museum were
    open.)

Compraría un carro, pero no   *I would buy a car, but I don't*
    encuentro uno que me guste.   *find one I like. (The action*
    would occur if the right car
    were found.)

   b. a future action, event, or situation with reference to a past action,
   event, or situation.

Yo creía que Francisco **iría** con   *I thought (that) Francisco would*
    nosotros.   *go with us.*
Pepe dijo que **viajaría**.   *Pepe said (that) he would travel.*

   c. a possible future action in a softened (mild) tone. In such cases, the
   conditional is considered more polite, whereas use of the present
   tense would be considered more informal.

—¿Te **gustaría** ir al cine?   *Would you like to go to the movies?*
—¿**Podría** servirle?   *Could I help you?*

E. Diga qué harían las personas y por qué no pueden hacerlo.

▶ Pepe / comer tamales / no en-   *Pepe comería tamales, pero no*
   contrar un restaurante mexicano   *encuentra un restaurante mexicano.*

   1. Aldo / vivir en Chile / no conocer a nadie allí
   2. Rosa y María / viajar a Francia / no saber francés
   3. nosotros / ir a la playa en enero / no tener vacaciones entonces
   4. yo / comprar un avión / no tener suficiente dinero
   5. tú / hacer una torta / no tener los ingredientes
   6. tú y Carlos / salir de aquí ahora / no saber adónde ir
   7. ustedes / dormir todo el día / tener clase
   8. Melba / montar en motocicleta con Luisa / tener que irse ahora

F. Soledad habla de sus planes para el futuro, pero Carlos no oye bien lo que ella dice. Pablo se lo repite a Carlos. Haga el papel de Soledad, de Carlos o de Pablo.

▶ vivir en un apartamento pequeño

Soledad: *Viviré en un apartamento pequeño.*
Carlos: *¿Qué dijo Soledad?*
Pablo: *Dijo que viviría en un apartamento pequeño.*

1. trabajar en un hospital para ganar experiencia
2. salir para Europa en julio
3. regresar a los Estados Unidos en agosto
4. asistir a otra universidad en septiembre
5. casarse con Adalberto Sánchez
6. comprar una casa muy grande
7. tener dos hijos
8. hacer un viaje todos los veranos

G. Ud. recibe toda clase de invitaciones maravillosas, pero no puede aceptarlas. Responda con mucha cortesía y diga por qué no las puede aceptar.

▶ ir al cine el jueves

S1: *¿Quieres ir conmigo al cine el jueves?*
S2: *¡Muchas gracias! Iría contigo, [pero no puedo ese día porque tengo que trabajar].*

1. comer en el café San Carlos el lunes
2. jugar al tenis el miércoles
3. montar a caballo el sábado
4. ir a la playa el domingo
5. bailar en el club el viernes
6. nadar en la piscina el martes

H. Haga frases lógicas, usando el condicional en la primera cláusula y una razón en la segunda cláusula.

▶ comprar un estéreo   *Compraría un estéreo, [pero no tengo dinero].*

1. visitar a mis abuelos
2. aprender a esquiar
3. pintar un cuadro
4. ir a la fiesta esta tarde
5. escribir una novela
6. salir todos los días

I. Suponga (*Assume*) que ganó medio millón de dólares. Diga lo que haría y lo que no haría bajo tales circunstancias.

▶ *Posiblemente, le daría mucho dinero al hospital de mi pueblo y compraría un automóvil nuevo. No gastaría (waste) mi dinero en ir al cine, comer tacos, etcétera.*

III. Future and conditional of probability

1. The future tense is frequently used in Spanish to express a conjecture or a probability of something occurring in the present. Some common expressions of conjecture or probability used in English are *I wonder, must be, can be, I suppose,* and *probably.*

—¿Quién **cantará** ahora?   *I wonder who's singing now?*
—**Será** Jorge.   *It must be Jorge.*

—¿Dónde **estará** Gloria?   *Where can Gloria be?*
—A estas horas **estará** en el   *At this hour she's probably in the*
gimnasio.   *gym.*

2. The conditional tense (mood) is frequently used in Spanish to express a conjecture or a probability of something occurring in the past.

—¿Quién **traería** esta torta?   *I wonder who brought this cake?*
—La **traería** Rosita, como siempre.   *I suppose Rosita brought it, as usual.*

—¿Dónde **estaría** David a   *Where could David have been at*
medianoche?   *midnight?*
—**Estaría** en la discoteca.   *He probably was at the discotheque.*
Siempre va los sábados.   *He always goes on Saturdays.*

J. Usted está solo/a en el dormitorio y contesta el teléfono. Dígales a las personas que llaman dónde Ud. supone que estén todos sus compañeros/as de dormitorio.

▶ Mónica   S1: *¿Está Mónica?*
            S2: *Lo siento, estará [en la biblioteca].*

1. Luis y Enrique   4. Gustavo
2. el señor Guzmán   5. Raúl y Beto
3. la señorita Ramírez   6. la señora de la Villa

K. Explique dónde estaban ayer, posiblemente, las siguientes personas y por qué. Use las expresiones indicadas y su imaginación.

▶ el señor Sánchez / trabajar en   *Ayer el señor Sánchez trabajaría en*
la oficina   *la oficina [porque tenía que escribir*
    muchas cartas].

1. mi mamá / ir de compras . . . .
2. mi hermana Julia / estudiar en la biblioteca . . . .
3. mi amigo Guillermo / viajar al aeropuerto . . . .
4. mi hermano Víctor / salir en tren . . . .
5. mis abuelos / venir a la universidad . . . .
6. los señores Álvarez / descansar en su casa . . . .

L. Son las diez de la mañana. Diga lo que posiblemente hacen en este momento algunos de sus amigos o algunos de los miembros de su familia.

▶ *Mi hermano Luis dormirá porque es muy perezoso. Mi amigo Ricardo arreglará su carro porque tuvo un accidente.*

M. Ayer usted vio a las siguientes personas. Diga por qué, posiblemente, se sentían de la forma indicada.

▶ Ernesto / de mal humor   *Ayer vi a Ernesto y parecía de mal humor. [El pobre pensaría en los exámenes].*

1. Alicia / triste
2. su profesora / agitada
3. su papá / cansado

4. su hermano / furioso
5. Miguel / alegre
6. tú y Marta / contentos/as

IV. Review of **ser** and **estar** with adjectives

Pepito no debe hacerlo; es muy joven.

¡Mira qué joven está Don Lucho!

1. **Ser** is used with adjectives to describe the normal attributes or characteristics of someone or something, when these attributes can be verified objectively by anyone.

Esa señora **es** vieja. Tiene noventa años.
La nieve **es** blanca.

That woman is old. She's ninety years old.
Snow is white.

2. **Estar** is used with adjectives when giving a subjective appraisal of the appearance, looks, or behavior of someone or something.

José **está** muy viejo.
¡Qué bonita **está** Rosa con su vestido nuevo!

José looks very old (to me).
How pretty Rosa looks in her new dress!

3. **Estar** is also used with adjectives to express a condition or state of being.

El autobús **está** lleno.	*The bus is full.*
¡Qué cansado **estoy!**	*How tired I am!*
Esta casa no **está** limpia.	*This house is not clean.*

4. Some adjectives have different meanings, depending on whether they are used with **ser** or **estar.**

Adjective	With ser	With estar
aburrido, -a	boring	bored
bueno, -a	good (character)	well (in good health)
listo, -a	smart, clever	ready
malo, -a	bad (character)	ill
oscuro, -a	dark (complexion)	dark (lack of light)

| Ese programa de televisión **es** muy aburrido. | *That television program is very boring.* |
| Tienes la cara muy triste. **¿Estás** aburrido? | *You have a very sad face (look). Are you bored?* |

N. Diga por qué algún pariente suyo actuaba de forma diferente a la normal la última vez que lo vio. Use adjetivos como **triste, alegre, amable, antipático, activo, perezoso,** etcétera.

▶ *Mi prima Inés es muy alegre; pero cuando la vi ayer, estaba triste porque estaba enferma.*

O. Complete los diálogos con la forma correcta de **ser** o **estar,** según el contexto.

1. —¿ _____ listo, Jaime? —Todavía no.
2. —¿ _____ ocupada la sala? —Sí, hasta las tres.
3. —¡Qué guapo _____ Fernando! —Es por el traje nuevo.
4. —¿Por qué estás aquí sola? —Porque _____ aburrida.
5. —¡Qué lista _____ la niña! —Es cierto, igual que su mamá.
6. —¿Qué le pasa a Pilar? —_____ triste porque no pudo salir con sus amigos.
7. —¿ _____ agradable el clima de España? —Sí, y _____ bastante seco.
8. —Las ensaladas siempre _____ enormes aquí. —Pues, no comeré nada más entonces.
9. —¿Puede salir Ramón hoy? —Lo siento. _____ malo todavía con un dolor de cabeza horrible.
10. —¿Por qué no come más el perro? — Porque _____ pequeño.

¡Exprésese usted!

La carta formal

Cuando se escribe una carta formal en español, se debe escribir con un estilo muy correcto *(formal)* y con un tono de mucha cortesía.

Lea la siguiente carta para obtener información sobre un curso de verano escrita por un alumno mexicano a una universidad española. Fíjese en las expresiones de saludo y de despedida para que pueda después escribir una carta.

México, D.F., 18 de abril de 1985

Sr. Prof. D. Manuel Abad
Departamento de Literatura
Facultad de Filosofía y Letras
5 Universidad de Córdoba
Córdoba, España

Muy apreciado profesor Abad:

Con gran interés leo los anuncios de los cursos de arte sobre el Barroco Andaluz dirigidos por Ud. en la Universidad de Córdoba durante el verano.
10 Mi especialización dentro del arte es precisamente el barroco, y me interesaría mucho recibir información detallada sobre los requisitos del curso, el costo del programa, vivienda y la posibilidad de obtener ayuda económica.

Estudio arte en la Universidad Autónoma de México y también con profesores particulares. Por eso me interesaría saber si sus cursos de verano

PRIEGO DE CORDOBA

II CURSO DE VERANO SOBRE

"EL BARROCO
EN
ANDALUCIA"

(80 Conferencias, Conciertos de música barroca,
Exposiciones, Excursiones y Actividades deportivas)

15 son de nivel elemental, intermedio o superior, porque me parece que estoy
preparado para seguir un curso intermedio.

Espero que Ud. pueda enviarme la información necesaria lo más pronto
posible, ya que falta poco tiempo para empezar el curso. Le agradezco su
atención.

20   Queda de Ud., muy atentamente,

Justino Ramírez de las Casas L.
Calle Constitución, No. 347 P-A
México 31, D.F.

A. Conteste las preguntas según el contenido de la carta.

1. ¿De qué se trata el curso?
2. ¿Cuándo y dónde tendrá lugar el curso?
3. ¿Por qué es de interés especial el curso para Justino Ramírez?
4. ¿Sobre cuáles detalles específicos pide información Justino
   Ramírez?
5. ¿Qué información personal ofrece Justino sobre sí mismo?

B. Suponga que Ud. desea asistir a un curso de verano en el Instituto de
Estudios Mexicanos en León, México. Escriba una carta a la directora
del instituto, Prof. Rosario Delgado G., pidiéndole información. Use
las fórmulas de saludo y despedida de la carta de Justino Ramírez o las
del *Estudio de palabras* de esta lección. Incluya la siguiente información
en su carta.

1. ¿Dónde se informó Ud. del curso?
2. ¿Por qué le interesa tomar el curso?
3. ¿Cuál es su preparación en el área de estudios del curso?
4. ¿Qué información necesita (el costo, la comida y vivienda, la
   duración del curso, etcétera)?

Lección 21
En México

Una imagen basada en estereotipos

Mercedes Hernández entra en una cafetería de la UNAM° para reunirse con sus amigos Victoria, Miguel y Luis. Los ve sentados en una mesa, y al acercarse se da cuenta de que discuten acaloradamente.

Universidad Nacional Autónoma de México

Victoria: Mira . . . no puede ser. ¡Es un horror, una vergüenza!

Mercedes: Oye, Viki, dime qué pasa. Gritan como si estuvieran locos. Oí sus voces desde la puerta.

Miguel: Hola, Meche. ¡Qué suerte! Llegaste a tiempo. Quisiéramos
5   saber tu opinión sobre este asunto.

Mercedes: Si me lo explicaran, tal vez podría darles mi opinión. ¿No les parece?

Luis: Tienes razón. Pues, hablamos de las telenovelas; de cómo representan la vida mexicana y particularmente de cómo
10   proyectan la imagen de la mujer mexicana.

Victoria: Mercedes, ¿qué te parece la mujer presentada en las telenovelas? ¿Crees que la mujer que llora por los actos de su

El público hispánico puede también leer su novela favorita además de verla en la televisión, como muestra esta fotonovela mexicana. Lea esta sección de la revista. ¿Qué estereotipos de la mujer y del hombre aparecen allí?

enamorado, que sufre y acepta pasivamente todas las discri-
minaciones de nuestra sociedad sea la imagen de la mujer
15   mexicana moderna?

  Mercedes: Claro que no. Si fuera así, tendríamos que decir que también
el hombre de las telenovelas es el típico hombre mexicano
moderno: el hombre macho, el hombre que hace lo que le da
la gana,° el déspota frío a quien no le importan los senti-   **le da** . . . feels like
20   mientos de la gente a su alrededor.

    Miguel: ¡Ea! La verdad es que yo me siento muy incómodo con ese
concepto del hombre. Hay que encontrar una solución para
cambiar esa imagen.

      Luis: Estoy de acuerdo. La imagen del hombre insensible, egoísta,
25   cruel y superficial no es muy lisonjera tampoco. No me gusta
pensar que yo sea parte de esa imagen.

  Victoria: Pues, no es suficiente despertar sólo la conciencia de ustedes.
Para encontrar una solución justa al problema, es necesario
despertar también la de los hombres y mujeres mexicanos de
30   todos los niveles sociales.

    Miguel: Sería interesante organizar un debate aquí en la universidad
misma e invitar a hombres y mujeres que tienen puestos de responsabilidad en todos los medios publicitarios.

      Luis: Excelente idea. También podríamos hacer un sondeo° entre los   poll, survey
35   estudiantes para averiguar cuál es su opinión sobre este asunto
tan polémico.° ¿No les parece?   controversial

Comprensión

1. ¿Dónde están los amigos de Mercedes?
2. ¿De qué hablan los amigos?
3. ¿Cómo se representa a la mujer mexicana moderna en las telenovelas?
4. ¿Cómo se representan a los hombres mexicanos?
5. ¿Qué tal les parece a Luis y a Miguel la representación de los hombres
   mexicanos en las telenovelas?
6. ¿Qué solución ofrece Miguel para resolver el problema de la imagen de
   la mujer y del hombre mexicano en las telenovelas?
7. ¿Qué solución ofrece Luis?

Conversación

1. ¿Qué tal le parece a usted el movimiento feminista?
2. ¿Conoce usted las ideas o los escritos de alguna feminista famosa?
3. ¿Piensa usted que los programas y los anuncios comerciales en la
   televisión se dedican con seriedad a mejorar la imagen estereotipada de
   la mujer? ¿y del hombre?

4. ¿Lee usted revistas femeninas? ¿cuáles? ¿Qué opina usted de ellas? ¿Qué piensa usted de los concursos de belleza?
5. ¿Mira Ud. telenovelas en los EEUU? ¿Qué opina de ellas? ¿Cómo es la imagen que proyectan del hombre y de la mujer?

Vocabulario

Palabras análogas

el concepto	estereotipado, -a	el movimiento	la publicidad
cruel	el/la feminista	particularmente	la responsabilidad
el debate	el horror	pasivamente	superficial
el déspota	la idea	presentado, -a	típico, -a
la discriminación	la imagen		

Sustantivos

el acto action
la belleza beauty
el/la enamorado/a sweetheart; person in love
el escrito writing
el sentimiento feeling
la telenovela soap opera
la vergüenza disgrace, shame
la voz voice

Verbos

acercarse to come near; to approach
gritar to shout
importar to matter
llorar to cry
opinar to think; to have an opinion
proyectar to project
representar to portray
sufrir to suffer

Adjetivos

egoísta selfish
incómodo, -a uncomfortable, uneasy
insensible insensitive
lisonjero, -a flattering
loco, -a crazy
macho, -a male; manly, virile
mismo, -a same, very; self *(with a pronoun)*

Otras palabras y expresiones

acaloradamente heatedly
los anuncios comerciales advertisements
como si as if
darse cuenta (de) to realize
dime qué pasa tell me what is the matter
estar de acuerdo to agree
los medios publicitarios mass media
el nivel social social level
tal vez perhaps

Práctica

A. Con un/a compañero/a de clase, prepare una lista de temas y problemas sobre la condición de la mujer en la sociedad contemporánea. Después compare su lista con la de otro grupo, y diga lo que se podría hacer para mejorar la condición de la mujer.

B. Piense usted en el uso de estereotipos femeninos y masculinos en los anuncios comerciales presentados por la televisión y la prensa y coméntelos con un/a compañero/a, dando *(giving)* algunos ejemplos.

Nota cultural La mujer mexicana

Según el estereotipo tradicional, la mujer mexicana se autorrealiza[1] en la familia en el papel de buena madre y buena mujer. Sus virtudes más apreciadas son la abnegación,[2] la sumisión y el sacrificio. Se cree que la mujer debe ser dependiente del hombre, ya sea[3] su padre o su marido. Pero el desarrollo económico del país trae cambios para toda la sociedad mexicana, y

_____
1. **se** . . . fulfills herself 2. self-denial 3. **ya** . . . whether

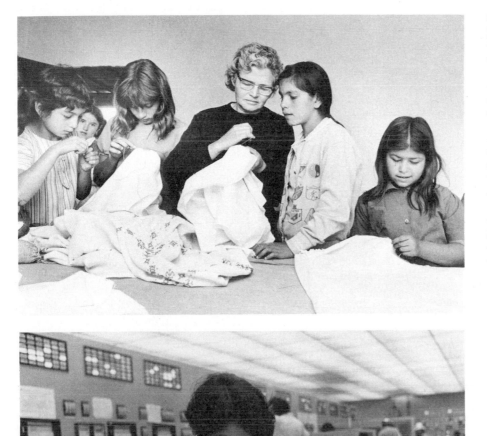

(Arriba) La costura ha sido la profesión femenina por excelencia de la mujer hispana en su papel tradicional. ¿Cree Ud. que haya algún tipo de labor que sólo la mujer deba hacer? ¿Sabe Ud. en qué culturas la costura es sólo una tarea para hombres? (Abajo) Ser ingeniera nuclear ya no es un caso extraordinario en la sociedad mexicana. La planta nuclear más importante de México está situada en Veracruz. ¿Cree Ud. que un accidente nuclear en esa planta podría afectar a la población en Estados Unidos? ¿Dónde está situada Veracruz?

estos cambios tienen un impacto también sobre las tradiciones familiares. Hoy en día, según las leyes mexicanas, la mujer tiene los mismos derechos civiles que el hombre, y el estado legal de la mujer mexicana está más adelantado[4] que en otros países hispanoamericanos.

Todavía la mayoría de las mujeres hacen trabajos que son considerados femeninos y por los cuales reciben un sueldo inferior al de los hombres. Sin embargo, hay un buen número de mujeres en profesiones tales como la medicina, el derecho,[5] la arquitectura, la ingeniería, la literatura y las artes. Hay también mujeres excepcionales que participan en la vida pública del país, como ministras, senadoras y embajadoras.[5]

---

4. advanced 5. law 6. ambassadors

Estudio de palabras

Ocupaciones y profesiones

el/la abogado/a lawyer
el/la auxiliar de vuelo steward, stewardess
el/la banquero/a banker
el/la bibliotecario/a librarian
el/la carnicero/a butcher
el/la carpintero/a carpenter
el/la cocinero/a cook
el/la conductor/a driver
la criada maid, female servant
el criado male servant
el/la ejecutivo/a executive
el/la escritor/a writer
el/la farmacéutico/a druggist

el hombre de negocios businessman
el/la médico/a medical doctor
el/la modisto/a women's tailor
la mujer de negocios businesswoman
el/la peluquero/a hairdresser
el/la periodista newspaper reporter, journalist
el/la piloto pilot
el/la sastre/a men's tailor
el/la vendedor/a vendor, salesman, saleswoman
el/la zapatero/a shoemaker; cobbler

Expresiones útiles

la agencia de colocaciones employment agency
las aptitudes qualifications (for a job)
el cargo post, charge
la carrera career
el deber duty, responsibility
el empleo employment, job
el empleo a tiempo completo full-time job

el empleo a tiempo parcial part-time job
la empresa firm
la especialización specialization
el salario wage(s)
solicitar empleo to apply for work
la solicitud de empleo job application
el sueldo salary
la tarea task, assignment

A. Complete cada oración con la palabra o expresión relacionada con la profesión u ocupación apropiada.

1. ¿Te gustan los artículos escritos por ese _____ en el periódico de hoy?
2. Fui a ver a mi _____ porque necesito un traje nuevo.
3. Anoche _____ de ese restaurante preparó unas comidas fabulosas.
4. Si te gusta tanto viajar en avión, ¿por qué no consideras la carrera de _____ ?
5. Uno de los _____ españoles más famosos es Miguel de Cervantes.
6. Tengo el pelo muy largo y mi _____ está enfermo. ¡Qué problema!
7. Su hermana es _____ , y trabaja en un hospital de la capital.
8. A mi amiga le interesa mucho el mundo de los negocios, así que va a ser _____ .
9. Su papá es _____ y trabaja en un banco en el centro comercial de la ciudad.
10. Mañana voy a ver al _____ para que me diga qué carne es mejor para este plato.
11. Voy a estudiar química porque me interesa la _____ de medicina.
12. Quiero conseguir un _____ para los fines de semana; así puedo ayudar a pagar mis estudios.

B. Usted busca trabajo. Escriba un anuncio para un periódico, indicando el tipo de trabajo que desea, sus aptitudes, su especialización y el sueldo que desea.

EMPRESA INTERNACIONAL
busca para Madrid
SECRETARIA BILINGÜE
(ESPAÑOL-INGLÉS)

- Con pleno dominio mecanografía. Valoraremos conocimientos de taquigrafía y otros idiomas.
- No importa edad ni estado. Preferible experiencia (no indispensable).
- Ofrecemos puesto estable en Empresa de primer orden. Ingresos elevados.

Concretar entrevista llamando al teléfono 231 59 02, lunes y martes.

PROGRAMADOR

Se requiere con:

- EXPERIENCIA EN COBOL-IMOS V.
- Incorporación inmediata.
- Salario a convenir.

Interesados, llamar al Teléfono 747 28 22. Sr. Salamanques.

EMPRESA DE ÁMBITO INTERNACIONAL
CONTABLE/ADMINISTRADOR

Se requiere: Personas jóvenes activas con capacidad de organización y trato humano. Libre servicio militar. Imprescindible inglés hablado y escrito.
Se ofrece: Condiciones económicas a convenir, según aptitudes del candidato. Formación permanente a cargo de la empresa. Incorporación inmediata a una gran firma.
Interesados, llamar por teléfono a la Srta. Johnson (733 76 39), donde les informará a partir de las 10 de la mañana.

C. Usted trabaja en una agencia de colocaciones. Prepare una lista de cinco empleos disponibles (available), indicando las aptitudes necesarias y el sueldo.

D. Complete la siguiente solicitud de empleo. Luego haga el papel de alguien que busca empleo en alguna oficina. Otro estudiante hará el papel del/de la director/a de la oficina.

I. Información personal   *Fecha* _____

Nombre _____

Dirección _____

Teléfono _____ Edad _____

Lugar de nacimiento[1] _____ Fecha _____

Carnet de conducir _____ Estado general de salud _____

Carnet de identidad _____ Nacionalidad _____

Personas que tiene a su cargo[2] _____

Parientes que trabajan en esta empresa _____

Estudios terminados _____

Idiomas extranjeros _____

Referencias (no familiares)

1. Nombre _____   2. Nombre _____
   Dirección _____   Dirección _____
   _____   _____
   Teléfono _____   Teléfono _____
   Ocupación _____   Ocupación _____

II. Empleo solicitado

Solicita el cargo de _____

Fecha en que puede empezar a trabajar _____

Sueldo a que aspira[3] _____

III. Empleo anterior

Nombre de la empresa _____

Dirección _____ Teléfono _____

Nombre y cargo de su jefe inmediato _____

Cargo desempeñado[4] _____

Fecha de ingreso[5] _____ Fecha de retiro[6] _____

Motivo del retiro _____

Sueldo inicial _____ Sueldo final _____

---

1. birth 2. **Personas** . . . persons dependent on you 3. **Sueldo** . . . desired wage
4. held 5. beginning 6. termination

Estructuras útiles

I. Commands with **tú** and **vosotros**

*¡Hola, Migdalia! **Entra, pon** tu abrigo allí y **siéntate** conmigo.*

1. The affirmative **tú**-command of regular verbs is formed by dropping the **-s** ending from the **tú-**form of the present indicative. The use of the pronoun **tú** is optional. If expressed, it occurs after the verb form.

   ¡Mira (tú) ese edificio!   *Look at that building!*
   Lee (tú) este artículo, por favor.   *Read this article, please.*
   Escribe (tú) una carta a Gabriel.   *Write a letter to Gabriel.*

2. The following irregular verbs have irregular affirmative **tú**-commands.

Infinitive	Tú-command	Examples
decir	**di**	**Di** la verdad.
hacer	**haz**	**Haz** la tarea.
ir	**ve**	**Ve** al correo.
poner	**pon**	**Pon** la mesa.
salir	**sal**	**¡Sal** de allí!
ser	**sé**	**Sé** más prudente.
tener	**ten**	**¡Ten** más paciencia!
venir	**ven**	**¡Ven** pronto!

3. The negative **tú**-command of all verbs is the same as the **tú-**form of the present subjunctive.

   No **comas** tanto chocolate.   *Don't eat so much chocolate.*
   No **pidas** nada.   *Don't ask for anything.*
   No **hagas** ruido.   *Don't make noise.*

4. A summary chart of affirmative and negative **tú**-commands of regular verbs is given at the top of page 390.

Infinitive	Affirmative	Negative
-ar verb	entra (tú)	no entres (tú)
-er verb	come	no comas
-ir verb	escribe	no escribas

5. Object pronouns used with **tú**-commands follow the same pattern as object pronouns used with other commands. In affirmative commands, object pronouns are attached to the end of the verb form, and a written accent is required on the stressed syllable. In negative commands, object pronouns precede the verb form.

Termina el trabajo.	Termína**lo.**
Pídele el periódico.	Píde**selo.**
No termines el trabajo.	No **lo** termines.
No le pidas el periódico.	No **se lo** pidas.

6. The affirmative **vosotros**-command of verbs is formed by replacing the final **-r** of the infinitive with **-d.** The **-d** is dropped in the reflexive construction. The negative **vosotros**-command of verbs is the same as the **vosotros**-form of the present subjunctive.

Affirmative	Negative
¡Entrad!	¡No entréis!
¡Preparádmelo!	¡No me lo preparéis!
¡Vendedlo!	¡No lo vendáis!
¡Sentaos!	¡No os sentéis!

A. Dé una orden a un/a compañero/a de clase, según las siguientes indicaciones.

▶ darme el diccionario   *[María], dame el diccionario, por favor.*

1. abrir la ventana
2. recordar nuestra tarea
3. volver conmigo a la cafetería
4. contarme lo que pasó
5. sentarte en esta silla
6. venir a la reunión
7. acercarte un momento
8. ser más paciente

B. Usted organiza una fiesta para uno/a de sus amigos/as. Conteste las preguntas de varios amigos/as que le están ayudando, dando una orden afirmativa o negativa.

▶ ¿Quieres que arregle la sala?   *Sí, arréglala, por favor.*
No, no la arregles hasta mañana.

1. ¿Quieres que yo traiga los platos y vasos?
2. ¿Quieres que ponga las mesas en la sala?
3. ¿Quieres que yo saque las fotos?
4. ¿Quieres que salga a comprar las bebidas?
5. ¿Quieres que te muestre lo que le compramos?
6. ¿Quieres que pida los sándwiches?

C. Roberto tiene 13 años. Él le pregunta a su padre si le permite hacer varias cosas. Su padre le responde con una orden afirmativa o negativa. Haga el papel del padre. Si usted da una orden negativa, dé una explicación apropiada.

▶ ¿Puedo ver la película de media-noche?

Sí, ve la película.
No, no la veas; [tienes clase mañana].

1. ¿Puedo invitar a mis amigos a cenar?
2. ¿Puedo pasar el fin de semana en casa de José?
3. ¿Puedo comprar unos esquís y botas nuevos?
4. ¿Puedo hacer mis tareas mañana en vez de hoy?
5. ¿Puedo ir al partido del domingo?
6. ¿Puedo aprender a conducir este verano?

II. Softening requests and criticisms

*¡Señor, Ud. **debería** conducir mejor!*

The verbs **poder, querer,** and **deber** are commonly used in making requests and criticisms. Use of the present indicative, the conditional, or the imperfect subjunctive of these verbs reflects the desire of the speaker to soften or make more polite a request or a criticism. The present indicative is the least soft or polite way of doing so, and the imperfect subjunctive is the most soft or polite manner.

—¿**Puedes** prestarme veinte pesos?

Can you lend me 20 pesos?

—¡No **debes** pedir eso!

You mustn't ask that!

—¿**Quiere** venir conmigo?

Do you want to come with me?

—**¿Podrías** prestarme veinte pesos?   *Could you lend me 20 pesos?*

—¡No **deberías** pedir eso!   *You shouldn't ask that!*

—**¿Querría** venir conmigo?   *Would you like to come with me?*

—**¿Pudieras** prestarme veinte pesos?   *Would you be able to lend me 20 pesos?*

—No **debieras** pedir eso.   *You really ought not to ask that.*

—**¿Quisiera** venir conmigo?   *Would you like to come with me?*

D. Pídales algunos favores a sus compañeros o amigos, usando **querer** o **poder** en el presente de indicativo y las expresiones indicadas.

► traerme un refresco   *[Jaime], ¿quieres traerme un refresco?*

1. comer conmigo hoy
2. llevarme al centro
3. enseñarme el artículo
4. decirme cómo hacer un pastel
5. esperarme después del concierto
6. dejarme tu carro mañana

E. Usted está en el Banco Nacional, y necesita usar los servicios de varias personas. Use el condicional o el imperfecto del subjuntivo de **poder** para pedir los servicios.

► señor / cambiarme este cheque   *Señor, ¿podría usted cambiarme este cheque?*

1. señor Martínez / comprobar el estado de mi cuenta
2. Sr. Director / informarme sobre su sistema de contabilidad
3. señoritas / explicarme cómo preparar este documento
4. señores / venderme unos cheques de viajero
5. señora Ruiz / cambiarme estos dólares por pesetas
6. señorita Jiménez / decirme el nuevo horario de servicio

F. Dígale a las siguientes personas lo que usted cree que deben o no deben hacer. Use el presente del indicativo, el condicional o el imperfecto del subjuntivo de **deber,** según el grado de cortesía que quiera mostrar.

► (a su profesor): darnos más tiempo para el informe   *Usted debiera darnos más tiempo para el informe.*

1. (a su hermana): leer mis cartas
2. (a un compañero): contar lo que ocurrió
3. (a su jefe): informarnos de los cambios
4. (a su senador): hacer más para mejorar la economía
5. (a una persona en la calle): tirar *(throw)* papeles al suelo
6. (a una joven que compra boletos): esperar su turno

III. Si-clauses

—¿Me prestas cien pesos?
—*Si los tengo,* te los presto.

—¡Caramba! No tengo, pero *si los tuviera* te los prestaría.

1. In a sentence containing a **si**-clause, the indicative is used in both the **si**-clause and in the main clause when the main clause describes a fact or a condition that is likely to exist or to happen, or that is habitual.

Si tú **vas** a la reunión, nosotros **vamos** también.	*If you go to the meeting, we're going too.*
Si **vienen,** seguramente **llegarán** tarde.	*If they come, they will surely arrive late.*
Si Carmen **estaba** en la fiesta, ¿por qué no **bailó?**	*If Carmen was at the party, why didn't she dance?*

2. To express a contrary-to-fact situation in the present or the future, the imperfect subjunctive is used in the **si**-clause. The conditional is generally used in the main clause to indicate the conclusion to the situation expressed in the **si**-clause.

Si nos **llamaran** por teléfono, **sabríamos** dónde están.	*If they would telephone us (but they won't), we would know where they are.*
Si **se sustituyeran** esos programas, **mejoraría** la imagen de la mujer.	*If those programs were replaced (but they won't be), the image of women would improve.*

3. **Si** + *imperfect subjunctive* is used in exclamations to express wishes that are impossible to fulfill.

¡Si **tuviera** un millón de dólares!	*If only I had a million dollars!*
¡Si yo **pudiera** viajar ahora!	*If only I could travel right now (but I can't)!*

4. Exclamations with **ojalá** (*I wish, I hope, may God grant, would that*) also express wishes. **Ojalá** followed by the present subjunctive indicates that

there is some hope that the wish will be realized. **Ojalá** followed by the imperfect subjunctive implies that there is very little hope of realization.

¡Ojalá nos **llegue** la carta mañana!

I hope the letter arrives tomorrow (it may)!

¡Ojalá nos **llegara** la carta mañana!

I wish the letter would arrive tomorrow (but it won't)!

G. Exprese cada oración con una cláusula con **si** y el indicativo para indicar que las situaciones son posibles o habituales.

▶ Siempre que salía, llovía.   *Si salía, llovía.*

1. Cuando comemos mucho, nos sentimos mal.
2. Cuando hago ejercicios, me canso mucho.
3. Cada vez que le preguntabas algo, te contestaba que no.
4. Siempre que Marta lo llama, dice que está ocupado.
5. Cuando vienen, me traen un regalo.
6. Cada vez que podía, lo ayudaba.

H. Hoy es un día en que todo sale mal *(turns out bad)*, y usted desea lo imposible. Exprese sus deseos.

▶ Tengo examen.   *¡Si no tuviera examen!*
▶ No sé la lección.   *¡Si supiera la lección!*

1. Hace frío.
2. No gano mucho dinero.
3. No funciona mi carro.
4. La tarea está difícil.
5. Tengo dolor de cabeza.
6. Todos nos sentimos mal.

I. Exprese cada oración con una cláusula con **si** contraria a la realidad.

▶ Si puedo, lo hago.   *Si pudiera, lo haría.*

1. Si cantas, te escucho.
2. Si comemos comida saludable, nos sentimos bien.
3. Si no comemos, nos morimos de hambre.
4. Si lo analizamos, lo entendemos.
5. Si Ud. llama al programa de radio, recibe un premio.
6. Si tengo tiempo y energía, termino pronto.

J. Conteste las preguntas y demuestre esperanza *(hope)* de que se cumplan *(fulfill)* sus deseos, o declare que son deseables pero imposibles, según su opinión. Use **ojalá** con el presente o el imperfecto del subjuntivo.

▶ ¿Hace buen día?   *No sé, pero ojalá haga buen día para el partido.*
                      ¡No! Ojalá hiciera buen día, pero llueve y hace frío.

1. ¿Comes en un restaurante esta noche?
2. ¿Sacas las mejores notas de la universidad?
3. ¿Recibes correo todos los días?
4. ¿Te llaman por teléfono tus amigos hoy?
5. ¿Vamos todos a México en el verano?
6. ¿Te eligen capitán del equipo?
7. ¿Viene alguien a visitarte en estos días?

K. Mencione dos o tres «sueños imposibles» que usted tiene. Empiece cada oración con una exclamación con **si** o con **ojalá**.

▶ *¡Si yo pudiera viajar por todo el mundo!*
▶ *¡Ojalá yo pudiera viajar por todo el mundo!*

IV. Como si-clauses

¡Hablas **como si fueras** Einstein!

Como si (*As if*)-clauses always introduce contrary-to-fact statements. The verb in the **como si**-clause is in the imperfect subjunctive or another past subjunctive form.

Esos jóvenes cantan **como si fueran** profesionales.	*Those young people sing as if they were professionals (but they aren't).*
Elisa habla **como si** lo **supiera** todo.	*Elisa talks as if she knew everything (but she doesn't).*

L. Las personas indicadas dan una impresión equivocada *(false)* de sus circunstancias o capacidades personales. Usted quiere corregir esa impresión. Exprese su opinión con una cláusula con **como si** y el imperfecto del subjuntivo.

▶ Ramiro no estudia mucho, pero saca buenas notas.
Saca buenas notas como si estudiara mucho.

1. Los estudiantes no viven mal, pero se quejan.
2. Tú no tienes mucho dinero, pero compras muchísima ropa.

3. No le gusta, pero siempre habla de ese programa de televisión.
4. No te interesa el arte, pero siempre hablas de los artistas famosos.
5. No la leen, pero siempre comentan esa revista.

M. Algunos de sus parientes y amigos actúan de una forma contradictoria. Haga oraciones apropiadas, usando las palabras y expresiones indicadas.

▶ vivir / ser millonario   *[Mis tíos] viven como si fueran millonarios.*

1. hablar de esos países / viajar mucho
2. comer / estar muerto de hambre
3. mirarme / tener miedo de mí
4. llorar / acabar el mundo
5. vestirse / ser más joven

¡Exprésese usted!
La autobiografía

Cuando se escribe una autobiografía, hay que considerar ciertas cosas:

a. el propósito de la autobiografía
b. quién la leerá
c. qué detalles enfatizar
d. qué detalles no mencionar

Josefina Salcedo J. escribió su autobiografía para enviarla con una solicitud para una beca *(scholarship)* en el extranjero ofrecida por el gobierno mexicano. Léala para comprensión general y prepárese a contestar preguntas sobre la vida de Josefina.

Autobiografía de Josefina Salcedo J.

Dicen que los hijos llegan con un pan debajo del brazo. Ésta es otra manera de decir que cada hijo que nace trae algo bueno para la familia. Los recuerdos que tengo de mi infancia son de una vida difícil para mi familia, pero feliz. Mi papá trabajaba a todas horas, me parece, hasta los domingos,
5 pero en mi casa siempre se sentía la alegría de mi mamá y de mis dos hermanos mayores, que siempre estaban en todo. Yo soy la menor, y como soy la única hija, siempre le ayudaba a mi mamá. Cuando no estaba en el colegio, estaba con mi mamá haciendo algo en la casa.

Mis papás querían que yo fuera a un buen colegio y por eso mi papá
10 trabajaba mucho, y luego también mis hermanos ayudaron al hacerse mayores. Algunas amigas mías no terminaron el colegio porque sus padres creían que eso era para los hombres nada más. Mi mamá decía que los

tiempos cambiaban y que las mujeres ya trabajaban en todo, especialmente
en la ciudad. Vivimos aquí en Guadalajara desde hace mucho, y en mi
15 opinión, es una ciudad que ofrece bastantes oportunidades para una mujer
como yo.

Después de terminar el bachillerato, entré a la Universidad de Guadalajara. Aquí estudio economía e inglés, y por las tardes trabajo en una academia de gimnasia y baile pues me gusta mucho la gimnasia y la practico
20 activamente. En la academia no me pagan mucho, pero al menos ya ayudo
a pagar mis estudios.

El mes entrante termino mis estudios de economía, y tengo la posibilidad de trabajar para la Compañía de Maquinaria Harrington de Inglaterra
aquí en Guadalajara. Me interesa mucho el puesto, pero creo que sería im-
25 portante viajar a Inglaterra o a los Estados Unidos por un año para perfec-
cionarme en economía y en inglés antes de comenzar a trabajar. Tengo una
buena base en inglés, pero un año de perfeccionamiento en los dos campos
me permitiría regresar a mi país realmente bien preparada.

A. Conteste en forma breve las siguientes preguntas sobre la autobiografía
de Josefina Salcedo.

1. ¿Qué quiere decir que los hijos llegan «con un pan debajo del
brazo»?
2. ¿Cómo fue la infancia de Josefina?
3. ¿Cuántos hijos hay en total en la familia?
4. ¿Qué ideas sobre la educación de las mujeres tenía la familia de
Josefina? ¿Cómo se comparaban estas ideas con las del resto de
su clase social?
5. ¿Cómo es la vida de Josefina en la universidad y en el trabajo?
6. ¿Qué posibilidades tiene Josefina para el futuro, y cuál le interesa
más?
7. ¿Qué le parece la autobiografía de Josefina? ¿Qué puntos son
más apropiados para la solicitud que hace?

B. Suponga que Ud. envió una solicitud para un programa de estudios
en México y que le piden su autobiografía. Escríbala en uno o dos
párrafos, considerando estos puntos:

1. ¿Cómo fue su infancia?
2. ¿Cómo era su ciudad y su educación? ¿Cambió su actitud hacia
los estudios en la universidad?
3. ¿Qué intereses y planes tiene para el futuro y cómo se relacionan
al programa?

Lengua en acción 7

A. Dime cómo se llega *(Lección 19)*

Imagínese que Ud. y un/a compañero/a de clase viven en diferentes calles del sector de Ciudad de México que aparece en el mapa. Marquen sus respectivas calles con una equis *(X)*. Su compañero/a le pregunta cómo llegar a su casa desde donde él/ella vive y Ud. se lo explica. Después, alternen los papeles.

Frases útiles

al oeste (este)	doblar a la izquierda	ir derecho *(straight ahead)*
cerca de	doblar a la derecha	una (dos, tres) cuadras
en la esquina	frente a	cruzar la calle

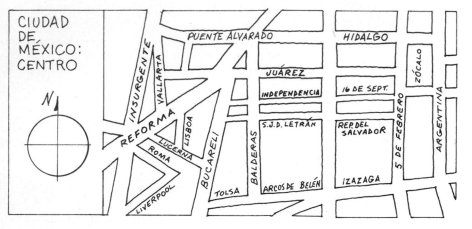

B. Una decoración fantástica *(Lección 19)*

Ud. entra por primera vez en el apartamento recién amueblado *(furnished)* de un/a amigo/a (su compañero/a de clase). Dígale cuánto

le gusta la decoración de su sala. Base sus comentarios en el dibujo e incluya lo siguiente:

a. Mencione un mueble o adorno *(decoration)* que Ud. considere particularmente interesante o atractivo.
b. Hágale varias preguntas sobre el artículo: ¿dónde lo consiguió?, ¿qué marca es?, ¿de qué es?, ¿quién es el artista?, etc., según sea apropiado.
c. Compare el apartamento con el suyo, diciéndole que Ud. no tiene una sala tan interesante.

Frases útiles

estilo único	tela bonita	madera maciza *(solid)*
cómodo	colores atractivos	ingenioso
útil	muy moderno	
de segunda mano	poco común	

C. Una bola de cristal *(Lección 20)*

Basado en lo que Ud. sabe de un/a compañero/a de clase, dígale cómo piensa que será su futuro. Su compañero/a comentará si está de acuerdo *(in agreement)* con su pronóstico: **Tienes razón, me gustaría**... Si él/ella no está de acuerdo, predirá *(predict)* su propio futuro: **No estoy de acuerdo, me gustaría...; No, no me casaré porque**.... Después, alternen los papeles.

1. *Futuro económico:* obtener un puesto muy bien pagado, heredar un millón, . . .
2. *Futuro romántico:* (no) encontrar el amor de su vida, casarse con un/a millonario/a, . . .
3. *Futuro profesional:* ser presidente de . . . , llegar a ser . . .
4. *Futuro familiar:* (no) tener . . . hijos, adoptar muchos hijos, . . .
5. *Futuro personal:* ser feliz, . . .

D. Un programa de estudios en México *(Lección 20)*

Ud. va a estudiar español en México este verano. Un/a compañero/a de clase está interesado/a en el programa. Conteste sus preguntas, basándose en el folleto *(brochure)* de la página 400.

Información que su compañero/a quiere saber

alojamiento en México	costo del alojamiento
compañeros de cuarto	excursiones
número de clases por día	localización
materias que se estudian	fechas del programa

UNIVERSIDAD INTERNACIONAL
Cursos de Verano para Extranjeros
Apartado Postal 569
Puebla, México

Curso de español para extranjeros
(Del 4 al 26 de agosto)

Clases

Tres horas diarias por la mañana, de lunes a viernes, durante tres semanas (total: 45 horas).

9–10 Lengua española
10–11 Conversación en español
11–12 Cultura mexicana

Actividades

1. Visitas a museos y monumentos locales
2. Presentaciones teatrales
3. Conferencias sobre la cultura mexicana
4. Excursiones a la capital, a las pirámides de Teotihuacán y a las ruinas de Tula

Alojamiento

Con familias mexicanas selectas. Incluye tres comidas diarias.
Estudiantes deben compartir algunas actividades de la familia. Dos estudiantes por cuarto.

Inscripción

El precio del curso es de:
    50.000 pesos mexicanos*
    200.000 pesos mexicanos (con alojamiento y comida)
*incluye clases, conferencias, acceso a instalaciones deportivas, admisión a actividades culturales y servicio médico.

Certificados

El día 26 de agosto se entregarán los Certificados de Asistencia a los alumnos que hayan completado las 45 horas de clase. Los Certificados de la Universidad Internacional han sido aceptados en varias universidades estadounidenses.

E. Un permiso especial *(Lección 20)*

Usted quiere que le acrediten el curso de verano en México. Necesita la firma del/de la director/a del departamento en la solicitud. Conteste las preguntas del/de la director/a (un miembro de la clase), basándose en el folleto.

Información que quiere saber el/la director/a

nombre y localización del programa
número total de horas de clase en
   el programa

los estudios que se hacen
si reciben certificado
actividades especiales

F. Un/a compañero/a de apartamento ideal *(Lección 21)*

Ud. comparte *(share)* un apartamento de tres habitaciones con un/a amigo/a (su compañero/a de clase). Necesitan encontrar otra persona para ocupar la tercera habitación. Explíquele a su amigo/a lo que cree que deben considerar al buscar una persona. Su amigo/a le dice si está o no está de acuerdo y por qué.

Consideraciones

hábitos de dormir	estado financiero *(financial)*
amistades *(friendships)*	hábitos de estudio
personalidad	conocimiento culinario
hábitos de limpieza	?

alguien que se acueste temprano.
¿Por qué? Cada persona tendrá su propio cuarto. (Sí, es muy importante. Yo me acuesto a las diez y no quiero que nadie me despierte.) Cree que debemos...

...ción 21)

...ción sobre las ambiciones de los *...ste a 2 ó 3 compañeros /as de* *...carreras piensan que son las* *...a escala de 1 a 7 los puntos que* *...a al seleccionar una carrera o* *...fesión para cada compañero/a.*

	S1	S2	S3
...on mejores			
...r			
...deal			
...n trabajo:			
6. Profesión/Carrera que Ud. le recomienda			

H. Lo siento, pero no puedo *(Wrap-up)*

Un/a compañero/a de clase le pide a Ud. un favor, pero Ud. no puede hacerlo. Resuelva el asunto, siguiendo los siguientes pasos. Use las sugerencias o cree una excusa original.

Paso 1: Su compañero/a le pide un favor a Ud.
Paso 2: Ud. le dice que no puede y le da una excusa cortés.
Paso 3: Su compañero/a insiste, dando razones.
Paso 4: Ud. da una sugerencia para resolver el problema.

Los favores	*Las excusas*	*Las sugerencias*
Quiere pedirle prestado *(borrow)* el libro de español porque . . .	Ud. tiene que estudiar para un examen y . . .	buscar el texto en la biblioteca
Quiere que Ud. llame a un/a profesor/a para decirle que él/ella no puede entregar un informe a tiempo porque . . .	Ud. no sabe su número de teléfono y . . .	dejarle una nota al/a la profesor/a en la oficina
Quiere que Ud. lo/la acompañe a la fiesta de un/a amigo/a porque . . .	Ud. no se siente bien y . . .	llamar a otro/a amigo/a

Unidad 8
En España

Los molinos de viento de Campo de Criptana, al sur de Madrid, evocan recuerdos de Don Quijote y Sancho Panza en el visitante a esta pintoresca región de España. Los molinos de viento eran una novedad (novelty) tecnológica en la época de Cervantes, el autor de Don Quijote, pero hoy los protege el gobierno por su valor pintoresco y como un símbolo del país. Observe a los hombres que, con su tradicional boina en la cabeza, se sientan a charlar al sol.

Lección 22
En España

Democracia bajo la monarquía

Después de casi cuarenta años de dictadura militar, desde el final de la
Guerra Civil en 1939 hasta la muerte del General Francisco Franco en 1975,
se instituyó en España una monarquía constitucional de carácter democrático bajo el rey Juan Carlos I de Borbón. El cambio no ha resultado tan
5 traumático como se había temido antes de la muerte de Franco. De hecho,
el rey ha apoyado el proceso democratizador° del país y ha ayudado a ace-   democratizing
lerar muchas de las reformas que el gobierno ha efectuado durante los últimos años. Su firme actuación, especialmente en los momentos de crisis, le
ha ganado la confianza y la admiración del pueblo.
10   Durante los años transcurridos desde la institución de la democracia en
España, el país ha atravesado etapas dificilísimas. El proceso de establecer
las instituciones democráticas, de reconciliar las fuerzas de la izquierda y de
la derecha, de formular y aprobar la nueva constitución y de afirmar las
autonomías regionales se ha visto complicado por serios problemas econó-
15 micos, un alto nivel de desempleo y repetidos actos terroristas. A pesar de
las dificultades, se han llevado a cabo importantes cambios, como la am-

*El rey de España, don Juan
Carlos I de Borbón, sale en su
coche a pasar revista a una
parada militar en Valladolid en
el día de las fuerzas armadas. Al
observar la expresión en la cara
de los espectadores, ¿qué
emociones parecen reflejar? ¿y
la del rey? ¿Qué piensa Ud. es el
papel del rey en la sociedad
española?*

pliación de las libertades de prensa, de palabra y de reunión, el reconocimiento de todos los partidos políticos y la celebración de elecciones libres. Con la democracia ha aumentado dramáticamente la actividad de la prensa,
20 ya que se han podido tratar abiertamente los problemas sociales, políticos y económicos del país sin temor a la censura.

Uno de los cambios más significativos ha sido la descentralización del poder; y, actualmente, varias de las regiones del país disfrutan de cierta autonomía del gobierno de Madrid. La autonomía les permite elegir sus
25 presidentes y parlamentos, administrar sus recursos y usar las lenguas regionales oficialmente. El uso de las lenguas regionales, que se había prohibido durante el régimen franquista,° ha resurgido en los medios de comunicación y en las escuelas, donde ahora se enseña tanto la lengua regional como el castellano.

Franco

Comprensión

1. ¿Cuántos años duró la dictadura de Francisco Franco?
2. ¿Qué hizo Don Juan Carlos de Borbón al tomar el control del gobierno?
3. ¿Qué problemas ha tenido que enfrentar el gobierno?
4. ¿Cuáles son algunos de los cambios efectuados bajo la democracia?
5. ¿Qué cambios ha habido en la prensa de España?
6. ¿En qué consisten las autonomías regionales?

Conversación

1. ¿Sabe usted qué países de habla española viven bajo dictadura militar?
2. ¿Sabe usted cuáles son los países europeos que viven bajo la monarquía?
3. ¿Hay clases privilegiadas en los Estados Unidos? Si las hay, ¿cuáles son?
4. ¿Cuáles son algunos de los problemas sociales, políticos y económicos de los Estados Unidos?
5. ¿Qué libertades existen en los Estados Unidos?

Vocabulario

Palabras análogas

acelerar	la democracia	oficialmente
el acto	democrático, -a	el parlamento
administrar	la descentralización	el/la presidente/a
la admiración	dramáticamente	privilegiado, -a
la autonomía	efectuar	el proceso
la celebración	las elecciones	reconciliar
civil	especialmente	el régimen
consistir	firme	repetido, -a
la constitución	formular	significativo, -a
constitucional	el general	terrorista
el control	militar	traumático, -a
la crisis	la monarquía	el uso

Sustantivos

la actuación   action, behavior
la ampliación   expansion
el carácter   character, nature
el castellano   Spanish language
la censura   censorship
la confianza   confidence
la derecha   right *(in the political spectrum);* right-hand side
el desempleo   unemployment
la dictadura   dictatorship
el final   end
la fuerza   force
la guerra   war
la izquierda   left *(in the political spectrum);* left-hand side
la libertad   freedom, liberty
la muerte   death
el partido   party *(political)*
el poder   power
la prensa   press
el reconocimiento   recognition
el rey   king
el temor   fear

Adjetivos

alto, -a   high
cierto, -a   some, certain

dificilísimo, -a   very difficult
efectuado, -a   brought about
libre   free
transcurrido, -a   passed, elapsed

Verbos

apoyar   to support
atravesar (ie)   to go through
aumentar   to increase
disfrutar   to enjoy
durar   to last
enfrentar   to face
establecer (zc)   to establish
instituir   to establish
resurgir   to rise up again
tratar   to deal with

Otras palabras y expresiones

abiertamente   openly
actualmente   at the present time
de habla española   Spanish-speaking
de hecho   in fact
la libertad de palabra   freedom of speech
llevar a cabo   to carry out

Práctica

A. Haga una encuesta *(poll)* sobre la opinión política de sus compañeros de clase, usando las siguientes preguntas. Trate también de averiguar por qué las personas opinan de una manera u otra.

1. Según usted, ¿cuál es el mayor problema económico de nuestro país hoy en día?

   _____ la inflación   _____ los altos impuestos *(taxes)*
   _____ los salarios bajos   _____ sin opinión

2. ¿Cuál debería ser la tarea más urgente del gobierno?

   _____ desarrollar las armas   _____ proveer *(provide)* al
   nucleares   pueblo más servicios sociales
   _____ mejorar la economía   _____ sin opinión

3. Según usted, ¿qué cualidad es la más importante en un líder político?

_____ inteligencia   _____ experiencia
_____ honestidad   _____ liderazgo (leadership)

4. ¿Qué considera usted que es más importante?

_____ la atención a los derechos individuales
_____ la atención a los derechos colectivos
_____ igual atención a los derechos individuales y colectivos
_____ sin opinión

5. Según usted, ¿se interesa la gente en la actividad política del país?

_____ sí, mucho   _____ a veces
_____ muy poco   _____ sin opinión

B. Prepare un resumen (summary) de los resultados de su cuestionario, indicando las opiniones de la mayoría. Explique también las razones dadas (given).

Nota cultural El cine español

Con los cambios políticos instituidos bajo la democracia en España, la industria cinematográfica española tiene mayor libertad y los directores del cine actual pueden analizar y comentar abiertamente la religión, la política y la sociedad españolas. Hoy día el público español puede ver películas como las de Luis Buñuel que fueron prohibidas durante la dictadura militar de Franco.

Buñuel se considera uno de los más importantes creadores del cine moderno con obras como *Viridiana, Los olvidados, Tristana* y *Ese oscuro objeto del deseo.* Su espíritu es siempre profundamente español. Aunque la mayoría de sus películas fueron producidas fuera de España, sus temas de tono antiburgués y anticonformista reflejan su visión de la realidad española.

Entre los directores contemporáneos del cine español figuran José Luis Garcí, José Luis Borau, Carlos Saura y Luis García-Berlanga, presidente de honor de la recién formada Academia de las Artes y las Ciencias Cinematográficas de España. El cine español recibe cada día más atención internacional como lo atestiguan[1] los premios otorgados[2] en los festivales internacionales, por ejemplo, el Oscar a *Volver a empezar* de José Luis Garcí como mejor película extranjera en 1982, y la mayor exportación de películas como *Furtivos* de José Luis Borau y *Mi prima Angélica, Carmen, Cría cuervos*[3] y *El amor brujo* de Carlos Saura.

---

1. **como** . . . as evidenced by 2. awarded 3. ravens (beginning of the Spanish proverb «Cría cuervos y te sacarán los ojos»)

En Madrid, como en todas las ciudades del mundo hispánico, hay infinidad de teatros de cine que exhiben películas de todo el mundo. Los hispanos son ávidos cineastas. ¿Ha visto Ud. la película que se exhibe hoy en el Cine Avenida? ¿Qué tipo de película es: una tragedia, una comedia, un documental, un misterio?

Estudio de palabras

La política

la campaña electoral electoral campaign
el/la candidato/a candidate
el consejo council
dimitir to resign
la elección election
el/la embajador/a ambassador
el gabinete cabinet
la junta council, board
la manifestación demonstration
el/la ministro/a minister
la papeleta voting paper, ballot paper

el/la partidario/a follower
el partido político political party
el/la presidente/a president
la publicidad publicity
la reina queen
el/la representante representative
la república republic
el rey king
el/la senador/a senator
la urna ballot box
votar to vote
el voto vote

A. Lea el siguiente volante (*flyer*) de propaganda política que anuncia la candidatura de Victoria Álvarez para senadora. Explique brevemente las razones por las que usted cree que se debe o no se debe elegir senadora a Victoria Álvarez.

Victoria Álvarez
¡La Mejor Para Senadora!

Es una mujer joven y enérgica, con demostrada experiencia en el servicio a la nación.

Licenciada en Economía y en Derecho Civil.

Directora por tres años del Banco de Comercio.

Conferenciante habitual en las universidades del país, conocida por sus ideas progresistas.

Miembro activo del Consejo de Planificación Económica del país, promovedora de medidas[1] para contrarrestar la inflación y el desempleo.

Presidenta actual del Colegio de Abogados de Sevilla, sustancial contribuyente al desarrollo de las leyes del país.

¡La mejor candidata por su dinamismo, su honestidad y su interés en el bienestar[2] de cada ciudadano!

¡Vote por Victoria Álvarez!

1. measures
2. well-being

B. Prepare un informe breve sobre un país de su preferencia. Hable de su tipo de gobierno (república, monarquía constitucional, etcétera), sus partidos políticos, el nombre del jefe de gobierno y otros aspectos políticos que usted considere importantes.

Estructuras útiles

I. Present perfect tense

In Spanish, the past participle (el participio pasado) is used with the auxiliary verb haber to form the perfect tenses.

A. The past participle

1. The past participle of most verbs is formed by adding -ado to the infinitive stem of -ar verbs, and -ido to the infinitive stem of -er and -ir verbs.

-ar	-er	-ir
hablado	comido	decidido
comprado	tenido	vivido
buscado	establecido	asistido

2. The following verbs have irregular past participles.

a. Forms ending in **-to**

abrir	**abierto**	opened
cubrir	**cubierto**	covered
escribir	**escrito**	written
morir	**muerto**	died
poner	**puesto**	put
romper	**roto**	broken
ver	**visto**	seen
volver	**vuelto**	returned

b. Forms ending in **-cho**

decir	**dicho**	said
hacer	**hecho**	made, done

c. Other irregular forms

ir	**ido**	gone
ser	**sido**	been

3. Compounds formed with the verbs listed above normally follow the same pattern.

describir	**descrito**	described
devolver	**devuelto**	returned
inscribir	**inscrito**	inscribed
prescribir	**prescrito**	prescribed
suponer	**supuesto**	supposed
suscribir	**suscrito**	subscribed

4. When the infinitive stem of an **-er** or an **-ir** verb ends in a vowel, an accent mark is required over the **i** of the **-ido** past participle ending.

caer	**caído**	fallen
leer	**leído**	read
oír	**oído**	heard
reír	**reído**	laughed
traer	**traído**	brought

B. Formation of the present perfect tense

*¡No entres! No **he arreglado** mi cuarto todavía.*

1. The present perfect (**el pretérito perfecto**) in Spanish is formed with the present tense of the auxiliary verb **haber** + *a past participle.*

Present of *haber* + past participle

---

he has ha hemos habéis han	hablado comido decidido

---

2. In general, the perfect tenses are used in a similar way in Spanish and in English. The present perfect is used to express a past action that the speaker sees as related to the present in some way.

Mi hermano **ha perdido** su cartera.	*My brother has lost his wallet.*
Los músicos **han tocado** dos horas sin parar.	*The musicians have played two hours without stopping.*
Hemos vivido en España diez años.	*We have lived in Spain ten years.*
He leído varias novelas de ese escritor.	*I have read a few novels by that writer.*
¿Han oído Uds. la noticia?	*Have you heard the news?*

3. Object and reflexive pronouns used with the present perfect precede the conjugated forms of **haber.**

—¿Has visto a mi hermano?
—No, no **lo he visto** por ninguna parte.

Have you seen my brother?
No, I haven't seen him anywhere.

—Dale la carta a tu hermana, por favor.
—Ya **se la he dado.**

Give the letter to your sister, please.
I have already given it to her.

—¿Te gustó la fiesta?
—Sí, **me he divertido** mucho, gracias.

Did you enjoy the party?
Yes, I (have) enjoyed myself a lot, thank you.

A. Diga si estas personas han hecho o no las siguientes acciones. Siga las indicaciones entre paréntesis y use el pretérito perfecto del verbo.

▶ Pilar / terminar / el trabajo de laboratorio (sí)

Pilar ha terminado el trabajo de laboratorio.

▶ tú / leer el artículo (no)

Tú no has leído el artículo.

1. ustedes / escribir / el informe (no)
2. Ramón / ir / a la manifestación (no)
3. Ángela y Luis / pedir / los billetes (sí)
4. José / sacar / el coche del garaje (sí)
5. usted / asistir a la conferencia (no)
6. Marta y tú / cancelar / las reservaciones (sí)
7. nosotros / comprender / la situación política de España (no)
8. yo / ver esa película / varias veces (sí)

B. Explíquele a un/a compañero/a que las siguientes personas ya han hecho lo que se pregunta. Use el pretérito perfecto en sus respuestas.

▶ ¿Visitará Ud. Madrid en abril? *No, ya he visitado Madrid.*

1. ¿Tus primos aprenderán a escribir cartas formales?
2. ¿Silvia y Felipe van a traer la tienda de campaña?
3. ¿Vas a oír las noticias de las elecciones?
4. ¿Carlos y su novia volverán a finales de mes?
5. ¿Irá tu prima Alicia de vacaciones esta semana?
6. ¿Ustedes van a preparar los cuestionarios hoy?

C. Diga tres cosas que usted y alguna/s persona/s que conoce han hecho en su vida, y tres cosas que no han hecho nunca.

▶ *Yo he viajado a Perú, he vivido en Colombia y he visitado Venezuela.*

▶ *Mi hermano nunca ha ido a un museo, ni ha asistido a un concierto ni ha votado en unas elecciones.*

D. Conteste las preguntas en el pretérito perfecto, usando pronombres para el objeto directo e indirecto.

▶ ¿Ya hicieron los trabajos de física?   *Sí, ya los hemos hecho.*
                                          No, no los hemos hecho todavía.

1. ¿Tus padres te regalaron un coche nuevo? ¿y a tu hermano?
2. ¿Le dijiste la verdad a tu novio/a?
3. ¿Yo les di a ustedes un examen difícil alguna vez?
4. ¿Y todos ustedes escucharon las noticias?
5. ¿Le prestaste el carro a una amiga recientemente?
6. ¿Me mostraron ustedes las fotografías del viaje en la clase?
7. Y yo, ¿les mostré a ustedes unas fotografías de mis viajes?
8. ¿Comprendieron ustedes la situación política perfectamente?

II. Pluperfect and conditional perfect

There are various perfect tenses in Spanish in both the indicative and subjunctive. Two indicative perfect tenses that are used most frequently are the pluperfect (**el pluscuamperfecto**) and the conditional perfect (**el condicional perfecto**).

A. *Pluperfect tense*

1. The pluperfect tense is formed with the imperfect of **haber** + *a past participle*.

Imperfect of *haber* + past participle	
había habías había habíamos habíais habían	hablado comido decidido

2. In general, the uses of the pluperfect are similar in Spanish and in English. The pluperfect is used to express an action that had taken place before another action in the past or before a specific moment in the past.

Mi hermano me dijo que **había perdido** su cartera.
My brother told me that he had lost his wallet.
Te aseguro que no le **habíamos dicho** eso ayer.
I assure you that we hadn't told him that yesterday.

B. Conditional perfect tense

1. The conditional perfect tense (**el condicional perfecto**) is formed with the conditional of **haber** + *a past participle*.

Conditional of *haber* + past participle

habría	
habrías	
habría	hablado
habríamos	comido
habríais	decidido
habrían	

---

2. The conditional perfect is used to express an action that would have taken place under certain circumstances, or that would have taken place but for some reason didn't.

—¿Te **habrías suscrito** a esa revista si fueras yo?

Would you have subscribed to that magazine if you were I?

—En tu lugar, lo **habría hecho.**

In your place I would have done it.

Habríamos ido a Colombia, pero no tuvimos tiempo.

We would have gone to Colombia, but we didn't have time.

E. Responda que las siguientes acciones o situaciones ya habían ocurrido cuando usted llegó a la reunión. Use el pluscuamperfecto del verbo.

▶ ¿Beatriz preparaba los refrescos?   *No, ya los había preparado cuando llegué.*

1. ¿Carolina mostraba las fotos de Costa Rica?
2. ¿Vicente y Julio hablaban con Tina?
3. ¿Los estudiantes organizaban la próxima reunión?
4. ¿Todos bebían o comían?
5. ¿Ricardo y Ernesto discutían los problemas económicos?
6. ¿Luis tocaba la guitarra?
7. ¿Los otros bailaban?
8. ¿Algunos jóvenes escuchaban discos?

F. Complete con frases lógicas, usando el pluscuamperfecto del verbo.

▶ Antes de ayer Pepe vino a   *[yo ya había salido].* visitarme, pero . . . .

1. Creo que Pedro no quiso venir a la fiesta porque . . . .
2. Cuando me encontré contigo, ...

3. Cuando me levanté, ...
4. El lunes, cuando llegaste a mi habitación, ...
5. No compré la motocicleta porque . . . .
6. Les dije a mis amigos que no quería ir con ellos porque . . . .
7. Cuando salimos del teatro, ...
8. No queríamos ver esa película porque . . . .

G. Diga lo que posiblemente habría ocurrido antes de 1975 en España con un gobierno democrático. Use el condicional perfecto.

▶ los partidos políticos / existir   *Los partidos políticos habrían existido antes.*

1. el país / celebrar elecciones libres
2. los ciudadanos / aprender las lenguas regionales
3. los periodistas / escribir sin temor a la censura
4. el pueblo / tener más libertad
5. las regiones del país / establecer las autonomías
6. el gobierno / hacer una nueva constitución

H. Usted y sus amigos lamentan no haber hecho todo lo que querían el fin de semana pasado. Explique lo que habrían hecho con más tiempo.

▶ yo / comprar zapatos nuevos   *Yo habría comprado zapatos nuevos.*

1. Marta / correr tres kilómetros más
2. Víctor y yo / reunirse para planear un viaje de esquí
3. tú / ver a tus padres
4. ustedes / ir a la manifestación
5. Pedro / leer otra novela de ciencia-ficción
6. yo / lavar el coche
7. Ana y tú / conseguir un nuevo apartamento
8. nosotros / pasar más tiempo en el campo

III. Superlatives with **sumamente** and **-ísimo**

—El abuelo de Julia es **sumamente viejo**, ¿no?
—¡Sí, es **viejísimo**! Tiene más de 100 años.

1. The suffix **-ísimo/a, -ísimos/as** is often used to give a superlative meaning to adjectives.

El hermano de Roberto es **altísimo.**

Roberto's brother is extremely tall.

Rosaura está **cansadísima.**

Rosaura is extremely tired.

2. Superlative meaning may also be expressed in Spanish with the adverb **sumamente** + *adjective.*

La comida está **sumamente buena.**

The food is exceedingly good.

Esta novela es **sumamente interesante.**

This novel is extremely interesting.

3. The chart below summarizes the formation of superlatives with **-ísimo**. In general, when a word ends in a vowel, the final vowel is dropped before adding the ending **-ísimo.** When a word ends in a consonant, the ending **-ísimo** is attached to the final consonant.

Base form	Type of change	Adjective in *-ísimo*
alto	final vowel **o** dropped	**altísimo**
alegre	final vowel **e** dropped	**alegrísimo**
amable	**ble > bil**	**amabilísimo**
loco	**c > qu**	**loquísimo**
largo	**g > gu**	**larguísimo**
fácil	**-ísimo** attached to final consonant	**facilísimo**

I. Ramón y Claudia acaban de conocerse en una fiesta y encuentran que tienen gustos parecidos *(similar).* Haga el papel de uno de los dos.

▶ La comida está buena. Ramón: *La comida está muy buena, ¿no?*
  Claudia: *Sí, está buenísima.*

1. Esos cantantes son muy malos.
2. El decorado es sumamente interesante.
3. El ambiente es sumamente agradable.
4. Esta fiesta está muy alegre.
5. La música es muy variada.
6. La noche está sumamente fresca.
7. Estos bailes son muy difíciles.
8. Esa chica es muy amable.

J. Piense en libros, películas, personas, etcétera, que le gustan mucho o que no le gustan nada. Descríbalos con un superlativo formado con **sumamente** o con un adjetivo que termina en **-ísimo**.

▶ *Me gusta mucho la novela «Crimen de invierno». En mi opinión es un libro interesantísimo y sumamente bien escrito.*

¡Exprésese usted!

Las invitaciones

Es de suma utilidad aprender a aceptar o a rechazar (*decline*) una invitación. Lea las siguientes respuestas a una misma invitación a pasar un fin de semana en casa de amigos, y observe las varias expresiones de cortesía usadas, tanto para aceptar como para excusarse por no aceptar la invitación.

Fuente Dorada, 14 de junio

Mi querido Manolo:

¡Cómo agradecerte tu amabilísima invitación a pasar el fin de semana en Soria! Nada me gustaría más que pasar unos días contigo y con los viejos amigos.

Desafortunadamente, para el fin de semana del 25 me será imposible. ¿Te imaginas la mala suerte? Ese fin de semana le prometí a mi madre que iría a verla a Madrid para ayudarle con la venta del apartamento. Ha decidido venirse a vivir conmigo en Fuente Dorada. Mi hermano no puede ir a ayudarle porque estará con la familia en Málaga. Fíjate, todo se ha combinado para impedir que yo vaya.

Espero que me invites otra vez cuando invites a los otros amigos. Y mientras tanto, ¿vendrás a verme en Fuente Dorada algún día pronto? Escríbeme cuando puedas venir, que me encantará verte por aquí. Recibe un abrazo muy grande y muy fuerte de tu amigo,

Carlos

Pinar del Río, 15 de junio

Mi queridísimo Manolo:

Me diste un gusto muy grande con tu carta. La invitación a Soria para el 24 y 25 me cae de maravilla. Precisamente esa semana voy a estar en Zaragoza y puedo ir a Soria antes de regresar a Pinar del Río.

Además, me alegro mucho de que vayan a estar allí Pepita y Julián, Paco y Carmen y posiblemente Carlos. También me parece estupenda la idea de pasar la tarde del sábado en el campo. ¿Vamos otra vez a la Taberna del Rey? No se me olvidará nunca la carne y el vino que nos sirvieron allí. Por mi parte pienso llevarte un jamón de Pinar, del que te gusta.

Te agradezco la invitación, y te la acepto con el deseo de verte nuevamente el 24 por la mañana. Te abraza tu prima,

María Dolores

A. Busque una palabra o expresión apropiada en las cartas anteriores para completar cada una de las siguientes oraciones.

1. _____ no puedo aceptar tu invitación.
2. Nada _____ que estar contigo el 3 de junio.
3. Tu invitación me cae _____ .
4. ¿Te imaginas _____? Estoy ocupado este fin de semana.
5. Todo se ha combinado para _____.
6. Te agradezco y te _____ la invitación con mucho gusto.
7. Esa idea me _____ .

B. Suponga que Ud. estudia en España y recibe una carta de Piedad, una amiga de su primo Pedro. Ahora Piedad quiere extenderle una invitación a Ud. para que pase una semana de vacaciones con ella y su familia en Sevilla. Usted puede pasar solamente tres días con ellos, de manera que acepta pero se excusa también porque no puede pasar toda la semana allá. Escriba una carta corta pero con mucha cortesía y entusiasmo. Use la forma de **tú** con Piedad.

Lección 23
En España

Las tunas

Las tunas son grupos de jóvenes universitarios que han mantenido vivas las canciones estudiantiles y tradicionales del país. Los grupos de tunos se organizan dentro de la universidad por facultades, de modo que las Facultades de Derecho, de Medicina o de Filosofía y Letras° tienen su propia tuna. Se visten al estilo medieval, de negro, con pantalones hasta la rodilla, calcetines largos y capa adornada con cintas de distintos colores. Tradicionalmente, las amigas les regalan esas cintas de colores después de una serenata.

Manuel Pineda y otros tres estudiantes de medicina de la Universidad de Santiago de Compostela están organizando un viaje a los Estados Unidos. Ellos forman parte de una excelente tuna, que visitará varias universidades norteamericanas que los han invitado a cantar su repertorio de canciones tradicionales.

Hace un mes que Manuel y sus compañeros se preparan para su estreno° estadounidense. Anoche se reunieron en casa de Manuel, donde estuvieron ensayando por dos horas. Entre las canciones que piensan presentar al público norteamericano se encuentra la «Tuna compostelana»,° cuyos versos se dan a continuación.° La canción habla del amor inconstante de un tuno de Santiago de Compostela, quien lleva en su capa una cinta por cada una de sus muchas conquistas amorosas.

Filosofía . . . Liberal Arts

debut

from Santiago de Compostela / **a** . . . next

Estos tres músicos son miembros de una tuna que en su totalidad puede tener quince o veinte músicos. Observe los trajes y los instrumentos (de izquierda a derecha: la bandurria, la pandereta y la guitarra). ¿Qué grupos musicales estudiantiles hay en su universidad? ¿Qué instrumentos tocan?

Tuna compostelana

Pasa la tuna en Santiago
cantando y tocando romances[1] de
  amor
luego la noche en sus ecos
25 los cuela de ronda[2] por todo
  balcón.
Y allá en el templo del Apóstol
  Santo[3]
una niña llora, ante su patrón,[4]
30 porque la capa del tuno que
  adora
no lleva la cinta que ella le
  bordó,[5]
porque la capa del tuno que
35   adora
no lleva la cinta que ella le bordó.

 *Estribillo:*[6]

Hoy va la tuna de gala[8]
cantando y tocando la marcha
  nupcial
suenan campanas[9] de gloria
50 que dejan desierta la
  universidad.
Y allá en el templo del Apóstol
  Santo
con el estudiante, hoy se va a
55   casar
la galleguita melosa y celosa[10]
que oyendo esta copla,[11] ya no
  llorará
la galleguita melosa y celosa
60 que oyendo esta copla, ya no
  llorará.

Cuando la tuna te dé serenata
no te enamores, compostelana
que cada cinta que adorna su
40   capa
es un trocito de corazón.[7]
Ay tralalara, etcétera . . .
no te enamores, compostelana,
y deja a la tuna pasar, con su
45 tralaralalá.

---

1. **ballads** 2. **los** . . . filters a serenade 3. **Apóstol** . . . Holy Apostle 4. patron saint 5. embroidered 6. Chorus 7. **trocito** . . . a bit of someone's heart 8. **de** . . . festively attired 9. **suenan** . . . bells ring 10. **galleguita** . . . sweet and jealous girl from Galicia 11. ballad, couplet

Comprensión

1. ¿Qué están organizando Manuel y otros tres estudiantes? ¿Por qué se reunieron?
2. ¿Qué es una «tuna»?
3. ¿Qué tipo de canciones cantan los tunos?
4. ¿Cómo se organizan las tunas?
5. ¿Cómo se visten los jóvenes?
6. ¿Por qué los tunos llevan cintas en sus capas?
7. ¿Qué hicieron anoche Manuel y sus compañeros? ¿Por cuánto tiempo estuvieron allí?
8. ¿De qué trata la canción «Tuna compostelana»?

Conversación

1. ¿Cree usted que la organización de un grupo como la tuna tendría éxito en las universidades de los Estados Unidos? ¿Qué obstáculos encontraría la formación de una tuna?
2. ¿Qué canciones tradicionales o estudiantiles existen en los Estados Unidos? ¿Sabe alguna?
3. ¿Sabe usted tocar la guitarra? Si no, ¿le gustaría saber tocarla? ¿Preferiría tocar canciones tradicionales o populares?
4. ¿Qué otro instrumento sabe o le gustaría saber tocar? ¿el piano? ¿la trompeta? ¿el acordeón? ¿el clarinete? ¿la flauta? ¿el tambor?
5. ¿Qué costumbres tradicionales existen en su universidad? ¿en su pueblo o ciudad?
6. ¿Qué ciudades de los Estados Unidos son famosas por sus tradiciones? Mencione las tradiciones que más le interesan.
7. ¿Pertenece Ud. a algún coro? ¿en la universidad? ¿en la iglesia? ¿Qué tipo de canciones cantan?

Vocabulario

Palabras análogas

el acordeón	el eco	el piano
adorar	la formación	el público
adornado, -a	formar	el repertorio
adornar	la gloria	la serenata
amoroso, -a	la guitarra	tradicionalmente
el balcón	el instrumento	la trompeta
la capa	medieval	universitario, -a
el clarinete	el obstáculo	el verso
desierto, -a	pasar	

Sustantivos
la cinta   ribbon
el derecho   law
la facultad   faculty, school in university
la flauta   flute
el tambor   drum
el templo   temple, church, chapel
la tuna   student musical group
el tuno   member of a student **tuna**

Adjetivos
corto, -a   short
inconstante   fickle

largo, -a   long
vivo, -a   alive

Verbos
ensayar   to rehearse
regalar   to give (a gift)
tocar   to play (a musical instrument)

Otras palabras y expresiones
ante   in the presence of
cuyo, -a / cuyos, -as   whose
la marcha nupcial   wedding march

Práctica

A. Imagínese que Ud. tiene que entrevistar a la estrella *(star)* de un programa musical en su universidad. Dé ocho preguntas que le haría en la entrevista.

B. El club de español quiere invitar a la tuna de la Facultad de Derecho de la Universidad Complutense de Madrid a cantar en su universidad. Escriba una carta al director del grupo. Usted quiere saber el programa que presentarían en su universidad si vienen a los Estados Unidos.

Nota cultural   El arte y la música en España

El museo del Prado de Madrid alberga[1] una de las mejores colecciones de obras maestras[2] del mundo, entre las que figuran obras de pintores[3] españoles como el Greco, Velázquez, Goya y Murillo. Las catedrales e iglesias y los museos de menor escala también son ricos repositorios del arte del país. Un gran número de galerías de arte exhiben cuadros de pintores jóvenes, nacionales y extranjeros. Estatuas de estilo renacentista[4] y clásico y esculturas contemporáneas adornan las plazas, parques y sitios públicos de las ciudades y de los pueblos.

Como en el arte, hay mucha variedad en la música española. Los conciertos de música clásica incluyen obras de compositores nacionales como

---

1. houses 2. **obras** ... masterpieces 3. painters, artists 4. Renaissance

La herencia cultural

Observe la doble cara de la herencia cultural
hispánica que se ve reflejada en la "Dama de Elche"
(abajo) y la "Máscara de guerrero" (arriba). La
primera es una escultura ibérica realizada hace
2.500 años. Está inspirada en los modelos griegos de
escultura y en joyas fenicias, dos culturas que
habitaron también el sureste español. En América,
las principales culturas indígenas precolombinas en
lo que es hoy día Colombia también crearon arte,
pero en metales preciosos, como esta máscara que se
conserva en el Museo del Oro de Bogotá, junto con
otras 27.000 piezas de oro.

Actividades

1. Imagine que Ud. habla con un hispano sobre unos
   bustos representativos de su cultura. ¿De qué
   bustos hablaría? ¿Dónde se encuentran? Descríbalos.
2. Dé por lo menos tres diferencias entre la Dama de
   Elche, la Máscara de guerrero y los bustos que
   Ud. describió. Hable de su forma, su tamaño y de
   lo que dicen de su cultura.

La antigüedad de la cultura hispánica puede verse en estos dos ejemplos. (Izquierda) Las pinturas prehistóricas de la Cueva de Altamira en España fueron realizadas en el Paleolítico. En los techos y paredes de la cueva se ven escenas de caza con unos 25 bisontes. (Abajo) Observe el Acueducto Romano de Segovia, realizado entre el siglo I y II. Tiene 118 arcos y sus piedras fueron esculpidas una a una. Los romanos construyeron teatros, templos, foros, carreteras y ciudades durante más de 500 años de dominación en España.

Actividades

1. Observe el Acueducto Romano de Segovia. ¿Cómo cree Ud. que corría el agua por ese acueducto? ¿Cómo son los acueductos de hoy?
2. Imagine que Ud. habla con un hispano sobre la herencia cultural de los Estados Unidos. ¿Qué culturas forman su historia? ¿Dónde hay ejemplos de esa herencia? ¿De qué época son?

La presencia árabe en España duró casi 800 años. Los árabes llegaron a la península ibérica en el año 711. Fueron expulsados de España por los reyes católicos, Isabel y Fernando, en el año 1492, año del descubrimiento de América por Cristóbal Colón. En estas fotos vemos un ejemplo de arte musulmán, la Alhambra, empezada en el siglo XIII como palacio y fortaleza. (Abajo) Desde sus balcones se contempla Granada y sobre su colina se ven los picos de Sierra Nevada. (Derecha) En un detalle de una puerta puede leerse en árabe la inscripción: Dios es Alá y Mahoma su profeta.

Actividades

1. Observe la foto de una puerta de la Alhambra. ¿Qué cree Ud. que hay detrás de la puerta? ¿Para qué cree que se usa la Alhambra hoy día?
2. ¿Qué elementos culturales cree Ud. que los hispanos heredaron de los árabes? ¿Sabe Ud. qué otros territorios fueron conquistados por los musulmanes?

Los españoles a su llegada a América encontraron una gran variedad de culturas. Una de las más desarrolladas era la inca que dejó espléndidos ejemplos artísticos y urbanísticos como el de la ciudad-fortaleza de Machu Picchu a 50 millas de Cuzco en Perú (izquierda). En términos generales podemos decir que el arte indígena de Hispanoamérica duró desde el siglo XII a.C. hasta el siglo XV. Otros pueblos indígenas, como los Huicholes, una de las tribus más antiguas de México, se distinguieron por su habilidad artesanal. (Derecha) Hoy se le da el nombre de la tribu al tejido de "huicholes", que se elabora con colores vivos y en representaciones mágicas o de animales.

Actividades

1. ¿Qué cree Ud. que interrumpió la evolución de la cultura inca en el siglo XV? Explique.
2. ¿A qué otra artesanía se parece el trabajo de los "huicholes"?

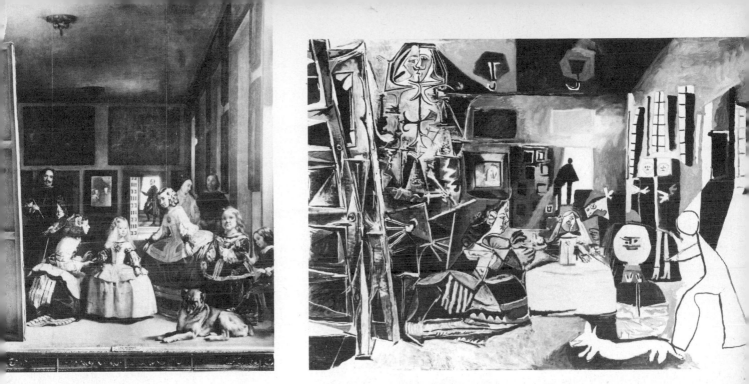

Manuel de Falla, Isaac Albéniz y Joaquín Turina. La guitarra clásica ha tenido un gran auge[5] en España gracias a intérpretes de fama mundial como Narciso Yepes y Andrés Segovia. Por otro lado, tienen mucho éxito las canciones de tradición folklórica, el flamenco, las canciones de carácter político que reflejan[6] los cambios políticos y sociales del país, y las canciones románticas de última moda.[7]

_____
5. popularity   6. reflect   7. **de** . . . of the latest fashion

(Izquierda) En el Museo del Prado de Madrid puede observarse el cuadro llamado «Las Meninas» de Diego Velázquez. El cuadro detiene por un instante la vida diaria de la corte del siglo XVII. Observe el autorretrato del pintor y el reflejo de los reyes en un espejo. (Derecha) Este cuadro de Picasso es parte de una serie titulada «Las Meninas», que se encuentra en la casa museo de Picasso en Barcelona. Encuentre Ud. los equivalentes de Velázquez en el cuadro de Picasso.

Estudio de palabras
El amor, el matrimonio y el divorcio

el anillo de compromiso
  engagement ring
el anillo nupcial   wedding ring
el aniversario   anniversary
el bautismo   christening; baptism
la boda   wedding
el compromiso   engagement
el divorcio   divorce
la edad   age

la luna de miel (el viaje de novios)   honeymoon
el matrimonio   married couple; marriage
el nacimiento   birth
el noviazgo   courtship
la pareja   couple
la separación   separation
el traje de bodas   wedding dress
la vida matrimonial   married life

Expresiones relacionadas
casarse to get married
dar a luz to give birth
divorciarse to get divorced
enamorarse to fall in love

estar comprometido, -a to be engaged
estar enamorado, -a de to be in love with
pedir la mano en matrimonio to propose

A. Conteste las siguientes preguntas.

1. ¿Está usted comprometido/a? ¿Cómo se llama su novio/a?
2. ¿Piensa usted casarse? ¿a qué edad?
3. En su opinión, ¿es bueno tener un noviazgo largo o corto? ¿por qué?
4. ¿Piensa usted que es importante que las mujeres casadas tengan una carrera? ¿por qué?
5. En su opinión, ¿cuáles son los lugares ideales para pasar la luna de miel? ¿por qué?
6. ¿Qué piensa usted del divorcio?
7. ¿Desea usted tener hijos? ¿cuántos? ¿Preferiría tener hijos o hijas? ¿por qué?

B. Complete estas oraciones con la forma correcta de una de las siguientes expresiones.

casarse	divorciarse	estar comprometido/a
dar a luz	enamorarse	estar enamorado/a

1. Mi amigo Pedro ——— de mi prima Luisa, pero todavía no ha pedido su mano.
2. Ayer la esposa del director del banco ——— a su primer hijo.
3. Dos de mis amigas ya ———; recibieron sus anillos de compromiso el catorce de febrero.
4. Mi hermano ——— el veinte de junio y pienso ir a la boda.
5. Nuestros padres no viven juntos ahora porque ——— hace seis meses.
6. Yo ——— muy fácilmente, pero nunca me he casado.

C. Termine usted las frases siguientes de una manera original.

1. La boda de Miguel y Carmen . . . .
2. El traje de bodas de mi abuela . . . .
3. Los suegros de mi hermana . . . .
4. Para el bautismo de su hijo . . . .
5. Según su hijo político . . . .
6. Para nuestro viaje de novios . . . .

D. Escriba una invitación para su boda, para el bautismo de su hijo/a o para la celebración del aniversario de sus padres.

Estructuras útiles

I. Present progressive tense

In Spanish, the present participle is used with the auxiliary verb **estar** to form the progressive tenses.

A. *Present participle*

1. The present participle of most Spanish verbs is formed by adding **-ando** to the infinitive stem of **-ar** verbs and **-iendo** to the infinitive stem of **-er** and **-ir** verbs. The English equivalent ends in -*ing*.

-ar	-er	-ir
habl**ando**	com**iendo**	decid**iendo**
compr**ando**	ten**iendo**	viv**iendo**
busc**ando**	recog**iendo**	asist**iendo**

2. When the infinitive stem of an **-er** or an **-ir** verb ends in a vowel, the **i** of **-iendo** changes to **y** and the ending becomes **-yendo**.

caer	**cayendo**	leer	**leyendo**
construir	**construyendo**	oír	**oyendo**
creer	**creyendo**	traer	**trayendo**

3. The **-ir** verbs that have a stem-vowel change **o > u** and **e > i** in the third-person singular and plural forms of the preterit also have the same stem-vowel change in the present participle.

Infinitive	Third person preterit (singular and plural)	Present participle
reír (e > i)	rió, rieron	**riendo**
dormir (o > u)	durmió, durmieron	**durmiendo**

4. The verbs **ir** and **poder** have the following irregular present participles.

ir	**yendo**
poder	**pudiendo**

B. Formation of the present progressive tense

—¿Qué hace Carlos?
—*Está escribiéndole* poemas a su
novia . . .

1. In Spanish, the present progressive tense **(la forma progresiva del tiempo presente)** is formed with the present tense of the verb **estar** + *a present participle.*

Present of *estar* + present participle	
estoy estás está estamos estáis están	hablando comiendo escribiendo

2. The present progressive in Spanish is used to express an action that is taking place at the moment of speaking. It cannot refer to something that is to take place later, as the present progressive can in English.

—¿Qué **estás haciendo?**   *What are you doing?*
—**Estoy leyendo** una novela.   *I'm reading a novel.*
But:
—¿Y qué **haces** mañana?   *And what are you doing tomorrow?*
—Creo que **voy** al cine.   *I think I'm going to the movies.*

3. Object pronouns used with the progressive may either precede **estar,** or be attached to the present participle. When they are attached to the present participle, a written accent mark is required to retain the original stress.

—¿Están ustedes haciendo las tareas?   *Are you doing the homework assignments?*
—No, no **las estamos haciendo.**
—No, no **estamos haciéndolas.**   *No, we aren't doing them.*

—¿Le estás explicando el asunto a Luis?

Are you explaining the matter to Luis?

—Sí, se **lo estoy explicando.**
—Sí, **estoy explicándoselo.**

Yes, I'm explaining it to him.

A. Cambie las oraciones a la forma progresiva del tiempo presente.

▶ Me lavo el pelo.   *Me estoy lavando el pelo.*

1. Toman el almuerzo.
2. ¿Escuchas la radio?
3. Leo una novela histórica.
4. Roberto corre en el parque.
5. Claudio echa una carta al correo.
6. Mi mamá prepara un gazpacho.
7. Marisa ve la exhibición de barcos.
8. Me visto para el teatro.

B. Alguien llama por teléfono a su residencia, y su hermano Fernando contesta el teléfono. Fernando le explica por qué nadie puede salir en ese momento.

▶ Isabel / dormir   *Isabel no puede salir porque está durmiendo.*

1. María Dolores / trabajar
2. Esteban y Luis / comer
3. nosotras / oír las noticias
4. yo / preparar la cena
5. Manolo y Teresa / analizar la encuesta política
6. Margarita y Oscar / lavar los platos
7. Carmen y yo / escribir un informe
8. Leonor / bañarse

C. La tuna de la Facultad de Derecho organiza los últimos detalles para un viaje a los Estados Unidos. En este momento usted está ayudando al director de la tuna con los preparativos. Conteste sus preguntas, usando la forma progresiva del tiempo presente. Use un pronombre de objeto directo o indirecto en su respuesta, si es posible.

▶ ¿Arregló Julio su capa?   *La está arreglando ahora.*
                             Está arreglándola ahora.

1. ¿Compró los billetes Raúl?
2. ¿Se despidió Paco de su novia?
3. ¿Ángel y tú ensayaron la nueva canción?
4. ¿Puso Miguel las maletas en el coche?

5. ¿Hizo Ignacio las reservaciones para el hotel?
6. ¿Buscó Ángel la nueva guitarra?
7. ¿Prepararon Julián y tú el itinerario?
8. ¿Cambiaron Ignacio y Raúl el dinero por dólares?

II. Preterit and imperfect progressive tenses

A. *Preterit progressive tense*

1. The preterit progressive tense (**la forma progresiva del pretérito**) is formed with the preterit of **estar** + *a present participle.*

Preterit of *estar* + present participle	
estuve estuviste estuvo estuvimos estuvisteis estuvieron	charlando leyendo describiendo

2. The preterit progressive tense is used to express an action in progress in the past that the speaker views in its beginning stage, in its final stage, or in its totality.

Estuve escribiendo cartas desde las cinco.	*I was writing letters from five o'clock on.*
Estuvimos charlando hasta las dos de la mañana.	*We were chatting until two o'clock in the morning.*
¿Estuviste cantando en el coro una hora?	*Were you singing in the choir for an hour?*

B. *Imperfect progressive tense*

1. The imperfect progressive tense (**la forma progresiva del imperfecto**) is formed with the imperfect of **estar** + *a present participle.*

Imperfect of *estar* + present participle	
estaba estabas estaba estábamos estabais estaban	charlando leyendo describiendo

2. The imperfect progressive tense is used to express an action in progress in the past that the speaker views in the midst of being performed. The imperfect tense may also be used to express the same action.

Estaban bailando (Bailaban)   *They were dancing when I came in.*
   cuando entré.
Estábamos charlando   *We were chatting at that moment.*
   (Charlábamos) en ese momento.

3. A habitual or repeated action in the past is usually expressed with the imperfect tense only.

Yo visitaba (*not* Estaba visitando)   *I used to visit Luis frequently.*
   a Luis frecuentemente.

4. Some verbs are rarely used in the progressive tenses in Spanish. The most common are **ser, estar, llevar** (*to wear*), **ir, venir,** and **salir.**

D. Diga que ayer estas personas estuvieron haciendo lo siguiente hasta la hora indicada.

▶ yo / bailar / la una   *Ayer estuve bailando hasta la una.*

1. Gregorio / estudiar / las diez
2. David y yo / trabajar en la cafetería / las tres
3. la nueva estudiante / charlar con Paco / las cinco
4. las candidatas / escuchar las noticias / las siete
5. su compañera de cuarto / escribir cartas / las ocho
6. el profesor / preparar los exámenes de español / las nueve

E. Describa lo que estaban haciendo hace una semana las personas mencionadas. Use la forma progresiva del imperfecto de los verbos en las respuestas.

▶ Andrés / estudiar en Puerto Rico   *Hace una semana Andrés estaba estudiando en Puerto Rico.*

1. Luisa / aprender a patinar
2. Roberto y tú / descansar en la playa
3. mi tía / buscar una nueva casa
4. su cuñada / traducir unos poemas de Martí
5. mi hermana / subir el Aconcagua
6. tú / viajar por Argentina
7. ustedes / participar en una conferencia
8. ese arquitecto / terminar los planos de un edificio

F. Describa lo que estaban haciendo hace unos ocho años algunas personas que usted conoce, comparado con lo que hacen ahora. Use la imaginación.

▶ *Hace unos ocho años Raquel estaba viviendo en una casa antigua, pero ahora vive en un apartamento moderno.*

G. Conteste las preguntas afirmativa o negativamente, usando los pronombres apropiados.

▶ ¿Uds. estuvieron viendo ese   *No, no lo estuvimos viendo.*
programa en la televisión?   *No, no estuvimos viéndolo.*

1. ¿Tus padres estuvieron hablándote mucho tiempo por teléfono?
2. ¿Estabas haciendo la comida cuando te llamé?
3. ¿Ustedes estuvieron discutiendo sus planes hasta tarde anoche?
4. ¿Pepe estaba dirigiendo la investigación?
5. ¿Estaban cantando la «Tuna compostelana» en la clase cuando llegaste?
6. ¿Estuviste pintando ese cuadro hasta tarde?

H. Diga cuándo estaban haciendo las cosas indicadas las siguientes personas. Use dos pronombres en sus respuestas.

▶ Ricardo le estaba escribiendo   *Se las estaba escribiendo [anoche].*
cartas a Julia.   *Estaba escribiéndoselas [anoche].*

1. María me estaba enseñando el trabajo.
2. Nosotros te estábamos preparando una sorpresa.
3. Yo te estaba arreglando la motocicleta.
4. Sara nos estaba describiendo unas costumbres españolas.
5. Tú les estabas cuidando el apartamento.
6. Mis amigos me estaban dando consejos (*advice*).

III. Use of reflexive verbs for unintentional actions

¡Ay! ¡Se me rompió el vaso!

1. Unintentional actions are sometimes expressed in Spanish with third-person reflexive constructions in which an indirect-object pronoun represents the person who unintentionally performs the action. The following verbs are often used in this construction.

caer	to drop	**quedar**	to remain
olvidar	to forget	**rasgar**	to tear
perder	to lose	**romper**	to break

2. Compare the difference in use of the non-reflexive and the reflexive structures in the following sentences.

Rompí el plato porque ya no servía.
I broke the dish because it was no longer useful.

Se me rompió el plato cuando lo lavaba.
The dish broke (I broke it unintentionally) when I was washing it.

Julio **rasgó** la camisa vieja porque ya no servía.
Julio tore the old shirt because it was no longer any good.

Se le rasgó la camisa en la fiesta.
He tore his shirt (unintentionally) at the party.

Dejamos los libros en casa porque no los necesitamos hoy.
We left the books at home because we don't need them today.

Se nos quedaron los libros en casa y tuvimos que regresar por ellos.
We left the books (unintentionally) at home and had to go back for them.

Dejé caer el plato porque estaba muy caliente.
I dropped (let go of) the dish because it was very hot.

Se me cayó el reloj y se rompió en mil pedazos.
I dropped the watch (unintentionally), and it broke into a thousand pieces.

I. Generalmente estas personas son cuidadosas, pero hoy tuvieron mucha prisa y por eso les fue mal en todo. Explique la situación, usando una construcción reflexiva.

▶ Antonio dejó los documentos en casa.
Se le quedaron los documentos en casa.

1. Yo rompí el espejo.
2. Tú perdiste los papeles.
3. Marta dejó caer la taza de café.
4. Pilar rasgó la falda.
5. Tú y Álvaro dejaron la carta en casa.
6. Nosotros perdimos los billetes.

J. Explique que a las siguientes personas les ocurrieron varios accidentes anteayer sin que ellos tuvieran la culpa *(blame)*.

▶ (nosotros): romper la cámara   *Se nos rompió la cámara anteayer. ¡No fue culpa nuestra!*

1. (tú y Jaime): perder el dinero
2. (los alumnos): quedar los libros en casa
3. (Luis): rasgar la chaqueta
4. (tú): olvidar la cita con el dentista
5. (yo): quedar la flauta en mi habitación
6. (mis hermanos): romper algunos discos
7. (tú): perder el bolígrafo
8. (Marta): caer el vaso de agua en la alfombra

¡Exprésese usted!

La descripción

La descripción del ambiente donde vive el protagonista de un escrito puede darnos tanta información sobre su personalidad como lo que se dice de él. Lea la siguiente descripción de una habitación y trate de encontrar toda la información posible sobre la persona que vive en ella. Luego haga el Ejercicio A y lea nuevamente la selección antes de hacer el Ejercicio B.

Su cuarto

El cuarto es grande, aun estando lleno de objetos en desorden: libros de filosofía, de matemáticas, de música, novelas clásicas y poesías contemporáneas. Una mesa muy grande está cubierta de planos de edificios y papeles llenos de números y jeroglíficos incomprensibles. La ventana, enorme pero
5 cerrada, deja entrar el sol de la mañana, pero no quita el mal olor de los cigarrillos a medio fumar, muertos sobre una mesa que lleva ya las marcas de infinitos cigarrillos. La papelera está llena de papeles y cartas sin terminar para mujeres que nunca las recibieron. En una pared, las fotografías de esas mujeres sonríen como si comprendieran que nunca van a recibir las cartas.
10 Otras fotografías de amigos distantes y de algún grupo universitario llenan otra pared. Dos o tres diplomas certifican habilidades matemáticas en varias especialidades. Y el teléfono suena, sin que nadie lo conteste.

A. Conteste las siguientes preguntas sobre la persona que vive en el cuarto.

1. ¿Es el dueño del cuarto un hombre o una mujer?
2. ¿Qué ocupación o profesión puede tener el dueño?

3. ¿Qué características tiene esta persona, en su opinión?
4. ¿Qué pasatiempos tiene?

B. Describa su habitación o la habitación de una persona que usted conoce bien, pero concéntrese en dos o tres detalles que reflejen la personalidad del individuo.

1. Primeras impresiones: Indique si el cuarto da la impresión de ser amplio o pequeño, oscuro o claro, ordenado o desordenado.
2. Detalles generales: Hable un poco del aspecto físico del cuarto. ¿Demuestra el estado del cuarto que la persona es alegre o triste, cuidadosa, desordenada?
3. Detalles específicos: Diga qué tipo de libros hay en los estantes, si los hay; qué cosas hay sobre los muebles y en las paredes. ¿Es posible deducir las cualidades o los defectos de la persona, su edad, sus pasatiempos, su pasado o su futuro a través de estos detalles?

"El Rastro" es un famoso mercado de las pulgas (flea market) en Madrid. Allí es posible encontrar de todo a precios razonables. ¿Qué le gustaría comprar? Escoja tres o cuatro cosas que reflejen su personalidad entre los objetos que ve en la foto o que se imagina que existen en este mercado.

Lección 24
En España

Un folleto sobre Barcelona

¡Gastronomía variada!

La gastronomía de Barcelona es sumamente variada, y el visitante encontrará platos para satisfacer cualquier gusto. Lleve a sus amigos a un restaurante y escójales algunos platos entre las especialidades de la región; por ejemplo, habas a la catalana,° un pollo al ast° o la riquísima zarzuela de
5 pescado y mariscos.° Si usted y sus amigos quieren conocer la comida catalana, vayan a uno de los restaurantes tradicionales del barrio gótico.°

habas . . . broad beans with
  sausage, Catalonian style
pollo . . . chicken roasted on a
  spit
zarzuela . . . assorted fish and
  seafood with sauce
barrio . . . old quarter

En Barcelona se come estupendamente en restaurantes de lujo o en "tascas" como ésta, con un ambiente popular. Los jamones que adornan la tasca tienen que estar en proceso de cura por varios meses antes de adquirir ese sabor que lo caracteriza. ¿Comería Ud. en un restaurante de lujo en Barcelona, o preferiría una tasca? ¿Por qué?

Una iglesia de gran imaginación

Es posible que usted haya visto en fotografías la iglesia de la Sagrada Familia, obra maestra de Antonio Gaudí. Todavía en construcción, le ofrecerá desde sus torres una vista espléndida de la ciudad. En 1891 Gaudí se en-
10 cargó de las obras ya iniciadas de esta iglesia monumental, pero murió en 1916 sin haber terminado los planes. Esta iglesia es una muestra de la gran

El templo de la Sagrada Familia es representativo de Barcelona y por eso vienen a visitarlo turistas de todo el mundo. Muchos ingenieros, arquitectos y artistas trabajan en la terminación de los planos del arquitecto Antonio Gaudí. Compare este templo con la catedral de Barcelona en la página 438. ¿Cómo son diferentes?

imaginación de su genial arquitecto. Es además prueba de la admiración de los que la ven, pues su construcción se debe a las contribuciones de los fieles° y visitantes.

faithful

Un museo fabuloso

15 Si usted es un aficionado de Picasso, encontrará cerca del Paseo de las Ramblas,° casi perdido entre los callejones° del barrio gótico, el Museo Picasso. Este museo alberga una colección representativa de las distintas fases en la obra del artista. Entre las obras merece especial atención su visión personal de *Las Meninas*° de Velázquez.

Paseo ... famous boulevard in Barcelona / side streets

Ladies-in-waiting

Vida nocturna animada

20 La vida nocturna de Barcelona es muy animada. Quien haya visitado la
ciudad de noche no la olvidará jamás. Asista a un concierto o a la última
función de un cine o teatro. Si quiere conocer el ambiente de la ciudad antigua, puede dar un paseo por las estrechísimas calles del barrio gótico o por
las Ramblas. Deténgase en un café al aire libre y tome una copa mientras ve
25 pasar la gente. Y para el trasnochador,° hay una multitud de clubs y disco-   ''night owl''
tecas que permanecen abiertos hasta la madrugada.

*La famosa avenida de Las Ramblas en Barcelona es un lugar predilecto de los
habitantes de esta encantadora ciudad. El centro de Las Ramblas es una amplia
acera donde se pueden admirar y comprar flores, plantas, libros, revistas y hasta pequeños animales domésticos en los atractivos quioscos. Los negocios, bares y teatros
a lo largo de la avenida también atraen a clientes de todas partes. ¿Necesita
comprar zapatos, o hacer una llamada telefónica, o tal vez obtener una medicina?
Busque el sitio apropiado en la fotografía.*

Comprensión

1. ¿Cómo es la comida de Barcelona? Nombre algunas de las especialidades de la región catalana.
2. ¿Dónde se encuentran restaurantes de comida tradicional en Barcelona?
3. ¿Quién fue el arquitecto de la iglesia de la Sagrada Familia en Barcelona? ¿Cómo se paga la construcción de esta obra?
4. ¿Qué cuadros alberga el Museo Picasso? ¿Dónde está este museo?
5. ¿Qué se puede hacer en Barcelona de noche?

Conversación

1. ¿Qué edificios o lugares de interés especial tiene la ciudad o el pueblo donde usted vive?
2. ¿Qué platos especiales recuerda de la ciudad o región donde Ud. vive?
3. ¿Se prepara en su casa algún plato especial? ¿Cómo es?
4. ¿Conoce usted algunas obras de Picasso, Velázquez o algún otro pintor famoso? ¿Qué opina de sus cuadros?
5. ¿Hay un museo en su ciudad o pueblo? ¿Qué obras alberga?
6. Nombre un pintor famoso de los Estados Unidos. ¿Cómo son sus obras?
7. ¿Qué diversiones nocturnas le gustan a usted?

Vocabulario

Palabras análogas

la atención
el catalán
la contribución
la discoteca
la diversión

espléndido, -a
la fotografía
la gastronomía
monumental

la multitud
representativo, -a
la visión
la zona

Sustantivos

la **especialidad** specialty
la **fase** phase
el **folleto** pamphlet, brochure
la **función** performance; function
el **gusto** taste
la **madrugada** dawn, early morning
la **obra maestra** masterpiece
el/la **pintor/a** painter
el **plato** dish (food)
la **prueba** proof
el **rascacielos** skyscraper
la **torre** tower

Adjetivos

animado, -a lively, animated
estrecho, -a narrow
genial brilliant

iniciado, -a begun
nocturno, -a night, nocturnal
perdido, -a lost
sagrado, -a sacred, holy
variado, -a diversified, varied

Verbos

albergar to house, contain
encargarse (de) to take charge (of)
escoger to choose
merecer (zc) to merit, deserve
satisfacer (zc) to satisfy

Otras palabras y expresiones

dar un paseo to go for a walk
en construcción under construction
tomar una copa to have a drink *(liquor)*

Práctica

A. Ud. va a hacer un viaje a Barcelona. Pida a su agente de viajes que le recomiende qué cosas debe ver y hacer en la ciudad. O entreviste a un/a amigo/a que haya estado allí y que pueda darle toda clase de información interesante.

B. Describa dos o tres aspectos interesantes de su propia ciudad o de otra que conozca. Compárela con la ciudad de Barcelona, si es posible.

Nota cultural La región de Cataluña

Una antiquísima tradición catalana es el baile de "la sardana" que muchos bailan hoy día los domingos al frente de la iglesia principal de pueblos y ciudades de la región. La plaza de la catedral de Barcelona atrae participantes y curiosos que observan este baile de apariencia fácil, pero en realidad simbólico y sofisticado. ¿Conoce Ud. algunos bailes en rueda (ring)? ¿Cómo son?

Cataluña, una región de España de gran importancia comercial e industrial, está situada al noreste del país en la costa mediterránea. Barcelona, su puerto principal, es el centro de la actividad cultural, comercial e industrial de la región. Cuenta con[1] industria química, eléctrica, metalúrgica, textil, de maquinaria y de automóviles. El turismo que inunda su costa y sus monumentos es también una importante fuente de ingresos[2] para la región.

En la política, Cataluña tiene una larga tradición de autonomía gubernamental, la cual perdió durante el régimen de Francisco Franco, y que se ha recobrado[3] con los cambios políticos actuales. El catalán, el idioma tradicional de los catalanes, florece[4] de nuevo en las escuelas, en la música y en los medios de comunicación.

Su cultura, abierta a las tendencias europeas que pasan por Francia a través de los Pirineos, refleja las influencias e innovaciones extranjeras. Muchos artistas de fama mundial son catalanes, entre ellos el arquitecto Antonio Gaudí, el músico Pablo Casals y los pintores Joan Miró y Salvador Dalí.

---

1. **Cuenta** . . . It has 2. **fuente** . . . source of income 3. recovered 4. flourishes

Estudio de palabras

Palabras análogas falsas

You have learned to recognize many Spanish cognates in this text. Nevertheless, some words that may seem to be cognates at first glance have different meanings in Spanish and in English when used in certain situations.

abrupto, -a rough (*terrain*)
actual present, current
asistir to attend
el disco record (*also,* disk)
la estación season (*also,* station)
la fábrica factory
el fútbol soccer
la historia story (*also,* history)
gracioso, -a funny

la lectura reading
la librería bookstore
molestar to bother, to annoy
particular private (*also,* particular)
pasar to happen (*also,* to pass)
el pastel pastry, pie (*also,* pastel)
recordar (uc) to remember
severo, -a strict (*also,* severe)

A. Complete las oraciones siguientes con una palabra apropiada de la lista.

fábrica	librería	pasó
discos	lectura	fútbol
particular	estación	asisten

1. Me gusta leer, pero esta ———— es demasiado difícil.
2. Sus hermanitos ———— a una escuela ———— .
3. ¿Qué te ———— anoche que no fuiste a la fiesta en casa de Flor?

4. En nuestra ciudad hay una _____ de automóviles alemanes.
5. Mis amigos fueron al estadio de la universidad para ver un partido de _____ .
6. ¿Te gusta escuchar _____ de canciones tradicionales españolas?
7. ¿Compraste estos libros en una _____ del centro?
8. ¿Qué _____ del año es la más agradable en España?

B. Complete las frases de la primera columna con un final apropiado de la segunda columna.

1. La señora de la Peña es muy buena profesora, pero . . .
2. A su papá le gustan mucho los pasteles . . .
3. ¿Quién es el jefe actual . . .
4. ¿Qué opinas de la historia . . .
5. Me molestan las personas que toman demasiado . . .
6. Nos gustaría practicar el alpinismo este verano . . .
7. Los padres de Rafaelito son muy graciosos porque siempre . . .
8. ¿Recordaste toda la letra (words) . . .

a. cuando van a las fiestas.
b. que nos contó mi amigo Raúl?
c. de esa canción de memoria?
d. es muy severa.
e. que viajan compran alcachofas.
f. que venden en esa pastelería.
g. pero las montañas que están cerca de aquí son muy abruptas.
h. de esa gran compañía internacional?

Estructuras útiles

1. Present perfect subjunctive

¡Es posible que el tren haya salido!

1. The present perfect subjunctive is formed with the present subjunctive of **haber** + a *past participle.*

Present subjunctive of *haber* + past participle

haya	
hayas	
haya	hablado
hayamos	comido
hayáis	venido
hayan	

2. The present perfect subjunctive is generally used in subordinate clauses that require the subjunctive to express an action that has taken place or is likely to have taken place before the action of the main verb. The main verb in the clause may be in the present indicative, future, or imperative. Note that the present subjunctive is also used in subordinate clauses after the same tenses to refer to present or future time.

Me alegro de que Ana **haya decidido** estudiar medicina.	*I'm glad that Ana has decided to study medicine.*
Tus nietos sentirán que no los **hayas visto.**	*Your grandchildren will be sorry that you haven't seen them.*
Apaga las luces cuando **hayas terminado.**	*Turn off the lights when you have finished.*

A. Diga que usted se alegra de que las siguientes situaciones o acciones hayan ocurrido.

► La situación política ha mejorado.   *Me alegro de que la situación política haya mejorado.*

1. La función ha empezado.
2. Has visitado el barrio gótico.
3. Mis padres han visto el Museo Picasso.
4. Tu amigo ha asistido a un concierto al aire libre.
5. Hemos encontrado una solución al problema de la vivienda.
6. Tú has escogido un candidato sumamente interesante.

B. El director de un gran almacén habla con el administrador y desea saber si las siguientes personas ya han cumplido (*fulfilled*) sus obligaciones. Haga el papel del director o del administrador. Use la expresión **es posible que** o **no creo que** en sus respuestas.

► S1: *¿Santiago llegó a la oficina?*   S2: *Es posible que haya llegado.*
                                                  No creo que haya llegado.

1. ¿Ustedes pidieron los armarios nuevos?
2. ¿Carmelo volvió del banco?

3. ¿La secretaria puso los anuncios en el periódico?
4. ¿Los vendedores abrieron las cajas (*cash registers*)?
5. ¿Vieron todos el nuevo horario?
6. ¿Llegaron los nuevos empleados puntualmente?

C. Usted acaba de recibir una carta de Patricia, una amiga que pasa el semestre en España. Explíqueles a sus amigos y compañeros lo que Patricia espera para todos.

▶ yo / no tener más accidentes   *Patricia espera que yo no haya tenido más accidentes.*

1. tú / aprobar química este semestre
2. ustedes / alquilar un apartamento para el semestre próximo
3. Ramón / ganar la competencia de natación
4. yo / comprar un nuevo coche
5. nosotras / divertirnos durante las vacaciones
6. tú / poder esquiar en Colorado
7. nosotras / no olvidarla

II. Past perfect subjunctive

1. The past perfect subjunctive is formed with the imperfect subjunctive of **haber** + *a past participle.*

Imperfect subjunctive of *haber* + past participle	
hubiera hubieras hubiera hubiéramos hubierais hubieran	hablado comido venido

2. The past perfect subjunctive is generally used in a subordinate clause requiring the subjunctive to express an action that had taken place before the action of the main verb. The main clause may be in the imperfect, preterit, or conditional. Note that the imperfect subjunctive is also used in subordinate clauses after the same tenses.

Sentía que no **hubieras venido** a vernos.	*I was sorry that you hadn't come to see us.*
No creyó que yo **hubiera dicho** tal cosa.	*He didn't believe that I had said such a thing.*
Dudarían también que Clara **hubiera tenido** la culpa.	*They would doubt too that Clara had been to blame.*

3. The past perfect subjunctive is frequently used in exclamations after **si** or **ojalá** to express a contrary-to-fact wish or desire about an action in the past.

¡Si **hubieras venido** a la fiesta!	*If only you had come to the party (but you didn't)!*
¡Ojalá que **hubieras venido**!	*I wish you had come (but you didn't)!*
¡Si no **hubiéramos visto** esa película!	*If only we hadn't seen that movie (but we did)!*
Ojalá que no **hubiéramos visto** esa película!	*I wish we hadn't seen that movie (but we did)!*

4. The past perfect subjunctive is also used in **si**-clauses that express a contrary-to-fact action or situation in the past. The conditional perfect or the conditional is used in the main clause to express the conclusion to the **si**- clause. Use of the conditional perfect means that the result of the situation has already occurred. Use of the conditional means that the result of the situation is still occurring or may still occur.

Si **hubieran llegado** antes, habrían visto el espectáculo.	*If they had arrived sooner (but they didn't), they would have seen the show.*
Si **hubiera vivido** en España, conocería Barcelona.	*If he had lived in Spain, he would know Barcelona.*

D. Exprese su deseo de que las situaciones descritas en las siguientes oraciones no hubieran ocurrido.

▶ Rompió el espejo.   *¡Si no lo hubiera roto!*

1. Se fue para Francia.
2. Tuvo una mala idea.
3. Dijo una mentira *(lie)*.
4. Se bebió los vinos.
5. Estuvo enferma.
6. Salió de la casa.

E. A todos nos gustaría que ciertas cosas hubieran ocurrido de una forma diferente. Responda a las preguntas, usando una exclamación con **si** o con **ojalá (que)**.

▶ ¿Tuviste vacaciones muy largas?   *¡Si las hubiera tenido!*
¡Ojalá que las hubiera tenido!

1. ¿Viajaste por Argentina?
2. ¿Recibió Luis un cheque de su casa?
3. ¿Ganaste la lotería?
4. ¿Terminaron las clases?
5. ¿Llenaste una solicitud de empleo?
6. ¿Conseguiste el empleo?

F. Graciela y su esposo César acaban de salir de viaje, y ahora César quiere saber si se hizo todo lo que se tenía que haber hecho en la casa antes de salir. Haga el papel de Graciela y conteste las preguntas de César.

▶ ¿Pusiste la alarma?   *¡No! ¡Ojalá la hubiera puesto!*

1. ¿Cancelaste el periódico?
2. ¿Emilio apagó todas las luces?
3. ¿Cerramos todas las ventanas?
4. ¿Recogieron las niñas las sillas?
5. ¿Habló Sara con el cartero?
6. ¿Te despediste de los vecinos?

G. Explique lo que habría ocurrido si la situación hubiera sido diferente. Use la información entre paréntesis, o conteste en forma original.

▶ Si (llover)/no habría ido al campo   *Si hubiera llovido, no habría ido al campo.*

1. Si (vivir en Argentina) / habríamos visitado Buenos Aires
2. Si (estudiar más) / habrías comprendido todo
3. Si (pensar en las consecuencias) / no lo habrían hecho
4. Si (ir a la reunión) / habría conocido al presidente
5. Si (hablar) / no habríamos tenido problemas

H. Diga cómo habría sido o cómo sería diferente su vida si estas cosas no hubieran ocurrido.

▶ nacer en California   *Si no hubiera nacido en California, no habría conocido a Juanita, mi mejor amiga.*

1. tomar este curso de español
2. venir a esta universidad
3. tener un talento musical
4. viajar a algún país extranjero
5. gastar el dinero en comida
6. enamorarse de alguien

III. **Pero** and **sino**

—*¿Quieres jugar al tenis?*
—*Ojalá pudiera, **pero** el examen de biología es mañana.*
—*Chico, ¡el examen no es mañana **sino** el viernes!*

Both **pero** and **sino** mean *but;* however, they are not interchangeable. **Sino** *(but, on the contrary)* is used to contradict and correct a preceding negative statement. **Pero** is used when no contradiction is implied, whether the preceding statement is affirmative or negative.

Sofía no piensa estudiar arte **sino** arquitectura.	*Sofía doesn't intend to study art but rather architecture.*
No viajamos en tren **sino** en autobús.	*We don't travel by train but by bus.*
Hoy no puedo verte, **pero** tal vez mañana sí.	*I can't see you today, but maybe tomorrow I can.*
Eduardo vive en los Estados Unidos, **pero** habla poco inglés.	*Eduardo lives in the United States, but he speaks little English.*

I. Conteste las preguntas de acuerdo con la realidad o según su opinión personal. Use **sino** en sus respuestas.

▶ ¿Hoy hace frío o calor?   *Hoy no hace frío sino calor.*
  Hoy no hace calor sino frío.

1. ¿Tu prima es alegre o triste?
2. ¿Para ti el español es fácil o difícil?
3. ¿Crees que la profesora habla muchas o pocas lenguas?
4. ¿Tu trabajo es muy interesante o es aburrido?
5. ¿Te gustan las personas extrovertidas o las personas introvertidas?
6. ¿Conoces a muchos o a pocos extranjeros?

J. Escoja la opción correcta para terminar cada oración.

▶ No voy a la fiesta, pero _____ .   *No voy a la fiesta, pero voy a bailar.*
  (voy a bailar, al cine)

1. Ojalá que Francisco no traiga los discos sino _____ . (la guitarra, que venga)
2. En este restaurante no sirven comida japonesa sino _____ . (es muy buena, china)
3. No conozco a tu amigo Miguel, pero _____ . (a Pablo, sé dónde vive)
4. Estudian francés, pero _____ . (alemán, no lo pronuncian bien)
5. No tengo cuatro hermanas sino _____ . (me gustaría tenerlas, dos)
6. No vamos a Inglaterra sino _____ . (a España, algún día pensamos ir)
7. Ellos salieron para el concierto, pero _____ . (se perdieron, al partido de baloncesto)

IV. Review of object and reflexive pronouns

A. Forms

Direct-object pronouns	Indirect-object pronouns	Reflexive pronouns
me	me	me
te	te	te
lo, la	**le (se)**	**se**
nos	nos	nos
os	os	os
los, las	**les (se)**	**se**

1. In Spanish, the forms of the direct-object, indirect-object, and reflexive pronouns are identical except for the third-person singular and plural.

2. Remember that when **se** is used with another pronoun, it may be a reflexive pronoun or the indirect-object pronoun **le(s)** that changes to **se** before **lo(s)** or **la(s)**.

Pepe **se escondió** en su cuarto.   *Pepe hid himself in his room.*
  (**se** = reflexive pronoun)
Todos **se divirtieron.**   *They all had a good time.*
  (**se** = reflexive pronoun)

—¿Le diste la información a   *Did you give Marta the*
  Marta?   *information?*
—Sí, **se la di. (se** = indirect-   *Yes, I gave it to her.*
  object pronoun)

—¿Les diste el dinero?   *Did you give them the money?*
—No, no **se lo di. (se** = indirect-   *No, I didn't give it to them.*
  object pronoun)

B. Position

1. Direct- and indirect-object pronouns normally precede conjugated verbs in affirmative and negative statements.

Yo **se lo digo** a usted.   *I'm telling it to you.*
No **me han llamado.**   *They haven't called me.*

2. With double-verb constructions and with the progressive tenses, object pronouns may precede the conjugated verb form or be attached to the end of the infinitive or present participle. An accent mark is required on the infinitive or the present participle to reflect the original stress when pronouns are attached.

—¿Puede **arreglarle** el coche a mi marido?			*Can you fix the car for my husband?*
—Sí, pero no **se lo puedo arreglar** (no **puedo arreglárselo**) ahora.			*Yes, but I can't fix it now.*
—¿Qué **le está contando** José?			*What is José telling you?*
—**Está contándome (Me está contando)** lo del accidente.			*He's telling me about the accident.*

3. In *affirmative commands*, object and reflexive pronouns are attached to the end of the command form of the verb. An accent mark may be required to reflect the original stress.

Aquí están las flores. **Véanlas,** ¡qué hermosas son!	*Here are the flowers. See (them) how pretty they are!*
Tráigame otro café, por favor.	*Bring me another (cup of) coffee, please.*
Ponte el abrigo y vamos.	*Put on your coat and let's go.*

4. In *negative commands*, object and reflexive pronouns precede the conjugated form of the verb.

No **los coman**.	*Don't eat them.*
No **me lo expliques.**	*Don't explain it to me.*
No **se sienten** allí.	*Don't sit there.*

5. Object pronouns are always used in the following sequence, whether or not they precede or follow the verb form.

(se)	me	lo(s)
	te	la(s)
	nos	le(s)
	os	

K. Diga lo que las primeras personas darán a sus amigos. Use el objeto indirecto en sus respuestas.

▶ Manuel / cinco pesetas / a Tomás   *Manuel le dará cinco pesetas.*

1. tú / una torta / a nosotros
2. yo / un disco / a Manuela
3. Margarita / una sorpresa / a Juan y a Elena
4. Eugenia y María / unas flores / a Tita
5. nosotros / una guitarra / a ti
6. ustedes / una radio / a nosotros

L. Diga si puede o no puede hacer lo siguiente y por qué.

▶ darme cien dólares   *No, no te los puedo dar porque [no tengo tanto dinero].*
Sí, puedo dártelos, [pero los voy a necesitar el mes que viene].

1. leerle las noticias a Juanita
2. ofrecernos una limonada
3. comprarles un estéreo a sus padres
4. conseguirme este libro
5. traerle un café a esta señorita
6. hacernos una comida española

M. Rechace *(Refuse)* cortésmente estas invitaciones o solicitudes, diciendo que prefiere hacerlas en otra ocasión.

▶ ¿Quieres visitarme mañana?   *Claro que quiero visitarte (te quiero visitar), [pero prefiero visitarte otro día].*

1. ¿Quieres invitar a Mario a tu casa el domingo?
2. ¿Quieres escuchar música clásica conmigo esta tarde?
3. ¿Quieres visitar a mis primas el martes?
4. ¿Quieres ver la exhibición de fotos con nosotros el lunes?
5. ¿Quieres llamar a Jorge por teléfono esta tarde?
6. ¿Quieres contarme hoy de tu viaje?

N. Conteste las preguntas de un(a) amigo(a) explicándole qué están haciendo las personas indicadas.

▶ ¿Dónde está Raúl? (lavarse el pelo)   *Está lavándose el pelo.*

1. ¿Dónde está Marta? (entrevistarse para un trabajo)
2. ¿Por qué no contestas el teléfono? (bañarse)
3. ¿Qué hacen ustedes? (prepararse la cena)
4. ¿Por qué no está listo Felipe? (ponerse guapo para su novia)
5. ¿Qué hacen Carmen y Víctor? (arreglarse para salir)
6. ¿Qué haces ahora? (vestirse para un concierto)

O. Usted está en una tienda exclusiva de Barcelona, y la vendedora ofrece enseñarle varios objetos. Acéptelos o recházelos *(refuse)*, según su interés personal.

▶ ¿Le muestro estas corbatas?   *Sí, muéstremelas.*
No, gracias, no me las muestre.

1. ¿Le muestro un sombrero?
2. ¿Le enseño los calcetines rojos?

3. ¿Le enseño otra camisa?
4. ¿Le enseño otros zapatos de un número más grande?
5. ¿Le muestro unos pantalones de color diferente?
6. ¿Le muestro una chaqueta de cuero?

P. El primer día en Barcelona usted y su amigo hablan con un guía *(guide)*. El guía les ofrece varios servicios, y ustedes los aceptan o los rechazan, según sus intereses.

▶ ¿Los llevo a la catedral? *Sí, llévenos a la catedral.*
No, no nos lleve a la catedral.

1. ¿Les muestro el Museo Picasso?
2. ¿Les explico la historia de Cataluña?
3. ¿Los llevo a un restaurante catalán?
4. ¿Les enseño el barrio gótico?
5. ¿Les hablo de la industria catalana?
6. ¿Los llevo al hotel ahora?

¡Exprésese usted!
El punto de vista

Para poder escribir claramente y convencer al lector hay que entender una situación desde varios puntos de vista.

Lea la siguiente anécdota contada por un español que vino a los Estados Unidos con ideas estereotipadas de los americanos. Trate de comprender a los protagonistas, especialmente al mendigo *(beggar)*, desde varios puntos de vista, usando su imaginación. ¿Necesitará realmente el dinero? ¿En qué pensará? ¿Será un borracho *(drunk)*?

El billete de diez dólares

No sé qué esperaba cuando llegué a los Estados Unidos. Mi imagen de Norteamérica era muy confusa por todos los libros que había leído y las películas norteamericanas que había visto en España. Pensaba que era un país rico y que era la tierra de las oportunidades. Por eso cuando me en-
5 contré con aquel hombre que tenía un fuerte olor a whisky, que me extendía la mano y me pedía dinero para *«something to eat»*, me sentí absolutamente desilusionado.

En España había encontrado mendigos, pero eso era comprensible en un país de menos oportunidades. Además yo sabía que unas cuantas pe-
10 setas les compraría en un restaurante algo que comer. En Estados Unidos, sin embargo, cualquier comida en un restaurante, según mi poca experien-

cia, costaba cantidades astronómicas. ¿Qué decirle, qué darle a este mendigo norteamericano, a esta persona que para mí era tan irreal, tan fantástica como uno de los fantasmas de mi juventud? Saqué mi billetera y
15 con absoluta consternación vi que solamente tenía un billete de diez dólares. Se lo di.

Póngase Ud. en el lugar del mendigo y escriba una composición en forma más corta, desde ese punto de vista. Piense en una de las siguientes posibilidades.

1. Si el mendigo en realidad necesita el dinero para comer, ¿qué piensa cuando recibe el dinero? ¿Qué hace con él? ¿Qué le dice al español? Explique también por qué se comporta *(behaves)* así.
2. Si el mendigo es un borracho, ¿qué actitud tiene hacia el español? ¿Qué piensa cuando ve el billete? ¿Qué dice? Explique por qué se comporta de esa manera.

Es imposible recorrer las calles de Barcelona sin sentirse atraído por alguna construcción del arquitecto Antonio Gaudí. Aquí puede verse la casa Batiló, que un artista copia fielmente en su lienzo (canvas).

Lengua en acción 8

A. Una elección *(Lección 22)*

Usted y unos/as amigos/as (2 ó 3 compañeros/as de clase) hablan
sobre los dos candidatos para el cargo de representante en el Senado
Estudiantil de su universidad. Discutan las cualidades de los candidatos. Luego explique por qué decidió votar por uno de los candidatos,
basándose en el perfil *(profile)* personal de los candidatos.

*Votar por Castillo es
votar por la experiencia*

Nombre: Andrés Castillo de Monterrey
Especialidad: Ingeniería química
Calificaciones: Promedio de B+
Honores: Miembro A△B, sociedad de estudiantes
de ingeniería
Experiencia: Vicepresidente del Consejo Estudiantil, escuela
secundaria; capitán del equipo de fútbol
Perspectiva personal: "Prometo cambiar la práctica actual de que los estu-
diantes tengan poco contacto con los profesores.
Organizaré seminarios y reuniones informales con
los profesores."

Una líder para el futuro

Nombre: Josefina Ávila-Torreón
Especialidad: Literatura y Derecho
Calificaciones: Promedio de A—
Honores: Premio como la mejor poeta, escuela
secundaria
Experiencia: Ayudante en una oficina privada de abogados
Perspectiva personal: "Prometo trabajar para garantizar la seguridad per-
sonal de todos los estudiantes, pero especialmente
la de las mujeres."

B. Un cambio de nota *(Repaso)*

Usted recibió una nota de C+ en una clase de sociología con el/la
profesor/a Martínez (un miembro de la clase), pero Ud. cree que
merece una B. Convenza al/a la profesor/a de que le cambie su nota,
siguiendo las indicaciones.

1. Descríbale qué actividades hizo bien en la clase.
2. Dígale por qué Ud. no obtuvo una B en el examen final: una
enfermedad, 4 exámenes el mismo día, . . .

3. Descríbale las consecuencias de recibir una C: sus padres, su beca (*scholarship*), . . .
4. Descríbale las circunstancias especiales de su caso: su abuela enferma, el número de clases, su trabajo, . . .
5. Pregúntele por qué le dio una C en la participación en clase e intente convencerle de que merece mejor nota.

Nombre del Estudiante _____	
Examen final	78=C+
Pruebas	81=B—
Informe final	83=B
Participación	75=C
Nota final	79=C+

C. Querido Corazón (*Lección 23*)

"Querido Corazón" es el nombre de un programa de radio que trata temas amorosos. Imagínese que Ud. es una de las personas descritas o invente otra situación. Llame a la radio y explíquele al/a la consejero/a cómo se llama y cuál es su problema. Escuche su consejo y, si está satisfecho/a, déle las gracias. Si no queda satisfecho/a, pida otra sugerencia.

Pedro Segundo: 28
Soltero; con una novia, Anita.
Un amigo, Pedro Amante, el ex-novio de Anita, ha invitado a Pedro Segundo a su boda. No sabe si es apropiado invitar a Anita a acompañarlo a la boda de Pedro Amante.

Bárbara Brilladoro: 24
Soltera; estaba comprometida. No sabe si debe devolverle el anillo de compromiso a su ex-novio.

Cindy Sinplata: 26
Casada; tres hijos.
Esposo acaba de abandonarla y no trabaja. No sabe qué hacer.

Nicolás Novás: 51
Casado por 20 años, luego divorciado.
Ex-esposa no quiere que él vaya a la boda de su hija. No sabe qué hacer.

D. ¿Cuánto cuesta este apartamento? *(Repaso)*

Usted tiene poco dinero y quiere alquilar un apartamento a un precio
económico. Regatee *(Bargain)* con el/la dueño/a del apartamento
sobre el precio que pide hasta llegar a un acuerdo.

El/La inquilino/a (Renter)

1. Descríbale al/a la dueño/a los problemas
   que tiene el apartamento.
2. Dígale qué arreglos tiene que hacer para que
   Ud. firme el contrato.

El/La dueño/a

Dígale lo que Ud. no considera necesario arreglar
en el apartamento.

Mencione lo que Ud. está dispuesto/a *(prepared)* a
arreglar. Sugiera que Ud. puede arreglar todo si
él/ella paga más o que Ud. puede bajar el
alquiler si acepta el apartamento sin reparaciones.

E. En el aeropuerto de Barajas, Madrid *(Lección 24)*

Usted se encuentra en la terminal internacional del aeropuerto de Madrid
y necesita comprar billetes para Nueva York. Pídale a un/a empleado/a
(un miembro de la clase) la información necesaria, según las indicaciones.

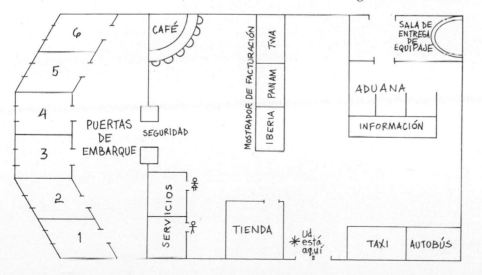

Información necesaria para el/la viajero/a

número de vuelos a Nueva York
hora(s) de salida
hora(s) de llegada
precio del vuelo
número de la puerta de salida (gate)
lugar donde está la aduana y sala de embarque,
un café, los servicios, . . .

Información necesaria para el/la empleado/a

nombre del/de la pasajero/a
número de billetes
pasaje de primera clase o clase turista
número de maletas para facturar
preferencia: sección fumadores/no fumadores
tipo de asiento: ventanilla o pasillo

F. En la aduana en Madrid (Repaso)

Usted llega de Francia a Madrid y tiene que pasar por la aduana en
España. Conteste las preguntas del/de la aduanero/a, según las
indicaciones. Al terminar la inspección, despídase del/de la adua-
nero/a.

Información que necesita el/la aduanero/a

nombre
ciudadanía
número de pasaporte
objetivo de su viaje a España

el contenido de sus maletas en
general
si tiene algo que declarar
si trae plantas, animales o comida

G. Una evaluación del semestre (Wrap-up)

Averigüe de otros tres miembros de la clase cómo evalúan en una
escala de 1 a 4 varios aspectos de su vida universitaria este semestre.
Después pregúnteles qué hubieran hecho de otra forma.

	S1	S2	S3
tus clases			
tus profesores			
tu progreso en español			
tu alojamiento			
tu vida social			
qué hubieras hecho de otra forma			

1 = excelente   3 = regular
2 = bueno   4 = malo

Otro mundo

I. La vida de los jóvenes

Estudio y profesiones

Hay grandes diferencias económicas y sociales entre los habitantes de los diferentes países hispánicos y estas diferencias influyen sobre las carreras escogidas por los jóvenes estudiantes. En los países más desarrollados, como España, Argentina y México, muchos jóvenes estudian profesiones modernas y sofisticadas como informática *(computer science)*, análisis de sistemas e ingeniería atómica. Sin embargo, las profesiones de prestigio continúan siendo las mismas a través del mundo hispánico: medicina, derecho *(law)* e ingeniería.

Al buscar empleo muchos de los nuevos médicos, abogados e ingenieros descubren que tienen que trabajar en otras actividades porque hay un excesivo número de esos profesionales. No es extraño por eso que muchos famosos escritores y filósofos hispánicos sean médicos, que casi todos los políticos sean abogados y que muchísimos ingenieros graduados trabajen en la banca o en el mundo de los negocios.

> *Para investigar y conversar:* Examine la base económica y el producto nacional bruto per cápita de algunos países hispánicos en las tablas de las páginas 459-460.

Estudio en el exterior

Más estudiantes de los países hispánicos vienen a estudiar a los Estados Unidos que a cualquier otro país del mundo. Los países hispánicos más representados en las universidades norteamericanas son Venezuela, México y Colombia.

Por lo general, los jóvenes del mundo hispánico desean viajar y estudiar en Estados Unidos y en Europa porque un título de una universidad extranjera da prestigio, mejores posibilidades de trabajo y buena posición social. Sin embargo, el alto costo de los estudios en el exterior limita el número de estudiantes que viajan al exterior. Algunos estudiantes de los países más desarrollados consiguen becas o préstamos *(loans)* a bajo interés que sus gobiernos nacionales ofrecen para fomentar el estudio en el exterior. Otros estudiantes que no tienen dinero propio tratan de conseguir becas ofrecidas por las universidades extranjeras.

> *Para investigar y conversar:* Averigüe cuántos estudiantes hispánicos hay en su institución, de qué países son y qué estudian. Hable con un estudiante hispánico y descubra por qué decidió estudiar en los Estados Unidos y qué piensa hacer después de graduarse.

Diversiones

Los hispanos que estudian en los Estados Unidos observan que los jóvenes norteamericanos bailan y se relacionan entre sí mucho menos que los hispanos. Los estudiantes norteamericanos observan que los jóvenes hispanos conversan más y salen más en grupo. Una diversión favorita hispánica es la de tener fiestas con baile los viernes y sábados por la noche. A estas fiestas se invitan amigos y amigos de amigos para hacer más grande el círculo de amistades. La actividad principal en estas fiestas es el baile. La comida y la bebida son secundarias.

También son secundarias la comida y la bebida en los bares que son muy populares en algunos países hispánicos como Argentina y España. Los jóvenes pasan largas horas conversando, bebiendo una cerveza o un vaso de vino y comiendo alguna cosa ligera que en España se conoce con el nombre de "tapas". Ir de tapas en España es una actividad popular de jóvenes y mayores. Por la noche un grupo de amigos pasan por los bares de moda y toman algo en cada bar mientras hablan de todo lo imaginable: política, estudios, amor, filosofía.

Otras diversiones son las fiestas de playa en los países tropicales, los "paseos" en grupo a un restaurante campestre (*country restaurant*) o a una villa o casa de campo. Las discotecas también son populares, aun cuando muchos prefieren los sitios que presentan alguna orquesta o grupo musical "en vivo".

El cine es una diversión favorita y económica para un público de todas las edades. Las entradas al cine cuestan la mitad o la tercera parte de su equivalente en los Estados Unidos y en todas las ciudades hispánicas se exhiben películas norteamericanas, hispánicas y europeas para todos los gustos. Las películas norteamericanas son muy populares entre los jóvenes, que copian la última moda de Hollywood y se forman una imagen (muchas veces estereotipada) de la vida en los Estados Unidos.

> *Para investigar y conversar:* Compare sus diversiones personales con las de los jóvenes hispanos de su edad. ¿Le gusta la música? ¿bailar? ¿el cine? ¿Cuándo y adónde sale de paseo?

II. Países y paisajes

Al ver la enorme variedad de los países hispánicos, conviene agruparlos por regiones para ver mejor las características del mundo hispánico. Empezando al norte están México y los países de Centroamérica: Guatemala, Honduras, El Salvador, Nicaragua, Costa Rica y Panamá. Tienen en común la posición geográfica, la cercanía a los EEUU, y para la mayoría de ellos, el fondo histórico de las importantísimas culturas maya y azteca. Se ve la influencia maya y azteca en el arte (murales, joyas, diseños textiles), en los nombres de lugares y ciudades (Tegucigalpa, Xochimilco), y en la religión y filosofía de vida.

Para investigar y conversar: En las tablas de las páginas 459-460, busque las diferencias étnicas y lingüísticas de los países de Centroamérica.

El Caribe hispanohablante incluye las islas de Cuba, la República Dominicana y Puerto Rico. Incluye también la costa caribe de Venezuela y Colombia. Es una región tropical de playas, cultivos de frutas, caña de azúcar, tabaco y coco. En esta región vive mucha gente de origen africano. Sus antepasados trajeron de África creencias religiosas (vudú, medicina espiritual), instrumentos musicales (bongoes, maracas) y festivales carnavalescos. Los ritmos de África se combinaron con la música española creando fandangos, rumbas y merengues, cumbias y salsas que han influido en la música de todo el mundo. La población indígena original desapareció por las enfermedades traídas de Europa y por la violencia de la conquista, pero contribuyó a la cultura hispánica moderna con algunas palabras (canoa), nombres de lugares y ciudades (Mayagüez, Higüey) y ciertos tipos de comida (ñame, malanga).

Para investigar y conversar: ¿Cuáles factores en las tablas de las páginas 459-460 unen a los países del área del Caribe?

Los países de Venezuela y Colombia participan del mundo suramericano de los Andes en su interior. En ambos países está la región de los llanos que se parece físicamente a las pampas argentinas y al oeste norteamericano y en sus crías de ganado. Cada país también ocupa una región de la selva amazónica donde aún existen hoy día tribus de indios no influidas por la civilización occidental. Difieren estos países en sus bases económicas (petróleo en Venezuela, café en Colombia) y en sus industrias, pero sus tradiciones, su música y su comida son muy semejantes.

Para investigar y conversar: Al comparar las estadísticas de estos dos países en las tablas de las páginas 459-460, ¿qué puede decirse de sus semejanzas y diferencias?

Continuando hacia el sur de Colombia, los países de Ecuador, Perú y Bolivia se consideran como área unida, sede *(seat)* antigua de la civilización incaica. Cuando los españoles se apoderaron *(seized)* del Inca, que así se llamaba el jefe de su sociedad, todo el imperio fue subyugado *(made subservient)*, como ocurrió con los aztecas en México. Una gran población indígena subsiste aún hoy día en esa región y se nota su influencia en la dieta (el maíz y la papa) y en la música que tiene cadencias indígenas.

Perú, siendo la sede inca, fue también la sede del gobierno español para la región en la época colonial. Lima mantiene muchos de sus monumentos coloniales, y Perú guarda gran riqueza de ruinas incaicas maravillosas.

Para investigar y conversar: Compare las estadísticas de población de esta región con Centroamérica y anote las semejanzas y diferencias.

El Paraguay parece único en Suramérica en su historia y tradición. Tiene una fuerte influencia india, como la región andina, pero la influencia es de los indios guaraníes, que no alcanzaron el desarrollo cultural de los incas.

Hoy día Paraguay tiene una población en gran parte bilingüe que habla español y guaraní. Aunque la población guaraní comprende el 65% de la población total, la lengua oficial es el español. El Paraguay no tiene las altas montañas de la región andina y tiene un clima entre tropical y subtropical.

Para investigar y conversar: Comparando las estadísticas y la posición geográfica del Paraguay en las tablas de las páginas 459–460 con las de cualquier otro país suramericano, explique los factores que hacen de Paraguay un país único, difícil de clasificar como parte de una región mayor.

El llamado cono sur de Suramérica comprende los países de Argentina, Uruguay y Chile. Esta área se conoce también con el nombre de "la América europea". El clima, la geografía y sobre todo la composición étnica de la región, separan al cono sur del resto de Hispanoamérica. La población indígena de la región pertenecía a tribus guerreras, de las cuales muy pocos sobrevivieron la conquista española. La composición étnica, en general europea, varía de un país a otro, siendo prevalentemente italiana en Argentina y Uruguay y alemana en Chile. Durante los años precedentes a las dos guerras mundiales muchos italianos y alemanes llegaron a esta región, mayormente entre los años 1880 y 1930. En las grandes ciudades de estos países se reconocen rápidamente las características de las capitales europeas en su arquitectura y en sus costumbres, como el horario y tipos de comida, arte y música y el uso social de los bares y cafés.

Para investigar y conversar: Compare las estadísticas sociales de los países del cono sur. Descubra sus semejanzas y diferencias en composición étnica, analfabetismo, lengua y otros puntos de interés para usted.

El país que descubrió y colonizó Hispanoamérica fue España. Al principio, España era un conglomerado de reinos separados como Castilla, Aragón, Asturias, Cataluña y muchos otros que se unían y se separaban por conveniencia política y económica. En 1492, año del descubrimiento de América, la unificación final de España se logró bajo los Reyes Católicos Fernando II e Isabel I.

Aunque llegaron a Hispanoamérica grandes números de inmigrantes de todo el mundo, la lengua, la religión y las bases culturales habían sido establecidas por los españoles. Así los ingleses, italianos, alemanes y las poblaciones de África y Asia que llegaron después se adaptaron a la cultura hispánica ya establecida. Los países hispanoamericanos ven a España aún hoy día con una mezcla de admiración y resentimiento, amor, y en algunos casos, odio por los recuerdos de la época colonial. A pesar de sus diferencias, España e Hispanoamérica han establecido lazos *(ties)* de unión cultural y económica mutuamente beneficiosos.

Para investigar y conversar: Usando las tablas de las siguientes páginas, contraste a España con uno de los países más ricos de Hispanoamérica (Argentina, Venezuela) y con uno de los más pobres (Bolivia, El Salvador).

México y América Central

País y Capital	Superficie en Km²	Población	Densidad Hab. por Km²	Grupos étnicos	Lenguas	Base económica	Producto nacional bruto*	Analfa- betismo
México Ciudad de México	1.972.547	77.094.000	39	M I C	español nahuatl maya	petróleo, gas, maquinaria, ali- mentos, agricultura, minería	1.800	17%
Guatemala Guatemala	108.889	7.746.000	71	I M	español maya	café, bananas, caña, petróleo	1.085	54%
Honduras Tegucigalpa	112.088	4.229.000	38	M C N I	español dialectos indios	bananas, coco, café, caña, textiles, cemento	590	43,1%
El Salvador San Salvador	21.041	5.395.000	256	M I C	español nahuatl maya	caña, algodón, tabaco, azúcar	854	32,7%
Nicaragua Managua	130.000	3.166.000	24	M C N I	español chibcha inglés	café, algodón, cacao, bananas, cemento, azúcar, carne	804	42,5%
Costa Rica San José	50.700	2.532.000	50	C M N I	español	café, bananas, cacao, tabaco, azúcar, carne	2.238	11,6%
Panamá Panamá	77.082	2.137.000	28	M I C N	español inglés chibcha	Canal, caña, cacao, café, bananas, azúcar, alcohol, refinería	1.116	14,4%

Las Antillas

País y Capital	Superficie en Km²	Población	Densidad Hab. por Km²	Grupos étnicos	Lenguas	Base económica	Producto nacional bruto*	Analfa- betismo
Cuba La Habana	110.861	9.995.000	92	C N M	español	caña, tabaco, café, arroz, azúcar, cemento, aceite	1.590	2,2%
República Dominicana Santo Domingo	48.734	6.110.000	125	M C N	español	caña, arroz, café, tabaco, azúcar, cemento	1.221	31,4%
Puerto Rico San Juan	8.897	3.401.000	383	C M N	español inglés	caña, tabaco, refinería petróleo, azúcar, ron, textiles	4.301	10,9%

Suramérica y España

País y Capital	Superficie en Km²	Población	Densidad Hab. por Km²	Grupos étnicos	Lenguas	Base económica	Producto nacional bruto	Analfabetismo
Colombia Bogotá	1.138.914	28.119.000	25	M C N I	español lenguas indias	café, tabaco, bananas, petróleo, petroquímica, textiles, cemento	1.112	14,8%
Venezuela Caracas	912.050	16.831.000	18	M C N I	español lenguas indias	petróleo, minería, hierro, petro-química, acero	4.716	15,3%
Ecuador Quito	283.561	9.116.000	32	I M C N	español quechua jívaro	petróleo, bananas, café, cacao, caña, tabaco, textiles, azúcar	1.428	19,8%
Perú Lima	1.280.216	19.201.000	15	I M C N	español quechua aymará	petróleo, minería, plata, cobre, zinc, café, papas, maíz, cereales	655	18,1%
Bolivia La Paz/Sucre	1.098.581	6.202.000	6	I M C	español quechua aymará	minería, estaño, plata, bismuto, oro, cereales, caña,	570	36,8%
Paraguay Asunción	406.752	3.573.000	9	I M C	guaraní español	forestal, caña, tabaco, algodón, aceites, cuero, carne	1.614	12,5%
Chile Santiago	756.945	11.865.000	16	C M I	español	minería, cobre, hierro, titanio, frutas, cereales, vino, lana, celulosa	1.950	5,6%
Uruguay Montevideo	176.215	2.994.000	17	C (M)	español	ganado, arroz, cereales, carne, lana, cuero	1.665	6,1%
Argentina Buenos Aires	2.766.889	30.070.000	11	C (M) (I)	español italiano inglés alemán	cereales, caña, frutas, ganado, carne, cuero, maqui-naria, textiles, vino	2.331	6,1%
España Madrid	504.782	38.335.000	76	C	español catalán vasco gallego	turismo, fruta, verduras, química, vino, textiles, maqui-naria, conservas, pesca	5.500	7,1%

Population, Area, Density, Illiteracy figures are from the *1986 UNESCO Statistical Yearbook.*
*Per Capita Income figures are expressed in U.S.$ and are from the *1987 World Almanac and Book of Facts.*
C, I, M, and N are equivalent to **Caucásico, Indio, Mestizo,** and **Negro,** respectively.
The main sources of income for each nation, ethnic groups, and languages are listed in order of importance.

Reference Section

Appendix A: English equivalents of basic texts (Units 2 and 3)   R2

Appendix B: Sound-spelling correspondences   R6

Appendix C: Glossary of grammatical terms   R8

Appendix D: Verb charts   R12

Spanish-English vocabulary   R21

English-Spanish vocabulary   R41

Index   R56

Appendix A: English Equivalents of Basic Texts (Units 2 and 3)

Lección 4: In Spain

How amazing!

Ricardo Solana and Marisol del Valle are students at Madrid's Complutense University. At this moment, Ricardo sees his friend Marisol in a bookstore in the downtown section of the capital.

Ricardo: Hi, Marisol. What are you doing around here?
Marisol: I'm looking for an art book. What about you? What are you doing?
Ricardo: Well, I'm looking for some books for my English course.
Marisol: Are there textbooks here?
Ricardo: Yes, but on the second floor.
Marisol: Oh, good (I see). And who is your English teacher this year?
Ricardo: Professor Duarte . . . Anita's father.
Marisol: Oh, yes. He's great, isn't he?
Ricardo: Yes, but very demanding.
Marisol: Is it true that he speaks French and German?
Ricardo: Yes, and also a little Italian and Russian.
Marisol: Five foreign languages! How amazing!

Lección 5: In Mexico

Is there a bank around here?

Carlos Guzmán, a young man from Venezuela, is in Mexico City, where he is going to spend his vacation. He's tired, but needs to go to the bank now to change bolívares for pesos before returning to the hotel. He speaks with a policeman on the sidewalk near the hotel.

Carlos: Excuse me, officer. Is there a bank around here? I need to change money.
Policeman: Yes, sir, there's one on Madero Street. It's called Nuevo Banco de Comercio.
Carlos: Is it nearby?
Policeman: No, it's quite far. About eight blocks from here.
Carlos: So far! Is it possible to go there by bus?
Policeman: Yes, of course. The bus goes by here, but there's a lot of traffic. It's easier to go by subway. The subway entrance is there at the corner.
Carlos: Then I'll go by subway. Thank you very much!
Policeman: You're welcome, sir.

Lección 6: In the United States
What's your cousin like?

Daniel Briceño and his fiancée Carolina Ortiz are in a coffee shop at Miami airport. They drink coffee and tea and eat sandwiches while waiting for the arrival by plane of one of Daniel's cousins who lives in Los Angeles.

Carolina: Do you like the sandwiches? They're delicious, don't you think?

Daniel: Yes, but, what terrible coffee! It's very strong . . . Waiter, a beer, please.

Waiter: Yes, sir, right away.

Carolina: Tell me, Daniel. What's your cousin's name?

Daniel: Enrique Briceño Cárdenas. He's a computer technician.

Carolina: How interesting! And what's he like? Tall and dark like you?

Daniel: No, on the contrary, Quique is short and blond, . . . but very nice, just like me.

Carolina: And also very humble like you, huh?

Daniel: Yes, of course. Like all the Briceños . . . Listen, Carolina, they're already announcing the arrival of the Los Angeles flight.

Carolina: And it's on time. What luck!

Daniel: Waiter, the bill, please.

Waiter: Right away, sir.

Lección 7: In Argentina
With or without you!

Sergio Ramírez has a date with his friend Carmen at the box office of Luna Park, a large stadium where they hold rock and popular music concerts in Buenos Aires. Now the two young people go to buy their tickets.

Scene 1

Sergio: Two tickets, please. Do you have inexpensive numbered seats?

Employee: No, there aren't any left. I only have some for the unnumbered seat area from row thirty.

Sergio: Then two of those, please.

Carmen: What a pity! I don't like that section.

Sergio: Well, Mencha, at least we have tickets . . . And, what about Luis and your cousin? Are they coming to the concert?

Carmen: No, they aren't coming. My cousin isn't well, and my brother has to study for his next philosophy exam.

Sergio: Hey, listen, we have to go in the stadium. (He pays for the tickets and they go in.)

Scene 2

Speaker: We now present the Spanish group Alas in "With or without you".

Alas group: I must talk with you, with you, with you.
I can't live without you, without you, without you.
If you don't want to spend your life with me, with me, with me,
The world is going to be awful for me, for me, for me!

(great applause)
Carmen: Terrific! What a great song!
Sergio: Fantastic! Another fabulous hit of the Alas group.

Lección 8: In Uruguay
Do you like that sailboat?

Eduardo García and Raúl Díaz are two young friends who live in Montevideo, capital of Uruguay. They are now in Punta del Este, an international tourist center near the capital. This weekend there is a colorful regatta with seventy sailboats, and the young people are watching them from the seashore.

Scene 1
Eduardo: Look. How incredible! Do you like that red sailboat, Raúl?
Raúl: Number forty-two? Yes, I like it, but I prefer that other one with blue sails.
Eduardo: I'm going to see if I can take some photos. Above all I want one of that red one.
Raúl: You can't take a good one (shot) from here.
Eduardo: We can go to the Club Marino where the official photographers and reporters are . . . but the tickets are very expensive.

Scene 2
Raúl: Look, there goes my neighbor Pilar. Do you remember her?
Eduardo: No, I don't remember her. Who is she?
Raúl: She is Pilar Guzmán, the reporter for *La Nación.* Shall we go to say hello to her? I think she could take us to the Club. That way, you can take your pictures from there with good light . . . And we don't have to pay for our tickets.
Eduardo: Great! What are we waiting for?

Lección 9: In Chile
A sociological survey

Patricia Torres is a sociology student at the National University of Santiago. This semester she has an interesting research project with other students. With them, she is trying to find out the standard of living of the middle class in one of the neighborhoods of Chile's capital. The students prepare a questionnaire and then go out to interview the neighborhood's inhabitants.

The answers to the questionnaire reveal interesting information about the living conditions of the people of that neighborhood. For example, among the residents interviewed, some families don't have either a telephone, a washing machine or a stereo. All have a television set, a radio and a refrigerator, but no family has more than two cars. The majority of mothers are housewives. Some mothers work as clerks or blue-collar workers; only two per cent of them have professions. All those interviewed need more economic help (aid) from the government.

Questionnaire

1. How many people in total live at home?   (one, two, three, more than three)
2. Who works in the family?   (father, mother, sons, daughters)
3. In which category does the father work?   (clerk, blue-collar worker, at home, professional)
4. In which category does the mother work?   (clerk, blue-collar worker, at home, professional)
5. Are there students at home?   (yes, no, how many?)
6. Where do the children study?   (in a public school, at the university, in a private school, in a technical institute)
7. Do you have a telephone?   (radio, TV set, refrigerator, stereo, washing machine, dishwasher, air conditioner, clothes dryer)
8. Do you have a car in the family?   (no, one, two, more than two)
9. Do you use public transportation?   (always, never, rarely)
10. In order to live well, do you need more economic help (aid) from the government?   (no; yes, a little; yes, a lot of help)

Appendix B: Sound-Spelling Correspondences

	Sound	Spelling	Examples
Vowels	[a]	a	casa
	[e]	e	peso
	[ɛ]	e	tengo
	[i]	i	vino
	[o]	o	cosa
	[ɔ]	o	orden
	[u]	u	luna
Diphthongs	[ay]	ai, ay	baile, hay
	[au]	au	Paula
	[ey]	ei, ey	reina, rey
	[eu]	eu	Europa
	[ia]	ia	piano
	[ie]	ie	reciente
	[io]	io	indio
	[iu]	iu	ciudad
	[oy]	oi,oy	oigo, voy
	[ua]	ua	guapo
	[ue]	ue	nuevo
	[uy]	ui, uy	ruina, muy
	[uo]	uo	antiguo
Consonants	[k]	c (before **a, o, u**) k (in a few foreign words) qu (before **e, i**)	casa, copa, cubano kilómetro que, quien
	[ch]	ch	chileno
	[d]	d (in initial position, and after **l, n**)	don, caldo, onda
	[ð]	d (between vowels, and final)	todo, usted
	[f]	f	fácil
	[g]	g (in initial position and after **n**)	grande, tango
	[ǥ]	g (between vowels)	luego
	[H]	g (before **e, i**) j (before all vowels) x (in a few words)	gente, región caja, jota, jurar México, Texas
	[l]	l	calma
	[ll]	ll	llama
	[y]	y, ll (in parts of S.A.)	yo, llama

Sound	Spelling	Examples
[m]	**m**	**m**úsica
[n]	**n**	**n**úmero
[ñ]	**ñ**	ma**ñ**ana
[p]	**p**	**p**ara
[r]	**r**	ca**r**ta
[rr]	**rr, r** (in initial position)	pe**rr**o, **r**ío
[s]	**s**	**s**alir
	c (before **e, i**)	**c**ero, **c**in**c**o
	x (before a consonant)	e**x**traño
	z	ca**z**a
[z]	**s** (before voiced consonants)	de**s**de, mi**s**mo
[t]	**t**	**t**iempo
[b]	**b** or **v**	am**b**os, **v**ino
[b̸]	**b** or **v**	ha**b**a, ca**v**a
[ks]	**x** (between vowels)	e**x**amen

Appendix C: Grammatical terms

Note: Examples in parentheses are not meant to be exhaustive.

adjective   a word used to modify a noun by qualifying, limiting, or specifying it. Qualifying or descriptive adjectives normally indicate the qualities of a noun (**bueno, malo**). Limiting or specifying adjectives can be demonstrative (**este, aquella**), numeral (**primero, uno**), possessive (**mi, tu**), and indefinite (**algún, ningún**) adjectives.

adverb   a word that modifies a verb (habla **bien**), an adjective (**muy** bueno), or another adverb (**muy** bien).

agreement   correspondence in gender, number, or person between words (ell**a es** alt**a**, ell**os son** baj**os**).

article   a word used to signal and specify nouns. It may be indefinite (**un, una**) or definite (**el, la**).

auxiliary verb   a verb that accompanies special forms of the main verb to form a unit expressing tense and mood (**ha** llegado, **pueden** venir, **debes** hacer, **estoy** leyendo).

clause   a group of words containing a subject and a predicate that forms part of a compound or complex sentence. A compound sentence normally consists of two independent clauses joined by a conjunction (**Habla español y escribe otras lenguas**). A complex sentence consists of a main clause and a subordinate clause. A *main clause* is the clause in a complex sentence that can stand grammatically by itself (**Es imposible** que yo no lo mire). A *subordinate clause* cannot stand grammatically by itself. It is introduced by a relative pronoun or a conjunction, and most commonly serves (a) as an *adjectival clause* (El hombre **que está ahí** es mi papá); (b) as an *adverbial clause* (Canta **como canto yo**); or (c) as a *noun clause* (Me dice **que no puede**).

conjugation   (a) forms of a particular verb for person, tense, number, and mood. (b) in Spanish, any of three major groups in which verbs are divided according to ending: 1st conjugation, verbs in **-ar**; 2nd conjugation, verbs in **-er**; 3rd conjugation, verbs in **-ir**.

conjunction   invariable word that joins words or sentences (**y, pero**).

digraph   a pair of letters representing a single speech sound (like **qu** in **qu**iero and **gu** in al**gu**ien).

diphthong   a complex speech sound beginning with one vowel sound and continuing to another vowel (or semivowel) sound within the same syllable (p**ue**de, s**ie**nte).

direct object the word or words that directly receive and complete the action of the verb (I read *two books*—Leí **dos libros**; I visited *my friends*—Visité **a mis amigos**).

gender a set of three categories (masculine, feminine, and neuter) into which words are divided and which determines agreement with modifiers. In Spanish, nouns are either masculine or feminine; in English, they are masculine, feminine, or neuter.

imperative a mood that expresses a command or request (Pepe, **come**, por favor).

imperfect the form of a verb that shows, usually in the past, an action or condition as incomplete, continuous, or habitual (Luisa **hablaba**). (See *preterit*).

impersonal construction a verbal construction that expresses the action of an unspecified agent. In English, an impersonal construction most often is expressed by the passive voice (*Bread is made* out of wheat), or by an unspecified subject pronoun (*you, one, they*) and the active voice (*One never knows!*; *You* can't grow by standing still; *They* invented a new machine). In Spanish, the most frequently used impersonal construction is formed with **se** (El pan **se** hace de trigo), but **uno** (¡**Uno** nunca sabe!) and the third-person plural without a subject pronoun (**Inventaron** una nueva máquina) are also possible. The passive voice is not used in impersonal constructions in Spanish.

indirect object the word or words that indirectly receive the action of the verb, often indicating *to whom* or *for whom* the action is performed (I give *them* a gift—**Les** doy un regalo; They offer *us* information—**Nos** ofrecen información).

infinitive the basic verb form that does not reflect tense, person, or number: in English, *to* + verb; in Spanish, the verb form ending in **-ar, -er,** or **-ir.**

intransitive a verb construction that does not require a direct object to complete its meaning (*I dream* often—**Sueño** a menudo). Note that a verb may be both transitive and intransitive. (See *transitive*.)

mood a set of verb forms used to indicate the speaker's attitude toward the factuality or likelihood of the action or condition expressed. The *indicative mood* is generally used to relate facts or supply information (Juan **vive** en San Diego; Marta **dice** que no **puede** ir con nosotros). The *subjunctive mood* is generally used (a) in dependent clauses after verbs that express emotion, doubt, denial, uncertainty, a subjective judgment, or attempt to influence someone's behavior or actions (Raquel quiere que yo **compre** las bebidas; Ojalá que **venga**); (b) in dependent adjective and adverbial clauses when the event, action, or situation is non-existent, hypothetical, or uncertain (No hay nadie que lo **sepa**; Terminamos pronto el trabajo a menos que no **vengan** todos los empleados).

nominalization the process by which a word such as an adjective (**bueno**), a phrase (**de madera**), or a clause (**que está ahí**) functions as a noun in a sentence: (Me gusta el pan bueno—Me gusta **el bueno**; Me gusta la mesa de madera—Me gusta **la de madera**; Me gusta la mesa que está ahí—Me gusta **la que está ahí**).

noun a word that designates any kind of being, idea, or object that can serve as subject or object of a verb or object of a preposition.

object (See *direct object* and *indirect object*.)

participle a form of the verb that is used with an auxiliary verb (such as a form of *to be* or *to have*) to indicate certain tenses. (See *past participle, present participle*.)

past participle the form of a verb used with the auxiliary *have* in English and **haber** in Spanish to form the perfect tenses. (¿Has **comprendido**? ¡No has **dicho** una palabra!) The past participle can also be used as an adjective in Spanish, in which case it agrees in gender and number with the noun it modifies (Son casas **construidas** en 1800).

perfect tense a verb form that generally expresses an action completed prior to a fixed point of reference in time (**he trabajado, había trabajado, habré trabajado**).

possessives (See *adjective* and *pronoun*.)

predicate that part of a sentence that expresses something about the subject and that normally includes a verb with its objects and modifiers.

preposition a word that comes before a noun or a pronoun to show its relation to another word in a sentence. The most common prepositions in Spanish are **a, con, contra, de, desde, en, entre, hacia, hasta, para, por, sin,** and **sobre,** plus a number of compound prepositions such as **antes de, detrás de.**

present participle (*gerundio* in Spanish) the form of the verb that ends in **-ndo** in Spanish (*-ing* in English), and that combines with the verb **estar** in Spanish (*to be* in English) to form the progressive (**Estoy leyendo** en este momento—*I am reading* right now). The present participle is not used as an adjective in Spanish as it is in English (The lady *standing* by the fire is the main character).

preterit the form of a verb that is generally used to express a completed action in the past and that views the past action in its beginning stage (El candidato **habló** desde las ocho), in its ending stage (El candidato **habló**

hasta las diez), or in its entirety (El candidato **habló** por dos horas). (See *imperfect.*)

progressive tense   a compound verb form that expresses an action in progress in the present, past, or future. (See *present participle.*)

pronoun   a word that functions as a substitute for a noun or other word or phrase. Pronouns in Spanish can be the subject of a verb (**yo, ella**), the object of a verb (**me, te**), the object of a preposition (**mí, ti**), or they can be possessive pronouns (**mío, tuyo**), and relative pronouns (**que, quien**).

reflexive construction   a construction in which a verb has a subject that is identical to (a) the direct object (I see myself—**Me veo**); or (b) the indirect object (I buy myself a suit—**Me compro** un traje).

relative pronouns   (See *pronoun.*)

tense   any of the forms in the conjugation of a verb that indicate the time (past, present, or future) in which the action or state occurs or is viewed.

transitive   a verb construction that requires a direct object to complete the meaning of the sentence (She *watches* me—Ella me **mira**). Note that a verb may be used both transitively and intransitively. (See *intransitive.*)

Appendix D: Verb Charts

Note: In the sections on stem-changing and spelling-changing verbs, only tenses in which a change occurs are shown.

Regular verbs

Infinitive	hablar	comer	vivir
Present participle	hablando	comiendo	viviendo
Past participle	hablado	comido	vivido

Simple tenses

	hablar	**comer**	**vivir**
Present indicative	habl**o**	com**o**	viv**o**
	as	**es**	**es**
	a	**e**	**e**
	amos	**emos**	**imos**
	áis	**éis**	**ís**
	an	**en**	**en**
Imperfect indicative	habl**aba**	com**ía**	viv**ía**
	abas	**ías**	**ías**
	aba	**ía**	**ía**
	ábamos	**íamos**	**íamos**
	abais	**íais**	**íais**
	aban	**ían**	**ían**
Preterit	habl**é**	com**í**	viv**í**
	aste	**iste**	**iste**
	ó	**ió**	**ió**
	amos	**imos**	**imos**
	asteis	**isteis**	**isteis**
	aron	**ieron**	**ieron**
Future indicative	hablar**é**	comer**é**	vivir**é**
	ás	**ás**	**ás**
	á	**á**	**á**
	emos	**emos**	**emos**
	éis	**éis**	**éis**
	án	**án**	**án**

	hablar	comer	vivir
Conditional	hablaría ías ía íamos íais ían	comería ías ía íamos íais ían	viviría ías ía íamos íais ían
Affirmative and negative commands	**tú:** habla, no hables **Ud.:** hable, no hable **Uds.:** hablen, no hablen **vosotros, -as:** hablad, no habléis	come, no comas coma, no coma coman, no coman comed, no comáis	vive, no vivas viva, no viva vivan, no vivan vivid, no viváis
Present subjunctive	hable es e emos éis en	coma as a amos áis an	viva as a amos áis an
Imperfect subjunctive	hablara aras ara áramos arais aran	comiera ieras iera iéramos ierais ieran	viviera ieras iera iéramos ierais ieran

Compound tenses

	hablar	comer	vivir
Present perfect indicative	he hablado has hablado, *etc.*	he comido has comido, *etc.*	he vivido has vivido, *etc.*
Pluperfect indicative	había hablado habías hablado, *etc.*	había comido habías comido, *etc.*	había vivido habías vivido, *etc.*
Future perfect	habré hablado habrás hablado, *etc.*	habré comido habrás comido, *etc.*	habré vivido habrás vivido, *etc.*
Conditional perfect	habría hablado habrías hablado, *etc.*	habría comido habrías comido, *etc.*	habría vivido habrías vivido, *etc.*
Present perfect subjunctive	haya hablado hayas hablado, *etc.*	haya comido hayas comido, *etc.*	haya vivido hayas vivido, *etc.*
Pluperfect subjunctive	hubiera hablado hubieras hablado, *etc.*	hubiera comido hubieras comido, *etc.*	hubiera vivido hubieras vivido, *etc.*

Stem-changing verbs

	-ar verbs: e > ie		-er verbs: e > ie	
Infinitive	**pensar** to think		**entender** to understand	
Present indicative	**pienso**	pensamos	**entiendo**	entendemos
	piensas	pensáis	**entiendes**	entendéis
	piensa	**piensan**	**entiende**	**entienden**
Affirmative commands	**piensa**	pensad	**entiende**	entended
	piense	**piensen**	**entienda**	**entiendan**
Present subjunctive	**piense**	pensemos	**entienda**	entendamos
	pienses	penséis	**entiendas**	entendáis
	piense	**piensen**	**entienda**	**entiendan**

	-ar verbs: o > ue		-er verbs: o > ue	
Infinitive	**contar** to count		**volver** to return	
Present indicative	**cuento**	contamos	**vuelvo**	volvemos
	cuentas	contáis	**vuelves**	volvéis
	cuenta	**cuentan**	**vuelve**	**vuelven**
Affirmative commands	**cuenta**	contad	**vuelve**	volved
	cuente	**cuenten**	**vuelva**	**vuelvan**
Present subjunctive	**cuente**	contemos	**vuelva**	volvamos
	cuentes	contéis	**vuelvas**	volváis
	cuente	**cuenten**	**vuelva**	**vuelvan**

	-ir verbs: e > i	
Infinitive	**servir** to serve	
Present participle	**sirviendo**	
Present indicative	**sirvo**	servimos
	sirves	servís
	sirve	**sirven**
Affirmative commands	**sirve**	servid
	sirva	**sirvan**
Present subjunctive	**sirva**	**sirvamos**
	sirvas	**sirváis**
	sirva	**sirvan**
Preterit	serví	servimos
	serviste	servisteis
	sirvió	**sirvieron**
Imperfect subjunctive	**sirviera**	
	sirvieras, *etc.*	

	-ir verbs: e > ie or i		-ir verbs: o > ue or u	
Infinitive	**sentir** to regret, to feel		**dormir** to sleep	
Present participle	**sintiendo**		**durmiendo**	
Present indicative	**siento**	sentimos	**duermo**	dormimos
	sientes	sentís	**duermes**	dormís
	siente	**sienten**	**duerme**	**duermen**
Affirmative commands	**siente**	sentid	**duerme**	dormid
	sienta	**sientan**	**duerma**	**duerman**
Present subjunctive	**sienta**	**sintamos**	**duerma**	**durmamos**
	sientas	**sintáis**	**duermas**	**durmáis**
	sienta	**sientan**	**duerma**	**duerman**
Preterit	sentí	sentimos	dormí	dormimos
	sentiste	sentisteis	dormiste	dormisteis
	sintió	**sintieron**	**durmió**	**durmieron**
Imperfect subjunctive	**sintiera**		**durmiera**	
	sintieras, *etc.*		**durmieras,** *etc.*	

Verbs with spelling changes

	Verbs in **-car:** c > qu before **e**		Verbs in **-gar:** g > gu before **e**	
Infinitive	**buscar** to look for		**llegar** to arrive	
Preterit	**busqué**	buscamos	**llegué**	llegamos
	buscaste	buscasteis	llegaste	llegasteis
	buscó	buscaron	llegó	llegaron
Affirmative commands	busca	buscad	llega	llegad
	busque	**busquen**	**llegue**	**lleguen**
Present subjunctive	**busque**	**busquemos**	**llegue**	**lleguemos**
	busques	**busquéis**	**llegues**	**lleguéis**
	busque	**busquen**	**llegue**	**lleguen**

	Verbs in -ger and -gir: g > j before a and o		Verbs in -guir: gu > g before a and o	
Infinitive	**coger** to pick up		**seguir** to follow	
Present indicative	**cojo**	cogemos	**sigo**	seguimos
	coges	cogéis	sigues	seguís
	coge	cogen	sigue	siguen
Affirmative commands	coge	coged	sigue	seguid
	coja	**cojan**	**siga**	**sigan**
Present subjunctive	**coja**	**cojamos**	**siga**	**sigamos**
	cojas	**cojáis**	**sigas**	**sigáis**
	coja	**cojan**	**siga**	**sigan**

	Verbs in consonant + -cer: c > z before a and o		Verbs in -zar: z > c before e	
Infinitive	**vencer** to conquer		**empezar** to begin	
Present indicative	**venzo**	vencemos		
	vences	vencéis		
	vence	vencen		
Preterit			**empecé**	empezamos
			empezaste	empezasteis
			empezó	empezaron
Affirmative commands	vence	venced	empieza	empezad
	venza	**venzan**	**empiece**	**empiecen**
Present subjunctive	**venza**	**venzamos**	**empiece**	**empecemos**
	venzas	**venzáis**	**empieces**	**empecéis**
	venza	**venzan**	**empiece**	**empiecen**

	Verbs in -eer: unstressed i > y	
Infinitive	**creer** to believe	
Present participle	**creyendo**	
Preterit	creí	creímos
	creíste	creísteis
	creyó	**creyeron**
Imperfect subjunctive	**creyera**	**creyéramos**
	creyeras	**creyerais**
	creyera	**creyeran**

Irregular verbs

	caer to fall	**conducir** to drive
Present indicative	caigo, caes, cae, caemos, caéis, caen	conduzco, conduces, conduce, conducimos, conducís, conducen
Preterit	caí, caíste, cayó, caímos, caísteis, cayeron	conduje, condujiste, condujo, condujimos, condujisteis, condujeron
Imperfect	caía, caías, *etc.*	conducía, conducías, *etc.*
Future	caeré, caerás, *etc.*	conduciré, conducirás, *etc.*
Conditional	caería, caerías, *etc.*	conduciría, conducirías, *etc.*
Present subjunctive	caiga, caigas, caiga, caigamos, caigáis, caigan	conduzca, conduzcas, conduzca, conduzcamos, conduzcáis, conduzcan
Imperfect subjunctive	cayera, cayeras, cayera, cayéramos, cayerais, cayeran	condujera, condujeras, condujera, condujéramos, condujerais, condujeran
Participles	cayendo, caído	conduciendo, conducido
Affirmative commands	cae, caed caiga, caigan	conduce, conducid conduzca, conduzcan

	conocer to know, be acquainted with	**dar** to give
Present indicative	conozco, conoces, conoce, conocemos, conocéis, conocen	doy, das, da, damos, dais, dan
Preterit	conocí, conociste, conoció, conocimos, conocisteis, conocieron	di, diste, dio, dimos, disteis, dieron
Imperfect	conocía, conocías, *etc.*	daba, dabas, *etc.*
Future	conoceré, conocerás, *etc.*	daré, darás, *etc.*
Conditional	conocería, conocerías, *etc.*	daría, darías, *etc.*
Present subjunctive	conozca, conozcas, conozca, conozcamos, conozcáis, conozcan	dé, des, dé, demos, deis, den
Imperfect subjunctive	conociera, conocieras, conociera, conociéramos, conocierais, conocieran	diera, dieras, diera, diéramos, dierais, dieran
Participles	conociendo, conocido	dando, dado
Affirmative commands	conoce, conoced conozca, conozcan	da, dad dé, den

	decir to say	**estar** to be
Present indicative	digo, dices, dice, decimos, decís, dicen	estoy, estás, está, estamos, estáis, están
Preterit	dije, dijiste, dijo, dijimos, dijisteis, dijeron	estuve, estuviste, estuvo, estuvimos, estuvisteis, estuvieron
Imperfect	decía, decías, *etc.*	estaba, estabas, *etc.*
Future	diré, dirás, *etc.*	estaré, estarás, *etc.*
Conditional	diría, dirías, *etc.*	estaría, estarías, *etc.*
Present subjunctive	diga, digas, diga, digamos, digáis, digan	esté, estés, esté, estemos, estéis, estén
Imperfect subjunctive	dijera, dijeras, dijera, dijéramos, dijerais, dijeran	estuviera, estuvieras, estuviera, estuviéramos, estuvierais, estuvieran
Participles	diciendo, dicho	estando, estado
Affirmative commands	di, decid diga, digan	está, estad esté, estén

	haber to have	**hacer** to make, to do
Present indicative	he, has, ha,	hago, haces, hace,
	hemos, habéis, han	hacemos, hacéis, hacen
Preterit	hube, hubiste, hubo,	hice, hiciste, hizo,
	hubimos, hubisteis, hubieron	hicimos, hicisteis, hicieron
Imperfect	había, habías, *etc.*	hacía, hacías, *etc.*
Future	habré, habrás, *etc.*	haré, harás, *etc.*
Conditional	habría, habrías, *etc.*	haría, harías, *etc.*
Present subjunctive	haya, hayas, haya,	haga, hagas, haga,
	hayamos, hayáis, hayan	hagamos, hagáis, hagan
Imperfect subjunctive	hubiera, hubieras, hubiera,	hiciera, hicieras, hiciera,
	hubiéramos, hubierais, hubieran	hiciéramos, hicierais, hicieran
Participles	habiendo, habido	haciendo, hecho
Affirmative commands	— — —	haz, haced
		haga, hagan

	huir to flee	**ir** to go
Present indicative	huyo, huyes, huye,	voy, vas, va,
	huimos, huís, huyen	vamos, vais, van
Preterit	huí, huiste, huyó,	fui, fuiste, fue,
	huimos, huisteis, huyeron	fuimos, fuisteis, fueron
Imperfect	huía, huías, *etc.*	iba, ibas, *etc.*
Future	huiré, huirás, *etc.*	iré, irás, *etc.*
Conditional	huiría, huirías, *etc.*	iría, irías, *etc.*
Present subjunctive	huya, huyas, huya,	vaya, vayas, vaya,
	huyamos, huyáis, huyan	vayamos, vayáis, vayan
Imperfect subjunctive	huyera, huyeras, huyera,	fuera, fueras, fuera,
	huyéramos, huyerais, huyeran	fuéramos, fuerais, fueran
Participles	huyendo, huido	yendo, ido
Affirmative commands	huye, huid	ve, id
	huya, huyan	vaya, vayan

	oír to hear	**poder** to be able, can
Present indicative	oigo, oyes, oye,	puedo, puedes, puede,
	oímos, oís, oyen	podemos, podéis, pueden
Preterit	oí, oíste, oyó,	pude, pudiste, pudo,
	oímos, oísteis, oyeron	pudimos, pudisteis, pudieron
Imperfect	oía, oías, *etc.*	podía, podías, *etc.*
Future	oiré, oirás, *etc.*	podré, podrás, *etc.*
Conditional	oiría, oirías, *etc.*	podría, podrías, *etc.*
Present subjunctive	oiga, oigas, oiga,	pueda, puedas, pueda,
	oigamos, oigáis, oigan	podamos, podáis, puedan
Imperfect subjunctive	oyera, oyeras, oyera,	pudiera, pudieras, pudiera,
	oyéramos, oyerais, oyeran	pudiéramos, pudierais, pudieran
Participles	oyendo, oído	pudiendo, podido
Affirmative commands	oye, oíd	— — —
	oiga, oigan	

	poner to put	**querer** to wish, to love
Present indicative	pongo, pones, pone, ponemos, ponéis, ponen	quiero, quieres, quiere, queremos, queréis, quieren
Preterit	puse, pusiste, puso, pusimos, pusisteis, pusieron	quise, quisiste, quiso, quisimos, quisisteis, quisieron
Imperfect	ponía, ponías, *etc.*	quería, querías, *etc.*
Future	pondré, pondrás, *etc.*	querré, querrás, *etc.*
Conditional	pondría, pondrías, *etc.*	querría, querrías, *etc.*
Present subjunctive	ponga, pongas, ponga, pongamos, pongáis, pongan	quiera, quieras, quiera, queramos, queráis, quieran
Imperfect subjunctive	pusiera, pusieras, pusiera, pusiéramos, pusierais, pusieran	quisiera, quisieras, quisiera, quisiéramos, quisierais, quisieran
Participles	poniendo, puesto	queriendo, querido
Affirmative commands	pon, poned ponga, pongan	quiere, quered quiera, quieran

	saber to know (how)	**salir** to leave
Present indicative	sé, sabes, sabe, sabemos, sabéis, saben	salgo, sales, sale, salimos, salís, salen
Preterit	supe, supiste, supo, supimos, supisteis, supieron	salí, saliste, salió, salimos, salisteis, salieron
Imperfect	sabía, sabías, *etc.*	salía, salías, *etc.*
Future	sabré, sabrás, *etc.*	saldré, saldrás, *etc.*
Conditional	sabría, sabrías, *etc.*	saldría, saldrías, *etc.*
Present subjunctive	sepa, sepas, sepa, sepamos, sepáis, sepan	salga, salgas, salga, salgamos, salgáis, salgan
Imperfect subjunctive	supiera, supieras, supiera, supiéramos, supierais, supieran	saliera, salieras, saliera, saliéramos, salierais, salieran
Participles	sabiendo, sabido	saliendo, salido
Affirmative commands	sabe, sabed sepa, sepan	sal, salid salga, salgan

	ser to be	**tener** to have
Present indicative	soy, eres, es, somos, sois, son	tengo, tienes, tiene, tenemos, tenéis, tienen
Preterit	fui, fuiste, fue, fuimos, fuisteis, fueron	tuve, tuviste, tuvo, tuvimos, tuvisteis, tuvieron
Imperfect	era, eras, era, éramos, erais, eran	tenía, tenías, *etc.*
Future	seré, serás, *etc.*	tendré, tendrás, *etc.*
Conditional	sería, serías, *etc.*	tendría, tendrías, *etc.*
Present subjunctive	sea, seas, sea, seamos, seáis, sean	tenga, tengas, tenga, tengamos, tengáis, tengan
Imperfect subjunctive	fuera, fueras, fuera, fuéramos, fuerais, fueran	tuviera, tuvieras, tuviera, tuviéramos, tuvierais, tuvieran
Participles	siendo, sido	teniendo, tenido
Affirmative commands	sé, sed sea, sean	ten, tened tenga, tengan

	traer to bring	**valer** to be worth
Present indicative	traigo, traes, trae, traemos, traéis, traen	valgo, vales, vale, valemos, valéis, valen
Preterit	traje, trajiste, trajo, trajimos, trajisteis, trajeron	valí, valiste, valió, valimos, valisteis, valieron
Imperfect	traía, traías, *etc.*	valía, valías, *etc.*
Future	traeré, traerás, *etc.*	valdré, valdrás, *etc.*
Conditional	traería, traerías, *etc.*	valdría, valdrías, *etc.*
Present subjunctive	traiga, traigas, traiga, traigamos, traigáis, traigan	valga, valgas, valga, valgamos, valgáis, valgan
Imperfect subjunctive	trajera, trajeras, trajera, trajéramos, trajerais, trajeran	valiera, valieras, valiera, valiéramos, valierais, valieran
Participles	trayendo, traído	valiendo, valido
Affirmative commands	trae, traed traiga, traigan	val, valed valga, valgan

	venir to come	**ver** to see
Present indicative	vengo, vienes, viene, venimos, venís, vienen	veo, ves, ve, vemos, veis, ven
Preterit	vine, viniste, vino, vinimos, vinisteis, vinieron	vi, viste, vio, vimos, visteis, vieron
Imperfect	venía, venías, *etc.*	veía, veías, veía, veíamos, veíais, veían
Future	vendré, vendrás, *etc.*	veré, verás, *etc.*
Conditional	vendría, vendrías, *etc.*	vería, verías, *etc.*
Present subjunctive	venga, vengas, venga, vengamos, vengáis, vengan	vea, veas, vea, veamos, veáis, vean
Imperfect subjunctive	viniera, vinieras, viniera, viniéramos, vinierais, vinieran	viera, vieras, viera, viéramos, vierais, vieran
Participles	viniendo, venido	viendo, visto
Affirmative commands	ven, venid venga, vengan	ve, ved vea, vean

Reflexive verbs

	levantarse to get up
Present indicative	me levanto, te levantas, se levanta nos levantamos, os levantáis, se levantan
Participles	levantándose, levantado
Affirmative **tú:**	levántate, no te levantes
and negative **Ud.:**	levántese, no se levante
commands **Uds.:**	levántense, no se levanten
vosotros, -as:	levantaos, no os levantéi.

Spanish-English Vocabulary

This vocabulary includes most of the words from the core materials, grammar and word-building sections, and non-guessable words from captions. The definitions are limited to the context in which the words are used in the book. A number after an entry refers to the lesson where the word first appears: the letter *P* refers to the *Lección Preliminar*.

The following abbreviations are used:

adj. adjective	*interj.* interjection	*pl.* plural
adv. adverb	*irreg.* irregular	*sing.* singular
f. feminine	*m.* masculine	*trans.* transitive
inf. infinitive	*n.* noun	

a to, at P; **al (a + el), a la** to the 5

a causa de because of 11

a eso de (las dos) at about (two o'clock) 10

a la (a las) + *number* at *(clock time)* 10

a la orden at your service; **a sus órdenes** *(pl.)* 2

a lo largo de along *(the length of)* 15

a menos que unless 18

a menudo often 17

a partir de from 7

a pesar de in spite of 17

a pie on foot 5

a propósito by the way 11

a tiempo on time 6

a través de through 17

a veces sometimes 17

la abeja bee 16

abiertamente openly 22

abierto, -a open 6

el/la abogado/a lawyer 21

abrazar to hug, embrace 14

el abrazo embrace 20

el abrelatas can opener 17

el abrigo coat 12

abril April 11

abrir to open 13

abrupto, -a rough *(terrain)* 12

absoluto: en ~ not at all 18

absurdo: es ~ it's absurd 18

la abuela grandmother 9

el abuelo grandfather 9; **los ~s** grandparents 9

abundar to be plentiful 9

aburrido, -a boring, bored 20

acabar de (+ *inf.*) to have just done something, to finish doing something 16

académico, -a, academic 18

acaloradamente heatedly 21

accesible accessible P

el accidente accident 10

la acción action 5

el aceite (de oliva) (olive) oil 13

acelerar to accelerate 22

el acento (tilde) accent 17

aceptar to accept 15

la acera sidewalk 5

acercarse to come near; approach 21

el acero steel 17

el acondicionador de aire air conditioner 9

aconsejar to advise 13

acordarse (ue) de to remember 12

el acordeón accordion 23

acostarse (ue) to go to bed 12

acostumbrado, -a accustomed 18

acostumbrarse a to get used to, be accustomed to 16

la actividad activity 18

activo, -a active 6

el acto action 21

el actor actor 13

la actriz actress 13

la actuación action, behavior 22

actual present, current 24

actualmente at the present time 22

acuerdo: de ~ agreed; **estar de ~** to be in agreement 21

adelantado: estar ~ to be running fast 10

además de in addition to 15

adiós good-by P

el adjetivo adjective 1

la administración administration 18

administrar to administrate 22

la admiración admiration 22

admirado, -a admired 13

el adobe adobe 17

¿adónde? (to) where? 5

la adopción adoption 10

adorar to adore 23

adornado, -a decorated 23

adornar to decorate 23

la aduana customs 12

el/la aduanero/a customs officer 12

la aerolínea (la línea aérea) airline 12

el aeroplano plane 8

el aeropuerto airport 6

afeitarse to shave 12

el/la aficionado/a fan P

afirmar to affirm 10

la agencia agency 12; ~ **de colocaciones** employment agency 21; ~ **de viajes** travel agency 12

el/la agente; ~**de prensa** press agent P ~ **de policía** police officer 5; ~ **de viajes** travel agent 12

agitado, -a agitated 19

agosto August 11

agradable pleasant 18

agradecido, -a: estar ~ to be grateful 20

la agricultura agriculture P

el agua *(f.)* water 6; **agua mineral** mineral water 13

el aguacate avocado 13

ahora now P; ~ **que** now that, since 18

el aire: al aire libre in the open air 16

aislado, -a isolated P

ajeno, -a foreign to 15

el ajetreo hustle and bustle 14

al *(+ inf.)* on *or* upon *(doing something)* 13

al contrario on the contrary 6

al fin finally 19

al final de at the end of 5

al lado de next to, beside 14

al mismo tiempo at the same time 12

al principio (de) at the beginning (of) 19

al tanto up to date 14

albergar to house, contain 24

la alcachofa artichoke 13

la alcoba (el cuarto de dormir, la habitación) bedroom 14

alegrarse (de) to be glad 13

alegre happy 3

alemán, -ana German 2

el alemán German *(language)* 3

la alfarería pottery 20

la alfombra rug 19

algo something 7

el algodón cotton 17

alguien someone, somebody 9

algún/alguno, -a some 8

alguna vez sometimes, on occasion 9

el almacén grocery store 5

el almanaque almanac P

las almejas clams 13

almorzar (ue) to have lunch 8

el almuerzo lunch, late mid-morning meal 13

alojarse to lodge 12

el alpinismo mountain climbing 8

alrededor de around 19

los alrededores outskirts 14

alto, -a tall 6; high 22

el altoparlante loudspeaker 7

la altura height, altitude 12

allí there 5

el ama de casa *(f.)* housewife 9

amarillo, -a yellow 6

el ambiente atmosphere 19

ambos, ambas both 21

americano, -a American 2

el/la amigo/a friend 4

amistoso, -a friendly 14

el amor love 3

amoroso, -a loving 23

la ampliación expansion 22

amplio, -a wide, full 16

analizar to analyze 10

análogo, -a similar 2

anaranjado, -a orange 6

andar to walk 11; ~ **en bicicleta (autobús, metro)** to ride a (go by) bicycle, bus 8

el anillo: ~ de compromiso engagement ring 23; ~ **nupcial** wedding ring 23

animado, -a lively, animated 24

el animal animal 16

animar to encourage, cheer 18

el aniversario anniversary 23

anoche last night 10

ante in the presence of 23

anteayer the day before yesterday 10

el antepasado ancestor 20

antes before 11; ~ **(de) que** before 18; ~ **de** *(+ inf.)* before . . .-ing 5

antiguo, -a ancient, old 14

antipático, -a unpleasant, disagreeable 6

la antropología anthropology 3

anunciar to announce 6

el anuncio announcement 13; **los anuncios comerciales** advertisements P

el año year P; ~ **pasado** last year 10; **en los últimos años** recently 15; **tener . . . años** to be . . . years old 17

apagar to turn off 13

el aparato equipment, apparatus 7

aparecer (zc) to appear 10

el apartamento apartment 5

aparte de besides, in addition to 20

el apellido last name 2

el aplauso applause 7

el apodo nickname 6

apoyar to support 22

apreciados señores (apreciada señora) Dear Sirs (Madam) 20

aprender to learn 3

aprobar (ue) to approve 8

apropiado, -a appropriate 19

las aptitudes qualifications *(for a job)* 21

aquel, aquella that (over there); **aquellos, aquellas** *(pl.)* those (over there) 8

aquí here 4; ~ **estoy a sus órdenes** I'm at your service 2

el árbitro referee 8

el árbol tree 19

el área *(f.)* area P

argentino, -a Argentinian 2

el armario wardrobe 19

la armonía harmony P

la arqueología archaeology 12

arqueológico, -a archaeological 12

el arquitecto architect 14

la arquitectura architecture 14

arreglar to fix 16

arrepentirse (ie) to repent, to be sorry 12; ~ **de** to be sorry to 17

arrogante arrogant 6

el arroz rice 13

el arte *(m. or f.)* art 3; ~ **dramático** dramatic arts 3

la arteria artery 8

la artesanía artisanry 15

el/la artesano/a artisan 15

el artículo article 10

el/la artista artist 8

la asamblea assembly 22

asegurar to assure 12

asesinado, -a assassinated 21

así (in) that (this) way, thus, so 8; **así, así** so-so 1

la asignatura course subject 3

asistir (a) to attend 6

el aspecto aspect 14

el asunto matter, business 11

la atención attention 24

atentamente courteously 20

el aterrizaje landing 12

aterrizar to land *(in a plane)* 12

el ático attic 14

el/la atleta athlete 18

el atletismo athletics 18

atrasado, -a: estar ~ to be running late 10

atravesar (ie) to go through 22

atreverse a to dare to 17

el atún tuna 13

aumentar to increase 22

aunque although 14

el autobús bus 5; **en (autobús)** by (bus) 5

el automóvil car 5

la autonomía autonomy 22

la autopista high-speed highway 14

la autoridad authority 15

autosuficiente self-sufficient P

el/la auxiliar de vuelo steward, stewardess, flight attendant 21

la avenida avenue 5

averiguar to find out; to verify 9

las aves de corral poultry 13

el avión airplane 5

la avioneta small plane 8

ayer yesterday 10; ~ **por la mañana** yesterday morning 10; ~ **por la noche** yesterday evening 10; ~ **por la tarde** yesterday afternoon 10

la ayuda help 9

ayudar to help 10; ~**se** to help each other 17

azteca Aztec 20

el azúcar sugar 13

azucarero, -a sugar 17

azul blue 6; ~ **claro** light blue 6; ~ **marino** navy blue 6

el bachillerato secondary school education; baccaulaureate 19

bailar to dance 3

el baile dance 3

bajo, -a short *(in stature)* 6; under 15

el balcón balcony 23

el balneario bathing resort 14

el baloncesto (el básquetbol) basketball 8

el ballet ballet 7

la banana banana 13

el banco bank 5

la bandera flag 24

el/la banquero/a banker 21

bañarse to take a shower, bathe 12

barato, -a cheap, inexpensive 8

bárbaro great 7

la barca small boat 8; **montar en barca (bote)** to go boating 8

el barco ship 8

el barrio neighborhood 9

el barro clay 20

basado, -a based on 24

la base basis 15

bastante bien quite well 2

el bautismo christening; baptism 23

el/la bebé baby 4

beber to drink 6

las bebidas drinks 13

el béisbol baseball 8

la belleza beauty 21

el beso; muchos besos many kisses 20

la biblioteca library 4

el/la bibliotecario/a librarian 21

la bicicleta bicycle 8

bien well 1; ~ **parecido** good looking 6

el bilingüismo bilingualism 15

el billete (boleto) de ida one-way ticket 12; ~ **y vuelta** round-trip ticket 12

la billetera wallet 12

la biología biology 3

biológico, -a biological 16

el/la biólogo/a biologist 16

el bistec beefsteak 13

blanco, -a white 6

la blusa blouse 12

la boca mouth 15

la boda wedding 23

la bodega (el sótano) cellar 14

el boleto ticket 12

el bolígrafo ballpoint pen 2

boliviano, -a Bolivian 2

los bolos bowling 18

la bolsa, el bolso purse, handbag 12

bonito, -a pretty, attractive 6

el bosque woods 16

las botas boots 12

el bote boat 8; ~ **de motor** motor boat 8; **montar en bote** to go boating 8

el boxeo boxing 18

brasileño, -a Brazilian 2

el brazo arm 15

buenas tardes (noches) good afternoon (evening, night) P

bueno, -a good 6; good *(character)*; in good health 20; okay 3; **bueno, bueno** good, good; okay, okay 3

buenos días good morning, hello P
la bufanda scarf 12
la burocracia bureaucracy 11
el burro donkey 16
buscar to look for 3
la búsqueda search 20
el buzón mailbox 20

el caballo horse 16; **montar a caballo** to ride horseback 14
caber (*irreg.*) to fit 20
la cabeza head 15
la cabra goat 16
el cacao cocoa (*bean*) 15
cada each P
caer (*irreg.*) to fall 15; **~se** to fall down 17
el café coffee; café 6; **(de color) café** brown 6
la cafetería cafeteria 21
el caimán alligator 16
el calamar squid 8
los calcetines socks 12
la calculadora calculator 2
el calor: hace calor it's very hot 11; **tener calor** to be warm (*persons*) 7
la calle street 5
la cama bed 16
la cámara (fotográfica) camera 7
el/la camarero/a waiter 6
el camarón shrimp 13
cambiar to exchange, change 5
el cambio change 15
caminar to walk 3
el camino: de camino on the way 14
el camión city bus (*Mexico*); truck 5
la camisa shirt 12
la campaña electoral electoral campaign 22
el/la campeón/ona champion 8
el campeonato championship 18
el/la campesino/a peasant 21
el campo field 11

canadiense Canadian 2
el canal canal P; channel 20
la canasta basket 15
cancelar to cancel 11
la canción song 3
la cancha (tennis, basketball) court P
el/la candidato/a candidate 22
el cangrejo crawfish, crab 13
cansado, -a tired 5
el/la cantante singer 7
cantar to sing 3
la caña de azúcar sugar cane 15
la capa cape 23
la capital capital city P
la cara face 15
el carácter character, nature 22
¡caramba! (*interj.*) hah! 16
los caramelos candy 13
el carbón coal 13
la cárcel jail 5
el cargo post, charge 21
la carne meat 13; **~ de cerdo** pork 13; **~ de res** beef 13
el carnet: ~ de conducir driver's license 21; **~ de identidad** ID card 21
la carnicería butcher shop 13
el/la carnicero/a butcher 13
caro, -a expensive 8
la carpeta file . 11
el carpintero carpenter 21
la carrera race 13
la carretera highway 12
el carro car 8
la carta letter 14; playing card 6
el cartero mailman 20
la casa house 5
casado, -a married 2; **estar ~** to be married 9
casarse to get married 15
la cascada waterfall 15
casi almost 18
el cassette cassette 2
castaño, -a (*for hair*) brown 6
el castellano Spanish (*language*) 22
el castillo castle 3

el catalán Catalan (*language*) 24
la catarata waterfall 15
la catedral cathedral 3
la categoría category 9
catorce fourteen 2
la causa: a causa de because of 11
causar to cause 13
la cebolla onion 13
la cebra zebra 16
la celebración celebration 22
celebrado, -a celebrated 10
célebre famous 23
el cemento cement 17
la cena supper, evening meal 13
cenar to have dinner 13
la censura censorship 22
el centavo cent 7
la central plant 17
central central 5
el centro downtown, center 4
centroamericano, -a Central American 18
cerca (de) near 5
el cerdo pig 16
los cereales cereals 13
cero zero 2
cerrado, -a closed 6
cerrar (ie) to close 8
la cerveza beer 6
el ciclismo cycling 18
las ciencias: ~ de computación computer science 3; **~ políticas** political science 1
el/la científico/a scientist 16
cierto, -a true 13; some, certain 22; **es cierto** it is true 13
el ciervo wild deer 16
cinco five P
el cine movie theater 5
la cinta ribbon 23
la cita date; appointment 7
la ciudad city P
el/la ciudadano/a citizen 13
civil civilian 22
la civilización civilization 15
civilizado, -a civilized 16
el clarinete clarinet 23
claro, -a light 6
claro of course 6

la clase class 2; kind 9
la clase media middle class 9
clásico, -a classical 7
clasificar to classify 16
el/la cliente/a client 15
el clima weather 18
el club club 3
el/la coautor/a coauthor 19
el cobre copper 16
la cocina kitchen 14
el/la cocinero/a cook 21
el coco coconut 15
el cocodrilo crocodile 16
el coche car 5
el codo elbow 15
coger to catch, get 17
el cognado cognate; ~ **falso** false cognate P
la colección collection 20
el/la coleccionista collector 15
el colegio elementary or high school P
colombiano, -a Colombian 2
el color color 6
el colorido: de gran colorido very colorful 8
la coma comma 17
el comedor dining room 14
comenzar (ie) to begin 10; ~ **a** to begin to 17
comer to eat 6
comercial commercial 11
comercializado, -a commercialized 12
comerciar to trade 15
el comercio commerce 5
el cometa comet 15
la comida meal; food 6; main meal of the day 13
las comillas quotes 17
la comisión commission 13
como like 6; ¡cómo no! of course! 5; ~ **si** as if 21; ~ **siempre** same as usual 1
¿cómo? how? what?; ¿~ es? what's he like? 6; ¿~ está? how are you? 1; ¿~ se dice ...? how does one say ...? 5; ¿~ se llama? what's your name? P

la cómoda chest of drawers 19
la comodidad comfort, facility 16
cómodo, -a comfortable 10
el/la compañero/a companion, pal 4
la compañía company 6
comparar to compare 12
la competencia competition 18
competitivo, -a competitive 18
complejo, -a complex 10
completamente completely 12
complicado, -a complicated 19
componer (irreg.) to make up; to compose 20
comprar to buy 3
comprender to understand 3
la comprensión understanding, comprehension 1
comprobar (ue) to check, verify 19
comprometido, -a: estar ~ to be engaged 23
el compromiso engagement 23
la computadora computer 6; ~ **personal** personal computer 2
común common 16
comunicarse (con) to communicate (with) 15
la comunidad community 19
la comunión communion 9
con with 5; ~ **frecuencia** frequently 14; ~ **mucho cariño** with much affection 20; ~ **permiso** excuse me P; ~ **tal que** provided, as long as 18
el concepto concept 21
la conciencia conscience 20
el concierto concert P
el concurso competition 7
la condición condition 9
conducir (zc) (also, **manejar**) to drive (a car) 12
el/la conductor/a driver 21
el conejo rabbit 16
la conferencia conference 11
la confianza confidence 22
confiar (en) to trust 12
el conjunto musical group 7
conmigo with me 7

conocer (zc) to meet, to know 9; ~**se** to know, to meet (one another) 17
conocido, -a well-known 13
la conquista conquest 20
conseguir (i) to get, obtain 9
el consejo council 22
conservar to keep, conserve 20
considerable considerable 10
considerar to consider 16
consistir to consist 22
la constitución constitution 22
constitucional constitutional 22
la construcción construction 12; **en construcción** under construction 24
construir to build, construct 18
consultar (con) to consult (with) 12
la contabilidad accounting 3
contacto: en contacto in touch
contar (ue) to count; to tell 8
contemporáneo, -a contemporary 2
contener contain P
contento, -a satisfied 5; happy 6
contestar to answer 3
el continente continent P
continuar to continue 10
continuo, -a continuous 20
contrario: al contrario on the contrary 6
el contraste contrast P
la contribución contribution 24
contribuir to contribute 20
el control control 22
la conversación conversation 1
la cooperación cooperation 13
cooperar to cooperate 19
el/la coordinador/a coordinator 11
la copiadora copier 7
el/la copiloto copilot 19
el corazón heart 7
la corbata tie 12
el cordero lamb 13
cordialmente cordially 20
la cordillera mountain range P

el coro chorus 7
el correo mail 16
correr to run; to jog 8
la corrida de toros bullfight 19
corriendo running 17
la cortesía courtesy P
la cortina curtain 19
corto, -a short 23
la cosa thing 2
coser to sew 21
la costa coast P
costar (ue) to cost 8
costarricense Costa Rican 2
la costumbre custom 15
la costura sewing 21
la creación creation 20
creativo, -a creative 9
creciente growing 18
creer to believe; to think 8
la crema cream 13
la criada maid, female servant 21
el criado male servant 21
criollo, -a Creole 13
la crisis crisis 22
el cristal glass, crystal 17
cristiano, -a Christian 15
cruel cruel 21
el cuaderno notebook 2
la cuadra (city) block 5
el cuadro painting 19
¿cuál (es)? which, what? 2
cualquier, -a whichever, what-
  ever, any 10
cuando when 7; whenever 18
¿cuándo? when? 5
cuanto: en ~ as soon as 18
¿cuánto, -a? how much?; **¿cuántos,
  -as?** (pl.) how many? 4
cuarto, -a fourth 16
el cuarto: ~ de baño bathroom
  14; **~ de dormir** bedroom 14
cuatro four 2
cubrir to cover 22
la cucaracha cockroach 16
la cuchara spoon 13
la cucharada tablespoon 13
el cuchillo knife 13
el cuello neck 15
la cuenta check, bill 6

la cuerda: música de cuerda
  string-instrumental music 13
el cuero leather 17
el cuerpo body 15
el cuestionario questionnaire 9
la culebra snake 16
el/la culpable guilty person 13
cultivar to grow, to cultivate 15
la cultura culture 20
cultural cultural 1
la cuñada sister-in-law 9
el cuñado brother-in-law 9
el curso course (of study) 4
cuyo, -a/cuyos, -as whose 23

la chaqueta jacket 12
charlar to chat 23
el/la chico/a boy; girl 4
chileno, -a Chilean 2
la chimenea chimney 14
chino, -a Chinese 2

dañarse to become damaged 16
dar (irreg.) to give 9; **~ a
  conocer** to show, make clear,
  reveal 9; **~ a luz** to give
  birth 23; **~ un paseo** to go for
  a walk 24; **~se cuenta (de)** to
  realize 21
de of, from 1; **~ hecho** in
  fact 22; **~ manera que** so that,
  in such a way that 18; **~ modo
  que** so that, in such a way that
  18; **~ nada** you're welcome, not
  at all P; **~ nuevo** again 10;
  ~ prisa quickly, hurriedly 17;
  ¿~ qué? from what? 5; what
  about? 7; **¿~ quién(es)?**
  whose? 4; **~ todos modos** at
  any rate, anyway 14
debajo de under, below 14
el debate debate 21
deber should, have to, must
  11; **se debe (a)** is due to 15
el deber duty, responsibility 21
la década decade 11
decidir to decide 3; **~se (a)** to
  make up one's mind 12

décimo, -a tenth 16
decir (irreg.) to say, to tell 5
la decisión decision 19
declarar to declare 10
la decoración decor 19
dedicar to dedicate 18; **~se (a)**
  to devote oneself (to) 17
el dedo finger or toe 15
definir to define 20
dejar to leave; forget 18; **~ de**
  to stop 17
del (de + el), de la of the, from
  the P,4
delante de in front of 5
el delegado delegate 10
delgado, -a slim, slender 6
delicado, -a delicate 15
delicioso, -a delicious 6
la demanda demand 10
lo demás the other, the rest of 18
demasiado, -a too much;(pl.) too
  many 18
la democracia democracy 22
democrático, -a democratic 22
dentro de within 12
depender (de) to depend (on) 15
el deporte sport 8
el/la deportista sportsman,
  sportswoman 8
deportivo, -a sporting (referring
  to sports) 13
la derecha right (in the political
  spectrum); right hand, side 22; **a
  ~ de** to the right of 22
el derecho law 23
derivado, -a derived 15
la derrota defeat 18
desaparecer (zc) to disappear 16
el desarrollo development 13
desastroso, -a disastrous 10
desayunar to have breakfast 13
el desayuno breakfast 13
descansar to rest 17
el descanso rest 19
la descendencia ancestry,
  lineage 15
la descentralización decentraliza-
  tion 22
descontento, -a dissatisfied 5

describir to describe 3
descriptivo, -a descriptive 6
el descubrimiento discovery 20
descubrir to discover 12
desde from 8; ~ **hace** + *time expression* for + *time expression* 11; ~ **que** since 18
desear to want; to wish 3
desempeñar to play (*a role*) 15
el desempleo unemployment 22
el deseo desire, wish 15
el desfile parade 24
deshabitado, -a uninhabited P
desierto, -a deserted 23
desilusionar to disappoint 18
desolado, -a desolate P
despacio slowly P
despedir (i) to say good-by 9
despegar to take off (*in a plane*) 12
el despegue takeoff 12
el despertador alarm clock 17
despertarse (ie) to wake up 12
el déspota despot 21
después after P; ~ **de** + *inf.* after (*doing something*) 13; ~ **de que** after 18
el destino destination 12
destruir to destroy 20
el desván attic 14
la desventaja disadvantage 12
el detalle detail 13
detenerse (*irreg.*) to stop 20
detrás de behind 5
devolver (ue) to return 22
el día day 1; **al día** daily 19; **hace un día estupendo** it's a great day 11
dibujar to draw, sketch 8
diciembre December 11
la dictadura dictatorship 22
diecinueve nineteen 2
dieciocho eighteen 2
dieciséis sixteen 2
diecisiete seventeen 2
los dientes teeth 15
la diéresis diaeresis 17
diez ten 2
difícil difficult 12; **es** ~ it is difficult 13

dificilísimo, -a very difficult 22
la dificultad difficulty 10
dime qué (te) pasa tell me what's the matter 21
dimitir to resign 22
el dinero money 5
el/la dios/a god, goddess 3
la dirección address 20
el/la director/a director 20
dirigir to direct 5; ~ **se a** to direct oneself, to be aimed (at) 17
la disciplina subject; discipline 9
el disco record 2
la discoteca discotheque P
la discriminación discrimination 21
el discurso speech 22
discutir to discuss 10
disfrutar to enjoy 22
distinto, -a distinct, different 12
distraer (*irreg.*) to distract 7
distribuir to distribute 19
la diversión entertainment 24
divertirse (ie) to have a good time, enjoy oneself 12
dividir to divide 6
la divinidad divinity, god 19
divorciado, -a: estar ~ to be divorced 9
divorciarse to get divorced 23
el divorcio divorce 23
doble double 13
doce twelve 2
el/la doctor/a doctor 1
el documental documentary 20
el documento document 9
el dólar dollar 7
doler (ue) to hurt 12
el dolor de cabeza headache 13
doméstico, -a domestic 16
domingo Sunday 1
dominicano, -a Dominican 2
donde where 5; wherever 18
¿dónde? where? 2; **¿a dónde?** (to) where? 5
dormido, -a asleep 6
dormir (ue) to sleep 8; ~ **se** to fall asleep 17
el dormitorio dormitory 5

dos two 2
el drama drama 15
dramáticamente dramatically 22
el dril denim 17
la ducha shower 16
dudar to doubt 13
dudoso: es ~ it is doubtful 13
el/la dueño/a owner 13
durante during 10
durar to last 22
el durazno peach 13
duro, -a difficult, hard 10

e and (*before words beginning with i or hi*) 16
el eco echo 23
la economía economics 3; economy 10
económico, -a economical 7
ecuatoriano, -a Ecuadorian 2
echar al correo to send in the mail 20
echar de menos to miss someone or something 16
la edad age 23; **de cierta edad** middle-aged 16
el edificio building 12
la educación education 19
educativo, -a educational 20
efectivo, -a effective 13
efectuado, -a brought about 22
efectuar to bring about 22
egoísta selfish 21
el/la ejecutivo/a executive 21
ejercer to exercise 15
el ejercicio exercise P
las elecciones elections 22
eléctrico, -a electric 9
el elefante elephant 16
elegir (i) to elect; to choose 9
la elocuencia eloquence 20
elocuentemente eloquently 20
el/la embajador/a ambassador 22
emocionante exciting 24
empezar (ie) to begin 7; ~ **a** to begin to 17
el/la empleado/a sales clerk, employee 7

el empleo work, job, employment 9; ~ **a tiempo completo** full-time job 21; ~ **a tiempo parcial** part-time job 21

la empresa firm 21

en in, at 1; by 5; ~ **absoluto** not at all 18; ~ **cuanto** as soon as 18; ~ **punto** sharp, exactly 10; ~ **seguida** right away 6

el/la enamorado/a sweetheart; person in love 21

enamorado, -a: estar ~ de to be in love with 23

enamorarse (de) to fall in love (with) 12

encantar to like something very much 12

encargarse (de) to take charge (of) 24

encender (ie) to turn on *(lights or equipment)* 8

encima de above, over 14

encontrar (ue) to find; to meet 8; ~ **se** to meet (one another) 17; to be located 12

el/la enemigo/a enemy 21

enero January 11

enfermarse to get sick, fall ill 12

el/la enfermero/a nurse 2

enfrentar to face 22

enfrente de facing, opposite 14

enojarse to get mad, to get angry 12

la ensalada salad 6

ensayar to rehearse 23

enseñar to teach 17

entender (ie) to understand 8

entero, -a entire, whole 12

entonces then 3

la entrada entrance 5; ticket 7

entrar to enter 3; to come in 17; ~ **se** to sneak in 17

entre between, among 7; ~ **sí** among themselves 15

entregar to deliver, hand over 10

el/la entrenador/a trainer, coach 18

entrenarse to train 18

la entrevista interview 13

el/la entrevistado/a person interviewed 9

entrevistar to interview 9

entusiasmarse (con) to get enthusiastic about 12

enviar to send 14

la época age, era 24

el equipaje baggage 12

el equipo team 8

la equitación horseback riding 18

equivocarse to make a mistake 12

las escaleras stairs 14

el escarabajo beetle 16

la escena scene 7

escoger to choose 24

escolar *(adj.)* school 18

la escolaridad schooling 18

escribir to write 6; ~ **se** to write to each other 17

el escrito writing 21

el/la escritor/a writer 20

el escritorio desk 2

escuchar to listen (to) 3

la escuela school 9

la escultura sculpture 1

ese, -a that; **esos, -as** *(pl.)* those (over here) 8

esencial essential 9

la esgrima fencing 18

el/la esgrimista fencer 18

el español Spanish *(language)* P

español, -a Spanish 2

especial special 20

la especialidad specialty 24

la especialización specialization 21

especialmente specially 22

la especie species 16

el espectáculo show 7

el/la espectador/a spectator 8

el espejo mirror 19

la esperanza hope 19

esperar to wait (for) 3; to hope (for) 13

las espinacas spinach 13

el espíritu spirit 18

espléndido, -a splendid 24

la esposa wife 9

el esposo husband 9

el esquí skiing P

esquiar to ski 8

la esquina corner 5

establecer (zc) to establish 22; ~ **se** to settle down 19

la estación season 11; station P; ~ **biológica** biological research station 16; ~ **de ferrocarril** train station 12

el estadio stadium 5

el estado state 2

los Estados Unidos United States 1

la estampilla stamp 20

el estante (la estantería) bookcase 19

el estaño tin 10

estar *(irreg.)* to be 1

estatal state 11

la estatura: de estatura (mediana) of (medium) height 6

el este east P

este, -a this; **estos, -as** *(pl.)* these 4

el estéreo stereo 7

estereotipado, -a stereotyped 21

el estilo style 14

estimado, -a esteemed 17; ~ **señor/a** Dear Mr./Mrs. 20

estimar to esteem, admire 14

el estómago stomach 15

estrecho, -a narrow 24

la estrella star 7

estricto, -a strict 17

la estructura structure 1

el/la estudiante student 1

estudiantil student 10

estudiar to study 3

el estudio study 1; study *(room)* 14; ~ **de palabras** word study 1

estupendo, -a great, wonderful 3; **hace un día estupendo** it's a great day 11

la etapa stage 4

el evento event 13

evidente evident 14

evitar to avoid 10

el examen exam 3

excelente excellent 15

exclusivo, -a exclusive 13

la excursión excursion 12

la exhibición exhibition 20

exhibir to exhibit 20

exigir to demand 10

existir to exist 19

el éxito hit, success 7; **tener éxito** to be successful 7

la experiencia experience 20

el/la experto/a expert 16

explicar to explain 14

el/la explorador/a explorer 12

exportar to export 17

expresar to express 13

la expresión expression P

expuesto, -a exposed to 15

exquisito, -a exquisite 6

exterior outside, exterior 15

extinto, -a extinct 15

la extracción extraction 19

extranjero, -a foreign 4

extraño strange 20

extraordinario, -a extraordinary 12

exuberante exuberant 18

la fábrica factory 2; **~ de automóviles** automobile factory 2

fabuloso, -a fabulous 7

fácil easy 5; **es ~** it is easy 13

la facultad faculty, school (in a university) 23

la falda skirt 12

falso, -a false P

la falta lack 10

faltar to need 12

la fama fame P

la familia family 4

famoso, -a famous 14

la fantasía fantasy 24

fantástico, -a fantastic 18

el/la farmacéutico/a druggist 21

fascinar to fascinate; to be fascinated by 12

la fase phase 24

fatal fatal; awful, terrible 7

la fauna wildlife 16

favorito, -a favorite 7

febrero February 11

la fecha date 11

federal federal 11

la felicidad happiness 16

el/la feminista feminist 21

¡fenomenal! phenomenal! 7

feo, -a ugly 6

el festival festival 13

la fiesta party 3

la figura figure 3

la fila row 7

la filmadora movie camera 7

la filosofía philosophy P

fin: al ~ finally 19

el fin: ~ de mes end of the month 10; **~ de semana** weekend 14

el final end 22; **al final de** at the end of 5

finalmente finally 20

financiado, -a financed 16

la firma signature 10

firme firm 22

la física physics 3

flaco, -a thin 6

el flan baked custard 13

la flauta flute 23

la flor flower 19

la flora vegetation, plant life 16

folklórico, -a folkloric 7

el folleto pamphlet, brochure 24

fomentar to promote, encourage 18

la forma: en forma in good shape 18

la formación formation 23

formar to form 23; **~ parte** to make up 20

formular to formulate 22

la foto photo 8

la fotografía photography 24

fotografiar to photograph 16

el/la fotógrafo photographer 8

el francés French (language) 3

francés, -esa French 2

la frecuencia: con frecuencia frequently 14

frecuente frequent 10

frecuentemente frequently 9

frente a facing 5

la fresa strawberry 13

el fresco: hace fresco it's cool 11

los frijoles kidney beans 13

el frío: hace frío it's cold 11; **tener frío** to be cold (person) 7

la frontera frontier, border P

la fruta fruit 6

la frutería fruit shop 13

el/la frutero/a fruit vendor 13

fuera de outside of 14

fuerte strong 6

la fuerza force 22

la función function 24

el fútbol soccer 8; **~ americano** football 8

el futuro future 20

el gabinete cabinet 22

las gafas glasses 6

la gallina hen 16

el gallo rooster 16

el ganado cattle 14

ganar to win 13; to earn 19; **~ se la vida** to earn one's living 17

las ganas: tener ganas (de) to want (to) 14

el garaje garage 14

las gaseosas soda pop 13

la gastronomía gastronomy 24

el gato cat 16

la gelatina gelatin 13

general general 10; **en ~** generally 15

el general general 22

generalmente generally 13

generoso, -a generous 6

genial brilliant 24

la gente people 9

gentilmente kindly 14

la geografía geography P

la geología geology 3

gigantesco, -a gigantic 12

el gimnasio gym 8

la gloria glory 23

el gobierno government 9

gordo, -a fat 6

el gorro cap 12
la grabadora tape recorder 7
gracias thanks, thank you 1
la graduación graduation 24
graduar(se) to graduate 19
la gráfica illustration; graph, diagram 3
grande (gran) big, large; great 6
gris gray 6
gritar to shout 21
el grupo group P
los guantes gloves 12
guapo, -a attractive 6
guatemalteco, -a Guatemalan 2
gubernamental governmental 10
la guerra war 22
el guión hyphen 17
los guisantes peas 13
la guitarra guitar 23
gustar to please 3; **me gusta(n)** I like 3
el gusto taste 24

haber (irreg.) to have 11
la habitación bedroom 14
el/la habitante inhabitant 9
el hábito habit 16
hablar to speak 3; **de habla (española)** (Spanish) speaking 22
hace + a time expression (+ que) + a verb in the preterit ago 11
hace + weather expression it's + weather expression 11
hacer (irreg.) to do; to make 4; ~ **escala** to make a stop (on the way to a destination) 12; ~ **las maletas** to pack the suitcases 12; ~ **reservaciones** to make reservations 11; ~ **un viaje** to take a trip 12
la hacienda ranch 14
hallan: se ~ are found 17
la hamaca hammock 15
el hambre (f.): **tener hambre** to be hungry 7
hasta until 2; ~ **la vista** see you later (I'll be seeing you) P; ~

luego see you later P; ~ **mañana** see you tomorrow 1; ~ **pronto** see you soon; ~ **que** until 18
hay there is, there are 3
el hecho: de hecho in fact 22
el helado ice cream 6
el hemisferio hemisphere 13
la herencia inheritance 15
la hermana sister 4
el hermano brother; **los hermanos** (pl.) brothers, brother(s) and sister(s) 4
hermoso, -a lovely 6
hidroeléctrico, -a hydroelectric 9
el hierro iron 17
la hija daughter 2
el hijo son; child (as related to parents) 2
los hijos children 2; sons, son(s) and daughter(s) 4
hispánico, -a Hispanic P
la historia history 1; story 24
histórico, -a historic 20
hola hi, hello P
el hombre man 4; ~ **de negocios** businessman 21
hondureño, -a Honduran 2
la hora hour; time 10; **¿a qué hora?** at what time? 10; **a última hora** at the last minute 11
el horario schedule, timetable 12
la hormiga ant 16
horrible: es ~ it is horrible 13
el horror horror 21; **¡qué horror!** how dreadful! 4
el hospital hospital 2
el hotel hotel 5
hoy today 1
la huelga strike 10
los huevos eggs 13
humano, -a human 15
humilde humble, modest 6

la idea idea 21
la identidad identity 20
identificar to identify 15
el idioma language 4

la iglesia church 5
igual que (yo) just like (me) 6
la imagen image 21
imaginar to imagine 11
imitado, -a imitated P
el impacto impact 15
el imperio empire 10
el impermeable raincoat 12
la importancia importance 10
importante important 10; **es** ~ it is important 13
importar to matter 21
imposible impossible 5; **es** ~ it is impossible 13
la impresión impression 14
impresionante impressive 20
impresionar to impress 12
la inacción inaction 5
incluso including 16
incómodo, -a uncomfortable, uneasy 21
incomprensible: es perfectamente ~ it is totally incomprehensible 18
inconstante fickle 23
increíble incredible 8; **es** ~ it's incredible 13
la independencia independence 12
indígena native, indigenous 20
el/la indio/a Indian; Native American 12
indulgente lenient 4
industrial industrial 2
la industrialización industrialization 14
la influencia influence 20
la información information P
informar to inform 20
el informe report 14
la ingeniería engineering 3
el/la ingeniero civil civil engineer 14
el inglés English (language) P
inglés, -esa English 2
iniciado, -a begun 24
inmediatamente immediately, right away 6
inmediato, -a immediate 10

el/la inmigrante immigrant 6
inminente imminent 10
inscribir to inscribe 22
el insecto insect 16
insensible insensitive 21
insistir (en) to insist (on) 13
la instalación deportiva sports facility 18
la institución institution 20
instituir to establish 22
el instituto institute 9
el/la instructor/a instructor P
el instrumento instrument 23
inteligente intelligent 6
interamericano, -a Interamerican 13
el interés interest 6; **tener interés (en)** to be interested (in) 6
interesado, -a interested 16
interesante interesting 6; **es ~** it's interesting 6
interesar to interest 12
internacional international 6
íntimo, -a intimate 14
la intranquilidad intranquility 10
la introducción introduction 15
la investigación survey, research, investigation 9
el invierno winter 11
invitar to invite 14
ir (*irreg.*) to go 5; **~ a** to be going to 17; **~ a pie** to go by foot 8; **~ de camping** to go camping 16; **~ de compras** to go shopping 12; **~se** to go (away) 12; to leave 17
la isla island P
el italiano Italian (*language*) 3
italiano, -a Italian 2
la izquierda left (*in the political spectrum*); left hand, side 22; **a ~ de** to the left of 5

el jaguar jaguar 16
el jai alai jai alai 18
jamás never, not . . . ever 9
el jamón ham 13
japonés, -esa Japanese 2

el jeep jeep 16
el/la jefe/a boss 11
la jirafa giraffe 16
joven young 5
el/la joven youth 4
las judías verdes stringbeans 13
el juego game 18
jueves Thursday 1
el/la jugador/a player 18
jugar (ue) (al + deporte) to play a sport 8
el jugo juice 13
julio July 10
junio June 11
la junta council, board 22
junto a next to 5
justo, -a just 13
la juventud youth 17

el kilómetro kilometer 17

laboral pertaining to work or labor 10
el laboratorio laboratory 16
el lado: al lado de next to, beside 14
el ladrillo brick 17
el lago lake P
lamentar to regret 13
la lámpara lamp 19
la lana wool 17
la langosta lobster 13
el langostino prawn 13
el lápiz pencil 2
largo: a lo ~ de along (the length of) 15
largo, -a long 23
lástima: es una lástima it's a shame 13
latino, -a Latin, Hispanic 3
la lavadora washing machine 9
el lavaplatos dishwasher 9
lavarse to wash oneself 12
la lección lesson 1
la lectura reading 24
la leche milk 6
la lechería dairy, creamery 13
el/la lechero/a milkman/woman 13

la lechuga lettuce 13
leer to read 3
las legumbres vegetables 13
lejos (de) far (from) 5
la lengua language P; **~ moderna** modern language 1
el lenguado sole 13
el león lion 16
levantarse to get up 12
la libertad freedom, liberty 22; **~ de palabra** freedom of speech 22
libre free 22; **al aire ~** in the open air 16
la librería bookstore 4
el libro book P; **~ de texto** textbook 4
el/la líder leader 10
el limón lemon 13
la limonada lemonade 13
limpiar to clean 16
lindo, -a pretty, attractive 6
la línea line 14; **~ aérea** (*also,* **aerolínea**) airline 12
el lino (hilo) linen 17
lisonjero, -a flattering 21
la lista list 10
listo, -a ready 11; smart, clever 20
la literatura literature 3
el lobo wolf 16
localizado, -a located 18
loco, -a crazy 21
el/la locutor/a speaker, announcer 7
la lotería lottery 13
luego then 9; **~ que** as soon as 18
el lugar place 2
la luna de miel (el viaje de novios) honeymoon 23
lunes Monday 1
la luz light 8

la llama llama P
llamar to call, to phone 3; **~se** to be called 12; **me llamo** my name is (*literally,* I call myself) P; **se llama** his/her name is 2

el llano plain 14

la llegada arrival 6

llegar to arrive 3; ~ **a ser** to become 13

lleno, -a full 6; ~ **(de)** full (of) 12

llevar to take; to carry 8; to wear 12; ~ **a cabo** to carry out 22

llorar to cry 21

llover (ue) to rain 8

la lluvia rain 3

macho, -a male; manly; virile 21

la madera wood 15

la madre mother 4

la madrina godmother 9

la madrugada dawn, early morning 24

magnífico, -a magnificent 14

el maíz corn 15

majestuoso, -a majestic 15

mal badly 3

la maleta suitcase 12

malo, -a bad 6; bad (character); ill 20

la mamá mother 2

mandar to send, to order 11

el mando command 15

manejar to drive (a car) 12

la manera: de manera que in such a way that; so that 18

la manifestación demonstration 22

la mano hand 2

¡manos a la obra! to work! 12

mantener (irreg.) to maintain, keep 14

la mantequilla butter 13

la manzana apple 13

la mañana: de ~ in the morning 10

el mapa map P

la máquina de escribir typewriter 7

el mar sea P

el maratón marathon 8

maravilloso, -a marvelous 18

la marca brand 9

marcar un gol to score a goal 18

la marcha nupcial wedding march 23

la margarina margarine 13

el marido husband 9

marino, -a pertaining to the sea, marine 8

la mariposa butterfly 16

los mariscos shellfish 13

marrón (invariable) brown 6

martes Tuesday 1

marzo March 11

más more 3; ~ **... que** more than 13; ~ **de** (+ noun phrase) more than + noun phrase 13

el/la más + adjetivo the most + adjective, the + an adjective ending in -est 14

lo más pronto posible as soon as possible 11

la máscara mask 15

las matemáticas mathematics 3

los materiales materials 17

materno, -a maternal 15

matriarcal matriarchal 15

el matrimonio married couple, matrimony, marriage 9

maya Mayan 20

mayo May 11

el/la mayor greater 14

mayor greatest 10; **el (hermano) mayor** older (brother) 4

la mayoría majority 9

el/la mecánico/a mechanic 2

medianoche midnight 10

las medias stockings 12

la medicina medicine P

el/la médico/a medical doctor 1

medieval medieval 23

el medio ambiente environment 16

mediodía noon 10

los medios de transporte means of transportation 8; ~ **publicitarios** mass media 21

mejor: es ~ it's better 13

el/la mejor best 14

el mejoramiento improvement 10

mejorar to better, improve 10

mencionar to mention 10

el/la menor smallest; smaller 14; **el (hermano) menor** younger (brother) 4

menos less, take away 2; except 7; ~ **... que** less than; ~ **de +** noun phrase less than, fewer than + noun phrase 13; **a menos que** unless 18

el/la menos + adjective the least + adjective 14

mentir (ie) to lie 8

el mercado market 5

merecer (zc) to merit, deserve 24

el mes month 10; ~ **pasado** last month 10; **al mes** monthly 19

la mesa table 2

la mesita de noche night table 19

el metro subway 5; meter 12

la metrópolis metropolis 5

mexicano, -a Mexican 2

el micrófono microphone 7

el miedo: tener miedo to be afraid 7

el miembro de la familia family member 9

mientras while 6; ~ **tanto** meanwhile 16

miércoles Wednesday 1

mil thousand 19

militar military 22

la mina mine 10

mineral mineral 10

el minero miner 10

un mínimo de a minimum of 11

el/la ministro/a minister 11

el minuto minute 10; **hace un minuto** a minute ago 11

mirar to look (at) 3

mismo, -a same, very, self (with a pronoun) 21; **a sí ~** himself, herself 20; **al mismo tiempo** at the same time 12

misterioso, -a mysterious 12

moderno, -a modern 14

el/la **modista** women's tailor 21

el **modo: de modo que** so that, in such a way that 18; **de todos modos** at any rate, anyway 14

moldear to mold 20

moler (ue) to grind 17

molestar to bother, to annoy 12

el **momento** moment 4; **en este momento** at this moment 4

la **monarquía** monarchy 22

monetario, -a monetary 13

el **mono** monkey 16

el **monólogo** monologue 1

monótono, -a monotonous 9

la **montaña** mountain P

montar (andar, ir) en bicicleta (en autobús, metro) to ride a (go by) bicycle (bus, subway) 8

monumental monumental 24

el **monumento** monument 12

morado, -a purple 6

moreno, -a dark-complexioned 6

morir (ue) to die 8; **~ se de hambre** to starve (*literally*, to die from hunger) 17

la **mosca** fly 16

el **mosquito** mosquito 16

mostrar (ue) to show 8

la **motocicleta** motorcycle 8

el **movimiento** movement 21

la **muchacha** girl 4

el **muchacho** boy 4

muchas gracias thank you very much P

mucho, -a much; **muchos, -as** many, a lot of 4

mucho gusto nice to meet you P

la **mueblería** furniture store 19

los **muebles** furniture 19

la **muerte** death 22

la **muestra** display, sample, example 20

la **mujer** woman 4; **~ de negocios** businesswoman 21

multicolor multicolor 15

la **multitud** multitude 24

mundial world 13

el **mundo** world P

el **mural** mural P

el **museo** museum 5

la **música** music P; **~ rock** rock music 7

musical musical 17

muy very 2; **~ bien** very well 1

nacer (zc) to be born 19

el **nacimiento** birth 23

la **nación** nation 8

nacional national 12

la **nacionalidad** nationality 2

nada nothing (at all) 9; **de ~** you're welcome, not at all 2

nadar to swim 8

nadie nobody, no one 9

la **naranja** orange 13

la **nariz** nose 15

la **natación** swimming 8

natural natural 16

navegar to sail 8

la **neblina: hay neblina** it's foggy 11

necesario, -a necessary 11; **es ~** it is necessary 13

la **necesidad** need, necessity 15

necesitar to need 3

negar (ie) to deny 8; **~ se a** to refuse to 12

la **negociación** negotiation 10

el **negocio** business 13; **el/la hombre/mujer de negocios** businessman/woman 21

negro, -a black 6

nervioso, -a nervous 5

la **nevera** refrigerator (*with freezer section*) 9

ni . . . ni neither . . . nor 9

nicaragüense Nicaraguan 2

la **nieta** granddaughter 9

el **nieto** grandson 9

los **nietos** grandchildren 9

nieva it's snowing 11

el **nilón** nylon 17

ningún/ninguno, -a no, not any; none 9

el/la **niño/a** small child 4

el **nivel: ~ de vida** standard of living 9; **~ social** social level 21

no no, not 1; **~ hay de que** don't mention it P; **~ . . . más que** only 13

nocturno, -a night, nocturnal 24

la **noche: de ~** in the late evening or at night 10

nombrar to name 18

el **nombre** name 8; **~ de pila** first name 6

el **noreste** northeast P

el **noroeste** northwest P

el **norte** north P

norteamericano, -a North American 2

nostálgico, -a nostalgic 3

la **nota** note 1

la **noticia** news 10

el **noticiero** newscast 13

noveno, -a ninth 16

la **novia** fiancée, sweetheart 6

el **noviazgo** courtship 23

noviembre November 11

el **novio** fiancé, sweetheart 6

la **nube** cloud 12

nublado: está ~ it's cloudy 11

la **nuera** daughter-in-law 9

nueve nine 2

nuevo, -a new 5; **de nuevo** again 10

el **número** number P; size (*of shoes*) 12

numeroso, -a numerous 15

nunca never, not . . . ever 9

o or 1; **~ . . . o** either . . . or 9

el **objeto** object; purpose 2

la **obra** work 20; **~ maestra** masterpiece 24; **¡manos a ~!** to work! 12

el/la **obrero/a** (*blue collar*) worker 9

observar to observe 16

el **obstáculo** obstacle 23

obtener (*irreg.*) to obtain 10

la ocasión occasion 15
occidental western 13
el océano ocean P
octavo, -a eighth 16
octubre October 11
la ocupación occupation 21
ocupado, -a busy 6
ocurrir happen; occur 7
ocho eight 2
el oeste west P
oficial official 8
oficialmente officially 22
la oficina office 10
ofrecer (zc) to offer 16
oír (irreg.) to hear 7
ojalá (I) hope 13
el ojo eye 15
olvidar to forget 3; ~se (de) to forget (about) 14
once eleven 2
opinar to think, have an opinion 21
la opinión opinion 6
la oportunidad opportunity 14
optimista optimistic 6
la orden: a ~ at your service; (pl.) a sus órdenes 2
la oreja ear 15
la organización organization 16
organizar to organize 16
orgulloso, -a proud 15
oriental eastern 15
el oriente eastern region (of Ecuador) 11
el origen origin P
la orilla del mar seashore 8
el oro gold 17
la orquesta orchestra 23
la ortografía spelling 1
oscuro, -a dark 6; dark (complexion) 20
el oso bear 16
el otoño fall, autumn 11
otra vez again 12
otro, -a other, another 1
la oveja sheep 16
¡oye! hey, listen! 6

el padre father; los ~ parents; fathers 4

el padrino godfather 9
págar to pay 7
la pagina page P
el país country P
el paisaje countryside 12
el pájaro bird P
la palabra word; ~ análoga cognate P
la palanca leverage, "pull" 11
el pan bread 13
la panadería bakery 13
el/la panadero/a baker 13
panameño, -a Panamanian 2
panamericano, -a Panamerican 18
el panorama panorama P
los pantalones pants 12
la papa potato 13
el papá father 4
el papel paper 2; role 15; ~ de carta letter paper 20; ~ de escribir writing paper 20
el papeleo "red tape" 11
la papelera waste basket 2
la papeleta voting paper, ballot 22
el paquete package 20
para for P; ~ fines de mes by the end of the month 10; ~ mí for me 7; ~ que so that, in order that (purpose, goal) 18; ~ servirle at your service 2
el parabrisas windshield 17
paraguayo, -a Paraguayan 2
paralizar to paralyze 10
parar to stop 14
pardo, -a brown 6
parecer (zc) to seem 11
la pared wall 14
la pareja couple 23
el paréntesis parenthesis 17
el/la pariente/a relative 9
el parque park 5
la parte part 10
participar participate 8
particular private 9
particularmente particularly 21
el/la partidario/a follower 22
el partido game 8; ~ político political party 22

partir: a ~ de from 7
pasado, -a last 10
el/la pasajero/a passenger 12
el pasaporte passport 12
pasar to spend (time) 3; to happen 13; to pass 23; ~ las vacaciones to spend one's vacation 5
el pasatiempo hobby 14
la pasión passion 13
pasivamente passively 21
el pastel pastry, pie 13; pastel 24
la pastelería pastry shop 13
el/la pastelero/a baker 13
el patinaje skating 8
patinar to skate 8
el patio patio 14
el pato duck 16
el/la patrón/a patron (saint) 4
el pavo turkey 13
pedir (i) to ask (for); to request 9; ~ la mano en matrimonio to propose 23
peinarse to comb one's hair 12
la película film 7
el peligro danger 16
pelirrojo, -a red-haired 6
el pelo hair 15; de pelo castaño brown-haired 6; de pelo negro black-haired 6
la pelota (el béisbol) baseball 18
el/la peluquero/a hairdresser 21
la península peninsula P
pensar (ie) to think; to intend 8; ~ + de to have an opinion of 8; ~ + en to think about 8
peor worse 14
el/la peor the worst 14
pequeño, -a small 6
la pera pear 13
perder (ie) to lose 8
perdido, -a lost 24
perdón excuse me 5
perezoso, -a lazy 6
perfectamente perfectly 4; es ~ incomprensible it's totally incomprehensible 18
el periódico newspaper 2

el/la periodista newspaper reporter, journalist 18
permanecer (zc) to remain 11
permitir to permit 13
pero but 3
el perro dog 16
perseguir pursue 12
la persona person 2
personal personal 14
pertenecer (zc) to belong to 15
peruano, -a Peruvian 2
la pesca fishing 15
la pescadería fish market 13
el/la pescadero/a fish vendor 13
el pescado fish 13
pescar to fish 12
pesimista pessimistic 6
el petróleo petroleum (n.) 11
petrolero, -a petroleum (adj.) 11
el piano piano 23
el pie foot 15; **a ~** on foot 5
la piedra stone 11
la pierna leg 15
la pieza piece 15
el/la piloto pilot 21
la pimienta pepper 13
pintar to paint 8
la piña pineapple 13
la pirámide pyramid 3
la piscina swimming pool 8
el piso floor 4
la pista ski slope; race track 8
la pista y campo track and field 8
la pizarra chalkboard P
el plan plan 11
el plano plan, diagram 11
la planta plant 15; **~ hidroeléctrica** hydroelectric plant 9
la plantación plantation 15
el plástico plastic 17
la plata silver 17
el plátano plantain 15
el plato plate 13; dish (food) 24
la playa beach 8
la plaza square 5
poblado, -a populated, inhabited P
pobre poor 6
poco: ~ a ~ little by little 15;

un ~ de a little (of) P
poco, -a little, few 5
el poder power 22
poder (irreg.) to be able; can 7
poderoso, -a powerful 15
el/la policía policeman/policewoman 5; **el/la agente de policía** police officer 5
el poliéster polyester 17
político, -a political 15; **el partido político** political party 22
el pollo chicken 13
poner (irreg.) to put 7; **~se** to put on (clothing) 12; **~se (a)** (+ inf.) to begin (to), to start (to) 17
popular popular 7
un poquito a little bit 4
por for, in exchange for 5; **~ aquí** around here 4; **~ ciento** percent 10; **~ ejemplo** for example 7; **~ eso** for that reason 16; **~ favor** please P; **~ fin** finally 14; **~ lo menos** at least 7; **~ parte de** on the part of 18; **~ todas partes** everywhere 14
¿por qué? why? 5
porque because 5
la posibilidad possibility 19
posible possible 5
la posición position 15
los postres desserts 13
el pozo well 15; **~ petrolífero** oil well 15
la práctica practice 1
practicar to practice 3
practicar los deportes to practice (go in for) sports 8
el precio price 10
el precipicio precipice, cliff 12
precisamente precisely 16
precisar to specify, state exactly 20
predecir (irreg.) to predict 11
preferible: es ~ it is preferable 13
preferir (ie) to prefer 8
el prefijo prefix 5

la pregunta question 1
preguntar to ask 3
el prejuicio bias, prejudice 14
preliminar preliminary 2
el premio prize 13
la prensa press 22
la preocupación worry 10
preocupado, -a worried 16
preocuparse (de) to worry (about) 12
la preparación preparation 14
preparar to prepare 15
prescribir to prescribe 22
la presentación introduction P
presentado, -a presented 21
presentar to present 7
la preservación del ambiente environmental conservation 16
preservar to preserve 16
el/la presidente/a president 22
prevenir (irreg.) to prevent 7
preventivo, -a preventive 10
la prima female cousin 6
primario, -a primary 19
la primavera spring 11
primer/primero, -a first 10
el primer plano foreground 22
primitivo, -a primitive 16
el primo male cousin 6
principal main 10
principalmente mainly 17
principio: al ~ de at the beginning of 19
prisa: de ~ quickly, hurriedly 17
privilegiado, -a privileged 22
probable probable 13
el problema problem 10; **¡qué problema!** what a problem! 4
la procesadora de palabras word processor 7
el proceso process 22
la producción production 10
el producto product 13
la profesión profession 6
profesional professional 8
el/la profesor/a professor 1
profundamente deeply, profoundly 20
el programa program P

prohibir to prohibit, forbid 13
prometer to promise 3
pronto quickly, soon 16; **tan ~ como** as soon as 18
la pronunciación pronunciation 1
propio, -a one's own 15
proponer (*irreg.*) to propose 7
el propósito: a propósito by the way 11
proteger to protect 16
protestar to protest 10
la provincia province P
próximo, -a next 7
proyectar to project 21
el proyecto project 9; **los proyectos de vivienda** housing projects 14
la prueba proof 24
la psicología psychology 3
la publicación publication P
la publicidad publicity 21
publicitario, -a pertaining to publicity 17
público, -a public 9
el público en general general public 20
el pueblo town 2; people, nation 20; **~ natal** home town 19
puede ser maybe; that can be 13
la puerta door 2
el puerto port 11
puertorriqueño, -a Puerto Rican 2
pues well P
el puesto position, appointment 11
puesto que because, since 18
el punto period 17; point 20; **~ y coma** semi-colon 17; **los puntos suspensivos** ellipses 17; **los puntos cardinales** points of the compass P; **~ de vista** point of view 15; **dos puntos** colon 17; **en punto** sharp, exactly 10

que that 4; **tener ~** to have to, must 7

¿qué? what? 1; **¿de ~?** from what? 5; what about? 7
¡qué . . . ! (+ *adjective* or *noun*) how . . . ! 6
¡qué barbaridad! how amazing! (how dreadful, etc., depending on context) 4
¡qué bien! how nice! 4
¡qué chévere! terrific! 6
¿qué esperamos? what are we waiting for? 8
¿qué hora es? what time is it? 10
¡qué lástima! what a pity 4
¿qué le pasó? what happened to him? 13
¡que le (te) vaya bien! have a good time! 12
¿qué quiere decir . . . ? what does . . . mean? P
¡que se (te) divierta(s) mucho! enjoy yourself! 12
¿qué tal? how are things? 1
quedar to remain; to be left 7
quedarle bien (grande, pequeño) to fit well (to be large, small) 12
quedo de usted (ustedes) atentamente cordially yours 20
quejarse (de) to complain (about) 12
querer (*irreg.*) to want; to wish; to love 8
querido, -a beloved, dear 3; **~ (Pedro, amigo/a)** dear (Pedro, friend) 20
el queso cheese 13
¿quién? who?; **¿quiénes?** (*pl.*) 4; **¿a ~?** who, to whom? 4; **¿de ~?** whose? 4
la química chemistry 3
quince fifteen 2
quinto, -a fifth 16
quitarse to take off (*clothing*) 12
quizás perhaps 14

rabioso, -a furious, very angry 5
el/la radio radio 9
el radioprograma radio program 17
el radiorreloj clock radio 17

la raíz root 20
la rana frog 16
raras veces rarely 9
el rascacielos skyscraper 24
rasgar to tear 23
el rato while, short time 23
el ratón mouse 16
la raya dash 17
la razón reason 18; **tener razón** to be right 7
realmente really 12
recibir to receive 3; **recibe un abrazo fuerte de tu (amigo/a)** receive a strong embrace from your friend 20
reciente recent 14
el recogedor (crop) picker 15
recomendar (ie) to recommend 10
reconciliar to reconcile 22
el reconocimiento recognition 22
recordar (ue) to remember 8; to remind 20
el recreo recreation 19
el recurso resource 10
redistribuir to redistribute 19
la reducción reduction 10
reelegir (i) to reelect 19
referirse (ie) to refer to 15
la refinería refinery 17
la reforma reform 10
el refrán proverb, saying 5
regalar to give (*a gift*) 23
la regata boat race, regatta 8
regatear to bargain, to haggle 15
el régimen regimen 22
la región region 10
regional regional 18
la regla ruler 2
regresar to return 5
el regreso return 16
regular not bad 1
la reina queen 22
reír (i) to laugh 9; **~se (de)** to laugh (about) 12
la relación relation 20
releer to reread 19
religioso, -a religious 15
el reloj watch, clock; **~ co-**

rriente regular watch (clock); ~ **digital** digital watch (clock); ~ **de pulsera** wrist watch; ~ **de pared** wall clock 10

el remitente sender 20

la repercusión repercussion 10

el repertorio repertoire 23

repetido, -a repeated 22

repetir (i) to repeat 9

el/la reportero/a reporter 8

la representación representation 12

el/la representante representative 9

representar to represent; to portray 21

representativo, -a representative 24

el reptil reptile 15

la república republic 22

el repuesto spare (part) 16

requerir (ie) to require, need 17

la reservación reservation 11

resistente resistant P

resolver (ue) to resolve, fix 10

responder to respond, answer 5

la responsabilidad responsibility 21

la respuesta answer 9

el restaurante restaurant 5

los restos remains 17

resultar to result 13

resurgir to rise up again 22

retener (irreg.) to retain 11

la reunión meeting 10

reunirse to get together 10

la revista magazine 2

la revolución revolution 20

el rey king 22

rico, -a delicious, rich 6

el río river P

riquísimo, -a very delicious; very rich 6

el ritmo rhythm 1

el rodaje shooting, filming 24

la rodilla knee 15

rogar (ue) to beg 13

rojo, -a red 6

romper to break 15

la ropa de (verano) (summer) clothing 12

rosado, -a pink 6

rubio, -a blond 6

el ruido noise 19

la ruina ruin 12

el ruso Russian (language) 4

sábado Saturday 1; **el** ~ **(domingo, etcétera) pasado** last Saturday (Sunday, etc.) 10; **los sábados** on Saturdays 3

saber (irreg.) to know (something) 9

sacar (fotos) to take (pictures) 8

sagrado, -a sacred, holy 24

la sal salt 13

la sala living room 14

el salario wage(s) 21

salir (irreg.) to leave, to go out 7; ~ **se** to leave, escape 17

el salón room, living room, hall 14

la salsa sauce 3

saludar to greet 1; ~ **se** to greet one another 17

el saludo greeting 14

salvadoreño, -a Salvadoran 2

salvaje wild 16

las sandalias sandals 12

el sándwich sandwich 6

el/la sastre tailor 21

satisfacer (zc) to satisfy 24

satisfecho, -a satisfied 10

la secadora de ropa clothes dryer 9

la sección section 11

el/la secretario/a secretary 13

secundario, -a secondary 19

la sed: tener sed to be thirsty 7

la seda silk 17

seguida: en ~ right away 6

seguir (i) to follow 9

según according to 3

segundo, -a second 4

la seguridad security 10

seguro, -a certain 17; **estoy** ~ I'm sure 13

seis six 2

la selva jungle 16

el sello stamp 20

la semana week 1; ~ **entrante** the coming week 13; ~ **pasada** last week 10; **este fin de semana** this weekend 8

el semestre semester 9

el senado senate 22

el/la senador/a senator 22

la sensación sensation 13

sentado, -a seated 6

sentarse (ie) to sit down 12

el sentimiento feeling 21

sentir (ie) to regret 13; ~ **nostalgia (por)** to be homesick (for) 19; ~ **se** to feel 12

la señal signal 20

el señor gentleman; **señor** (+ last name) Mr. (+ last name) 1

la señora lady; **señora** (+ last name) Mrs. (+ last name) 1

la señorita young lady; **señorita** (+ last name) Miss (+ last name) P

la separación separation 23

septiembre September 11

séptimo, -a seventh 16

ser (irreg.) to be 1

la serenata serenade 23

la serie series 20

la seriedad seriousness 18

serio, -a serious 13

serio: tan en ~ so seriously 18

la serpiente snake 16

el servicio service 12

el/la servidor/a servant 20; **su servidor/a** at your service 20

la servilleta napkin 12

servir (i) to serve 9

severo, -a strict, demanding 4

sexto, -a sixth 16

si if 5

sí yes; **ah, sí** oh, yes 1

siempre always 7

siento: lo siento I'm sorry P

la sierra sierra (mountain range) P

siete seven 2

el siglo century 12

significativo, -a significant 22

los signos: ~ **de exclamación (admiración)** exclamation points 17; ~ **de interrogación** question marks 17; ~ **de puntuación** punctuation marks 17

siguiente following 12

la silla chair 2; ~ **mecedora** rocking chair 19

el sillón armchair 19

el símbolo symbol 15

similar similar 12

simpático, -a attractive, nice, friendly 6

sin without; ~ **ti** without you (*fam.*); ~ **embargo** nevertheless 10; ~ **que** without 18

el sindicato syndicate, labor union 24

el sinnúmero endless number 18

sino but 24

el sistema system 15

el sitio place 2

la situación situation 10

situado, -a located 16

sobre about 1

sobre todo especially, most of all 3

el sobre envelope 20

el sobrenombre nickname 6

sobrevivir survive P

la sobrina niece 9

el sobrino nephew 9

social social 15

la sociedad society 15

la sociología sociology 3

sociológico, -a sociological 9

el sofá sofa 19

el sol: hace sol it's sunny 11

solamente only 9

solicitar trabajo (empleo) to apply for work 21

la solicitud de empleo job application 21

solo, -a alone 7

sólo only 7

la soltera single woman 9

el soltero bachelor 9

soltero, -a single, unmarried 2

la solución solution 13

el sombrero hat 12

sonreír (i) to smile 9

sorprender to surprise 13

el sótano basement 14

subir to go up 17; ~**se** to climb with effort 17

la suegra mother-in-law 9

el suegro father-in-law 9

el sueldo salary 10

el suelo floor 14

el sueño: tener sueño to be sleepy 7

la suerte: tener suerte to be lucky; **¡qué suerte!** what luck! 6

el suéter sweater 12

suficiente enough, sufficient 19

el sufijo suffix 3

sufrir to suffer 21

sugerir (ie) to suggest 8

sumamente very 14

superficial superficial 21

superfluo, -a superfluous 9

suponer (*irreg.*) to suppose 22

el sur south P

el sureste southeast P

el suroeste southwest P

suscribir to subscribe 22

el sustantivo noun 1

tacaño, -a stingy 6

el taco heel of shoe 6

tal such (a) 20; ~ **vez** perhaps 21

la talla size (*of clothing*) 12

el tamaño size (*general term*) 12

también also, too 1

el tambor drum 23

tampoco neither, not . . . either 9

tan so 12; ~ . . . **como** as (so) . . . as 15; ~ **en serio** so seriously 18; ~ **pronto como** as soon as 18

el tango tango (*dance*) 3

¡tanto! so much! so far! 5; **al** ~ up to date 14; **tanto/a, tantos/ as** + *noun* + **como** as much (many) . . . as 15

tardar (en) to be late (in) 12

tarde late 10; **de la** ~ in the afternoon or early evening 10; **esta misma** ~ this very afternoon 11; **es** ~ it's late 1

la tarea task, assignment 21

la tarjeta postal postcard 20

el taxi taxi 5

la taza cup 13

el té tea 6

el teatro theater 5

el técnico en computadoras computer technician 6

técnico, -a technical 9

tecnológico, -a technological 20

el techo roof 14

la tela cloth 15

la teleducación educational TV 20

el teléfono telephone 9

el telegrama telegram 11

la telenovela soap opera 21

el/la televidente TV viewer 20

televisado, -a televised 7

el televisor (en blanco y negro, a colores) (black-and-white, color) TV 7

temer to fear 13

el temor fear 22

el templo temple, church 23

temprano early 10

la tendencia tendency 9

el/la tendero/a grocer 13

el tenedor fork 13

tener (*irreg.*) to have 2; ~ **que** + *inf.* to have to + *inf.*; must 7

tener . . . años to be . . . years old 7; ~ **calor** to be warm (*persons*) 7; ~ **ganas (de)** to want, to feel like 14; ~ **hambre** to be hungry 7; ~ **interés (en)** to be interested (in) 6

el tenis tennis 8

tercer/tercero, -a third 10

terminar to end, finish 7; ~ **(de)** to finish 17

la ternera veal 13

el terreno land P

terrible terrible 6

el **terror**   terror   7
terrorista   terrorist   22
el **texto**   text   4
la **tía**   aunt   9
el **tiempo**   time   11; weather   11;
  hace buen (mal) tiempo   the
  weather is good (bad)   11
la **tienda**   store   5; ~ **de cam-**
  paña   tent   16; ~ **de comesti-**
  bles   grocery store   13
la **tierra**   land, earth   3
el **tigre**   tiger   16
el **tío**   uncle   9
típico, -a   typical   21
el **tipo**   type   P
el **título**   title   P
el **tocadiscos**   record player   4
tocar   to play (a musical instrument)   23
el **tocino**   bacon   13
todavía   still   14
todo, -a   all, everything   6;
  todos/as (pl.)   everybody   9;
  todo el mundo   the whole world,
  everybody; **de todos modos**   at
  any rate, anyway   14; **todo el**
  país   the whole country   13
tolteca   Toltec   20
tomar   to take; to have (food, drink),
  to eat   3; ~ **el tren**   to take the
  train   12; ~ **una copa**   to have a
  drink (liquor)   24
el **tomate**   tomato   13
tonto, -a   stupid   6
el **toro**   bull   16
la **toronja**   grapefruit   13
la **torre**   tower   24
la **torta**   cake
el **total: en total**   in total   19
trabajar   to work   2
el **trabajo**   work   10
el **trabalenguas**   tongue twister   6
la **tradición**   tradition   15
tradicional   traditional   15
tradicionalmente   traditionally   23
traducir (irreg.)   to translate   9
traer (irreg.)   to bring   7
el **tráfico**   traffic   19
el **traje**   dress, suit   12; ~ **de**

bodas   wedding dress   23
tranquilo, -a   calm   2
transcurrido, -a   passed, elapsed
  22
el **tránsito**   traffic   5
transmitir   to transmit   10
el **transporte público**   public
  transportation   9
tratar   to deal with   22; ~ **(de)**
  to try to   9
traumático, -a   traumatic   22
trece   thirteen   2
treinta   thirty   7
tremendo, -a   tremendous   7
el **tren**   train   7; **en tren**   by
  train   7
tres   three   2
la **tribu**   tribe   15
triste   sad   5; **es** ~   it's sad   13
triunfante   triumphant   13
el **triunfo**   triumph   18
la **trompeta**   trumpet   23
tropical   tropical   16
la **tuna**   student musical group
  composed of guitarists and
  singers   23
el **tuno**   member of a student
  tuna   23
el **turismo**   tourism   8
el/la **turista**   tourist   12

u (= **o** before **o** or **ho**)   or   9
último, -a   last   15; **a última**
  hora   at the last minute   11
la **universidad**   university   P
universitario, -a   pertaining to a
  university   23
uno, una   one   2
urbanístico, -a   referring to the
  city   14
urbano, -a   city, urban   19
urgente: es ~   it's essential   10
la **urna**   ballot box   22
uruguayo, -a   Uruguayan   2
usar   to use   3; to wear   12; ~
  gafas   to wear glasses   6
el **uso**   use, usage   22
los **utensilios**   utensils   13
útil   useful   1

utilizar   to use   P
las **uvas**   grapes   13

la **vaca**   cow   16
las **vacaciones**   vacation   5
vacío, -a   empty   6
valer (irreg.)   to be worth   20
el **valor**   value   15
vamos a + infinitive   let's + verb   5
el **vapor**   steamship   8
la **variación**   variation   1
variado, -a   diversified, varied   24
la **variedad**   variety   16
varios, -as   several   10
el **vaso**   glass   13
las **veces: a veces**   sometimes   17;
  raras veces   rarely   9
el/la **vecino/a**   neighbor   8
la **vegetación**   vegetation   18
los **vegetales**   vegetables   13
veinte   twenty   2
la **vela**   sail   8
el **velero**   sailboat   8
el/la **vendedor/a**   vendor,
  salesman, saleslady   21
vender   to sell   6
venezolano, -a   Venezuelan   2
venir (irreg.)   to come   7
la **venta**   sale   15
la **ventaja**   advantage   12
la **ventana**   window   2
ver   to see   4; **al** ~   on seeing   12;
  verse   to see each other   17
el **verano**   summer   11
el **verbo**   verb   1
la **verdad: es** ~   it is true   13;
  ¿verdad o falso?   true or false?   3
verde   green   6; ~ **oscuro**   dark
  green   6
la **vergüenza**   disgrace, shame   21
el **verso**   verse   23
el **vestido**   dress   12
vestirse (i)   to get dressed   12
la **vez: una vez al mes**   once a
  month   19; **otra vez**   again   12;
  tal vez   perhaps   21
viajar   to travel   3; ~ **en avión**
  (tren, barco)   to travel by plane
  (train, boat)   8

el viaje: ~ **de negocios** business trip 11; ~ **de novios (la luna de miel)** honeymoon 23; **¡buen viaje!** have a good trip! 12

el viajero traveler 12

la vicuña vicuna P

la vida life 4; ~ **matrimonial** married life 23

el vídeo video 7

el videodisco videodisk 7

la vieja old woman 4

el viejo old man 4

viejo, -a old 6

el viento: hace viento it's windy 11

viernes Friday 1

el vino wine 6; **el** ~ **(tinto o blanco)** (red or white) wine 13

el/la violoncelista cellist 23

el violoncelo violoncello, cello 23

la visión vision 24

la visita visit 20

el/la visitante visitor 15

visitar to visit 3

la vista view; **a** ~ **de pájaro** a bird's-eye view P; ~ **parcial** partial view 18

la vivienda housing 9; **los proyectos de vivienda** housing projects 14

vivir to live 2; ~ **juntos** to live together 9

vivo, -a alive 23

el vocabulario vocabulary 1

volar (ue) to fly 12

el vólibol (voleibol) volleyball 18

volver (ue) to return 7

votar to vote 22

el voto vote 22

la voz voice 21

el vuelo flight 6

y and 1

ya already; now 6; ~ **no** no longer 7; ~ **no quedan** there aren't any left 7; ~ **que** now that, since 18

la yegua mare 16

el yerno son-in-law 9

¡yo sí! I do! 3

la zanahoria carrot 13

el/la zapatero/a shoemaker; cobbler 21

los zapatos shoes 12

la zona zone 24

el zorro fox 16

English-Spanish vocabulary

This vocabulary contains a selected listing of common words presented in the lesson vocabularies. Many word sets, such as foods, sports, animals, months of the year, are not included. Page references to word sets are given in the index.

Abbreviations used:

adj.	adjective	*m.*	masculine
adv.	adverb	*n.*	noun
f.	feminine	*pl.*	plural
inf.	infinitive	*sing.*	singular
irreg.	irregular	*trans.*	transitive

a lot   mucho *(adv.)*
able: be able   poder *(irreg.)*
about   sobre
above   encima de, sobre
accent   el acento (tilde)
according to   según
accounting   la contabilidad
action   la acción, el acto
actor   el actor
actress   la actriz
admire   estimar
advantage   la ventaja
advise   aconsejar
afraid: be afraid   tener miedo
after   después; **after** *(doing something)*   después de (+ *inf.*)
afternoon   la tarde; **in the afternoon**   de (por) la tarde
again   de nuevo, otra vez
age   la edad; **age (era)**   la época
ago   hace + *time expression* (+ que) + *preterit*; **a minute ago** hace un minuto
agree   estar de acuerdo
agreed   de acuerdo
air conditioner   el acondicionador de aire
airline   la aerolínea, la línea aérea
airplane   el avión, el aeroplano
airport   el aeropuerto
alarm clock   el despertador
alligator   el caimán

almost   casi
alone   solo/a
already   ya
also   también
although   aunque
always   siempre
ambassador   el/la embajador/a
among   entre
ancestor   el antepasado
ancestry   la descendencia
and   y, e *(before* i *or* hi*)*
angry   rabioso/a
announce   anunciar
announcer   el/la locutor/a
annoy   molestar
answer   contestar *(v.)*, responder *(v.)*; la respuesta *(n.)*
ant   la hormiga
anyway   de todos modos
apartment   el apartamento
appear   aparecer (zc)
apple   la manzana
appointment   la cita
April   abril
are you going to be in . . . ?   ¿va a estar en . . . ?
arm   el brazo
armchair   el sillón
around   alrededor de
around here   por aquí
arrive   llegar
art   el arte *(m. or f.)*

artist   el/la artista
as (so) . . . as   tan + *(adj. or adv.)* + como
as if   como si
as much (many) . . . as   tanto/a, tantos/as + *(noun)* + como
as soon as   en cuanto, tan pronto como, luego que
as soon as possible   lo más pronto posible
ask   preguntar; **ask (for)**   pedir (i)
asleep   dormido/a
assure   asegurar
at   en; **at** *(clock time)*   a la (a las) + *number*
at any rate   de todos modos
at least   por lo menos
at the last minute   a última hora
at the same time   al mismo tiempo
at this moment   en este momento
at what time?   ¿a qué hora?
at your service   a la orden; *(pl.)* a sus órdenes
athlete   el/la atleta
atmosphere   el ambiente
attend   asistir (a)
attractive   guapo/a
August   agosto
aunt   la tía
automobile factory   la fábrica de automóviles
autumn   el otoño

avenue   la avenida
avoid   evitar

baby   el/la bebé
bachelor   el soltero
bacon   el tocino
badly   mal
baggage   el equipaje
ballot box   la urna
bank   el banco
baseball   el béisbol, la pelota
basket   la canasta
basketball   el baloncesto, el básquetbol
bathing resort   el balneario
bathroom   el cuarto de baño
bay   la bahía
be   ser (irreg.), estar (irreg.)
be afraid   tener miedo
be cold (persons)   tener frío
be hungry   tener hambre
be interested in   tener interés en
be lucky   tener suerte
be right   tener razón
be sleepy   tener sueño
be thirsty   tener sed
be warm (persons)   tener calor
be wrong   no tener razón
beach   la playa
bear   el oso
beautiful   hermoso/a
beauty   la belleza
because   porque; because of   a causa de
become   llegar a ser
become damaged   dañarse
bed   la cama; go to bed   acostarse (ue)
bedroom   la alcoba, el cuarto de dormir, la habitación, el dormitorio
beef   la carne de res
beefsteak   el bistec
beer   la cerveza
before   antes (de) que; before ... (+ -ing)   antes de (+ inf.)
beg   rogar (ue)
begin   empezar (ie), comenzar (ie); begin to   empezar a, comenzar a
believe   creer

belong to   pertenecer (zc) a, ser de . . .
below   debajo de
beside   al lado de
better   mejor
between   entre
bicycle   la bicicleta
big   grande
bill   la cuenta
bird   el pájaro
birth   el nacimiento
black   negro/a
black-haired   de pelo negro
block   la cuadra
blond   rubio/a
blouse   la blusa
blue   azul; navy blue   azul marino
boat (small)   la barca; motor boat   el bote de motor
boat race   la regata
body   el cuerpo
book   el libro
bookcase   el estante, la estantería
bookstore   la librería
boots   las botas
border (frontier)   la frontera
boring   aburrido/a
born: be born   nacer (zc)
boss   el/la jefe/a
bother   molestar
bowling   los bolos
boy   el muchacho, el chico
brand   la marca
bread   el pan
break   romper
breakfast   el desayuno
brick   el ladrillo
brilliant   genial
bring   traer (irreg.)
brochure   el folleto
brother   el hermano
brother-in-law   el cuñado
brown (for color)   café, marrón, pardo/a; brown (for hair)   castaño/a
brown-haired   de pelo castaño
build   construir
building   el edificio
bull   el toro

bullfight   la corrida de toros
bus   el autobús, el camión (México)
business   el negocio
business person   el/la hombre/ mujer de negocios
business trip   el viaje de negocios
busy   ocupado/a
but   pero, sino
butcher shop   la carnicería
butter   la mantequilla
butterfly   la mariposa
buy   comprar
by the end of the month   para fines de mes
by the way   a propósito
by train   en tren
by!   ¡chau!, ¡adiós!

cabinet   el gabinete
cafe   el café
cafeteria   la cafetería
cake   la torta
calculator   la calculadora
call   llamar (por teléfono)
called: be called   llamarse
camera   la cámara (fotográfica)
camping: go camping   ir de camping
canal   el canal
cancel   cancelar
candy   los caramelos
capital city   la capital
car   el automóvil, el carro, el coche
carpenter   el carpintero
carrot   la zanahoria
carry   llevar
carry out   llevar a cabo
cassette   el cassette
cat   el gato
catch   coger
cattle   el ganado
censorship   la censura
century   el siglo
cereals   los cereales
certain   seguro/a, cierto/a
chair   la silla
chalkboard   la pizarra
champion   el/la campeón/ona
change   cambiar (v.); el cambio (n.)
channel   el canal

character   el carácter
cheap   barato/a
check   comprobar (ue) *(v.)*; la cuenta *(n.)*
cheese   el queso
chemistry   la química
chicken   el pollo
child *(small)*   el/la niño/a
children   los hijos, los niños *(pl.)*
chimney   la chimenea
choose   escoger, elegir (i)
chorus   el coro
church   la iglesia
citizen   el/la ciudadano/a
city   la ciudad
class   la clase
classmate   el/la compañero/a (de clase)
clean   limpiar
clever   listo/a
clock radio   el radiorreloj
close   cerrar (ie)
closed   cerrado/a
cloth   la tela
clothes dryer   la secadora de ropa
clothing *(summer)*   la ropa (de verano)
cloudy: it's cloudy   está nublado
coast   la costa
coat   el abrigo
coffee   el café
cognate   la palabra análoga
cold: it's very cold   hace mucho frío; be cold *(persons)*   tener frío
colon   dos puntos
color   el color
comb one's hair   peinarse
come   venir *(irreg.)*
comfort   la comodidad
comfortable   cómodo/a
comma   la coma
companion   el/la compañero/a
company   la compañía
competition   el concurso, la competencia
complain   quejarse
computer   la computadora
computer science   las ciencias de computación
confidence   la confianza

continue   continuar
contribute   contribuir
cook   el/la cocinero/a
cool: it's cool   hace fresco
cordially yours   quedo de usted (ustedes) atentamente
corn   el maíz
cost   costar (ue)
council   el consejo, la junta
count   contar (ue)
country   el país
countryside   el paisaje
couple   la pareja
course *(of study)*   el curso
court *(tennis, basketball)*   la cancha
cover   cubrir
cow   la vaca
crazy   loco/a
cream   la crema
cry   llorar
cup   la taza
curtain   la cortina

decade   la década
decide   decidir
deeply   profundamente
defeat   la derrota
delicious   rico/a
deliver   entregar
demand   exigir

demonstration   la manifestación
deny   negar (ie)
describe   describir
deserve   merecer (zc)
desire   el deseo
dessert   el postre
destroy   destruir
detail   el detalle
development   el desarrollo
dictatorship   la dictadura
die   morir (ue)
different   distinto/a, diferente
difficult   difícil, duro/a
difficulty   la dificultad
dine   cenar
dining room   el comedor
direct oneself   dirigirse (a)
disadvantage   la desventaja
disappear   desaparecer (zc)
disappoint   desilusionar
discover   descubrir
discovery   el descubrimiento
discuss   discutir
disgrace   la vergüenza
dishwasher   el lavaplatos
display   la muestra
dissatisfied   descontento/a
distinct   distinto/a
distract   distraer *(irreg.)*
divide   dividir
divorce   el divorcio
divorced: get divorced   divorciarse
do   hacer *(irreg.)*
do you know how to . . . ?   ¿sabe Ud. . . . ?
doctor   el/la doctor/a, el/la médico/a
dog   el perro
donkey   el burro
door   la puerta
dorm(itory)   el dormitorio, el colegio mayor
double   doble
doubt   dudar
downtown   el centro
draw   dibujar
dress   el vestido
dressed: get dressed   vestirse (i)
drink   beber *(v.)*; la bebida *(n.)*

drive (a car) conducir, manejar
driver el/la conductor/a
drum el tambor
duck el pato
during durante

each cada
ear la oreja
early temprano
earn ganar
east el este
easy fácil
eat comer; tomar
economics la economía
economy la economía
educational educativo/a;
  educational TV la teleducación
eggs los huevos
either . . . or o . . . o
elect elegir (i)
employee el/la empleado/a
employment agency la agencia
  de colocaciones
empty vacío/a
end el final
engineer el/la ingeniero/a
engineering la ingeniería
English inglés/esa
enjoy disfrutar
enough suficiente
enter entrar
entire entero/a
enthusiastic: get enthusiastic
  (about) entusiasmarse (con)
entrance la entrada
environmental conservation la
  preservación del ambiente
especially sobre todo
essential: it's essential es urgente
everything todo; everybody
  todos/as; all todo/a; the
  whole world todo el mundo;
  the whole country todo el país
everywhere por todas partes
exactly en punto
exam el examen
except menos
executive el/la ejecutivo/a
exercise ejercer

expensive caro/a
explain explicar
eye el ojo

face enfrentar (v.); la cara (n.)
facility la instalación
facing enfrente de
factory la fábrica
fall caer (irreg.) (v.); fall down-
  caerse (v.); fall el otoño (n.)
fall asleep dormirse (ue)
fall in love (with) enamorarse (de)
false falso/a
family la familia
famous famoso/a
fan el/la aficionado/a
fantastic fantástico/a
far (from) lejos (de)
fascinate fascinar
fat gordo/a
father el padre, el papá
father-in-law el suegro
fear temer (v.); el temor (n.)
February febrero
feel sentirse (ie)
feeling el sentimiento
fencing la esgrima
fiancé(e) el/la novio/a
field el campo
film la película
finally al fin, finalmente, por fin
find encontrar (ue); find out a-
  veriguar
finger el dedo
finish terminar, acabar; have just
  finished (doing something) acabar de (+ inf.)
first primer/primero/a
fish el pescado
fishing la pesca
fit caber (irreg.); fit well (to be
  large, small) quedarle bien
  (grande, pequeño)
fix arreglar
flattering lisonjero/a
flight el vuelo
flight attendant el/la auxiliar de
  vuelo
floor el piso
flower la flor

flute la flauta
fly volar (ue)
foggy: it's foggy hay neblina
follow seguir (i)
follower el/la partidario/a
following siguiente
food la comida
foot el pie
for para, por; for me para mí;
  for example por ejemplo; for
  that reason por eso
forbid prohibir
force la fuerza
foreign extranjero/a; foreign
  to ajeno a
foresee anticipar
forget olvidar; forget (about) ol-
  vidar(se) (de)
fork el tenedor
fourth cuarto/a
fox el zorro
free libre
freedom la libertad
friend el/la amigo/a
friendly amistoso/a, simpático/a
frog la rana
from desde; a partir de; de
fruit la fruta
fruit vendor el/la frutero/a
full (of) lleno/a (de)
furious rabioso/a
furniture store la mueblería

game el juego; el partido
garage el garaje
generally generalmente
generous generoso/a
gentleman el señor
German alemán/ana
get conseguir (i)
giraffe la jirafa
girl la muchacha, la chica, la niña
give dar; give (a gift) regalar
give birth dar a luz
glad: be glad alegrarse de
glass el vaso; el cristal
gloves los guantes
go ir (irreg.); go by foot ir a pie
go for a walk dar un paseo
go out salir (irreg.)

go shopping   ir de compras
go through   atravesar (ie)
go to bed   acostarse (ue)
go up   subir
godfather   el padrino
godmother   la madrina
good   bueno/a
good afternoon (evening, night)
   buenas tardes (noches)
good-looking   bien parecido
good morning   buenos días
good-by   adiós
government   el gobierno
grandchildren   los nietos
granddaughter   la nieta
grandfather   el abuelo
grandmother   la abuela
grandparents   los abuelos
grandson   el nieto
grapefruit   la toronja
grapes   las uvas
grateful: be grateful   estar
   agradecido/a
gray   gris
great   estupendo/a, bárbaro, gran
   (before a noun)
green   verde
greet   saludar
greeting   el saludo
grocery store   el almacén, la tienda
   de comestibles
growing   creciente
guilty person   el/la culpable
gym   el gimnasio

hair   el pelo
hairdresser   el/la peluquero/a
hall   el salón
ham   el jamón
hand   la mano
happen   pasar
happiness   la felicidad
happy   alegre, contento/a,
   satisfecho/a
hard   duro/a
have   haber; tener (irreg.); have to
   (+ inf.) tener que (+ inf.); have
   to deber
have a drink (liquor)   tomar una
   copa

have a good time   divertirse (ie)
have a good trip!   ¡buen viaje!
have an opinion of   pensar de
have been doing something
   for + a time expression
   hace + time expression
   + que + present tense
have breakfast   desayunar(se)
have dinner   cenar
have just done something   acabar
   de (+ inf.)
have left   quedar; I have (ten
   days) left   me quedan (diez días)
have lunch   almorzar (ue)
head   la cabeza
headache   el dolor de cabeza
hear   oír
height   la altura
help   ayudar (a) (v.); la ayuda (n.)
hen   la gallina
here   aquí
hi!   ¡hola!
high   alto/a
highway   la carretera; la autopista
history   la historia
hit   el éxito
holiday   la fiesta, el día festivo, las
   vacaciones
holy   sagrado/a
home: be home   estar en casa
homesick: be homesick   sentir
   nostalgia por
home town   el pueblo natal
honeymoon   la luna de miel, el
   viaje de novios
hope: hope (for)   esperar (v.), la
   esperanza (n.)
horse   el caballo
horseback riding   la equitación
hot: it's very hot   hace mucho calor
hotel   el hotel
hour   la hora; an hour   una hora
house   albergar (v.); la casa (n.)
housewife   el ama de casa (f.)
how?   ¿cómo?; how (what)
   ...!   ¡qué (+ adj., adv., n.)!
how does one say ...?   ¿cómo se
   dice ...?
how much?   ¿cuánto/a?; how
   many?   ¿cuántos/as? (pl.)

hug   abrazar (v.); un abrazo (n.)
human   humano/a
humble   humilde
hungry: be hungry   tener hambre
hurt   doler (ue)
husband   el esposo, el marido

I   yo
I don't either   yo tampoco
I hope   ojalá
I'm not sure   (no) estoy seguro/a
I'm traveling in ...   viajo en ...
ice cream   el helado
if   si
impressive   impresionante
improve   mejorar
improvement   el mejoramiento
in   en
in addition to   además de, a parte
   de
in exchange for   por
in fact   de hecho
in front of   delante de
in good shape   en forma
in spite of   a pesar de
in the open air   al aire libre
increase   aumentar
inexpensive   barato/a
inhabitant   el/la habitante
inheritance   la herencia
insensitive   insensible
insist (on)   insistir (en)
intelligent   inteligente
intend (+ inf.)   pensar (+ inf.)
interest   el interés (n); interesar (v.)
interested: be interested in   tener
   interés en
interesting   interesante
interview   entrevistar (v.); la
   entrevista (n.)
introduce   presentar
introduction   introducción
invite   invitar
iron   el hierro
it's cloudy   está nublado
it's cool   hace fresco
it's foggy   hay neblina
it's snowing   nieva
it's sunny   hace sol
it's very cold   hace mucho frío

it's very hot hace mucho calor
it's windy hace viento

jacket la chaqueta
jail la cárcel
January enero
job el empleo; **full-time job** el empleo a tiempo completo; **part-time job** el empleo a tiempo parcial
job application la solicitud de empleo
juice el jugo
jungle la selva
just justo/a

keep conservar, mantener *(irreg.)*
kidney beans los frijoles
kitchen la cocina
knife el cuchillo
know *(a fact, information)* saber *(irreg.);* **know** *(someone or something)* conocer (zc)

lack faltar
lady la señora
lake el lago
lamb el cordero
land *(in a plane)* aterrizar *(v.);* **land** *(earth)* la tierra *(n.)*
landing el aterrizaje
language el idioma, la lengua
last durar *(v.);* pasado/a *(adj.)*
last name el apellido
last night anoche
last year el año pasado
late tarde; **be late** llegar tarde; **it's late** es tarde
law el derecho, la ley
lazy perezoso/a
learn aprender
leather el cuero
leave dejar; irse; **(escape)** salirse; **(go out)** salir *(irreg.)*
left izquierda; **to the left of** a la izquierda de; **left-hand side** la izquierda
leg la pierna
lemon el limón

lenient indulgente
less menos; **less . . . than** menos . . . que, menos de
let's vamos a (+ *inf.*)
letter la carta
lettuce la lechuga
leverage *("pull")* la palanca
library la biblioteca
lie mentir (ie)
life la vida; **married life** la vida matrimonial
light la luz *(n.);* claro/a *(adj.)*
like gustar *(v.);* como *(adv.)*
lion el león
listen (to) escuchar
little poco; **little by little** poco a poco; **a little (of)** un poco de; **a little bit** un poquito
live vivir; **live together** vivir juntos
lively animado/a
living room la sala, el salón
lobster la langosta
located situado/a; **be located** encontrarse (ue)
long largo/a
look (at) mirar; **look for** buscar
lose perder (ie)
love encantar *(v.),* querer *(v.);* el amor *(n.)*
lovely hermoso/a
lucky: be lucky tener suerte
lunch el almuerzo

mad: get mad enojarse
magazine la revista
magnificent magnífico/a
mail el correo
main principal
maintain mantener *(irreg.)*
majority la mayoría
make hacer *(irreg.)*
make a mistake equivocarse
make a stop *(on the way to a destination)* hacer escala
make reservations hacer reservaciones
make up one's mind decidirse (a)
make up componer *(irreg.)*

male macho/a
man el hombre
map el mapa
mare la yegua
market el mercado
marriage el matrimonio
married casado/a; **get married** casarse
married couple el matrimonio
marvelous maravilloso/a
mass media los medios de comunicación
mathematics las matemáticas
matter importar *(v.);* el asunto *(n.)*
maybe puede ser; tal vez
meal la comida
means of transportation los medios de transporte
meanwhile mientras tanto
meat la carne
medicine la medicina
meet conocer (zc); encontrar (ue); **meet one another** encontrarse
meeting la reunión
middle class la clase media
middle-aged de cierta edad
midnight la medianoche
milk la leche
miss (someone or something) echar de menos
money el dinero
monkey el mono
month el mes; **monthly** al mes
more más; **more . . . than** más . . . que, más de
morning la mañana; **in the morning** de (por) la mañana
mother la madre, la mamá
mother-in-law la suegra
motorcycle la motocicleta
mountain la montaña
mountain climbing el alpinismo; **go mountain climbing** practicar el alpinismo
mountain range la cordillera
mouse el ratón
mouth la boca
movie camera la filmadora
movie theater el cine

much mucho/a *(adj.)*; mucho *(adv.)*
museum el museo
music la música
must deber

name el nombre; **first name** el nombre de pila; **my name is . . .** me llamo . . .
napkin la servilleta
narrow estrecho/a
nationality la nacionalidad
native indígena, nativo/a
near cerca (de)
necessary necesario/a
neck el cuello
need faltar *(v.)*; necesitar *(v.)*; requerir (ie) *(v.)*; la necesidad *(n.)*
neighbor el/la vecino/a
neighborhood el barrio
neither tampoco
nephew el sobrino
never jamás, nunca
nevertheless sin embargo
new nuevo/a
news la noticia
newscast el noticiero
newspaper el periódico
next próximo/a; **next to** junto/a; al lado de
nice simpático/a
nickname el apodo, el sobrenombre
niece la sobrina
night la noche; **at night** de (por) la noche; **night table** la mesita de noche
no longer ya no; **there aren't any left** ya no quedan
no (not any) ningún/ninguno/a
nobody nadie
nocturnal nocturno/a
noise el ruido
noon el mediodía
nose la nariz
not at all en absoluto
notebook el cuaderno
nothing (at all) nada
now ahora; **now that** ahora que; ya que

number el número
nurse el/la enfermero/a
nylon el nilón

object el objeto
of de; **of course** claro, cómo no; **of medium height** de estatura mediana
offer ofrecer (zc)
office la oficina
often a menudo
old viejo/a; **old man, woman** el/la viejo/a
older (younger) brother el hermano mayor (menor)
on foot a pie
on *(doing something)* al (+ *inf.*); **on seeing** al ver
on the contrary al contrario
on the way de camino
on time a tiempo
one's own propio/a
onion la cebolla
only no . . . más que, solamente, sólo
open abrir *(v.)*; abierto/a *(adj.)*
optimistic optimista
orange la naranja *(n.)*; anaranjado/a *(adj.)*
order mandar
other otro/a; lo demás
our nuestro/a
out: go out salir *(irreg.)*
outside of fuera de
outskirts los alrededores
over encima de, sobre
owner el/la dueño/a

pack the suitcase hacer las maletas
package el paquete
paint pintar
painting el cuadro
pamphlet el folleto
pants los pantalones
paper el papel
parents los padres
park el parque
party la fiesta; **party (political)** el partido (político)

pass pasar
passenger el/la pasajero/a
passport el pasaporte
pastry shop la pastelería
pay pagar
peach el durazno
pear la pera
peas los guisantes
pen el bolígrafo
pencil el lápiz
people la gente; **people** *(nation)* el pueblo
pepper la pimienta
perfectly perfectamente
perhaps tal vez
person la persona
pessimistic pesimista
pie el pastel
pig el cerdo
pineapple la piña
pink rosado/a
pity: it's a pity es una lástima
place el lugar, el sitio
plane el aeroplano, el avión
plantain el plátano
plate el plato
play *(a musical instrument)* tocar; **play** *(a role)* desempeñar; **play (a sport)** jugar (ue) (al + deporte)
player el/la jugador/a
please por favor
points of the compass los puntos cardinales
police officer el/la agente de policía, el/la policía
political science las ciencias políticas
poor pobre
port el puerto
position el puesto
possible posible
post el cargo
potato la papa
power el poder
powerful poderoso/a
practice practicar
prawn el langostino
prefer preferir (ie)
prejudice el prejuicio

prescribe prescribir
present presentar *(v.)*; actual *(adj.)*
press la prensa
pretty bonito/a, lindo/a
prevent prevenir *(irreg.)*
price el precio
private particular
prize el premio
problem el problema
prohibit prohibir
project proyectar
promise prometer
promote fomentar
propose pedir la mano en matrimonio; proponer *(irreg.)*
protect proteger
proud orgulloso/a
proverb el refrán
purple morado/a
purpose el objeto
purse el/la bolso/a
put poner; **put on** *(clothing)* ponerse; **begin to** ponerse a

queen la reina
question la pregunta
quickly de prisa; **(soon)** pronto
quite well bastante bien

rabbit el conejo
race la carrera; **race track** la pista
rain llover (ue)
raincoat el impermeable
ranch la hacienda
rarely raras veces
read leer
ready listo/a
realize darse cuenta (de)
really realmente
reason la razón
receive recibir
record el disco
record player el tocadiscos
recreation el recreo
red rojo/a
red tape el papeleo
red-haired pelirrojo/a
referee el árbitro
refrigerator la nevera

refuse to negarse (ie) (a)
regret lamentar
rehearse ensayar
relative el/la pariente/a
remain permanecer (zc); quedar
remember acordarse (ue) de; recordar (ue)
repeat repetir (i)
reporter el/la periodista, el/la reportero/a
representative el/la representante
require requerir (ie)
resource el recurso
respond responder
rest descansar *(v.)*; **the rest of** lo demás
restaurant el restaurante
return regresar *(v.)*; devolver (ue) *(trans. verb)*; volver (ue) *(v.)*; el regreso *(n.)*
ribbon la cinta
rice el arroz
rich rico/a; **very rich** riquísimo/a
ride a *(go by)* **bicycle (bus, subway)** montar (andar, ir) en bicicleta (en autobús, metro)
right away en seguida
right derecha; **to the right of** a la derecha de; **right** *(in the political spectrum)* la derecha; **right-hand side** la derecha
rise up again resurgir
river el río
rocking chair la silla mecedora
roof el techo
rooster el gallo
root la raíz
ruler la regla
run correr

sacred sagrado/a
sad triste
sail la vela
sailboat el velero
salad la ensalada
salary el sueldo
sale la venta
sales clerk el/la empleado/a

sales person el/la vendedor/a
salt la sal
same mismo/a
same as usual como siempre
satisfied contento/a, satisfecho/a
satisfy satisfacer (zc)
say decir *(irreg.)*
say good-by despedir (i)
scarf la bufanda
schedule el horario
school la escuela; **school** *(elementary or high)* el colegio
school department *(university level)* la facultad
scientist el/la científico/a
score a goal marcar un gol
sea el mar
seashore la orilla del mar
season la estación
seated sentado/a
second segundo/a
see ver
see you Monday hasta el lunes
see you later hasta luego, hasta la vista
see you soon hasta pronto
see you tomorrow hasta mañana
selfish egoísta
sell vender
send enviar, mandar
serious serio/a
servant el/la criado/a
serve servir (i)
settle down establecerse (zc)
several varios/as
shame la vergüenza
sharp en punto
shave afeitarse
sheep la oveja
shellfish los mariscos
ship el barco
shirt la camisa
shoes los zapatos
shopping: go shopping ir de compras
short corto/a; **short** *(in stature)* bajo/a
should deber
shout gritar

show dar a conocer *(v.)*; mostrar (ue)*(v.)*; el espectáculo *(n.)*
shower la ducha
shrimp el camarón
sick: get sick enfermarse
silk la seda
similar análogo/a
since desde que, puesto que, ahora que, ya que; **since yesterday** desde ayer
sing cantar
singer el/la cantante
single el/la soltero/a *(n.)*; soltero/a *(adj.)*
sister la hermana
sister-in-law la cuñada
sit down sentarse (ie)
size *(of clothing)* la talla; **size** *(of shoes)* el número
skate patinar
skating el patinaje
ski esquiar
ski slope la pista
skirt la falda
skyscraper el rascacielos
sleep dormir (ue)
sleepy: be sleepy tener sueño
slim delgado/a
small pequeño/a
smaller menor
smart listo/a
smile sonreír (i); sonreírse (i)
snake la culebra, la serpiente
sneak in entrarse
snow la nieve
snowing: it's snowing nieva
so tan; **so that (in order that)** para que; **so that (in such a way that)** de manera que; de modo que
soap opera la telenovela
soccer el fútbol
social level el nivel social
socks los calcetines
soda pop las gaseosas
sofa el sofá
some algún, alguno/a
somebody alguien
something algo

sometimes a veces; **sometimes (on occasion)** alguna vez
son el hijo
son-in-law el yerno
song la canción
soon pronto
sorry: be sorry to arrepentirse (ie)
Spanish *(language)* el español, el castellano
Spanish-speaking de habla española
spare (part) el repuesto
speak hablar
speaker el/la locutor/a
specify precisar
spectator el/la espectador/a
spelling la ortografía
spend *(time or money)* gastar
spinach las espinacas
spoon la cuchara
sport el deporte; **sports facility** la instalación deportiva; **go in for sports** practicar los deportes
sporting deportivo/a
square la plaza
stadium el estadio
stairs las escaleras
standard of living el nivel de vida
start (to) ponerse a *(+ inf.)*
starve *(literally, to die from hunger)* morirse de hambre
state el estado
station la estación
steamship el vapor
steel el acero
stereo el estéreo
still todavía
stingy tacaño/a
stockings las medias
stop detenerse *(irreg.)*; parar; **stop** *(+ –ing)* dejar de *(+ inf.)*
store la tienda
story la historia, el cuento
strait el estrecho
strawberry la fresa
street la calle
strict severo/a, estricto/a
strike la huelga
stringbeans las judías verdes

strong fuerte
structure la estructura
student el/la estudiante *(n.)*; estudiantil *(adj.)*
study estudiar
stupid tonto/a
subject *(course)* la asignatura, la disciplina
subscribe suscribir
subway el metro
success el éxito
suffer sufrir
sugar el azúcar
sugar cane la caña de azúcar
suggest sugerir (ie)
suit el traje
suitcase la maleta
Sunday el domingo
sunny: it's sunny hace sol
support apoyar
suppose suponer *(irreg.)*
survey la investigación
sweetheart el/la enamorado/a; el/la novio/a
swim nadar
swimming la natación
swimming pool la piscina

table la mesa
tailor el/la sastre
take llevar; *(have food or drink)* tomar
take (pictures) sacar (fotos)
take a shower bañarse
take a trip hacer un viaje
take charge (of) encargarse (de)
take off *(clothing)* quitarse
take off *(in a plane)* despegar
take the train tomar el tren
tall alto/a
task la tarea
taste el gusto
tea el té
teach enseñar
team el equipo
tear rasgar
teeth los dientes
telephone el teléfono
tell contar (ue)

tent la tienda de campaña
terrible terrible
textbook el libro de texto
thank you gracias; **thank you very much** muchas gracias
that (this) way así
theater el teatro
then entonces, luego
there allí
there is (there are) hay; **there isn't any . . .** no hay ningún . . .
thin flaco/a
thing la cosa
think pensar (ie); **think about** pensar en; **think (have an opinion)** opinar, creer
thirsty: be thirsty tener sed
through: go through atravesar (ie)
Thursday el jueves
ticket el billete, el boleto; **one-way ticket** el billete de ida; **round-trip ticket** el billete de ida y vuelta
tie la corbata
tiger el tigre
time el tiempo
tin el estaño
tired cansado/a
title el título
to a; **to the** al (a + el), a la
toast la tostada
today hoy
toe el dedo
together: get together reunirse
tongue twister el trabalenguas
too también
too much (many) demasiado/a, os/as
tower la torre
town el pueblo
track and field la pista y campo
trade comerciar
traffic el tránsito
train entrenarse
train station la estación de ferrocarril
translate traducir (irreg.)
transportation (public) el transporte (público)

travel viajar; **travel by plane (train, boat)** viajar en avión (tren, barco)
travel agency la agencia de viajes
tree el árbol
tribe la tribu
triumph el triunfo
trousers los pantalones
truck el camión
true cierto/a
true or false? ¿verdad o falso?
trust confiar (en)
try to tratar (de)
turkey el pavo
turn off apagar
turn on (lights or equipment) encender (ie)
TV (black-and-white, color) el televisor (en blanco y negro, a colores)
TV viewer el/la televidente
typewriter la máquina de escribir

ugly feo/a
uncle el tío
uncomfortable incómodo/a
under bajo; debajo de
under construction en construcción
understand comprender; entender (ie)
unemployment el desempleo
unless a menos que
unpleasant antipático/a
until hasta, hasta que
up: go up subir
urban urbano/a
use usar
used: get used to acostumbrarse
useful útil

vacation las vacaciones
value el valor
varied variado/a
variety la variedad
vegetables las legumbres
vendor el/la vendedor/a

very muy; sumamente; **very well** muy bien; sumamente
visit visitar
volleyball el vólibol (voleibol)
vote votar (v.); el voto (n.)

wage(s) el salario
wait (for) esperar
waiter el camarero
waitress la camarera
wake up despertarse (ie)
walk andar, caminar; **go for a walk** dar un paseo
wall la pared
wallet la billetera
want tener ganas (de), desear; querer (irreg.)
war la guerra
warm: be warm (persons) tener calor
wash (oneself) lavar(se)
washing machine la lavadora
waste (time) gastar
watch el reloj
water el agua (f.); **mineral water** agua mineral
wear llevar; **wear (glasses)** usar (gafas)
weather el clima, el tiempo; **the weather is nice (bad)** hace buen (mal) tiempo
wedding la boda
wedding dress el traje de bodas
wedding march la marcha nupcial
week la semana; **the coming week** la semana entrante
weekend el fin de semana
well bien, pues
well-known conocido/a
western occidental
what? ¿qué?, ¿cuál?
what are we waiting for? ¿qué esperamos?
what is (the article) about? ¿de qué trata (el artículo)?
what is (your) phone number? ¿cuál es (su) número de teléfono?
what time is it? ¿qué hora es?

what's he like? ¿cómo es él?
what's your name? *(formal)* ¿cómo se llama usted?
when cuando; **when?** ¿cuándo?
where donde; **where?** ¿dónde?
which? ¿cuál?
while mientras
white blanco/a
who? ¿quién, quiénes? *(pl.)*; **to whom?** ¿a quién?
whole entero/a
whose cuyo/a, cuyos/as; **whose?** ¿de quién, de quiénes?
why? ¿por qué?
wide amplio/a
wife la esposa
win ganar
window la ventana
windy: it's windy hace viento
wine el vino; **(red or white) wine** el vino (tinto o blanco)

winter el invierno
wish desear *(v.)*, querer *(irreg.) (v.)*; el deseo *(n.)*
with con; **with me** conmigo; **with you** contigo
within dentro de
without sin
wolf el lobo
woman la mujer
wonderful estupendo/a, bárbaro/a, maravilloso/a
wood la madera
woods el bosque
wool la lana
word la palabra
word processor la procesadora de palabras
work trabajar *(v.)*; la obra *(n.)*, el empleo *(n.)*, el trabajo *(n.)*; **apply for work** solicitar trabajo
worker *(blue collar)* el/la obrero/a

world el mundo
worried preocupado/a
worry preocuparse
worse (worst) (el/la) peor
write escribir
wrong: be wrong no tener razón

year el año; **be . . . years old** tener . . . años
yellow amarillo/a
yes sí
yesterday ayer; **yesterday afternoon** ayer por la tarde; **yesterday evening** ayer por la noche; **yesterday morning** ayer por la mañana
you're welcome de nada
young joven
young lady la señorita

zero cero

Index

a
  personal 80
  for emphasis/clarification 133
  with indirect-object pronouns 206
  + infinitive 324
acabar de + infinitive 294
accent marks 21
adjectives 107
  forms: 4-way 107
  forms: 2-way 107, 108
  clauses with subjunctive 336
  comparison 248
    más . . . que 249
    menos . . . que 249
    tan . . . como 280
  demonstrative 145
  descriptive 104, 107
  irregular 266
  nationality 44
  possessive 78
  long form 307
  shortened 192
  superlative 264
    el/la más joven, etc. 264
    -ísimo 415
    sumamente 415
    with **ser** and **estar** 114, 378
adverbial clauses
  with subjunctive 338
adverbs
  comparison 248
  irregular comparison 267
  in **-mente** 112
  position 112
affirmative vs. negative counter-parts 164
al and **del** 94
al + infinitive 236
alphabet, Spanish 51
alphabetization 51
animals and insects 297
article (marker)
  definite, singular 58
  definite, plural 58

  definite with days of week 59
  indefinite, singular 40
  indefinite, plural 42
  neuter article **lo** 221, 282
  omitted after **tener** 43
  omitted after **ser** before nouns of occupation and nationality 43
  plural = *some* 42
  used in general sense 59
  used with titles 59

body, parts of 276
buildings 89

capitalization
  days of week 50
  months 50
  nationality 50
  titles (**Sr.,** etc.) 34
  yo 50
cardinal numbers: *see* numbers
classroom objects 38
clothing 216
cognates 5, 23, 277
  false cognates 439
colors 106
commands
  nosotros-commands 318
  order of two pronouns used with commands 341
  tú-commands 389
  usted-commands 318
  vosotros-commands Appendix D, 389
  negative commands 389
  position of object pronouns 390
  "let's"-commands 319
como si-clauses 395
comparisons
  equality 280
  inequality 248
  de = *than* 248
  irregular adjectives 266

  of adverbs 267
  superlative in **-ísimo** 415
compound nouns 317
compound prepositions 259
conditional
  forms 374
  uses 375
  for probability 377
  in result-clauses 375
  to express politeness 375
conmigo, contigo 133
conocer 168
conocer vs. **saber** 168
construction materials 317
contractions **al** and **del** 94
courtesy titles 34
¿cuál? vs. **¿qué?** 362

dar Appendix D
  preterit 203
  present subjunctive 243
dates (year) 201
dates (months) 200
days of week 22
de = possession 77
  origin 26
  materials 317
  + infinitive 324
deber, poder, querer in requests 391
decir Appendix D
  present indicative 135
  preterit 203
definite articles 58
  singular forms 58
  plural forms 58
  with days of week 59
  with titles 59
del and **al** 94
demonstrative adjectives 145
demonstrative pronouns 146
dependent infinitives 56
diaeresis 316
diminutives 76
diphthongs 71, 142

direct-object pronouns
forms 147
position 148
pre-verbal 148
after commands 447
with double-verb constructions 148
position in negative sentences
446
disjunctive pronouns 133
drink and food 238

estar Appendix D
meaning changes with **ser** and
estar 379
present indicative 90
preterit 203
present subjunctive 243
uses 90
vs. **ser** 114
with **-ndo** forms 426
vs. **ser** with adjectives 115, 378
exclamations
with ¡**qué!** 112
expressions of time 184, 208

fabrics 317
false cognates 439
faltar 225
family vocabulary 75, 161
food and drink 238
food shops 241
furniture 356
future
forms of future tense 372
regular 372
irregular stem 373
regular use 372
for probability 377
ir a + *inf.* for future 93
expressed by present 55

geographical terms 6
government and administration
408
greetings and leave-takings 19, 371
gustar 61, 225
gustar-like verbs 225

haber Appendix D
the invariable form **hay** 81
preterit 204
present subjunctive 278, 441

hacer Appendix D
present indicative 135
present subjunctive 279
preterit 204
to express duration of time 208
hace . . . que 208
desde hace . . . = ago 208
in weather expressions 201
hay que 131

imperfect indicative
forms 301
uses 302
vs. preterit 304, 323
imperfect progressive 428
imperfect subjunctive
forms 357
use of imperfect subjunctive for
politeness 391
use in **si**-clauses 393
impersonal reflexive construction
359
indefinite article
singular 40
plural 42
omission of, after **tener** 43
un with certain nouns in **-a** 40
indicative vs. subjunctive in
adjective clauses 336
adverbial clauses 338
indirect-object pronouns
forms 206
with **a**-phrases 206
infinitive
infinitive forms and stems 53
dependent infinitive 56
intonation 36
questions 36
exclamations 36
statements 36
commands 36
ir Appendix D
present indicative 92
present subjunctive 278
preterit 203
+ **a** + *inf.* for future 93

linking 36, 37
lo
as neuter pronoun 282
+ adjective 221, 282
lo vs. **le** 148
lo de, lo que 283

locatives 89
love, marriage and divorce vocabulary 423

mail vocabulary 370
mayor, menor 267
me gusta, me gustan 60
menor, mayor 267
metals 317
months 199

names
use of first names and courtesy
titles 34
nationalities 44
negation with **no** 26
double negatives 164
nominalization
of adjectives 220
el de, la de 220
nosotros for mixed gender 24
nosotros-commands 318
nouns
compound nouns 317
ending in **-ma** or **-ta** 277
singular and plural forms 42
gender in **-o, -a, -e** 40
gender of nouns in **-e** 40
nouns in **-ad, -ión** 40
nouns of occupation 386
nouns representing persons 74
masculine plural for mixed gender
groups 75
numbers
cardinals
0–20 37
21–30 128
31–199 128
200 to 10,000,000 162
ordinals 299
mil, millón 163

objects
classroom 38
useful modern 127
household 258
occupations and professions 386
ojalá 393
orthographic *h* 126

para 189
meanings 189
vs. **por** 189

participles
  present participle (**-ndo** forms)
    425
  use in progressive   425
  past participles
    regular   409
    irregular   410
  use of past participle in present
    perfect tense   409
perfect tenses   413
  present perfect   409
  pluperfect   413
  present perfect subjunctive   440
  past perfect subjunctive   442
  conditional perfect   413
pero and **sino**   444
personal **a**   80
personal characteristics   104
persons (**niño, niña,** etc.)   74
place names   89
poder   Appendix D
  imperfect and preterit   323
  present tense   152
  preterit   204
  for requests   391
poner   Appendix D, 135
  present subjunctive   279
  preterit   204
por
  meanings   190
  vs. **para**   189
possession with **de**   77
possessive adjectives   78
possessive pronouns   308
prefixes   90, 357
prepositions   259
  as word set   259
  compound prepositions   259
  use of **a** before *inf.*   324
  use of **de** before *inf.*   324
present perfect   409
present subjunctive tense
  irregular   278
  regular   242, 260
  with impersonal expressions
    246, 262
  with verbs of wish, will   244, 262
  with expressions of emotion,
    doubt, denial   245, 262
present tense
  regular **-ar**   54
  regular **-er**   110

regular **-ir**   110
  with irregular **yo-**forms   134
preterit
  regular forms   186
  irregular forms   202
  spelling-changing verbs   186
  stem-changing verbs   218
  vs. imperfect   304, 323
progressive tenses   425
  imperfect progressive   428
  present   426
  preterit progressive   428
  with object pronouns   426
pronouns
  demonstrative   145
  direct object   147
  disjunctive (prepositional)   133
  indirect object   206
  interrogative pronouns **¿cuál?** vs.
    ¿qué?   362
  in affirmative sentences   148, 446
  in commands   447
  in negative sentences   446
  after infinitive   148
  position of indirect object **-se** vs.
    reflexive or reciprocal **-se**
    341
  position of object pronouns   148
  possessive   308
  prepositional   132
  reflexive   223, 446
  relative   361
    que   361
    el que   361
  se for **le** or **les**   341
  subject pronouns   23
    masculine plural forms for
      mixed genders   24
    omission of subject pronouns
      25
  two object pronouns   340
  with the progressive   426
pronunciation
  vowel sounds   20
  [r]   87
  [R]   103
  [ñ]   125
  [b] vs. [β]   141
  [d] vs. [đ]   160
  [p], [t], [k]   182
  [h]   198
  [s], [ks], [gs] = *x*   238

  [z] and [s]   215
  [g] vs. [ǥ]   257
  [L] vs. [y]   275
punctuation
  accent marks   21
  upside-down exclamation and
    question marks   22
  dashes and quotes   316
  diaerisis   316

¿qué? vs. **¿cuál?**   362
¡qué! in exclamations   112
querer   Appendix D
  preterit   204
  imperfect vs. preterit   323
  present tense forms   150
  use for politeness   391
questions   96

reflexive verbs or structures
    Appendix D, 222, 321
  reflexive pronoun forms   223
  with articles of clothing   224
  impersonal **se**   359, 430
  reflexive for passive   359
  reciprocal   321
  unintentional actions   430
relative clauses   361
rooms in house   258

saber   Appendix D
  imperfect vs. preterit   323
  preterit   204
  present subjunctive   278
saber vs. **conocer**   168
salir
  present indicative   135
  present subjunctive   279
seasons   199
ser   25
  indicate membership in a group
    26
  indicate nationality   26
  meaning changes with **ser** and
    estar   379
  present indicative   25
  preterit   203
  present subjunctive   278
  uses   26
  vs. **estar**   114

vs. **estar** used with adjectives 114, 378
si-clauses
  in the imperfect subjunctive 393
  in the indicative 393
  as exclamations 393
sino and **pero** 445
spelling-changing consonant
  sounds 296
spelling-changing verbs Appendix
  D, 135
spelling problems
  g and **j** 296
  g and **gu** 296
  z, s, c 296
  h 126
sports 144, 332
stem-changing verbs Appendix D
  e > **ie** 150, 261
  o > **ue** 152, 261
  e > **i** 166, 218, 261
  o > **u** 218
storepeople/owners 241
stores and businesses 241
stress 73
subjects (courses) 52
subjunctive
  imperfect subjunctive 357
  indicative vs. subjunctive in ad-
    verbial clauses 338
  past perfect subjunctive 442
  present subjunctive 242, 260,
    262, 334
  present perfect subjunctive 440
  verbs with special stem 278
  after conjunction **que** 242
  after expressions of influence
    244
  after expressions of emotion 245
  after expressions of opinion 245

after expressions of hope 245
after expressions of doubt or
  uncertainty 245
after impersonal expressions 246
ojalá que with subjunctive 393,
  443
in adjective clauses 336
in noun clauses 244, 334
in adverbial clauses 338
in **como si**-clauses 395
in **si**-clauses 393, 443
to express politeness 391
commands 318, 390
vs. indicative 338
stem-changing verbs 260
suffixes 52, 76, 112, 277
superlative 264
  of adjectives 264
  in **-ísimo** 415
surnames, Spanish 16
syllabication 72

tan . . . como 280
tanto . . . como 280
tanto como 280
tener Appendix D
  omission of definite article after
    tener 130
  present indicative 130
  present subjunctive 279
  preterit 204
  tener años 130
tener que vs. **hay que** 131
time
  regular clock time 183
time expressions 184, 208
titles 34
traducir Appendix D, 168
traer Appendix D

transportation 143
travel terms 217
tú vs. **usted** 24

venir Appendix D
  present indicative 135
  present subjunctive 279
  preterit 203
ver Appendix D, 70
verbs
  double-verb constructions 56
  regular **-ar** 54, Appendix D
  regular **-er** 110, Appendix D
  regular **-ir** 110, Appendix D
  spelling-changing 135, Appendix
    D
  stem-changing Appendix D,
    150, 152, 166, 218, 135
  e > **ie** Appendix D, 150, 261
  o > **u** Appendix D, 218
  o > **ue** Appendix D, 152, 261
  e > **i** Appendix D, 166, 218, 261
  verbs that require no preposition
    before a noun 55
  with special subjunctive stem
    279
  verbs that take a preposition
    before infinitive 324
  irregular verbs Appendix D
  verb tenses: *see individual tenses
    and Appendix D*
vosotros-forms Appendix D, 24
vowel sounds 20

weather expressions 201
word families 333
word order
  in interrogative sentences 96

Credits

Black and White Photographs

Unit 1: page 13, Stuart Cohen; 14, left, Paul Conklin; 14, right, Peter Menzel; 17, Beryl Goldberg; 19, Victor Englebert; 29, top, Peter Menzel; 29, bottom, Stuart Cohen; 30, right, Paul Conklin; 30, left, Peter Menzel; 32, Peter Menzel; 47, Stuart Cohen; 63, Paul Conklin. **Unit 2:** page 67, Owen Franken/Stock, Boston; 68, Paul Conklin; 83, 84, 98, Beryl Goldberg; 99, 101, Peter Menzel; 102, Alan Carey/The Image Works; 117, Ulrike Welsch. **Unit 3:** page 121, Pat Canova; 122, 137, 138, Peter Menzel; 141, top right, Andrew Sacks/Art Resource; 141; top left, Peter Menzel; 155, 156, Peter Menzel; 160, Victor Englebert. **Unit 4:** page 177, Peter Menzel; 178, Victor Englebert; 181, Beryl Goldberg; 195, 211, Peter Menzel; 214, Vautier/DeCool, Click/Chicago; 228, Peter Menzel. **Unit 5:** page 233, Peter Menzel; 234, 237, Victor Englebert; 252, Chip and Rosa Peterson; 253, Stuart Cohen; 256, 270, Peter Menzel; 271, D. J. Variakojis/Nawrocki; 274, Robert Frerck/Odyssey Productions; 285, Susan Van Etten. **Unit 6:** page 291, Peter Menzel; 292, Susan Van Etten; 295, 311, Peter Menzel; 312, Lemoine/Gamma-Liaison; 315, left, Peter Menzel; 315, right, Nigel Nicholson/The Image Bank; 328, Diego Goldberg/Sygma; 331, Fred Ward/Black Star; 344, Laffont/Sygma. **Unit 7:** page 351, Peter Menzel; 352, Beryl Goldberg; 355, Andrew Sacks/Art Resource; 364, Stuart Cohen; 366, 369, Peter Menzel; 385, top, Ulrike Welsch; 385, bottom, Peter Menzel. **Unit 8:** page 403, Peter Menzel; 404, Wide World; 408, Paul Conklin; 419, Robert Frerck/Odyssey Productions; 423, right, Alinari/Art Resource left, Giraudon/Art Resource; 433, 434, 435, 436, bottom, Paul Conklin; 436, top, Peter Menzel; 438, Paul Conklin; 450, Susan Van Etten.

Color Photographs

El mundo hispánico: page 1, top, Robert Frerck/Odyssey Productions; 1, bottom, Peter Menzel; 2, top left, Robert Frerck/Odyssey Productions; 2, top right, Stuart Cohen; 2, bottom, Robert Frerck/Odyssey Productions; 3, top, Peter Menzel; 3, bottom, Robert Frerck/Odyssey Productions; 4, left, Robert Frerck/Odyssey Productions; 4, top right, Ulrike Welsch; 4, bottom, right, Peter Menzel. **La vida diaria:** page 1, top and bottom, Stuart Cohen; 2, top, © 1981 John Littlewood/Littlewood Communications; 2, bottom, Robert Frerck/Odyssey Productions; 3, David Kupferschmid; 4, top, Peter Menzel; 4, bottom, Robert Frerck/Odyssey Productions; 5, top, Ulrike Welsch; 5, bottom, Robert Frerck/Odyssey Productions; 6, Robert Frerck/Odyssey Productions. **Festivales y celebraciones:** page 1, © 1983 Peter Menzel/Stock Boston; 2, top, Victor Englebert; 2, bottom, Ulrike Welsch; 3, top, Robert Frerck/Odyssey Productions; 3, bottom, Ulrike Welsch; 4, top and bottom, Robert Frerck/Odyssey Productions; 5, top, Owen Franken; 5, bottom, Robert Frerck/Odyssey Productions; 6, Robert Frerck/Odyssey Productions. **Música, baile y teatro:** page 1, Robert Frerck/Odyssey Productions; 2, Stuart Cohen; 3, top, Peter Menzel; 3, bottom, Cary Wolinsky/Stock, Boston; 4, top, Ulrike Welsch; 4, bottom, Peter Menzel; 5, top, Jeff Slocomb/The Picture Group; 5, bottom, Cameramann International; 6, Peter Menzel. **La herencia cultural:** page 1, top, Chip and Rosa Peterson; 1, bottom, Scala/Art Resource; 2, top and bottom, Robert Frerck/Odyssey Productions; 3, top, Peter Menzel; 3, bottom, Robert Frerck/Odyssey Productions; 4, Robert Frerck/Odyssey Productions; 5, top and bottom, Robert Frerck/Odyssey Productions; 6, left, Ulrike Welsch; 6, right, Kal Muller/Woodfin Camp.

Art

Drawings by George M. Ulrich

Page 6, left, *Tú Internacional*, Panamá, Panamá; 6, right, *Tiempo Libre*, Guayaquil, Ecuador; 217, Aeromexico Airlines, Miami; 217, Avianca, La Aerolínea de Colombia, Miami Springs; 217, Viasa Airlines, Miami; 217, Iberia Airlines, Regal Park.

Student Evaluation: *En contacto, 3/e*

The authors and editors of this textbook would like to have your opinion about your experience with this edition of *En contacto*. Please express yourself freely and add any additional comments you may have.

1. College or University _____

2. What did you like best about the book? _____

3. Which parts did you find to be the most difficult or uninteresting?
   _____

4. In which areas did your professor place more emphasis?

   _____ Grammar   _____ Culture

   _____ Conversation   _____ Reading and Writing

5. Did you watch videos as part of your Spanish course? _____

6. If yes, in what way did you find the videos valuable for learning Spanish? _____

7. Did you use the laboratory tapes or purchase your own audio tapes?
   _____

8. Did you use the DASHER computer program? _____ If you did, how useful was it? _____

9. What changes would you recommend for future editions of *En contacto?* _____

10. Will you be taking a second year of Spanish? _____

You do / do not have my permission to use the above statements for advertising purposes.

_____   _____
(signature)   (date)

Please send your evaluation to:
   Houghton Mifflin Company
   Foreign Language Department-Spanish
   1 Beacon Street
   Boston, MA 02108

Barranquilla
Cartagena
Maracaibo
San Carlos
Caracas
Río *Orinoco*
GUYANA
GUAYANA
FRANCESA
Río *Magdalena*
VENEZUELA
Medellín
☆ Bogotá
COLOMBIA
SURINAM
Cali
Popayán
Río *Negro*
ECUADOR
Amazonas
☆ Quito
Río
ECUADOR
Guayaquil
PERÚ
BRASIL
CORDILLERA
Machu
Picchu
Lima
Callao ☆
DE
Cuzco
Puno
La Paz
☆
Brasilia
☆
Lago Titicaca
BOLIVIA
Sucre
LOS
Potosí
Río *Paraná*
PARAGUAY
São Paulo
TRÓPICO DE
CAPRICORNIO
Salta
Asunción
Río de Janeiro
OCÉANO
CHILE
ANDES
San Miguel
de Tucumán
PACÍFICO
ARGENTINA
▲ *Aconcagua*
OCÉANO
Valparaíso
URUGUAY
ATLÁNTICO
Santiago ☆
Buenos Aires ☆
☆ Montevideo
La Plata
Río de la Plata
Concepción
PAMPAS
Río Colorado
Mar del Plata

0	400	800 km
0	200	400	600 mi

PATAGONIA

Punta Arenas
TIERRA DEL FUEGO
Estrecho de Magallanes
CABO DE HORNOS

AMÉRICA DEL SUR